HISTORY OF THE CHURCH

III

HISTORY OF THE CHURCH

Edited by
HUBERT JEDIN
and
JOHN DOLAN

Volume III

THE CHURCH
IN THE
AGE OF FEUDALISM

by

FRIEDRICH KEMPF

HANS-GEORG BECK

EUGEN EWIG

JOSEF ANDREAS JUNGMANN

Translated by

Anselm Biggs

Burns & Oates • London

1980

BURNS & OATES LONDON

2-10 Jerdan Place, London SW6 5PT

Translated from the *Handbuch der Kirchengeschichte,* edited by Hubert Jedin,

Vol. III, "Die mittelalterliche Kirche",

Part 1, "Vom kirchlichen Frühmittelalter zur gregorianischen Reform."

Herder, Freiburg

ISBN 0 86012 085 6

CONTENTS

PREFACE

This third volume of the *Handbuch der Kirchengeschichte* begins with the turn of the seventh century and concludes with the Concordat of Worms (1122) and the Ninth General Council (1123). In the original planning of the *Handbuch* it was intended that this volume should go to the end of the thirteenth Century and that the next volume should treat the Late Middle Ages, the Reformation, and the Counter Reformation, but circumstances led to a change in plan. In principle there is no objection to the new arrangement, which is also to be found in other historical treatments. The period 700 to 1123 is clearly distinct from the preceding and the following epochs. The earlier and the present plan are about equal in merit; each has much in its favour. Volumes III, IV, and V deal with two especially exciting themes: the Schism between the Eastern and Western Churches and the split in the unity of Western Christendom. One who is chiefly interested in the history of the Western Church will regard the Late Middle Ages and the Reformation as a separate period ending with the Counter Reformation and will want to have them included in a single volume. In the history of the Latin-Greek *oikumene*, on the other hand, the Late Middle Ages constitute the end of a process that began with the turn of the seventh century, reached its climax in the Schism of 1054, and finally expired in the negotiations for union that extended into the fifteenth century. Hence it makes good sense to devote a special volume to this period.

This is precisely the plan followed by the German original. Volume III covers the whole period from *ca.* 700 to *ca.* 1500, but it appears in two half-volumes. In the English version it was decided to call them Volumes III and IV. Thus the English Volume III corresponds to the German Volume III/1. It is divided into two periods: the Early Middle Ages (700–1046) and the Gregorian Reform (1046–1124).

To avoid misunderstanding it is necessary to explain the term "Early Middle Ages", which in the German original is *Kirchliches Frühmittelalter*. Actually, the Middle Ages, as commonly understood, began before 700. Whether one prefers to see the beginning of the Middle Ages in the fifth or the sixth century, in any event there existed a German-Roman, and hence an early medieval, civilization in the newly established Germanic kingdoms in addition to the already present Roman civilization. Although the Church was affected by it, she still clung to her ancient Roman tradition; she was able all the more easily to do so when she could continue to live according to the Roman Canon Law. Only when, from the turn of the seventh century, three great powers — the Byzantine, the Muslim, and the Carolingian states — confronted one another, did the Western Church and early medieval civilization coalesce. The age then beginning, that of Canon Law under strong Germanic influence, marks the start of the *Kirchliches Frühmittelalter* — the "Early Middle Ages" as applied to the period covered by the first part of this volume. Among its characteristic features are: an intimate relationship between *Regnum* and *Sacerdotium,* royal theocracy, the proprietary church system, lay investiture, and new forms in liturgy, piety, and the care of souls. The elements that then became a part of the life of the Church were to a great extent conditioned by the time. Once the West had passed through its early medieval phase and had moved into the Classical Middle Ages, the Church had to do something about her early medieval externals. She did so in the age of the Gregorian Reform and thereby released the forces that were to develop in the next two centuries. The Church's "Classical Middle Ages" began with the Gregorian Reform.

From the viewpoint of Western history, then, it would seem natural to end this volume with the dividing line between the "Early" and the "Classical" Middle Ages and to postpone the Gregorian Reform to the next volume. But the period of the Gregorian Reform is of decisive importance also for the history of the Greek Church, especially for her relationship with Western Christendom. And in Byzantium this did not mark the start of a new period but rather the close of a long process whose outcome was virtually inevitable. There is no room for doubt that only a few persons were basically affected when in 1054 the papal legates and the Patriarch Michael Caerularius hurled anathema at one another. Of itself this conflict could not have definitively separated the Eastern and the Western Churches; it was only the immediately succeeding period that widened the break into a real schism. If, from the turn of the seventh century, the Greek Church, rigid in her tradition, and the Latin Church, buoyant with the influx of newer peoples, went more and more their separate ways, this process reached its final stage in the epoch of the Gregorian Reform. Confronting a Western Christendom which called into being the crusading movement and enabled the papacy to assume the leadership of the Christian world, the apprehensive Greeks regarded the prolonged separation as quite proper. An exact knowledge of the Gregorian Reform is the prerequisite to an understanding of the Schism. Hence, its course is appropriately included in this volume.

Several authors collaborated in this volume. Hans-Georg Beck undertook the history of the Greek Church — he will continue it into the fifteenth century in Volume IV — and the General Bibliography for Byzantine Church

History. Eugen Ewig wrote the sections on the Carolingian period. Josef Andreas Jungmann treated liturgy, pastoral activity, and piety in the Early Middle Ages. The writer of these lines dealt with the Saxon and Early Salian periods and the Gregorian Reform, compiled the General Bibliography for the Western Church, and edited the volume as a whole.

In regard to the bibliography, the crux of every handbook, it is to be noted that the individual chapters were produced in a period of about five years. The authors made every effort to add to the already completed chapters studies that appeared later. Special care was devoted to the General Bibliography.

Sincere thanks are extended to those already mentioned and to Herder Publishers for an appreciative and devoted cooperation.

Friedrich Kempf

PREFACE TO THE ENGLISH EDITION

Few periods in the history of Western civilization are of greater significance than the era which witnessed the emancipation of the papacy from the influence of Byzantium and its *rapprochement* with the newly emerging Carolingian *imperium*. In a sense the perduring characteristics of the next millennium were solidified during this epoch, universalism, feudal social structure, and a deep penetration of Latin Christian cultural elements.

While the Church in the West adjusted itself to the Muslim conquests and the conversion of the Germanic peoples, the East grappled with the problems of Iconoclasm, Adoptianism, the challenge of secular Hellenism, and the conversion of the Slavs. In spite of the differences which led to the Great Schism of 1054, cultural and theological interchanges produced affinities which lasted until the time of the Crusades, a revival of hagiography and mysticism, the struggle against the proprietary church, and the domination of religio-monasticism in literary and artistic traditions.

What differentiates the present volume of the *Handbuch der Kirchengeschichte* from similar works is the close integration it achieves in its account of the affairs of the East as well as West during this critical period. It deftly avoids the traditional over-emphasis on the activities of the Church of Rome and offers a new answer to the ancient Hellenic query: Ἕλληνες ὄντες βαρβάροις δουλεύσομεν. At the same time its treatment of the new relationship of the Church and Western Christendom, the background of the Gregorian reform and the great debate on the essentials of a Christian society sheds new light on this central problem of medieval history. The detailed account of the new forms of devotion and the *vita evangelica* movements place medieval piety and liturgy in a new perspective. The study of the origins of Canon Law and Scholasticism reflect the research that has been made in these fields in recent decades. Rounding out the picture of the inner structure and life of the Church during this period are the lucid accounts of the evangelization of Northern and Eastern Europe. With its wealth of source material and its succinct treatment of a wide range of subjects from the Carolingian Renaissance to the First Crusade, the English edition of the *Handbuch* will, it is hoped, fill a *lacuna* not only for the Church historian but for the serious student of secular and cultural history as well.

John P. Dolan
University of South Carolina

LIST OF ABBREVIATIONS

The bracketed references pertain to the General Bibliography of this volume.

AAB   *Abhandlungen der Deutschen* (till 1944: *Preussischen*) *Akademie der Wissenschaften zu Berlin*. Phil.-hist. Klasse, Berlin 1815 seqq.

AAL   *Abhandlungen der Sächsischen Akademie der Wissenschaften in Leipzig* (till 30, 1920 *AGL*), Leipzig 1850 seqq.

AAM   *Abhandlungen der Bayerischen Akademie der Wissenschaften*, Phil.-hist. Klasse, Munich 1835 seqq.

AAMz   *Abhandlungen* (der geistes- und sozialwissenschaftlichen Klasse) *der Akademie der Wissenschaften und der Literatur*, Mainz 1950 seqq.

ActaSS   *Acta Sanctorum* [Gen. Bib. I, 10].

ADipl   *Archiv für Diplomatik, Schriftgeschichte, Siegel- und Wappenkunde*, Münster-Cologne 1955 seqq.

ADRomana   *Archivio della Deputazione Romana di Storia Patria*, Rome 1935 seqq. (1878 till 1934: *ASRomana*).

AGG   *Abhandlungen der Gesellschaft der Wissenschaften zu Göttingen* (from Series III, 27, 1942: *AAG*), Göttingen 1843 seqq.

AHD   *Archives d'Histoire doctrinale et littéraire du Moyen-âge*, Paris 1926 seqq.

AHPont   *Archivum Historiae Pontificiae*, Rome 1963 seqq.

AHR   *The American Historical Review*, New York 1895 seqq.

AHVNrh   *Annalen des Historischen Vereins für den Niederrhein, insbesondere das alte Erzbistum Köln*, Cologne 1855 seqq.

AkathKR   *Archiv für Katholisches Kirchenrecht*, (Innsbruck) Mainz 1857 seqq.

AKG   *Archiv für Kulturgeschichte*, (Leipzig) Münster and Cologne 1903 seqq.

AMrhKG   *Archiv für mittelrheinische Kirchengeschichte*, Speyer 1949 seqq.

AnBoll   *Analecta Bollandiana*, Brussels 1882 seqq.

Andrieu OR   *Les ordines romani du haut moyen-âge* [Gen. Bib. I, 9].

ASRomana   *Archivio della Reale Società Romana di Storia Patria*, Rome 1878–1934 (from 1935: *ADRomana*).

AstIt   *Archivio storico Italiano*, Florence 1842 seqq.

AUF   *Archiv für Urkundenforschung*, Berlin 1908 seqq.

BAL   *Berichte über die Verhandlungen der Sächsischen Akademie der Wissenschaften zu Leipzig* (till 71, 1, 1919: *BGL*), Leipzig 1846 seqq.

BÉCh   *Bibliothèque de l'École des Chartes*, Paris 1839 seqq.

Beck   H.-G. Beck, *Kirche und theologische Literatur im byzantinischen Reich*, Munich 1959.

BÉH   *Bibliothèque de l'École des Hautes Études, Sciences philologiques et historiques*, Paris 1869 seqq.

BeitrGPhMA   *Beiträge zur Geschichte der Philosophie des Mittelalters* [Gen. Bib. I, 11].

Benedictina	*Benedictina,* Rome 1947 seqq.
BHG	*Bibliotheca hagiographica graeca, ed. socii Bollandiani,* Brussels, 2nd ed. 1909.
Bibl	*Biblica,* Rome 1920 seqq.
BIStIAM	*Bollettino dell'Istituto Storico Italiano per il Medio Evo e Archivio Muratoriano,* Rome 1886 seqq.
BJRL	*The Bulletin of the John Rylands Library,* Manchester 1903 seqq.
BLE	*Bulletin de littérature ecclésiastique,* Toulouse 1899 seqq.
BM	*Benediktinische Monatsschrift* (1877–1918: *St. Benediktsstimmen),* Beuron 1919 seqq.
Bouquet	*Recueil des historiens des Gaules et de la France* [Gen. Bib. I, 3].
Braun	J. Braun, *Der christliche Altar,* 2 vols., Munich 1924.
ByZ	*Byzantinische Zeitschrift,* Leipzig 1892 seqq.
Byz(B)	*Byzantion,* Brussels 1924 seqq.
ByzNGrJb	*Byzantinisch-Neugriechische Jahrbücher,* Athens-Berlin 1920 seqq.
CahArch	*Cahiers Archéologiques. Fin de l'Antiquité et Moyen-âge,* Paris 1945 seqq.
CambrHJ	*The Cambridge Historical Journal,* Cambridge 1923 seqq.; since 1958: *The Historical Journal.*
Caspar	*Geschichte des Papsttums* [Gen. Bib. II, 5].
Catholicisme	*Catholicisme. Hier — Aujourd'hui — Demain,* dir. par. G. Jacquemet, Paris 1948 seqq.
CCivMéd	*Cahiers de la Civilisation Médiévale,* Poitiers 1958 seqq.
ChartDipl	*Académie des Inscriptions et Belles Lettres: Chartes et diplômes relatifs à l'histoire de France* [Gen. Bib. I, 3].
CHR	*The Catholic historical Review,* Washington 1915 seqq.
CivCatt	*La Civiltà Cattolica,* Rome 1850 seqq. (1871–87 Florence).
ClassHist	*Les classiques de l'histoire de France au moyen-âge* [Gen. Bibl. I, 3].
CollText	*Collection de textes pour servir à l'étude et l'enseignement de l'histoire* [Gen. Bib. I, 3].
DA	*Deutsches Archiv für Erforschung des Mittelalters* (1937–43: *für Geschichte des Mittelalters,* Weimar), Cologne–Graz 1950 seqq. (cf. *NA*).
DACL	*Dictionnaire d'archéologie chrétienne et de liturgie,* ed. by F. Cabrol and H. Leclercq, Paris 1924 seqq.
Dahlmann-Waitz	*Quellenkunde der Deutschen Geschichte* [Gen. Bib. I, 2].
DDC	*Dictionnaire de droit canonique,* ed. by R. Naz, Paris 1935 seqq.
DHGE	*Dictionnaire d'histoire et de géographie ecclésiastiques,* ed. by A. Baudrillart and others, Paris 1912 seqq.
Dölger Reg	*Corpus der griechischen Urkunden des Mittelalters und der neueren Zeit. Reihe A: Regesten. Abt. 1; Regesten der Kaiserurkunden des oströmischen Reiches von 565–1453,* rev. by F. Dölger, 5 Fasc., Munich 1924–65.
DOP	*Dumbarton Oaks Papers,* ed. by Harvard University, Cambridge, Mass., 1941 seqq.
DSAM	*Dictionnaire de Spiritualité ascétique et mystique. Doctrine et Histoire,* ed. by M. Viller, Paris 1932 seqq.
DThC	*Dictionnaire de théologie catholique,* ed. by A. Vacant and E. Mangenot, cont. by É. Amann, Paris 1930 seqq.
Duchesne LP	*Liber Pontificalis* [Gen. Bib. I, 5].
DVfLG	*Deutsche Vierteljahresschrift für Literaturwissenschaft und Geistesgeschichte,* Halle 1923 seqq.
ECatt	*Enciclopedia Cattolica,* Rome 1949 seqq.
EHR	*English Historical Review,* London 1886 seqq.

EI¹   *Enzyklopädie des Islams,* Leipzig 1913–38.
ELit   *Ephemerides Liturgicae,* Rome 1887 seqq.
ÉO   *Échos d'Orient,* Paris 1897 seqq.

Feine RG   *Kirchliche Rechtsgeschichte* [Gen. Bib. II, 6].
Fliche-Martin   *Histoire de l'Église* [Gen. Bib. II, 3].
FlorPatr   *Florilegium Patristicum* [Gen. Bib. I, 11].
FontiStIt   *Istituto Storico Italiano, Fonti per la Storia d'Italia* [Gen. Bib. I, 3].
Fournier-LeBras   *Histoire des collections canoniques en Occident* [Gen. Bib. I, 4].
FZThPh   *Freiburger Zeitschrift für Theologie und Philosophie* (before 1914: *Jahrbuch für Philosophie und speculative Theologie;* 1914–54: *Divus Thomas*), Freiburg.

García Villada   Z. García Villada, *Historia eclesiástica de España* [Gen. Bib. II, 4].
GdV   *Die Geschichtsschreiber der deutschen Vorzeit* [Gen. Bib. I, 3].
Gebhardt-Grundmann   *Handbuch der deutschen Geschichte* [Gen. Bib. II, 2].
Geiselmann   J. R. Geiselmann, *Die Eucharistielehre der Vorscholastik,* Paderborn 1926.
GGA   *Göttingische Gelehrte Anzeigen,* Berlin 1738 seqq.
Giesebrecht *Geschichte der deutschen Kaiserzeit* [Gen. Bib. II, 2].
Glotz   *Histoire Générale,* ed. by G. Glotz: *Le Moyen Âge* [Gen. Bib. II, 1 a].
Gr   *Gregorianum,* Rome 1920 seqq.
GRM   *Germanisch-Romanische Monatsschrift,* Heidelberg 1909–42 and 1951 seqq.
Grumel Reg   V. Grumel, *Les Regestes des actes du patriarcat de Constantinople,* Fasc. 1–3, Kadiköy 1932–47.

Haller   *Das Papsttum. Idee und Wirklichkeit* [Gen. Bib. II, 5].
Hartmann   *Geschichte Italiens im Mittelalter* [Gen. Bib. II, 2].
Hauck KD   *Kirchengeschichte Deutschlands* [Gen. Bib. II, 4].
Hefele-Leclercq   *Histoire des conciles* [Gen. Bib. II, 5].
Hesbert   R. J. Hesbert, *Antiphonale Missarum sextuplex,* Brussels 1935.
HJ   *Historisches Jahrbuch der Görres-Gesellschaft,* (Cologne 1880 seqq.), Munich 1950 seqq.
HS   *Hispania Sacra,* Madrid 1948 seqq.
HThR   *The Harvard Theological Review,* Cambridge, Mass., 1908.
HV   *Historische Vierteljahresschrift,* Leipzig 1898–1937 (till 1898: *DZGw*)
HZ   *Historische Zeitschrift,* Munich 1859 seqq.

IER   *The Irish Ecclesiastical Record,* Dublin 1864 seqq.
Ital. Pont. P. Kehr, *Regesta Pontificum Romanorum: Italia Pontificia* [Gen. Bib. I, 5].

Jacob-Hohenleutner   *Quellenkunde der deutschen Geschichte* [Gen. Bib. I, 2].
Jaffé   *Regesta Pontificum Romanorum* [Gen. Bib. I, 5].
JbbDG   *Jahrbücher der deutschen Geschichte* [Gen. Bib. II, 2].
JEH   *The Journal of Ecclesiastical History,* London 1950 seqq.
JLW   *Jahrbuch für Liturgiewissenschaft,* Münster 1921–41 (now *ALW*).
JÖByzG   *Jahrbuch der österreichischen byzantinischen Gesellschaft,* Vienna 1951 seqq.
Jungmann LE J. A. Jungmann, *Liturgisches Erbe und pastorale Gegenwart,* Innsbruck–Vienna–Munich 1960.
Jungmann MS *Missarum sollemnia* [Gen. Bib. II, 10].

KRA   *Kirchenrechtliche Abhandlungen,* intro. by U. Stutz, Stuttgart 1902 seqq.
Künstle   K. Künstle, *Ikonographie der christlichen Kunst,* 2 vols., Freiburg 1926–28.

Lietzmann SG   H. Lietzmann, *Das Sacramentarium Gregorianum nach dem Aachener Urexemplar* (*Liturgische Quellen* 3), Münster 1921.

LQF   *Liturgiegeschichtliche Quellen und Forschungen,* Münster 1909–40, 1957 seqq.

LThK   *Lexikon für Theologie und Kirche,* ed. by J. Höfer and K. Rahner, Freiburg, 2nd ed. 1957 seqq.

LuM   *Liturgie und Mönchtum, Laacher Hefte,* (Freiburg i. Br.) Maria Laach 1948 seqq.

MA   *Le Moyen-âge. Revue d'histoire et de philologie,* Paris, then Brussels: 1. Series: 1888–96; 2. Series: 1897–1929; 3. Series: 1930–41; 4. Series: 1946 seqq.

MAH   *Mélanges d'archéologie et d'histoire,* Paris 1880 seqq.

Manitius   *Geschichte der lateinischen Literatur im Mittelalter* [Gen. Bib. II, 11].

Mansi   *Sacrorum conciliorum . . . collectio* [Gen. Bib. I, 4].

Martène R   E. Martène, *De antiquis Ecclesiae ritibus,* I–IV, Antwerp 1736–38.

MG   *Monumenta Germaniae Historica* [Gen. Bib. I, 3] *inde ab a. C. 500 usque ad a. 1500;* indices by O. Holder-Egger and K. Zeumer, Hanover–Berlin 1826 seqq. Sections:

MG Auct. ant.   *Auctores antiquissimi.*

MGCap   *Capitularia.*

MGConc   *Concilia.*

MGConst   *Constitutiones.*

MGDD   *Diplomata.*

MGEp   *Epistolae.*

MG Ep. sel.   *Epistolae selectae.*

MG Font. jur.   *Fontes iuris germanici.*

MGLiblit   *Libelli de lite.*

MGLL   *Leges.*

MGNecr   *Necrologia.*

MGPoetae   *Poetae.*

MGSS   *Scriptores.*

MGSS rer. Germ.   *Scriptores rerum Germanicarum in usum scholarum ex Monumentis Germaniae historicis recusi* or *separatim editi* (octavo).

MGSS rer Germ. NS   *MG, Scriptores rerum Germanicarum, Nova series* (octavo).

MGSS rer. Lang.   *Scriptores rerum Langobardicarum.*

MGSS rer. Mer.   *Scriptores rerum Merovingicarum.*

MIÖG   *Mitteilungen des Instituts für österreichische Geschichtsforschung,* (Innsbruck) Graz–Cologne 1880 seqq.

Mirbt   *Quellen zur Geschichte des Papsttums und des römischen Katholizismus* [Gen. Bib. I, 4].

Misc Mercati   *Miscellanea Giovanni Mercati,* 6 vols., Rome 1946.

Mitteis   *Lehnrecht und Staatsgewalt* [Gen. Bib. II, 8a].

Mohlberg   C. Mohlberg, *Das fränkische Sacramentarium Gelasianum in alamannischer Überlieferung* (*Liturgiegeschichtliche Quellen* 1/2), Münster, 2nd ed. 1939.

MS   *Medieval Studies,* ed. by Pontifical Institute of Medieval Studies, Toronto 1939 seqq.

Muratori   *Rerum Italicarum Scriptores* [Gen. Bib. I, 3].

NA   *Neues Archiv der Gesellschaft für ältere deutsche Geschichtskunde zur Beförderung einer Gesamtausgabe der Quellenschriften deutscher Geschichte des Mittelalters,* Hanover 1876 seqq. (from 1937: *DA*).

NZM   *Neue Zeitschrift für Missionswissenschaft,* Beckenried 1945 seqq.

ÖAKR   *Österreichisches Archiv für Kirchenrecht,* Vienna 1950 seqq.

OGE   *Ons Geestelijk Erf,* Antwerp–Thielt 1927 seqq.

OrChrP	*Orientalia Christiana periodica,* Rome 1935 seqq.
OstKSt	*Ostkirchliche Studien,* Würzburg 1951 seqq.
Ostrogorsky	G. Ostrogorsky, *Geschichte des byzantinischen Staates* (= *Byzantinisches Handbuch,* Pt. I, vol. II), Munich, 3rd ed. 1962.

PG	*Patrologia graeca* [Gen. Bib. III, 3].
Pitra S	J. B. Pitra, *Spicilegium Solesmense,* 4 vols., Paris 1852–58.
PL	*Patrologia latina* [Gen. Bib. I, 3].
Plöchl	*Geschichte des Kirchenrechts* [Gen. Bib. II, 6].
Potthast R	*Regesta Romanorum Pontificum* [Gen. Bib. I, 5].

QF	*Quellen und Forschungen aus dem Gebiet der Geschichte,* ed. by the Görres-Gesellschaft, Paderborn 1892 seqq.
QFIAB	*Quellen und Forschungen aus italienischen Archiven und Bibliotheken,* Rome 1898 seqq.

RAC	*Reallexikon für Antike und Christentum,* ed. by T. Klauser, Stuttgart 1941 (1950) seqq.
RAM	*Revue d'ascétique et de mystique,* Toulouse 1920 seqq.
RBén	*Revue bénédictine,* Maredsous 1884 seqq.
RE	*Realencyklopädie für protestantische Theologie und Kirche,* intro. by J. J. Herzog, ed. by A. Hauck, 24 vols., Leipzig, 3rd ed., 1896–1913.
RÉB	*Revue des Études byzantines,* Paris 1946 seqq.
RÉG	*Revue des Études Grecques,* Paris 1888 seqq.
Rep Font	*Repertorium fontium historicorum medii aevi* [Gen. Bib. I, 2].
RET	*Revista Española de teología,* Madrid 1941 seqq.
RevSR	*Revue des Sciences Religieuses,* Strasbourg 1921 seqq.
RH	*Revue historique,* Paris 1876 seqq.
Rhallis	*Rhallis and Potlis,* Σύνταγμα τῶν Θειῶν καὶ κανόνων ... ἐκδοθὲν ὑπὸ T. A. Ῥάλλη καὶ M. Πότλη, 6 vols., Athens 1852–59.
RHE	*Revue d'histoire ecclésiastique,* Louvain 1900 seqq.
RHÉF	*Revue d'histoire de l'Église de France.* Paris 1910 seqq.
RHR	*Revue de l'histoire des religions,* Paris 1880 seqq.
Righetti	*Manuale di storia liturgica* [Gen. Bib. II, 11].
RivAC	*Rivista di archeologia cristiana,* Rome 1924 seqq.
RMab	*Revue Mabillon,* Ligugé 1921 seqq.
RNPh	*Revue néoscolastique de philosophie,* Louvain 1894 seqq.
Rolls Series	*Rerum Britannicarum medii aevi Scriptores* [Gen. Bib. I, 3].
RQ	*Römische Quartalschrift für christliche Altertumskunde und für Kirchengeschichte,* Freiburg i. Br. 1887 seqq.
RQH	*Revue des questions historiques,* Paris 1866 seqq.
RSIt	*Rivista storica Italiana,* Naples 1884 seqq.
RSPhTh	*Revue des sciences philosophiques et théologiques,* Paris 1907 seqq.
RSR	*Recherches de science religieuse,* Paris 1910 seqq.
RSTI	*Rivista di storia della chiesa in Italia,* Rome 1947 seqq.

SA	*Studia Anselmiana,* Rome 1933 seqq.
SAB	*Sitzungsberichte der Deutschen* (till 1944: *Preussischen*) *Akademie der Wissenschaften zu Berlin.* Phil.-hist. Klasse, Berlin 1882 seqq.
Saeculum	*Saeculum. Jahrbuch für Universalgeschichte,* Freiburg i. Br. 1950 seqq.
SAM	*Sitzungsberichte der Bayerischen Akademie der Wissenschaften.* Phil.-hist. Abt., Munich 1871 seqq.
Santifaller NE	L. Santifaller, *Neuere Editionen mittelalterlicher Königs- u. Papsturkunden:*

Österr. Akad. d. Wiss., Mitt. d. Wiener Dipl. Abt. der Mon. Germ. Hist. 6, Vienna 1958.

SAW   *Sitzungsberichte der* (from 225, 1, 1947: *Österreichischen*) *Akademie der Wissenschaften in Wien,* Vienna 1831 seqq.

SC   *Scuola Cattolica,* Milan 1873 seqq.

Schnürer   *Kirche und Kultur im Mittelalter* [Gen. Bib. II, 1 c].

Schubert   *Geschichte der christlichen Kirche im Frühmittelalter* [Gen. Bib. II, 3].

SE   *Sacris Erudiri. Jaarboek voor Godsdienstwetenschapen,* Bruges 1948 seqq.

SM   *Studien und Mitteilungen aus dem Benediktiner- und Zisterzienserorden bzw. zur Geschichte des Benediktinerordens und seiner Zweige,* Munich 1880 seqq. (since 1911 new series).

Speculum   *Speculum. A Journal of Medieval Studies,* Cambridge, Mass., 1926 seqq.

SteT   *Studi e Testi,* Rome 1900 seqq.

StGThK   *Studien zur Geschichte der Theologie und Kirche,* Leipzig 1897–1908.

StudGreg   *Studi Gregoriani,* ed. by G. B. Borino, 7 vols., Rome 1947–61.

StudiBiz   *Studi Bizantini e Neoellenici,* Rome 1925 seqq.

StudMed   *Studi Medievali,* Turin 1904 seqq.; N. S. 1928 seqq. (Nuovi Studi Medievali, Bologna 1923–27).

ThGl   *Theologie und Glaube,* Paderborn 1909 seqq.

ThQ   *Theologische Quartalschrift,* Tübingen 1819 seqq.; Stuttgart 1946 seqq.

ThZ   *Theologische Zeitschrift,* Basle 1945 seqq.

Tr   *Traditio,* New York 1943 seqq.

TThZ   *Trierer Theologische Zeitschrift* (till 1944: *Pastor Bonus*), Trier 1888 seqq.

Ueberweg   *Grundriß der Geschichte der Philosophie* [Gen. Bib. II, 12].

Veit   *Volksfrommes Brauchtum und Kirche im Mittelalter* [Gen. Bib. II, 1 c].

VIÖG   *Veröffentlichungen des Instituts für österreichische Geschichtsforschung,* Vienna 1935 seqq.; 1946 seqq.

WaG   *Die Welt als Geschichte,* Stuttgart 1935 seqq.

Wattenbach   *Deutschlands Geschichtsquellen im Mittelalter* [Gen. Bib. I, 2].

Wattenbach-Holtzmann   *Deutschlands Geschichtsquellen im Mittelalter. Deutsche Kaiserzeit* [Gen. Bib. I, 2].

Wattenbach-Levison   *Deutschlands Geschichtsquellen im Mittelalter. Vorzeit und Karolinger* [Gen. Bib. I, 2].

Watterich   *Pontificum Romanorum Vitae* [Gen. Bib. I, 5].

ZBLG   *Zeitschrift für Bayerische Landesgeschichte,* Munich 1928 seqq.

ZGObrh   *Zeitschrift für die Geschichte des Oberrheins,* Karlsruhe 1851 seqq.

ZKG   *Zeitschrift für Kirchengeschichte* (Gotha), Stuttgart 1876 seqq.

ZKTh   *Zeitschrift für Katholische Theologie* (Innsbruck), Vienna 1877 seqq.

ZRGG   *Zeitschrift für Religions- und Geistesgeschichte,* Marburg 1948 seqq.

ZSavRGgerm   *Zeitschrift der Savigny-Stiftung für Rechtsgeschichte, Germanistische Abteilung,* Weimar 1863 seqq.

ZSavRGkan   *Zeitschrift der Savigny-Stiftung für Rechtsgeschichte, Kanonistische Abteilung,* Weimar 1911 seqq.

ZSKG   *Zeitschrift für Schweizer Kirchengeschichte,* Fribourg 1907 seqq.

PART ONE

The Church under Lay Domination

The Papacy's Alienation from Byzantium and Rapprochement with the Franks

CHAPTER 1

Christendom at the Beginning of the Eighth Century

Dark clouds hung over the Christian world as the seventh century gave way to the eighth. The entry of the Anglo-Saxons into the circle of Christian peoples must have been of little significance to contemporaries, compared with the loss of the two ancient and highly civilized Christian lands which were buried in the second Muslim flood: Africa and Spain. The great age of Latin Africa was past when the catastrophe loomed. Justinian had recovered for the Empire provinces much reduced in size, but they had experienced an "Indian Summer" under Byzantine rule. In the controversies over the Three Chapters and Monothelitism the African Church had still had something important to contribute and many successes among the Berbers to record. The expansion of Islam, which at first had come to a standstill in Tripolitania, was resumed in 669. The Arabs occupied the province of Byzacena, where they founded Kairawan, the future capital of Muslim North Africa. Carthage fell in 698. Resistance by the Christian Berbers and the last imperial strongholds in the West was broken in the first years of the eighth century, and Africa withdrew from the Christian cultural community. What was left of the Christian minority grew smaller and lost all historical significance.

The Visigothic Kingdom had occupied a leading position in the Germano-Roman civilization of the seventh century. But domestic conflicts facilitated the adventure of the Berber Tarik, who crossed over to Spain in league with the Gothic claimants to the throne from the family of Witiza. At the battle on the Guadelete, at Jérez de la Frontera, on 19 July 711, the last Gothic King, Roderick, lost crown and life. The conquest of the kingdom was the work of Musa, Muslim governor of Africa. While the Arabs were also occupying Septimania, the Gallic province of the Visigothic Kingdom (719–21, 725), Pelagius, a swordbearer of King Roderick, tried to reorganize the Christian resistance in Asturias. Pelagius's victory at Covadonga in 722 assured the permanence of the small Asturian principality, but it did not acquire any real importance until the second half of the ninth century. The

Church continued to exist in Muslim Spain, whose governor resided at Córdoba, but more and more lost contact with free Christendom.

The main power of the caliphate was, meanwhile, directed against the imperial city on the Bosphorus. The Byzantine Empire, convulsed since 695 by anarchy around the throne, seemed about to become an easy prey. The fall of Constantinople would, so far as one can judge, have opened up the pagan world of Central and Eastern Europe to Islam and thereby presented a mortal threat to Latin Christendom. The Arabs assaulted the walls of the imperial city for a solid year (15 August 717, to 15 August 718) but, contrary to all expectations, Constantinople held out. Its defender, the Emperor Leo III, became the saviour of Christendom. Fifteen years later, in the Battle of Poitiers (733),[1] Charles Martel brought the Arab advance to an end in the west also. Free Christendom had lost Africa and Spain but had repulsed the great offensive of the Muslim world and protected Central and Eastern Europe from Islam. The loss of provinces in the Mediterranean area was compensated by a mission in the interior of Europe. The centre of gravity of the Christian world began to shift "to the inner West" (ἐπὶ τὴν ἐσωτέραν χώραν τῆς δύσεως).[2]

A presupposition for this change was the dissociation of Rome from the ancient Empire, which had become a Greek state and had its centre of gravity on the Bosphorus. But to contemporaries this was an idea that could hardly be realized, since the Empire was not only a political but also a spiritual reality in which the Popes lived no less than the Emperors, despite the conflicts constantly breaking out since the *Henoticon* of 482. These conflicts were chiefly religious and ecclesiastical in nature, even if an Italian-Greek opposition stood out ever more distinctly in them. The Popes became Italy's spokesmen, but at the same time they spoke for a religious and ecclesiastical group which still saw the Empire as a unity. It should not cause surprise that Greek and oriental influence reached its zenith at Rome with the restoration of peace in the Church in 681. Of the thirteen Popes between 678 and 752, eleven were Sicilians, Greeks, or Syrians. Under Eastern influence the feast of the Exaltation of the Cross and the four great Marian feasts, Purification, Annunciation, Assumption, and Birthday, were introduced at Rome; they are first attested under Pope Sergius I (687–701). The *monasteria diaconiae,* all of them foundations of the sixth and seventh centuries and first mentioned under Pope Benedict II (684–85), displayed mostly Greek and oriental liturgical practices. They gathered in great numbers around the ancient *palatium* of the Emperors, which had become the Roman residence of the

---

[1] The traditional date of the battle of Poitiers is 732, but M. Baudot, "Localisation et datation de la première victoire remportée par Charles Martel contre les Musulmans" in *Mémoires et documents publiés par la Société de l'École des Chartes* XII, 1 (1955), 93–105, proves that the date was 733.

[2] Gregory II to the Emperor Leo III; cf. footnote 4.

Byzantine Exarch. The centre of the Greek colony was the Forum Boarium, with Santa Maria in Cosmedin. Other Greek quarters were near Santa Maria Antiqua *(Graecostadium)* and in the Suburra, near Santi Sergio e Bacco *(Graecostasis)*. There were Greek churches and monasteries on the Capitoline (Santa Maria in Aracoeli), on the Palatine (San Cesario), on the Aventine (San Saba), on the Caelian (Sant' Erasmo), and on the Esquiline (Santa Lucia Renati). Pope John VII (705–07) had an *episcopium* built at Santa Maria Antiqua, and his successors seem to have lived there until Zachary, who had the Lateran palace renovated.

The directors of the *monasteria diaconiae* probably played a role in the group of papal advisers, although they had not yet been admitted to the circle of deacons. The college of seven regionary deacons, which had constituted the papal council up to Gregory the Great, was no longer the only influential body. No deacon succeeded to the papacy from John V (685–6) to Gregory II (715–31). The group of seven of the later cardinal bishops is first encountered in 732. Stephen III (768–72) regulated their duties in the liturgical celebrations in the Roman basilicas, probably in conformity with an already existing rite. The number of titular churches, whose rectors constituted the group of later cardinal priests, seems to have been raised from twenty-five to twenty-eight at this moment. Thus the circle of the future cardinals became gradually more distinct in the early years of the eighth century.

In addition to the clergy, the high bureaucracy of the *iudices* became much more prominent in the latter part of the seventh century. Already ancient dignitaries were the *primicerius* and *secundicerius notariorum,* who managed the chancery, and the *primus defensorum,* head of the Church's attorneys. These were joined by the *arcarius* (income), the *saccellarius* (expenditure), and the *nomenculator* (care of the poor and pilgrims). The *vicedominus* directed the papal household, while the treasury and the wardrobe were administered by the *vestararius;* neither of these belonged to the group of higher *iudices.* The *bibliothecarius,* in charge of the archives and the library and first mentioned toward the end of the eighth century, also remained outside this board, whose number was only raised to seven in the ninth century with the admission of the *protoscriniarius,* director of the city notaries. All the *iudices* belonged to the Roman nobility, which also naturally included the members of the imperial official nobility of non-Roman origin.

The Greek and oriental Popes were loyal subjects of the Emperor, but they represented the Roman viewpoint in ecclesiastical questions no less firmly than Popes of Roman or Italian origin. The Syrian Sergius I rejected the Quinisext Council of 692, which attached ecumenical validity to such Greek and oriental customs as clerical marriage and various details of fasting and liturgy. When the Emperor Justinian II planned the fate of Martin I for him, the imperial troops in Italy sided with the Pope. For the first time an imperial warrant for arrest was inoperative in Italy. The anarchy in the

5

imperial office, breaking out in 695, further weakened the imperial authority. Pope Constantine did, it is true, go to Constantinople in 710 to make peace with Justinian II, but this was to be the last papal journey to the Bosphorus. The Monothelite Philippicus Bardanes (711–13) was not recognized as Emperor in Rome. At Ravenna the Exarch named by Justinian II was assassinated, and the government of Byzantine Italy was assumed by George, who transformed the imperial troops into Italian militias. The overthrow of Philippicus Bardanes brought an end to the Italian interregnum, but the chaos in the Empire lasted until the repulse of the Arabs by the Emperor Leo III.

Leo, founder of the Syrian Dynasty, energetically set about reorganizing the Empire. But when he proclaimed a new tax he encountered at Rome strong opposition from Pope Gregory II (715–31), who as a Roman had a better grasp of Italian interests than his Greek and oriental predecessors and at the same time was also fighting for the property of his Church. The arrest of the Pope, ordered by the Emperor, again foundered on the resistance of the Roman militia, which was supported by the Lombards of Spoleto and Benevento. The troops of Venetia and the Pentapolis also mutinied, and in 726 or 727 the Exarch Paul was murdered. His successor, Eutychius, allied with the Lombard King Liutprand, who subdued the rebellious Dukes of Spoleto and Benevento. Eutychius was able to enter Rome in 729, but the King supported the Pope, and, since the situation in Byzantine Italy had been exacerbated by Iconoclasm, the Exarch had to give up any further measures against Rome.

Iconoclasm, which, appealing to the divine transcendence, attacked the pictorial representation of God and the saints, emanated from the East, where in 723 the Caliph Yazid II ordered the removal of all icons from the churches. It then spread to Asia Minor. Germanus, Patriarch of Constantinople, opposed Iconoclasm, but the Emperor Leo III, who came from the borderlands between Cilicia and Syria, had meanwhile joined the opponents of images. He had the celebrated icon of Christ at the Chalke Gate pointedly destroyed in 726, thereby provoking a storm of indignation from the iconodule Greeks. A part of the army mutinied and set up an anti-emperor. But the rebellion was put down on 28 April 727. The Emperor now sought to gain the Pope for his idea. Their correspondence, which was protracted through 728 and 729, led to no agreement. Gregory II ranged himself by the side of the Patriarch Germanus, who, following an express prohibition of images on 17 January 730, obtained a successor who was submissive to the Emperor.

The prohibition of 730 led to a bloody persecution of the opposition. John Damascene, a high-ranking Christian official at the court of the Caliph, became the theological spokesman of the iconodules. In 736 he entered the monastery of Saint Sabas at Jerusalem. In the eyes of John Damascene, who justified sacred art and the veneration of icons by means of the Incarnation, Iconoclasm was a final offshoot of Monophysitism. In Ostrogorsky's words, "The Emperor was unable to impose Iconoclasm on alienated Italy". But the Pope firmly kept the ecclesiastical opposition in line and prevented the setting up of an anti-emperor by the troops of Italy. He did not give a thought to an alienation from the Empire. Nothing irrevocable had yet happened when Gregory II died on 11 February 731.

His successor, the Syrian Gregory III (731–41), again got in touch with the Emperor, but Leo III could no longer be diverted from the path he had taken. A Roman synod in November 731, at which appeared the metropolitans of Ravenna and Grado, "cum ceteris episcopis istius [He]speriae partis", expelled from the communion of the Church the despisers of ecclesiastical custom, who refused to honour sacred images and profaned them. What ensued is obscure. Perhaps, after a fruitless effort to subject Rome, Ravenna, and Venetia to his will by means of a naval demonstration, Leo III in 733 hit upon a decree which aimed to condemn Rome to insignificance. While confiscating the papal patrimonies in South Italy and Sicily, he cut off from Rome Sicily, Calabria, and the prefecture of Illyricum, comprising Thessalonica along with Macedonia and Greece, which had hitherto belonged to the Roman metropolitan and patriarchal jurisdiction, and attached them to the patriarchate of Constantinople.[3] Or perhaps he simply disregarded the Italian opposition as unimportant and abandoned Old Rome, fallen from its former height, to its fate. Whatever it may have been, the Emperor took no notice of the warning already directed to him by Gregory II: ὅτι οἱ ἄγριοι καὶ βάρβαροι ἥμεροι ἐγένοντο ... πᾶσα ἡ δύσις καρποφορίας πίστει προσφέρει τῷ ἁγίῳ κορυφαίῳ.[4]

Of course, it remained to be seen whether the "Western" basis would bear the strain.

CHAPTER 2

The Revival of the Frankish Kingdom
and
The Crossing of the Anglo-Saxons to the Continent

The great Western power that united the Teutonic and the Latin genius was the Frankish Kingdom. At the beginning of the seventh century it had reached the first climax in its history, but from the end of the century

---

[3] This is the older view, still prevalent in German and Italian scholarship. The opinion of V. Grumel is different. He connects this measure with the "apostasy" of the papacy from the Empire, that is, with the Frankish alliance of Stephen II in 753–54. *Ostrogorsky,* 142 and n. 1, accepts the date proposed by Grumel.

[4] "That the savages and barbarians had become civilized ... The entire West offers fruits in faith to the holy prince [Peter]." (Gregory II to the Emperor Leo III; see Caspar in *ZKG* 52 [1933], 83).

it was menaced with inner dissolution because of the decay of the Merovingian Dynasty. This serious crisis was brought on by the assassination of King Childeric II in 675. Victor in the power struggle of the magnates was Pepin of Herstal. In the male line he descended from Arnulf of Metz and in the female line from Pepin of Landen; he united in his own hands the dynastic property of both families along the Meuse and the Moselle. The victory of Tertry in 687 made him master of the entire kingdom, with control of the kingship itself, which he made completely powerless around 700. Though Aquitaine and the duchies on the right bank of the Rhine went their separate ways, the kingdom was reinvigorated. But the premature deaths of his sons, Drogo and Grimoald, placed the work of the Arnulfing in jeopardy. This first *princeps Francorum,* dying at the end of 714, left no legitimate heir who had attained to his majority and who could have continued his father's lifework. And so the *Regnum Francorum* had to pass through the iron age of the bastard Charles Martel before reaching the great climax of its history under the Carolingians.

After Pepin's death three factions opposed one another in the Frankish Kingdom: Pepin's widow, Plectrudis, who was fighting for her grandson, Theudoald, a minor; the illegitimate Charles Martel, who was joined by a part of the Arnulfing supporters; and Raganfred, chosen mayor of the palace by the Neustrians and in control of the Merovingian King. Charles defeated the Neustrians at Vincy near Cambrai in March 717. In 717–18 he subjugated his stepmother Plectrudis at Cologne. In 719 there occurred a new war with the Neustrians, who were overcome this time near Soissons. Charles ruled Neustria to the Loire, but had to recognize Aquitaine as an independent principality. Only the victory over the Muslims near Poitiers in 733 opened up southern Gaul to him. In 733–36 he occupied Burgundy. Provence, whose governor Maurontus even asked for Muslim help, was conquered in 737–38. Thus the Frankish Kingdom was again constructed, and beyond the Rhine it was possible to incorporate Thuringia and much of Frisia. An effort was made to include Alemannia too, but it was not completed. In regard to Bavaria, like Aquitaine, Charles had to be content with a more or less effective suzerainty.

A second Frankish wave flowed over Gaul and Germany in the wake of the Carolingian reconquest of the Frankish Kingdom. The mayor's vassals from the Meuse, the Moselle, and the Rhine assumed the leading positions in the conquered territories and formed the matrix of the "Carolingian imperial aristocracy". The *princeps Francorum* provided new means of power for the central government. Since the crown lands and the confiscated property of opponents did not suffice, he had recourse to Church property, which had greatly expanded in the sixth and seventh centuries. The "secularization" was effected by direct confiscation or by the nomination of trusted laymen as bishops and abbots; they then placed the property of their churches at the disposal of the mayor for the equipping of troops. These brutal usurpations produced nothing less than chaos in the Church, and the metropolitan organization fell completely into ruins. Not the least consequence of the secularization was a powerful moral deterioration. Of course, it did not operate everywhere in the same way. The damage was least in the lands which constituted Charles's oldest center of support; worst in the territories which had been subjugated only after severe struggles. Charles's encroachments did not originate in an anti-ecclesiastical attitude. The Frankish *princeps* and his vassals were permeated with a strong religious emotion, which was powerfully stimulated by the struggle against the Muslims. They obtained their victories with Christ's help. Avignon, like Jericho, fell at the sound of trumpets. The chronicle which was compiled at the direction of Charles's brother, Childebrand, saw the *princeps Francorum* in the image of Joshuah. Some day the conqueror would have to be followed by the legislator.

In the 730's Charles's position had become established to such a degree that he could leave the throne unoccupied and before his death divide the realm among his sons. Carloman and Pepin the Short buried their father, who died on 22 October 741, in the royal vault of Saint-Denis and excluded their half-brother, Grifo, from the paternal inheritance. The first critical period of the change of authority was quickly overcome. In 743 the brothers again elevated a Merovingian to the vacant throne, but they quite frankly regarded the kingdom as their own. The subjugation of the Alemanni was completed in 746. Carloman, who had harshly sat in judgment over the adherents of Theudebald, last Duke of Alemannia, at Canstatt, renounced the government in 747. He founded a monastery on Monte Soracte near Rome and eventually became a monk at Saint Benedict's abbey of Monte-cassino. Not political but religious motives prompted Carloman's decision. Since the death of his father he had cooperated with the work of Boniface, and, according to Schieffer, "only those Anglo-Saxon Kings, who had preceded him on this path, could have been the decisive examples".

Roman missionaries had once journeyed to Anglo-Saxon Britain *via* the Frankish Kingdom, and since the mid-seventh century Anglo-Saxon pilgrims, churchmen, and kings had travelled the same road in the opposite direction. They usually crossed to Quentovic (Boulogne) or Rouen and proceeded from there on the Roman roads which led by way of Lyons to Italy. Wilfrid of York in 678 for the first time selected another route, by way of the mouths of the Rhine, since he was on bad terms with Ebroin, mayor of the palace of Neustria and Burgundy. He spent the winter of 678–79 with King Aldgisl in Frisia, where he preached the Gospel. Though Wilfrid's activity was a mere episode, it became the starting point for the Frisian mission which his pupil Willibrord undertook more than a decade later.

Willibrord, born in Northumbria around 658, grew up in Wilfrid's monastery of Ripon. When in 678 his master was deposed from the see of

York, the pupil left Ripon and spent the next twelve years in Ireland. There the Anglo-Saxon Egbert, who also had missionary ambitions, became his teacher. Since the Anglo-Saxon territories offered no further opportunities for missionary work following the conversion of Sussex and the Isle of Wight (681–86), Egbert in 688 sent his companion Witbert to the Frisians. The ultimate aim was missionary work among the closely related Saxons. But after only two years of frustration Witbert left. Radbod, who was anti-Christian, had replaced Aldgisl as King of the Frisians. But Egbert did not become discouraged. At his bidding Willibrord sailed for the continent in 690 with eleven companions.

Willibrord went, not to Radbod, but to Pepin of Herstal, who had just re-established Frankish suzerainty over southwest Frisia. The earlier Frankish mission of Amandus, apostle of Flanders, had reached as far as Antwerp, which now became Willibrord's first base. Around 692 he went to Rome and obtained the Pope's blessing on the work he had begun. The mission then spread to other areas bordering on the Frankish Kingdom. Willibrord's companion, Swithbert, during his master's absence, had himself consecrated a bishop by Wilfrid and undertook to preach among the Bructeri south of the Lippe. Two other Anglo-Saxons, both named Ewald, proceeded to the Saxons in western Münsterland. But this was a premature move. Both Ewalds were slain and a Saxon expedition destroyed the mission among the Bructeri before the turn of the century. Swithbert obtained from Pepin an island in the Rhine near Neuss, the present Kaiserswerth, where he died in 713.

In these circumstances the Anglo-Saxon mission at first confined its attention to Frisia. At Pepin's suggestion Willibrord returned to Rome, where on 21 November 695, he was consecrated a missionary archbishop and given the name Clement by Pope Sergius I. The fortress of Utrecht, which had been again in Frankish hands since the beginning of the seventh century, became the seat of the Archbishop. Willibrord saw to the rebuilding of the Frankish church of Saint Martin, that had been destroyed, and to the construction of a cathedral, which, following the example of Canterbury, he consecrated to the Redeemer. As bases to the rear he obtained the recently founded abbey of Echternach near Trier and the monastery of Süsteren near Maastricht. During Pepin's lifetime the mission prospered, but on his death it completely collapsed. Only after Radbod's death in 719, when Charles Martel had restored Frankish rule in southwest Frisia, could Willibrord resume the interrupted work. The church of Utrecht revived and was again endowed. Charles Martel's charter of 1 January 723, issued in regard to it, introduced a second phase of permanent missionary work, which, it is true, achieved enduring successes only within the Frankish frontiers west and south of the Zuyder Zee as far as the Yssel. His base was too restricted for a new ecclesiastical province such as the apostle of the Frisians had dreamed of. But when Willibrord died on 7 November 739, the foundations of the future see of Utrecht had been laid.

By that time Winfrid-Boniface was already the dominant figure among the Anglo-Saxon churchmen in the Frankish Kingdom. He came not from Anglian Northumbria but from Wessex. Born near Exeter in 672 or 673, he was sent for his education to the monastery of Exeter around 680. He later entered the abbey of Nursling near Winchester and was there ordained a priest. In mature life he decided upon the *peregrinatio propter Christum*. From the outset his aim was the conversion of the related Saxons of the continent, but only a mission land bordering on Saxon territory could provide the initial steps in this direction. And so in 716 Winfrid crossed from London to Dorestad near Utrecht. Meanwhile, the attempt to establish a mission there had failed because of Radbod, just as had Witbert's efforts in 688–89. Winfrid returned home again, but in 718 he left once more, this time forever.

It was just at that moment that Charles Martel had established his control of Frankish Austrasia. In February 718 Willibrord obtained a privilege from the new mayor. Winfrid, however, did not contact Charles; instead, he went *via* Neustria to Rome, where on 15 May 719, Pope Gregory II gave him a missionary mandate and at the same time the name Boniface, which from now on he used exclusively. For the moment the Frisian mission field seemed closed off. The situation looked more favourable along the southern frontier of the Saxon lands. In 704 and 717 Heden, Duke of the Thuringians, had sent rich presents to Willibrord and had thereby shown his interest in the Anglo-Saxon missionaries. And so Boniface went to Thuringia by way of Bavaria, where he apparently gained his disciple Sturmi at this time. In Thuringia he encountered resistance from the clergy who were already on hand. The conflict brought about a journey to Frankland, during which Boniface learned of the death of the Frisian King Radbod. Once again he devoted himself to the mission in Frisia, labouring there for two years under Willibrord's guidance.

In 716 and 718 Boniface had gone it alone, and so it should cause no surprise that in 721 he again left Willibrord. By way of Trier, where a young Frank, Gregory, joined him, he proceeded to the upper Lahn in order to evangelize the still pagan Hessians around Fritzlar and Kassel on the Saxon frontier. He found support in the commanders of the Frankish fortress of Amöneburg, where he established a first monastic cell. His preaching among the Hessians brought his first great success. He now went to Rome for the second time and on 30 November 722, he was consecrated a bishop by Gregory II. On this occasion he took the oath of obedience which the suffragan bishops of the Roman province were accustomed to take to the Pope as their metropolitan. The obligation of loyalty to the Emperor, which was included in this oath, was replaced by the engagement not to be in communion

11

with bishops who acted contrary to the *instituta sanctorum patrum* and to take action against them, or, if this was not possible, to report them to the Pope. Thus Boniface's missionary diocese was intimately linked to Rome. Gregory II dismissed the new bishop with a recommendation to Charles Martel, who issued a safe-conduct for him at the beginning of 723. Boniface was now on the same footing as Willibrord.

Under the protection of the *princeps Francorum* the mission in Hesse made rapid progress. In 723 Boniface felled the "thunder oak" of Geismar and from its wood constructed the first church of Fritzlar, around which gathered a second monastic settlement. In 725 he went through the forest to northeastern Thuringia, where, following the extinction of the ducal family, pagan Saxon influence had gained ground. Ohrdruf, on the eastern slope of the forest, arose as the third monastery. After a decade missionary work in Hesse and Thuringia was completed. The time seemed ripe for establishing a new ecclesiastical province, and in 732 Pope Gregory III raised Boniface to the rank of archbishop by the bestowal of the pallium.

Should the projected province comprise only Boniface's missionary territory? Even the Thuringian territory along the Main, which had been Christian for some time, still had no ecclesiastical autonomy. A papal letter of 738 mentions among the tribes in Boniface's diocese the Thuringians, Hessians, Borthari (Bructeri?), the Nistresi (the Nister or Diemel area?), the Wedrecii (around Wetter or Wetterau?), the Lognai (Lahngau), the Suduodi (?), and the Graffelti (Grabfeld). Hence it may be surmised that the new province was to include the greatest part of the lands "in Germany", to the right of the Rhine, under direct Frankish rule, excluding the politically autonomous duchies of the Alemanni and the Bavarians. Then it is possible to explain the strong opposition evoked by the great project. Boniface had already encountered local opposition from the clergy. Until now he had dealt successfully with it. So long as he was working in remote frontier areas as the director of a mission, there had been few sources of friction with the Frankish episcopate. But the new plan was bound to provoke the Rhenish bishops against him, for they regarded the spacious territories of transrhenane "Germany" as their spheres of interest. The projected province failed to materialize, for, as Schieffer says, the necessary aid of Charles Martel, "which would have had to go far beyond the previous relationship of protection, was lacking".

The Archbishop utilized the next years in consolidating his position. The arrival of Anglo-Saxon helpers made new foundations possible. In the Thuringian territory along the Main arose the Anglo-Saxon convents of Tauberbischofsheim, Kitzingen, and Ochsenfurt. A great success for Boniface was the establishing of contact with the Bavarian Duke Hucbald (d. 736) and his successor Odilo. And Charles Martel's Saxon campaign, set for 738, even opened up the prospect of the longed for Saxon mission. In these years Boniface may have been tossed between hope and disillusionment until finally his third journey to Rome in 737–38 seemed to confirm all his hopes. Not only Thuringia and Hesse but also Bavaria and Saxony were entrusted to him. Gregory III extended the Archbishop's commission by making him his legate in Germany. In addition to the general credentials, the Pope gave him letters to the peoples of the transrhenane lands ruled by the Franks and to the bishops of the Bavarians and the Alemanni (Augsburg) and a missionary summons to the "Old Saxons".

The hope for an opening up of Saxony was premature and soon had to be buried. But in 739, with the aid of Duke Odilo, Boniface was able to regulate the Bavarian situation and to establish the bishoprics of Regensburg, Freising, Salzburg, and Passau, which had been envisaged long before. Bavaria did not yet obtain its own ecclesiastical metropolis; Boniface retained the supreme authority. Ecclesiastical organization in Thuringia and Hesse was now an especially urgent question. Boniface had probably not been able to undertake it while Charles Martel was alive, but the death of the *princeps Francorum* gave him a free hand.

Carloman, heir of Frankish Austrasia, at once sought a close cooperation with the Anglo-Saxon Archbishop in Germany, but Boniface had to pay for this cooperation by renouncing his position in Bavaria. Even in the last years of Charles Martel the emancipation of Bavaria from Frankish suzerainty had begun anew. The exclusion of the half-brother Grifo, whose mother was a Bavarian princess, led to the break between the Carolingians and Duke Odilo. Boniface had at first counted upon Grifo, but he promptly took hold of Carloman's hand, for there now opened up for him the prospect of a reform of the Church in the Frankish Kingdom. In 742 occurred the founding of the "Bonifatian" sees of Würzburg, Büraburg (Fritzlar), and Erfurt, to which was soon added Eichstätt in the Bavarian border districts of the Swalafeld and the Nordgau, ceded to the Franks. The first Frankish reform council met on 21 April 743. It was followed in March 744 by the reform councils of Les Estinnes in Hainaut (Carloman's territory) and Soissons (Pepin's territory).

The three Bonifatian reform councils sought the restoration of law and order in the Frankish Church and the renewal of moral and religious order among clergy and laity. Carloman subordinated the episcopate of his portion of the kingdom to the Archbishop-Legate Boniface. In Pepin's lands the ancient ecclesiastical provinces of Rouen, Reims, and Sens were to be restored. Annual provincial councils were to strengthen the inner structure of the provinces and promote moral reform.

Other decrees related to the restoration of diocesan structure. The subjection of the clergy to the diocesan bishop was reimposed. Priests were to report regularly to their bishop in regard to their conduct and the carrying out of their functions, while itinerant bishops and priests were not to be instituted

13

without examination by a synod. But the ticklish question of the proprietary church was not taken up.

The restoration called for a guaranteeing of the material bases. The full restitution of ecclesiastical property, which Carloman had decreed in his first enthusiasm in 743, was toned down at Les Estinnes and Soissons. A portion of Church property — the greater part — was excepted from the restitution because of the military necessities, but thereafter it was to be regarded as "tribute-paying loan land". This decree was of far-reaching significance for the development of Frankish feudalism.

Moral prescriptions for clergy and laity promoted inner reform. Priests were forbidden to carry arms and thus to engage in the chase and in war and they were required to practise celibacy. The prohibition of heathen practices and the enjoining of the canon law on marriage concerned the laity. Only those belonging to the lower clergy were removed from office. The renewal of the personnel in the episcopate could not be undertaken abruptly but only as the occasion arose in a long-range plan.

The reform inaugurated in 743–44 profited not only the Church but also the reorganizations of the kingdom, as the regulations for the secularized Church property make clear. The two Carolingians acted as kings: they convoked and directed synods, appointed bishops, and created ecclesiastical provinces. "The principle of the territorial Church began to consolidate itself even in a monarchical and theocratic sense, not least under the stamp of Anglo-Saxon models . . . It corresponded to the usages of English legislation that the decrees of councils should no longer be promulgated as episcopal decrees, as in the Merovingian period, but as enactments of the ruler, as capitularies . . Furthermore, it was something new that Carloman and . . . Pepin . . . combined their first synods with an assembly of the secular magnates of the kingdom . . No really active role pertained to the Pope. He stood in the background as guardian and witness of the true faith and ancient morality, as the highest tribunal, to which respect was due . . . The task looming before Boniface corresponded to the role which Archbishop Theodore had been once called upon to play in the Church of his homeland" (Schieffer).

In these years Boniface was at the height of his creative activity. But the three reform councils meant only a beginning, not a completion, and the completion of the job was not granted to the Archbishop-Legate. Apart from the "Bonifatian" bishops, only those of Cologne and Strasbourg took part in the first reform synod. The opposition in the Austrasian episcopate was thus still strong. The names of those present at Les Estinnes are not known. Twenty-three bishops appeared at Soissons, all of them from the provinces of Reims, Rouen, and Sens. The reorganization of the province of Tours and of the sees in Burgundy and Provence could thus not yet be undertaken, and Aquitaine, like Bavaria, held aloof.

The programme of 743 was not to be entirely implemented, even in

Francia. The restoration of the three Western ecclesiastical provinces did not take place. The application for the grant of the *pallium* was sustained only for Grimo of Rouen. At first the restoration seemed to make better progress in Austrasia. A council of the whole Frankish Kingdom in 745 assigned Cologne to Boniface as a metropolitan see and deposed Bishop Gewiliob of Mainz, who had become guilty of shedding blood. The province of Cologne was to comprise the Rhenish sees from Speyer to Utrecht and the Meuse see of Tongres-Liège. Thus the province of Trier was excluded. Apart from this concession to the principal opponent, Milo of Trier, nothing else was done. The restoration of the metropolitan organization foundered also in Austrasia. The synod which met in 747 under the presidency of the Archbishop-Legate was indeed an imposing exhibition by the friends of reform in Austrasia and Neustria, but it did not obtain ratification by the Carolingians. In the same year Boniface lost his strongest support through Carloman's retirement. Pepin had all along represented a more cautious ecclesiastical policy. Now, having pushed aside his nephew Drogo and assumed the government in the entire kingdom, he had all the more to avoid opposition by the magnates. Boniface withdrew into the background.

Boniface remained Archbishop and Legate, but the Frankish realm was no longer the scene of his activity. The closing years of his life were devoted to the care of the more restricted sphere of Hesse and Thuringia and of his mainly Anglo-Saxon assistants. More prominent now were the abbey of Fulda, founded in 744, and the bishopric of Mainz, given to him in 746–47 on the collapse of the Cologne project. Fulda had been planned from the start as a great monastic civilizing center and had been organized on the model of the Benedictine archabbey of Montecassino by Boniface's pupil, Sturmi. Fulda lay in the diocese of Würzburg but on the extreme northern edge, and, in accord with the intention of the founder, it was to serve especially for the Christian penetration of the dioceses of Büraburg-Fritzlar and Erfurt "prope marcam paganorum". Hence in 751 Boniface obtained from Pope Zachary a privilege of exemption for the abbey, which freed it from the authority of the Bishop of Würzburg.[1] He thereby created in his old sphere of activity an "archiepiscopal enclave" with which he kept in closest touch from Mainz. As his successor at Mainz he chose his Anglo-Saxon pupil Lul. Pope Zachary acquiesced in Boniface's designs and allowed him in 748 to appoint a coadjutor bishop with a view to the succession. But it was not until 752 that Boniface consecrated him. For his plan he needed Pepin's consent; it was finally obtained through the good offices of Fulrad, Abbot of Saint-Denis. Apparently he then sought to establish in law the union of Mainz and Hesse-Thuringia, which for the time being was merely a personal

---

[1] According to W. Schwarz, *Jurisdicio und Condicio*, 91 ff., there was question of a papal privilege of protection, which assured the abbey's autonomy but did not infringe on the diocesan bishop's right of consecration.

union, by having Büraburg and Erfurt recognized as suffragans of Mainz. He was thus preparing the way whereby his successor Lul would later achieve the inclusion of the two fields of Boniface's missionary activity within the diocese of Mainz.

The Anglo-Saxon mission territory of Frisia also remained subject to Boniface. In 741 the Archbishop-Legate had here appointed a bishop as Willibrord's successor and had given the abbey of Saint Martin at Utrecht to his Frankish disciple Gregory. When the see of Utrecht again fell vacant in 752–53, Hildegar of Cologne wanted to incorporate it into his diocese. But Boniface was able to defeat the claim of Cologne with the aid of Pepin, who in 753 committed the direction of the Frisian Church to him personally. In the very same year Boniface set out on the Frisian journey on which his life was to reach fulfillment. In the exercise of his office of shepherd of souls in Frisia, when on 5 June 754, within the Pentecost octave, he was intending to confirm some neophytes in central Frisia, the eighty-year-old apostle met a martyr's death near Dokkum in a pagan surprise attack. His remains were recovered by a Frankish punitive expedition and, in accord with his desire, were deposited at Fulda. His martyrdom brought about a complete *volte-face* in the Frankish magnates, who now paid to the saint the reverence they had denied to the living Archbishop.

CHAPTER 3

The Founding of the Carolingian Monarchy
and
The Progress of the Reform

From 747 the destiny of the Frankish Kingdom was in the hands of the Mayor Pepin. Born in 714, this second son of Charles Martel had been educated at Saint-Denis. His father had decided that he should inherit Burgundy and Neustria and in 740 had sent him to Burgundy with his uncle Childebrand. The young prince grew up in a Frankish *milieu* — he was a stranger to the Anglo-Saxons.

The men who directed Pepin's education at Saint-Denis are unknown to us. But under Charles Martel we encounter a churchman who can be compared with Willibrord and Boniface as a typical representative of the religious forces still alive in the Frankish Church — Pirmin, "apostle of the Alemanni". Pirmin's "earthly homeland" has been a subject of controversy for years, but it is of no importance in comparison with his intellectual world, which was certainly stamped by the monastic culture of southern Gaul and displayed a clearly Spanish element. Perhaps the father of Alemannian monasticism, who, in the manner of the Irish, had received episcopal con-

secration but represented the Benedictine rule and founded a monastic congregation resembling those of Fructuosus of Braga, was a refugee from
Spain or Septimania. It seems that the Burgundian abbey of Flavigny, in the
diocese of Autun, was one of the stops on his route. He emerged into history
in 724, when, with the cooperation of Charles Martel, he founded the abbey
of Reichenau. Strained relations with the Duke of the Alemanni, and perhaps
also with the Bishop of Constance, led to his expulsion. He went to Alsace,
where in 728 he established the abbey of Murbach, to which Charles Martel
granted a charter of protection. From Reichenau was founded the Rhaetian
monastery of Pfäfers in the diocese of Chur; from Murbach, the Leodegarcella
at Lucerne. Pirmin himself worked thenceforth in the dioceses of Strasbourg
and Metz. His pupil Eddo became Bishop of Strasbourg in 734. The monasteries of Neuweiler and Hornbach in the diocese of Metz owed their origin
to Pirmin. When the see of Basel was revived on the dissolution of the
Alsatian duchy in 739 and Strasbourg was compensated for the loss of the
Sundgau by means of the Ortenau, Pirmin emerged as a monastic founder
in the Ortenau too, with the establishing of Gengenbach (after 748) and the
reform of Schwarzach (before 749) and Schuttern. He resided in the abbey
of Hornbach, and there he died in 753.

Hornbach was the principal monastery of the Wido, a powerful Frankish
noble family, to which belonged Milo of Trier, the chief opponent of Boniface
in Austrasia. The founding and reform of the Ortenau monasteries was made
possible by the assistance of another Frankish magnate from the Moselle
country, Duke Rothard, who after 746 functioned with Warin as governor
in Alemannia and introduced there the Carolingian county organization. For
his part, Rothard was on intimate terms with the men who, under Pepin,
were to assume the leadership of the Frankish Church — with Chrodegang of
Metz, who came from the Meuse homeland of the Pepinids, and Fulrad of
Saint-Denis, a Moselle countryman of the Arnulfings. Fulrad belonged to
Pepin's chapel. Chrodegang had served as *referendarius* under Charles Martel
and in 742 had received the see of Metz. As Bishop of Metz he founded the
model abbey of Gorze in 748, from which monks were sent to Gengenbach
and in 764 to Lorsch, a foundation of Chancor, Count of the Rheingau.

Fulrad first became prominent at a decisive turning point in Frankish
history. Following his brother Carloman's retirement, Pepin had assumed the
government of Austrasia without opposition, but he had to proceed once
more against his half-brother Grifo, who, having been pardoned, was plotting
revolts with Saxon and Bavarian help. Quiet did not ensue until after two
victorious campaigns against Bavaria (747) and Saxony (748). "Quievit terra a
proeliis annis duobus", remarked the semi-official chronicle of Pepin's uncle
Childebrand, alluding to the Book of Joshuah, thereby underlining the
providential character of this peace. Then Pepin dispatched his chaplain
Fulrad and Bishop Burchard of Würzburg to Pope Zachary with the cele-

brated question: "de regibus in Francia, qui illis temporibus non habentes regalem potestatem, si bene fuisset an non". The two envoys returned with the papal answer: "ut melius esset, illum regem vocari, qui potestatem haberet, quam illum qui sine regali potestate manebat, ut non conturbaretur ordo ..."[1] At the end of 751 Pepin was elected King by the Franks, raised to the throne, and anointed by the Frankish bishops. The last Merovingian was sent to a monastery.

Scarcely ninety years earlier the Pepinid Grimoald had snatched at the crown for his son, but the *coup d'état* had failed. Grimoald had kept to the forms of the secular law, having his son adopted into the royal Merovingian family. Pepin's election and enthronement also complied with Germanic law, which, however, was now complemented and reinforced by the royal anointing, borrowed from the Old Testament. The recourse to the Old Testament may have occurred spontaneously, and it was also suggested by the liturgy. But anointing had already been customary among the Visigoths in Spain, and it is by no means impossible that the Visigothic model may have had an impact in the Frankish Kingdom. In the early Carolingian age it was not only Pirmin's circle, which was connected with Chrodegang, that attested the Spanish cultural stream. Another witness was the spread of the great Spanish canonical collection, the *Collectio Hispana,* which was copied in 787 on the orders of Bishop Rachis of Strasbourg and was then revised at Autun. On the other hand, the inquiry made to the Pope presupposes the influence of the Anglo-Saxons, their regular exchange of correspondence with Rome, which, since the beginning of the Bonifatian reform, extended also to the mayors of the palace. According to the *Annales Regni Francorum,* compiled under Charles the Great, Pepin was anointed by Boniface, but this report is not confirmed by contemporary sources. The papal reply was based on the patristic notion of *ordo,* according to which name and thing corresponded to each other in the divine order of the world. It was, according to Büttner, an "award, clothed in the traditional forms of correspondence", made by the highest religious authority and not associated with any political conditions. The patristic idea of *ordo* thus came into a meaningful relationship with the Germanic idea that real kingship had to prove itself by means of a charism, "the royal healing".

The anointing of Pepin as King was of decisive importance for the development of the Christian notion of the king in the West. The ruler's position in the Church was thereafter sacramentally justified, for the royal anointing was regarded as a sacrament until the Investiture Controversy. The formula *Dei gratia rex* is first met under Charles the Great. The royal liturgy soon appeared not only at the king's anointing but also on great feasts, when he wore his crown. It acquired an imposing expression in the royal *laudes,* which may

---

[1] *Contin. Fredegarii,* 32, *MGSS rer. Mer.,* II, 182.

first have resounded for Pepin, even though they too are first attested for Charles the Great. The triumphant "Christus vincit, Christus regnat, Christus imperat" began and concluded in the *laudes* the acclamations of Pope, King and Queen, royal family, and *exercitus Francorum,* joined with invocations of Christ, the angels, and the saints. In the basic version, determined under Charles the Great, the apostles were called upon for the Pope, Mary and the angels for the King, and the martyrs for the army. These groups corresponded in Visigothic Spain to the three divine Persons — the angels as the retinue of the Father, the apostles as that of the Son, the martyrs as that of the Holy Spirit. And so, despite the basically Christological character of the *laudes,* they symbolically expressed that the kingship belonged to the order of creation (God the Father), while the priesthood pertained to the order of redemption (God the Son).

In this symbolism the *exercitus Francorum* occupied the place of the Christian people, the *ecclesia* — the sphere of the Holy Spirit. Appealed to on its behalf were the great old Gallic bishops, Hilary of Poitiers and Martin of Tours, and the old Gallic martyrs, regarded as national patrons. Thus the Franks clearly appeared to be the new Israel. The same idea was expressed in Pepin's prologue to the *Lex Salica,* with its emphasis on the divine election, the proficiency in arms, and the orthodoxy of the Frankish people, which, even in its pagan days, sought wisdom through divine inspiration, aspired to *iustitia* "according to the degree of its moral sense", and preserved *pietas.* This eulogy of the Franks corresponds to that of the Visigoths, composed more than a century earlier by Isidore of Seville, and seems to have been directly influenced by it.

Pepin's prologue of 763–64 was drawn up in the Carolingian chancery by Baddilo, who is seen from 757 as director of the scribes and from 760 to 766 as sole chancellor. Baddilo was a royal chaplain. Like vassals, the chaplains entered the service of the Carolingians by means of commendation, which obliged them, not to military service, but to liturgical service at court. To this "basic function" were soon added other tasks, such as responsibility for charters and diplomacy. With Pepin's coronation the chapel became the most important instrument of Christian kingship. Pepin gave it a more stable organization by appointing as *summus capellanus* the chaplain Fulrad, to whom in 750 he had given the abbey of Saint-Denis, the most distinguished royal monastery. And the chancery, as the chapel's field of activity, was more tightly organized. In 760 Baddilo became its first head.

Church reform was taken up again from 754, when Chrodegang had succeeded Boniface as head of the Frankish episcopate. The Council of Ver in 755 was followed by those of Verberie (756), Compiègne (757), Attigny (c. 760–62), and Gentilly (767). In the last named the Franks were first concerned with the question of Iconoclasm. At Ver a new effort was made to restore the metropolitan organization, but once again with no apparent success. In 769 only Wilchar of Sens was *archiepiscopus*. In addition to questions concerning episcopal authority in dioceses, the law of marriage was especially discussed. In order to provide material assistance again to the churches of the kingdom, Pepin imposed the tithe by law in 765. It was to be used exclusively for the care of souls; one-fourth was to go to the bishop, three-fourths to the parish clergy. The universal introduction of the tithe was of great moment for ecclesiastical organization, for, through the delimitation of tithe-areas, "the foundation was laid for a new system of small parishes". Chrodegang's rule for canons, composed around 754 for the clergy of the Metz cathedral, promoted the reform of clerical morals. In it Chrodegang followed the Roman model but also borrowed most of the regulations of the rule of Saint Benedict and relied on the Frankish synodal law. In contrast to monks, canons retained the use of their private property. At the Council of Ver the *ordo clericorum,* based on the *canones,* was for the first time placed alongside the *ordo monachorum.* Chrodegang and Pepin also began the Romanization of the Gallican liturgy and chant, which was realized under Charles the Great. Here were already seen the effects of the close relations with Rome, brought about by Pepin's Italian expeditions.

CHAPTER 4

The Beginnings of the Papal State

Since the conflict with the Emperor Leo III, Rome and Ravenna, though still parts of the Empire, had to depend on their own strength and devices in the face of the expanding Lombard Kingdom. The restoration of Rome's city walls, begun as early as 708 and resumed under Gregory II, was completed under Gregory III (731–41). Thereafter the basis of Roman politics remained that solidarity with Ravenna, Spoleto, and Benevento which had developed under Gregory II. The papacy found a more effective protection than city fortifications and alliances in the esteem which Peter, the prince of the apostles, was held in the Germanic-Roman world, not least by the Lombard King Liutprand, who sought not only to incorporate the exarchate and the duchies of Spoleto and Benevento into his kingdom, but also to protect the Roman Church. Thanks to Saint Peter's reputation, Gregory III was able to procure the restoration of Ravenna, occupied in 732–33, to the Exarch. Friendship with Spoleto led the Pope in 739 to the edge of the abyss, since the King, after subjugating the Roman duchy, appeared before Rome. Gregory III decided to invoke the aid of Charles Martel, but the *princeps Francorum,* to whom the Lombard King had given help against the Muslims in Provence in 737–38, sent the Abbot Grimo to negotiate peace. The immediate danger was exorcised, but the Lombard sword of Damocles continued to hang over Rome.

Gregory's successor, the Greek Zachary, in 742 again sent notification of his election and his profession of faith to the Emperor and the Patriarch of Constantinople. Leo III's son and successor, Constantine V, was at that moment threatened by an iconodule anti-emperor, but in 743 he became master of the situation. The Lombard King utilized the opportunity to neutralize Rome by a twenty-years peace. In 742 Zachary had to give up the alliance with Spoleto and recognize the royal conquests at the expense of the exarchate. In return, Liutprand restored papal patrimonies and even four frontier fortresses of the Roman duchy that had been seized in 739. He also once again refrained from an attack on Ravenna because of papal intervention. The peace was maintained under Liutprand's successor, Ratchis (744–49). But it could hardly be kept secret from the Lombards that the independence of Ravenna and Rome depended entirely on their good will. King Aistulf, who in 749 overthrew his brother Ratchis, was determined to finish the job. He occupied Ravenna in 750–51 and in the spring of 752 inaugurated economic warfare against Rome.

When the Lombard's intentions in regard to Rome became clear, Pope Zachary was dead. His successor, the Roman Stephen II, engaged in negotiations and in June-July 752 concluded an armistice. Aistulf expected the Pope to advocate the recognition of the Lombard conquests by the Emperor. But Stephen II sympathized with the people of Ravenna and implored the Emperor to send military help. When the Lombard King learned this news, he sent the Romans an ultimatum in October 752 — to recognize his sovereignty and to pay a heavy tribute to Pavia. The Emperor sent, not an army, but an embassy under the *silentiarius* John. It reached Rome probably in November 752 and was then received by Aistulf at Ravenna. Negotiations continued. Envoys of King and Pope accompanied the *silentiarius* on his return to the imperial court.

The Pope understood that he could no longer expect any real aid from the Emperor. Constantinople was preparing for a new council, that could only aggravate the religious conflict with Rome. In this emergency Stephen II turned to Pepin. A first message, transmitted secretly by a pilgrim in March 753, depicted the precarious situation of Rome. Soon after the Pope sought an official invitation to the Frankish Kingdom. Pepin's return-embassy reached Rome in June and July. Aistulf now proceeded to a military attack on Rome, probably intending to present the Franks with a *fait accompli*. But he acted too late. In September the invitation to Frankland was delivered by two very exalted Frankish dignitaries. Archbishop Chrodegang and Duke Autcar, Pepin's brother-in-law. At the same time appeared the imperial *silentiarius* with an order to the Pope to negotiate with the Lombard King in the Emperor's name.

On 14 October 753, Stephen II, accompanied by the *silentiarius* John and the Frankish escort, left the Eternal City for Pavia. The Lombard King continued to be inflexible, but dared not prevent the Pope from continuing his journey into Frankland; the imperial envoy seems to have given his consent to this. Stephan II left Pavia on 15 November. He was welcomed on Frankish soil at the abbey of Saint-Maurice by Abbot Fulrad of Saint-Denis and Duke Rothard. The King awaited the Pope at the royal villa of Ponthion, southeast of Châlons, but sent his twelve-year-old son Charles to meet him. Stephen II reached Ponthion on the Epiphany 754. Pepin rode toward him, paid him the homage of *proskynesis* prescribed also by imperial etiquette, and escorted him, leading the Pope's horse by the reins. The discussions began the next day. Stephen appeared as a suppliant before Pepin, who, in his own name and the name of his sons, promised *defensio* on oath. Thus was the decision made. Details of the agreement were left for later. Stephen II spent the winter at the royal abbey of Saint-Denis, while the King sought to achieve his goals first through negotiations with Aistulf.

No fewer than three Frankish embassies went to the court of Pavia in 754, but the Lombard King proved to be an obstinate and dangerous opponent. He knew that among the Frankish magnates there was strong opposition to a military intervention in Italy. And, as a matter of fact, no agreement between Pepin and the magnates was reached at the March assembly at Berny-Rivière. Aistulf backed up the opposition by getting Pepin's brother, Carloman, to undertake a journey into the Frankish Kingdom. This danger brought the Pope and the Frankish King even closer together. Stephen loaned Pepin his spiritual authority so that he could relegate Carloman and his sons to a monastery. And at Easter 754, at the assembly of Quierzy near Laon, Pepin obtained a decision for the Italian campaign. The King apparently gave the Pope in writing a promise to guarantee the territorial status of Rome and Ravenna, of Venetia and Istria, and the autonomy of Spoleto and Benevento.[1] The two partners concluded a pact of friendship. Shortly before the departure for the campaign, Stephen at Saint-Denis solemnly anointed Pepin and his sons Charles and Carloman as Kings. He excluded the collateral line of the Pepinids from the kingship and bestowed upon the three Kings of the Franks the title of *patricius* as the expression of their protectorate over Rome, but it is uncertain whether he did so by virtue of an imperial commission or on his own authority.[2]

[1] E. Griffe, *Aux origines de l'État pontifical,* incorrectly regards the *donatio* of Quierzy, given only in extracts in the *Vita Hadriani* in the *Liber pontificalis,* as an interpolation. The only point debatable is whether, with the promise of Quierzy, there was also included the grant to Saint Peter of specified territories and of the island of Corsica, without prejudice to their belonging to the *Imperium* or to the *Regnum*. It is certain that "the Popes (from Stephan II) claimed the sovereignty of Saint Peter over all lands freed by the Franks from Lombard rule", and "that Pepin and Charles . . . made promises that to a great extent were never fulfilled" (R. Classen, *Karl der Grosse, das Papsttum und Byzanz,* 543, 542).

[2] Besides Dannenbauer, F. Dölger (*ByZ* 45 [1952], 187–90) and E. Stein defend the view that the Pope granted the title of *patricius* by order of the Emperor. On this question cf.

While Pepin was moving into Italy *via* the Mont-Cenis in August 754, his brother Carloman died in a monastery at Vienne. The attempted revolution in the Frankish Kingdom collapsed. Aistulf began negotiations for peace when the Franks besieged him in Pavia. In the treaty of peace he recognized Frankish suzerainty over the Lombard Kingdom and obliged himself to give up Ravenna "cum diversis civitatibus".

Peace was concluded between "Romans, Franks, and Lombards", though neither the Emperor nor the city of Rome was represented at Pavia. Aistulf evacuated Venetia and Istria and turned over Ravenna to the metropolitan of the city. But he retained parts of the exarchate and likewise did not entirely carry out the restorations due to Rome. The undefined constitutional situation of Rome and Ravenna allowed him to defer fulfilling his engagements and play off Ravenna against Rome. And as Iconoclasm flared up again at that very moment, a Lombard-Byzantine coalition moved into the realm of the possible.

But the Lombard King was lacking in patience. In December 755 he marched on Rome, which was completely invested on 1 January 756. Only the sea-route was still open. This the Frankish *missus* Warnehar took, together with three papal envoys, who in March delivered to the Frankish King a desperate appeal for help in the name of Saint Peter. In May an imperial embassy *en route* to Pepin arrived in Rome. It likewise took the sea-route to Marseilles, but when it got there Pepin was already before Pavia. The envoy George proceeded on to the King and made known his master's demand — the handing over of Ravenna and the exarchate to the Emperor. Pepin replied that he had embarked on the campaign only "pro amore beati Petri et venia delictorum", but he offered the Emperor a pact of friendship. The envoy conveyed the offer to Byzantium.

Aistulf capitulated at the end of June 756. The stipulations of the second peace of Pavia were substantially more severe than those of the earlier treaty. The Lombards had to surrender one-third of their royal treasury, renew the annual tribute of Merovingian times, and make the restitutions to the Pope through the agency of deputies of the Frankish King. Thus did the "Papal State" become a reality. It comprised the duchy of Rome and the exarchate of Ravenna with the Pentapolis. Officials and people took an oath to the Pope, and a papal administration was set up. In law the Papal State belonged, as

J. Deér, "Zum Patricius Romanorum-Titel Karls des Grossen" (*AHPont* 3 [1965], 31–86, with the other literature), and P. Classen (*Karl der Grosse, das Papsttum und Byzanz*, 552). In the form of the title *patricius Romanorum* Classen sees the determining argument against a grant by the Emperor, since, in imperial law, the patriciate was a dignity conferred by the Emperor with no territorial connection. With Dölger, Deér assumes that the territorial connection was first made by the Pope in regard to the *Ducatus Romanus* (*patricius*, protector of the Romans in the strict sense); in the Emperor's view the addition *Romanorum* expressed only in general the connection with the *Imperium Romanum* (*patricius* in the Roman Empire).

before, to the Empire. Pepin did not use the title *patricius Romanorum;* he probably did not want to prejudice an agreement with the Emperor. And Stephen II and his successors made it clear by their coinage and the dating of their charters that they recognized the imperial sovereignty.

The events immediately following seemed to favour the realization of the full Roman programme. King Aistulf died in December 756. His successor, Desiderius, was elevated to the throne in 757 in agreement with the Pope and with Abbot Fulrad of Saint-Denis, who had to supervise the implementation of the restitutions. Desiderius promised, in addition, to cede Bologna, Ferrara, Imola and Faenza, Ancona, Numana, and Osimo. The Dukes of Spoleto and Benevento commended themselves to the Pope. But Rome's exaggerated expectations were not realized. Paul I, who succeeded his brother Stephen on the papal throne on 19 May 757 and sent notification of his election to the Frankish King after the manner of the earlier notices sent to the Exarch, soon had to tone down his demands. Desiderius did not give a thought to observing his promises. In 758 he subjugated Spoleto and Benevento and got into contact with Byzantium, but King Pepin declined to make another expedition to Italy. He was wholly absorbed in completing the Frankish state, to which Septimania was added as early as 759 and reluctant Aquitaine in 768 after long struggles. Pepin was obliging to Desiderius in order to prevent a Lombard-Byzantine coalition. Paul I gave in and in his demands for restitution agreed essentially to the stipulations of the second peace of Pavia. He had to yield also at Ravenna, where a direct papal administration was replaced by an indirect one conducted by the metropolitan.

A *modus vivendi,* unstable though it was, had been discovered with the Lombards. Then relations with Constantinople became Paul I's great concern. In the fateful year 754 there had met at Hiereia on the Bosphorus an imperial iconoclast council, which brought on the flood-stage of Iconoclasm in the Empire. A new wave of Greek emigrants reached Italy, and the Pope placed at the disposal of the Greek monks the monastery of San Silvestro in Capite, founded in his own home in 761. After the Frankish-Byzantine discussions of 756–57 concerning friendship had failed, it was not until 763 that Frankish and papal envoys again proceeded to the imperial court. On this occasion Paul protested against the persecution of iconodules. He got into touch with the three oriental Patriarchs, who in the same year had taken a stand against the iconoclasts in a synod in Palestine. A Frankish embassy, which in 765 made the first journey to the Abbasid court of Baghdad, seems to have been suggested by the Pope and the Patriarch of Alexandria. Toward the end of this year the royal and papal mission returned after an unusually long stay at the imperial court. It was accompanied by Greek envoys, who proposed a matrimonial alliance to Pepin. The Emperor was apparently seeking to woo the Franks away from Rome. Pepin turned down the marriage proposal but did not let the ties with Byzantium break. When, after a rather long interval, due to the Aquitanian war, another synod of the kingdom met again in 767 at Gentilly, there occurred at it a religious discussion in regard to images between Greeks and Romans. Paul's apprehensions were proved to be groundless, for the Franks remained on the Roman side.[3]

Paul I died on 28 June 767, soon after the Synod of Gentilly. During his pontificate he had excessively favoured the *proceres ecclesiae* — the high ecclesiastical bureaucracy — and so his death was followed by a reaction on the part of the *iudices militiae*. The Roman military aristocracy was grouped around Duke Toto of Nepi; the *primicerius* Christopher became his adversary. Toto did not shrink from a *coup d'état*. Without even preserving the appearance of an election, he had his brother Constantine acclaimed as Pope by his friends and dependants. Constantine received the various orders *per saltum* and on 5 July 767, mounted the throne of Peter. The new Pope, elevated under such doubtful circumstances, worked zealously but vainly to obtain recognition by the King of the Franks. Meanwhile, he was the unchallenged master of Rome for more than a year. His opponent, Christopher, had to leave the city after Easter 768, but instead of entering a monastery at Spoleto, as he had promised, he went to the Duke of Spoleto and to King Desiderius, asking their help. The Lombards did not have to be entreated for long. The *primicerius* had friends in the city, and with their assistance a *coup de main* on Rome at the end of July succeeded. He was able to get rid of his Lombard confederates, who had riotously sought to set up a Pope, and, as *servans locum sanctae Sedis,* convoked a regular election-meeting for 1 August. In this the priest of Santa Cecilia, Stephen, was unanimously elected Pope. Constantine was conducted about the city in a mock-parade and on 6 August was condemned by a synod at the Lateran. On 7 August Stephen III was consecrated Bishop of Rome.

Against the will of the new Pope the victorious faction let itself be carried into shameful excesses. Constantine, interned in the monastery of San Saba, was blinded by a gang. The same fate was visited on the Lombard envoy, Waldipert, who died as a result of the brutality. These revolutionary occurrences made Stephen decide it was advisable to convoke a new synod, to which the Franks were also invited. An embassy set out for the Carolingian court at the beginning of September, but it did not find Pepin among the living. He died on 24 September; on the following day he was interred at Saint-Denis in the royal vault. The protection of the Roman Church in an extremely critical moment now devolved upon the young Kings, Charles and Carloman.

[3] In this context reference must again be made to the disputed dating of the exclusion of the Pope from the imperial sphere of sovereignty with the confiscation of the Roman patrimonies and the subjection of South Italy, Sicily, and the vicariate of Thessalonica to Constantinople, which is interpreted by some scholars as the imperial reply to the "apostasy" of Stephen II and the establishing of the Papal State; see Chapter 1, footnote 3.

The Greek Church in the Epoch of Iconoclasm

CHAPTER 5

The First Phase of Iconoclasm (730 to 775)

Iconoclasm shook the Byzantine Empire to a degree that is comparable only to the Arian troubles after Nicaea I or the Monophysite struggles of the fifth and sixth centuries. But, differing from these, it ended without a new denominational split coming into existence as a lasting consequence. Despite its effects on the West, which were especially political in nature, it was to a certain degree a special characteristic of an Orthodox world which was closing and isolating itself.

It did not occur by chance and cannot be dismissed as the fruit of imperial caprice in matters of faith. The hostility of the early Christian world to images was, it is true, appeased in the course of centuries as people learned how to make distinctions and to distribute emphasis, and the historical picture and the memorial led without violence to the cult of icons. But the voices which rejected this development or at least warned against it and saw the present trend as a departure from the primitive Christian ideal were never entirely silenced. It was only in the sixth and seventh centuries that icons entered on their victorious progress as cult images to any great degree, a progress which was powerfully accelerated by rampant popular credulity, legends, and miracles. Numerous miraculous icons appeared, images of Christ not made by human hands *(acheiropoieta)*, of Mary by the painter-evangelist Luke, icons which had fallen from heaven, which bled, which resisted the enemies of the cult, which guarded cities, cured the sick, brought back the dead.[1] If this development impresses us as being a straight and undisturbed growth, this is only partly correct, because the opposing literature was almost entirely destroyed at the command of Nicaea II in 787.[2] But we can still hear voices calling for restraint and sobriety in scattered fragments of *catenae,* in Monophysite works, in citations from orthodox writings against Jewish propaganda, and so forth. There were whole areas

[1] Still best summarized in E. von Dobschütz, *Christusbilder* (Leipzig 1899).
[2] Nicaea II, canon 9.

in the Church which were opposed to images, notably Armenia, and it is significant that the most important Armenian sect which originated at that time, the Paulicians, made hostility to images their standard, apparently for the sake of the "pure Christian doctrine".[3] The great Iconoclasm of the eighth and ninth centuries meant only the effort to clarify this complex of controversial questions precisely and to enable Orthodoxy to arrive at a pure understanding of its own nature. Hence, at the beginning of the eighth century we have to inquire not so much into the causes of the controversy as into the external occasion for it.

The contemporary pious chroniclers and later historians — all of them iconodules — regarded as the initiator of the movement the Emperor Leo III the Syrian (717–41). According to them, he was already subject, by virtue of his antecedents, to Islamic or Jewish influences, and hence he was predisposed to hostility to images, and his closest advisers had been recruited from this intellectual milieu. And, especially in modern literature, much has been made of the influence of the Paulicians on him. But all this is conjecture, for which there is no striking historical proof. In other words, such explanations are accepted because there is not enough willingness to admit the demonstrable existence of an ancient current which rejected the cult of images and the garland of legends and marvels creeping over it. Even the assumption of Monophysite ideas as coming from the Emperor's Syrian homeland is a mere hypothesis. The familiar search for the filiation of heresies and heretics clearly yields only a godfather.[4]

What we really know from unobjectionable contemporary testimonies, the letters of the Patriarch Germanus I (715–30), is the fact that the initiative lay, not with the Emperor, but with ecclesiastical circles — the bishops of Asia Minor. Again, there is no basis for the insinuation that these prelates were, for their part, influenced by any "Phrygian" heresies and that the ancient parallel tradition, hostile to images, of the Orthodox Church and concern

---

[3] N. H. Baynes, "The Icons before Iconoclasm" in *HThR* 44 (1951), 93–106 (the same article appears in *Byzantine Studies and Other Essays* [London 1955], 226–39); S. Der Nersessian, "Une apologie des images du VIIe siècle" in *Byz(B)* 17 (1944–5), 58–87; id., "Image Worship in Armenia and its Opponents" in *Armenian Quarterly* 1 (1946), 67–81; E. Kitzinger, "The Cult of Images in the Age before Iconoclasm" in *DOP* 8 (1954), 83–150; J.-B. Frey, "La question des images chez les Juifs à la lumière des récentes découvertes" in *Bibl* 15 (1934), 265–300.

[4] N. Jorga, "Les origines de l'iconoclasme" in *Bulletin Sect. Hist. Acad. Roumaine* 11 (1924), 143–56; G. Ostrogorsky, "Les débuts de la querelle des images" in *Mélanges Ch. Diehl*, I (Paris 1930), 235–55; L. Bréhier, "Sur un texte relatif au début de la querelle iconoclaste" in *ÉO* 37 (1938), 17–22; J. Starr, "An Iconodulic Legend and its Historical Basis" in *Speculum* 8 (1933), 500–3. In regard to the famous edict of the Caliph Yazid II against the veneration of images by Christians in his empire, which Theophanes reports in his chronicle (AM 6215, 401 f., de Boor), even in the history of the caliphate it was a mere episode and, according to Theophanes himself, of no real significance; cf. also Levi della Vida, in *EI*, 1st ed., IV, 1257 f.; A. Vasiliev, "The Iconoclastic Edict of the Caliph Yazid II" in *DOP* 9/10 (1956), 23–47.

for the purity of doctrine and worship were not sufficient to explain their activity. Most prominently mentioned were Bishop Constantine of Nacolia in Phrygia, Metropolitan Thomas of Claudiopolis, and Metropolitan Theodore of Ephesus. Whether these bishops were in contact with the future Emperor Leo while he was still *strategos* in Asia Minor is entirely unknown. Early in the 720's they went to Constantinople in order to induce the Patriarch Germanus to take steps against the cult of images. Germanus refused but did not attribute any particular significance to the matter. Perhaps on this occasion the bishops also called on the Emperor and found a more sympathetic ear. Back in their dioceses, they began to remove cult images on their own responsibility and to forbid their veneration, apparently without encountering any great opposition.[5] A first imperial announcement occurred most probably in 726; it consisted of, not a decree, but an exhortation to the people no longer to honor icons but rather to get rid of them.[6] The Emperor set the example and had a celebrated icon of Christ at the Chalke Gate of the palace removed. The sequel was a popular riot; some of the soldiers directed to remove the image were killed. The Emperor's measures were limited to corporal chastisement of the guilty and to banishment and fines. There were no martyrs in defense of icons, and the Patriarch Germanus continued in office, despite his discreet opposition. It is scarcely conceivable that the Emperor's exhortations and first fumbling measures could have had an effect throughout the Empire, so that, for example, the entire Helladic Theme would have arisen against Leo III and set up an anti-emperor in defense of orthodoxy. The revolt in Greece is indeed a fact. But the short period of time between the Emperor's proceedings against icons and the Helladic Theme's naval expedition against Constantinople does not permit us to relate these events as cause and effect. However, it is not to be ruled out that the rebels, who were very quickly suppressed, took upon themselves, in the course of the revolt, the struggle against the Emperor's Iconoclasm, to the extent that this was at all familiar to them. Just what is the point of Theophanes's report, not known to the Patriarch Nicephorus, that the Emperor then "did away with the schools and the pious method of education that had prevailed since the days of Constantine the Great",[7] is difficult to determine. Only a later legend exaggerated the story into a report of the burning of the professors of the higher school at Constantinople and of its library.

One cannot speak of an official Iconoclasm until 17 January 730, when the Emperor, after a final vain effort to gain the Patriarch Germanus to his

---

[5] Correspondence of the Patriarch Germanus on this in *PG* 98, 147 ff.

[6] Theophanes, AM 6217 (404 de Boor): ". . . ἤρξατο τῆς κατὰ τῶν ἁγίων καὶ σεπτῶν εἰκόνων καθαιρέσεως λόγον ποιεῖσθαι . . ." *Vita Stephani Junioris:* ". . . καὶ τὸν ὑπ' αὐτοῦ λαὸν ἐκκλησιάσας μέσον πάντων λεοντοειδῶς βρύξας . . . εἶπεν . . ." (*PG* 100, 1084 C).

[7] Theophanes, AM 6218 (405 de Boor).

policy, published an edict against the cult of images.[8] Germanus had to abdicate but was able to end his days in peace on an estate. Anastasius, his former *synkellos,* was made Patriarch in his stead and supported the imperial Church policy. The theological justification of this policy was apparently restricted essentially to the charge that iconodules were guilty of idolatry. It is only from this edict that the Patriarch Nicephorus dated the persecution by the iconoclasts. Theophanes speaks of many clerics, monks, and devout lay persons, who obtained the martyr's crown, but he seems to be condensing some decades. The hagiographical evidence scarcely leaves place for the supposition that under Leo III martyrdom was the rule, but there were individual cases.

Iconoclasm entered upon an acute and politically dangerous stage by virtue of the dispute with the Holy See. To be sure, economic and financial questions were crucial here alongside the religious, and these probably first brought the religious question to its special importance for Italy. In any case, the Emperor's intransigent attitude contributed essentially to alienate Italy from the Empire, to promote the *rapprochement* with the Franks, and to shatter the ancient Constantinian Imperial Church-*Oecumene.*

The intellectual basis for the dispute over Church practice very quickly appeared.[9] The most weighty contribution to the iconodules came from a Syrian monk, John Damascene. His friends in the Empire enabled him to find a powerful response, while he provided the iconodules with the Christological and soteriological arguments on behalf of icons. In addition, the admonition of George of Cyprus may also be mentioned, whereas the observations of the Patriarch Germanus can hardly be counted as really controversial literature. The icon-theology of this period did not confine itself to reasons drawn from liturgy and morality but immediately lifted the subject to the highest dogmatic plane. It fought the war by means of arguments from the theology of creation and from Christology, against Manichaeism and Monophysitism respectively. The opponents were soon unable to remain content with pointing to the danger of idolatry. What Germanus had already called for, a general council, appeared as a necessity.

Leo's son, the Emperor Constantine V (741–75), decided to hold the council, but in his own way. But at first he had his hands full, with the Empire's militant foreign policy and with maintaining himself against revolt.

---

[8] *Dölger Reg,* no. 294; on the date see Ostrogorsky, *loc. cit.* (footnote 4).
[9] On the Theology of Iconoclasm, see pp. 48 ff.; also, G. Ostrogorsky, "Der Zusammenhang der Frage der heiligen Bilder mit der christlichen Dogmatik" (Russian) in *Seminarium Kondakovianum* 1 (1927), 35–48; id., "Die gnoseologischen Grundlagen des byzantinischen Streites um die heiligen Bilder" (Russian), ibid. 2 (1928), 47–52; G. Ladner, "The Concept of the Image in the Greek Fathers and the Byzantine Iconoclastic Controversy" in *DOP* 7 (1953), 1–34; L. Koch, "Zur Theologie der Christusikone" in *BM* 19 (1937), 375–87; 20 (1938), 32–47, 168–75, 281–8, 437–52.

Soon, however, perhaps after John Damascene's arguments had become known to him, he came forth himself as a theologian. He denied the possibility of an adequate icon of Christ, an εἰκών, which would not be an εἴδωλον, with reference to the impossibility of portraying Christ's divine nature. Only the Eucharist, he said, was a true image of Christ, living by the equality of nature between prototype and copy.[10] What else there was of iconoclast literature at this time has been lost. In any event, the ground had now been made ready for the general council.

It met on 10 February 754, at Hiereia, an imperial palace on the Asiatic side of the Bosphorus. Whether the Pope and the oriental Patriarchs had been invited is unknown. They were not represented, and in 787 this fact would constitute a chief argument against the ecumenicity of the synod. The Metropolitan Theodore of Ephesus, one of the first champions of Iconoclasm, presided. The number of participants — 338 Fathers — was amazingly high. The sessions continued until 8 August. It seems that the synod was not under any imperial pressure in regard to time and that its freedom of debate was not curtailed. In addition to the Emperor's theological works a *florilegium* of patristic passages hostile to images was apparently laid before the synod, and it seems to have made an impression. A whole generation later the iconodules still had to reckon with the arguments of the synod of 754, without being entirely capable of dealing with them. That some converts of 787 who had taken part in the discussions of 754 felt obliged to find fault with the *modus procedendi* of Hiereia should not cause surprise.

The synodal decree[11] is extant and shows clearly that the way of dogmatizing in the question of images, once entered upon, could not be abandoned. Christ is not capable of being represented; in fact, every image of Christ, according to what it intends to represent, presupposes either a Monophysite or a Nestorian Christology. Both the making and the honouring of icons were condemned. But the council warned against an indiscriminate destruction of existing works of art. Like the Emperor, the synod also discovered in the Eucharist alone an adequate image of Christ. On the other hand, the Fathers avoided the too bold ideas and formulas of the imperial theologian — another argument against the alleged subservience of the council.

Iconoclasm, hitherto supported by an imperial decree, was now a dogma of the entire Eastern Church. This is hardly saying too much. For whereas previous dogmatic decisions were always connected with the excluding of a group of the episcopate, for the most part of some importance, this does not seem to have been necessary at Hiereia — there is no mention anywhere of any noteworthy resistance by groups of bishops. And one could venture the opinion that the Church would have been on the road to that indifference

[10] Fragments of the imperial theology in G. Ostrogorsky, *Studien zur Geschichte des byzantinischen Bilderstreites* (Breslau 1929), 7 ff.

[11] The decree was read at the Second Council of Nicaea; see *Mansi* XIII, 204–364.

toward images which the Carolingian theologians displayed, had not the Emperor Constantine V forced the issue, slowly, it is true, but ever more energetically, by going far beyond the conciliar decrees.

The fact that the slowly hardening opposition proceeded from the monks so embittered him against them that before long it was impossible to determine whether the persecution was directed chiefly against monasticism or against the cult of icons. The conjecture that the monastic world attacked the conciliar decrees for economic reasons — because they ruined its lucrative icon market — cannot be proved. It may perhaps be supposed that monks were closer to popular devotion, more attached to icons, than were the bishops, and hence, then at least, they did not so much carry out the will of the people but rather formed it. For to all appearances monasticism did not from the start have behind it the overwhelming majority of the people. Instead, the monks' opposing stand *vis-à-vis* the executive authority of the state probably first obtained for them a following among the masses. Much of what the iconodules said about the Emperor was probably only a logical inference from what he actually stood for. But other charges correspond closely with the character sketch of that powerful but hot-tempered and unpredictable ruler, with his wrath and his animosity, which he gradually displayed. He is said to have refused Mary the sacred title of Theotokos, to have denied the saints even the term "holy", and to have forbidden the cult, not only of icons, but also of relics. Where he encountered resistance, he confiscated the monasteries, transformed them into barracks, and enrolled the monks in the army.[12] An occasional provincial governor went even further, forcing monks and nuns to abandon celibacy. The government went to extremes in inflicting torture and banishment and did not shrink from the death penalty.

Considerable time elapsed, however, before the Emperor drew the ultimate conclusions. It was only about ten years after the Synod of Hiereia that the persecution broke out in all its harshness. Leader of the opposition was Abbot Stephen the Younger of Mount Auxentius in Bithynia. The Emperor tried in every way to break his resistance, and his trial was long protracted. It is possible that Stephen was actually not condemned to death but met death by being handed over to the rage of a mob. The monasteries of Bithynia, then the most important monastic settlement in the Empire, were depopulated, because the monks were either in exile or in prison. Churches were wrecked and profaned, and the monastic way of life was exposed to ridicule. But monasticism did not remain passive. From its circles proceeded violent pamphlets against the Emperor, such as the treatise *Ad Constantinum Caballinum*,[13] incorrectly attributed to John Damascene. Despite the persecution, monasticism built up a certain self-assurance and was recognized as the basic

---

[12] Cf. *Dölger Reg,* nos. 324, 327, 333, 337.
[13] *PG* 95, 309–44.

force of the whole Church, as a power which had the duty and the ability to represent the conscience of the Church in view of the lethargy of the episcopate.

The number of martyrs in the strict sense was probably not very great, even under Constantine V. The people's support of the monks left much to be desired. And the army stood beside the Emperor with unfailing loyalty. His policy, however, had become so clearly ill-advised in the course of time that at his death in 775 a reaction was not an impossibility.

CHAPTER 6

The First Restoration of the Icons

At the death of the Emperor Constantine V the tide of the persecution of the iconodules had begun to ebb at last, though the position of the iconoclasts was not lost. Bound up with the name of the dead Emperor and of his father, Leo III, in the minds of many self-assured Byzantines in the army and in the high bureaucracy was the memory of a period of energetic national self-defence against Islam and the barbarian world. Besides, the recollection of the iconoclastic persecution ceased to endure, however deep it may have been, and was interpreted, not so much as a struggle for "purity of faith" as a parallel to the fight for national self-assertion. Constantine's measures in the recruiting of monks, for example, may have made all the more sense in these circles, if the Arabs, as was the case, pressed on into the Bithynian monastic centres. Be that as it may, the memory of these Emperors remained green, and all the more when their successors had hardly any noseworthy successes in foreign policy to their credit. In addition, at least one generation of Byzantine Christians had now grown up under Iconoclasm and had perhaps been able to establish that Church life had suffered no particular harm through the removal of icons. Thus, a restoration of the cult of images could be accomplished only with the utmost discretion and with consideration for the memory of the dead Emperors.

Constantine V's son, Leo IV (775–80), apparently did not envisage any such restoration. Nevertheless, he seems to have abolished his father's excessive measures of persecution. Following his death, his widow, Irene, came to power for her minor son, Constantine VI, by outmaneuvering the brothers of Leo IV. She was determined to make the most of it. The cult of images was very close to her heart and no one doubted that she would work to restore it. *Rebus sic stantibus,* such a policy was pro-monastic, and Theophanes noted from the outset that "the adherents of orthodox piety gradually acquired confidence again".[1] If anyone wanted to become a monk, he could

---

[1] Theophanes, AM 6273 (455 de Boor).

do so without hindrance, and monasteries were reopened. At this time there was established in Bithynia the monastery of Sakkudion,[2] first ruled by Abbot Plato, uncle of Theodore of Studion. It became the source of an ecclesiastico-political movement of large proportions.

But in reality any restoration of pre-iconoclast conditions was illusory, so long as the decrees of the Synod of Hiereia were in force, for the council had regarded itself as ecumenical. Restoration could be effected only by another council, and it also required, not only in law but in fact, a new and uncompromised Patriarch. The Patriarch in office, Paul, was certainly not an iconoclast of any great importance, but he had once sworn to obey the decrees of Hiereia. Was it a mere coincidence that he now asked to resign because of sickness and recommended the holding of a new synod? As always, no one forced him to stay in office, though it seems that even the Empress esteemed him highly. But now she had the opportunity of placing a new man at the head of the Church. It is a testimony to her good sense and her grasp of the actual difficulties of the situation that she did not select a representative of the monastic faction, despite its heavy pressure, but a high official who was still a layman, the *protoasecretis* Tarasius. He seemed to assure the Empress a course that was politically sensible and moderate, and he did not disappoint her.[3] Well briefed, Tarasius also called for a new general council and made this a condition of his accepting his election as Patriarch. A large gathering at the Magnaura palace agreed to the demand, even though not without opposition.[4] Tarasius was thereupon consecrated Bishop of Constantinople *per saltum* on 25 December 784.

Probably in the spring of 785 he contacted the Holy See by sending notification of his elevation in the so-called synodical. The letter explained his promotion to the patriarchal dignity from the lay state, included a profession of faith which contained the orthodox doctrine of images, mentioned his demand for an ecumenical council, and asked the Pope to send two representatives.[5] About this same time Irene also made known to the Pope her plans for a council and asked him, probably in a second letter, to accept Tarasius's peaceful overtures.[6] Pope Hadrian took exception to certain points in the letters which he received. In the Empress's letters there was indeed expressed the good intention of restoring orthodoxy, but not the readiness to annul the injustice done by her predecessors to the Holy See in the seizure of Illyricum. The promotion of Tarasius from the lay state to the episcopacy was certainly in need of a dispensation because it was

---

[2] Cf. *infra*, p. 52.

[3] *DThC* XV, 1, 54–57 (R. Janin); J. Andreev, *German i Tarasij* (Sergiev Posad 1907); Beck 489.

[4] Tarasius's procedure and discourse in Theophanes, AM 6277 (458 ff. de Boor); for the opposition, see *Mansi* XII, 990.

[5] *Grumel Reg,* no. 351.   [6] *Dölger Reg,* nos. 341, 343.

uncanonical, and the use of the expression "Ecumenical Patriarch" was still offensive to the Roman view. But the prospect of an ecumenical council that would destroy the memory of the pseudo-ecumenical Synod of Hiereia and could energetically restore an awareness of the papal primacy caused Hadrian to make light of his hesitations, recognize Tarasius with qualifications, and hail the Empress's plan for a council. He had all the more reason for this because he could probably scarcely afford to jeopardize by a refusal the projected marriage of Charles the Great's daughter Rotrudis to Constantine VI. Be that as it may, he named two delegates for the coming synod in a letter which contained an exposition of his faith on the subject of the cult of images. His representatives were Peter, Abbot of the Roman monastery of San Saba, and the Archpriest Peter. He expressly emphasized his right to confirm the decrees of the council.[7] The oriental patriarchates were likewise invited to participate. But their position *vis-à-vis* the Islamic authorities was such that Alexandria and Antioch could only manage to be represented by two *synkelloi* — and it is open to question whether these were really invested with full authority by their Patriarchs — while Jerusalem was unable to do even that much.

The iconoclasts must have been worried about their position but they did not give up. We hear of heated conferences among their bishops, and this agitation had its effect. Tarasius felt obliged to threaten with punishments such gatherings as took place without his authorization, on the ground that they were uncanonical.[8] Then, when the council met in the church of the Apostles on 1 or 17 August 787, imperial guards invaded the building during the very opening session, at which Irene and her son were present, and put an end to the meeting, with the approval of some of the bishops. The Empress had to start over again. She first removed the guards from the capital on the pretext of an expedition against the Arabs and replaced them with line troops from Thrace, who in her opinion were more reliable. Finally, she considered it advisable to transfer the council to the country. As its site she selected Nicaea in Bithynia, probably in the hope of surrounding her synod with the lustre of the first ecumenical council. Here, with no further obstacles, the council could be solemnly opened on 28 September 787.[9]

In name the papal representatives occupied the presidency, but in the very first session the Sicilian bishops asked Tarasius to assume the direction of the discussions. The Empress was represented by observers. Statements in regard to the number of participants vary between 258 at the beginning of the synod and 335 at its conclusion. The number of bishops was supplemented by a considerable crowd of monks and abbots, who were apparently entitled to vote — compensation for their services in the preceding struggle

[7] *Mansi* XII, 1078–83.
[8] *Grumel Reg,* no. 354.
[9] Acts in *Mansi* XII, 951–1154; XIII, 1–485.

in the Church. The most illustrious were Abbot Plato of Sakkudion, Theophanes Confessor, Nicetas and Nicephorus of the monastery of Medikios, and Abbot Sabas of Studion. The majority of the bishops came from Asia Minor, Thrace, and Macedonia. South Italy was represented by eight Sicilian and six Calabrian bishops. It is clear that a high percentage of the bishops, apart from the Italians, had come to some sort of terms with the preceding Iconoclasm. If they had all been excluded from the synod, it could not have met at all. It may be supposed that those were admitted without difficulty who had at once conformed to the changed situation in 780. Apparently the opposition first took action against all who had postponed their *recantatio* until the opening of the council. To this group belonged the prelates of such important metropolises as Iconium, Nicaea, Rhodes, Pessinus, Neocaesarea, and others. It goes without saying that the question of the validity of ordinations conferred by iconoclast bishops was also brought up. The monks vigorously opposed the admittance of these bishops, and it required all the skill of Tarasius, who was here loyally supported by the papal represent-atives, to avoid any wholesale condemnation. Whoever could show convinc-ingly that he had changed his mind was to be admitted to the synod. Only those bishops who had taken part in the persecution of iconodules were to be de-posed, but it seems that no particularly noteworthy number was so dealt with.

Among the Fathers of the Council there seems to have been no theologian of rank. Only the *vita* of Theodore of Studion states that Tarasius made special use of the advice of Abbot Plato. The bold speculations of John Damascene's first discourse on images were not taken into consideration. Both the handling of the *ratio theologica* and especially that of the proof from tradition were appallingly inadequate in comparison with the Council of 680. The manner of using the Old Testament would scarcely have obtained the approval of a single Council Father of the seventh century. In the demon-stration of the Church's tradition all possible legends and miracle stories made a significantly deeper impression than the well-stated skeptical remarks of older Fathers, who were either not considered at all or were easily pushed aside. Hence it is also not surprising that, in contradistinction to the synod against the Monothelites, the adherents of the previous iconoclast doctrine did not lift a finger to make their earlier viewpoint even intelligible. The opposition maintained total silence, despite the call for a free exchange of views that was proclaimed at the beginning of the synod. In the history of theology the discussions of this synod mark the nadir for the Eastern Church. It may be assumed that those theologians who occupied themselves in a really "theological" manner with the cult of icons were in a dwindling minority and that any decision was prejudiced by religious emotion.

If the result of the debates in the *horos*,[10] that is, the conciliar definition,

[10] *Mansi* XIII, 373–79.

seems so much more sound, theologically moderate, and worthwhile, this is one of those marvels encountered so often in the history of the councils. One must not forget that Pope Hadrian`s letter, which was read and applauded at the beginning of the synod, represented that Western theology of images which had developed, not on the basis of dogmatic speculation, but of considerations of moral theology. It was the special merit of Tarasius, gathered from his incidental remarks in the discussions, that he tried time and again to shake the complacency of his fellow bishops in regard to legends and again and again brought the terminology back to the precise distinction between λατρεία (adoration) and προσκύνησις (veneration).

The *horos* declared the veneration of icons to be the orthodox doctrine, condemned Iconoclasm as a heresy, and ordered the destruction of iconoclast writings. The definition of "cult" itself was restricted essentially to its characteristic as "a mark of honour" (τιμητικὴ προσκύνησις), a term which includes lights and incense. This veneration was sharply distinguished from *latreia,* or real adoration. Veneration itself was justified by its relation to the person represented by the image. The moral value of cult was properly stressed, but no distinction was made between the Cross, images of Christ, and images of the saints. The Christological argument was touched on, but it was in no sense penetrated in depth.

The Empress invited the Fathers to hold the closing session at Constantinople in the Magnaura palace. On 23 October 787, the *horos* was again read, this time in the presence of Their Majesties. After the Empress's question as to whether it met with universal consent had been answered in the affirmative, the Empress, in defiance of protocol, signed ahead of her son and then had him sign. The twenty-two disciplinary canons, with which the acts end, were probably passed at this session. Some of them dealt with the situation created by Iconoclasm, such as the command not to dedicate churches without the deposition of relics and the prohibition of keeping heretical works or of using monastic buildings for profane purposes. Other canons attacked simoniacal abuses and called for simplicity and austerity of morals in the lives of clerics and monks.

The Patriarch Tarasius furnished Pope Hadrian with a brief report of the synod.[11] He obtained the acts through his legates, but in Rome they were wretchedly translated, and it was the defects of the translation that were taken over by the *Libri Carolini* and made the misunderstanding worse. Tarasius does not seem to have asked Rome to confirm the decrees.

Peace seemed to have been restored in the Orthodox Church. But Iconoclasm was not yet dead, and the Patriarch's wise attitude toward the *lapsi* of the preceding period created among the monks a resentful opposition which waited only for an opportunity to break forth.

---

[11] *Grumel Reg,* no. 359.

CHAPTER 7

Interlude in Church and State

The Second Council of Nicaea was, not least of all, a triumph for the Empress Irene. She had managed to neutralize the army's opposition, bind the party of the monks to her, and find a Patriarch on whom she could rely. Her rule was based on the reconciliation of her Church with Rome. And even though the engagement of Charles the Great's daughter Rotrudis and her son Constantine VI was not realized, she was now able to renounce such an outside support for her policy in the Empire's domestic affairs; in fact, she could precipitate a break on her own initiative, since Byzantine national pride seldom esteemed highly such foreign connections.[1]

Irene's exertions were directed ever more clearly toward sole rule. Her actually extraordinary position as ruling coempress was no longer sufficient, and Constantine VI had now reached an age which qualified him to assume the government. Since he could not expect that his mother would retire, he allied with army circles and elements of the official aristocracy in order by their aid — and this meant the help of iconoclasts — to enforce his claims. But the Empress-mother discovered the plot and took vigorous action. She demanded of the army an oath that guaranteed her position as coruler. The troops of the capital were persuaded to acquiesce, but the troops in the themes offered a bitter resistance and in 790 proclaimed Constantine VI as sole ruler. Irene yielded and withdrew. But only two years elapsed before her influence over her son had been re-established and her position as coempress was again a reality. Since Constantine VI did not live up to the expectations of the troops but performed without success, and to a certain extent with severe losses, on both the Bulgarian and the Eastern fronts, and likewise more and more sacrificed his adherents to the will of his mother, he so isolated himself that the troops sought to raise his uncles, brothers of Leo IV, to the throne. The attempt was suppressed in blood. Now the young Emperor had nothing more to hope for, from either his mother or the army. It was his mother's intrigues — the monastic chronicler Theophanes is the witness[2] — that maneuvered him into conflict with the monastic party and thereby gave the *coup de grâce*.

The juridical situation is less clear than has usually been assumed. According to Theophanes there is no doubt that Irene in 788 brought about the marriage of her unwilling son with Mary the Paphlagonian, forcing him to break off his engagement to Rotrudis. To what extent his mother then calumniated the young Empress cannot now be determined, but there was talk of an

[1] Irene's role in cancelling the engagement to the Carolingian princess is clear from her son's reaction.

[2] Theophanes, AM 6282 (464 de Boor), AM 6287 (469 de Boor).

attempted poisoning. In any event, the Emperor felt justified in divorcing Mary and inducing her to take the veil — and he was even more ready to do so, since he had decided to marry Theodota, one of his mother's ladies-in-waiting. Three canonical problems were thereby raised: the question of the grounds for divorce, that of the right to remarry, and that of the Church's treatment of successive bigamy. The development of the Byzantine matrimonial law was not yet final, even as far as the Church was concerned, and each of the three questions could be variously answered. In addition, there was also the Emperor's exceptional position in regard to the canons; it had been brought up on occasion but had never been peremptorily settled. The precise legal situation can hardly be reconstructed now.

Confronted with the complex of questions, the Patriarch Tarasius had two alternatives — to prevent the Emperor from remarrying and hence to make the Emperor's iconoclast advisers his own declared opponents, with the risk of starting the Church conflict again, or of practising dissimulation, thereby pushing a part of the zealot monastic faction, which had not agreed to his moderate policy at the Council of 787, into open opposition. At first he refused his permission for a remarriage of the Emperor and threatened excommunication. Nevertheless, Constantine VI married Theodota with the proper solemnities, the priest Joseph blessing the union. It can no longer be determined whether Joseph was so authorized by Tarasius, but, in any event, the Patriarch did not take any very important steps. In other words, he did not impose ecclesiastical censures on the Emperor but only on Joseph, and then only after the Emperor's fall, and he let *oikonomia* prevail.[3]

Considering the situation of the Byzantine Church, such a procedure is understandable. But the previous Church quarrel had made clear the ambiguity of this situation; the monks who had borne the burden of the recent struggle were no longer willing to subordinate to this new Church system the prestige they had gained and, like the Patriarch, to let *oikonomia* supersede the law. Abbot Plato of Sakkudion and his nephew Theodore assumed the leadership of the resistance, but not all monks fell into line behind them. Even the highly esteemed monk-chronicler, Theophanes Confessor, displayed scarcely any sympathy for or approbation of the intransigent attitude of this group of monks. He aimed to keep aloof from the political involvement of the Studites — all the more emphatically as time passed — and he even hinted that the Studites aimed at schism. And in all this the Patriarch was to be affected every bit as much as the Emperor. They branded the Emperor's remarriage as adultery — hence the label of "Moechian Controversy", — accused the Patriarch of laxity, and withdrew from his communion. Both the Emperor and the new Empress did everything

---

[3] *Grumel Reg*, no. 368. A brief account of the "Moechian Controversy" in R. Devreesse, "Une lettre de S. Théodore Studite relative au synode moechien (809)" in *AnBoll* 68 (1950), 44–57. Further details in the bibliography on Theodore of Studion; see *infra*, 53.

to bring the monks over to their side. When they failed, Plato and Theodore were imprisoned and banished. Thus the Emperor had alienated not only the army but also the ecclesiastical reform circles.

Irene's hour had struck. In 797 she had her son blinded — he lived only a few more years — and assumed the government as sole ruler of the Empire.[4] Plato and Theodore, restored to liberty by her, failed to speak against the murderess with a vehemence like that they had used against Constantine VI. Perhaps it was just this circumstance that rendered them unreliable in the eyes of Theophanes. Tarasius was compelled to excommunicate Joseph. The Empress Theodota was branded an adulteress and her child was disinherited.[5]

Tarasius died in 806, but the priest Joseph long continued to be the victim of the ambivalence which always characterized the notion of *oikonomia* in Byzantium. Tarasius's successor was another layman, the imperial chancellor Nicephorus,[6] well known as chronicler and saint of the second period of Iconoclasm. Nicephorus, Patriarch from 806 to 815, belonged to a family that had supplied defenders of the cult of images under Constantine V. He apparently needed time to determine his position in the ecclesiastical controversy of the day. The elevation of this layman again angered the Studites, and thus they again exposed themselves to criticism by Theophanes. Even worse was the fact that the Emperor Nicephorus I induced the new Patriarch to call a synod to restore the priest Joseph to the communion of the Church. The Emperor was probably acting out of resentment toward his predecessor, Irene. The Patriarch obeyed the imperial order and the synod agreed,[7] despite the protest of Theodore of Studion,[8] who explained that he was not against recourse to *oikonomia* in principle, but in this case the use of *oikonomia* would only lead to a great schism in the Church. Of course, the great schism was once again only a Studite schism. Actually the case was unimportant and obsolete, but Theodore could not bear that an affair in which he had long been most vigorously involved should now be settled affably. A new synod in 809 condemned the principles which Theodore had invoked.[9] Unfortunately, we know the guiding principles which the synod is supposed to have laid down only from Theodore's own pen,[10] and it is unquestionable that he formulated them too subtly. Be that as it may, he had to go into exile again. He then appealed, in great agitation, to Pope Leo III.[11] The Pope, who had only a short time before crowned the "anti-Emperor" Charles, declined to intervene and, with pastoral prudence, urged patience on

---

[4] On this point see W. Ohnsorge, "Das Kaisertum der Eirene und die Kaiserkrönung Karls des Grossen" in *Saeculum* 14 (1963), 221–47.

[5] Theodore of Studion, *Ep.* I, 31 (*PG* 99, 1012).

[6] P. J. Alexander, *The Patriarch Nicephorus of Constantinople* (Oxford 1958), with a detailed listing of the earlier literature.

[7] *Grumel Reg,* no. 377. [8] *Epp.* I, 21; I, 22; I, 24 (*PG* 99, 969–88).

[9] Ibid. [10] *Ep.* I, 33 (*PG* 99, 1017–21). [11] Ibid.

Theodore.[12] With the change on the imperial throne in 811 this exile too came to an end.

The Emperor Michael I (811–13) was apparently more influenced by Studite monachism than by the Patriarch Nicephorus, to whom he owed the crown. Just the same, the Patriarch now had the opportunity of sending his synodical[13] to Pope Leo III — something not permitted by the Emperor Nicephorus because of his bitterness over the coronation of Charles the Great. The embassy which delivered the synodical was the one which at Aachen recognized Charles as *basileus*.[14] In all probability the embassy also sought to obtain at Rome an expression of opinion in regard to the "Moechian Controversy". This would have been due less to the initiative of the Patriarch than to that of the Emperor, influenced by Theodore of Studion, since Theodore's petition to the Pope had so far had no result. Whether now the Pope actually spoke out in support of the Studites' attitude, as the *vita* of Theodore claims, or the imperial pressure was sufficient, in any event the Patriarch in 812 had to humble himself to the extent of deposing the priest Joseph again and making peace with the Studite opposition.[15] With this the nasty "Moechian" business was laid to rest.

It was not the only point causing trouble between Patriarch and monks. Already during the Second Council of Nicaea it had become evident that the mild attitude of the Patriarch Tarasius toward the bishops of the iconoclast period had not pleased the monks. Apart from a very few exceptions, the bishops had remained in possession of their sees. It seems that the monks sought another legal title in order to renew the episcopate according to their own views, whereas Tarasius steered a different course in this matter also. He was no friend of the iconoclasts, but he did not want in the Church a powerful group of deposed bishops, which would have made possible the survival of Iconoclasm and the restoration of the policy of the Emperor Constantine V.

The point at issue was the question of simony. A perusal of the canons of the Seventh Ecumenical Council would cause one to believe that a great number of the bishops of that day had acquired their sees through simony. But if the canons are compared with later statements of the Patriarch Tarasius on this point, such as the decree of 787–88, mentioned by the *Vita Tarasii*,[16] it seems to follow that the monks energetically labelled as simony all ordination fees, offerings made to the consecrating prelate, and the like. In any case, here too Tarasius first sought a *via media*. Bishops guilty of simony were not to be deposed forever, but, following a penance, that is, suspension for at least one year, they could be restored to office. The relevant decree was in keeping with the desire of the Empress Irene and was published in

---

[12] *Ep.* I, 34 (*PG* 99, 1021–8).   [13] *Grumel Reg,* no. 382.
[14] *Dölger Reg,* no. 385.   [15] *Grumel Reg,* no. 387.   [16] Ibid., no. 361.

787 or early in 788 — in any event, with the participation of the papal representatives at the Council.[17] The zealots among the monks, on the other hand, led by a certain Sabas, raised a storm and appealed to Pope Hadrian I. Eventually the Patriarch Tarasius had to give in. He was still, even now, accommodating to penitent simonists to a degree — and this too was taken amiss — but they were no longer allowed to exercise their office again.[18] This is evident toward the end of 790, that is, after Irene had been forced into retirement, in a letter to the anchorite and Abbot John and in a further letter to Pope Hadrian I, in which he submitted the matter to the Pope's judgment.

The quarrel between the Patriarch and the monks had to do, not with the bases of the orthodox faith, but rather with questions of *oikonomia,* that is, considerations of equity in applying the canon law. The fact that again and again the monks went to the point of schism in this matter shows how power-ful their self-assurance had become in the meantime. The legal questions under discussion were questions of judgment — and to this extent the proceedings of the monks against their bishops were unprecedented. The image of the Patriarchs, both of whom are highly venerated by the Orthodox Church as saints, is not lacking in vacillation and imprecision, for their action was also always determined by the Emperor's will. To what extent this was an integral component of the training of the will of the "Church" in Byzantium was not clarified in this generation, since even the Studites had different ideas in regard to the Emperor's competence when he was on their side.

The Church-State aspect of the conflicts consists in this, that the monastic party was apparently unwilling to recognize the real motive of the Patri-archs — not to expose the precarious peace of the post-iconoclast period to any excessively strong tests. The Patriarchs, men of public life, could scarcely fail to note how weak was the consistently iconodule majority and how great the danger of a new flare-up of Iconoclasm. In this situation a firm alliance of the monastic party with the iconodule hierarchy would have been the need of the moment. It was not realized.

CHAPTER 8

The Second Phase of Iconoclasm (815 to 843)

The faith of the Byzantine nation almost always saw the destiny of its Empire intimately linked with its religion, with God's blessing or displeasure. From this point of view the divine mercy had apparently been rather on the side of the iconoclasts and their Emperors than on that of their successors,

---

[17] Ibid., no. 360.   [18] Ibid., nos. 363f.

especially of the Empress Irene and the Emperor Michael I Rhangabe. One who did not share this popular belief could still make use of it for political ends, circumstances permitting. This seems to have been exemplified in the conduct of the Emperor Leo V. How did this come about? The iconodule predominance had obviously been most closely connected with Irene's government. No matter how she was extolled by monastic hagiography and chronicles, the reign of this Empress was a calamity for the Empire. Her unfortunate relations with the army, her military failures, the squandering of the revenues, and the misguided favouritism at court led to revolt. Irene's authority and coterie were swept away rapidly and pitilessly and the throne was given to Nicephorus I (802–11). The stern rule of the new Emperor brought him, in the eyes of many of the pious, close to the iconoclasts, and he was certainly no friend of monks. He did not halt iconoclast propaganda and in some respects his cynicism recalled Constantine V. But in 811 the Bulgars inflicted on him a severe defeat, which brought about his death and cost his seriously wounded son Stauracius his throne.

The new Emperor, Michael I (811–13), was plagued with extremely bad luck in his dealings with the Bulgars, and, according to Theophanes, most of the blame for this was due to the advice which the Emperor accepted from Theodore of Studion.[1] Commanders in Asia Minor allowed themselves to be seduced into a revolt which was clearly motivated by a hostility toward monks and icons as well as by the *restauratio memoriae* of Constantine V. The latter's still living sons were to be raised to the throne and the decrees of the Synod of 754 were to be revived. But apparently it was not possible to gain the entire army to the cause, and the revolt misfired. But when the Bulgars drew their lines more tightly around the approaches to the capital and the Emperor's maneuvers in Thrace became ever more unfortunate, the agitation against him in Constantinople became all the more intense. The iconoclasts broke open the tomb of Constantine V with the cry: "Arise and aid the city that is perishing!" They spread the report that the dead Emperor had bounded from the grave on horseback to ride out to a struggle of annihilation against the Bulgars.[2] Another severe defeat by the Bulgars caused Michael I to seek refuge behind the walls of the capital, whereupon the commanders in camp chose as Emperor the *strategos* of the Anatoliac Theme.

Leo V (813–20) thus rose to power on a wave which clearly suggested the mentality prevailing under the first two Syrian Emperors, and he regarded it, if not as right, at least as advisable to undertake an attempt at a restoration in this direction. But at first he was completely preoccupied with the Bulgar peril. When a treaty of peace had been made with the new Bulgar Khan, Omurtag, in 814, Leo felt that his time had come.

---

[1] Theophanes, AM 6305 (498 de Boor).   [2] Theophanes, AM 8305 (501 de Boor).

His most important advisers in this matter were Theodotos Kassiteras, related to the Syrian Dynasty, the Bishop Antony of Sylaion, and the learned grammarian, John Hylilas, allegedly of the family of the Morocharzanioi. The theological approach that was assumed held that the cult of images was permissible only if it was ordered by the Bible; since this was not the case, it could not be allowed. The really appealing argument, already referred to, was that the rule of the iconoclast Emperors had been a blessing for the Empire. But it was desired to elaborate the theological proofs and so search was made in libraries, with the result that the acts of the Synod of 754 were soon discovered. After this preparation, an approach was made to the Patriarch Nicephorus, probably in the late fall of 814. The imperial order to the Patriarch was at first to the effect that he should remove the icons from direct veneration by the people; hence no general destruction of images was ordered.[3] The Emperor felt that he could rely on the majority of the population. The Patriarch's reply was a decided negative.[4] The veneration of images, he said, was an ancient Church tradition and so needed no express order in the Bible. The Patriarch also refused to have the question again discussed by a synod or an episcopal conference. However, he probably had a presentiment of the danger and sought to have the iconodules close ranks firmly. A number of bishops and abbots, the most prominent of the latter being Theodore of Studion, joined the Patriarch and swore to maintain their unity and to withstand the iconoclasts even at the cost of their lives.[5]

It was especially important that at this moment of danger factionalism among the orthodox was resolutely put aside and peace was restored between the Studites and the hierarchy. The iconodules proceeded into the conflict armed with experience and enlightened by history. A part of the bishops who had associated themselves in this agreement soon bowed to the imperial will again, since Leo V apparently knew how to minimize his demands. He required only that the Patriarch should make one small concession — to remove from the immediate contact of the faithful the low-hanging icons in the church; there the matter should rest. As Nicephorus refused to agree even to this, he was deported to Asia Minor, where, in order not to become an obstacle to the peace of the Church, he resigned his office.

As early as 1 April 815, the Emperor appointed as the new Patriarch Theodotos Kassiteras (815–21), previously mentioned, and in the same month there met at Hagia Sophia a synod which renewed the decrees of the Synod of 754, sharply criticized Nicaea II, and again forbade the manufacture of images of Christ and the saints.[6] But there was intentionally no further

---

[3] *Scriptor incertus de Leone Armeno,* 352 (Bonn).

[4] Ibid.

[5] *Grumel Reg,* no. 391.

[6] Reconstruction of the *definitio* and of the accompanying *florilegium* in D. Serruys, "Les actes du concile iconoclaste de l'an 815" in *MAH* 23 (1903), 345–51; substantially improved in

reference to icons as idolatrous images, "for there are degrees of wickedness". Likewise, the Christological arguments were touched on only in passing. The patristic *florilegium,* which apparently served the participants in the synod as the basis of discussion, probably placed emphasis on the argument of "holiness". According to it, holiness is a quality imparted by God to the elect. No artist can, without blasphemy, claim to bestow similar properties on a material image. The practical implementation of the conciliar decrees provided for the removal of low-hanging images, which were too close to the devotion of the faithful, but to leave those higher up alone, in so far as no handling for religious purposes was attempted in their regard. They were left alone as γραφή *(scriptura)*. Most probably no special declarations of submission nor even an oath to the synod was demanded; it was enough to maintain communion with the Patriarch.

The council knew some success. In contradistinction to the first phase of Iconoclasm, however, monasteries and monks no longer formed the core of the opposition to the same degree. The letters and laments of Theodore of Studion are clear — many abbots joined the iconoclasts.[7] On the other hand, a considerable number of bishops can be named who now energetically represented the iconodule viewpoint. Alexander found the reason for this in the fact that since the time of the Emperor Leo IV monks had more and more been admitted to the episcopate; the prospect of an episcopal see was able to break the resistance of probable candidates in the monasteries.[8] This can be expressed in different words: the best in monastic circles had already become bishops and as such had offered resistance. It may be added that the strong intervention of the Studites under Theodore's leadership in political and ecclesiastical matters, which was not a part of the traditional role of Byzantine monasticism, had somewhat hurt his cause. And, finally, no explicitly iconoclast declarations were demanded, so that many monks were in the position of pursuing their own type of devotion without any real cost. The officials seem often to have been satisfied if they were assured that persons would neither hold meetings nor publicly propagate the cult of images. Only a few paid for their attachment to the cult of images with their lives. More common penalties were flogging and banishment. The most famous exiles were the Patriarch Nicephorus and, once again, Theodore of Studion, whose relations to each other improved under the force of circumstances without becoming cordial. Despite the assignment of a compulsory residence, Theodore was able to make the most of his very widespread

G. Ostrogorsky, *Studien zur Geschichte des byzantinischen Bilderstreites* (Breslau 1929), 48–51; also P. J. Alexander in *DOP* 7 (1953), 37–66. Bibliography in *Hefele-Leclercq* III, 2, 741–98; M. Anastos, "The Ethical Theory of Images formulated by the Iconoclasts in 754 and 815" in *DOP* 8 (1954), 151–60.

[7] Cf. G. A. Schreiber, *Der heilige Theodor von Studion* (Münster 1900), 84.
[8] *The Patriarch Nicephorus* (Oxford 1958), 144f.

intelligence service; he was in contact with Rome and the oriental patriarchates, but the response was rather faint.

Emperor Leo V, inaugurator of the persecution, was assassinated during the Christmas festivities of 820. The ex-Patriarch Nicephorus commented with the remark that the Roman Empire had lost a godless but otherwise important ruler.[9] Theodore exulted that the winter was past, even if spring was still slow in coming.[10] Leo was succeeded on the throne by Michael II the Amorian (820–29), whose character and religious standpoint were painted in dark colours by later chroniclers hostile to the Amorian Dynasty. According to them, he was more favourable to Judaism than to Christianity. The few objective contemporary reports do not support these spiteful remarks. He was not a friend of the cult of icons, but in this he was acting less in accord with religious convictions than with the *status quo* in which he had grown up and which he felt unable to change without wrecking the Empire. To persecute was not in his nature, and besides he first had to consolidate his authority. Thus the exiles, such as Theodore of Studion, could return. Even Nicephorus would have been able to recover his patriarchal see, if he had only made up his mind not to touch the question of icons again. But Nicephorus was not prepared for this.

The Emperor issued a *thespisma,* whereby the entire dispute was to be buried in silence and everyone was to follow his own conscience.[11] If Michael did not consistently follow this policy thereafter, this was probably because there soon occurred a revolt which adopted as its own the catchwords of the iconodules. This was the revolt of Thomas, a Slav by birth. He had himself crowned Emperor by the Patriarch of Antioch, rallied to his standard the discontented, those behind in their tax payments, destitute peasants, beggars, and vagrants, and also clerics and dissatisfied provincial aristocrats, proceeded across Asia Minor, and laid siege to Constantinople.[12] The social revolutionary character of the movement seems to me to be secondary. There is much to support the thesis that its origins were in the imperial court, of a dynastic and political nature, and connected with the overthrow of Leo V. In no sense was it a question of a rising of iconodules as such; rather, this movement was, along with others, incorporated into a disparate programme which made use of every opportunity. It was only in 823 that the revolt could be suppressed. But the Muslim power, with which Thomas had allied, had again become fully active and did serious damage to the Empire.

Michael's son, Theophilus (829–42), witnessed the catastrophe of the fall of the strongest fortress in Asia Minor, Amorion, in 838. Theophilus was a more severe persecutor of iconodules than his father. He was a pupil of that John the Grammarian who in 815 had prepared the decrees of the

[9] Genesios, I, 17 (Bonn).   [10] *PG* 99, 1397.
[11] *Dölger Reg,* no. 402.   [12] See *Ostrogorsky* 171 f.

45

iconoclast synod and who soon became the Patriarch John VII (837–43).[13] He was the most efficient personality among the iconoclast bishops, and the defamatory hatred of the orthodox was directed at him to a much greater degree than at the Emperor. On instructions from the Patriarch, the persecution, especially of monks, was intensified. The Emperor himself was not consistent in his attitude. His wife Theodora was apparently able to practise the cult of images without any great hindrance. But Theophilus had an iconodule like the Sicilian monk Methodius first flogged and imprisoned; then, very soon, he procured for him an honourable abode, even though it was secluded within the imperial palace, because he liked the man's knowledge and scholarship.

When Theophilus died Iconoclasm crumbled. The reasons for this collapse are complex. But first of all it must not be assumed that the entire Empire had meanwhile been converted to the cult of icons. Even as late as the time of Photius there was mention of iconoclasts. But, keeping in mind the uniquely political theology of the Byzantines, for whom the prosperity of the Empire represented God's reward for the orthodox faith, the political failures of especially the last iconoclast Emperors had presented the iconodules with impressive arguments. The sources make known that precisely these political misfortunes were thoroughly exploited against Iconoclasm. In addition, the iconoclasts of the second phase did not follow any strict line. Their *laissez-faire* deprived their policy of persuasive force, smoothed out the differences, and brought about a fatal indifference in their own circles. Another point must also be considered. If in the first period of Iconoclasm one gropes in total darkness in the effort to fix responsibility for the outbreak of the struggle on Paulicians, Saracens, Monophysites, or Jews, the influence of Paulician politicians, of Armenian sectarians and theologians, to whom iconoclastic ideas were natural, cannot be mistaken for the years 815 to 820 and perhaps even to 829. A certain infiltration of court society by such foreign elements, it seems, cannot be ruled out. But Theophilus, despite all borrowing from the greatly admired Caliphs of Baghdad, was making ready in what pertains to the history of civilization a self-realization of Greek thought that again rolled back the foreign influences. Furthermore, the catastrophe of Amorion awaked in him crusade projects which embraced all of Christendom and presupposed its oneness in faith. And, finally, the group of iconodules was more united and no longer so theologically defenceless in the face of the outbreak of hostilities in 815 as had been the case in 730. The period of peace between 780 and 815 had procured for the monks the esteem of the people; they were able to regard themselves as the religious leaders of the masses. And even if these masses, as such, ceased to be their adherents in the

---

[13] V. Grumel, "Jean Grammatikos et saint Théodore Studite" in *ÉO* 36 (1937), 181–89; Alexander, *op. cit.* 235f.

period of the second persecution, this happened, not because of conviction, but out of weakness, and the masses were ready, at the very moment when the pressure was eased, again to make common cause with them. And so the government had no choice but to revise its current policy. The question whether such a revision, in the sense of a legally established *laissez-faire* and not merely of one acknowledged on occasion, would not have achieved its goal as well as would a complete *volte-face* can hardly be decided in the present state of the sources.

At his death Theophilus was succeeded by his three-year-old son, Michael III (842–67). The direction of the regency was assumed by the widowed Empress Theodora, a long-time devotee of icons. But the initiative for the restoration proceeded, not directly from her, but from her adviser and minister, Theoctistus. The Empress gladly allowed herself to be convinced by the political necessity, just so long as the memory of her dead husband was not disparaged. A way was found to oblige her. The Patriarch John VII was induced to abdicate, and his place was taken by the Sicilian Methodius (843–47). Then in March 843 a solemn synod was held which re-established the cult of icons.[14] Thus was ended a battle which had drained off the energies of the Orthodox world for generations. A peace was inaugurated which would no longer be troubled by this point. Orthodoxy was reunited in a new self-understanding, but at the price that religious attitudes which in the older Church had been entirely possible and lawful, even though perhaps not obligatory, now had to leave the inclosure of the Church.

Orthodoxy was reunited, but it also went into seclusion. In the whole of Church history the controversy over the cult of icons constitutes a divisive element, not by its nature but because of the attendant phenomena. The decision of 787 in favour of the cult of images can be understood formally as a common achievement of the Holy See and the Byzantine Church. But in 843 the Orthodox Church imposed the settlement without the assistance of the West. In between lay the papacy's difficulties with the theological ideas of Charles the Great and his compilers of theological *florilegia*. Theodore of Studion appealed to Rome, but, in the final analysis, to no purpose, although he and the Patriarch Nicephorus had learned to esteem the importance of the Apostolic See as the tribunal of the faith in the very heat of the battle. But their theoretical understanding was no longer honoured. Not the least reason for this was the fact that the first iconoclasts, even if they did not expel the First Bishop of their Empire from the Mediterranean ecclesiastical world, had, however, turned him around toward the northwest. In 787 the papacy had fallen into a painful situation, between Eastern Orthodoxy, to which it knew itself to be still closely bound up, and the unique theological concept

[14] The *horos* is not in print; cf. *Beck* 56.

of the "orthodoxus imperator" Charles. The theological opposition which here burst forth could be played down in later centuries by outstanding theologians, such as the Carolingians, but the political consequences of the opposition were on the scale of world history and could not be eliminated again. Hence, Iconoclasm consolidated the special life of the Orthodox Church, but at the same time it is one of the great milestones on the road leading to the separation of the Churches — not on the road of dogmatic controversy, but the road of a slow transformation and re-formation of rite and worship, leading to new emphases, to new contrasting effects, which no longer allowed the maintaining of the ancient East-West *koine* in civilization and Church.

CHAPTER 9

Theology and Monasticism in the Age of Iconoclasm

In order to do justice to the intellectual situation of the Byzantine Church in the first phase of Iconoclasm it is necessary to proceed from the impression that the resistance of theologians and bishops to Iconoclasm was meagre. This impression cannot be removed by pointing to the powerful pressure exerted by the Emperors and the imperial police, for in the second phase of the struggle such pressure was unable to prevent the flowering of an iconodule theology. It seems to me to be far more reasonable to point out that the rest of eighth-century theology, like the profane literature of the age, was in no way distinguished for its richness — in other words, the "dark centuries" had not yet been left behind, and Iconoclasm was not responsible for them.[1]

The single celebrity of the age was John Damascene,[2] an Arab of distinguished family. He grew up at the court of the Caliph and eventually responded to the call to the monastic life at Mar Saba in Jerusalem. He died before 754. His work forces us to assume at Damascus, at Jerusalem, and in the lauras in the vicinity of the Holy City educational opportunities, especially a wealth of manuscripts, which surpass anything we know of the other metropolises of the caliphate. As the theologian of the cult of icons, John, like his successors, certainly took as his point of departure in his argumentation the questionable existence of authentic portraits of Christ and the saints and certainly confused the metaphysical image with the pictorial image. Thus for him the image

---

[1] On the famous question, or rather hypothesis, of the hostility of Iconoclasm to culture, an hypothesis which can be refuted by an Emperor like Theophilus, cf. B. Hemmerdinger, "Ḥunain ibn Isḥâq et l'iconoclasme byzantin" in *Actes XIIe Congr. Intern. d'Études Byzant. 1961,* II (Beograd 1964), 467–69; id.,"La culture grecque classique du VIe au IXe siècle", *Byz(B)* 34 (1964), 125–33.

[2] For his life and work in general, see J. M. Hoeck, "Johannes von Damaskus" in *LThK* V, 1023–26, which made all earlier accounts of his life out of date. His writings in *PG* 94–96; critical estimate in J. M. Hoeck, *OrChrP* 17 (1951), 5–60.

became revelation and means of grace. Whatever one may think of these speculations, with John the totality expanded into a grandiose system of cosmic liturgy, into a hymn to the transfigured matter and world that God had created, into the visible expression of a theandric law which governs the whole redeemed world. Without realizing it and in a different connection he was thus continuing Maximus Confessor.[3]

In the history of theology John's name is, of course, especially linked with his *Sources of Knowledge* (Πηγὴ γνώσεως). In addition to a synopsis of the history of heresy, which presents many problems for the history of literature, this consists of a compendium of dialectics and of a compact exposition of the content of the orthodox faith ("Εκθεσις ἀκριβής).[4] In this work John turns out to be, not an original thinker, but probably the most original mosaicist within the art of theology. To refuse him on this account a prominent place in the development of theology,[5] as has usually been the case, is to overlook the theme of this mosaic, for which the *depositum fidei* is a model. It likewise undervalues in principle the importance of "summarizing" for scholarship in general and for theology in particular, the importance of a cross-coordinator and of a reliable compass-card. In its first stages Western scholasticism, which had early become acquainted with John through translations,[6] esteemed this work highly. And on closer examination one can also understand how deep are John's tracks in Byzantine theology. His work, which, significantly, had its home beyond the frontiers of the Empire, did not constitute the winding up of the development achieved by the Fathers. But it did summarize this achievement with special skill, with real erudition and theological instinct, and passed it on for use in a poorer age. It must not be forgotten that the separation of philosophical and purely theological topics, apparently first made by John, was a contribution to systematization, which was able to facilitate substantially the self-realization of theology on the philosophical bases of its thought.[7] The influence of this theologian on the succeeding generations of Byzantine theologians can only be fully appreciated when one pictures to oneself the great importance attaching to liturgical reading in introducing young students of divinity to the world of thought of the theology of the past — the *vitae* of the saints sufficiently prove this. In these liturgical readings, however, the numerous sermons, hagiographical texts, and hymns of this saint play no slight role, even if the critical study of

---

[3] H. Menges, *Die Bilderlehre des heiligen Johannes von Damaskus* (Münster 1938); cf. also *Beck* 300f.

[4] B. Kotter, *Die Überlieferung der Pege gnoseos des heiligen Johannes von Damaskos* (Ettal 1959).

[5] In particular most recently, B. Studer, *Die theologische Arbeitsweise des Johannes von Damaskus* (Ettal 1956), whose impressive work does not, of course, lose its importance because of this criticism.

[6] Bibliography in *Beck* 480.

[7] Cf. G. Richter, *Die Dialektik des Johannes von Damaskos* (Ettal 1964).

them is far from being completed. In the words of J. Hoeck, John Damascene "realized his own ideal perfectly".

The theology of the iconoclasts themselves is substantially less well known to us. However, from the extant fragments of the Emperor Constantine V and of the great Synod of 754 can be sifted trains of thought which are not without importance for the history of theology. This theology, too, made use of the works of the past, as has already been indicated in a general way. The following is deserving of special note. The Quinisext Council of 692, and hence the orthodox complement to the great imperial Councils of 553 and 680–81, had in its Canon 82 attacked the pictorial representation of Christian symbols, such as the Lamb of God, because in these symbols it saw "shadows" of the New Testament fulness but not the fulness itself. It seems as though, for the iconoclast theologians, this train of thought, that is, the full reality of grace of the New Testament, was the decisive element. Only in this way can we understand why again and again they pointed out that images in the Church caused persons to forget that in the Church there is *the* authentic image of Christ, the Eucharistic Bread, and that, in comparison with it, nothing else can claim any true reality.[8] The slight regard paid by the iconodule theologians of the second phase to this perhaps clumsily advanced argument may not have been without effect on the later and rather superficial Byzantine theology of the Eucharist. A synthesis was no longer sought in the heat of battle.

No slight role in the second phase was played by the Abbot of Studion, Theodore (759–826). His works on Iconoclasm have come down to us only in truncated form. Theodore was a person who united the exaltation of the martyr with the vehemence of the politician — of a politician who, even in times of peace in the Church, was almost always driven into opposition or else forced himself into it. He took up John Damascene's ideas, but sharpened them, brought them to too fine a point, and made the cult of icons an essential element in the theology of the Incarnation. In this, in accordance with an old characteristic of the Greek mind, which dominated, for example, most treatises of Byzantine sacramental theology, the element of light and of sight, hence something optical, was brought predominantly to the fore. However, Theodore's importance lay not in the field of speculative theology but in that of monasticism, to be discussed later.[9]

The greatest theologian of the second phase of Iconoclasm was certainly Nicephorus, Patriarch from 806 to 815; he died in exile in 828. It only rarely occurred to the iconoclasts of the second phase to label the cult of images idolatry. All the more, then, they emphasized the patristic basis of their doctrine, which was now in fact not too complicated. Nicephorus did not

[8] Constantine V, fragment 21, in G. Ostrogorsky, *Studien zur Geschichte des byzantinischen Bilderstreites* (Breslau 1929), 10.
[9] Bibliography *infra,* footnote 15.

always display skill in this connection and put aside patristic texts, notably those of Epiphanius of Salamis, in a few cases where modern criticism cannot possibly follow him. He certainly did so not out of lack of philological scruples, but because his concept of ecclesiastical tradition was in no position to help restore the actual break in tradition. For what was characteristic of him was precisely that he, to a greater extent than John Damascene even, introduced this notion of tradition into the argumentation. The cult of images had to be lawful because it is the Church's tradition. It is worthy of note that from this very argument the concept of the Universal Church and the theological recourse to Rome come into their own. However, as in the case of Theodore, in Nicephorus also the "viewing" as a basic theological element pushed itself to the fore; the Gospel of hearing was substantially perfected in a Gospel of seeing. For the first time there is decidedly encountered in Nicephorus the condemnation of Iconoclasm as an heretical political theology, which sought to substitute the image of the Emperor, on coins, for the image of the heavenly *Pantokrator*.[10]

In connection with John Damascene mention was made of the importance of the contemporary homiletics and hymnography. Representative of the age at its very beginning was Andrew of Crete (d. 740), with some fifty homilies, which enjoyed great popularity in the collections of the Byzantine Church for liturgical use. But Andrew also played a significant role in liturgical poetry as an early representative of that *Kanon*-poetry, which replaced the old *kontakion* and in which the poetic genius of the Byzantine Church found a congenial form.[11] The bulk of the liturgical texts in the official books of the Church was contributed by Andrew and, in addition, by Cosmos the Melode, foster-brother of John Damascene, Joseph, brother of Theodore of Studion, and Joseph the Hagiographer (d. 886).

The hagiography of the period began with the first *vitae* of the defenders of images, whereas canon law and exegesis attracted scarcely any notice.

Byzantine monasticism and its development are of particular importance in the period of Iconoclasm. The struggle of the Emperors against the monks played no part in the beginning of the movement, but when the orthodox resistance solidified it was the monks who assumed the leadership. This circumstance gave them an ecclesiastical and political importance which they did not again achieve until the late Byzantine period. The great centre of monasticism in the iconoclast epoch was, first of all, Bithynian Olympus, the holy mountain of the middle Byzantine period, and the adjacent districts from Kara Dagh (Sigriane) on the Propontis by way of the district of Atroa,

---

[10] Nicephorus's work is not yet published in full; what has been published is easiest found in *Beck* 490f. On his doctrine of images see A. J. Visser, *Nikephoros und der Bilderstreit* (The Hague 1952); a reliable monograph which takes into account the unpublished material is P. J. Alexander, *The Patriarch Nicephorus of Constantinople* (Oxford 1958).

[11] *Beck* 500–02.

southwest of Prusa, to the Gulf of Mundania (Apamea). The centre which furnished the archimandrite, or archabbot of the whole group, was, at least for a time, the Agauron monastery on the Plain of Prusa, the highest located (1430 m), the Photeinodios monastery, but even more important was the monastery of the Symbola. A group of settlements came into existence between the two phases of Iconoclasm. Among these were the monastic colony of Sigriane, of the celebrated Theophanes, confessor and chronicler; the monastery of Eustachios, founded by Joannikios; and the monastery of Abramites, established by the Patriarch Tarasius in the vicinity of the Agauron monastery. The monastery of Stephen the Younger, who died in 764 as a martyr in defence of icons, on Mount Auxentius near Chalcedon, may also be mentioned. Constantine V's persecuting measures did serious damage to some of these monasteries but were unable to prevent a rapid recovery. In this connection it is clear that we must not imagine these monasteries, apart from a few exceptions, as a solid complex of "imperial abbeys", but as loose settlements consisting of primitive lauras or mountain caves, hence as institutions which were not firmly established in one particular place but claimed all the mobility that so long characterized the Byzantine form of monasticism.[12] From this Bithynian monastic settlement proceeded also the new impulses of monasticism in the capital. The Abbot of the monastery of the Symbola, a seventh-century foundation, was that Saint Theosterictus who gave the habit to Plato, a citizen of distinguished family in Constantinople.[13] Plato succeeded Theosterictus as Abbot and then built the monastery of Sakkudion (781) on a family property in the plain. It was at Sakkudion that his nephew Theodore, the future Studite, began his monastic career. When Plato resigned in 794, Theodore took charge of the abbey, but in 798 he transferred the community, threatened by Muslim attacks, to the virtually abandoned monastery of Studion in Constantinople. Studion thereby became the headquarters of a circle of monks who were active and extremely interested in ecclesiastical and political affairs in the capital. After a few years their number was reported as more than 700, but this figure probably includes the remaining settlements in Bithynia and other *metochia*.

The norm for Byzantine monachism as regards organization was Justinian's legislation, which, with a few exceptions, had made the cenobitic ideal binding.[14] But this ideal had long been violated by the principle of freedom

---

[12] B. Menthon, *Une terre de légende, l'Olympe de Bithynie* (Paris 1935) and then various articles by A. Hergès in *ÉO* 1 (1898–99), (1899–1900), and *Bessarione*, a. 3, vol. 5 (1898–99); cf. also L. Laurent, *La vie miraculeuse de saint Pierre d'Atroa* (Brussels 1956).

[13] Cf. O. Volk in *LThK* VIII, 554f.

[14] Of the bulky literature, let it suffice to mention here: B. Granić, "Die Rechtsstellung und Organisation der griechischen Klöster nach dem justinischen Recht" in *ByZ* 29 (1928–29), 6–34; A. Tabera, "De ordinatione status monachalis in fontibus justinianeis" in *Commentarii pro Religiosis* 14 (1933), 87–95, 199–206; 15 (1934), 412–18.

of movement and by the permanently present ideal of the anachoretic life, as well as by the institute of the spiritual direction of the novices by Πατέρες πνευματικοί, charismatically gifted elderly monks, whose influence sharply reduced that of the abbots. Theodore now tried to restore the purest form of the cenobitic ideal. This goal was promoted by his monastic instructions, by the brief rules, composed in verse, for the individual offices and occupations in his monastery, and above all by his rule, which we no longer possess in the original. Theodore, the type of the aristocratic Byzantine from the high official hierarchy, thereby transferred his qualities of leadership to the cloister and created for himself an instrument of the ecclesiastical policy already discussed.[15] But it would be wrong to think that he thus reformed Byzantine monasticism and gave it new commitments. One has rather the impression that most of the other monasteries were not prepared to follow him in this respect. The effort was limited to Studion and its success must have ended after a couple of generations. It was only two centuries later that Athanasius, the founder of the laura on Mount Athos, stirred the rule of the Studite to new life, but in an area remote from the capital and hence lacking the possibilities of excessively direct political ambitions.

[15] There is no critical edition of his works; most are in *PG* 99. The (revised) monastic rule is in *PG* 99, 1681–1824; the epigrams, ed. by A. Garzya, in Ἐπετ. Ἑταιρ. Βυζ. Σπουδῶν 28 (1958), 11–64. Monographs: G. A. Schneider, *Der heilige Theodor von Studion* (Münster 1900); I. Hausherr, *S. Théodore Studite* (Rome 1926). For further bibliography see K. Baus in *LThK* X, 45f.

The Age of Charles the Great (768 to 814)

CHAPTER 10

Charles the Great and Italy

At Pepin's death in 768 his older son, Charles, was twenty-six, while the younger, Carloman, was seventeen. The magnates did homage to Charles at Noyon, to Carloman at Soissons, where in 751 Pepin had been made King. Charles obtained the Atlantic provinces, from Gascony to Frisia; Carloman, the central and Mediterranean territories. Both Frankish Kings sent a delegation of bishops to the Roman synod which met on 12 April 769. In addition to thirteen Frankish bishops, there were represented seven Lombard bishops, twenty-one from the Roman duchy, and eleven from the exarchate. The blinded Constantine was sentenced to do penance and his elevation to the papacy and his ordinations were declared to be invalid. Other decrees determined the procedure of subsequent papal elections. An active vote was limited to the clergy; a passive vote, to the cardinal priests and cardinal deacons. To the laity was left only acclamation, but it was a legal requirement, for only after the acclamation was it possible to draw up the document of election, which had to be signed by the laity also. The election procedure thus determined continued to be an ideal. Practice quite often departed from it, but reformers had recourse to it later. Finally, the synod again expressed its views in regard to the question of icons, probably at the urging of the three oriental Patriarchs, who had condemned Iconoclasm.

The Roman synod put the seal on the triumph of the *proceres ecclesiae* over the *iudices militiae*. The *primicerius* Christopher was master of the city; his son Sergius became *secundicerius* and *nomenculator,* and his son-in-law Gratiosus was made *dux* of Rome. This faction represented, *vis-à-vis* the Lombards, the Roman maximum program. The intervention of King Desiderius had worked to his own disadvantage, but he did not remain idle. When the see of Ravenna fell vacant at the end of August 769 he successfully supported the candidate of the *militia* and occupied parts of Istria, which he sought to withdraw from the authority of Grado and attach to the Lombard ecclesiastical province of Aquileia. Very useful to the Lombard King was the conflict within the Frankish Kingdom which was known as early as the spring of 769 and quite obvious in the summer of 770.

After a new attempt by the Queen-Mother Bertrada to bring about a settlement had proved unavailing with Carloman in June 770, Charles sought allies against his brother. Bertrada effected a pact of friendship between Desiderius and Charles. Charles married a daughter of the Lombard King, thereby becoming at the same time the brother-in-law of Tassilo of Bavaria and of Arichis of Benevento, who had shortly before married other daughters of Desiderius. Charles certainly had no intention of allowing his father-in-law a free hand against Rome. In Italy he pursued a policy of maintaining a balance of power, just as Pepin had done after the second peace of Pavia. At his suggestion the *patrimonium Samniticum* in the duchy of Benevento was restored to the Pope. And Desiderius had to yield in regard to Ravenna. The archdeacon Leo, the Pope's candidate, was elected metropolitan and consecrated in Rome by Stephen III himself.

Stephen had by no means agreed to Charles's Lombard marriage. He drew closer to Carloman, for whose son Pepin, born in 770, he planned to act as godfather. The *primicerius* Christopher definitely favoured the connection with Carloman, from whom an anti-Lombard policy could be anticipated. But the Pope aspired to throw off the influence of the all-powerful *primicerius* and his faction, whose excesses he had never approved. The *cubicularius* Paul Afiarta, who had a secret understanding with Desiderius, worked to undermine Christopher. On his advice Stephen agreed to a conference with the Lombard King, who appeared before Rome with an army in the Lent of 771. At their meeting in Saint Peter's, Desiderius declared that he was prepared to make very generous restitutions if the Pope would abandon the *primicerius*. Stephen let himself be imposed upon and sacrificed Christopher, who was handed over by Desiderius to Paul Afiarta. He was savagely mutilated and died of his injuries three days later. The hopes which Stephen III had of his understanding with the Lombard came to nothing. Desiderius evaded his pledges with the scornful remark that Rome would still need his aid against Carloman. The Lombard King had become Rome's protector, and Stephen III had merely exchanged the tutelage of Christopher for that of Afiarta. He did not long survive this humiliation, dying on 3 February 772. Inspired by the best motives, he was unequal to the great things required of his office in an unscrupulous environment. His pontificate was a complete failure.

One can well imagine with what feelings Charles received the report of these happenings at Rome, which his *missi* had allowed to take place by their inactivity. The policy of the Lombard King had led him into a blind alley, for Charles could no more tolerate a Lombard protectorate over Rome than he could allow Carloman to intervene in Italy. If the tension between the brothers did not lead to war in 771, the Roman occurrences may have been the reason. Apparently even before the end of the year Charles dismissed his Lombard Queen and thereby broke completely with her father. Shortly before there had occurred an event which completely altered the situation and gave Charles all the trump-cards — his twenty-year-old brother Carloman died on 4 December 771 in the villa of Samoussy near Laon and was buried in the monastery of Saint-Remi at Reims. Before Christmas the magnates swore allegiance to the older brother at Corbeny. But Carloman's widow, Gerberga, fled with her two sons and a few *fideles* to the King of the Lombards.

While Charles was reuniting the Frankish Kingdom, a change was also in process at Rome. As successor of Stephen III there was chosen the deacon Hadrian, who belonged to the city nobility of the Via Lata and, by origin and career, gave promise of bridging the opposition between the *proceres ecclesiae* and the *iudices militiae*. Very soon after Hadrian's consecration, which took place on 9 February 772, the Lombard King sent to the new Pope a demand for a pact of friendship with him. As a *sine qua non* Hadrian stipulated the fulfilling of the promise of restitution which Desiderius had made to his predecessor. At the end of March he sent Afiarta to Pavia as his envoy, thus removing that dangerous man from Rome. Even before the arrival of the papal embassy, Desiderius had launched an attack on the exarchate; he seized Ferrara, Comacchio, and Faenza and laid siege to Ravenna.

The Pope protested against this violation of peace. Desiderius conspired with Afiarta for a repetition of the game of the previous year and demanded a personal meeting with Hadrian; the Pope would break with Charles and anoint as kings Carloman's sons, who were of minor age. But Hadrian, who had "a heart of diamond", did not let himself be intimidated. He insisted on his condition and began an investigation into the death of Sergius, who had been killed by Afiarta's associates while Stephen III lay dying. Afiarta's guilt quickly became clear. This lackey of the Lombard King was arrested on his return trip through the exarchate. Hadrian requested Leo of Ravenna to send Afiarta to Greece and to deliver him to the Emperor. But the metropolitan did not comply with this direction. On his own authority he eventually commanded Afiarta to be executed.

The crisis came to a head in the succeeding months, as the Lombards moved against the Pentapolis and finally against the Roman duchy itself. When they besieged Rome in the winter of 772–73, Hadrian, "necessitate compulsus", decided to appeal to Charles. Once again the papal envoy went by sea. He met the Frankish King at Thionville at the end of February or the beginning of March 773. Not until Charles had inquired of Desiderius about the Pope's complaints did he send an embassy to Rome. The Franks made known the papal demands for restitution at Pavia on their return journey but encountered a refusal. Thereupon Charles offered the Lombard King financial compensation in return for restitution. When Desiderius still persisted in refusing, Charles summoned the magnates to Geneva for a general assembly and a campaign. After the army had deployed in the Alps, he repeated his last offer —

but this time probably with the intention of containing the Lombard King until he could carry out his own strategic plan.

Like his predecessor, Desiderius drew up his forces in the defiles of the Mont Cenis, where Charles himself faced him. But the Frankish King had ordered a second army under his uncle Bernard to the Mons Jovis, or Great Saint Bernard. It went through the pass without much opposition and advanced to the Plain of the Po. Desiderius's army, seized with panic, fled in the direction of Pavia. The events of 754 and 756 were repeated, except that now was displayed the "Iron Charles", who abandoned his father's methods and demanded unconditional surrender from the Lombards. In September 773 he prepared for a long siege of the Lombard capital. Lombard resistance in the other cities of North Italy soon collapsed. At Verona Gerberga and her children fell into Charles's hands and were sent to a monastery, probably Corbie. Desiderius's son, Adalgis, who had also retired to Verona, escaped and finally got to Byzantine territory.

Meanwhile, defections from Desiderius had also begun in Central Italy. At the very outbreak of the war Lombards had fled from Spoleto and Rieti to Rome. After the first Frankish successes not only Città di Castello, Fermo, Osimo, and Ancona, but also the Lombards of Spoleto commended themselves to the Pope, who installed the new Duke, Hildebrand, at Spoleto. Only Arichis of Benevento, son-in-law of Desiderius, remained loyal to the Lombard King.

The course of events in Central Italy appears to have worried Charles, and so he decided on a further step that led beyond what his father had done. With a large retinue he made a pilgrimage to Rome at the end of March 774. The Pope, taken by surprise, made hurried preparations to receive him. When, on Holy Saturday (2 April), Charles reached the thirtieth milestone at the stop of Ad Novas, near Trevignano, there awaited him the Roman military nobility with the standards — a special mark of honour proper to the King. The succeeding acts followed the ceremonial customary in regard to the Exarchs. At the first milestone, at the foot of Monte Mario, Charles was met by the *scholae* of the *militia* under their *patroni* (officers) and by the children. The King dismounted and went on foot, as a pilgrim, to Saint Peter's, where the Pope with the clergy welcomed him. After entering the basilica and praying before the *confessio Sancti Petri,* the King requested permission to enter the city of Rome, "sua orationum vota per diversas Dei ecclesias persolvenda."[1] After Franks and Romans had sworn oaths of security to each other before the tomb of Peter, Pope and King proceeded together to the Lateran, where the Pope administered the Sacrament of baptism. The King then went back to Saint Peter's. He took up his lodgings, not in the imperial palace on the Palatine, but near Saint Peter's, where the *scholae peregrinorum,* the foreign

[1] *Liber Pontificalis* I, 497.

quarters, were. In this may be seen consideration for the Emperor or even for the Pope and the Romans, for residence on the Palatine would have pertained to Exarchs in office.

On Easter Sunday, Monday, and Tuesday the King of the Franks participated in the solemn papal liturgy, traditionally celebrated at Santa Maria Maggiore, Saint Peter's, and Saint-Paul-outside-the-Walls respectively. On Easter Monday were heard for the first time in Rome the Frankish royal *laudes,* which Hadrian ordered sung in honour of his guest.

But Charles had not come to Rome merely to pray. On Easter Wednesday the decisive political agreements, which had certainly already been under discussion, were reached. The Pope, attended by the *iudices cleri et militiae,* went to Saint Peter's and asked the King to implement the *promissio* of Quierzy, which was now clearly interpreted as a promise of donation. The *promissio* was read. It received Charles's approval, whereupon he had his chancellor draw up a second promise of donation similar to the first *(ad instar anterioris).* In this Charles promised to Saint Peter and to his vicar, besides the duchy of Rome, which was not expressly mentioned, the island of Corsica, the exarchate of Ravenna, the provinces of Venetia and Istria, and also the duchies of Spoleto and Benevento. The northern frontier of the papal territory was designated by the line Luni–Sorgnano–La Cisa Pass–Parma–Reggio–Mantua–Monselice, which was probably borrowed from a treaty of *ca.* 600 and had been adopted for the *promissio* of Quierzy. The passage is probably to be understood to mean that the section from La Cisa to Monselice was to form the frontier of the exarchate, which then, though this is not said in so many words, ran to the southeast, following the ridge of the Apennines. Perhaps, in addition, the Lunigiana between La Cisa and Luni was also granted to the Pope, but hardly all of Lombard Tuscany. Charles's *promissio* was deposited in Saint Peter's in two copies. A third, drawn up by the papal chancery, was taken along by Charles when he returned to Pavia.

No less significant than the *promissio* were the consequences in regard to constitutional law that Hadrian drew from the new situation. Until Charles's Italian expedition Hadrian, like his predecessors, had dated his charters according to the Emperor's regnal years. Now the imperial regnal years disappeared from papal documents, and the Emperor's name and image from Roman coins. The years of the pontificate and the Pope's name and image replaced them.[2] The importance of this change is clear: the Papal State seceded from the Empire, the Pope became a sovereign.

[2] The new manner of dating first appears in 781–82, since no papal letters and charters have come down from the preceding years. Classen, *op. cit.* 545, points out that the dating according to the Emperor's years was first omitted at the Roman Synod of 769. In his view the new papal dating was perhaps not introduced until 781, when the Empress Irene was seeking an understanding with the West (ibid. 559).

This change may have been agreed upon with Charles, since about the same time he assumed an expanded title. The Lombard King surrendered to the Frankish ruler on 5 June 774; with his family he shared the lot of Gerberga and her children. Charles made his entry into Pavia on 7 June. On 16 July is first encountered the triple style of *Rex Francorum et Lango-bardorum atque Patricius Romanorum* to express the constitutional structure of Charles' expanded realm. If Charles officially assumed the designation of *Patricius Romanorum,* which had already been conferred on his father by the Popes but which Pepin had never used, he was thereby making known that the protection of the Papal State had now moved from the moral into the juristic sphere and had gained a new constitutional importance.

The old conflict between Lombard and Roman Italy was not, of course, ended merely because Charles had become *Rex Langobardorum* and *Patricius Romanorum.* Before his return to Frankland the King had indeed fulfilled Desiderius's promise of restitution, but not his own *promissio donationis.* He also permitted the Archbishop of Ravenna to establish himself as the intermediate court in the exarchate, which was expanded to include Imola and Bologna. The Pope was put off with the prospect of a later adjustment. But in 775 the whole newly erected structure of Carolingian Italy seemed to be tottering. The Lombard national opposition found support at Benevento, whose Duke, after the fall of Pavia, had assumed the title of Prince as a sign of his independence. Hadrian learned of an alliance of Benevento with the Dukes of Spoleto, Chiusi, and Friuli, with Adalgis, the claimant of the Lombard throne, and with the Byzantines. Then the death of the Emperor Constantine V, on 14 September 775, caused confusion in the ranks of the allies. Only Hrodgaud of Friuli rebelled at the end of 775, but this rebellion was still so serious that in December 775 Charles proceeded to Italy for the second time and remained there till July 776. He now instituted a reorganization of the Lombard Kingdom along Frankish lines, but still did nothing in regard to carrying out his *promissio.* Hadrian waited in vain for him to visit Rome.

The Pope was disappointed and annoyed, and his relations with the Frankish King cooled noticeably. Ravenna continued to be troublesome, and a papal effort to establish control of Istria failed. Hence in 777 Hadrian finally decided on a new embassy to Charles, who promised to visit him at Easter of 778. The baptism of the King's son Carloman was to take place on this visit. But the Spanish campaign rendered a new postponement necessary. In May 778 Hadrian tried a last time to bind the Frankish King to his *promissio* by holding up to him the example of Constantine. With his letter he inclosed charters in regard to the property of the Roman Church in Tuscany and the Sabine district, Corsica, Spoleto, and Benevento. The claims to the *patri-monium* in these areas should act as the basis for the claim of the Roman Church to the lands mentioned in the *promissio.* At the same time, however, there was thereby set up a face-saving device in the event that the political demands could not be implemented.

The mention of Constantine must not be overlooked. The text of the papal letter is reminiscent of the so-called *Constitutum Constantini,* for the dating of which, in our view, Hadrian's letter provides a *terminus ad quem.* The famous forgery made use in its *narratio* of the legend of Silvester, which can be shown to go back to *ca.* 500. According to the *Constitutum* Constantine the Great handed over to Saint Peter and his vicars, whose universal primacy he sanctioned by imperial law, the imperial *palatium* of the Lateran, the insignia of imperial sovereignty, and "Romae urbis et omnes Italicae seu occidentalium regionum provincias, loca et civitates". The Roman clergy obtained the dignities and prerogatives of the Senate. The Emperor transferred his residence to Byzantium and abandoned Rome and the West to the Roman Church, "quoniam, ubi principatus sacerdotum et christianae religionis caput ab imperatore celeste constitutum est, iustum non est, ut illic imperator terrenus habeat potestatem".[3] The imperial ratification of the Roman primacy could only have been directed at Constantinople, for this point was not contested in the West. It was, of course, already in the Silvester legend. In addition, the *Constitutum* emphasized the quasi-imperial position of the Pope in the West, that is, the papal sovereignty, first claimed by Hadrian after 774, as well as the sovereign rights to the provinces of Rome and Italy "seu occidentalium regionum", which are probably to be interpreted as a claim to a large Italian ecclesiastical principality. The formal criteria of the forgery permit an even earlier stage in the time of Hadrian's three predecessors, but the legal content points clearly to the pontificate of Hadrian, more particularly to the years 774–78.

Hadrian was probably under no great illusions any more as to the success of his final appeal to Charles. The King of the Franks, who, following the set back at Roncesvalles, had to suppress a new Saxon revolt, was unable to undertake his third Italian journey until the end of 780 and paid the long projected visit to Rome at Easter, 5 April 781. The time was ripe for an adjustment of the Italian question, especially since at Constantinople the Empress Irene, after the premature death of Leo IV on 8 September 780, had assumed the regency for her son, Constantine VI, who was under age. The Empress had resumed contact with the West. Solemn ceremonies, which served to secure the Carolingian Dynasty and to exonerate Charles, demonstrated at the same time the concord of Pope and King. Hadrian acted as godfather for the King's son Carloman, who was baptized as Pepin; he anointed the boy as King of Italy and his younger brother Louis as King of Aquitaine. The King's daughter Rotrudis was engaged to the young Emperor Constantine VI.

[3] *Const. Const.,* ed. W. Gericke, *ZSavRGkan* 43 (1957), 88 (K. Zeumer, *Festschrift für R. von Gneist* [Berlin 1888], 47 ff.).

Hadrian and Charles together sent an embassy to the Duke of Bavaria, Tassilo, with the admonition to remain loyal to the Frankish King. The Pope interred his dream of a large Papal State. He renounced Terracina, which was disputed between him and Byzantium, or rather Naples, and his claims to Tuscany and the duchy of Spoleto. In return, Charles gave him the Sabine district, whose frontiers with regard to Spoleto were defined by Frankish *missi,* and the revenues paid to Pavia from Tuscany and Spoleto. Further frontier rectifications were probably held out to Hadrian, but they were not formally granted until 787, when Charles awarded to him southern Tuscany (Viterbo, Orvieto, and Soana) with the maritime cities of Grosseto (Rosellae) and Piombino (Populonia), the Liris frontier with Sora, Arpino, and Arce opposite Benevento, and the cities of Aquino, Teano, and Capua. The Benevento cessions could not, it is true, be fully realized, but the Papal State now acquired its definitive shape.

CHAPTER 11

The Completing of the Frankish Empire

Pepin had left to his sons a Saxon problem as well as an Italian one. The original Saxons made their home in Holstein. In the third century they had united with the Chauci, who lived between the Ems and the Elbe, and then they had advanced triumphantly to Britain as well as southward. Together with the Franks they had destroyed the Thuringian Kingdom in the sixth century and occupied the area south of Hanover between the Weser, the Elbe, the Unstrut, and the Saale. Finally, around 700 they conquered the territory of the Bructeri south of the Lippe, which belonged to the Frankish Kingdom. On the eve of Charles's Saxon wars the Saxon "state" appeared as a loosely organized aristocratic republic, with a strict class distinction between the chieftains of the original Saxon stock on the one hand and the *frilingen* and *laten* of the subjugated districts on the other.

Only more or less incidental features of Saxon paganism are known. The divine trinity, already transmitted by Tacitus, appears in the Saxon formula of abjuration as Wodan, Donar, and Saxnot (Ziu). Wodan and Saxnot occur also in the Anglo-Saxon genealogies, as ancestors of the royal houses. The "Saxon steed" played an important role as a cult animal; it followed the chieftain to his grave, and its flesh was eaten in the ritual meal. A very dark chapter in Saxon religious history has to do with belief in witches, which included a ritual cannibalism.

The earlier Carolingians put a stop to Saxon expansion and subjected the frontier areas of Westphalia and Eastphalia to tribute. Alongside the Frankish frontier fortresses churches were to be found quite early. Willibrord, Swith-

61

bert, and Boniface had started out here but had soon established new churches in the border zone. Important missionary centers were Utrecht, Swidberts-werth (today Kaiserswerth, precursor of the abbey of Werden), Amöneburg, Büraburg-Fritzlar, Fulda, and Hersfeld. At the time of Pepin the Anglo-Saxon centres of Frisia, Hesse, and Thuringia were often in competition with the old Frankish sees of Cologne, Mainz, and Worms. In the northern sector Utrecht, as the Anglo-Saxon centre, continued to exist independently of Cologne. But in the Rhine-Main sector the rivalry was partly appeased in Pepin's last years by the uniting of Büraburg-Fritzlar and Erfurt with Mainz. Charles the Great also intervened here by the grant of privileges which made Lorsch (772–73), Fulda (774), Hersfeld (775), Fritzlar (775–82), and perhaps also Amöneburg royal monasteries.

In the Hessian and Thuringian frontier districts there was no longer any possibility of a "non-political" mission, that is, one not directed by the Frankish King. But in the northern section the situation had not yet hardened to the same degree. The Utrecht mission extended in Charles's first years into the Frisian-Saxon frontier area around Deventer, where the Anglo-Saxon Lebuin built a church. Through Saxon friends he gained access to the tribal assembly at Marklo, where he urged the Saxons to accept Christianity voluntarily. But the Saxons' hour of destiny had already struck; it was now too late for a real decision in regard to accepting the Christian faith. The political and ecclesiastical incorporation of Saxony into the Frankish Kingdom must have been one of Charles's first aims. He set about realizing it in 772, immediately after the uniting of the two parts of the Frankish realm, and again took it up in 775 right after the conclusion of the Italian campaign. The Saxons formally submitted in 776 at Lippspringe and repeated this submission in 777 at the Diet of Paderborn, the first general assembly of the kingdom to be held in Saxony. They pledged their loyalty, according to their law, in exchange for their liberty and property. The beginnings of the Frankish march system in southern Westphalia (Dortmund) and in Angria (Paderborn) probably go back to this period. The first mass-baptisms took place. Abbot Sturmi of Fulda assumed charge of the Eresburg and the direction of the mission in the Paderborn area. No doubt the Cologne mission was also established in Westphalia south of the Lippe, and perhaps that of Mainz in the Eichsfeld and the Leine valley (Göttingen and Nörten) and that of Hersfeld in the district between the Saale, the Unstrut, and the Bode.

Outside the march areas Frankish rule seems to have rested especially only on the pro-Frankish faction of the nobility. But there was also an anti-Frankish party and to it belonged the Westphalian Widukind, of a noble family native to the district of Münster and Osnabrück. Instead of appearing in Paderborn, he had fled to the land of the "Northmen". He returned in the autumn of 778, after the Franks' defeat at Roncesvalles, and stirred up the revolt that brought on the second phase of the Saxon war. Up to this time Charles had not advanced beyond Osnabrück–Minden and Wolfenbüttel–Schöningen, but now he proceeded for the first time all the way to the Elbe, where he made contact with the neighbouring Slavonic tribes. The inhabitants of the Bardowiek around Lüneburg and the Northmen accepted baptism in 780. In that year all of Saxony was divided into mission jurisdictions. In July 782 a second general assembly of the Frankish Kingdom was held in Saxony, this one at Lippspringe. Here for the first time appeared envoys of the Danes and the Avars.

Charles felt that the time had now come to bring all of Saxony under the Carolingian government. The country was divided into counties, most of which were entrusted to the pro-Frankish nobles. Probably at that time the King also extended to Saxony the ecclesiastical legislation of the Frankish state and issued the *Capitulatio de partibus Saxoniae,* which L. Halphen reduced to the dreadful formula: acceptance of Christianity or death. With terrible monotony the words "morte moriatur" occurred again and again — not only for refusal of baptism or violence to clerics or other Christians, but for violations of ritual prescriptions, such as the Lenten fast, or of the command to tithe. The only moderating effects were connected with the decrees on the right of asylum in churches and the rule that offences that were not public could be a matter of ecclesiastical penance.

Critics of Christianity and of the Church since the age of the *Aufklärung* have, again and again, quoted the *capitulatio,* which, as a matter of fact, is contrary to the basic principles of Christianity. The historian, however, must not stop with this absolute statement, but must put the question in accordance with the historical context. The death penalty was not something foreign to the Saxons — it was inflicted for marriage of persons of different classes and for trespass. Among the Franks death was the punishment of high treason, and for Charles the service of God and that of the King could not be separated. The King demanded obedience not only to himself but also to God, and by the same means and in the same spirit. Christians no less than pagans of that period were impressed especially by the *tremendum* in connection with religion. As in the Old Testament, *timor Dei* came before *amor Dei.* Religious and ecclesiastical precepts were generally understood as a whole, without making any finer distinctions between *ethos* and *ritus.* This is the explanation of what to the modern understanding is an incredible discrepancy between offence and punishment in the *capitulatio.* To be sure, churchmen were not lacking even in the eighth century who opposed the harshness of the law and the crude religious ideas upon which it was based. Criticism of the *capitulatio* and of the missionary methods of these years is an imperishable title to fame for Alcuin and for Paulinus of Aquileia, and it had an effect on Charles.

The *capitulatio,* which could only appear to the Saxons as a violent enforcement of a foreign faith and a foreign law, caused revolt to flare up again. An army, to which the King, called back to Frankland, had entrusted the subjection of the Sorb tribes, was wiped out on the Süntel, where the Franks suffered the worst defeat in the Saxon war. Nevertheless, the Saxons did not risk battle when Charles himself appeared on the scene. Widukind again fled to the Northmen, and the pro-Frankish nobles surrendered many rebels, who were now dealt with according to the *capitulatio*. In the autumn of 782 was held the criminal court of Verden, which the *Annales Regni Francorum* claim took a toll of 4,500 Saxon victims. The tradition in regard to this figure cannot be explained away, but the number must not be taken any more seriously in the literal sense than are other medieval statistics. The annalist merely intended to state that an unusually large number of Saxons were executed.

The execution at Verden had an effect opposite to that intended. The Saxon war reached its climax in 783–85 and in 784 even spread to Central and Eastern Frisia. When, finally, in the spring of 785 Charles advanced to the Bardowiek, negotiations took place with Widukind and Abbio, who met Charles at the palace of Attigny and were baptized there. Like other Saxon nobles, Widukind was presumably appointed to govern a Frankish county. According to a tradition which is credible, even though it cannot be traced back beyond 1100, he was buried in the church he had founded at Enger near Herford. His family continued to be prominent in West-phalia into the eleventh century, and from it came Queen Mathilde, mother of Otto the Great. With Widukind's submission the second and bloodiest phase of the Saxon war ended. The King prescribed thanksgiving throughout his dominions. The peace was unbroken for seven years, during which the foundations were laid for Saxony's ecclesiastical organization.

The sees of Mainz and Würzburg and the monasteries of Fulda, Hersfeld, and Amorbach became the chief agents of the evangelizing of southern Saxony. The mission field around Göttingen was incorporated into the diocese of Mainz. Hersfeld maintained a commanding position between the Unstrut, the Saale, and the Bode. On Sturmi's death in 779, Fulda relinquished the mission station of Paderborn to Würzburg and under Abbot Baugulf (780–802) took charge of the stations of Hameln and Minden. Amorbach obtained that of Verden.

The care of western Saxony was exercised by the sees of Cologne and Liège and the monasteries of Echternach and Corbie. The territory south of the Lippe was attached to the diocese of Cologne. Echternach assumed charge of the Münsterland; Liège, of Osnabrück; Corbie, of the stations of Meppen and Visbeck. The clergy of Utrecht were unable to supply any personnel for the early work in Saxony, for the conversion of Frisia had not yet been completed. But two Utrecht clerics did finally transfer from the Frisian to the Saxon mission: the Anglo-Saxon Willehad, who went to the county of Wigmodia (Bremen) in 780, and the Frisian Liudger, who took charge of Münster in 792. Each received a base of his own in the rear — Willehad the Cella Jüsten near Jülich, Liudger the Cella Leuze in Brabant. Closer to his mission territory Liudger founded the abbey of Werden.

The ecclesiastical personnel on the front did not suffice for the evangelization of eastern Saxony, and so the King applied to the bishoprics inside the Frankish Kingdom. The station of Elze–Hildesheim was attended to by Reims, the station of Seligenstadt–Halberstadt by Châlons. Traces of Trier's influence around Hamburg and of that of Metz around Magdeburg can be ascertained.

Gradually there grew up self-sufficient bishoprics in the mission areas, but not before the beginning of the ninth century. The earliest to be established were those in Westphalia and Angria — Münster, Osnabrück, Bremen, Paderborn, and Minden, in the years 803–07. The Eastphalian sees of Hildesheim, Halberstadt, and Verden apparently did not obtain their autonomy before the time of Louis the Pious. The sees of Münster, Osnabrück, and Bremen were assigned to the province of Cologne, which also acquired the Angrian see of Minden that grew out of the Fulda mission field. The sees of Paderborn, Verden, Hildesheim, and Halberstadt were allotted to the province of Mainz. Cologne and Mainz, which shared Saxony, were not by mere chance the ecclesiastical metropolises of the two great deployment areas in the Saxon wars.

While the Saxon wars were in progress Charles was also faced with a Spanish problem. Ever since the annexation of Septimania (or Gothia) to the Frankish Kingdom in 759, the Pyrenees had formed a strong frontier between Franks and Muslims. The Muslims had internal problems of their own. In 750 the Umayyad Dynasty had been supplanted by the Abbasids, who transferred the seat of the caliphate from Damascus to Baghdad. Abd-ar-Rahman, the only surviving Umayyad, fled to Spain, where he established the Emirate of Córdoba, independent of Baghdad. But throughout his life he had to contend with opposing factions.

There appeared before Charles at the Paderborn Diet of 777 Suleiman Ibn al Arabi, *wali* of Barcelona and Gerona, to request the King's aid against the Emir of Córdoba. He was allied with Hussain Ibn Yahya and Abu Thawr, *walis* of Zaragoza and Huesca, and presented the King with the keys of his cities in token of their symbolic surrender. As victor over Lombards and Saxons, Charles was then at a first climax of his power. He accepted the offer and probably expected that success would come to him as easily in Spain as it had in Italy. He seems to have envisaged the establishing of a Muslim Spanish vassal state.

The mobilization became a grand-scale undertaking. Not only all the peoples of the old Frankish realm but also Lombards and Bavarians were summoned, and in 778 the King in person led one army of Franks and Aquitanians via the western passes of the Pyrenees toward Pamplona. The second army marched via Septimania and Le Perthus toward Barcelona. The two armies united before Zaragoza around the middle of June. Thus far everything had proceeded smoothly, but now, for reasons unknown, the *Wali* Hussain refused to surrender the city. Charles finally gave up the enterprise and decided to withdraw. After destroying Pamplona, the Franks crossed the Pyrenees. On 15 August the army was attacked by Basques in the pass of Roncesvalles. Apparently the King was hurrying on ahead with a part of the troops. But the attack did not affect only the rear-guard, as Einhard claimed. The entire army was thrown into confusion and many leaders fell. Sixty years later their names were still on everyone's lips, including that of Roland, Margrave of Brittany, glorified in legend.

The assailants were not Muslims but Christian Basques of Navarre or possibly Gascony, and Charles apparently feared a revolt in Aquitaine. He decided to make his son Louis sub-King of Aquitaine in order to oblige the separatist feelings of the Aquitanians and at the same time to relieve the central government. The sub-kingdom was established in 781, together with the sub-kingdom of Italy.

An attack by the Muslims across the Pyrenees was not to be feared, but Abd-ar-Rahman undertook campaigns into the Ebro basin and in 781–3 re-established his authority as far as the Pyrenees. These expeditions also involved measures of retaliation against the Christian population, among whom Charles's ill-fated expedition had aroused the hope of deliverance. Many Christians who had been compromised with the Franks emigrated during the next years, among them persons such as Theodulf and Agobard, who were to play a leading role in the Carolingian Renaissance. In the view of this circle the enterprise of 778 assumed the character of an expedition to liberate Christians. The King himself never lost sight of Spanish Christianity from now on. In 782 Archbishop Wilchar of Sens conferred episcopal consecration on the priest Egila and commissioned him to work in Spain for "reform", that is, for a conformity of morals and customs with those of the Roman-Frankish Church. Behind this project stood King and Pope. At first the establishing of a religious and ecclesiastical influence was enough; the liberation of the Spanish Christians was postponed *secundum temporis opportunitatem*.

On the inclusion of the Lombard Kingdom into Charles's empire the future of Bavaria and of Benevento was left undecided. Tassilo of Bavaria had managed to strengthen his position within his duchy by means of the synods of Dingolfing (770) and Neuching (772). In 772 he won a decisive victory over the Carinthians, who now obtained a new Christian Duke and were evangelized from Salzburg. The ups and downs of Frankish power could for the future be clearly read in Frankish-Bavarian relations. The crisis did not mature until 787. Tassilo asked the Pope to mediate with the Franks, but Hadrian was already too closely bound to Charles, who rejected any mediation. A royal-papal embassy went to the court of Regensburg and demanded compliance with the obligations of a vassal, threatening excommunication. Tassilo submitted only as a result of a concentric deployment of the Franks around Bavaria. But he was unable to make the best of his lot. On the advice of his wife Liutberga, daughter of Desiderius, he got into contact with the Avars. Thereupon, the Frankish party among the Bavarian magnates instituted a process for high treason. It was deliberated in 788 at Ingelheim, where Tassilo had appeared. The indictment referred to disloyalty, threatening of royal vassals, and an understanding with the pagan Avars. Earlier cases of disloyalty to King Pepin were also adduced in support. The judges called for the death penalty, which Charles commuted to imprisonment in a monastery. The adherents of the ducal house were also sent to monasteries. Bavaria was placed under Charles's brother-in-law Gerold as prefect, but the ducal property went to the King.

Charles tackled the Beneventan question at almost the same time that he dealt with the Bavarian. When the Lombard Kingdom had been incorporated into the Frankish state, Duke Arichis had assumed the title of *princeps,* thereby claiming a royal position. He further expressed this claim by erecting palaces at Benevento and Salerno and in his charters and on his coins. He was able to maintain this policy for a time, due to Byzantine backing. But when the Empress Irene, who assumed the regency in the Empire after the death of the Emperor Leo IV, sought an understanding with the Franks and arranged the engagement of her young son, Constantine VI, to Charles's daughter Rotrudis in 781, Benevento was isolated. On the conclusion of the second Saxon war, Charles went to Italy in the winter of 786, and in January 787 he moved against the South Italian duchy. When he had advanced as far as Capua, Arichis made a peace proposal which the King accepted. Arichis took an oath of loyalty to Charles, furnished hostages, probably bound himself to pay tribute, and ceded to the Pope the territory west and north of the Liris, with a number of cities. At Capua appeared also an imperial embassy, which was to discuss the projected marriage of the young Emperor with Charles's daughter. But the marriage alliance had been concluded under different presuppositions. Not only the Beneventan question but also the new ecclesiastical policy of the Empress Irene, who had broken with Iconoclasm in 784, gave occasion for friction between her and the Western ruler. For Irene had invited the Pope, but not the Franks, to the council summoned by the imperial court to restore the cult of icons in the East and thereby ecclesiastical unity in Christendom.

At the end of March the King returned to Rome, where he kept Easter with Hadrian. Arichis was unwilling to preserve the peace. Hadrian learned that he had established contact with the imperial court. The Byzantines wanted to restore the pretender Adalgis to the Lombard Kingdom, and Arichis was to receive the dignity of *patricius* and become Duke of Naples. But the Duke died at Salerno on 26 August 787. The Frankish King came to terms with the Beneventans in the early summer of 788, appointing Arichis's son Grimoald as Duke, under the supervision of the Frankish *missus* Winigis. Grimoald had to include Charles's name on his charters, seals, and coins. In November 788 Winigis repelled an attack by the enraged Greeks. Since King Pepin quickly occupied Istria, the Byzantines, left with only Venetia, Naples, and a few maritime cities of Calabria and Apulia, were actually excluded from Italy.

After the ending of the Saxon war in 785 and the suppression of the Thuringian, or Hardrad's, revolt in the Main region in 786, the Frankish Kingdom experienced five years of relative quiet which were decisive for the progress of the Carolingian Renaissance. In this period Charles had secured the frontiers against the Bretons, the Wilzi of the Elbe, and the Greeks in Benevento and Istria and had annexed Bavaria. The incorporation of Bavaria made the Franks the immediate neighbours of the Avars and gave them new tasks.

A Turkish people like the Huns and the Bulgars, the Avars had emigrated from Siberia around 400 to the East European steppe, where they defeated Hunnic and Bulgar tribes and carried them along with them. Modern Hungary became the centre of their empire. After their abortive siege of Constantinople in 626, their power declined in the seventh century through the emancipation of Slavonic tribes and of the Bulgars, but it recovered in the eighth century. When Tassilo was deposed in 788, the dreaded nomads invaded Bavaria and Friuli, but they were driven back. Charles brought to maturity a plan for definitively warding off the danger by a great enterprise.

The campaign was carried out by three armies in the late summer of 791, and Charles advanced to Komárno. He spent the following winter and the spring of 792 at Regensburg, at which time the Rhine–Danube canal via the Rezat and the Altmühl (Bamberg–Regensburg) was planned. But the great operations contemplated for 792 could not be carried out. At the end of 791 Grimoald of Benevento deserted to the Byzantines, and the Lombard troops had to be sent to the south Italian frontier. On 6 July 792, the Saxons suddenly fell upon the recently assembled northern army. And in the autumn Charles was apprised by the Lombard Fardulf of a plot of his oldest son Pepin, whose right of succession had been put in doubt, with a large number of the Frankish high nobility. The Saxon revolt, apparently still restricted locally, was suppressed, and Pepin's conspiracy was nipped in the bud. The King reacted harshly. Some of the conspirators were executed, others were banished; these last included Pepin, who was interned at Prüm. But the crisis still had not been surmounted. A severe famine occurred. The campaign of the young Kings, Pepin of Italy and Louis of Aquitaine, against Benevento collapsed in the spring of 793. The Spanish Muslims exploited the situation, crossed the Pyrenees for the first time in forty years, and inflicted a heavy defeat on Margrave William of Toulouse near Orbieu. The Saxon revolt flared up again and became a serious conflagration. The Frankish state was in great peril.

It is amazing how calmly and quickly the King mastered the great crisis of 792–93. He saw correctly that possibly setbacks but not catastrophes could occur on the Beneventan front and in the Pyrenees, and so he entrusted the defensive in both sectors to his sons. Charles did not interrupt the Avar war but confided its management to Margrave Eric of Friuli and Gerold, prefect of Bavaria. The Frankish offensive was resumed in 795, and its success exceeded all expectations. Exploiting the chaos among the Avars, Eric of Friuli contrived to press as far as the "Ring" in the Theiss plain and to conquer this centre of Avar power, where the treasure amassed during the preceding two centuries fell into his hands. The immense booty even caused a rise in the price of food in the Frankish Kingdom during the next decade. Although guerilla warfare continued until 805, the hour of the Avar Kingdom had struck. In 796 King Pepin proceeded to Pannonia in order to accept the homage of the defeated. The Avar Prince Tudun went to Aachen and was baptized at the royal court. As with Widukind, Charles himself acted as godfather.

In 794 the King had assumed the direction of the Saxon war. The revolt once again involved all of Saxony and eastern Frisia. Charles amassed his troops at Mainz; his son and namesake did so in the Cologne area. The rebels were surrounded in the territory of the Eresburg and laid down their arms. Thereby southern Saxony, where the Saxon demesnes of the German Kings were later situated, was definitively pacified. Only the northern counties persisted in the revolt. The King led the campaigns in person until 798. He turned over the further operations, which went on until 804, to his son Charles. The Franks behaved ruthlessly. Many Saxons were transplanted to the interior of the empire. Temporarily, Nordalbingia was abandoned to the allied Slavonic Obodrites.

Within just about five years all the dangers that had appeared so menacing in 792–93 had been exorcised. The peaceful pursuits of the 780's could now be taken up again. During the crisis Charles had not lost sight of the intellectual problems, and in 794 at the Synod of Frankfurt he had forcefully expressed the Frankish claim, *vis-à-vis* Byzantium and Toledo, to have a decisive voice in theological matters also. The *Regnum Francorum* was being transformed into the *Imperium Christianum*.

CHAPTER 12

Reform of Empire and Church: The Carolingian Renaissance

In the first decade of his reign Charles the Great was so preoccupied with the great questions of "foreign policy" that little leisure for the inner order of his realm was left to him. Not until the second decade of his rule was he able to resume his father's legislative activity. His earliest extant capitulary dates from 779; three capitularies for Italy and the *Capitulatio de partibus Saxoniae* have come down to us from the succeeding decade. Three capitularies of 789, including the *admonitio generalis* to the clergy, which represents a first climax, bring this early legislation to a close. What has survived of the capitularies does not exhibit all the legislation of these years but does make known the growing intensity of Charles's domestic political activity.

The word *capitulare* was new; it refers to the dividing of the text into *capitula* and was probably adopted from Lombard-Italian usage. In content the capitularies corresponded to the old decrees and edicts. They included laws of permanent validity, such as administrative and executive decrees, details of criminal law, public law, administrative and canon law, but before 800 not the details of private law (personal and family law, property law apart from that affecting *beneficia,* compensations, procedural law). Their juridical basis was the royal ban — the King's right to command under penalty. Following preparation by commissions of *legislatores,* the planned capitularies were submitted to the assembly of the magnates, which, however, had only a right to advise and recognize, not to consent in the modern sense. Purely ecclesiastical matters were often discussed by purely ecclesiastical commissions, which were then acting also as councils. Promulgation was made by the King orally *(verbum regis),* often in the form of solemn address *(adnuntiatio).* Hence the surviving capitularies are not legally binding law texts in the late Roman or the modern sense, but caption outlines of projects, *adnuntiationes* or circulars, in most cases informally jotted down by secretaries *ad hoc.* Only in special cases were capitularies drawn up by the chancery.

The great capitulary of Herstal of 779 was intended to foster peace in the kingdom. It contained severe decrees against robbery and brigandage. Even private retinues and sworn associations in gilds were forbidden. Counts and royal vassals who were negligent in administering justice were to forfeit their *beneficia;* judges in immunities who did not surrender fugitive criminals were to be removed from office. The King ordered the settlement of feuds by means of compensation. He confirmed his father's law on tithes and definitively regulated the question of Church *beneficia* by the introduction everywhere of the double tithe — *decima* and *nona* — as well as of a recognition rent.

The idea of peace again appeared in the *admonitio generalis,* probably formulated by Alcuin. Peace and order were promoted by organizational reforms of fundamental importance, which were implemented at this time, though the texts of the corresponding capitularies have not survived: the introduction of *scabini* in the counties, the earliest known case occurring in 780, and of *advocati* in the immunities before 792. The Carolingian *scabini*, like the earlier *rachimburgi*, were assessors and judges in the county court. Also like the *rachimburgi*, they were appointed from established landed proprietors of good repute, no longer from case to case but for life, under the supervision of royal *missi*. The *advocati* were chosen in an analogous manner. The place of the former *advocati*, named only *ad hóc*, was taken by permanently appointed *advocati*, selected in agreement with the count. Within the immunity they looked after the same functions — low justice — as did the *centenarii* or *vicarii* in the counties, represented the lord of the immunity and his peasants before the county court, and were responsible to the count for criminals who had taken refuge in the immunity. The counts were bound more closely to the ruler by becoming royal vassals. They were subordinate to the royal *missi*, who played a role in their appointment.

Missi are referred to in connection with this function as early as 779. There had long been *missi dominici*, but now they were sent out regularly. Charles divided the entire kingdom into *missatica*, based on tribal areas, marches, and ecclesiastical provinces and dioceses. *Missi* were selected from the higher clergy — bishops and abbots — and the chaplains, from counts and vassals, not resident in the district, in each case a cleric and a layman, whose cooperation was intended to strengthen the *concordia* of the two classes in the state. Not only the supervision of law and administration but also the promulgation of the capitularies pertained to their duties. The intensification of legislative activity certainly speeded up the constituting of the *missatica* in the 780's. Supervision of the carrying out of their functions by resident bishops, abbots, and counts fostered the development of the method of inquest in law.

In the *admonitio generalis* Charles appears as a Church reformer of the type of King Josiah of Israel, who exerted himself, *circumeundo, corrigendo, ammonendo,* to lead back the kingdom entrusted to him by God to true religion. Apparently the capitulary was drawn up by Alcuin. The first part of its decrees is based on the canonical collection of Dionysius Exiguus, given to the King by Pope Hadrian in 774. It constitutes a sort of summary of canonical regulations for the clergy in the framework of diocese and province. The restoration of discipline among monks and clergy by means of the renewal of the diocesan law of the early Church had been a fixed goal of all Frankish synods since Boniface. In the capitulary of Herstal Charles had first made the subordination of bishops to metropolitans a programme again. In addition to Wilchar of Sens, who after the death of Chrodegang of Metz seems to have been the only archbishop in the Frankish Kingdom, Tilpin of Reims, Possessor of Tarantaise, and Weomad of Trier around 780 and Lull of Mainz in 782 became archbishops. The elevating of Erembert of Bourges to be archbishop and metropolitan between 784 and 791 shows that the restoration included Aquitaine also, where, it is true, Erembert was probably the only metropolitan for a while. The establishing of ecclesiastical provinces could proceed rapidly since the Roman-Merovingian arrangement was maintained and a clear outline was available in the *Notitia Galliarum*. The reform seems to have faltered only in the south-east of Gaul, since the old quarrel between Vienne and Arles was revived in 794 and there also existed at that time uncertainties in regard to the rank of Tarantaise in Alpes Graiae, Embrun in Alpes Maritimae, and Aix in Narbonensis Secunda. Responsible for Germany and Rhaetia were still Cologne (for Frisia and Westphalia) and Mainz. Bavaria alone became autonomous as the province of Salzburg in 798.

Despite this recourse to the juridical arrangement of the earlier Church, the re-establishing of the ecclesiastical provinces in the Frankish Kingdom was no mere restoration. New was the combining of the archiepiscopal dignity with the office of metropolitan, which spread from England (Canterbury and York) first to the Frankish West (Sens) and then to the entire kingdom. In earlier times prelates superior in rank to metropolitans, such as patriarchs and papal vicars, were termed archbishops. Boniface and Chrodegang of Metz, as leaders of the Austrasian Church, were indeed archbishops but not metropolitans. Even under Charles the Great the archiepiscopal dignity was bestowed upon Angilram of Metz and Theodulf of Orléans as a personal distinction. But thereafter it was regularly given to the bishops of the metropolitan sees. The archiepiscopal pallium became the sign of the metropolitans,[1] who were now obliged to fetch the insignia from Rome within three months, presenting on this occasion a profession of faith. Before receiving the pallium they were not allowed to consecrate their suffragans. Thus the new archbishops were more closely attached to Rome than were the old metropolitans. At the same time, as sharers in papal authority they acquired a stronger position in their provinces. Alongside the Roman concept of the metropolitan power as a sharing in the universal primacy there persisted also the notion, coming from an earlier period, of a metropolitan constitution not created by the papacy.

The decrees of the second part of the *admonitio generalis* were very greatly modelled on the Ten Commandments, which were interpreted in the sense of the public peace. In one special chapter Charles imposed on the clergy the duty of preaching on faith and morals. The two groups, secular and regular clergy *(canonicae observantiae ordines vel monachici propositi congregationes)*, are mentioned in the chapter on the conduct of ecclesiastics but are not distinguished in any detail. The *cantus Romanus* was prescribed for the liturgy,

---

[1] The pallium was originally a scarf proper to imperial officials. Gregory the Great still obtained the imperial consent for conferring it. Cf. T. Klauser, *Der Ursprung der bischöflichen Insignien und Ehrenrechte* (Krefeld 1949), 19 ff.

with reference to the regulations of King Pepin, which, to be sure, had by no means eliminated the existing confusion in the Gallican liturgy. Success was achieved only as a result of Charles's exertions. The liturgical books — sacramentary, lectionary, *ordines,* homiliary, antiphonary — were revised on the basis of Roman or Franco-Roman texts by the Carolingian court theologians and disseminated everywhere. Charles himself had asked the Pope for an authentic sacramentary and in 785–86 had received from Hadrian the *Gregorianum.* This, of course, contained only text for the papal liturgical rites; it had to be completed by Alcuin with recourse to the *Gelasianum* of Pepin. In Alcuin's recension this *Gregorianum* or *Hadrianum* obtained in regard to the Western liturgy the same importance that the *Dionyso-Hadriana* did in regard to Western canon law. Thus the consideration of Charles's liturgical reform leads in turn to the great teacher of the Carolingian Renaissance, who also had a decisive share in drawing up the *admonitio* of 789. It was not mere chance that the first allusion of certain date to Charles's concern for education is in the same *admonitio generalis.*

Charles's special gift for creating something new out of earlier modest beginnings appears also in an examination of the Carolingian Renaissance. At the Frankish royal court there had long been an "academy of pages", consisting of *pueri palatini,* youngsters of the royal family and of the higher nobility. According to Hincmar of Reims, the *pueri palatini* constituted a special *ordo.* At the time of Pepin they seem to have been under the patronage of Queen Bertrada, who was probably the first to stress learning in the proper sense in the training of the boys. The "academy of pages" was not identical with the chapel, to which belonged only men who had completed their education. However, under Charles the *pueri palatini* seem to have occasionally performed the function of court secretaries.

The teachers at the court school in Pepin's time are unknown. At the beginning of Charles's reign we find two "foreigners", pupils of Alcuin of York: the Anglo-Saxon Beornrad, who obtained the abbey of Echternach in 777, and the Irishman Joseph the Scot. Dungal, another Irishman, famed for his knowledge of astronomy, may also have been in the King's circle at that time. To these men from England and Ireland were added Italians from the time of Charles's second visit to Italy: the Lombard Fardulf, who came to Gaul as an exile in 776, and the grammarians Paulinus and Peter of Pisa in 776 or soon after. The year 782 saw the arrival at court of the Lombard Paul the Deacon; he came to ask pardon for his brother, who, like Fardulf, had taken part in Hrodgaud's rebellion. That was an epoch-making year, for in it Alcuin, who had directed the cathedral school of York since 767, took up residence at the Frankish court. He assumed the direction of the court school; when he departed for Tours in 796 it passed to Einhard and thereafter was held by Frankish court chaplains. The last great representative of the early Carolingian Renaissance, the Visigoth Theodulf, may have come into the Frankish Kingdom with the wave of Spanish emigrants in 780. Some time before 790 he was admitted to the circle of the court scholars.

The early Carolingian Renaissance came to an end with Alcuin's removal to Tours. By then the older teachers at the court school had already departed. Paul the Deacon had stayed in Frankland only a short time; in 785 or 786 he had gone back to Montecassino. In 787 Paulinus became Patriarch of Aquileia. Peter of Pisa also was back in Italy in the late 780's. Fardulf received the abbey of Saint-Denis in 793; Theodulf, the see of Orléans in 798.

The education imparted at the court school was based on the *Septem Artes,* handed down from late antiquity. The emphasis lay on the *trivium* (grammar, rhetoric, dialectic) but the *quadrivium* (arithmetic, geometry, astronomy, music) was not entirely neglected. In the words of Fleckenstein, the instruction was "not restricted to rigid . . . lessons, but grew . . . organically out of the close association of teachers and pupils". It comprised both the elementary and the higher levels, but was constituted differently according to the several groups of individuals. Only one group of them was being prepared for an ecclesiastical career; another group, for a career in the world. Teachers and outstanding pupils were gathered under the presidency of the King into a sort of "academy" with regular meetings. In these they had common discussions on learned topics, solved riddles, and read poetic letters.

The members of this intimate circle bore pseudonyms, marks of *familiaritas,* but not selected by caprice. First of all was Charles, known as King David. Then came the Archchaplain Hildebald, Archbishop of Cologne (*ca.*791–819), who, as the foremost ecclesiastic of the realm, represented the High Priest Aaron. Einhard, inspector-general of the royal buildings, was called Beseleel, after the builder of the tabernacle. The abbots bore the names of ancient monastic Fathers — Adalard of Corbie was Antony, Richbod of Lorch was Macarius — or of prophets — Beornrad of Echternach was Samuel. Paulinus was called Timothy, after the disciple of the Apostle Paul. Charles's sister Gisela was called Lucy, his daughter Rotrudis Columba, after saints occurring in *the Laudes regiae.* Literary pseudonyms were borne by Alcuin (Flaccus), Angilbert (Homer), Modoin, later Bishop of Autun (Naso), an unknown Maro, and perhaps also Theodulf (Pindar). From poetry were taken the names of the high secular court dignitaries — of the seneschal Audulf (Menalcas), of the chamberlain Meginfrid (Thyrsis), of the cup-bearer Eberhard (Nemias); to this category belonged also the name of the deacon Reculf (Damoetas). If one looks more carefully, it is seen that, despite the numerical superiority of classical pseudonyms, the emphasis was on biblical names. The classical pseudonyms of the secular dignitaries had no importance of their own, but were merely taken from Virgil's *Eclogues.* The same is not true, however, of the literary pseudonyms. Horace, Homer, Ovid, and Virgil indicated scholars and poets. These nicknames expressed not only a veneration for the classical authors, but also ambition to reproduce them in a changed world, out of a Christian spirit. As Fleckenstein says, "Alcuin did not want to be an ancient pagan with Horace but that Horace should be a Christian Flaccus in him".

The renewal of the *Septem Artes* was undertaken, not as an end in itself, but in subordination to Charles's concern for reform. The study of the *Septem Artes* was the indispensable prerequisite for the emendation and exegesis of the sacred texts and for the proper ordering and organization of the liturgy. Reform had to begin with the simplest things — handwriting and orthography. Thus it appears in the *admonitio generalis*. It is said elsewhere that, while knowledge without works is dead, the prerequisite for right acting is right knowing.

Hence the first fruit of Charles's exertions for the reform of education was the new Carolingian script, which was distinguished from the older scripts by the clarity of the letters and the preciseness of words and sentences. Its first example — the poetic dedication of the Godescalc evangeliary, produced at court in 781–83 — is a landmark in the history of the Carolingian Renaissance. Refining of script and refining of language were intimately connected. The linguistic emendation led, not to a revival of classical Latin, but only to an elimination of vulgarisms. Latin and the Romance languages definitely separated. From the Carolingian reform proceeded Mediaeval Latin, based on the Bible and the Fathers and already foreshadowed in England. Flexible enough to express the new intellectual content, it became the language of the educated classes in the West. Apart from the literary works of the court circle there must be mentioned as the first document of the linguistic reform Part II of the *Annales Regni Francorum,* covering the period 794 to 807.

Around the same time began the wider manuscript transmission of classical authors. It testifies to the revival of the *Septem Artes,* in particular of the *trivium,* in which the study of the classics had been pursued in the schools since antiquity. But the pagan authors were not merely literature for study in school; they also provided a ready form for the expressing of secular values. Thus, for his biography of Charles in the ninth century Einhard went back to Suetonius, since the plan of the lives of saints was not applicable to a king's life. Hence it should not cause surprise "that the writings and poems dealing with Charles the Great reveal ancient forms in a far greater degree than do other works" (Fleckenstein). Later, in a similar manner, Aristotle unlocked for the Christianity of the thirteenth century a good bit of the "world". But David, as well as Solomon, as the Anglo-Saxon Cathwulf wrote to Charles in 775, was "in sapientia divina et sæcularibus litteris inbutus".[2] Fleckenstein says that "when [the court] made itself, alongside and apart from the monas-

[2] *MGEp* IV, 503.

teries, the bearer of what had hitherto been a monastic education, this could indeed maintain its Christian but not its monastic character". There was no change in the subordination of the *litterae saeculares* to the *sapientia divina*. Charles did not long for a new Virgil but for just twelve Church Fathers like Jerome and Augustine. More important to him than the classical texts were the ecclesiastical, the *libri canonici veraces*.

The "authentic text" of canon law, presented to Charles in the *Dionyso-Hadriana* in 774, inaugurated the series of these *libri canonici*. Shortly afterwards other canonical collections of the "Gelasian Renaissance" found admittance into the Frankish Kingdom. The *Hispana* too was circulated. Archbishop Riculf of Mainz seems to have spread the *Hispana Gallica,* which his suffragan, Rachis of Strasbourg, had transcribed in 787. In various manuscripts the *Dionyso-Hadriana* was bound with the *Hispana*. Analogous connections with the capitularies, on the other hand, cannot be proved. The old canonical texts were apparently to constitute *the* norm, as being the authentic law.

The "authentic" sacramentary, the *Gregorianum* or *Hadrianum* sent to Charles in 786, which Alcuin completed by recourse to Pepin's *Gelasianum,* has already been mentioned. Alcuin also published a lectionary containing the Mass readings, which was in accord with the *Hadrianum*. The Roman *ordines,* containing the instructions for the rites, were revised by an unknown scholar. Charles entrusted to Paul the Deacon the task of compiling a homiliary — patristic readings for the Office — which was introduced universally by the *Epistola generalis*. Between 758 and 763 Pope Paul I had sent King Pepin a Roman antiphonary. It was edited by Amalarius and published under Louis the Pious — the last liturgical book to be prepared. Thus Roman texts were the basis of the *libri canonici* in canon law and liturgy. In this context must be mentioned also the *Rule* of Saint Benedict, since from as early as the seventh century it was regarded in Gaul as the "Roman" monastic rule. In 787 Charles had an "authentic" copy of it made at Montecassino. The Roman calendar of saints was also received, along with the Roman liturgical books. Alcuin inserted it into the *Hadrianum*. The cults of Roman saints pushed aside the Gallo-Frankish saints during the ninth century and dominated the field into the eleventh century. It was only during the crusades that they were complemented by oriental cults.

Charles the Great was also concerned about the text of the Bible, but, contrary to what has been maintained, he did not commission Alcuin to prepare a revised standard text. What Charles was mostly concerned with was to have manuscripts that were correct in regard to orthography and grammar. A first example of such exertions was the Maurdramnus Bible, produced at Corbie before 781. The same motives prompted Alcuin later, as Abbot of Tours (796–804), to have the entire Bible transcribed. A real textual revision was the work, not of Alcuin, but of Theodulf, who in this connection even made what was for the age "an unprecedented attempt to correct Jerome's work by the Hebrew text".[3] But none of the Bibles produced at Corbie, Tours, Orléans, and many other places was accepted and circulated as authentic by the court. The court had greater importance only for the spread of the psalter which Jerome had revised according to the Greek text. It had apparently been received under Pepin and, as the *Gallicanum*, established itself in the whole of Western Christendom. On the other hand, the Gospel text used in the court school was supplanted by that of the Alcuin Bibles from the second half of the ninth century.[4]

From the court proceeded the initiative for the renewal of cultural life. The Carolingian Renaissance spread from the court, and new centres of culture took their place beside the older ones. Teachers and pupils carried the spirit of the court school to the places where they assumed new duties. In the old and the new centres *sapientia saecularis* and *divina* were not cultivated only for their own sake. The pastoral care of souls was also to be renewed from the great churches. Extant is a corresponding decree of Theodulf for the diocese of Orléans: "Presbyteri per villas et vicos scholas habeant."[5] There had been parish schools as early as the sixth century. They gave elementary instruction in reading, writing, and arithmetic, and in particular a catechetical instruction. That the faithful should learn the creed and the "Our Father" by heart was a demand made by the Carolingian capitularies ceaselessly from the *admonitio* of 789.

Preaching and catechetical instruction could take place only in the vernacular. Hence it should not cause surprise that the baptismal vows, "Our Father", and creed, and later the doxology, the list of sins, and formulas of confession are among the oldest texts in the German language. In general, the *admonitio generalis* forms the *terminus a quo* in dating them. Earlier Old High German boundary descriptions of 777 and 779 from Fulda and Würzburg point to Anglo-Saxon models, and the alliterative religious poetry was probably also stimulated by the Anglo-Saxons; its oldest witnesses are the Wessobrunn Prayer and the Muspilli. The oldest glossaries go back to a very early time; they probably originated at Freising with Bishop Arbeo (764–83) and at Fulda and testify to scholarly efforts. From them developed a literature of translation, which included the psalter, hymns, and the Benedictine *Rule* (interlinear glosses), and reached their climax in a translation of works which were grouped around Isidore's *De fide catholica*.

If Old High German literature began earliest in Bavaria and Fulda, its development took place in a clear relationship to the Carolingian Renaissance. To be sure, none of the extant linguistic monuments came from the court itself. The centres of early German literature were Fulda, Lorsch and Mainz, Freising and Regensburg, Reichenau, Murbach, and Weissenburg. Without exception

---

[3] Fischer, *Bibeltext und Bibelreform,* 178.

[4] Ibid. 193 ff. (psalter) and 174 and 195 (Gospels).

[5] *PL* 105, 196 C. — Fleckenstein, *op. cit.* 44.

they lay in the area connected with Boniface, with Bavaria, and with Pirmin's Alemannia. Old High German was given its phonetic characteristics by an older Bavarian and a younger Rhine-Frankish linguistic movement. The Rhine-Frankish was not the speech of the court but of Mainz, whose importance as the ecclesiastical *metropolis Germaniae* becomes clear in a consideration of the beginnings of the German language and literature.

The mother tongue of the Carolingians was the Frankish of the Cologne-Maestricht district, which determined the Carolingian language of law and administration. In the old Frankish districts between the Rhine and the Seine the word *theodisk* was coined to specify the old Frankish language; it was used for the Germanic languages as a whole, the earliest examples dating from 786 and 788, when, in the age of Charles the Great, the existence of a Germanic family of languages became known. Since at the same time the Romance language was separating from Latin, the existence of a Romance family of languages also entered into men's consciousness. The recognition of the division of the Christian West into two great linguistic communities — they are called "rustica Romana lingua aut theotisca" in the synodal acts of Tours of 813 — thus arose from Charles the Great's reform of education, from the Carolingian "Renaissance".

CHAPTER 13

Iconoclasm, Adoptionism, and Filioque

With astonishing rapidity the Frankish Kingdom rose to the position of the ranking Christian political power from the middle of the eighth century, and at the end of the century it was also about to assume intellectual leadership in the West. The *Imperium*, still involved in difficult struggles with the caliphate and overrun by Slavonic immigrants in its European provinces, was relegated to the frontier of the *orbis christianus*. But the Emperors had maintained their claim to be the rulers of this *orbis*. As had once happened in the Frankish Kingdom, so now in Christendom itself *auctoritas* and *potestas* had separated. So long as Iconoclasm kept Rome and Constantinople apart, this may have seemed unimportant, especially since the imperial claim was scarcely recognized in the West any more. The reconciliation of Pope and Emperor at the Council of Nicaea in 787, however, could not fail to pose the question of the position of the Frankish King in Christendom. The attitude of the Franks to the decrees of Nicaea was thus encumbered with this question from the outset.

The acts of Nicaea reached Charles in a poor Latin translation that had been made in Rome. In 790 the King commissioned the Visigoth Theodulf to undertake a detailed refutation. Theodulf's first draft was discussed at court. Then Charles sent the Pope a memorandum in which he bluntly rejected the Council; this was the *Capitulare de imaginibus,* drawn up in the form of theses. Hadrian replied with a defense of Nicaea. His answer was also discussed at court and taken into account in the final redaction of Theodulf's work, but the viewpoint peculiar to Theodulf's treatise was maintained essentially unchanged. Thus originated in 791 the *Libri Carolini* — the embodiment of the Frankish view of the quarrel over images, composed by Theodulf, discussed and corrected in the court circle, and bearing the name of the King himself.[1]

Theodulf had not contented himself with a superficial refutation of the Latin translation of the acts. He had developed a theology of word and image of real value, and in addition he had taken up the question of the Emperor's position in the Church. In the question of images he established the Western view, following Gregory the Great. At the outset he defined its limitations against the iconoclasts, who confused image and idolatry. Essentially Theodulf completely agreed with the authentic acts of Nicaea, when he clearly distinguished *adoratio,* belonging to God alone, from *veneratio,* the honouring of the saints and their relics. But he was unwilling to allow even *veneratio* to images. The Platonic notion of art held by the Greeks, who honoured the prototype in the copy, was foreign to him. He understood the plastic art as a craft, the work of art as mere adornment, in its quality dependent on the worth of the material and on the skill and experience of the artist. It may indeed be able to make past deeds and happenings present, but not to represent adequately a religious content, in contradistinction to the revealed word. Hence, such revealed signs as the ark of the covenant and the cross were, in his view, superior to the religious picture. Thus Theodulf's rationalistic notion of art ended in a spiritualism based on the revealed word.

In the very first chapter the *Libri Carolini* sharply attacked the forms of the imperial cult that had been passed on to the Christian world. The polemic was aimed at the formula "per eum qui conregnat nobis deus", for God reigns in us, not with us. It was directed against the designating of the Emperors as *divi,* of their *gesta* as *divalia,* for these are *gentilia vocabula.* Not least, it rejected the epithet ἰσαπόστολος, for "tanta est distantia inter apostolos et imperatores, quanta inter sanctos et peccatores".[2] The honouring of images of the Emperor was directly connected with the theme of the cult of images, "nullam enim hoc scelus fecisse legimus gentem, nisi Babylonios et Romanos". Here the ancient equation Rome-Babylon for the *Imperium* was again dragged out. But the imperial authority as such was not for this reason to be depreciated. In another passage it was explained that, according to Scripture, emperors, like kings, are to be honoured, but in due form and not *propter se vel*

---

[1] A. Freeman, *Speculum* 40 (1965), 203–89, has definitively clarified the question of authorship and reaction in a dispute with L. Wallach.

[2] *Libri Carolini,* IV, 20, 212.

propter ordinem.[3] In the attack on the Empress Irene, whose right to speak at the Council was severely criticized because of her sex, the question of the legitimate imperial authority could perhaps be faintly heard.[4]

Connected with the polemic against the imperial office was that against the universal character of the Second Council of Nicaea. According to the *Libri Carolini* the universality of a council could be determined quantitatively and qualitatively. Quantitatively, a council should be regarded as universal if the totality of Christian churches was represented or consulted; qualitatively, if two or three churches (Mt. 18:20) issued decisions in the framework of the Catholic tradition. But the authoritative guarantee of tradition was the Roman Church, which "nullis synodicis constitutis ceteris ecclesiis praelata est, sed ipsius Domini auctoritate primatum tenet".[5] Thus was the ground cut from under the older view of the ecumenical council as convoked by the Emperor and justified by the participation of Rome and of the four eastern patriarchates. Charles, in whose name the *Libri Carolini* were issued, stressed with pride that the Church in his realm had never swerved from the "sancta et veneranda communio" with Rome; that this bond had been recently strengthened by the acceptance of the Roman liturgy; that he not only ruled Gaul, Germany, and Italy, but had also led the Saxons to the faith. Thereby, indirectly but unmistakably, was registered a Frankish claim to a voice in the great affairs of Christendom.

The fact that the *Libri Carolini* sharply emphasized the Roman primacy and at the same time challenged the validity of the Nicene decrees, which had been issued in agreement with the Pope, is not without irony. Charles sent the final redaction to the Pope, but shortly thereafter the great crisis broke and the matter was not pursued further for the time being. The King did not take it up again until 794, together with the question of Adoptionism, which ran parallel to it.

After his failure at Zaragoza Charles did not completely lose sight of Spanish affairs. Around 782 a certain Egila, whose name was Gothic and who had been consecrated by Wilchar of Sens as a bishop without a fixed see, went to Spain with the errand of propagating the Frankish ecclesiastical reform

[3] Ibid. III, 29, 166.

[4] Ibid. III, 13. Freeman, *loc. cit.* 218, comments: "Implicit in this issue is the further question of imperial dignity: may it be vested in a woman? At this point pre-eminently in the *Libri Carolini* the nascent ambitions of Charlemagne come into collision with Byzantium." Of importance also in this connection is the reference of Beckwith (*Karl der Grosse. Lebenswerk und Nachleben,* III: *Karolingische Kunst,* 297) that the first generation of Carolingian artists — the Godescalc Evangeliary of 781–3 and even the Dagulf Psalter of 795 — was under the influence of the art of Rome, but then the East Roman-Byzantine influence became clearly discernible. Beckwith first identifies "the atmosphere of an imperial audience in the great palace of Constantinople" in the Ada group (*c.* 800), and then especially in the group of manuscripts on the Vienna Evangeliary.

[5] *Libri Carolini,* I, 6, 20.

beyond the Pyrenees and of uniting Spain more firmly to Rome. Egila's mission was compromised by his overzealous helper, Migetius, who not only attacked mixed marriages between Christians and Muslims but also eating with Muslims and who by his Trinitarian doctrine made himself vulnerable to attack. The Spanish Primate, Elipandus of Toledo, who is said not to have been himself favourable to the intermingling of Christians and Muslims, had Migetius condemned by a synod at Seville before October 785. At this synod Elipandus described the relationship of the man Jesus to God by means of the image of adoption: "Christus adoptivus filius Altissimi humanitate, et nequaquam adoptivus divinitate".[6]

Elipandus's formula should not be understood as an echo of older heresies. In the Spanish Church the struggle against contrary heretical doctrines — Arianism and Apollinarianism, Priscillianism, Monophysitism, and Monothelitism — had led to a sharp contrasting of the two natures of Christ, and hence among the Spanish Church Fathers there appeared formulas similar to that of Elipandus for explaining the Man Jesus. The key expression was transmitted by the Mozarabic liturgy, which bore the stamp of Elipandus's predecessors, Eugene II, Ildefonso, and Julian. The problem in which the Metropolitan of Toledo was in sympathy with Nestorius was the safeguarding of Jesus's true manhood, perhaps because of the association with Muslims, for whom the God-Man was a stumbling block. The distinguishing of the two natures of Christ in the image of *filius adoptivus* (humanity) and *filius proprius* (divinity) was not heterodox, but outside Spain it could be misunderstood, for in Germanic law adoption signified a very loose bond, in contradistinction to the *Lex Romana Visigothorum*.

The formula of Elipandus would hardly have been attacked had there not developed in Spain itself an opposition between the free Christians of Asturias and those of the Emirate of Córdoba. The conflict originated with Abbot Beatus of Liébana, famed for his commentary on the Apocalypse, and his pupil, Bishop Etherius of Osma, who accused Elipandus of destroying the unity of the person of Christ and of denying the divinity of the Redeemer. Both were closely associated with the faction of Alfonso II, who was later to lead the struggle for Asturian self-assertion against the emirate. In 785 Elipandus replied with anathema against his opponents. Thereupon Beatus and Etherius composed a polemic, which they published in March 786. The Pope, who had been informed by adherents of Beatus and regarded Elipandus as a Nestorian, called upon the Spanish episcopate to bring the Primate back to the unity of faith. But, except for Teudila of Seville, the

---

[6] W. Heil ("Der Adoptianismus, Alkuin und Spanien" in *Karl der Grosse, Lebenswerk und Nachleben,* II, 95–155), following Spanish scholars, derives Adoptionism from the tradition of the Antiochene theology, which remained alive in Spain, where there long persisted an opposition to the Second Ecumenical Council of Constantinople. Migetius's sect, in his view, was in the Pelagian tradition.

bishops of the Emirate of Córdoba ranged themselves behind the Metropolitan of Toledo.

The Franks were also dragged into the conflict by the Asturians, who around 790 denounced the adoptionist attitude of Felix, Bishop of Urgel, an esteemed prelate in the area under Frankish rule south of the Pyrenees. The formula of Elipandus could not fail to give special offense in the Frankish sphere, for in the Carolingian view of Christ the stress lay on the divine nature, and the Roman notion of adoption, with its strong bonds, was unfamiliar to the Franks. In the summer of 792 Felix was summoned to a synod at Regensburg. Paulinus of Aquileia seems to have been entrusted with the refutation. Felix recanted at Regensburg and a second time at Rome. He then returned to his see but fled to Muslim Spain, where he again professed the formula of Elipandus. The Muslim attack of 793 enabled him to return to Urgel, and now the adoptionist propaganda reached formerly Visigothic Septimania.

In 792–93 Elipandus and the episcopate of the emirate protested to Charles and the Frankish episcopate against the treatment of the Bishop of Urgel. Charles sent the Spaniards' documents to Hadrian, who condemned them, whereupon the King summoned a general assembly and synod of his realm to meet at Frankfurt on 1 June 794. The meeting, presided over by the King and two papal legates, included the bishops of the entire Frankish dominion and possibly delegates from England and Asturias. The Council of Frankfurt was content, in so far as the Greeks were concerned, with condemning one proposition, which was indeed heterodox in the completely distorted Latin translation. Clearer and more comprehensive was the rejection of the Toledo adoptionist formula. A detailed refutation of Adoptionism was provided in two memoranda of the Frankish and Italian episcopates. That of the Italians was drawn up by Paulinus. The Frankish memorandum and a related letter from the King were composed by Alcuin, who had just returned from a rather long stay in England. Alcuin countered Elipandus's formula "Filius adoptivus" with the formula "Homo assumptus", which was intended to express that the human nature of Jesus had never had an autonomous existence. Whether or not the Toledans grasped the nuance is doubtful, since *adoptivus* and *assumptus* were very often used synonymously in Spain.

In regard to images the Council of Frankfurt did no more than condemn *adoratio,* and hence it did not touch the real kernel of the Nicene decrees. The *Libri Carolini* were never officially promulgated and were not even ratified at Frankfurt, probably out of regard for the Pope. For the moment the controversy over images was concluded by the Frankfurt decree; it did not flare up again in the West until the reign of Louis the Pious.

The case was different with regard to the procession of the Holy Spirit, which Theodulf had used against the Greeks, presumably for the first time, in the *Libri Carolini*. At issue was the *Filioque* in the Creed of Nicaea-Constantinople, "qui ex Patre Filioque procedit", which was lacking in the original text but had appeared from time to time, first of all with Ambrose. It was present especially in the Creed of the Council of Toledo of 589, adopted probably as a clarification of the Catholic view *vis-à-vis* Arianism. From the Mozarabic Creed the *Filioque* had passed into the Gallican, and was in Charles's Creed of 794 with which the royal letter to Elipandus concluded. Essentially there was involved, not a novelty, but an elucidation: "c'était affirmer d'une autre manière la Trinité consubstantielle".[7] But Theodulf had incorporated the question of the procession of the Holy Spirit in his polemic, and Hadrian's rejection of the polemic had included this point also. The question had played no role at Frankfurt. But Paulinus of Aquileia took up the matter again at a provincial synod at Cividale in 796–7, which justified the Frankish stand in greater detail. What was involved at the moment was a mere echo of the Frankish-Byzantine confrontation. The explosive force of the disputed question would not take effect until later.

Adoptionism was likewise treated again at Cividale, and afterwards Paulinus also composed a polemic against Felix. It was especially important to win back the adoptionists in Septimania and in the district south of the Pyrenees, reconquered since 798. Pope Leo III condemned Adoptionism at a Roman synod in October 798. As a result of the transalpine polemics, Alcuin in the spring of 798 sent a treatise to the monasteries of Septimania, wrote to Elipandus again in 799, and composed against Felix a new polemic, which he published in 800. The situation in Septimania was adjusted in 799 by the *missi,* Theodulf of Orléans and Leidrad of Lyons. Felix, whose see had again been incorporated into the Frankish Kingdom, was summoned to Aachen in the spring of 800, and there he disputed with Alcuin.[8] Having again recanted, he died around 818 after an exemplary life in exile at Lyons. Following his death, Agobard of Lyons composed a new and final refutation of his view.

In Asturias the circle around Beatus and Etherius won out with the accession of Alfonso II to the throne in 791. The Frank Jonas, later Bishop of Orléans, toured the country at this time, and at the latest in 799 Beatus was in friendly contact with Alcuin. With the establishing of the archiepiscopal see of Oviedo in 811 the small Christian Kingdom of Asturias withdrew from the obedience of Toledo. Adoptionism lingered on for a while in the Emirate of Córdoba, but basically its fate was sealed here too with the death of Elipandus.

---

[7] *Histoire de l'église,* VI, 175.
[8] Reverting to the older opinions Heil dates the letter to Elipandus as 798 and the Synod of Aachen as May 799.

CHAPTER 14

From Frankish Kingdom to Christian Empire

The Carolingian Kingdom had survived the crises of 778 and 792–93; it came out of the last and most severe crisis stronger and greater than it had been previously. The efforts of the 780's for inner order and the intellectual renewal could be taken up again and bear fruit. The King's "project for a capital" show that after the crisis he again addressed himself to the plans and measures of 786–91. Until 784 Herstal was the favourite villa in which the King spent most of his time, when he was not claimed by military and political enterprises in Saxony and Italy. But from the conclusion of the Saxon War in 785 Aachen took the place of the previously favoured villa. It was not the change from Herstal to Aachen that was of historical significance, but rather the related plan of building the new residence as a stable centre of the empire. On his Italian journey of 786–87 Charles took the preliminary steps for realization of this intention. The Avar war and the crisis of 792–93 must have delayed the completion of the residence, but from the end of 794 Aachen clearly and unambiguously appeared as the centre of the empire, even though the buildings had not yet been finished.

In legislation too Charles continued to build on the foundations laid in the 780's. The Frankfurt Capitulary of 794 took up again to a great extent the regulations of the two great capitularies of 779 and 789, especially the prohibition of *coniurationes,* the rules for the payments for benefices established out of secularized Church property *(decima, nona, census),* the regulations on Church discipline, which were stated in more detail, the directions for the setting up of schools and on the care of souls. In the Frankfurt Capitulary there occurred for the first time a regulation in regard to the proprietary Church law, which the Carolingians had not previously dared to touch. Charles did not infringe on the right of alienation belonging to the lords of churches, but he ruled that churches once erected had to be maintained and that the divine worship conducted in them must not be jeopardized. The proprietary church system was indirectly affected by the prescriptions on ecclesiastical discipline. Thus already in 743 Carloman and Pepin had decreed the universal obligation of the clergy to give an accounting to the bishop, to receive him on the occasion of the visitation and of his confirmation journey, and to get the chrism from him every year. At Herstal Charles had prescribed, without detailed comment, the episcopal authority to govern the clergy *secundum canones.* At Frankfurt he forbade his court clergy to have any dealings with refractory clerics. In a letter sent by Charles in 779–81 to his counts and vassals in Italy it was presupposed that lords of churches had to present their clerics to the bishop for their installation. At Frankfurt was published the universal prohibition for clerics to abandon one church for another without the consent of the local bishop.

Charles's efforts in regard to the economic resources of the empire are seen in the great ordinance for the demesne, the *Capitulare de villis,* which more recent study assigns to the last years of the eighth century. It prescribed an inventory of the royal property, contained regulations on the stocking of the royal manors, and specified the tasks and duties of the demesne officials. It also indirectly influenced ecclesiastical economic management and served as an example for the describing of the Church's property.

A circular letter of 794–800, the *Epistola de litteris colendis,* imposed on the cathedrals and abbeys of the empire the obligation of establishing schools. But the finest sign of the maturing process of these years was the new missionary method, which was defined at a synod held in Bavaria in 796 under the direction of Arn of Salzburg and Paulinus of Aquileia. At the outset the bishops mentioned that conversion is God's work, not man's. They demanded an accommodation to a *gens bruta et inrationalis,* which needed instruction. Mass baptisms and force were rejected. The instruction which had to precede baptism should aim at understanding and not at fear of man. The new principles were based on old insights of Gregory the Great. They were intended for the mission among Avars and Slavs, which belonged to the sphere of the Archbishops of Salzburg and Aquileia, but they were also to be applied to the Saxon mission. In this connection Alcuin's criticism of the previous mission, including the condemnation of the overhasty introduction of the tithe, brought about a change. The *Capitulare Saxonicum,* issued at Aachen in 797, introduced the new policy of reconciliation.

The age of the great conquests was concluded with the Avar war; it was now necessary to assure the gains against external attacks. Frankish might did not suffice to take possession of the entire Avar Empire. The Theiss became the frontier against the Bulgars, who annexed the eastern part of the former Avar realm. But even on the other side of the Theiss the Avars and the Moravians, Slovenes, and Croats, once ruled by the Avars, were now only under the supervision of the Prefect of Bavaria and of the Margraves of Friuli and Istria. In 796 King Pepin of Italy specified the Drave as the frontier between Bavaria and Italy, between the ecclesiastical provinces of Salzburg and Aquileia, and Charles ratified this in 803 and 811. While there were already two marches in the Italian sector, a real march organization was lacking in the Bavarian sector until the end of the century. It was created after the death of the Prefect Gerold in 799. Charles then founded the East March, attached to the see of Passau, and the March of Carinthia-Pannonia, attached to that of Salzburg.

There were no changes in Italy. As earlier, the Dukes or Margraves of Spoleto provided the border patrol *vis-à-vis* Benevento and the Byzantines. In the Pyrenees, on the other hand, the situation was not stabilized until the turn of the century. Envoys sent by Spanish Muslims to ask Charles's aid against the Emir Al Hakam of Córdoba turned up in Aachen in 797 and 798, but the King had become cautious. The Frankish offensive, resumed in 798, had only limited goals, which were achieved when Barcelona fell into the hands of the Franks in 801 after a two years' siege. The conquered strip of Spain, later the County of Catalonia, was attached to the existing March of Septimania (or Toulouse) and subjected ecclesiastically to Narbonne.

The expanded Frankish realm, now strengthened on its frontiers, did not have an equal in the Christian West. Only the British Isles, the Kingdom of Asturias, and the Principality of Benevento were not included in it. In Ireland and Britain there was a rather large number of small kingdoms. But the Irish and Anglo-Saxons were familiar with the institution of a hegemonic high kingship, which belonged to the Kings of Meath and Connaught in Ireland, to the Kings of Mercia in England.

In regard to Benevento Charles claimed a real suzerainty as successor of the Lombard Kings, but it remained illusory; in regard to the other Christian *regna* he claimed merely the recognition of a pre-eminence expressed in the forms of *amicitia*.

Irish history is quite obscure at this period. The see of Armagh, founded by Saint Patrick, achieved a sort of primatial rank in the Emerald Isle around 800 but it is uncertain whether it also entailed a political concentration. A remark of Einhard's that cannot be checked is our only indication of political relations between the Frankish King and Ireland.

Charles's claim to pre-eminence encountered resistance in England from the self-assured King Offa of Mercia (757–96). In 784 Offa assumed the style of *Rex Anglorum*. Following the Carolingian example he put the royal name on his coins. In 787 he had his son Egfrith raised to the throne as co-ruler and, again imitating the Carolingians, had him anointed as King. He also succeeded in securing the Pope's consent to make Mercia a separate ecclesiastical province with Lichfield as the metropolitan see. In his diplomatic relations with Charles Offa emphasized their equal partnership. This led to a break around 789, which, however, was patched up a few years later. In 796 Charles sent gifts, taken from the Avar booty, to the Pope, to King Offa, and to Aethelred of Northumbria. Mercia's high kingship declined soon after Offa's death and the province of Lichfield was abolished. The Kings of Northumbria and Wessex maintained friendly relations with the Franks, but not on the basis of equality. There was no longer a king among the Anglo-Saxons who could be compared with Charles even remotely.

Frankish-Asturian relations were determined by the common opposition to the Emirate of Córdoba and to the adoptionists. The Kingdom of Asturias first took shape under Alfonso II (791–843). He had himself anointed in the style of the former Visigothic Kings, and made Oviedo his capital and the ecclesiastical metropolis. He was thereby clearly laying claim to the succession to Toledo. In him Charles encountered a King who was as self-assured as Offa was, but the community of interests against Córdoba was too strong to permit dissension between Charles and Alfonso, and the actual predominance of the Frankish monarch in this partnership could certainly not remain unknown to the Asturian King. The *Annales Regni Francorum* report two Asturian embassies of 798, whereby Alfonso delivered gifts to the Franks, including a share in the great spoils gained in a surprise attack on Lisbon in 797.

The *amicitia* of the Frankish ruler with the other Christian kings of the West had become a reality, even though it might often have appeared in a somewhat different light beyond the Frankish frontiers from the way it appeared at Aachen. Efforts were made to explain the new reality in new words. As early as 776 the Anglo-Saxon Cathwulf had spoken of the Frankish state as "Regnum Europae"; and in 799 Charles seemed to the author of the "Paderborn Epic" to be "Pater Europae".

The ancient territorial name was certainly not unfamiliar to Alcuin also, but he thought in other categories. The designation *Imperium christianum* is found in his letters for the first time in 796–97; he used it also in his edition of the Gregorian Sacramentary to denote the *Imperium Romanum*. In 794 Paulinus of Aquileia had already referred to Charles as *Gubernator omnium Christianorum*. The name David, which Charles had occasionally used in his intimate circle since the 780's, now acquired a different importance, as the epithet *Novus David* shows, first used by Alcuin in a letter of 794. The Frankish monarch now appeared as Christendom's David, and the royal throne at Aachen was an imitation of that of Solomon.

The new expressions, meanwhile, were exclusively bound up with the religious and literary spheres. The special position assumed by the Frankish ruler was not juridically specified even by the name David. In Christendom the Emperor alone took precedence over kings. Charles had trodden the way of *imitatio imperii,* borrowing from the imperial office the monogram at the very beginning of his reign and later the metal *bulla.* The range of his dominion was specified, first in the *Libri Carolini* and then also in the letter issued by the Frankish episcopate at the Council of Frankfurt and by Alcuin, with the ancient geographical names: Gaul, Germany, Italy. Charles appeared as lord of the central provinces of the former Western Empire, successor of the Emperors. Imperial characteristics appeared in the court art in the last decade of the eighth century. In constructing the court chapel at Aachen Charles probably had in mind the imperial buildings in Constantinople and the imperial mausoleum of the Theodosian Dynasty at Rome. But the juridical step to the imperial office had not yet been taken. It was only in the final climax which the *imitatio imperii* achieved in the "Paderborn Epic" around 799 that a poet dared to seize upon the special titles reserved to the Emperor: Charles appears as Augustus, Aachen as *Roma secunda.* By then the crisis in

Constantinople and Rome was already evident to all the world: the gates to the imperial dignity had opened.

A state of war had existed since 788 between Byzantium and the Franks. Support at the imperial court enabled Duke Grimoald of Benevento to evade Frankish sovereignty in 791. The campaigns conducted against him in 791–93 by King Pepin of Italy were fruitless. A considerable part of the Italian army was involved in the Avar war, but the victories of Eric of Friuli on the Avar front in 795 and 796 made likely a new Frankish offensive in South Italy. Hence it is not surprising that in 797 the Emperor Constantine VI commissioned the Patrician of Sicily, Nicetas, to extend peace feelers. The young ruler, who was weary of the tutelage exercised by his mother Irene, reverted in the ecclesiastical sphere to Iconoclasm. It has been suggested that his new policy towards the Franks was determined by his religious policy.

The conflict between mother and son ended in tragedy. On 15 August 797, Irene had Constantine VI deposed and blinded. She assumed the government herself and thereby created a precedent in the history of the *Imperium* that was extremely vulnerable from the point of view of constitutional law. Since the internal political situation remained precarious, Irene also needed peace. In the autumn of 798 there appeared at Aachen an embassy sent by the Empress to offer the renunciation of Istria, then under Frankish occupation, and the surrender of Benevento. Although the deposition and blinding of Constantine VI were regarded in the Frankish state also as an unprecedented crime, Charles accepted the offer. The peace still awaited ratification, but before this came about a new and dramatic event occurred — the revolt against Pope Leo III.

Leo III had succeeded Hadrian I on 27 December 795. Einhard relates that Charles mourned the dead Pope as a brother. Relations between Charles and Hadrian had not always been untroubled. The Pope had had to give up his dream of a large Papal State in Italy and had stood up to the King when the latter attacked the Second Council of Nicaea. But throughout his life Hadrian had been loyal to the Frankish alliance and in particular he had maintained order in the Papal State. The King probably did not forget this.

The change in the Holy See in December 795 was the first since the incorporation of the Lombard Kingdom into the *Regnum Francorum*. The Romans carried out the election and consecration of Leo III without apprising the King of the Franks, thereby declaring their sovereignty. The new Pope sent to the *Patricius*-King not only the document of election, but also the keys to the *confessio Sancti Petri* and the standard of the city, with the request that the Romans' oath of obedience and loyalty be received by a representative. It may be doubted whether Hadrian would have offered the oath-taking in this form. But Leo, not belonging by birth to the city nobility, needed the support of the royal protector, since, probably from the outset, he had to deal with a powerful opposition, which included the family of his predecessor.

Charles's reply to Leo III contained fundamental statements regarding the duties of the two powers. They show to what a great extent power had shifted to the side of the King, whom Paulinus of Aquileia had panegyrized as *Rex et Sacerdos* in 794. The often quoted passages run as follows: "It is incumbent upon us, with God's help, to defend Holy Church outwardly with weapons everywhere against attacks by pagans and devastations by infidels, and to consolidate her inwardly through the understanding of the true faith. It is your task, Holy Father, like Moses, to lift up your arms in prayer and so to aid our army that by your intercession the Christian people, under God's guidance and guarantee, may always be victorious over the enemies of his holy name, and the name of our Lord Jesus Christ may be glorified in the whole world."[1]

This passage certainly must not be considered in isolation; it must be seen together with the expressions of the *Libri Carolini* on the Roman primacy. By his remarks on the inner strengthening of the Church Charles certainly meant first of all his concern for ecclesiastical order, for the education of the clergy and the religious instruction of the people, just as Alcuin explained the *Rex et Sacerdos* formula by *Pontifex in praedicatione*. But concern for the inner consolidation of the Church had extended at Frankfurt also to questions of faith and it did not exclude the Pope, as the admonition shows: "Hold fast to the holy canons and carefully observe the rules of the Fathers . . . in order that your light may shine before men." It may be assumed that Charles had already heard complaints about Leo personally, for the instruction to the *missus* Angilbert contains the following sentences: "Admonish the Pope to lead an honourable life, to observe the sacred canons zealously, and to rule Holy Church in piety . . . Above all he should fight the simoniacal heresy, which only too often stains the body of the Church . . ."[2]

Gregory the Great had once written in a similar vein to the Frankish Kings, but now the roles were reversed.

It can be noticed that in these years the influence of the *patricius* was increasing also in the Papal State. In 798 Leo III adopted Charles's regnal years in papal dating. He also had the cooperation of Pope and King represented pictorially in Rome. The founder's mosaic in the apse of Santa Susanna shows the Pope on the right, the King on the left of Christ. More significant were the two great mosaics which were set up by Leo in the *triclinium* of the Lateran, the papal hall for the holding of synods, legal proceedings, and receptions. The first of these showed Christ with Peter and Constantine the Great; the second, Peter with Leo and Charles, in the same arrangement as

[1] *MGEp* IV, *Epp. Alcuini,* no. 93, 137f.
[2] Ibid., no 92, 135f.

at Santa Susanna. That the King was admitted in pictorial representations in Rome was a novelty, comparable to the acceptance of his regnal years in dating. In regard to constitutional law there was, it is true, no change, for in documents as well as in pictures the King occupied the second place. Also like his predecessors, Leo III coined as sovereign of Rome.

The leaders of the Roman opposition to Leo were the *primicerius* Paschal and the *saccellarius* Campulus, relatives of Hadrian I. An inquiry from Alcuin to Arn of Salzburg in June 798 reveals that there was anxiety in the Frankish Kingdom in regard to events in Rome. The revolt broke out on 25 April 799. *En route* from the Lateran to the stational church of San Lorenzo in Lucina, the Pope was suddenly attacked in front of the monastery of San Silvestro in Capite. He was ill treated and stripped of the pontifical vestments. There is evidence that a deposition took place before the altar of San Silvestro. Mutilation — blinding and tearing out of the tongue — was probably ordered but not carried out. The same night Leo was transported to the monastery of Sant'Erasmo near the Lateran. The conspirators had probably condemned him to confinement in the monastery, the punishment for deposed dignitaries of both the ecclesiastical and the lay state. San Silvestro and Sant'Erasmo belonged to the Greek monasteries in Rome. For this reason relations between the conspirators and the imperial court have been alleged, but this is scarcely correct, for at that moment the Empress needed peace with Charles and there is not a trace of any Byzantine intervention.

A new papal election did not take place, perhaps from fear of the Franks, who were already presented with the *fait accompli* of the revolution against Leo. The Frankish Duke Winigis of Spoleto hurried to Rome, accompanied by the royal *missus,* Abbot Wirund of Stablo-Malmédy. Matters took an unexpected turn for the conspirators, since Leo succeeded in fleeing from Sant'Erasmo to Saint Peter's, where he met the Franks. After a Frankish attempt at mediation had failed, Winigis took the Pope with him to Spoleto and reported to the King.

Charles was at Aachen when he received the first news of the Roman happenings. He did not cancel a Saxon expedition that had already been announced, but dispatched an embassy with an invitation to the Pope to come to Paderborn. There he solemnly received Leo at the end of July. It was obvious that the King did not recognize the deposition, but the Pope was followed by envoys of the rebels, who now lodged a formal charge before Charles. It accused the Pope of adultery and perjury.

Events had taken a course which seriously endangered the papal sovereignty in Rome. The dramatic turn is clear from a letter of Alcuin to the King in June 799:[3] "Until now there were three men who counted in Christendom: The Vicar of Peter, Prince of the Apostles, and you have apprised me of what

---

[3] Ibid., no. 174, 288.

has happened to him; the holder of the imperial office, the temporal ruler of New Rome, and how he was toppled, not by outsiders, but by his own, is in all mouths; and finally you, the King, whom our Lord Jesus Christ has appointed head of the Christian people and who surpass the other two in power, wisdom, and dignity. See, the safety of the Church of Christ depends entirely on you alone."

The question was how the King could help. A mere restoration of Leo seemed impossible in view of the accusation. The Pope could have taken an oath of purgation according to Germanic law or declared his abdication. But it was not only Alcuin who had misgivings in regard to these solutions. Only the Emperor, if anyone at all, could act as judge of the Pope. But even the Emperor's competence was questionable according to the canonical principle formulated at the beginning of the sixth century: "Prima sedes a nemine iudicatur." And so Charles finally postponed a decision. He had Leo conducted back to Rome and through his *missi* introduced a process for gathering information.

The "Paderborn Epic", already mentioned, describes the reception of the Pope by the Frankish King according to imperial etiquette and thus shows that the imperial question was in the air. Soon after the Pope's departure, an envoy sent by the Patrician Michael of Sicily met the King in September. Unfortunately, the subject of their conversations is unknown. The next Byzantine embassy, delegated by the Empress *propter pacem confirmandam,* did not reach the Frankish Court until the beginning of 802.

The Pope was back in Rome on 29 November. In December royal agents, headed by the Archchaplain Hildebald of Cologne and Arn of Salzburg, held a *placitum* in the Lateran *triclinium,* to which Paschal and Campulus were invited. Arn complained to Alcuin *de moribus apostolici* in such a manner that Alcuin burned the letter. But the accusers had, in accord with Roman law, the burden of the proof, and apparently they were unable to adduce adequate evidence. The royal agents had no authority to render a final decision of the case, and so they restored Leo temporarily. The accusers were arrested and sent across the Alps "on the basis of a verdict of unjustified violence and violation of the peace", to quote Zimmermann.

The King took his time. He spent the winter at Aachen and in 800 at the beginning of spring set out for the North Sea. Here he took preventive measures of security against the Vikings, who shortly before had directed their first raids against Northumbria, Scotland, and Ulster. At the end of April he went via Rouen to Tours, where he received the submission of the Bretons and discussed with his son Louis the progress of the operations in Spain and the protection of the coasts of Aquitaine and Septimania from Muslim pirates. He surely also conferred here with Alcuin on the Roman question. His stay was prolonged because of the illness of Queen Luitgardis, who died at Tours on 4 June. Alcuin accompanied Charles back to Aachen, where in mid-June occurred the synod at which he overcame Felix of Urgel. The synod probably also afforded an opportunity of discussing the Roman question again in detail with the Frankish bishops.

The journey to Rome was not arranged until the general assembly of Mainz at the beginning of August. Again time elapsed before it got under way. At the middle of November Charles was in Ravenna. On November 23 he arrived at Mentana, twelve leagues from Rome. The Pope welcomed him at Mentana with a banquet. At the first milestone a solemn procession was formed, the mounted cavalcade of ruler and court, passing amid the acclamations of the Roman corporations and the foreign *scholae,* which had stationed themselves along the King's route. The ceremonial accompanying Charles's first entry into Rome in 774 had been quite different. This time it displayed the marks of honour rendered to the Emperor, and Charles could not but know that.

In Rome the King convoked a council on the model of the Frankish general synods. In addition to the higher clergy of Rome and of the Frankish Kingdom, the Roman Senate and the Frankish magnates were also invited to take part. The council held plenary sessions in Saint Peters's under the King's presidency on 1 and 23 December. But the first plenary session had already been preceded by preliminary discussions. The members of the council were not in agreement: a part upheld Alcuin's viewpoint, that the Pope could not be judged, while the others demanded that Leo exculpate himself. The outcome of the preliminary discussions was a compromise. In the opening address on 1 December the King declared that the purpose of the meeting was to examine the accusation against the Pope. The assembly replied that it was unwilling to sit in judgment on the Pope, whereupon Leo declared his readiness "to purge himself of the false charges in the presence of the assembly, following the example of his predecessors". At the plenary session of 23 December the Pope took an oath of purgation, which referred only to the points of the accusation. To quote Zimmermann again, "the other objections that had been made against Leo remained undiscussed".

Following the conciliar session the participants, according to the *Annals of Lorsch,* demanded the transfer of the imperial dignity to Charles on the ground that the imperial throne among the Greeks was vacant, while Charles already possessed the imperial city of Rome as well as all the other imperial capitals in Italy (Ravenna was meant and perhaps also Milan), Gaul (Trier and Arles), and Germany (probably Mainz), so that he was really already an Emperor without the title. Charles is said to have agreed. There is no reason to doubt this report. For ten years already the court theologians and the higher clergy had been expounding Charles's imperial position by referring to his possession of Italy, Gaul, and Germany. Was it mere chance that on that same 23 December the court chaplain Zachary returned from an embassy to Jerusalem accompanied by two monks of the monasteries of Mount

Olivet and Saint Sabas, who, on the orders of the Patriarch, delivered the keys of the Holy Sepulchre and of the City of David as well as a banner, thereby recognizing Charles as the protector of the Christians of the East? The imperial position of the great Frankish King could not have been more clearly demonstrated.

According to custom, the Pope celebrated the third Mass of Christmas 800 in Saint Peter's, where the conciliar session of 23 December had taken place. After the *oratio,* during which all bowed low, the *laudes* were intoned on solemn festivals. But before they were begun, Leo III took a crown and placed it on the King's head with a brief formula of blessing. At once the Romans acclaimed Charles as Emperor, and the imperial title was also included in the *laudes* by the congregation: "Carolo Augusto, a Deo coronato, magno et pacifico imperatori Romanorum, vita et victoria!"[4] Some sources report also the investing of Charles with the purple imperial mantle and the presentation of a scepter. Leo III rendered *proskynesis* to the new Emperor, just as it had been due to the former Emperors. It was the first and last *proskynesis* of a Pope before an Emperor of the mediaeval West.

Still controverted is the interpretation of the celebrated passage in Einhard's *Vita Caroli,* that Charles felt such an aversion for the *nomen imperatoris* that, despite the great feast day, he would not have gone into the church, if he had foreseen the Pope's intention.[5] In the present state of research it can no longer be held that Charles had been surprised by the act as such and was absolutely opposed to the imperial office. The context in Einhard permits us to suppose that Charles's expression was uttered in irritation over later complications with Constantinople. However, it must be recognized that the transfer of the Roman imperial office to the King of the Franks also posed internal constitutional problems, which could not become clear until later. Perhaps Charles, following the model of the council of 23 December, intended a greater role for his Franks in the act of his elevation and took offence at the manner in which the Pope and the Romans had pushed themselves into the foreground.[6] A proclamation as Emperor by the Franks with the exclusion of the Romans or even an autocratic assumption of the

---

[4] *Annales regni 801.* In the *Liber Pontificalis* the formula is given thus: "Karolo, piissimo Augusto, a Deo coronato, magno et pacifico imperatore, vita et victoria!" According to Classen, *op. cit.* I, 588, the version of the *Liber Pontificalis* corresponds to the "only text spoken by the Romans".

[5] *Vita Caroli,* 28.

[6] Thus Folz, *Couronnement impérial,* 172 ff. But this supposition is still problematic. In no sense may the opinion be held which claims that in 800 Leo appeared in the role of a Pope who himself possessed the rank and attributes of an Emperor. Opposed to this opinion is the *proskynesis* which Leo exhibited to the new Emperor. As Classen says, personal motives may have been decisive for Leo III at this moment. "It was probably more important for him to render harmless his Roman opponents for all time than to insist on the postulate of the *Constitutum Constantini* that no earthly Emperor might rule in Rome" (*op. cit.* I, 574).

imperial title could, of course, not have been considered, since a "Frankish" empire would have been juridically insignificant and would have impressed no one. If Charles wanted the imperial office — and today this is certain — then he also had to accept the only possible form in which it could have been validly created: that of Roman constitutional law. The sources indicate that various nuances were possible within the prescribed form. The context of Charles's remark as reported by Einhard cannot be more precisely ascertained, despite all the exertions of scholars.[7]

A few days after the imperial coronation Charles sat in judgment on the Roman opposition. The leaders of the rebels were, in accordance with Roman law, condemned to death as *rei maiestatis,* but then, on Leo's intercession, the sentence was commuted to exile. The judgment on the Roman opposition shows that, as Emperor, Charles had become overlord of Rome and of the Papal State. In the dating of papal charters the year of the Emperor took precedence over the year of the Pope. A testimony from the end of the ninth century makes known that the same change occurred in the matter of pictorial representation. The papal coins hereafter bore Charles's name and title on the obverse, Leo's monogram on the reverse.

That the Roman-Christian imperial ideology was adopted along with the imperial dignity appears from the imperial style, which was determined at the latest during Charles's stay at Ravenna in May 801. The old royal title — *Rex Francorum et Langobardorum atque Patricius Romanorum* — expressed the triple constitutional nature of Charles's authority. After the assumption of the imperial office the Roman reference had to move to first place. There could result constitutional difficulties, since the royal nation of the Franks was pushed into second place. These were evaded by adopting the formula *Romanum gubernans imperium,* customary in Italy, so that the imperial title was now: "Karolus serenissimus Augustus, a Deo coronatus, magnus et pacificus imperator, Romanum gubernans imperium, qui et per misericordiam Dei rex Francorum et Langobardorum". The *Imperium Romanum* is to be understood here, in the sense of a theology of history, as "an institution with a mandate from God as the Ruler of the World".[8] The King of the Franks and Lombards executed the mandate as Emperor. The position of the Franks as the predominant people in the state was thereby maintained, and at the same time the imperial office was defined as dominion over Christendom.

The imperial title was not the only thing new in the symbolism of the state. Into his charters Charles introduced the solemn invocation of God, the years of the Emperor and of the indiction, and, in the case of bulls, a special eschatocol with a Byzantine-type chancery signature. He had an imperial seal cut, which bore on the obverse the image of the ruler, the imperial title,

---

[7] The best summary of the problem is given by Classen, *op. cit.* I, 589–91.
[8] Schramm, *Karl der Grosse im Lichte der Staatssymbolik,* 37.

and the imperial epithets of the old type, on the reverse a symbol of the city of Rome, with the circular legend *Renovatio Romani imperii*. The image of the ruler on the new imperial coinage followed a medallion of Constantine; on the reverse was a church, with the inscription *Religio christiana*. Thus the symbolism of gold seal and coinage stressed the Roman and Christian imperial ideology; the image on the coins seems to indicate that Charles saw in Constantine his imperial exemplar.

CHAPTER 15

The Development of the Carolingian Theocracy

The imperial years of Charles the Great were a time of relative external peace for the Frankish world. The Emperor had Holstein organized as a march against the Danes. In the Slavonic foreland of Eastphalia the Wilzi, who were allied with the Danes, and likewise the Obodrites and the Sorbs finally had to acknowledge Frankish suzerainty. Supervision of the Danish-Slavonic frontier was assumed by the Emperor's oldest son, Charles, who from 798 had directed the last struggles against the Saxons on his own and in 800 had been anointed King by the Pope. The same tasks were thus assigned to him which his younger brothers were performing on the frontiers of Italy and Aquitaine.

Much greater anxiety was certainly caused the Emperor by the piratical raids of Spanish and African Muslims, who regularly visited the islands and coasts of the western Mediterranean from 806 to 813. Charles's security measures extended also to the North Sea and Atlantic coasts. However, the Viking peril was not yet apparent in these years. The Emperor's chief task lay in the sphere of domestic politics. Virgil had once described the historical task of the *Imperium* as a mission to establish peace, based on dominion. To the Roman notion of peace had been added the Christian concept, based on charity. It stood at the centre of Augustine's *Civitas Dei. Iustitia,* which realized *ordo, ordo,* whose fruit is *pax,* and *pax* itself were no longer understood as referring to the static internal life but were related to Christ; they were capable of increase, open to God.

The Germans did not know the universal peace of the Roman and Christian type. Their peace was of various forms and degrees, like the circles of law in which the German lived. The law circles of the house, the kinship, the confederation were regarded as autonomous communities, not derived from the state, which the King must not violate. Hence even the King's peace had no universal validity. It referred to definite aspects of public life — worship, court of justice, army. The King could not exclude the feud *infra patriam;* at most he could settle it. If he wished to impose universal peace, this was possible only by means of the *pax christiana*. The Christian peace, basically the concern of the Church, thereby became the business of the ruler. Thus is explained the remarkable admixture of religious, political, and social aspects of peace in the Carolingian capitularies.

The Christian royal dignity had made the ruler the representative of the *pax christiana*. But the transfer of the imperial office now provided new impulses and once again considerably intensified Charles's exertions for *iustitia, ordo,* and *pax*. The majority of the extant capitularies of the great monarch are from his imperial years, and the most important of these are from 802–03 and 805–06. The new ethos is most eloquent in the oath to the Emperor of 802. After the conspiracy of 786 Charles had reintroduced the Merovingian oath required of the subjects, and following the crisis of 792–93 he had required a second swearing. The older formula of the oath contained only the obligation of refraining from acts of *infidelitas* against the King. The instruction to the royal *missi* of 802 shows that this obligation was now transformed and extended. The oath to the Emperor obliged positively to active preparedness in the service of God, to active willingness for the realization of *aequitas*. Negatively, it obliged to a renunciation of any attack on the group of the defenceless especially protected by the Emperor — orphans, widows, the Church, pilgrims, strangers — and of any act against the Emperor's regulations. The duty of fidelity was formally reinforced by the acceptance of the formula of vassalage into the oath to the Emperor. After a renewed prohibition of all "private" sworn associations in 803 and 805, the taking of the oath as such was restricted in 805 to the oath to the Emperor — the oath of the subjects — the oath of vassals, which involved the Emperor, and the oath in court, that is, to the obligation toward God and the ruler.

The inclusion of God and his commandments in the oath-taking had as a consequence the extending of the cases of *infidelitas* and *periurium* to attacks on the defenceless, the usurping of royal property and the exploitation of *beneficia* for private ends, the misuse of representation in court, and disregard of military duty. Offences against the decalogue ranked thereafter as *infidelitas* and could be punished with corresponding penalties. The *latro* appears as "infidelis noster et Francorum". In this way a prohibition of the feud also became possible. The instructions to the *missi* of 802 and 805 contained such prohibitions and ordered the settlement of feuds by compositions: "distringantur ad pacem, etiamsi noluerint".[1] The instruction of 805 forbade the bearing of arms — *scuti, lanceae, loricae* — *infra patriam*. Thus was inaugurated the struggle of the mediaeval crown against the feud, even though it took centuries for it to have definite success.

The ruler's sphere of jurisdiction was considerably expanded by the

---

[1] *MGCap* I, no. 44, 123, of 805. Cf. also *MGCap* I, no. 33, 32, of 802.

acceptance of the *pax christiana,* and memories of the ancient imperial office probably contributed to a further expansion. In Charles's imperial capitularies the *Lex scripta* was stressed in a novel way as the basis of justice. The *Lex Saxonum* and the *Lex Thuringorum* were drawn up, and the publishing of the *Lex Frisionum* was prepared for. Even more significant was the inclusion of matter taken from tribal law in the legislation of the capitularies and the effort to create a uniform Frankish law. But after the first stimulus of 802–3 this attempt broke down.

A special importance attaches to the Imperial Assembly of Aachen of October 802 in both secular and ecclesiastical legislation. Just as the relevant tribal law was prescribed for the laity, so the *Dionyso-Hadriana* and the Benedictine *Rule* were prescribed for the clergy. The *Dionyso-Hadriana* was, then, to occupy in Church life the same position as tribal law in secular life. But within the ecclesiastical sphere a clearer distinction was made between the diocesan and the regular clergy. The *vita canonica,* modelled on Chrodegang's *Rule,* was set off more clearly than before from the Benedictine *lex* of monasticism. The introduction of the Roman Office among the diocesan clergy and of the Benedictine Office among the regular clergy brought about a separation also in the liturgical sphere. At first, it is true, none of this went beyond decrees. The implementation of the new order was reserved for Louis the Pious, who again took up the work of the synod of 802.

The dogmatic discussions had come to rest. Only the controversy over the *processio Spiritus Sancti* flared up again in 809, since in Palestine there had occurred dissensions between the Frankish and oriental monks on this question. Theodulf of Orléans and Abbot Smaragdus of Saint-Mihiel submitted opinions, and Charles once again involved the Pope in the matter. But the usually weak Leo clung to the position of his predecessor and refused to admit the *Filioque* into the Roman Creed.

In these years the capitularies were further concerned with questions of law, of ecclesiastical discipline, of education and pastoral activity. Legislation in regard to the proprietary church was further developed. While the bishop's participation in the nomination of the clergy serving such churches and his right of direction had already been established, now the episcopal right of supervision of the buildings belonging to proprietary churches was laid down (803–13), the simoniacal granting of such churches was forbidden, and the removal of the clerics serving them was subjected to the bishop's approval (813). In order to enhance the effectiveness of the legislation by capitulary and to put an end to graft and to oppression of the people by the *missi,* from 802 on Charles chose his *missi* only from the ranks of the bishops, abbots, and counts, no longer from the simple vassals. He then proceeded to set up definite *missatica.*

There are indications that the monarch's strength waned after 806; a grave chronic illness befell him in 811. In the capitularies of this period there were complaints that the *concordia* between the spiritual and the temporal magnates left very much to be desired. Clerical immunities on the one hand and the proprietary church system and ecclesiastical *beneficia* on the other gave rise to conflicts. In 809 the Emperor planned to resume ecclesiastical legislation on a more elaborate scale but the Danish peril of 810 forced him to put it aside. In 813 he convoked synods of the entire Empire to Mainz, Reims, Tours, Chalon, and Arles, which were to correct deficiencies and discuss the prosecution of the reform. In this connection he raised the question of the penitential discipline and thereby supplied impetus to the struggle against the insular penitentials under the auspices of canon law. But the completion of the work was not to be granted to him; it became the task of his successor.

The question of the succession had been most intimately connected with the constitutional formation of the Empire since Christmas of 800; for its part, the constitution of the Empire was inseparable from the development of relations with the Greek East. Charles's imperial coronation could only be regarded on the Bosphorus as an unprecedented usurpation and an immediate threat. The war between the Franks and the Beneventans was not yet ended, and in Byzantium it was feared that the Franks would attack Sicily. Furthermore, the relations which Charles had established at the end of 797 with the Caliph Harun-ar-Raschid of Baghdad could have been aimed at Constantinople and Córdoba. Meanwhile a peaceful solution was being sought in the West. When a Greek embassy arrived in Aachen at the beginning of 802, Charles is said to have tried to effect the union of the two Christian Empires by an offer of marriage to the Empress Irene.[2] Irene was dethroned on 31 October 802, soon after the arrival of the Frankish embassy, and relegated to a convent, where she died on 9 August 803. The new Emperor Nicephorus I sent Charles an embassy, which reached Salz in the summer of 803. But the negotiations collapsed. Charles apparently insisted on a recognition of his imperial dignity; his counter-proposals received no reply.

War eventually broke out, and the coasts of the Adriatic Sea became the scene of the conflict. The Patriarch Fortunatus of Grado, the highest ranking ecclesiastic in Venetia, had presented himself to Charles in August 803 to have his privileges confirmed. He probably urged the reconstituting of the ancient ecclesiastical province of Venetia (Aquileia), which had been divided for 200 years into the Lombard province of Aquileia (Cividale) and the imperial province of Venetia (Grado). As a matter of fact, in January 805 Emperor and Pope reached an agreement at Aachen "de Aquileiense ecclesia velut una, quae suam sedem haberet". The Patriarch's Frankish policy at first encountered resistance from the people of Venetia, who expelled him;

[2] The fantastic plan was probably based only on rumours then current in Constantinople (cf. Classen, *op. cit.* I, 596–98).

but then around the turn of 805–6 they appeared before Charles with the Dalmatians (Zara) to do homage to him. In 806 Nicephorus dispatched a fleet to recover the lost districts. After struggles which lasted until 810 and in which success varied from one side to the other, King Pepin succeeded in partially subjecting Venetia, but the Frankish attack on the Dalmatian maritime cities failed.

The Frankish monarch certainly regarded Venetia only as a dead pledge. When the Byzantine Emperor sent an envoy to Pepin in 810, Charles seized the opportunity to end the war. The envoy, who found that Pepin was dead, was invited to come to Aachen, where Charles offered the renunciation of Venetia and the Dalmatian cities in exchange for the recognition of the western imperial office. A Frankish embassy went to Byzantium in the spring of 811 to negotiate on this basis. Nicephorus fell in battle against the Bulgars in July, but his successor, Michael I, accepted the proposal. A Byzantine embassy which reached Aachen in April 812 proclaimed the recognition of the Western Emperor, and at the beginning of 813 a new Frankish embassy went to Constantinople for the ratification of the peace. In the negotiations of 811–12 Charles had agreed to renounce the Roman setting of his imperial dignity, as demanded by the Greeks. The authentic "Roman" imperial office, which alone was anchored in the classical and the Christian theology of history as the world Empire, was reserved to the Eastern Emperor, who, after the peace with the Franks, adopted the expanded title of Βασιλεὺς τῶν Ῥωμαίων *(Imperator Romanorum)*.

Peace with Constantinople brought also peace with Benevento in the summer of the same year 812. Grimoald II, who had lost his Byzantine support, acknowledged Frankish suzerainty and obliged himself to pay tribute. The third peace of this year was concluded around the same time with the Emir of Córdoba. The Western Empire had discovered a *modus vivendi* with the Eastern Empire and the neighbouring Islamic state, and so it was hardly an accident that relations between Aachen and Baghdad were thereafter discontinued.

The peace treaties of 812 crowned the work of Charles the Great. The future of the Western Empire was first definitely assured by the Byzantine recognition. A settlement had been found on the basis of the twofold imperial office, which remained from now on a fact in the history of Christendom. The renunciation of the universality of his imperial dignity, which was implied by the surrender of the Roman setting, was probably not difficult for Charles to make, for he was especially concerned for a position of equality with Constantinople, and this seemed to have been achieved with the recognition of the Western imperial office. It was hardly perceived at Aachen that the twofold emperorship could not but deepen the cleavage in Christendom, but was probably sensed at Rome.

The imperial coronation of 800 had proceeded, on the part of the Franks and of the Romans, from the assumption that the imperial throne was vacant. And the fantastic project of a marriage between Charles and Irene was based on the notion that there could be only one Emperor in Christendom. Irene's deposition, which could scarcely have become known in the West before the beginning of 803, compelled a rethinking of the imperial question. For Rome a solution certainly lay along the same lines as for Constantinople, since the Roman and Christian imperial idea was still a living reality in both cities: if it was necessary to come to terms with a second Emperor, he was permitted to be only an Emperor of a lesser order. But of course the omens were opposed: If the Greeks intended to reserve the authentic "Roman" imperial office for themselves, then the Pope was concerned to present the ruler of the West as the real world-emperor in the meaning of the theology of history. It has been surmised that in this connection Leo III made use of the Donation of Constantine, in which the precedence of Old Rome over New Rome was clearly stressed. As a matter of fact, evidence upholds this conjecture. However, the *Constitutum Constantini* was certainly not composed for this purpose; rather it was reinterpreted. In it could be read that Constantine had given the imperial crown to Pope Silvester, who, however, had declined to wear it. If the forger was concerned about the theoretical justification of the papal sovereignty in a new age with no Emperor, similarly after the reconstitution of the Western Empire a papal power to dispose of the genuine imperial crown of Constantine and of Old Rome could be deduced from the same text. Perhaps Leo III interpreted the passage in this sense after 802 and explained this interpretation to "his" Emperor on the occasion of a second visit to Frankland (November 804 to January 805).[3]

If this assumption is correct, Charles the Great did not go along with Leo's suggestion. He was unwilling to base the pre-eminence of the western imperial office on an interpretation of the *Constitutum* whereby that office would have been derived from the Pope; furthermore, he was neither able nor willing to consider the imperial question apart from the Frankish royal and dynastic law. His reply, given at Thionville on 6 February 806, was the regulation of the succession, the *Divisio imperii,* in which, following Frankish law, he divided the *imperium vel regnum* equally among his three sons. The already existing subkingdoms of the younger sons, Pepin and Louis, were enlarged in view of the succession: Italy by the addition of Rhaetia, Bavaria, and Alemannia south of the Danube; Aquitaine by means of the larger part of Burgundy to the line Auxerre-Chalon-Mâcon-Lyons-Savoy. The oldest son, Charles, was to receive the heart of the immediate ancestral area of dominion: *Francia* between the Loire and the Rhine, with northern Burgundy and northern Alemannia, with Frisia, Saxony, and Thuringia. The nucleus of

---

[3] Schlesinger, *Kaisertum und Reichsteilung,* 36 ff.; see also Ohnsorge, *Abendland und Byzanz,* 90 ff.

this portion of the Empire was *Francia,* so that it is possible to speak of a division of the Empire into three subdivisions: Frankland, Italy, and Aquitaine. The pre-eminence of the oldest son was expressed by the allotting of *Francia* to Charles. A further characteristic of the *Divisio* lay in the uniform assignment of the most important Alpine passes to the three sons, who were to aid one another and to undertake together the protection of the Roman Church and of the other churches.

Older studies held that in the *Divisio* Charles had entirely disregarded the imperial office, but it has recently been demonstrated by Schlesinger that this view is incorrect. Out of regard for the still unclarified situation produced by the war with Byzantium, the ruler of the West left open two possibilities: a withdrawal to a hegemonic imperial office of a Frankish colouring and an imperial office in the succession to Constantine but disregarding the *Constitutum.* The expectation of the imperial office was made ready for the three sons by their elevation to be *consortes.* Charles thereby reserved to himself the possibility "of designating one of the *consortes* as sole bearer of the *nomen imperatoris"* or, "after the example of Constantine, of making all three the holders of the imperial title" (Schlesinger).

Charles the Great's two oldest sons died before the conclusion of the negotiations with Constantinople, which brought Byzantine recognition of the Western Empire. Only Pepin of Italy left a son, Bernard, to whom his grandfather assigned the Lombard Kingdom in 812. Bernard could not rank as an equal partner in the succession with the Emperor's only surviving son; he was also invested only with the subkingdom of Italy, not with the expanded inheritance of his father Pepin. Now only King Louis of Aquitaine was considered as successor in the imperial office and in the entire Empire. Charles intended to make him coemperor in his own lifetime, following the imperial practice of Constantinople. After he had obtained the consent of the magnates to this project, he had Louis come to Aachen. On 11 September 813, the Emperor, in his robes of state and attended by his son and the magnates, proceeded to the chapel at Aachen. After they had prayed together, he committed his son before the altar to the duties of ruler and lord. He then crowned Louis with a crown that had been laid on the altar[4] and had him acclaimed as *Imperator et Augustus* by the people. There was no religious coronation. The act of 813 shows that, despite his renunciation of the Roman setting of his title, Charles regarded himself as a "genuine" Emperor in

---

[4] According to Thegan, *Vita Hludowici* in *MGSS* II, 592, Charles commanded his son Louis to put on his own head the crown that had been laid on the altar. In this statement Thegan is in opposition to all other sources, which speak of a coronation by the father. A self-coronation would have been without parallel at this period. If one nevertheless follows Thegan's account, the explanation is that the seriously ill and aged Emperor was, physically, in no condition to crown his son himself — as Eichmann and von Fichtenau agree — but the act was regarded as performed by the father.

101

succession to Constantine. At the same time the imperial office was now firmly bound up with Aachen und *Francia;* the polarity of *Imperium christianum* and *Regnum Francorum* was neutralized at least for the next reign.

The Empire was provided for. As early as the beginning of 811, when Charles fell gravely ill, he had arranged by testament a division of the treasure of the *camera.* On 22 January 814, the Emperor, who was almost seventy-two years old, was attacked by a high fever. Pneumonia developed, and the Emperor died on 28 January. His remains were laid to rest, not at Saint-Denis with his parents and his grandfather, but in the Marienkirche at Aachen.[5]

There has been talk of a crisis in the last years of Charles's reign. According to this, the Emperor achieved no real success in regard to Benevento and Brittany, the Elbe Slavs and the Bohemians, the North Sea Vikings and the Mediterranean Saracens. In particular, the great impulse of 802 petered out ineffectually. The *Divisio* of 806 stood in sharp contrast to the concept of Emperor and Empire as expressed in 802. There was no institutional sub-structure to support the gigantic Empire; only the unusual qualities of its creator enabled it to endure for a while. But as early as 811 the cracks in the building were already clear, and Louis the Pious inherited an *Imperium* that was already in a state of internal decay.

This sharp criticism is not without justification in individual points, but on the whole it goes too far. No danger threatened the Empire from Benevento, Brittany, or the Slavs, and the Viking and Muslim pirates became really dangerous only after the death of Louis the Pious. Today the *Divisio* of 806 is no longer regarded as a denial of the imperial idea of 802. The gigantic Empire did indeed lack an established officialdom, and it may be correct that, as a whole, it had to collapse sooner or later. But it long held its own, "thanks to its inherent solidity and tenacity" (Schieffer). But, above all, its distinctive force did not disappear with its break-up: none of the successor states could deny its Carolingian origin. The order of the Church, the feudal system, the reform of currency and courts, the new Christian concept of ruler and state, the Carolingian reform of education — all these outlived Charles's Empire. Through these accomplishments Charles became one of the great builders of Europe: with all his "desire to rule and to exercise power" still not extravagant in conquest, in the prudent use of elements at hand, in the arranging and binding of these elements into a new comprehensive whole, he is quite comparable to Augustus.

[5] In regard to the place of burial cf. Kreusch, "Kirche, Atrium und Porticus der Aachener Pfalz" in *Karl der Grosse. Lebenswerk und Nachleben,* III, 499, with the bibliography: "under the ambo between the two eastern piers of the octogon".

SECTION FOUR

Climax and Turning Point of the Carolingian Age
(814 to 840)

CHAPTER 16

Reform in Empire and Church from 814 to 828

When his father died, the thirty-five-year-old Louis of Aquitaine was in his prime. He was seriously inclined and did not care for noisy good fellowship. He early encountered the great reformer of his realm, who was to be closely associated with him throughout life, the Visigoth Witiza, who as a monk took the name Benedict.

Witiza was born in 751, son of a Visigothic Count of Maguelonne, who had joined the Franks. He became a page at Pepin's court and cupbearer of Queen Bertrada. In 774 he distinguished himself at the siege of Pavia. An accident that befell his brother made him reflect seriously, and in 780 he entered the abbey of Saint-Seine near Dijon, where he studied the oriental, Greek, and Latin monastic rules. When he realized that the complete observance of the Benedictine Rule was not possible at Saint-Seine, he founded the monastery of Aniane on his ancestral property in his Septimanian homeland. The new monasticism made a deep impression on the members of the social class to which Witiza-Benedict belonged. With his assistance the Margrave William of Toulouse established the monastery of Gellone in 804. At the royal court of Aquitaine the Chancellor Helisachar was one of the friends of the Abbot of Aniane. Up to 814 twenty-five monasteries are said to have been reformed or founded in Louis's kingdom. The reform also affected the neighbouring districts. Alcuin of Tours, Theodulf of Orléans, and Leidrad of Lyons caused the renewal of abbeys subject to them. The bishops meeting at Chalon-sur-Saône in 813 decided that the pure Benedictine Rule was to be observed throughout their jurisdictions. Charles the Great himself was impressed by the Aniane reform, but its great hour did not strike until the reign of his successor.

Although Louis was already coemperor, he seems to have expected opposition to his succession. He feared Charles's cousins, Abbot Adalard of Corbie and Count Wala, and took measures against his sisters' lovers, probably not only for reasons of morality. Charles's daughters were not permitted to choose between marriage and the veil, as their father had directed; they were thrust into convents. Louis conscientiously carried out the stipulations in regard to material things in his father's last will. He even maintained his half-brothers, Drogo, Hugh, and Theuderich at court and had his sisters' sons raised as befitted their station. Bernard of Italy came to do homage and was dismissed graciously. Of Louis's own children, Lothar and Pepin, who had already attained their majority, received Bavaria and Aquitaine as subkingdoms. The third son, Louis the German, was still a minor and remained in the company of his father.

The Emperor reorganized the Aachen *ministeria* by a new palace order and thereby introduced a stricter discipline along the court magnates. The palace school, the library, and the supervision of construction remained, but the poets vanished from Aachen for the time being. Louis did not have his father's versatility; his interests lay especially in theology and Church reform. Benedict of Aniane was summoned to the imperial court. He first received the abbey of Maursmünster in Alsace, but soon moved to the abbey of Inden, now Cornelimünster, which was consecrated in 817 as an imperial foundation near the *sedes* of Aachen. Alongside the Aachen palace school, whose brilliance faded in comparison with the later flourishing cultural centres of the Carolingian Renaissance in the Empire, stood the Benedictine abbey as the dominant reform centre.

Of the advisers and friends of Charles the Great several survived the old Emperor — his cousins Adalard of Corbie (d. 826) and Count Wala (d. 836), the Archchaplain Hildebald (d. 818), Theodulf of Orléans (d. 821), and Arn of Salzburg (d. 821). So did Jesse of Amiens (d. 837) and Einhard (d. 840), but in regard to age they belonged to the new Emperor's generation. Even before the end of 814 there came a break between Louis and the collateral Carolingian line of Adalard. The Abbot of Corbie was banished to Noirmoutier at the mouth of the Loire, while Count Wala became a monk at Corbie. There existed points of opposition connected with monasticism between Adalard and Benedict of Aniane. But personal and family differences between Louis the Pious and the Abbot of Corbie were probably the decisive factors. In Charles's last years Adalard and Wala had been closely associated with Bernard of Italy. They may have looked after his interests more energetically than was to the liking of the new ruler.

In other respects the new Emperor brought his own confidants to court without removing his father's advisers. Hildebald of Cologne retained the direction of the court chapel, which passed only after his death to Hilduin of Saint-Denis. Einhard gave up the direction of the palace school and of construction but he remained in the Emperor's council. Louis assigned him a number of important abbeys and in 815 the Mark Michelstadt in the Odenwald. More significant was the change in the chancery, where the chancellor of Aquitaine, Helisachar, replaced Charles's last chancellor, Jeremias. But Jeremias in no sense fell into disgrace; he soon accepted the archiepiscopal see of Sens, one of the most important churches in the Empire. Under Helisachar the business of the chancery was managed by Durandus. Both men seem to have come from Septimania, Benedict's native land. Durandus retained the conduct of business when in 819 Fridugis, an Anglo-Saxon pupil of Alcuin, replaced Helisachar as chancellor. He probably created the new formulary for charters, which expressed the spirit of the Carolingian Renaissance in the official documents and at the same time served the new ruler's ecclesiastical policy. In the direction of the palace school Einhard's successor Clement was followed by the chaplains Aldric, Thomas, Gotabert, and Walafrid Strabo. Aldric became Abbot of Ferrières in 821, chancellor of Pepin of Aquitaine in 827, and Archbishop of Sens in 829. Besides Jeremias and Aldric of Sens there were other outstanding representatives of the new generation in the episcopate: Agobard of Lyons (d. 840), Ebbo of Reims (d. 851), Hetti of Trier (d. 847), Modoin of Autun (d. c. 843), and Jonas of Orléans (d. 843). The Spaniard Agobard and the Aquitanian Jonas, together with Witiza-Benedict, Helisachar, and Durandus, represented the Aquitanian-Spanish element among Louis's advisers.

The laymen in the retinue of the new Emperor belonged almost exclusively to the Frankish imperial aristocracy. Louis seems to have increased the number of court functions at Aachen rather than to have made new appointments. The most influential councillors were counts from western *Francia*. The greatest influence in the first decennium of the reign was exercised by Matfrid of Orléans. In 821 Lothar's father-in-law, Count Hugh of Tours, also entered the circle of the highest ranking advisers. The contact of this Frankish aristocracy with its native country along the Meuse and the Scheldt, the Moselle and the Rhine, was at that time still quite vital. People knew that the Empire had been re-established from there and felt pride in being the representatives of this Empire.

But Louis the Pious did not rule only with a narrow circle of men of confidence. He also sought uninterrupted contact with the rest of the magnates. Imperial assemblies, which had hitherto met once a year only, were soon convened two or even three times a year. However, not all the magnates of the Empire always attended them. There were also smaller assemblies, which considered a specific question and rather resembled a great council. Government in council was a characteristic of the new style. It was successful so long as a leading personality was able to combine the divergent opinions and interests of the various groups. Leading personalities of this sort were apparently Benedict of Aniane and Wala of Corbie, who in succession had a decisive influence in determining imperial policy.

The change on the imperial throne took place at a time of peace, and so the real tasks of the new Emperor lay in the field of domestic policy. Louis and his advisers energetically set about these tasks. As early as 814 movement

105

appeared in an imperial policy that had been stagnating for some years. *Missi* were sent to all parts of the Empire to inquire into and correct abuses in the administration of justice. At the same time the Emperor had ecclesiastical privileges called in for the purpose of reconfirmation. The confirmations were issued in accord with a new formula in which immunity and royal protection, two hitherto separate institutions, were merged. Immunity was an institution of public law and until the ninth century had been always granted to episcopal sees. It accorded to the immunist a certain autonomy in regard to taxation and courts of justice. Royal protection, on the other hand, was connected with entry into the sphere of the royal *mundeburdis;* royal proprietary monasteries in particular enjoyed it. By virtue of the union of immunity and protection episcopal sees and royal monasteries were assimilated: the latter obtained the greater internal freedom of movement of the old immune churches, while the former were admitted to the circle of royal churches. Thus Louis the Pious created a uniform Imperial Church, with a comprehensive Church reform as his aim.

After the constitutional presuppositions had been created, a great reform council met at Aachen in August 816. Its decrees affected clerics, monks, and nuns. For monks not only the Benedictine Rule but a uniform observance was prescribed; this observance assured a life apart from the world and, in Loewe's words, "directed [monasticism] to its proper tasks, particularly in liturgical prayer". Strict regulations in regard to inclosure relegated the laity to the periphery of claustral life. Manual labour was again enjoined, and monastic schools were restricted to the *oblati*. The Benedictine liturgy supplanted not only the Roman but also the *laus perennis*[1] and the *cursus Scotorum*. The lawgiver of monks was Benedict of Aniane. "Monasteria ita ad formam unitatis redacta sunt, acsi ab uno magistro et in uno imbuerentur loco. Uniformis mensura in potu, in cibo, in vigiliis, in modulationibus cunctis observanda est et tradita.[2]

Like the monastic reform, that of the canonical life also had recourse to the Aachen decrees of 802. The *Institutio canonicorum* that was now determined did not originate simply in Chrodegang's Rule for the clergy of Metz. It was inspired by the same ideal as Chrodegang's Rule, even though it was milder. It was based on statements from the Fathers of the Church. Clerics attached to cathedral and collegiate churches were allowed to retain their private property, but they were bound to the *vita communis,* including refectory and dormitory. The "uniformis mensura in cibo et potu" was also introduced here, but graduated in accord with the property of the churches. The Roman liturgy took care of the prayer life. Analogous regulations were contained in the *Institutio sanctimonialium,* or Rule for canonesses, which prescribed a

---

[1] The unceasing celebration of the Divine Office, starting at the Burgundian royal abbey of Saint-Maurice at the beginning of the sixth century.

[2] *Vita Benedicti abb. An.* in *MGSS* XV, 215 ff.

regular liturgy and a limited common life. Benedict and Helisachar were probably the initiators of the reform.

Ordo saecularis and *ordo regularis* had received their basic statutes at Aachen. The *vita canonica* of the diocesan clergy was clearly distinguished from the *vita regularis* of the monks in 816. The rules for canons and canonesses were sent to the bishops of the Empire, and their introduction within a year was made obligatory. Supervisory committees were announced to the monasteries for 1 September 817. After the close of the Council of Aachen the Emperor went to Reims for a personal discussion with the new Pope Stephen IV.

Leo III had died at Rome on 12 June 816. Stephen IV was elected as his successor and consecrated on 22 June. This was the first papal election to take place after the establishment of the Western Empire. In the Byzantine period papal elections had been ratified by the Emperor or Exarch before the consecration, though since the election of Zachary there had been no imperial approval. In 816 the Romans did not revert to the old imperial law, and Louis the Pious had nothing to do with the election. Stephen IV merely sent him a notification. But he had the Romans swear loyalty to the Emperor and requested a meeting with him.

Emperor and Pope met at Reims at the beginning of October 816. During a festive Mass in the cathedral Stephan IV anointed and crowned the Emperor and the Empress. For this purpose the Pope had brought the "crown of Constantine" from Rome, thereby underscoring the Roman notion of the imperial office. However, the events at Reims must not be overestimated — the Pope's biographer does not mention them at all. The coronation at Reims was not a constitutive act. Louis probably interpreted it as a "consolidating" of his imperial dignity. He renewed the *pactum amicitiae* with the Pope and allowed the opponents of Leo III, banished to Frankland sixteen years previously, to return to Rome. His other arrangements with the Pope were expressed in the privilege of 24 January 817, for the Roman Church, in which Louis confirmed in writing the freedom of papal elections and the autonomy of the Papal State in regard to administration and justice. The notification of the papal election was to be made only after the consecration, and the Emperor was to act as judge in the Papal State only in the event of a denial of justice. Stephen IV died on the very day on which the *Ludovicianum* was issued. The elevation of his successor, Paschal I, took place according to the form customary since Zachary and Stephen II and now formally recognized in the privilege.

Louis was content with a minimum of rights in Rome. But the exalted notion entertained by himself and his councillors in regard to the imperial office, which was characterized on the gold *solidi* as *munus divinum*, was not thereby affected. A reformulation of the imperial title had been rendered necessary because of the settlements with the Byzantines. With its concise simplification in the formula *Imperator Augustus*, not only the Roman but also the Frankish and Lombard relationship disappeared. The *Ordinatio imperii* of 817 expressed unambiguously that the Emperor should stand above the nations.

On Holy Thursday 817 the Emperor had an accident which impressed on him the transitory nature of earthly things. Magnates in his retinue besought him to promulgate a regulation of the succession, by which they meant a division of the Empire according to Frankish law. However, they afforded the opportunity for a new sort of imperial arrangement, which, following a triduum, was discussed and decided. The oldest son, Lothar, was elected and crowned coemperor "as a result of divine inspiration". The younger brothers, Pepin of Aquitaine and Louis, who obtained Bavaria, were made Kings, but both they and their areas of rule *(potestates)* remained subject to their father and his successors in the imperial dignity. Further divisions of the inheritance were forbidden even to the subkings. If there existed several heirs, election by the people should decide the succession.

In the *ordinatio* Empire and Church were understood as a unity. Hence the *unitas imperii* was regarded as willed by God. It must not be rent "by human division" to accomodate children, in order that no vexation may rise in Holy Church. On the unity of the Empire rested the eternal peace of the entire Christian people , the preservation of which the *ordinatio* claimed to foster. The office of Emperor and that of King were understood on the analogy of the office of bishop. Lothar was raised to the office of coemperor in an inspired election after a triduum, and this manner of election was provided for specific cases in the future, even for the subkings. The Emperor's penal law in relation to the Kings was copied from the Church's penal law: a threefold admonition *secreto per fideles legatos,* then *monitio et castigatio coram altero fratre,* and finally enforcement by the Empire after an interrogation of the imperial assembly.

In its impressive inclusiveness and its cold rationalism the *ordinatio* marks without any doubt a climax of Carolingian legislation and also of the Carolingian Renaissance, by whose leaders it was drawn up. At first the question remained open as to whether the daring imperial edifice would stand the test of history, even though it survived its first ordeal, the rebellion of Bernard of Italy. The legislators had assigned to the Italian *regnum* the same position as that accorded to Bavaria and Aquitaine. Thereby Bernard's rise to the rank of joint-king according to the old law was blocked. The Emperor's nephew had recourse to arms, but his fight for the old dynastic law ended in a complete debacle. In March 818 the unlucky prince, in whose ruin Theodulf of Orléans was also included, was condemned to death in an imperial assembly at Aachen. The Emperor commuted the sentence to blinding, as a result of which Bernard died. Italy received no new subking, and the unity of the Empire was assured for the immediate future.

Once the basic law of the *Imperium* had been secured against all opposition, the reform of 816 was again taken up. An imperial assembly met at Aachen after Christmas 818 to define the Church's ties to the Emperor and the Church's obligations to the Empire. The preface of the capitulary of 818–19 is a second significant document revealing the new concept of the Empire. It distinguishes the mortal person of the ruler from the imperial office, which stands on a lonely elevation. The Emperor is *adiutor Dei;* his sphere of duty embraces *ecclesiastica negotia* and *status rei publicae.* The Christian people are divided into three classes — canons, monks, and laity. The Emperor directs them and manages the reins of the Empire *aequissimo libramine.*

The filling of prelacies by the ruler had been an essential element in the administration of the Frankish Church since the sixth century. Most sees formally possessed the right to elect their bishops, whereas the abbots of the monasteries were in most cases determined by the founder or lord of the proprietary church. But the discrepancy between practice and law was here especially strong. In 818–19 Louis the Pious granted the right of election to all sees and to imperial monasteries of the *ordo regularis,* but he retained the right to confirm and invest, which involved a review of the election. The chapters of canons in the Empire did not obtain the privilege of election; here the direct nomination of the abbot or provost by the ruler continued to be possible, including the grant of the office to a lay abbot. Since, as a result of the distinction of the *vita canonica* and the *vita regularis,* many of the old monasteries of monks transformed themselves into canonries, the number of churches of which the monarch had the direct disposal remained considerable.

The contributions of the bishops to the Empire were of a public sort rather than of the nature of proprietary churches, and they continued basically as before. Unless it was otherwise determined in individual privileges, the bishops thus had also their court duties to fulfill — attendance at imperial assemblies and synods and the undertaking of the commission of *missi* — and to pay taxes and lodge the ruler and his envoys on journeys. The vassals of bishops owed military service to the monarch.

Besides their public burdens, the monasteries had to render in kind the *servitium* due from proprietary churches. In 818–19 Louis graded their burdens. In the first degree the full service was maintained, consisting of military levy, annual gifts, and prayer. A second degree was dispensed from the military levy, and a third from the annual gift as well, so that only the obligation of prayer for the Emperor remained. The determining of the three groups was made in accord with the current state of resources. A general invenventory of monastic property was ordered in connection with this definition.

Nonetheless, their imperial obligations were a heavy burden on the churches thereafter. In the hope of avoiding a disruption by them of the inner life of the Church a distinction was made between the property of the bishop or abbot and that of the chapter or monastery. The imperial burdens were laid on the property of bishop or abbot, while the goods of the chapter or monastery, the *mensa fratrum,* was to be reserved for the maintenance of the ecclesiastical community and its buildings as well as for the care of the poor. The episcopate was directed to place property at the disposal of ecclesiastical communities "ad claustra perficienda"; such land was freed from contributions to the ruler. These measures determined the development of the Church's organization for centuries and established the dualism of prelate and chapter. At the same time the reform inaugurated a new phase of architectural history, leading in the case of episcopal churches to the great cathedral.

The *capitulare ecclesiasticum* of 818–19 also regulated the situation of the lesser and the proprietary churches. Charles the Great had already decreed that the bishop should control the installation and removal and the conduct of the clergy of proprietary churches and prohibited the destroying of existing proprietary churches. Now, on the analogy of monastic and canonical reform, there was concern for the economic and social security of the clergy of proprietary churches, which was to be guaranteed by three fundamental rules. First, the ordination of the unfree to the priesthood was forbidden. Next, a minimum livelihood was fixed, consisting of one hide free of manorial burdens; for it, as well as for house and garden, tithes and offerings, only spiritual service was due. Finally, it was stipulated that a priest was to be appointed for every church with a legal minimum income. These principles were soon communicated from proprietary churches to parish churches under the bishop's immediate supervision, which were coming more and more to be regarded as the bishop's proprietary churches. Then two further regulations secured the rights of the manorial lords: bishops were obliged to ordain the clerics presented to them for proprietary churches if they were unobjectionable in their conduct and education and to assign the tithe to proprietary churches that were properly endowed and occupied.

The reform activity of these years was not confined to the ecclesiastical sphere. The administration of the court and of the finances at Aachen was reorganized early in the new reign. In addition to the holders of the old court offices there appeared under Louis *magistri ostiariorum, mendicorum, mercatorum, Iudaeorum* and a *mansionarius,* who was responsible for the residences of the magnates. Following the measures taken in Charles's last years, the *missatica* were erected as specified areas, in imitation of the ecclesiastical provinces. Within these jurisdictions a definite system for the transmission of orders was created. The capitularies were more clearly formulated, better arranged, more fundamentally justified, and more carefully preserved. Material from the tribal laws had already been introduced into the capitulary legislation under Charles. Louis the Pious went a step farther by having material from royal legislation adopted into the tribal laws, thereby conferring on royal law the enhanced prestige of *lex*.

Legislation by capitulary seems to have come to a temporary halt in 821. The Emperor's mentor, Benedict of Aniane, died on 11 February 821, and the Carolingian Empire moved into a new phase of its history.

The most conspicuous occurrence after the death of Benedict of Aniane was the reconciliation of the Emperor with Adalard and Wala and the amnesty granted to the rebels of 817 at the imperial assembly of Thionville in October 821. This was followed at Attigny in August 822 by the reconciliation of Louis with his three half-brothers, Drogo, Hugh, and Theuderich, who had been removed from court in 818 and forced to enter the clergy. At Attigny the Emperor made a public confession of his misdeeds against Adalard, Wala, and Bernard of Italy and did penance for all the wrong done perhaps by himself or his father. The bishops associated themselves with the confession and the penance. In this there has been a tendency to see a humiliation of the ruler by the proud Abbot Adalard, but such a view is wrong. Actually, it was a proving of the sincerity of the Emperor, who gave an example in the spirit of the new ruler-ethos. The work of 814–21 was not overthrown; rather it was ratified by the swearing of the magnates to the *ordinatio* at Nijmegen and Thionville in May and October 821. As Schieffer says, "What seemed to be regulated by statute and secured with regard to power was also to be consolidated morally in the spirit of justice, peace, and reconciliation".

Adalard gained a leading position in the Emperor's council, alongside the Archchaplain Hilduin, Abbot Helisachar, and Count Matfrid. Hardly noticeable as yet was the influence of the Empress Judith, whom Louis had married in 819 after the death of his first wife. One of the strongest personalities in the episcopate was Agobard, a man with a keen sense of duty, a clear and consistent, though not always realistic, thinker. His demand, made in 822 and repeated in 823, for the integral restitution of the property of the Church was disavowed by Adalard and Hilduin out of regard for the internal peace of the Empire. Nor would the two leading councillors allow a purely ecclesiastical consideration of the Jewish problem, which Agobard raised as a pastor of souls. Agobard had as little success in his attack on ordeals, which he launched in the spirit of Carolingian "rationalism", and in his proposal for making the *Lex Salica* the basis of a uniform imperial law. Obstacles insurmountable at that time were raised against this final bold demand, made in the spirit of unity.

In 822 Adalard left court for his abbey of Corbie, where he composed his *De ordine palatii,* probably as a sort of political testament. Meanwhile, his younger brother, Wala, had been appointed tutor of the coemperor Lothar. Lothar and Pepin, the two oldest sons, had grown up and married in 821 and 822 respectively, while the younger Louis was still at his father's court. When in 822 Lothar was sent to Italy to implement the Carolingian legislation, he was accompanied by Wala, who was of all the councillors the most conversant with the Italian situation. The young Emperor's measures in Italy were probably Wala's work essentially. Lothar stayed south of the Alps until 825. In 823, however, he returned to his father's court for two months, and while there he acted as godfather for his youngest brother, Charles. During these three years Italy was firmly incorporated into the Empire. But Lothar was not satisfied with the mere implementation of the Carolingian legislation. Beyond that he took a really unique step for this period in the field of culture by founding nine schools with corresponding school districts in the Lombard Kingdom.

The presence of the coemperor in Italy could not fail to have an effect on Rome. An invitation from Paschal I reached the young Emperor in the spring of 823. He accepted and was crowned by the Pope at Easter, like his father almost seven years earlier at Reims. But the meeting in Rome did not turn out entirely to Paschal's taste, since Lothar and Wala now took a firmer hold of the reins in the Papal State. After the departure of the Franks, some of the Pope's men killed two high papal functionaries "because in every respect they had shown themselves to be loyal to the young Emperor Lothar". Louis the Pious appointed an investigating committee. Paschal, however, checkmated it by taking an oath of purgation in regard to his role and shielding the ones responsible by a declaration that the dead men had been lawfully executed as traitors.

But the tables were turned when Paschal died in the spring of 824 and Wala procured the election of Eugene II, the candidate of the nobility. Thereby were established the preconditions for a new regulation of Frankish-Roman relations, which was published on 11 November 824 in the *Constitutio Romana*. In this Lothar declared that all persons under papal and imperial protection were unassailable, thereby putting his adherents for the future beyond the reach of a one-sided prosecution for treason. He introduced the principle of personality of law in the Papal State, where hitherto Roman law had prevailed. Even more decisive was the instituting of a supervisory tribunal officiating in Rome, composed of one papal and one imperial *missus*. They were to superintend the administration of the Papal State and make an annual report to the Emperor. The *mos canonicus* of the papal election was confirmed, but at the same time it was decreed that for the future the Pope-elect, before his consecration, had to take an oath *pro conservatione omnium* before the imperial *missus,* following the form of the oath first taken by Eugene II.

The Papal State was attached more firmly than ever to the Carolingian Empire by the *Constitutio*. At a Roman Synod in 826 Eugene II adopted also the Frankish legislation on proprietary churches in summary form. The bonds created by the *Constitutio* were lasting. Lothar strengthened them further in 844 by making the papal election dependent on a special imperial *iussio* and prescribing that it take place in the presence of imperial *missi*.

John IX approved this regulation at a Roman Synod of 898, although it actually went beyond the Byzantine imperial law.

Nevertheless, the *Constitutio Romana* did not affect the Pope as spiritual head of the Church. This point was made clear when on 17 November 824 an embassy from the Eastern Emperors Michael II and Theophilus appeared before Louis the Pious at Rouen. Its purpose was not only to re-establish relations, interrupted since the death of the Emperor Michael I in 813, but also to interest the Franks in a compromise with Rome in regard to the question of images. For Iconoclasm had flared up again at Constantinople under the Emperor Leo V (813–20). Michael II was inclined toward it but wanted to maintain internal peace. The attitude of the Franks, who allowed images but forbade any *adoratio,* seemed to him to provide a compromise solution. A Frankish embassy actually presented a petition in this sense at Rome. Eugene II maintained the decrees of Nicaea II, but granted the Emperor authorization to convoke a synod of the Empire in regard to Iconoclasm.

The synod met at Paris on 1 November 825, near or perhaps in the abbey of Saint-Denis, which was ruled by the Archchaplain Hilduin. As archchaplain he was the Emperor's first adviser in ecclesiastical questions, besides being personally interested in Greek theology. The participants in the synod, to which were submitted the letters of Pope Hadrian, the *acta* of Nicaea II, and the *Libri Carolini,* upheld the Frankish viewpoint, but aimed their polemic chiefly at the iconoclasts. They even outlined relevant replies from the Emperor to the Pope and from the Pope to the *Basileus,* which, however, Louis the Pious did not send on. He had the letter to the Pope rewritten and offered to Eugene II the sending of a common embassy to Byzantium, but nothing came of this. In regard to a second Byzantine embassy, that came to Compiègne in 827 *propter foedus confirmandum,* we know only that it delivered the works of the pseudo-Dionysius, certainly at the request of Hilduin. Iconoclasm had a journalistic epilogue in the Frankish Empire, evoked by the extremely iconoclastic writings of Bishop Claudius of Turin. Participants in the controversy included the Irishman Dungal and Bishop Jonas of Orléans. In the East Iconoclasm collapsed with the death of the Emperor Theophilus, and Orthodoxy was restored in 843.

Legislation in the Empire had come to a temporary halt in 821. The activity of the succeeding years centered rather on the enforcing of existing capitularies than on the introducing of new ones. Capitularies are not again extant until the years 825–26, and Abbot Ansegis of Saint-Wandrille probably began at that time his semiofficial collection of capitularies, which he completed in 827. Among the pieces from 825 belongs the *Admonitio ad omnes regni ordines,* the third and final document dealing with the concept of Emperor and Empire. It resumed and continued the ideas of the preface of 818–19. Here, for the first time, the imperial office is described as a *ministerium,*

113

on the analogy of the episcopal office. The two spheres appear under the terms *ecclesia* and *regnum*. New is the idea that every magnate in his post and his position participates in the Emperor's *ministerium*. The Emperor is the *admonitor,* the magnates are the *adiutores,* obliged among themselves to mutual support. The task of the clergy is to teach by word and example, to care for church, worship, and education. The task of the secular magnates is the realization of peace by just judgment, by the maintenance of public safety, by the protection of the defenceless.

The *admonitio* was issued at the Aachen imperial assembly in August 825, at which Wala seems to have reported on the government of Italy. Lothar's coregency was from now on expressed officially in charters and other documents, which for the future were published in the name of the two Emperors. After the Aachen assembly Wala returned to the monastery of Corbie, where at the beginning of 826 he succeeded his brother Adalard as Abbot. On this occasion Corbie's daughter house, Corvey on the Weser, the first great monastery in Saxony, became autonomous under Abbot Warin Wala, whose mother was from a Saxon family, had played a prominent role in the founding of Corvey in 821–22. Relations between mother and daughter houses did not cease after 826. On the contrary: through Wala Corvey was to acquire an important involvement in the Scandinavian mission, which began to develop just at this moment.

The Scandinavian mission grew out of the Saxon. It was started by Archbishop Ebbo of Reims, who sought a new field of activity when the Reims missionary territory in Saxony became independent with the founding of the see of Hildesheim in 815. Following the example of Boniface, Ebbo in 822 was appointed by the Pope legate for the North; in 823 the Emperor gave him Münsterdorf in Holstein as his base. The hour for the conversion of the North seemed to have struck when in 825 the strife in Denmark between Horik, son of King Göttrik, and the pretender Harold was ended. Harold, who presumably obtained modern Schleswig as a subkingdom, came to Ingelheim in 826 to do homage and on 24 June was baptized at Sankt Alban in Mainz. Louis the Pious invested him with the Frisian County of Hriustri at the mouth of the Weser as a Frankish fief. At Wala's suggestion the Fleming Anschar, *scholasticus* of Corvey, was appointed director of the mission in Harold's territory.

The high hopes of 826 were unfulfilled. In 827 Harold was expelled from Denmark. Anschar returned with some Danish neophytes, who were educated at Corvey and other Saxon monasteries. When envoys of the Swedish King Björn appeared in the Frankish Empire in 829, Wala urged the beginning of a new mission. Anschar accompanied the Swedish envoys to their country and now had more success. In 831 the see of Hamburg was founded for the mission among the Danes, the Swedes, and the Obodrites. Anschar was consecrated Bishop of Hamburg by the Emperor's brother,

Drogo of Metz, and the Metropolitans of Mainz, Trier, and Reims. The Pope sent him the pallium and appointed him legate. Gauzbert, a relative of Ebbo of Reims, became Bishop of the Swedes in 832. Thus in these years the Frankish Church reached out for the first time beyond the frontiers established by Charles the Great. But it was the misfortune of the Nordic mission that it was getting started at the very moment when the collapse of the Frankish Empire was under way because of inner chaos.

CHAPTER 17

The Carolingian Renaissance under Louis the Pious

The beginnings of the Carolingian Renaissance go back to the palace school and the learned circle around Charles the Great. The palace school and library continued under Louis the Pious, and more and more men of the intellectual *élite* came forth from the school. The annals of the Empire were carried on, and Louis's court astronomer wrote the Emperor's biography. Poems were dedicated to the Emperor by Theodulf, Ermoldus Nigellus, and Walafrid Strabo, the only poet among the teachers at the palace school. Fréculf of Lisieux wrote a universal history for the instruction of young Prince Charles. The Irishman Dicuil dedicated his four books on the *computus* to Louis. But on the whole the *artes* gave place to theology. Rhabanus, Agobard, Dungal, Hilduin, Jonas, Prudentius, Amalarius, and Smaragdus dedicated works dealing with religion, the Church, and theology to the Emperor and the Empress.

It was in the very nature of the Carolingian cultural movement that the palace school at Aachen should not remain the sole centre of education. The courts of the subkings were not strangers to education. The Irishman Dungal was enabled by the Carolingians to go to Pavia, which occupied a central position in Lothar's educational legislation. Ermoldus Nigellus was at the court of Pepin of Aquitaine before being banished to Strasbourg. In addition to the courts, important regional centres had made their appearance under Charles the Great, and under Louis the Pious there were many more of them. Most of these centres lay between the Loire and the Rhine, but even so Burgundy (Lyons), German Franconia (Würzburg and Fulda), Swabia (Reichenau), and Bavaria (Salzburg and Freising) did not lack centres for the cultivation of the mind. It can be observed not infrequently that the first impulses came from the imperial court. Members of the Carolingian family, archchaplains, and archchancellors governed sees and abbeys which occupied an honourable place in the Carolingian Renaissance. From the court clergy proceeded many bishops with famous names.

The most distinguished cathedral school was probably that of Lyons.

115

From it came Agobard, his deacon and assistant Florus, the later Archbishop Amolo, and Bishop Claudius of Turin. Lyons represented the southern European school of thought with strong ties to Spain. The city was a centre of the Carolingian reform party and of Carolingian "rationalism". Agobard and Florus opposed lay domination in the Church and fought for free episcopal elections and the *privilegium fori*. To justify his demands in regard to Church and state, Florus made use of texts from Roman law, something that otherwise was encountered only in Italy (Pavia and Bobbio). He thereby became a chief witness for the *canonisation progressive du droit romain*. Agobard's political ideas and his fight against ordeals have already been considered. Agobard and Florus allowed only texts from the Bible in the liturgy. They rejected not only religious poetry in divine worship but also liturgical allegorizing. Agobard was also unenthusiastic about the cult of relics. He distinguished the shrines of the saints *(memoriae)* from the real houses of God *(templa)*. The *enfant terrible* of the school was the Spaniard, Claudius of Turin, whose extreme hostility to images even evoked opposition in the Frankish Empire.

The chief opponent of the Lyons theologians in liturgical matters was Amalarius of Metz, a pupil of Alcuin at Tours. He perhaps went first to the diocese of Metz in 805, where he probably received the abbey of Hornbach. For a while he presided also over the Church of Trier, but his contemplative nature was not equal to the organizational tasks thereby imposed. Since the days of Chrodegang Metz had been the most important liturgical centre in the Frankish realm. In 836–37 Amalarius completed the series of canonical books of Charles the Great with an antiphonary compiled from texts of Rome and Metz. His renown as a liturgist had been established long before. It was based on the *Liber officialis,* first published in 821, then several times reissued and enlarged. In it were summarized his liturgical studies in a vast allegorical explanation of the chief part of the Church year (Septuagesima to Pentecost), ecclesiastical consecrations, liturgical vestments, the Mass, and finally the readings. His allegorical method was based on Bede, but it had first been applied to the liturgy by Alcuin. Amalarius handled it as a master and with originality, and he even claimed direct inspiration for his theories. He understood the Mass as a drama. Although he suffered defeat in his controversy with Agobard and Florus, his works became standard for the further development of the liturgical symbolism of the Middle Ages. But even before then Walafrid Strabo made use of them in his *Libellus de exordiis et incrementis ecclesiasticis.*

Amalarius was a scholar secluded from the world and living only for his theological and liturgical interests. The political and ecclesiastical controversies of the time found not the faintest echo in his writings. Hence he was a failure as Bishop of Trier, for a bishop could not ignore these questions. The episcopate was preoccupied with protecting the Church's rights *vis-à-vis* the magnates and with implementing the revived canon law. An irenical character like Jonas of Orléans not only took a stand in regard to images but also wrote *De institutione laicali* for Matfrid of Orléans and a mirror for princes for Pepin of Aquitaine. He drafted the acts, of great ecclesiastical significance, of the Synod of Paris of 829, using as their basis an *admonitio* to Pepin. To Jonas's predecessor Theodulf were due the first episcopal capitularies, which were followed by others at Liège, Basel and Freising. They contained the essential regulations for parish administration. In addition, their goal was the consolidation of episcopal authority in regard to the clergy and monks of the diocese, the enforcement of the Church's matrimonial and penitential law in regard to the laity, and the prevention of lay encroachments within the Church. In this connection the struggle against the insular penitentials was also stepped up. Since the existing canonical collections were too bulky and hence could be consulted only with difficulty, special collections, such as that of Laon, were compiled, or new penitentials appeared, drawn up in the spirit of the ancient ecclesiastical discipline of Rome. Of these last, the earliest went back to Halitgar of Cambrai (817–31). Not least of the tasks of the episcopate was that of assuring the material bases of ecclesiastical life, which were often still inadequate, especially in areas hardest hit by the secularizations of the early eighth century. Concern for the Church's property led to an examination of the property titles in archives and then to the narrating, by recourse to documents, of the history of bishops, including the acceptance of both authentic and forged charters, as at Le Mans under Bishop Aldric (832–57).

The school system, which formed only one part of the great field of activity of the bishops, occupied a central position in the monasteries. Hence it should cause no surprise that the main centre of book production and of literary culture was in the monasteries. It is true that Saint-Martin de Tours lost its rank as a central home of learning after Alcuin's death, but it became the great publishing centre of the ninth century, sending manuscripts and richly illuminated books to all parts of the Frankish Empire. Alongside Saint-Martin, the Reims *scriptoria* of Saint-Remi and Hautvillers became more prominent under Louis the Pious. No new central school sprang up at Aniane, the motherhouse of the Benedictine reform. Among the intellectual centres of *Francia* were Saint-Denis, where the Archchaplain Hilduin even fostered Greek and translated the writings of pseudo-Dionysius in 832–35, and Corbie, where in 831 Paschasius Radbertus launched the Eucharistic controversy of the ninth century with his *De corpore et sanguine Domini*. At Ferrières in the diocese of Sens Abbot Aldric (821–29) prepared the ground for his monastery's fame in the succeeding period.

Fulda was the leading monastic school in the reign of Louis the Pious. This foundation of Saint Boniface owed its position to the Abbots Eigil (818–22) and Rhabanus (822–42). Rhabanus Maurus, a Frank from Mainz, had been, like Amalarius of Metz, a pupil of Alcuin at Tours. He was not an original thinker like Amalarius, but the ranking expert in early Christian literature, in which he even surpassed his teacher, Alcuin. His literary productivity was extraordinary and included the *artes* as well as theology, in which field most of his work lay. These special talents made Rhabanus the *praeceptor Germaniae*. No other school in Germany could be compared with that of Fulda. Even Reichenau, which began its rise under Abbot Tatto and in Walafrid produced an important poet and scholar, lagged behind. At Fulda efforts were made to translate substantial portions of the Bible; here Tatian's harmony of the Gospels was translated into Old High German. Whether the *Heliand* and the Old Saxon Genesis, both of which were influenced by the Anglo-Saxon biblical poetry in spirit and form (alliteration), originated at Fulda or Werden is disputed. Rhabanus was aware of the existence of a Germanic group of languages, the *lingua theodisca,* and from him this knowledge passed to his pupils. But the word *theodiscus* established itself as a designation of the Germanic linguistic community at the same time also in other authors of the Romance-speaking West.

The development of the Carolingian Renaissance under Louis the Pious presents an imposing picture. It is true that the theological and ecclesiastical literature now occupied very much more room than it had under Charles the Great. But this orientation to Church themes must not be one-sidedly attributed to the Emperor's interests. A maturing is also expressed by it, since the preceding period would not yet have been capable of so comprehensive a discussion of the politics of Empire and Church. Meanwhile, the *artes,* it is true, received less emphasis than before, but they did not therefore lose their role in education as a whole. The ideas and demands of the leading men were not always in accord with historical reality. The great concept of the unity of Christendom in the Carolingian Empire was soon to prove to be an illusion. But in the discussion of Church reform and imperial unity, of the duties of ruler and magnates, the notions of dominion and service, of Church, Empire, and law were deepened and clarified. This clarification and this preoccupation with objectivity were enduring gains.

CHAPTER 18

The Crisis of Empire and Church (828 to 840)

Following a long period of peace there went forth a cry of alarm from the two Emperors to the magnates of the Empire in February 828: "Undique inimicos sanctae Dei ecclesiae commoveri et regnum . . . infestare velle cognoscimus."[1] The occasion for this alarm was provided by reverses on the

---

[1] *MGCap* II, no. 185, 5.

frontiers: in Holstein, in the marches of Pannonia and Friuli, and in Catalonia. Viewed from a distance, none of this gave cause for panic, and the situation on the frontiers soon stabilized itself again. Charles the Great would hardly have been disturbed, but concern and anxiety prevailed at the imperial assembly which met at Aachen in February 828. Hugh of Tours, Matfrid of Orléans, and Balderic of Friuli were relieved of office. The cashiering of three great dignitaries produced a government crisis. General complaints in regard to imperial administration were heard in Aachen. Proposals for reform were to be submitted to the next imperial assembly. But the assembly summoned to Ingelheim for June found no opportunity to discuss reforms because of the military situation. Such discussion could not take place until December, at a rather small winter *placitum* in Aachen, which was prolonged to February 829. On this occasion Wala came forward with a great reform memorandum.

This former paladin of Charles the Great began with a sharp criticism of the court, in particular the absence of energetic leadership and the pursuit of *beneficia* by the courtiers, of the lack of pastoral activity and of discipline on the part of the clergy, and of the corruption, feuds, and factions among the secular magnates. He found the causes of the abuses in the passivity of the central authority and the unlawful intermingling of the ecclesiastical and secular spheres. The Emperor was urged to greater activity in upholding the law and to greater care in choosing his officials. Now as earlier, Wala regarded him as the *totius stabilimentum regni,* on which both the *ordo disciplinae* and the *status rei publicae* reposed. But in regard to the Church he attributed to him only a right of supervision and no real governing power. Like his trusted friend and biographer, Paschasius Radbertus, he probably saw the Emperor in the image of Theodosius rather than of Constantine.

For Wala the Church was an *altera res publica,* established as such on the Sacraments and the Church property and ruled by the bishops. He regarded Church property as a fief committed by God to the clergy; Christ had the sole disposition of it. The Church should carry out its own tasks within the framework of canon law and give an account of its work at annual provincial councils. Since chaplains had no canonically sanctioned superiors and did not fit into the order of the Christian classes of canons, monks, and laity — the canonical rule had not been prescribed for them — in Wala's view the chapel had nothing to justify its existence. The Abbot of Corbie demanded the freedom of ecclesiastical elections and denied the Emperor the disposal of Church offices, while allowing him a right of supervision that was still to be defined as regards its details. He did not exclude the granting of Church property in cases of public necessity. But such grants should be made "ob defensionem magis quam ad rapinam" and by the bishops, not by the direct action of the ruler.

As a testimony of the imperial idea Wala's memorandum was related

119

to the preface of 818–19 and the *admonitio* of 825. The Abbot of Corbie did not deviate from the prevailing fundamental idea. His specific concern was to separate the spiritual and secular spheres so that the two estates of the Empire could thereafter devote themselves to their proper tasks. Bastard institutions such as lay abbacies and court chapel were the main targets of his attack. But Wala did not get bogged down in isolated phenomena and he furthermore distinguished the imperial right of supervision of the Church from the imperial right of ruling the *res publica*.

Although the memorandum unleashed a storm among all factions, it still left a lasting impression. Louis the Pious announced weekly court sessions at Aachen and summoned four synods at Paris, Mainz, Toulouse, and Lyons to investigate abuses in Empire and Church. The *missi,* who were sent out during the octave of Easter in 829, were to question *scabini* and people in regard to abuses. The synods met during the octave of Pentecost. Only the acts of that of Paris, drawn up by Jonas of Orléans, are extant. The first two books, which preceded the decrees, had probably already been sketched by Jonas beforehand. In addition to the episcopate's self-criticism, a real mirror of the official duties of bishops in the spirit of the reform of Louis the Pious, they contained fundamental statements concerning the proper order in Christendom. The Church, it is said, forms a body, which is organized in two classes, here described as *persona sacerdotalis* and *persona regalis*. The King thereby moved to the side of the laity, and this was further emphasized by appeal to Gelasius — "gravius pondus sacerdotum". However, Jonas did not deny the inclusion of the Church in the Empire; he declared at the outset that the Church was confided to the two Emperors for government and protection. The ruler holds his Empire from God, not from his ancestors. In Book II his ecclesiastical task is designated as *defensio*.

Like Wala, the other participants in the Council of Paris saw in the fusion of the spheres a basic evil, which kept them from their ecclesiastical duties, among other things from the convoking of annual provincial councils. However, in this matter there had been a continual improvement since King Pepin's time. Like Wala, the Paris Fathers pressed for the suppression of the court chapel as a bastard institution. But in the acts is to be found no attack on the lay abbacy. Lay abbots, it is said, should lead an honourable life, just like regular abbots. It was conceded that the Emperor had the right to appoint ecclesiastical dignitaries, and he was asked to exercise the greatest care "in bonis pastoribus rectoribusque constituendis". The same care was urged upon him in choosing his secular assistants ("in eligendis adiutoribus vestris et rei publicae ministris"). Here a fine distinction was made between the *constitutio* of the spiritual magnates and the *electio* of the secular magnates by the Emperor. This was in accord with Wala's ideas. But the Fathers of Paris refrained from any polemics. The difficult question of the separating of the spheres and of the *libertas episcopalis* was to be discussed at a later time, "suo tempore". Wala's influence is probably to be seen in the recommendation that public schools be established in three suitable cities of the Empire. Lothar had already set up corresponding schools in Italy.

In August 829 the magnates gathered at Worms for the imperial assembly. The episcopate submitted a full report, which followed the Paris decrees in all respects. But the Emperor did not at all agree with the *relatio episcoporum*. He suspended reform and by a unilateral decree established an inheritance for the now six-year-old Prince Charles, son of the Empress Judith. Swabia, Rhaetia, Alsace, and parts of Burgundy were constituted a duchy for him. This complex of territories did not correspond to any old unity, as did the Kingdoms of Aquitaine, Bavaria, and Italy. Nevertheless, the Emperor intended to make this area a subkingdom. The older sons were clearly surprised by the edict. Following the end of the assembly, Lothar was sent to Italy and his coregency was ended.

The opposition gathered at Corbie. Abbot Wala, now fifty-six years old, represented the glorious Carolingian past, which seemed jeopardized by the suspension of reform and the unilateral disposition of the inheritance. He coined the slogan *pro principe contra principem*. The conspirators, to whose numbers belonged almost all the previously leading personalities, exploited for their ends the expedition against the Bretons which the Emperor and his new adviser, Bernard of Barcelona, had set for Holy Thursday, 14 April 830, with no regard for Holy Week. The *coup d'état* succeeded. The Emperor again took Lothar, who was hurrying back from Italy, as coemperor. The Empress Judith and her brothers were sent to monasteries and their adherents were banished.

The change of government of 829 had been annulled, but new rivalries erupted among the victors. The Abbot of Corbie, who strove honourably for the continuation of the great reform work in Empire and Church, lost control of events. The upshot was a complete *volte-face* at the imperial assemblies of Nijmegen in October 830 and Aachen in February 831. The leaders of the conspiracy were imprisoned and Lothar was sent back to Italy. Wala's "imperial revolution" had been shattered on the person of the Emperor and the egoism of the magnates.

The imperial authority had been compromised by the events of 830–31, while the inner conflicts had been aggravated. But the die was not cast until 831, when Louis abandoned the *ordinatio* and divided the Empire outside of Italy among his three younger sons, Pepin, Louis, and Charles, on the basis of the kingdoms of 817 and the duchy of 829. The result was a fragmentation of *Francia*, which Charles the Great had left intact in 806. Although appeal was made to Charles in order to justify the principle of division — the text of the *divisio* of 831 closely followed that of the *divisio* of 806 — the specific details offended against a basic conception of the first Emperor of the Franks. A stabilizing of the situation did not follow from the new disposition of the inheritance. Instead there were new conflicts with Pepin of Aquitaine and Louis of Bavaria, who now allied with Lothar.

Differing from Wala's *coup d'état* of 830, the revolt of the sons in 833 could only be turned directly against the old Emperor. Lothar, as coemperor, assumed the leadership of the opposition and succeeded in involving Pope Gregory IV as guarantor of the *ordinatio*. The legal basis was provided by the right of resistance, justified in both Christian and Germanic thought. For by annulling the *ordinatio* and disinheriting Pepin, as he planned to do in 832, Louis the Pious had violated dynastic and imperial law. The aim of the opposition was to restore the *ordinatio* and Lothar's coregency and to guarantee the hereditary rights of Pepin and Louis, whose portions were to be enlarged in comparison with the arrangement of 817. The Pope envisaged his role as one of arbitration between the father and the sons. In April he sent an embassy across the Alps to act in accord with this idea.

Louis the Pious had learned of the conspiracy in February 833. He left Aachen for Worms in order to be ready for an attack from Italy and Bavaria and summoned there the higher clergy and the host. But the movement of revolt spread quickly. Lothar marched into Burgundy, where Archbishops Agobard of Lyons and Bernard of Vienne joined him. Even Wala, who was again at Corbie since the revolt of King Louis, decided after much hesitation to follow Lothar's embassy. Agobard wrote a manifesto in defence of the right of the sons against their father. Meanwhile, the bishops who had gathered round the old Emperor sent a sharp resolution to the Pope. They declared the papal intervention to be unlawful and reminded Gregory IV of his oath of loyalty. The Emperor, they said, had modified the *ordinatio* "iuxta rerum opportunitatem", and this modification was irrevocable. The Emperor would explain its justification to the Pope. Finally, they threatened a renunciation of obedience. At the same time the Emperor called upon his sons to submit to him. He placed the chief blame on Lothar. Louis the Pious and his magnates cited the paternal power of coercion and the oath of vassalage taken by the sons and the magnates.

The mutual recriminations made the Pope hesitate. Wala had to remind him that he was a judge only and could not himself be judged. This applied, of course, only to the religious sphere, but the old Emperor had actually rendered himself guilty of sin in the eyes of the conspirators by annulling the *ordinatio,* issued "divina inspiratione". In his rejoinder to the bishops Gregory IV stressed that he had come, not as a partisan of Lothar, but on his own initiative as an arbiter of peace. He justified this by his ecclesiastical office, whose special task and higher dignity he underscored in the spirit of Gelasius. To the duty of unconditional obedience as understood by the bishops loyal to Louis he contrasted the Christian view of the oath of loyalty, which obliged him also to rebuke the Emperor for offences against the unity of the Church and Empire. A decision in regard to the *ordinatio,* he said, could not be rendered by one faction, but only by all, who had also the right to recon-sider unilateral decisions of the Emperor. But a withdrawal of obedience from the Pope would mean schism.

It is beyond doubt that the arguments in the papal reply corresponded to the spirit of the imperial legislation preceding the crisis — but Louis the Pious had abandoned just this foundation. An award by battle seemed inevi-table. The two armies faced each other near Colmar on 24 June 833. In this situation the papal mediation now became appropriate. The Pope proceeded to the Emperor and returned with peace proposals to the sons' camp. But it was too late. In the meantime the rebels' propaganda had its effect, and the army of Louis the Pious deserted to the other side. The old Emperor went with the Empress to the camp of the sons. Before long Gregory IV could not fail to understand that he had been used, and he returned, "grief stricken", to Rome.

There occurred what Wala had foreseen with resignation: the loss of all power by the old Emperor. The three older brothers disposed of the Empire as they pleased in a new division which excluded the ten-year-old Charles. He was supposed to become a monk at Prüm. This time there was a real division, with an immediate taking of possession. The shares of Pepin and Louis did not correspond to the *divisio* of 831 but were larger than had been the case in 817. The strict subordination of the Kings to the Emperor ceased, but a loose imperial suzerainty was maintained. The family of their father was naturally turned over to Lothar. He had Louis the Pious taken to Saint-Médard de Soissons, the Empress Judith to Tortona, and young Charles to Prüm.

Lothar held a general assembly of the Empire at Compiègne in October. The leading men in his council still included Hugh, Matfrid, and Lambert, but not Wala and Hilduin, whose places had been taken by Ebbo of Reims and Agobard of Lyons. They urged the deposition of Louis the Pious, which could not be avoided after all that had happened, even if Wala and Hilduin refused to have anything to do with such a sentence. Since there was no precedent for the deposition, the legal basis had to be first created. For almost twenty years the imperial office had been understood, in Schieffer's words, "as a divine commission and as an ecclesiastical function". A legal basis for a process existed, so it could be concluded, if the Emperor denied the duties of his *ministerium,* the realization of *pax et concordia* in the Christian world. Whether this was actually the case could be determined only by the bishops as the "appointed representatives of the Church". And so, during the assembly of Compiègne, the episcopate assembled at nearby Soissons. The accusations, which were made by Ebbo of Reims, comprised *sacrilegium, homicidium,* and *periurium.* Louis the Pious, it was said, had broken the promise made to Charles the Great in 813 by his evil treatment of his relatives and by allowing the killing of Bernard in 818. He had cancelled the *ordinatio* and frivolously made sport of the divisions of the Empire and the oaths of the people. He had profaned Lent, disregarded the obligations he had assumed in 830, permitted the Empress to commit perjury, and led his army against Christians. The Emperor confessed that he had unworthily administered the office of ruler that had been entrusted to him. He handed the clergy a list of his failures, laid aside his arms, and was garbed as a penitent. The purpose of this procedure was to render the Emperor unqualified for his office.

The proceedings were a logical development from the idea of the *Imperium christianum,* but the indictment was a distortion by factional politics. By piling up the charges, the Emperor's enemies were depriving the decisive arguments of any weight. Louis could not be reproached with the events of 814 and 818, for which he had long before done voluntary penance. The combination of ecclesiastical penance and deposition in the proceedings was open to attack. In his *Liber de reverentia filiorum* Rhabanus Maurus put his finger on the critical points. Excommunication, he said, could not result from crimes which the Emperor had not committed, for the punishment of traitors was imperial law; ecclesiastical penance could never lead to deposition, for he who performed it was by that very fact restored to the communion of the Church. Rhabanus dodged the central problem — the revocation of the *ordinatio* and the disinheriting of Pepin. But his explanation of ecclesiastical penance hit the mark. In actuality there was only one way of rendering the Emperor disqualified for office, and that was entrance into the cloister. Lothar's faction wanted to persuade Louis the Pious to take this step. But the old Emperor refused to acquiesce by declining to come to a decision before his personal liberty had been restored. Lothar could not agree to this condition, since the deposition of the father had produced a change of mood in the Empire, and so Louis the Pious remained for the moment in the custody of his oldest son.

The situation became the more intolerable, the longer it endured. Pepin and Louis the German did not recognize the deposition of their father. They were in an easy situation, since without prejudice to their own interests they could evade the final consequences of the revolt of 833. And so all the odium of the rebellion fell ultimately on Lothar. In addition, new rivalries broke out between Lothar's advisers, Matfrid and Lambert. Wala sought in vain to set the reform of the Empire in motion again.

The adherents of the old Emperor gathered around Louis the German, who in December 833 demanded the release of the father. Once more there was a full reaction. Lothar was forced back to Italy in 834, and Wala and the leading spiritual and secular magnates followed. Louis the Pious, after his solemn restoration to the throne in February 835, had the archbishops who were the most seriously compromised deposed — those of Reims, Lyons, Vienne, and Narbonne — but refrained from any new disposition of the inheritance. He sought peace with Lothar, which Wala especially advocated on the part of the coemperor. But the Abbot of Corbie was not to witness the reconciliation of the two Emperors, for he died in an epidemic in 836. His death, even under the changed circumstances, was another serious loss for the Carolingian Dynasty and Empire. The tragedy of the Empire was fundamentally the tragedy of Wala, since from the place where he was standing he was not able to halt fate, but rather by his initiative accelerated it. "Virum magnum fuisse constat", said Leibniz concerning him, "sed Catonis fato mala publica acrioribus remediis exasperasse".

The establishing of a portion for his youngest son Charles remained a chief concern of the old Emperor. The death of Pepin of Aquitaine opened the way for a new arrangement of the inheritance. At Worms in 839 Louis the Pious divided the Frankish Empire between Lothar and Charles. Pepin's sons were disinherited, and Louis the German was restricted to Bavaria. Peace did not thereby return, for the injured parties revolted. But the opposition was clearly defeated, and had to remain defeated, if Lothar and Charles stayed together. In this expectation Louis the Pious died on 20 June 840, on an island in the Rhine near Ingelheim.

The Western Church from the Death of Louis the Pious to the End of the Carolingian Period

CHAPTER 19

The Frankish Empire from 840 to 875

The judgment that history would render on the future of the Frankish Empire lay with Lothar I. The Emperor could have been satisfied with the partition of 839 and, so far as can be ascertained, could have enforced it even against Louis the German. Thus the Carolingian Empire would have been spared the rude shocks of the next years. But Lothar, who was then forty-five years old and a mature man, was not inclined to recognize his brother Charles, scarcely seventeen years old, as an equal partner and resumed the struggle over the *ordinatio*. In this struggle he met defeat. On 25 June 841 Louis the German and Charles the Bald gained the upper hand on the bloody field of Fontanet near Auxerre, concerning which Regino of Prüm said later that it broke the power of the Franks. The higher Frankish nobility pressed for an understanding. The three brothers met on 5 June 842 at Mâcon, where they concluded an armistice. Long and stubborn negotiations at Metz and Koblenz finally produced the Treaty of Verdun at the beginning of August 843. The *regna* of Italy, Bavaria, and Aquitaine constituted the point of departure for the partition of Verdun. The other territories of the *Imperium* were distributed on the basis of *aequa portio,* but probably from the start it had been settled that Lothar, as Emperor and head of the dynasty, should receive the *sedes* of Aachen. Such was the origin of Lothar's Middle Kingdom, which comprised Italy, the Provençal-Burgundian districts between the Alps, the Rhone, and the Saône, *Francia media* between the Rhine, the Meuse, and the Scheldt, and Frisia. Louis received Germany, except for Frisia, and, to the left of the Rhine, the districts of Mainz, Worms, and Speyer, with their rich domains.

The kingdoms created at Verdun lacked internal cohesion. This has always been stressed with reference to Lothar's Middle Kingdom, but it is true also of the East and the West Frankish Kingdoms. For the great linguistic families were not yet relevant to nationality; important in this regard were rather the older tribal and territorial communities of which the Carolingian Empire was composed. Their amalgamation into larger nationalities was now a task rather than a fact. The East Frankish Kingdom possessed a relatively archaic structure, as yet hardly affected by the Carolingian theocracy. In various sections an abandonment of Carolingian institutions, termed a "process of de-Frankization" by Tellenbach, can be ascertained. Louis the German and his successors issued no East Frankish capitularies, the *missatica* and the comital organization decayed and were transformed. The episcopate, still preoccupied with missionary work in Saxony, appeared as assistant to the kingship but not as an autonomous political factor. A change here did not get under way until toward the end of the ninth century.

In contrast to the East Frankish Kingdom, the Middle Kingdom and the West Frankish Kingdom had extensive coasts, which from the outbreak of war among the brothers became more and more the goal of Viking and Muslim pirates. The instability of both these kingdoms was in contrast to the relative stability of the East Frankish Kingdom. The West Frankish Kingdom had the most difficult start. Nowhere was the position of the Frankish imperial aristocracy and of the episcopacy so strong as it was in western *Francia* and in western Burgundy, where the ideas of the days of Louis the Pious made their strongest impact. The West Frankish Kingdom took shape in conflicts between King, episcopate, and secular magnates. Here the peace-concept of the older capitularies was developed further into the peace agreement among the magnates and between the King and the magnates. Even in 843 Charles the Bald had to conclude the Treaty of Coulaines with the magnates, in which the *honor ecclesiae,* the *honor regis,* and the *honor fidelium* were defined and guaranteed in writing. The West Frankish Kingdom became a juridical association based on the totality of the *fideles*. The consent of the magnates to the capitularies became obligatory.

Charles sought to compensate for the weakness of the royal authority by a new religious enhancement of the kingship. When he decided to recover Aquitaine he had himself anointed at Orléans in 848 by the Archbishop of Sens. This anointing was followed by a second in 869, performed by the Archbishop of Reims at Metz and regarded as consolidating Charles's claims to the Kingdom of Lothar II. The Carolingian notion of Empire and State acquired a profound expression in the rich symbolism of the coronation ritual. Hincmar of Reims drew up this ritual and gave it its definitive form in the coronation *ordo* of 877. According to Schramm, "The King was thereafter a *christus Domini,* separated from the laity, anointed like a priest". Nevertheless, he was not an absolute ruler, for Hincmar included in the *promissio* of his ritual the obligations of the King as first specified at Coulaines; in this *promissio* the King bound himself to the duties of his office. The *ordo* of 877 continued in use for more than two centuries; even later it was merely adjusted to circumstances rather than changed in its basic features. It became the exemplar for the drawing up of the coronation ritual in Spain, England, and Germany.

127

"De-Frankization" in the East, elaboration of the Carolingian political theory in the West, stagnation in the Middle Kingdom — these were the characteristics of a process of individuation. But it must not be forgotten that, despite this, the Frankish *Imperium* was still regarded as a unity even in the late ninth century. The treaty sealed the defeat of the Carolingian imperial office, but people still held to the idea of one *Imperium* and of one *populus christianus*. The brothers ruled, not separate states, but parts of the one Empire, which was henceforth represented by the *corpus fratrum*. The juridical connection that ensued was expressed in the Treaty of Verdun by the words *amicitia, pax,* and *mutuum adiutorium*. It consisted in a mutual right of succession and in a common domestic and foreign policy, which should be determined from time to time at the "Frankish Diets", regular meetings of the Carolingian partners in government. Furthermore, the community of the several kingdoms was expressed also in the gatherings of the episcopate and in the possessions, rights, and relationships of the imperial aristocracy, which at first encompassed the entire *Imperium*.

Lothar did not straightway in 843 inter the idea of a supremacy of the Emperor. In the West the situation was not yet calm, and so the Emperor aspired to isolate the Western King by diplomatic means and to renew his own supremacy in a roundabout way by exploiting the Church. At Lothar's request Drogo of Metz in 844 obtained the post of papal vicar north of the Alps with the right to convoke councils of the three kingdoms, control provincial councils, supervise all bishops and abbots, and act as intermediate tribunal in appeals to Rome. However, the papal delegation remained ineffectual and the attempt to separate Louis the German from Charles the Bald miscarried. The Frankish Diet of Thionville of October 844 was due to the initiative of Louis. In their *communiqués* the three Carolingian rulers stressed the notion of *fraternitas;* they ordered the restoration of Church property and of the Church's rights and threatened the Western opposition with a common enforcement.

Charles the Bald gathered in the harvest of Thionville by arranging the election in April 845 of the monk Hincmar of Saint-Denis as Archbishop of Reims. The election was a masterstroke. Earlier, on the occasion of Wala's *coup d'état,* Hincmar had remained loyal to Louis the Pious. But he had also stood up for his teacher and friend, Abbot Hilduin of Saint-Denis, to whom Lothar had given the archbishopric of Cologne in 842 and the office of archchancellor in 843. Thus the new Archbishop of Reims may have appeared as the proper intermediary between Charles and Lothar. As a matter of fact, Lothar dropped Ebbo in 845, but again took up his complaints the next year. He obtained from the Pope the convoking of an imperial synod to Trier (846), where the problem of Reims should be treated again. The Carolingians met for a second Frankish Diet at Meersen in February 847. After the Meersen meeting Lothar gave up any idea of an imperial restoration and at Péronne in 849 became definitely reconciled with Charles the Bald.

The Viking peril, which threatened equally the Middle and the West Frankish Kingdoms, may have been one reason for the reconciliation of the brothers. But there were other reasons too. Lothar I was growing old and thinking of putting his affairs in order. In 850 he had his oldest son, Louis II, crowned Emperor by the Pope. He needed the agreement of his brothers for the regulation of the inheritance that he was planning. The third Frankish Diet, held at Meersen in 851, marked the climax of the *fraternitas*. In their common capitulary the brothers spoke only of the one *Regnum Francorum*. Each of them bound himself not to disturb the authority of the partners, by propaganda or interference, in the future, and the agreement was expressly extended to include the heirs of each. The twenty-year-old strife seemed definitely to have been laid to rest. The clergy in particular placed great hopes on the Diet of Meersen, for they anticipated a renewal of ecclesiastical life in the entire Empire and the resumption of the reform of Louis the Pious.

In the late summer of 855 Lothar I divided his dominions among his three sons, Louis II, Lothar II, and Charles. The coemperor Louis had to be content with Italy, which he had been governing since 840. Lothar II received *Francia media* with the capital Aachen and neighbouring Frisia and northern Burgundy (the ecclesiastical provinces of Besançon and Geneva). Charles obtained southern Burgundy (provinces of Lyons and Vienne) and Provence. By this partition of his inheritance Lothar I set the seal on his renunciation of the idea of imperial unity. Following the disposal of his lands he entered the monastery of Prüm, where he died a few days later, on 29 September 855. In the same year occurred the deaths of Pope Leo IV and Drogo of Metz, imperial archchaplain and papal vicar beyond the Alps. Lothar's Archchancellor Hilduin, former Abbot of Saint-Denis, entered Prüm with the Emperor and thereby withdrew from the stage of the great world. He did not long survive his imperial master at Prüm. Thus with Lothar I disappeared the last fighters for one *Imperium Francorum*. It now had to be seen whether *fraternitas* could supply for the *Imperium*.

The years between the Treaty of Verdun and the death of Lothar I later seemed to be an interlude in the process of Frankish decay. Lothar I was both Emperor and senior member of the dynasty, but his death completely altered this situation. The partition of his inheritance wrecked the equilibrium of the partner-kingdoms and complicated the relations of the partner-kings. Imperial dignity and seniority parted company. The senior member of the dynasty was now Louis the German. The imperial office, having passed to Louis II, King of Italy, forfeited all authority within the Carolingian family, though its influence on the papacy persisted.

Of the five partner-kings Lothar I's youngest son, the sickly Charles of

129

Provence, retired from any real activity, leaving the political game to be played by two uncles, Louis the German and Charles the Bald, and two nephews, Louis II of Italy and Lothar II of Lotharingia. Doubtless the most powerful of the four was Louis the German, although the rising Moravian state gave him trouble from 855. In 858 he received an appeal from a faction of the West Frankish nobility, who, in agreement with Archbishop Wenilo of Sens, invited the head of the dynasty into the country against Charles the Bald. Charles's position seemed desperate at first, but the loyalty of the episcopate of the provinces of Reims and Rouen finally saved his crown. Louis the German had to withdraw in January 859 — the abortive effort ruined his prestige in the entire Empire. At a synod held at Metz in May 859 and comprising the West Frankish and Lotharingian episcopates, his action was sharply condemned as a breach of *fraternitas* and an attack on the unity of the Church. Hincmar of Reims and Gunthar of Cologne delivered the synodal letter to the East Frankish King. Louis the German fell back upon his own episcopate and counteracted a complaint lodged with the Pope by his imperial nephew. Lothar II effected a reconciliation between the uncles. At Koblenz on 5 June 860, *fraternitas* was restored at a Frankish Diet on the basis of the Meersen decrees of 851. The attempt of the senior Carolingian to establish his pre-eminence in the *Imperium* had failed.

The marriage of Lothar II produced further confusion. Lothar II seems to have married Theutberga, sister of the powerful Duke Hubert of Transjurane Burgundy — the districts of Geneva, Lausanne, and Sion — for political reasons only. The marriage remaining childless, he soon returned to his former mistress, Waldrada, by whom he had a son, Hugh, and a daughter, Gisela. Hugh and Gisela were to be legitimated by his marriage with Waldrada, for in the course of the reform the ecclesiastical view had been upheld — that only legitimate children were entitled to inherit. The dispute over the royal marriage first took place before Lotharingian courts in 858 and 860. After an extorted confession of guilt, Queen Theutberga was condemned by the episcopate of Lothar's kingdom to public penance for incest. But in the fall of 860 she succeeded in fleeing to Charles the Bald. Once free, the unhappy Queen appealed to Rome, whereupon Lothar also sent an embassy to the Pope.

The marriage case had, as mentioned, not only a religious and ecclesiastical but also a political aspect. Lothar II could count on the sympathy of his brothers, who were likewise without male heirs, especially since he approached them with territorial cessions in 858–59. He thought he had bound his two uncles to himself by his mediation of peace in 859–60. But Charles the Bald wrecked the Carolingian solidarity and supported Theutberga's appeal. The papal reply was some time in coming, and Lothar II decided to act. A third Synod of Aachen, in April 862, authorized him to remarry. He communicated the decision to the Pope and requested papal sanction also. He did not, however, await the papal decision, but married Waldrada in the same year, 862.

The West Frankish King continued to support Theutberga. He agreed to the demand of Hincmar of Reims that the question of the marriage should be examined at a general Frankish synod. Pope Nicholas I did not intervene in the marriage case until November 862. He delegated Bishops Radoald of Porto and John of Cervia to investigate the matter at a new synod at Metz, in which the kingdoms of Louis the German, Charles the Bald, and Charles of Provence should each be represented by two bishops. Since Charles of Provence died in January 863 and the partition of his lands between his brothers, the Emperor Louis II and King Lothar II, took time, the March date that had first been decided could not be adhered to. Meanwhile, the Pope had received news of Lothar's remarriage. In a letter he called upon the Frankish episcopate in Gaul and Germany to condemn the King to ecclesiastical penance. But events at first followed an entirely different course. The synod convened at Metz in June 863, but no bishops represented the East and the West Frankish Kingdoms. The legates, bribed by Lothar, published the papal instructions only in a distorted form. The synod ratified the annulment of Lothar's marriage with Theutberga and declared the lawfulness of his marriage with Waldrada. Archbishops Gunthar of Cologne and Theutgaud of Trier were commissioned to convey the synodal decrees to the Pope.

Nicholas I could not but have been furious at the course of events, but he prepared his countermeasures in the greatest secrecy, perhaps out of concern about complications with the Emperor Louis II. In October 863 the two archbishops were summoned to an assembly of clergy and laity at the Lateran. There the Pope delivered a staggering blow. Not content to annul the Metz decrees, he deposed the Archbishops of Cologne and Trier and forbade the filling of the now vacant sees without his consent.

The Pope's sentences hit the two archbishops like a bolt from the blue. They had recourse to the Emperor, who appeared in Rome with troops at the beginning of 864. Nicholas I had formally put himself in the wrong, since his summary procedure against Cologne and Trier was irregular from the point of view of canon law. But the moral position of Lothar II's accusers was extremely weak. Hence Louis II gave up the idea of using force against the Pope, who, however, had to accept the imperial man of confidence, Arsenius of Orta, as permanent *apocrisiarius* in Rome. The two archbishops remained deposed.

The two uncles were not observing the course of events idly. On 9 February 865 they met at Thuzey near Toul, where they confirmed the Koblenz *fraternitas* and in a common message advised their nephew to make his peace with the Church. But they also turned down the papal invitation to a Roman synod. It was clear that Lothar for his part must now submit to the Pope. He again took back Theutberga and handed over Waldrada to the papal legate.

Waldrada, to be sure, escaped and returned to Lothar. The game was resumed, but the Pope remained firm and excommunicated Waldrada. In May 867, or possibly June 868, Louis the German and Charles the Bald met again, this time in the old royal city of Metz. Here they not only renewed the decrees of Thuzey; they also came to an agreement in regard to the eventual partition of the kingdoms of both nephews and their common assumption of the protection of the Roman Church. The days of the imperial office and of the Middle Kingdom seemed numbered. The East Frankish and the West Frankish Kings, who had once allied for defence against the imperial aspirations of the lord of Aachen and of Rome, now joined to partition the kingdoms of Rome, or at least of Pavia, and of Aachen.

The situation of their northern nephew looked desperate. Lothar II announced a journey to Rome. The Pope stated his preconditions: dismissal of Waldrada, full rights for Theutberga, and canonical elections at Cologne and Trier. At this dramatic moment the unexpected occurred: on 13 November 867 Pope Nicholas I died. His successor, Hadrian II, was regarded as being a rather saintly man, and it was expected that his hand would be gentler in the great ecclesiastical affairs. By the mediation of the Emperor Louis II and of the Empress Engelberga, Lothar met Hadrian at Montecassino on 1 July 869. The Pope even gave him communion — but in a manner equivalent to an ordeal. A Roman council, attended by the episcopate of all the Frankish kingdoms, was to take up the whole question anew in the spring of 870. But this did not happen, for Lothar II died at Piacenza on 8 August 869, on his return from Italy.

The death of the unfortunate prince ended a long conflict, but sealed the fate of the line of Lothar I, which was now represented only by the Emperor Louis II, who had no son. The Emperor was fighting against the Muslims in South Italy. Even before he could lay claim to his brother's inheritance, his uncle, Charles the Bald, appeared in Metz, where he had himself crowned King of Lotharingia on 9 September 869. Louis the German, immobilized by illness, did not put in an appearance until 870. At Meersen in August 870 the two uncles partitioned the inheritance of Lothar II, in conformity with the agreement of 867. The Emperor's protest against the *fait accompli* was seconded by the Pope but remained ineffective. In a personal discussion with the Empress Engelberga in May 872 Louis the German did indeed cede his share of Lotharingia to his imperial nephew, but this purely formal concession, probably made with an eye to the succession to Italy, did not affect the actual situation. To the Emperor a united Christian front in South Italy appeared finally as more important than a quarrel over inheritance in his own family. He consumed his strength in the struggle against the Muslims and died on 12 August 875. With him expired the male line of the family of Lothar I, in which the imperial dignity had been hereditary. The Frankish kingdoms entered a new phase of their history.

CHAPTER 20

Spain and the British Isles
The Muslim and Viking Attacks on the West

The Frankish *Imperium* represented Western Christendom into the ninth century. Not that its boundaries embraced the entire West. But even under Louis the Pious Carolingian influence still extended to Spain and England. It was the crisis of the *Imperium* that first produced a decline of Frankish prestige.

King Alfonso II of Asturias (791–842), who rejected the claim of the Emir of Córdoba to tribute, had to resist serious Islamic attacks in 791–96, which placed the very existence of his state in peril. He had to rely upon the friendship of the Franks. The Frankish alliance proved good in the years from 797 to 822; Islamic attacks slackened and finally ceased entirely. At this time the Franks were able to push their frontier beyond the Pyrenees. They established the March of Spain and a suzerainty of Basque Navarre, annexing Pamplona around 796–98. Frankish rule in Pamplona remained precarious, it is true, and in 824 Navarre became independent under Iñigo II of the House of Asturias. Thus arose a second, though very small, Christian kingdom in Spain. But even in 828 the Christians in remote Mérida applied not only to the Asturians but also to Louis the Pious for help in a revolt against the Emir of Córdoba. The Christians of Asturias had then withstood a second Islamic offensive (823 – c. 828), which was to be followed by a third (839–41). Both tides of this holy war sent waves also against the Franks. But they died down before the Pyrenees and the Asturo-Cantabrian mountains. Alfonso II had saved Asturias.

Sources from the late ninth century report that the King re-established the *ordo Gothorum*. Alfonso II restored the capital, Oviedo, following its destruction by Islamic troops in 794 and 795. He had himself anointed as King in 791 on the model of the Visigothic Kings, the first Asturian ruler to do so. He reorganized the central administration in imitation of the former royal court at Toledo and set up a provincial administration under *comites* and *iudices*. The *Lex Visigothorum* again became the national law, and the *Collectio Hispana* formed the basis for the reorganizing of the Church. Even the beginnings of the great sanctuary of Santiago go back to the time of Alfonso II. Relics of the Apostle James the Greater had perhaps been carried to safety from Mérida to the church of Our Lady at Compostela near the Galician episcopal city of Iria in 711–12. James the Greater became the patron of the Christians in the struggle for the existence of Asturias against Córdoba, and Alfonso II had the first church of Santiago de Compostela built.

The King left his successors a still small but already firmly established kingdom, which laid claim to all of Spain as the continuation of the Visigothic

Kingdom. The realization of this claim was, of course, in the still distant future. *Al Andalus,* the Emirate of Córdoba, was then experiencing its summertime under the Umayyads Abd-ar-Rahman II (822–52) and Muhammad I (852–86). The Arabic civilization of Andalusia was in flower and attracted many Christians, so that conversions to Islam increased. The Mozarab Christians enjoyed religious freedom, but as a tolerated ghetto community to which any public activity was prohibited. While the religion of the numerically relatively small conquering class was subject to no restrictions, all propaganda was forbidden to the Church. The death penalty was inflicted for efforts at conversion.

The bishops, who had to be confirmed by the conquerors, submitted, but toward the end of the 840's there was opposition in the ranks of the lower clergy, the monks, and the laity of Córdoba, the capital, to the increasing assimilation. Between these groups and the Muslims there occurred spirited confrontations in the decade 850–59. The integralist Christians did not evade discussions on the divinity of Jesus and Muhammad's office as a prophet. They even provoked them and accepted death in return. The episcopate of the province of Seville condemned their actions in 852 at a synod in Córdoba under the presidency of the metropolitan, Reccafrid. The leader of the Córdoba opposition, which had the sympathy of the overwhelmingly Christian population of Mérida and Toledo, was the priest Eulogius. He was imprisoned for having concealed a Muslim woman who had become a Christian and was finally executed in 859, after the Toledans had pointedly elected him their metropolitan, useless though this was. The Córdoba martyrdoms reverberated even in the Frankish Empire. Audradus of Sens expected a Frankish intervention under the patronage of Saint Martin of Tours to liberate Spanish Christianity, but of course Charles the Bald was unable to appreciate such hopes and maintained peace with the emirate. On the strength of this peace the monks of Saint-Germain-des-Prés asked and obtained relics of the Córdoba martyrs.

In default of the Franks, it was the Asturians who continued to embody the *Reconquista.* Under Alfonso III (866–910) they reached beyond the Asturo-Cantabrian mountains and, despite the resistance of the Emirs, resettled the no-man's-land, created as a defensive measure by Alfonso I (739–57), as far as the Douro. Viseu and Lamego, León, Zamora, Simancas, and Burgos came to life again as cities or strongholds. Among the colonists were many Mozarabs from the emirate, especially from Toledo. The size of the kingdom was doubled by the newly erected Marches of León and Castile, which soon became the chief protagonists of the *Reconquista.* Alfonso III did not remain content with this, but turned his court into an intellectual centre of the country, in this imitating the Carolingians. Still, one cannot speak of a Spanish branch of the Carolingian Renaissance, since the Spanish development was overwhelmingly focused on its Visigothic past. This clearly appears in the court historiography, which resumed the historiography of the Visigothic period, interrupted around 700, and strongly emphasized the continuity of the Kingdoms of Toledo and Oviedo. Alfonso III established a new policy of friendship for Navarre, but still insisted on the recognition of the Asturian hegemony. He thought of acquiring a *corona imperialis* from the treasure of Saint-Martin de Tours, which would have given a symbolic expression to his position of leadership. In a letter of 906 to the abbey he styled himself *Rex Hispaniae*. It cannot be decided with certainty whether he introduced the imperial title to express his claim to all of Spain.

The continuous rise of Asturias in the ninth century was unparalleled in Western Christendom. England at this time shared the fate of the Carolingian Empire. The supremacy of the Kings of Mercia had reached its climax under Offa (757–96) and came to an end in 825. Like the Carolingians, the Mercian Kings had convoked assemblies composed of both ecclesiastics and laymen, which met usually at the royal residences from 746 to 816 and regulated especially gifts of land to the Church, but also questions of the ecclesiastical order — the bishops' right and duty of supervision, monasticism, the proprietary church, liturgy and feast days, marriage and economic morality. Offa fostered the shrine of the chief British martyr, Alban of Verulam, which lay within his narrow sphere of power. The Mercian ecclesiastical province of Lichfield that he established lasted only a short time, from 788–802. And an attempt by his successor, Cenwulf (796–821), to transfer the southern English metropolitan see to London failed. Canterbury remained the metropolis of the southern province, which extended to the Humber. The assimilation of the Anglo-Saxon to the Frankish Church, which was inaugurated under Offa by a papal legation of 786–87, made further progress after Offa's death. Archbishop Wulfred of Canterbury (805–32) introduced the *vita canonica* in his cathedral. Vernacular religious literature, which had begun with Caedmon in Bede's time, was continued by the Mercian Cynewulf in the ninth century and thematically enriched by the incorporation of legends, homilies, biblical commentaries, and liturgical poetry. However, the promising development of the Anglo-Saxon Church came to a premature end because of the invasions of the Vikings.

Mercia's great age was past when the fury of the Vikings hit England. At the middle of the ninth century four independent Anglo-Saxon kingdoms coexisted: Wessex, Mercia, Northumbria, and East Anglia. The first Viking expeditions, proceeding from politically fragmented Norway in the late eighth century, had only grazed England. The main storm centre of the Norwegian Vikings had fallen upon the group of islands in the North Sea and had flooded over to Scotland and Ireland. Lindisfarne was sacked in 793, Jarrow in 794. In 795 the Vikings destroyed the grave and church of Saint Columba on the island of Rechru; in 798 they ruined Saint Patrick's in Galloway and in 820 occupied the Isle of Man. Thereafter arose Viking states on the Orkneys, the Hebrides, and in Ireland at Dublin, from which the Norwegians also attacked the Scottish and British western coasts. They soon sailed the old sea-routes from Ireland to the west coast of Gaul and appeared early at the mouths of the Loire and the Garonne. Here they encountered the Danes.

Unification of the state had begun earlier in Denmark than in Norway. King Göttrik had opposed Charles the Great. King Horik (c. 825–54), a descendant of Göttrik, showed himself to be well disposed toward Anschar's mission, though he himself remained a pagan. But in 854 he fell in battle against his nephew Guthrum, and with him the Danish Kingdom came to an end for the time being. The Scandinavian mission, already badly hurt by the destruction of Hamburg in 845, now suffered a second and seemingly mortal blow. Archbishop Anschar, to whom Louis the German had assigned Bremen as see, clung to his missionary assignment until his death in 865, but the few mission stations which continued to exist in Denmark and Sweden under his successor Rembert (865–88) were doomed to destruction.

The great Viking expeditions of the Danes began in 834–35 and were directed against both the Frisian-Frankish and the Anglo-Saxon coastal districts. In Britain it was Kent that was the most exposed, but the Vikings soon extended their operations to East Anglia and Lindsey. The situation was aggravated when around 850 they proceeded to winter in their areas of activity. The crisis reached its height when the various enterprises were coordinated under the leadership of Ivar and Halfdan, sons of Ragnar Lodbrok, and the "Great Army" prepared to overwhelm England in 865. One after the other, Northumbria, East Anglia, and Mercia fell into the hands of the Danes, who proceeded to settle down and established kingdoms of their own. Only Wessex stood firm. Alfred the Great (871–99) assumed the government of Wessex at the beginning of the crisis. Matters hung by a thread for almost a decade until 879, when Alfred achieved the decisive victory of Edington over the Viking King Guthrum, who had himself baptized as an admission of defeat. The mutual boundaries were established in the peace of 886. Alfred claimed the territories south of the city of London, but north of the Thames only the southwestern part of the former Kingdom of Mercia, which now became a province of Wessex. The reconquest of the Danish part of England, the Danelaw, began only with the victory of Tettenhall in 910 under Alfred's son Edward.

After a half-century of struggle and of the occupation of extensive parts of England by the Danish Vikings, complete chaos reigned in the ecclesiastical sphere. The Northumbria of Bede, Willibrord, and Alcuin no longer existed, and in the other territories also the cathedrals were burned and the monasteries destroyed. Bishops and abbots, with their clergy and communities, often led a fugitive existence for years, and many sees remained vacant for years, some for decades. Still, in the end the Church did not perish, even in the Danelaw, and only a few episcopal sees, such as Lindisfarne, were so thoroughly destroyed that they could not be reoccupied. The immigrant Scandinavian pagans could be gradually assimilated. But the intellectual and moral retrogression was enormous, for the dispersal of chapters and religious communities meant the disappearance of the *élite* that had taken care of the candidates for the clerical state.

Alfred the Great recognized this critical situation and sought to remedy it. He summoned men to his court from areas that had been least affected by the devastation: his friend and biographer Asser from Wales; Waerferth and Plegmund, who became Bishops of Worchester and Canterbury, from eastern Mercia; and from the continent the Gallo-Frank Grimbald and the Old Saxon John. To the last mentioned he entrusted the abbey of Athelney, his "Saint-Denis". The King, who felt it to be a defect that in his youth he had received no training in the *artes* and theology, had fundamental texts of Christian literature translated into Anglo-Saxon: the *Regula pastoralis* and the *Dialogi* of Gregory the Great, *De consolatione philosophiae* of Boethius, Augustine's *Soliloquia,* which was expanded into an anthology on immortality, and finally the historical works of Orosius *(Adversus paganos)* and Bede *(Historia ecclesiastica)*. In the prologue of his law code Alfred referred to the Jewish-Christian law. Bede and other sources formed the basis for the *Anglo-Saxon Chronicle,* a history of Britain from Caesar to Alfred in Old English. What was here hinted in its basic idea — the claim to an imperial hegemony in Britain — was stated *expressis verbis* by Asser in his Latin biography of the King.

Alfred the Great became the founder of Old English prose literature through the literary work of his court circle, in which, like his contemporary, Alfonso III of Asturias, he personally participated. In his translations the King had in mind the free youth of his kingdom, who in the future were to acquire a knowledge of reading and writing in the vernacular at the schools. The higher Latin education was prescribed for the clergy. In this field the Wessex court circle produced nothing, and hence its limits become visible here. Wessex did not experience a comprehensive intellectual and spiritual reform, such as that of Charles the Great; it lacked the external presuppositions in an age which had not yet recovered from severe struggles.

The sufferings of the Frankish Empire were not less than the trials of Britain and Ireland, especially since at the same time the Carolingians had to fight also against the Muslims, who, like the Vikings, made their appearance in pirate bands and launched their attacks against the mouths of the great rivers. The Vikings who invaded the Frankish Empire were entirely of Danish origin, like those operating in England. At times there were even mutual relations between the enterprises in the Frankish Empire and in Britain: the plundering bands concentrated at a given time at the points of least resistance.

137

The first goal of the Danish Vikings on the continent was Frisia. Dorestad was plundered annually from 834 to 837. Following a brief pause, caused by the last effective defence measures of Louis the Pious, new plundering raids began in 841 during the war among the royal brothers. Lothar I handed over the County of Zeeland to the Dane Rorik and thereby made him "custodian" of the mouths of the Meuse and the Scheldt. In the same year another Danish band appeared at the mouth of the Seine and burned Rouen. In 842 it was the turn of Quentovic, the most important centre for the transit trade to and from England. The Danes established themselves at the Seine mouth in 845 and at the Loire mouth in 846. From the latter place they dislodged a Norwegian group that had already destroyed Nantes in 843. Bordeaux went up in flames in 848. An iron ring extended along the Frankish coast from the Rhine to the Garonne.

At first the Frankish defence broke down completely. Lothar I did not succeed in ridding himself of his troublesome Danish vassal in Zeeland after the Treaty of Verdun. Dorestad, the chief Carolingian centre for commerce with Scandinavia, was ruined in these struggles, having endured its seventh and final sack in 863. Rorik established a Dano-Frisian domain, which on his death passed to his countryman Gotfrid, possibly a relative.

In the years 856–62 western *Francia* experienced a great invasion staged by the Seine Vikings. Paris, already sacked in 843, was taken again in 856 and 861. The invasion first centred on the territory between the Loire and the Seine, then on the districts on the Somme, where its effects were particularly severe, since these areas had received the fugitives from the Seine. The great Carolingian abbeys of Saint-Wandrille, Saint-Riquier, Saint-Bertin, and Saint-Omer went up in flames. Only with the aid of a group of Vikings whom he recruited was Charles the Bald finally able to redress the situation.

In the meantime, however, other Viking bands, which had returned from a Mediterranean expedition, fell upon the districts between the Loire and the Garonne and in 862–6 pushed deep into the interior, to Orléans and Clermont. Especially hard hit was Aquitaine, where numerous episcopal sees were abandoned and long remained vacant, including the metropolitan see of Bordeaux. On the Loire the Franks were more successful under the leadership of Robert the Strong, ancestor of the Capetians. In the Edict of Pîtres in 864 Charles the Bald ordered the building of fortresses in the country and established marches on the Seine and the Loire. When the Frankish resistance stiffened, the Vikings departed for England, and the West Frankish Kingdom knew a full decade of quiet.

The final and most difficult trial for the Carolingian kingdoms began when numerous Vikings, with their wives and children, streamed back again to the continent from England after the victories of Alfred the Great. The chief blow by the "Great Army" was first directed at the area between the Rhine and the Somme. In 879 the "Great Army" entered the Scheldt. In 880 the Saxons suffered a severe defeat and toward the end of 881 the chief Viking forces pushed up the Meuse to Liège, Maestricht, and Aachen. From there they moved on to the Rhine and destroyed Cologne, Andernach, and Koblenz. But the news that the East Frankish King was massing troops in the district of Mainz caused them to proceed up the Moselle. Trier fell in ruins at the beginning of 882. The resistance of Count Adalard and of Bishop Wala of Metz at Remich induced the Vikings to withdraw to the middle Meuse. In 885 they transferred the centre of their attack to Paris. The Emperor Charles the Fat purchased their departure by assigning them areas in Burgundy for the winter of 886–87 and thereby delivering a hitherto untouched land for plunder. Only the victory of the East Frankish King Arnulf near Louvain in November 891 brought a turning point and induced the chief groups to depart for England. From there in 896–97 a group again moved to the continent; their leader, Rollo, became the founder of Normandy.

On their voyages between 859 and 862 the Vikings also advanced far into the Mediterranean. They sacked Nîmes, Arles, and Valence in 860, Pisa and Fiesole in 861. But the Mediterranean remained the domain of the Muslims, who from Spain and Africa terrorized the Christian lands. Their first expeditions were aimed at the Byzantine Empire. They got under way with an accidental success of the Spanish Muslims, who occupied Crete in 825. In 827 began the officially organized attack of the Aghlabids of Tunis on Sicily, a struggle that was protracted for a half-century. The Muslims' first success was the conquest of Palermo in 831. Messina fell in 843, but the old Sicilian capital, Syracuse, held out until 878. Palermo became the seat of the Arabic administration. Toarmina continued until 902 as the final, but isolated, Greek base.

Even before the Sicilian war had ended, Muslim bands also crossed to South Italy, at first as mercenaries in the pay of the mutually hostile Christian states. Internal struggles weakened the Lombard Principality of Benevento from 839 and led in 847 and 858 to the separation of the Duchies of Salerno and Capua. During these disturbances the Muslims seized Bari and then also Taranto. Muslim vessels appeared before Ancona in 840, before Ostia in 846. The amazing attack on Rome was of no particular consequence, and a second attack on the capital of Christendom in 849 was successfully warded off. But at the same time a Muslim state with Bari as capital arose in Apulia. Emperor and Pope contrived to stabilize the situation in Central Italy, but in South Italy all the exertions of the Emperor Louis II finally foundered on the disunity of the South Italian principalities. After the death of Louis II in 875 the Western Empire ceased to count as a factor for order. The Muslims entrenched themselves between Capua and Gaetà on the Garigliano, and from there they devastated Central Italy and the Papal State. They destroyed Montecassino in 882. As during the Viking attacks on England and Aquitaine, so now also many sees and abbeys in South and Central Italy were left desolate. Effective assistance came only from the Greeks, who under the important general, Nicephorus Phocas, recovered Calabria in the 880's and in addition conquered the parts of Apulia and Lucania that had been occupied by the Muslims. Under papal leadership the Christians in Central Italy finally formed a coalition, which liberated the countryside in the decisive victory on the Garigliano in 915.

While African Muslims were afflicting South and Central Italy, Spanish Muslims were operating on the Gallic and North Italian coasts. More serious raids began here too around 840, but the brigands did not become a real threat until toward the end of the 860's, when they proceeded to establish permanent centres on La Camargue. In the 890's the Muslims erected La Garde-Freinet, their most famous fortress, in the diocese of Fréjus. From here they desolated Provence and the district around Genoa, took possession of the Alpine passes, and extended their expeditions into the Valais and Sankt Gallen. The trials of the regions afflicted by them only reached their climax in the 920's. Here too many churches and monasteries were destroyed. Sees of the provinces of Aix, Embrun, and Arles remained vacant for decades.

Only North Italy, the East Frankish Kingdom, and southern Lotharingia were spared serious devastations by the Vikings and Muslims in the second half of the ninth century. But these regions were to fall prey to the Magyars, who broke into the Western world in the tenth century. Thus the storm created by Muslims, Vikings, and Magyars well nigh left the whole German-Roman West desolate. Of course, not all lands were equally affected. Naturally, the interiors had less to suffer than the coastal and frontier provinces. But even in the districts which were directly exposed to the fury there were differences of degree in proportion to the effectiveness of the defence. Thus the starting point of reconstruction differed at any given moment when the great storm let up. The differing situations led to a displacing of the political and cultural centres of gravity within the West. Another circumstance, however, was of still greater importance for the future. While in southern Europe the Christian and Islamic worlds remained strictly separated and in consequence the Muslim invasion had a purely destructive effect, in northern Europe there finally resulted a symbiosis with the Vikings, who accepted Christian civilization. In Central Europe a similar situation occurred, since missionaries soon found a way to reach even the Magyars. The men and the forces which kept alive the substance of German-Roman civilization in the catastrophe of the late ninth and early tenth centuries made ready, under severe trials, the incorporation of Scandinavia and East Central Europe into the Western world.

CHAPTER 21

The Papacy and the West from 840 to 875

The history of the Roman Church reached a climax in the ninth century in the pontificates of Nicholas I (858–67), Hadrian II (867–72), and John VIII (872–82). Fundamental changes in the relations between the papacy and the imperial office were under way. They were conditioned by the partition of Verdun and later by the extinction of the male line of the family of Lothar I.

The Emperor's suzerainty of the Papal State, the basis for which was the *Constitutio Romana* of 824, continued unaltered. Efforts at Rome to loosen imperial control were fruitless. When there was the threat of a double election in 844, Sergius II was consecrated before the imperial confirmation had been obtained. But Lothar I dispatched his archchaplain, Drogo of Metz, and his son Louis to Rome with a large escort, and Drogo insisted on a reexamination of the proceedings by a synod. Thereafter a papal election was to take place only when authorized by an imperial *iussio* and in the presence of imperial *missi*. This method was actually not followed in 847 on the plea of the danger from the Muslims, but for the future it was observed. The imperial consent was even noted in the official biographies of the *Liber pontificalis*. The imperial authority was also made good within Rome. The throwing of a wall around the Leonine City was ordered by Lothar I in 846 and carried out by Pope Leo IV in 848–52.

The Emperor Louis II intervened in papal elections even more vigorously than had Lothar I. In 855 his *missi* tried to procure the elevation of the Cardinal Priest Anastasius the Librarian to the papacy; he was a highly cultured man but had been deposed by Leo IV. The effort failed, since Anastasius, on account of his having been deposed by the dead Pope, was unacceptable even to Roman circles that were amenable to compromise, and so Benedict III was chosen. The election of Nicholas I in 858 took place in the Emperor's presence. Hadrian II was not the Emperor's candidate in 867, but he was chosen following a reconciliation with Louis II. We have no precise information as to the election of John VIII.

A change of great importance set in as a result of the connection of the elevation to the imperial office with the imperial coronation by the Pope, a connection that made its appearance after the Treaty of Verdun. When the Frankish "monarchy" fell apart and the Emperor became only one sectional ruler among others, the protectorate over Rome remained the only sign which distinguished the Emperor from the Kings. The sanction afforded the Carolingian imperial line by the Pope thereby acquired an enhanced importance. Lothar I's oldest son, Louis II, was crowned King of Italy by Sergius II in 844 and coemperor by Leo IV in 850. Since, unlike his predecessors, Lothar I had not himself been crowned, the coronation at Rome

had a legalizing effect, and Nicholas I regarded it as the decisive juridical element. In 871, in a polemic exchange with the Greeks, Louis II
appealed to his dominion over Rome and his anointing at the hands of the
Pope. Thus the imperial coronation by the Pope became a constitutive
element of the elevation of the Western Emperor, which, of course, took
effect historically only after the extinction of the family of Lothar I.

In Frankish politics the Popes and the Emperor disagreed in the marriage case of King Lothar II. Like other great imperial decrees, the Treaty
of Verdun seems to have been sent to Rome. Sergius II bestowed the
office of papal vicar on Drogo of Metz. Leo IV likewise supported the
imperial policy. Benedict III ratified the Emperor's settlement with Reims,
and he mediated the quarrel among the sons of Lothar I in regard to the
inheritance.

South Italy had been a field of common papal and imperial interest since
the days of Charles the Great. Great changes occurred here when Muslim
mercenaries were employed in the conflict between Benevento and Naples
(834–39) and in the struggles over the succession to Benevento (839–47) and
eventually established the Sultanate of Bari. At this same time the Carolingians
were disabled by their own succession quarrels, and so the earliest steps
toward arranging a united Christian front came from the Greeks. In 839,
842, and 843–44 they negotiated with the Western Emperors in regard to
an alliance against the Muslims, that was to be confirmed by the marriage
of a Byzantine princess to Lothar's son Louis II. Although Lothar I accepted
these offers in a friendly manner, they came to nothing. The Franks did not
become active until the Muslims suddenly attacked Rome in 846. In 847
Louis expelled the Arabs from the city of Benevento and mediated a peace
between the two Lombard pretenders, which led to the definite division of
the principality into the Duchies of Benevento and Salerno. But the Arabs
maintained themselves in much of South Italy and before long Capua detached
itself from Salerno to become the third Lombard principality. Renewed
Frankish interventions in 852, 860, and 863 were only partial successes.

It was not until 866 that Louis II succeeded in regulating matters in South
Italy and in establishing a united Christian front. In 867–68 there were further
negotiations for an alliance with Byzantium, but they ended in new dis-
agreements in 871. Just the same, Louis II managed to take Bari in February
of that year. The son of Lothar I was at the height of his power, when a
conspiracy of the South Italian princes imperilled all the successes he had
achieved. On 31 August the conspirators arrested the Emperor at Benevento
and did not set him free until 17 September, after he had sworn not to attack
them. From Taranto the Muslims again poured into the South Italian
principalities. From Salerno and Capua requests for aid again reached the
Emperor, who rescued both cities in 873. But Benevento and Naples
continued to be hostile to him. The Duke of Benevento sought and found

142

help among the Byzantines. In 873 he acknowledged the suzerainty of the Eastern Emperor Basil I, to whom the Lombards even delivered Bari. The power of Louis II was broken. He left South Italy in the autumn of 873 and died on 12 August 875. The Byzantines came forward in the place of the Franks as the leading power in the defence against the Muslims.

In South Italian politics the Popes staunchly supported Louis II, in particular his exertions for the establishing of a united Christian front, even though they continued to distrust the Greeks. On the other hand, the marriage case of Lothar II led to dissension between Emperor and Pope when, at the end of 863, Nicholas I quashed the acts of the Synod of Metz and deposed the Archbishops of Trier and Cologne. Louis II increased his control of the Papal State but avoided imposing any solution of the crisis by force, even though in 867, at the height of the quarrel with Photius, the Byzantines suggested that he depose the Pope. For his part, Nicholas I abstained from any intervention in the secular sphere. He held to the Gelasian theory of the two powers, which had been roused to new life by the Frankish episcopate in 829. It is true that he understood the imperial coronation as the autonomous right of the Roman Church and thus, according to Knabe, he "regarded the papal authority as being the equal of legitimate birth as a source of imperial power", but he recognized the crowned Emperor as his temporal ruler and claimed no *potestas in temporalibus*.

The death of Nicholas I on 13 November 867 resolved the crisis in the relations between Emperor and Pope. Close cooperation was resumed under Hadrian II, who in 872 released Louis II from his oath to the South Italian rebels and repeated his imperial coronation in order to wipe out the ignominy of the imprisonment at Benevento. Hadrian also supported his imperial master in the question of the inheritance of Lothar II. Only in one point did the views of Emperor and Pope differ: whereas Louis II destined as his successor Louis the German or the latter's oldest son, Carloman, at the papal court the succession of Charles the Bald was favoured.

After 840 and *a fortiori* after 855 the imperial office no longer corresponded to the Frankish Empire, but the Frankish Empire, now as earlier, constituted the nucleus of Western Christendom and, as such, continued to be the Pope's proper field of action. Rome's relations with the non-Frankish states of the West were not intense or frequent. Nothing is known of contacts with Ireland. On the separation of Brittany from the Frankish Empire the Breton ecclesiastical province of Dol was established against the will of the Popes. When Asturias grew strong under Alfonso III, Pope John VIII may have consented to the elevation of Oviedo to metropolitan status in 876 and ordered the consecration of Santiago de Compostela and the holding of a Spanish council.[1] The old connections between Rome and England did not

[1] The letter of John VIII referring to this is probably not authentic. See *Wattenbach-Levison* 4, 454, no. 291.

cease, but they were impeded by the Viking attacks. Papal letters to the Archbishops of Canterbury and York of around 874 and to Canterbury of 878 and 891–96 are extant. They came from a period when Wessex was surmounting the crisis and the situation in South England was gradually re-establishing itself. Around 875 Burgred of Mercia retired to the city of the Apostles, after he had lost his kingdom in the struggle against the Danes. As early as 853 King Aethelwulf of Wessex (839–58) had sent his son Alfred to Rome, where Pope Leo IV honoured the boy with the insignia of the consulship. Alfred accompanied his father when, two years later, he undertook a pilgrimage to the tombs of the Apostles because of the Viking peril. In 884, at the request of Alfred the Great, Pope Marinus I freed the *Schola Saxonum* near Saint Peter's from tolls and taxes. But in the great mass of papal charters and letters the items for England and Spain are not of great importance. The consolidation of the papal primacy of jurisdiction was completed within the Western *Imperium*. Initial efforts in this direction appeared under Leo IV (847–55) but were first developed under Nicholas I.

Ravenna, former residence of the Emperors, the Ostrogothic Kings, and the Exarchs, formed a counterpole to Rome within the Papal State. The capital of the provinces of Emilia and Flaminia had probably once belonged to the Roman ecclesiastical province, but, in any event, in the fifth and sixth centuries it was in closer dependence on Rome than were other metropolises. In the Byzantine period the prelates of Ravenna sought to throw off this dependence. The Emperor Constans II, during the Monothelite controversy, granted them in 666 a privilege making their see autocephalous, but they naturally had to renounce this at the restoration of ecclesiastical peace in 680–82. Thereafter, as before, the metropolitans of Ravenna were again consecrated at Rome, but they acquired greater freedom in the governing of their province. When the Franks intervened in Italy, they endeavoured with Carolingian aid to establish an ecclesiastical state of their own. They were unsuccessful, but thereafter the old rivalries were intensified by "the new political envy . . . in regard to possessions and territorial rights in Romagna and the Pentapolis" (Brandi). Under Leo IV there was open conflict in 853, since the exarchate was virtually autonomous politically under Duke George, brother of Archbishop John, and the Archbishop was usurping Roman ecclesiastical property. The question was regulated at a synod which the Pope held in the Emperor's presence in Ravenna. The controversy flared up again in 861. Nicholas I summoned the Archbishop to Rome, excommunicated him in March 861, and subsequently went to Ravenna. Archbishop John submitted at the Roman synod in November. He had to oblige himself to come to Rome every two years henceforth, to consecrate his suffragans only with papal assent, and not to prevent their going to Rome. According to Brandi, "If the submission of [861] was merely a sacrificing of autonomy, . . . it extended, in the case of this second

144

serious defeat, according to the mind of the ninth century, especially to the suffragan sees, whose relationship to Ravenna was weakened, while it was strengthened in regard to Rome".

Brandi felt that at Ravenna Rome "first tested her own supremacy and the forms of subordination". This is to be taken *cum grano salis,* for the canonical presuppositions for the papal jurisdiction over Ravenna and over the Frankish metropolises were of different sorts. In the case of Ravenna it was possible to appeal to an historical right. In the case of the Franks it was necessary to go back to the inalienable right of the primacy of Peter. For the traditional canon law was not acquainted with a central ecclesiastical government, such as Nicholas worked for — as a system it was first developed by pseudo-Isidore. It is true that the bond between Rome and the metropolitan sees was strengthened in the West by the introduction of the archiepiscopal pallium, and even before pseudo-Isidore the canonical effects of the papal primacy were familiar and hardly to be distinguished from basic statements of the False Decretals. "Sunt qui Gallicanos canones aut aliarum regionum putent non recipiendos, eo quod legati Romani seu imperatoris in eorum constitutione non interfuerint", wrote Agobard of Lyons in his *De dispensatione rerum ecclesiasticarum*.[2] If the Emperor were here expunged, which was very natural, then one would obtain the statement of pseudo-Isidore that all conciliar decrees need Roman authorization.

The determining of the moment when the False Decretals first became known in Rome is made more difficult by the circumstance that one must reckon with the fluctuating interpretations of things of this sort. A papal letter of January 865 to the West Frankish episcopate, containing clear references to pseudo-Isidore, establishes the *terminus ad quem*. But since Nicholas remarks in this "that the Roman Church 'penes se in suis archivis et vetustis rite monumentis recondita veneratur' the papal letters, including forged letters".[3] Hauck suspects that the False Decretals had been in Rome for some time. Haller feels that the first traces of a use by Leo IV can be demonstrated. It is not impossible that the opposition to Hincmar at Reims in 853 may have brought the forgeries to Rome, but the papal letter to Hincmar that refers to this matter does not contain an unequivocal allusion to pseudo-Isidore. Hence it must remain on open question whether Nicholas already knew the forgeries when in 863 he deposed the Archbishops of Cologne and Trier.

More probable is the assumption that Rothad of Soissons first brought the *corpus* of pseudo-Isidore to Rome. Rothad was one of the bishops of the Reims province who had acknowledged the deposed Archbishop Ebbo during his temporary restoration by Lothar I in 840–41. Open conflict between him and Hincmar broke out in 861, when Hincmar demanded the

[2] *PL* 104, 241, A/B. Cf. *Fournier-LeBras* 124 ff.
[3] *MGEp* VI, 394.

145

reinstallation, after the performance of penance, of a cleric whom Rothad had deposed. The Archbishop had his recalcitrant suffragan excommunicated at a provincial synod. Rothad appealed to Rome, but then agreed to answer to an episcopal tribunal, which in 862 deposed him and sentenced him to detention in a monastery. The matter was nevertheless brought before the Pope and in the autumn of 863 Nicholas finally demanded that Rothad be sent to Rome. In January 865 he annulled the deposition at a Roman synod. The proceedings were conducted entirely according to the rules of the False Decretals, to which Nicholas alluded in his letter to Hincmar.

It was to no purpose that Hincmar pointed out that, according to the existing canon law, the Pope could indeed accept an appeal, but the case had to be referred back to an episcopal tribunal. The Archbishop and the King, who had likewise opposed Rothad, bowed to Rome's judgment. Around the same time there occurred an estrangement between Hincmar and Charles the Bald. Wulfad, one of the clerics of Reims who had been ordained by Ebbo, had won favour at court, and the King wanted to promote him to the archiepiscopal see of Bourges. Since the episcopate did not lightly regard the synodal decision of 853, Charles the Bald sought to force the restoration of Wulfad through Rome. In the spring of 866 Nicholas I gave the Archbishop of Reims the alternative of pardoning Ebbo's clerics or of submitting the case to a new synod, by which Wulfad's appeal would be accepted. Hincmar, who perceived that the canonical grounds of his own position would thereby be jeopardized, was willing neither to grant the amnesty nor to set in motion a new process. The synod, meeting at Soissons in August, declined, under his influence, to take up the case again and recommended that the Pope himself grant the amnesty. Charles the Bald did not even wait for the papal decision and had Wulfad consecrated Archbishop immediately. In December 866 Nicholas I decreed the restoration of Ebbo's clerics. In a very ill-humoured letter he left it up to Hincmar to prove within a year the lawfulness of the depositions decreed by him and called for all of Ebbo's records. The Pope or his advisers apparently intended to force a Roman process on Hincmar. The Archbishop of Reims had no difficulty in proving the lawfulness of his election and of his official activity, but he did so with bitterness of heart. A second memorandum, based on the records, was drawn up at the imperial synod which met at Troyes on 25 October 867. The assembled Frankish bishops urged the Pope to determine anew the rights and duties of metropolitans and their suffragans and to explain the principle of the competency of the Roman court in the cases of bishops. The juxtaposition of the old and the new law had produced so much perplexity that a papal statement of principles seemed necessary. But this did not take place. Nicholas did not receive the message of the council. Just before his death he had declared himself satisfied with Hincmar's justification and had thereby ended the conflict.

The third and last quarrel between Reims and Rome occurred in the pontificate of Hadrian II. The Archbishop's nephew and namesake, Hincmar of Laon, was summoned before a royal tribunal in the summer of 868 for having deprived royal vassals of fiefs belonging to his see of Laon. The Archbishop of Reims at first intervened in support of his nephew and brought it about that the younger Hincmar was cited before an ecclesiastical court and took an oath of loyalty to the King. But before his uncle's intervention, the nephew had already appealed to Rome. Before the end of the same year Hadrian II demanded the annulment of the confiscation of the property of the church of Laon, as ordered by the King, and the dispatch of the appellant to Rome. The King did not yield, but in April 869 summoned the Bishop to the Synod of Verberie. Hincmar of Laon decreed as a precautionary measure an interdict on his diocese in the event that he should be arrested. Just the same, Charles the Bald had Hincmar of Laon arrested, while Hincmar of Reims lifted the interdict that had been ordered. Again the old and the new canon law confronted each other. The correspondence with Rome assumed a very bitter form, but King and Archbishop did not budge. The Bishop of Laon was deposed at the Synod of Douzy in August 871. Finally, Charles the Bald played off the Pope against the papal chancery. He decided that it was not Pope Hadrian but Anastasius the Librarian who was speaking in the sharp notes. When in 872 he applied directly to the Pope through his *missus,* he received a conciliatory reply in a secret letter: The King might send Hincmar of Laon to Rome, and the Pope would then appoint judges according to the old canon law. In addition, Hadrian declared that after the death of Louis II he would accept no one but Charles "in regnum et imperium Romanum". The Pope not only yielded; he had made an amazing change of course. The ten-year-old struggle between Rome and Reims ended with a victory for the old canon law — the hour for a centralized papal government of the Church had not yet struck.

Ecclesiastical conflicts of the type of the collisions with Cologne, Trier, and Reims did not take place between Rome and the East Frankish episcopate. In the East Frankish Kingdom there were, it is true, only three metropolitan sees, and of these only two, Mainz and Salzburg, really counted. The church of Hamburg was seriously damaged by the destruction wrought in 845. Louis the German hoped to provide for the missionary work by giving Anschar also the see of Bremen, a suffragan of Cologne. The union was decreed at the Synod of Mainz in 848, and a few years later it received the consent of Archbishop Gunthar of Cologne. Pope Nicholas I approved the uniting of the two sees in 864 and at the same time detached Bremen from the Cologne province. Archbishops Anschar (d. 865) and Rembert maintained the mission stations of Schleswig and Rügen in Denmark and of Birka in Sweden. But the Scandinavian mission was lacking in any power of expansion, and in the 880's it completely collapsed.

147

Quite different was the situation with regard to the Slavic mission in the southeast, which was maintained by Regensburg, Passau, Salzburg, and Aquileia. Since the 830's it had expanded to Bohemia and Moravia and also included Croatia, where the Roman Christian influence had earlier been recognized *via* Dalmatia. The Slavonic princes who acknowledged Frankish suzerainty also accepted Christianity. The Moravian Prince Pribina had himself baptized in 835 at Traismauer in the diocese of Salzburg and received from Louis the German a Slovene domain on the Zala and on Lake Balaton. Ten Bohemian *duces* received baptism at Regensburg in 844–45. The Serbo-Croatian region south of the Drave was a mission territory of Aquileia. We learn that the Archbishops of Salzburg in the 840's and 850's built thirty-two churches in Pannonia, including Pettau, Szalavár (Moosburg), and Pécs, for the most part in Pribina's Slovene principality. In his Moravian homeland Pribina founded the church of Neitra. The mission must also have made much progress in Moravia proper, for at the Synod of Mainz in 852 the Moravian people were regarded as newly converted. In the same year the Croatian bishopric of Nic, in Aquileia's mission field, first emerged into the light of history.

Meanwhile, it had not been possible to incorporate all of the wider area of the former Avar realm into the Frankish Empire. In the 830's there arose a new Slavonic state on the March River. The union of the Moravian tribes was probably the work of the Duke Moimir, from whom the Moravian Prince Pribina fled to the Franks between 830 and 835. The overthrow of Moimir and the installing of his Christian nephew Rastislav (846–70) were achievements of Louis the German, who thereby re-established Frankish suzerainty over Moravia. But Rastislav did not intend to put up with Frankish overlordship, and in 855 there began under his leadership a war for Moravian independence. In 861 Rastislav was in possession of the area as far as the Gran with Neitra, but in 870 he fell into the hands of Louis the German, who had him blinded and sent him to a monastery. The new Duke of the Moravians, Svatopluk (870–94), who had taken the place of his uncle, Rastislav, by virtue of an agreement with the Franks, quickly shook off Frankish suzerainty again. In 871 Bohemia also came within the Moravian sphere of influence. In the Peace of Forchheim in 874 Louis the German recognized the independence of Moravia in return for tribute, while in 890 King Arnulf also admitted Moravian domination of Bohemia in the Peace of Omuntesberg. Thus was there created north of the Danube a great Moravian state, which included the Slavonic tribes as far as Silesia and Galicia within its frontiers.

The Moravian Duke Rastislav was a ruler of importance. He recognized that the new state would be consolidated by the acceptance of Christianity. Were Moravia, as a Christian kingdom, to be admitted into the Western community, its permanence could no longer be questioned. On the other hand, however, complete independence could not be achieved so long as Moravia remained a part of the Bavarian ecclesiastical province of Salzburg. And so it was that in 862–63 Rastislav applied to the Byzantine Emperor for priests.

The Greek missionaries arrived in the Moravian state in 863–64. At their head were two brothers from Thessalonica, Constantine-Cyril and Methodius. Constantine, the younger of the two, had been born in 827. In 842 he had gone to study at Constantinople, where Leo of Thessalonica and Photius were his teachers. When Photius was summoned to court, Constantine took over his professorship. But the younger scholar soon entered the service of the Church and became a deacon and perhaps a priest. In 860 he went as imperial envoy to the Chazars in what is today the Ukraine. After his return he received the commission to proceed to the Moravians. His brother Methodius, who accompanied him, had been born in 815. Around 840 he had been made imperial *strategos* on the Strymon, but had then entered a monastery and had been made abbot. As natives of Thessalonica, the brothers were familiar with the Slavonic language; this was true especially of the former *strategos,* Methodius. Since as yet the Slavonic dialects differed little among themselves, they were able to address Rastislav's Moravians in their mother tongue. Unlike the Western Church, the Byzantine Church did not know any single ecclesiastical language, and so Constantine and Methodius had no hesitation about translating, not only the Bible, but the liturgical texts, including the Roman Mass, known as the Liturgy of Saint Peter, into the vernacular. For this purpose they created the Glagolithic script, which was based on the Greek minuscule with the addition of a few signs for specifically Slavonic sounds.

For three full years the brothers taught in Rastislav's realm, and their successes soon pushed the Bavarian mission into the background. But, since they were not bishops, they were unable to confer ordination on the Slavonic candidates for the priesthood whom they were training. Hence they decided to journey to Constantinople and proceeded to Venice, where in 867 they received from Nicholas I an invitation to come to Rome. When the brothers reached Rome, Nicholas was dead, but Hadrian II prepared a triumphal reception for them, since Constantine was bringing along the relics of Saint Clement of Rome, which he had found in the Crimea at the time of his journey to the Chazars.

But opposition to the Greek missionaries was not wanting. It was not especially the Greek liturgy that was contested — in Rome there were plenty of Greek monasteries, which followed their own way of life — but rather the introduction of the vernacular into the Mass. Already in Venice Constantine had had to defend himself on this score, and the same charges were heard in Rome. Some circles would admit only three sacred languages — Hebrew, Greek, and Latin, sanctified by the inscription on Christ's cross.

149

But Pope Hadrian was free from any narrow-mindedness. He had the Slavonic liturgy celebrated in Roman churches, ordained Methodius a priest, and had some of the Slavonic disciples of the brothers ordained priests and others deacons. Constantine died in Rome on 14 February 869, and Methodius returned to the Slavonic mission lands with papal recommendations. The only restriction imposed on him was that he should read the Epistle and the Gospel in Latin before proclaiming them in Slavonic.

Since a political change had taken place in Moravia in 869–70, Methodius at first laboured in the Slovene principality on Lake Balaton, where Kocel had succeeded his father, Pribina, in 861. Methodius very soon returned to Rome, where in 870 Hadrian II consecrated him Archbishop of Sirmium (Mitrovitza near Belgrade). The new ecclesiastical province was to embrace the entire Serbo-Croatian, Slovene, and Moravian mission territory. It was an event of special importance, for just at that moment Bulgaria was threatening to slip away from Rome, since Nicholas I had, for canonical reasons, denied the Khan's wish that Formosus of Porto be made missionary bishop of the Bulgars. Bulgaria returned to the Byzantine obedience in February 870. By making Methodius Archbishop of Sirmium, Pope Hadrian was underlining Rome's right to Illyricum, whose capital had once been Sirmium. But actually Methodius was unable to establish himself in the destroyed late Roman capital of Illyricum. He returned to Kocel and for the time being resided in his chief fortress, Szalavár.

The Archbishop's moving into a territory which belonged to the East Frankish Pannonian March, had been assigned by Leo III to Salzburg, and was already being evangelized by Salzburg could not but lead to a collision with the Metropolitan of Bavaria. The Salzburg archpriest who was functioning in Pannonia returned home in 870. Methodius was apparently arrested in the Moravian part of his diocese by Carloman, son of Louis the German, and in November 870 brought before a Bavarian synod, meeting probably at Regensburg. The Archbishop of Salzburg saw to the composing of the *Libellus de conversione Bagoariorum et Carantanorum,* a comprehensive account of the founding and missionary activity of his church. Methodius appealed to the Pope's inalienable right, but was taken to Swabia, possibly to Ellwangen, and imprisoned. The protests of Hadrian II were fruitless, but John VIII intervened energetically. He demanded and obtained the release of the Archbishop but forbade him to use Slavonic in the liturgy. Methodius departed for the Moravians, who achieved their independence in 874. He became the Apostle of the Moravians, although John VIII also subjected to him in ecclesiastical matters the Serbian Duke Montemir of Slavonia. The principality of Kocel, who died at this same time, remained under East Frankish suzerainty and a mission district of Bavaria.

It is not unthinkable that the papal *rapprochement* with Charles the Bald already effected by Hadrian II was motivated by the clashes between Rome and the Bavarian episcopate in 870–73. The great project of making good the loss of Illyricum, of the papal vicariate of Thessalonica, by the establishing of an extensive Slavonic ecclesiastical province had been conceived by Nicholas I and pushed forward on a grand scale by Hadrian II. It was hurt by the loss of Bulgaria and the Bavarian opposition in Pannonia. But the founding of a Moravian Church was an important success. Methodius must be placed alongside Boniface in his effectiveness. In the Moravian Prince Svatopluk (870–94), whose morals he severely criticized, he did not find the support which Rastislav had given him, but he enjoyed the confidence of Pope John VIII, who upheld him against Svatopluk and the latter's favourite, Bishop Wiching of Neitra, and who lifted the prohibition of the Slavonic liturgy in 880. In 882 Methodius journeyed to Constantinople, where he was cordially received by Emperor and Patriarch. He died on 6 April 884.

The death of the Apostle of the Slavs brought about a crisis. Pope Stephen V summoned to Rome Gorazd, whom Methodius had recommended as his successor, forbade the Slavonic liturgy, and named Wiching administrator of the metropolitan see. The small group of Methodius's disciples were unable to maintain themselves and in 885 they escaped to Bulgaria. There they reverted to the Byzantine rite, but in the Slavonic language. By a new adaptation to the Greek alphabet they transformed the Glagolithic script into the Cyrillic, which is still used by the Orthodox Slavs.

Meanwhile, in Moravia Wiching fell out with Svatopluk, who expelled him in 893. The ecclesiastical reorganization, for which Pope John IX (898–900) sent legates, collapsed, since in 906 the Moravian state fell to pieces under the blows of the Magyars. Ecclesiastical centres were maintained in Bohemia, which had again come under East Frankish suzerainty in 895, and apparently also at Cracow and in parts of Hungary (Slovakia and Esztergom). The Croats, whose Prince Domagoj threw off Frankish suzerainty on the death of Louis II, also remained loyal to the Slavonic Roman liturgy. When in 925 their Prince Tomislav was elevated to the royal dignity, their churches were attached to the Dalmatian province of Spalato.

CHAPTER 22

The Degradation of the Papacy and the Empire (875 to 904)

The death of the Emperor Louis II presented contemporaries with difficult problems of law. The revived Western Empire was hereditary in the senior Carolingian line until 875, though since 850 coronation by the Pope had played a constitutive role. In this regard the *ordinatio imperii* of 817 retained its validity — even in the Frankish domestic chaos the right of Lothar I and his heirs to the imperial crown was never debated. Only on the extinction of the line of Lothar did the question come up: Who was to award the imperial crown? At the same time the succession to the Kingdom of Italy was opened. At Metz in 867 or 868 the royal uncles, Louis the German and Charles the Bald, had reached an understanding in regard to the eventual partition of the inheritance of Lothar and the common assumption of the protectorate over the Roman Church. But in 872 Louis II had designated as his successor Louis the German's son, Carloman of Bavaria, while at the same time Pope Hadrian II had held out the prospect of the imperial crown to Charles the Bald. In so doing the Pope may have been relying not only on the ancient right of the *populus Romanus* and the papal right of coronation but also on the regulation of the *ordinatio imperii* that, in the event of Lothar I's death without sons, the *populus christianus* should appoint a successor in the imperial office from the surviving brothers.

At the death of the Emperor Louis II the Holy See was occupied by John VIII, third and last of the important Popes of the ninth century. John had already exercised great influence as archdeacon under Nicholas I. By convoking the clergy and senate of Rome in August 875 and having them acclaim Charles the Bald as Emperor he created a *fait accompli*. On 29 September Charles appeared at Pavia, where a part of the Italian magnates did homage to him. He proceeded to Rome, and there on Christmas 875 John VIII gave him the imperial crown. On 2 January 876 the Pope made Archbishop Ansegis of Sens his vicar for Gaul and Germany. As Lothar I had once done, so now Charles the Bald apparently contemplated the gaining of new importance for the imperial office throughout the Frankish Empire by means of the Church. The Pope was especially interested in greater independence in the Papal State and defence against the Muslims. Charles the Bald annulled the stipulation that the papal election had to take place in the presence of imperial *missi* and turned over the direction of the policy in regard to South Italy to John VIII. Louis II had already given seven cities of the Duchy of Spoleto and Byzantine Gaetà to the Roman Church and had promised to restore the papacy's South Italian and Sicilian *patrimonium*. Charles the Bald made over to the Pope the revenues of the three great monasteries of Farfa, Rieti, and Sant'Andrea on Monte Soracte, subjected to him the Duchies of Spoleto and Benevento, and "gave" him the Byzantine Duchies of Naples and Calabria.[1] In February 876 he received the homage of the Italian magnates at Pavia, entrusted the government of Italy to his brother-in-law Boso, and then returned to the West Frankish Kingdom.

It soon became plain that, despite the concessions of Charles the Bald, the Pope could not control the situation in South Italy, and so John VIII did what he could to make possible an effective imperial operation against the Muslims. A general Frankish synod was to meet at Ponthion and restore

[1] For the concessions made by Charles the Bald, which can only be reconstructed from later versions of the imperial privileges, cf. E. E. Stengel, *Die Entwicklung des Kaiserprivilegs*. See ibid. also for the concessions made by Louis II.

harmony in the Empire. But of the bishops of the kingdom of Louis the German only Willibert of Cologne appeared, and the opposition of Hincmar of Reims obstructed the vicariate of the Archbishop of Sens even in the West Frankish Kingdom. Despite everything, Charles the Bald managed to have himself recognized as Emperor by the West Frankish magnates by their selection of him as their imperial *advocatus*.

The death of Louis the German on 28 August 876 delivered the new Emperor from his most dangerous adversary. The sons of the East Frankish King partitioned their father's kingdom: the oldest, Carloman, received Bavaria, Louis the Younger acquired Franconia, and the third son, Charles the Fat, obtained Swabia. Since the three East Frankish Kings were by no means in harmony, it would now have been possible for Charles the Bald to intervene in Italy. But the Emperor thought that the opportunity had come for him to restore the unity of the Empire, and so, in September 876, he marched against Louis the Younger by way of Aachen and Cologne. But his exaggerated hopes were quickly dashed to the ground: on 8 October nephew routed uncle at Andernach, and the imperial prestige received a staggering blow. But the defeat had no political repercussions, for the opposition among the East Frankish brother-kings was greater than the opposition of uncle and nephew.

A second journey to Rome could not be avoided, because of the turbulent state of Italy. In April 876 John VIII condemned *in absentia* the leaders of his opponents among the nobility and the Cardinal Bishop Formosus of Porto, who was connected with this faction. In South Italy Naples and Benevento, which were unwilling to submit to papal direction, were secretly supported by the Spoletans. The governor of Italy, Boso, was recalled by Charles the Bald after he had eloped with Irmingard, only legitimate descendant of the line of Lothar I, in the summer of 876, following an understanding with the Dowager Empress Engelberga. Carloman of Bavaria had already invaded Italy in September 875 and was now preparing a new campaign. At the beginning of August 877 John VIII held a large synod at Ravenna, at which 150 bishops ranged themselves behind him and the Emperor. Soon afterwards Charles the Bald crossed the Alps. Emperor and Pope met at Vercelli and at the beginning of September proceeded to Pavia, where they received the news that Carloman of Bavaria had crossed the Alps with a large army. Since the Emperor had brought along only a small retinue and the requested reinforcements from the West Frankish magnates had not arrived, he found himself compelled to return to the West Frankish Kingdom. *En route* he died on 6 October 877.

In this situation the Pope had no choice but to establish contact with Carloman, to whom the Italian magnates had already done homage at Pavia. However, the King of Bavaria postponed his journey to Rome till the following year. He was never to see the Eternal City. Taken seriously ill on his return across the Alps, this oldest son of Louis the German continued to be incapacitated until death freed him from his sufferings in 880. John VIII left Rome at the end of April 878 and went by ship to Genoa. From there he invited the Carolingians to a general Frankish synod. His original plan was probably to offer the imperial dignity to Louis the Stammerer. But while he was in Provence, where he had proceeded from Genoa, he discovered that the health of the West Frankish King was poor. At that time the Pope seems to have given serious consideration to the candidacy of Boso as a possible solution. By virtue of his marriage to the Princess Irmingard, Boso had become the representative of the line of Lothar I and he was in possession of solid political power in Provence. John supported Boso's candidacy until March 879, when the sickness and, on 10 April, the death of Louis the Stammerer gave events another twist. On 15 October 879 Boso had himself proclaimed King by his vassals and the episcopate of the provinces of Vienne, Lyons, Besançon, Tarentaise, Aix, and Arles, following the rules of the *ordinatio* of 817. And so the line of Lothar I turned up again — not in Italy, but in Burgundy.

The question of the succession threw the West Frankish Kingdom into internal confusion, since the East Frank, Louis the Younger, also came forward as a candidate. This favourable moment gained for him western Lotharingia, while Louis III and Carloman, sons of Louis the Stammerer, finally divided the remainder of their father's inheritance. The West Frankish and the East Frankish Carolingians united against Boso and Lothar II's bastard Hugh, who had been claiming Lotharingia since 878. The common action against the two pretenders of the line of Lothar I eventually prepared the way for the devolution of the entire Carolingian Empire on the youngest son of Louis the German, Charles III the Fat, who fell heir to his brother, Louis the Younger, in 882 and to his West Frankish cousins in 885. Boso alone maintained his independence in his firmly unified Burgundian-Provençal kingdom.

John VIII had turned to the East Frankish line in April 879 and had first of all approached Charles the Fat. But the situation in *Francia* did not at the outset permit any of the sons of Louis the German to intervene in Italy. Not until the autumn of 879 did Charles the Fat appear in Pavia; he met the Pope at Ravenna in January 880. This move yielded to the King of Swabia only the Italian royal crown. Only on his second Italian journey, lasting from December 880 to March 881, was there found time for his imperial coronation at Rome on 21 February 881. The Pope obtained as little real assistance then as he did on the occasion of a third encounter at Ravenna in February 882. At that very moment the Muslims were establishing themselves on the Garigliano, from where they terrorized Rome. The ghastly murder of John VIII on 15 December 882 indicates how low the imperial authority had fallen. It was also an omen of an approaching dark epoch in papal history.

John VIII was followed in rapid succession by Marinus I (882–84), Hadrian III (884–85), and Stephen V (885–91). Marinus was the first Pope to have been a bishop before his accession to Saint Peter's see. This violation of the canons was also a sign of the breakdown of the old rules. The new Pope pardoned the opposition of 876 and gave back to Formosus his see of Porto. In 883 Marinus obtained from the Emperor the deposition of the Margrave Guy of Spoleto, but this merely produced further confusion. In the pontificate of Hadrian III it seemed as though the situation of the Empire was finally improving. The Emperor obtained successes against the Vikings and sought to profit from this to assure the succession of his bastard, Bernard. The Pope — such is the irony of history — was ready to assist him in this project but died *en route* to the East Frankish Kingdom, and matters took a turn for the worse again. Hadrian's successor, Stephen V, was selected against the will of the Emperor. When Charles the Fat in 887 demanded his cooperation in regulating the succession in the Empire — the still underage grandson of Louis II, Louis of Vienne, Boso's son, was selected as heir — the Pope declined and perhaps thereby hastened the dissolution of the Empire. The fall of Charles the Fat must have left Stephen V indifferent.

The deposition and death of the Emperor Charles the Fat mark an epoch in the history of the Carolingian Empire. Regino of Prüm underscores this turning point with the statement that now for the first time non-Carolingians were raised to the kingship in the subkingdoms. Under Carolingian rule remained only the East Frankish Kingdom, including Lotharingia, and the lower Burgundian Kingdom of Vienne, whose King Louis, still a minor, represented the line of Lothar I by virtue of his being a grandson of the Emperor Louis II. The new East Frankish King, Arnulf of Carinthia, was a bastard of Carloman of Bavaria. The Robertian Eudes established himself as King of the West Franks; the Welf Rudolf, as King of Upper Burgundy, the province of Besançon. The Italian crown was disputed between Berengar of Friuli and Guy of Spoleto. Empire and dynasty had parted company. A last but weak bond of imperial unity remained in the suzerainty of the East Frankish King, which was recognized by all the partner-kings except Guy of Spoleto. For the moment Arnulf could not give a thought to the imperial dignity, because of the Viking peril and the struggle now being resumed with the Moravians. In 890 Stephen V did ask his aid against "mali christiani" and "imminentes pagani", but on 21 February 891 he had to give the imperial crown to Guy of Spoleto.

Stephen's successor in the Holy See was Formosus of Porto (891–6), even though his elevation was likewise contrary to the ancient rule that no bishop was allowed to pass from his see to another. His opponents accused Formosus of ambition; his personal conduct was above reproach, and he was a man of strict, even ascetical life. He too had put up with the Spoletan Dynasty; in fact, he even had to crown Guy's son Lambert as coemperor on 30 April 892.

But Formosus was not happy with this state of affairs and as early as the fall of 893 a first appeal for help was sent to Arnulf. Arnulf's Italian expedition did not materialize. The Emperor Guy died in 894, and in September 895 a new papal appeal for help was sent to the East Frankish King. Arnulf appeared in Pavia in December 895 and from there moved against Rome. The East Franks took the Leonine City by storm, and the Empress-Mother Agiltrudis evacuated Rome. In mid-February 896 Arnulf received the imperial crown from Pope Formosus. But the campaign planned against Spoleto had to be cancelled, for the new Emperor was suddenly overtaken by the hereditary illness of the East Frankish Kings. Arnulf returned northward, as though in full flight, in April, but even before he had reached the Alps, Pope Formosus died on 4 April 896.

Death spared Formosus severe trials but not a *damnatio memoriae* of a gruesome sort. In January 897 his corpse was disinterred and, in full pontificals, brought before a synod, where a deacon, as his proxy, confessed his guilt. The synod acknowledged the nullity of his elevation to the papacy and of his official acts. Finally, his corpse was cast into the Tiber. It was recovered by a hermit, who reinterred it. The gruesome trial was not unavenged. In the same year 897 the adherents of Formosus in Rome rose and Pope Stephen VI was deposed and eventually strangled. But the Formosans were not very lucky with the next two Popes: both Romanus and Theodore II died in quick succession. Encouraged by this, the anti-Formosans seized the initiative and in the spring of 898 brought about the election of Bishop Sergius of Caere as Pope. The fact that, by this change of see, Sergius was violating an ancient ecclesiastical prohibition probably did not much concern the Romans, for three promotions of bishops to the papacy within a brief period had virtually nullified the opposing rule. Hence it was not for canonical reasons but for reasons of party politics that the Formosans forcibly expelled the newly elected Sergius and elevated John IX (898–900). John's first efforts were directed to the restoration of order in conjunction with the Emperor Lambert. A Roman Synod, attended also by North Italian bishops, condemned the sentence passed against Formosus, anathematized those who violated corpses and the leaders of the anti-Formosans, especially Sergius, and sought to guarantee future papal elections by decreeing, among other things, that, as earlier, they must take place in the presence of an imperial *missus*. Then the Emperor Lambert and John IX held another synod at Ravenna, which confirmed the Roman decrees and provided for appeal to the Emperor in the event of conflicts among the Romans, thus renewing the *Constitutio Romana* of Lothar I.

All that was expected of the future was frustrated by the sudden death of the young Emperor. In Lambert the Roman Church lost its last support. No help could be expected from the Emperor Arnulf, who succumbed to his incurable illness on 8 December 899 at Regensburg, nor from his successor as King of Germany, Louis the Child. John IX's successor, Benedict IV (900–3), did, it is true, give the imperial crown to young King Louis of Provence in 901, but the latter was defeated in his struggle with Berengar of Friuli; blinded, he returned to Provence in 905. But, before this, important events had occurred at Rome. On the death of Benedict IV there ensued a split in the still dominant Formosan faction. After about two months, in September 903, the priest Christopher overthrew the legitimate Pope Leo V and usurped his place. But the intruder was not to enjoy his success. At the beginning of 904 Sergius of Caere marched on Rome with an armed force and seized power. His pontificate marked an epoch, not so much because of the now final elimination of the Formosans as because of the connections which Sergius had with influential families. With him began a new period of Roman history, that of the domination of the city and the papacy by the nobility.

CHAPTER 23

Reform, Theology, and Education under the Later Carolingians

The Carolingian Renaissance did not come to an end with the end of imperial unity, but achieved its third and final climax under the grandsons of Charles the Great. Its effects were first clearly discernible in Rome in this phase. In the Frankish Empire decentralization, which had begun under Louis the Pious, made further progress after the Verdun partition. Instead of the single imperial court there now existed three and later even five courts of equal rank; but these were in no sense the only or even the outstanding centres of education in the partner-kingdoms. Only the court of Charles the Bald, at which was the great Irish scholar, John Scotus (before 845 to after 867), polarized the cultural life of the West Frankish Kingdom to a certain degree.

An adherent of Lothar I celebrated in song the battle of Fontanet. The history of the war among the royal brothers was written by Nithard, who was not only a vassal of Charles the Bald but, through his mother, a grandson of Charles the Great. There are also other testimonies of the education of the lay aristocracy, such as the *Manuale* of Dhuoda, wife of Bernard of Barcelona, for her son William, and the catalogues of the libraries of the Margrave Eberhard of Friuli and Count Eckehard of Mâcon. But war and inner chaos led in the next decades to an ever growing barbarism among the imperial aristocracy. Nithard's work had no sequel, and the initial efforts for a lay education atrophied.

The sons of Louis the Pious, who had had the benefit of a first-rate education, were, like their father, interested in theological questions. The Emperor Lothar I, to whom Walafrid dedicated two works in 841 and Wandalbert of

157

Prüm his martyrology in 848, asked Rhabanus and Angelomus of Luxeuil for scriptural commentaries. The *praeceptor Germaniae* dedicated some of his writings also to Louis the German, who, following the estrangement during the war among the brothers, made him Archbishop of Mainz in 847. The East Frankish King consulted Hincmar of Reims on Genesis and the Psalms and acquired the works of Saint Ambrose. Sedulius Scotus, who was closely connected with the court of Aachen but also had ties with the other Carolingians, probably wrote his "mirror for princes" for Lothar II. The widest range of intellectual interests was possessed by Charles the Bald, to whom some fifty contemporary writings were dedicated. The West Frankish King himself commissioned authoritative theological opinions.

The most important link between the court and the great ecclesiastical centres of culture at this time was still the royal chapel. The chapels at Aachen, Frankfurt, Regensburg, and Compiègne were made collegiate churches. Thereby the Kings fulfilled a long-standing desire of the Church reformers. The canons continued to be members of the palace clergy, but, in contradistinction to the chaplains, who were from now on bound to service in the immediate retinue of the King, they had a fixed residence and an ecclesiastical status. Moreover, in Lotharingia and Provence a closer connection between the chapel and the most outstanding ecclesiastical metropolises was in preparation. In the East Frankish Kingdom the same process appeared in the latter part of the reign of Louis the German. Likewise, with the assigning of the highest spiritual functions at court to the most distinguished metropolitans in their realms the Kings seem to have acceded to the desire of the reformers for the inclusion of the palace clergy in the existing Church order. In the West Frankish Kingdom, as earlier, the archchaplains and archchancellors were provided with abbeys, such as Saint-Denis, Saint-Germain-des-Prés, and Saint-Martin de Tours. In Italy at this time no association of specific churches with court officers can be determined.

A number of large monasteries were closely attached to the several royal courts as the endowment of queens, princes, and princesses. From the chapels and the royal monasteries abbots and, especially in the West Frankish Kingdom, bishops thereafter proceeded. But new educational centres seldom arose as a result of direct action by the court clergy. More clearly than in the preceding period the episcopate appeared as the representative of education. The bishops even took charge of the quasi-official historiography, which had hitherto been the province of the chapel.

The various lands of the Frankish Empire did not all participate in equal measure in the later Carolingian Renaissance; in an age of growing external perils several older centres ceased to be active. Saxony had not yet fully opened itself up to Carolingian culture. Provence remained on the fringes and had to suffer early from the attacks of Muslim pirates. Aquitaine was disturbed by inner confusion, and its coasts were afflicted by the Vikings. Only the sees of Bourges and Poitiers continued to have rather close relations with *Francia*. But even in *Francia* the ecclesiastical provinces of Tours and Rouen, severely tried by the struggles with Vikings and Bretons, became less prominent. In the third quarter of the ninth century the centres of intellectual life were in the provinces of Sens and Reims, Lyons and Vienne, Trier and Cologne, Mainz and Salzburg. And, alongside the Frankish centres, Rome emerged again as an intellectual centre in this period.

Compared with the age of Louis the Pious, the third phase of the Carolingian Renaissance was full of variety and colour. The *artes* were represented not only by grammarians but also by philologists and "humanists" of universal knowledge, such as Lupus of Ferrières (diocese of Sens), Heiric of Auxerre, and John Scotus. Nor was the age lacking in gifted poets: Sedulius Scotus, Milo of Saint-Amand, Gottschalk, and Wandalbert of Prüm. Most writers did not confine themselves to the *artes* but also tried their hand at scriptural exegesis. Even Otfrid's poem on the life and sufferings of Christ, which introduced the fourfold final rhyme of the contemporary Latin poetry into Old High German, was a scholarly and to a great extent exegetical work. History and hagiography were likewise cultivated. The new type of "historical" martyrologies originated at Lyons and Vienne, where Florus and Ado revised Bede's martyrology. Recourse to them was had by the Paris monk, Usuard of Saint-Germain-des-Prés, whose martyrology, compiled in 875 at the request of Charles the Bald, was soon widely circulated and finally became the basis of the *Martyrologium Romanum*.

A mastery of Greek was acquired by two Irishmen, John and Sedulius Scotus, at the West Frankish and the Lotharingian courts, and by the papal librarian, Anastasius. John Scotus and Anastasius translated into Latin the writings of pseudo-Dionysius, which were to be of the greatest importance for the later intellectual formation of the West and already inspired the philosophical and theological concepts of John Scotus. This teacher at the court of Charles the Bald had no equal as an original thinker in his day. In his chief work, *De divisione naturae*, composed in 867 at the request of Archbishop Wulfad of Bourges, he describes the creation of the world, *natura creata et non creans*, by God, *natura creans et non creata*, through the agency of ideas, *natura creans et creata*, and its return to God as its final end, *natura nec creans nec creata*, through the mediatorship of Christ. The Christian teaching on creation and redemption was here given a Neoplatonic interpretation with no toning down of its dogmatic content.

For John God remains ultimately inaccessible — theology of negation — to the extent that he has not revealed himself directly or indirectly by means of ideas and creation. Man ascends to him by his senses, reason, and intellect. Sense knowledge became a necessary preliminary to rational knowledge only because of the fall; but it is at the same time a remedy for sins in so far as it leads from the sensuous external to the intellectual. *Ratio* is not comprehended as separate from faith, but as a God-given force for the illuminating of faith. It conducts to intellectual knowledge, that is, to the vision of God, which for its part presupposes a theophany. The return of man to God is possible only through Christ, God's self-revelation, and his grace. Sin is explained neoplatonically as perseverance in the present state; its punishment lies in itself. Death appears as progress to the higher form, as return to the ideas, which are to be understood, not as emanations from God, but as an expression of the divine will, and which have their eternity in the Logos. To the extent that ideas exist virtually also in man's mind, the entire creation is also redeemed together with man by Christ.

John Scotus was one of the most important representatives of Carolingian intellectual life in the West Frankish Kingdom, but he was not its only witness. Carolingian theology reached its climax simultaneously in the discussion on the Eucharist and on predestination. In Christian antiquity the Eucharist had been understood as the "representation *(anamnesis)* of Christ's real person and of the salvation connected with it". The great mystery was left undefined. The presence of the Redeemer in the Sacrament was referred to the Logos, to the historical Jesus, and to the *Corpus Christi mysticum,* all at the same time, but the various theological schools stressed different aspects. The occasion for the Eucharistic controversy of the ninth century may have been provided by Amalarius, who in his explanation of the Mass in 821 interpreted also the *fractio panis,* relating the parts of the Host to the *triforme corpus* of the Lord — that is, the body born of Mary and glorified in the resurrection, the *ecclesia militans,* or community of the living, and the *ecclesia triumphans,* or community of the dead. This concretizing of the mystery was attacked by Florus and condemned at the Synod of Quierzy in 838.

But even before Quierzy Paschasius Radbertus of Corbie had composed his *De corpore et sanguine Domini* in 831–33 for the edification of his confrères at Corvey. In this he stressed the full identity of the Eucharist with the body of Christ that was born of Mary and expounded the reality of the Mass as the repetition of Calvary. The work did not attract the interest of theologians until Radbertus offered it in a revised and expanded form to Charles the Bald. The Abbot of Corbie followed Ambrose, whereas Carolingian theology was under the standard of Augustine, who had, it is true, understood the Eucharist as the "substantial image of the *res ipsa*", but at the same time stressed its "function of sign as *sacramentum corporis* at a distance from the *res ipsa*". The first opposition to Radbertus came after 845 from Rhabanus Maurus, who defined communion as union with Christ into one body by faith. Likewise the Saxon monk Gottschalk, otherwise an opponent of Rhabanus, adopted a stand against the Abbot of Corbie in a work composed around 850. He likened the presence of Christ in the bread and wine to the hypostatic union of the two natures of the Son of God, just as John Damascene had done a century earlier. Hence Gottschalk saw in it an objective reality, but only

160

in the form of a divine power inherent in the Eucharist. He rejected the interpretation of the Mass as a real repetition of Calvary. Gottschalk's fundamental notion was shared by his friend and teacher, Ratramnus of Corbie, who, like several early Christian theologians, compared the presence of Christ in the Eucharist to the operation of the Holy Spirit in the baptismal water.

Paschasius Radbertus defended his doctrine in his commentary on Matthew, resumed after 853, and in a letter to Fredegard of Saint-Riquier. He again maintained his explanation of the Mass, but defended himself against misinterpretations springing from a far too materialistic idea of the Lord's glorified body, and especially rejected the thesis attributed to him of a dismembering of Christ's body in communion. He wanted transubstantiation to be understood as a mysterious re-creation, repeated at any given moment, of the body and blood of the Lord. With this the controversy came to an end and was only taken up again, under different circumstances, in the eleventh century.

The discussion of the Eucharist had been confined to a relatively small group. Matters were far more stormy in the controversy over the teaching of the monk Gottschalk on predestination, in which even the episcopate took sides. Son of a Saxon Count Bern, Gottschalk was born around 804 and as a child was offered to the monastery of Fulda. Before 824 he was sent to complete his studies at Reichenau, returning to Fulda around 827 in the company of Walafrid, his fellow student. He now met Lupus of Ferrières, who was then studying in the foundation of Saint Boniface. Before long the Saxon monk came into conflict with his Abbot Rhabanus, since he demanded his release from the monastery and the return of the property donated by his father. In June 829 at a synod at Mainz Archbishop Otgar granted him a release on condition of his renouncing the dowry presented to the monastery. Neither party was satisfied, and Rhabanus appealed to the Emperor. The decision of Louis the Pious has not come down to us, but the Saxon must have been released from the vows made as an *oblatus*.

Gottschalk thereupon left Fulda but then returned to the monastic life. The stops on his journey might quite well have been Corvey, Corbie, Hautvillers, and Rebais. Finally he entered the monastery of Orbais, in the diocese of Soissons, where he was ordained a priest between 835 and 840. After a pilgrimage to Rome he went *via* Friuli, where he stayed for a while at the court of the Margrave Eberhard, as missionary to the Croats and Bulgars. In 848 he returned to *Francia*.

Already in Italy Gottschalk, as a biased but highly gifted interpreter of Augustine, had expounded his doctrine of double predestination to salvation and to damnation, of the limitation of the redemption to the elect, as appears from letters written by Rhabanus in 840 and 845–46. After his return to *Francia* he was summoned in October 848 before a synod at Mainz, which was presided over by Louis the German. Here he defended his teaching against Rhabanus, now Archbishop of Mainz, but was condemned as a heretic and a vagabond monk, whipped, and sent back to Orbais. Rhabanus notified the metropolitan, Hincmar, who the next year summoned the monk to the Synod of Quierzy, which had been convoked by Charles the Bald. Here too Gottschalk refused to retract, was again flogged, perpetually silenced, and conveyed to the monastery of Hautvillers in the archdiocese of Reims, since Hincmar distrusted the proper local Ordinary, Rothad of Soissons.

Detention in a monastery was not the same thing as imprisonment. It is true that Gottschalk lived in a penitentiary apart from the monastic community proper, but in regard to maintenance and clothing he seems to have been treated like his confrères. He continued to write and found friends who would circulate his works. Hincmar opposed them with a brief treatise on predestination, and thereby began the great controversy. Ratramnus of Corbie entered the lists on behalf of his pupil and friend. Hincmar turned to five highly esteemed theologians, among them Amalarius of Metz, Prudentius of Troyes, and Lupus of Ferrières. But Prudentius and Lupus ranged themselves, apart from slight differences in detail, on the side of Gottschalk, who for his part dispatched a lengthy memorandum to the participants in the Synod of Quierzy. Even the court took notice, and Charles the Bald asked Lupus and Ratramnus for their opinion. Both complied in 850 with detailed discussions, Lupus in *Liber de tribus quaestionibus,* Ratramnus in *De praedestinatione.* Rhabanus and Hincmar had admitted only a predestination to good. Lupus adhered to double predestination, even though he made a distinction between *praedestinatio ad gloriam* and *praedestinatio ad poenam* and expressed himself cautiously on the question of the limiting of the redemption to the elect. Ratramnus characterized predestination to glory as a free act of the divine mercy, predestination to punishment as a being left in the state of reprobation.

Hincmar, theologically isolated, sought help from John Scotus. But Neoplatonic philosophy proved unable to solve the great theological mystery, and John's inadequate effort called the metropolitans of Sens and Lyons into the fray. Wenilo of Sens entrusted the refutation of the Irishman to his suffragan Prudentius, who presented his views in a new treatise written in 851–52. In the name of the Church of Lyons, whose Archbishop Amolo had thus far occupied an intermediate position, Florus attacked the doctor of the West Frankish court. Hincmar thereupon sought to play off Amolo against Florus, but Amolo died in 852 and was succeeded by Remigius. The new Archbishop of Lyons had a second treatise written, and this was directed chiefly against his fellow Archbishop of Reims.

Gottschalk was now almost forgotten as the quarrel moved to another plane. The controversy centered on the four *capitula* which Hincmar, with the aid of Charles the Bald, had had ratified by a small group at Quierzy.

In these *praedestinatio ad poenam* was interpreted as *praescientia,* the recovery of free will was explained, in accord with tradition, as a gift of the grace of redemption, and God's salvific will and the redemption were expressly referred to all mankind, in opposition to the prevailing Augustinianism. Hincmar's *capitula* encountered criticism in a new polemical work from Lyons and in the Synod of Valence in 855, the canons of which specified the viewpoint of the episcopate of Lyons, Vienne, and Arles, which in many respects differed from that of Hincmar. In 856 the episcopate of the province of Sens expressly committed the newly elected Aeneas of Paris to the tradition-al Augustinian doctrine. A collision between the Lyons and the Reims factions occurred at the Frankish Diet of Savonnières in 859. The question had to be removed from the agenda. Hincmar again expressed himself in a third and final treatise, into which he incorporated the teaching of the Greek Fathers, who were more in accord with his view than was Augustine. And so the discussion was resumed in 860 at the Frankish Diet of Thuzey, whose irenic *communiqué* adopted some of Hincmar's views but did not reconcile the funda-mental differences. In 859 the Rhône bishops had referred the question to the Pope. Nicholas I had Hincmar and Gottschalk summoned to the Synod of Metz in 863, but neither of them appeared. The initiative of the Pope, who was apparently inclined toward the Augustinian view, aroused the hopes of Gottschalk's friends, and in 866 the monk Guntbert secretly left Hautvillers for Rome with Gottschalk's writings. But the fronts had already become obscured in the West Frankish Kingdom, and Hincmar commissioned Archbishop Egilo of Sens to act as his proxy. Nicholas I, at that time heavily burdened with other kinds of anxieties, issued no decision — he died in the autumn of 867.

Around the same time, between 866 and 870, the monk Gottschalk also died. He was a fascinating personality of great brilliance. No innovator, he was a man of the most profound inner fervour, to whom worship and doctrine became so personal an experience that even deep mysteries appeared to him as evident truths. The bluntness which is frequently found in the nature of men of his type grew in the course of his detention into a psychosis. But the experience of divine grace also strengthened the unhappy monk at the height of his sufferings, and Gottschalk gave expression to this in poetry that will never die.

The Eucharist and predestination were not the only problems occupying the theologians of the third Carolingian generation. The doctrine of the Trinity and questions referring to the nature of the soul and the vision of God were likewise discussed — and by the same persons: Gottschalk, Hinc-mar, and Ratramnus. More important apparently was the movement stimula-ted in the West by the Synod of Constantinople of the summer of 867 with its excommunication of Pope Nicholas I. The Pope mobilized the Frankish episcopate also against Byzantium. He applied to Hincmar of Reims, who entrusted Eudes of Beauvais with the refutation of the traditional Greek accusations against the Latins. On behalf of the province of Sens Aeneas of Paris wrote *Adversus Graecos*. The East Frankish Kingdom expressed itself at the Synod of Worms in 868. But Ratramnus of Corbie eclipsed the bishops with his *Contra Graecorum opposita,* in which he replied to the grievances of the East in detail. He especially took up the old controverted question of the *processio Spiritus Sancti* and defended the papal primacy against Byzantium. The renewed Greek-Latin controversy of 867–68 formed the final act of the great theological discussions which had begun after the Treaty of Verdun and had been conducted from the start predominantly, and, after the death of Rhabanus, exclusively, by the diocesan and regular clergy of Western *Francia* (the provinces of Reims and Sens) and of the Rhône region (the province of Lyons).

It was also in the West Frankish episcopate that the political impulses in questions of Empire and Church, coming down from the days of Louis the Pious, produced their strongest effects. The last great representative of the Carolingian "great church" was Hincmar of Reims, the most loyal assistant of Charles the Bald and his successors, for whom, nevertheless, the unity of the Empire in the form of a *fraternitas* continued to possess validity. The intimate cooperation of the Archbishop with the crown began early in the 850's, when Charles wanted to free himself from the at first overpowering influence of his lay aristocracy. It survived the difficult crisis of confidence between King and Archbishop in 865–67 and eventually also the tension evoked a decade later by Charles's Italian policy. The theocratic political ideology of the Carolingian period received its final formulation from Hincmar. The Archbishop proceeded from the Gelasian teaching of the two powers, which had impressed itself on the consciousness of the Franks in the reign of Louis the Pious. He clearly distinguished the political sector, the *res publica,* from the ecclesiastical. He defined the royal power, which in his view occupied the central place, as a *ministerium* instituted by God. But he rejected the unconditional duty of loyalty, especially for bishops, whom he wanted to keep uninvolved by feudal ties. Bishops, he said, owed fidelity to the King not "in omnibus" but "iuxta ministerium", on the basis of their office. That Hincmar was not concerned to challenge the obligations of the episcopate to the state is seen in his conduct in the conflict between the King and his suffragan of Laon, in which the Archbishop acknowledged the ruler's competence in matters of ecclesiastical feudalism.

In his doctrine of the two powers Gelasius had attributed more importance to the *auctoritas sacrata pontificum,* with respect to its greater responsibility before God, than to the *regalis potestas.* Hincmar also based the higher authority of the bishops on the anointing of the King, the ritual for which he himself composed. The anointing was not only an external sign of the divine institution of the royal office but also a raising of the King above the laity. To attack the Lord's anointed was an especially serious crime. But by virtue of his anointing the King became no more irremovable than was the bishop, who, like him, was a *christus Domini*. The question of whether, in the case of tyranny, of serious offences by the ruler against the law of God, the bishops were competent to act as judges had been posed as early as 833. Hincmar answered affirmatively in principle. As appears from his attitude toward Louis the German in 858–60 and Lothar II in 860–83, he saw in the imperial synod, that is, in the all-Frankish council, the court before which Kings had to answer and which, in a case of necessity, could even depose a King. Whether Hincmar ever concretely considered deposition proceedings remains very doubtful.

In all the subkingdoms Kings and bishops continued to depend upon one another. Following the end of the war among the royal brothers the episcopate expected a resumption of the reform endeavours of the days of Louis the Pious. The higher clergy again met regularly at the Frankish Diets, at the assemblies of individual kingdoms, and at the imperial synods. In the West Frankish Kingdom there was soon a considerable amount of ecclesiastical legislation, while in the East Frankish Kingdom the death of Rhabanus marked a turning point. But great reform gatherings with a program of significance no longer took place in the West either. Among the regularly recurring themes were the questions of ecclesiastical property, the proprietary church, the penitential discipline, and the Church's matrimonial law. In their totality they dealt with the inner improvement of dioceses and the authority of the episcopate *vis-à-vis* clerics, monks, and laity.

In addition to imperial assemblies and councils there were also provincial and diocesan synods, which dealt with a group of themes that were on the whole similar. It seems that the many claims made on the episcopate by the imperial service interfered with provincial synods to a great extent. However, synods of the great ecclesiastical provinces, in whose convocation or decisions the King had a direct share, were hardly different from imperial councils. The detailed activity in the dioceses was probably more noteworthy than the meagre sources would indicate. Diocesan statutes were issued in the bishoprics of Reims, Bourges, Tours, Toul, Le Mans, Orléans, Châlons, and Soissons. The network of parishes was further extended in the second half of the ninth century, and the struggle against the *chorepiscopi* was successful. The former large parishes under an archpriest had already been replaced here and there in the West by deaneries. The deans supervised the life and official acts of the clergy of their districts and thereby strengthened the authority of the bishop over the rural proprietary churches. The name is first attested in the diocese of Le Mans around 840, but the institution was soon found in Champagne. In 852 Hincmar of Reims had instructions compiled for the deans of his diocese. Around the same time regional archdeaconries were also established, which often probably conformed to the former territories of *chorepiscopi*. The archdeacons supervised the delimiting and financial administration of parishes and controlled the archpriests and deans. The first evidence for them comes from the sees of Langres (870), Orléans (871), and Reims (874). With deanery and archdeaconry the mediaeval diocese acquired its shape. But it still required.considerable time before these institutions were everywhere established.

If one's glance shifts from the parochial and diocesan organization to the monasteries and chapters, the balance is far less favourable. The abuse of the lay abbacy increased first in the West Frankish Kingdom under Charles the Bald and then in the subdivisions of the Middle Kingdom, and many an old *abbatia* was ruined, either temporarily or even permanently. But it must not be overlooked that many of these churches, even if not exactly the richest and most famous, remained in the possession of the episcopate. The reform introduced under Louis the Pious did not die out entirely, and the later Carolingians also confirmed free abbatial election and the division of the *mensa*. Charles the Bald in 853 and the Emperor Louis II in 865 ordered their *missi* to undertake a monastic visitation.

Although provincial synods were largely supplanted by synods of the several kingdoms, still the metropolitans played an important role in the ninth century. Since the time of Charles the Great they bore the title of archbishop and wore the pallium as the insignia of their rank. The assemblies and synods of the various kingdoms were dominated by certain archbishops — those of Sens and Reims in the West Frankish Kingdoms, those of Cologne and Trier in Lotharingia, of Lyons in Provence, of Mainz in the East Frankish Kingdom, and of Milan and Aquileia in Italy. The typical archbishop of the day, who energetically defended the rights of metropolitans against both rebellious suffragans and Rome, was Hincmar of Reims.

According to the ancient canon law the metropolitan was not the superior of the bishops of his province; he exercised over them only a right of supervision. He convoked and directed provincial synods. He confirmed the elections of his suffragans, thus possessing a right of veto, and had a right to be asked for his approval of the important decisions of his suffragans. From the time that metropolitans wore the pallium as archbishops, a right originally belonging only to the Metropolitan of Arles as papal vicar, they were also regarded as representatives of the Pope — competent *in partem sollicitudinis* in a sense not defined in more detail in law. On the other hand, they were also intermediaries between the episcopate and the Emperor and were frequently appointed *missi* in their provinces. As such they had the task of publishing the capitularies and supervising their implementation in their provinces. But their powers were encroached upon in regard to the choosing of bishops, in which they had been concerned since the sixth century.

Strengthened by the reform of Empire and Church, the archbishops of the ninth century had frequently exerted themselves to transform the old right of supervision into a power of direction. Hincmar made a distinction between metropolitans with and those without the pallium. According to him, metropolitans without the pallium were on occasion subject to a patriarch or primate, whereas those with the pallium were directly subject to Rome. The archbishops of the Frankish Empire, he said, had obtained, along with the pallium, the rights of the Vicar of Arles: they were answerable to no one in instituting their suffragans and in convoking provincial synods. Thus were the ancient rights of metropolitans in the Frankish Empire defined and extended. According to Hincmar, an archbishop had the right to convoke provincial synods, which he directed, to a place of his choice and to punish absent bishops, to appoint visitors during the vacancy of sees, to arrange the new election and consecration, to examine and confirm the bishop-elect, and to decide a disputed election. The suffragan was to be bound by the arch-bishop's authorization not only for the alienation of Church property but also for the acceptance of functions and for journeys outside the province. Appeal could be made to the archbishop from the decisions of the bishop or of the diocesan synod. According to Hincmar the archbishop could also summon cases to his own tribunal and interfere at will in the administration of his suffragans. Appeal to Rome, however, was possible only after a provincial synod had passed sentence. The Pope had to look into it, but, according to the ancient canon law as determined by the Council of Sardica, he had to refer the case to the synod of a neighbouring province. In Hincmar's view ecclesiastical legislation was the business of general councils; he conceded to the decretals only a function of clarifying and implementing.

The exalted opinion which Hincmar had of his office led to conflicts with his suffragans, Rothad of Soissons in 856–64 and Hincmar of Laon in 869–72. The tensions in the province of Reims were aggravated by the opposition of the clerics and monks who had been ardained by Ebbo during his temporary restoration in 840–41 and whom Hincmar had suspended. To all appearances the Reims opposition was intimately connected with the great forgery *atelier,* from which proceeded the capitularies of pseudo-Benedictus Levita and the decretals of pseudo-Isidore. Of course, the intentions of the forgers were not simply identical with the aims of Hincmar's opponents; they were far more comprehensive and sought to guarantee the Carolingian reform work, threatened as it was by political developments.

The Carolingian reform had produced a uniform organization in the dioceses and provinces and had elevated the level of intellectual and religious education and moral consciousness, but it had been unable completely to disengage the Church from its involvement in the world. The restoration of the secularized Church property ceased. The proprietary church was regulated by law but thereby legalized. The lay abbacy was merely checked, not abolished.

167

Despite the privileges granted by Louis the Pious, elections to high ecclesiastical offices were not really free. Since the confusion of the 830's retrogression was again noticeable in all these spheres. The moral deterioration of the lay aristocracy threatened the Church's marriage law, and episcopal authority over the clergy belonging to proprietary churches remained problematic. New secularizations struck at the material foundations of the Church, and in wide areas of the Empire the lay abbacy was again gaining ground. The higher clergy were deeply implicated in the Carolingian factions, and political passions and accusations jeopardized legal safeguards. The main items of the reform program of the forgers corresponded to the ever recurring themes of the imperial assemblies: security of Church property from usurpation and secularization, freedom of the clergy for their religious and ecclesiastical duties, legal safeguards for the episcopate and the lower clergy by means of respect for canonical processes, and the extending of the *privilegium fori* to all clerics. But the forgers emphasized that the guarantor of the reform was no longer the Emperor since the Treaty of Verdun but the Pope. For them he ranked as the supreme judge in all *causae maiores,* that is, especially in the cases of bishops. In their view all synods received their authority from Rome, so that no conciliar decree possessed validity without the express or tacit consent of the Pope.

It is only possible to understand the forgeries when they are inserted into their historical context. Already in the ninth century Rome was regarded as the mother of many Gallic churches. Legends of apostolic foundations had spread from Arles throughout the south of Gaul in the fifth and sixth centuries, while in the early eighth and the early ninth centuries they can be traced in the Gallo-Frankish north, at Paris, Châlons, Trier, and Cologne. The Roman Church had supplied the doctrinal, liturgical, and canonical norms for the reforms of Pepin and Charles the Great. Persons had rights confirmed and exemptions granted by the Holy See. As Ullman says, "The forgers invented, not the ideology, but the decrees which were to act as the historical basis for the ideology". In the Middle Ages reform was always understood as a return to the ancient law. And so the ninth century forgers regarded themselves, not as innovators, but as renewers. And so also they dressed up their ideas in capitularies of the great Carolingians and in decretals of the ancient Popes. The hand of the forgers is to be detected first in the interpolated *Hispana* of Autun. Then from the same *atelier* proceeded in quick succession: the *Capitula Angilramni,* allegedly sent by Hadrian I to Angilram of Metz; the *Capitularies* compiled allegedly by Benedictus Levita at the suggestion of Archbishop Otgar of Mainz; and the *Decretals* of the so-called Isidorus Mercator.

The forgeries were made between 847 and 852. For in 847 occurred the death of Archbishop Otgar of Mainz, already referred to as dead in the *Capitularies,* and 1 November 852 is the date of the diocesan statutes of

168

Hincmar of Reims, in which some of the False Decretals are quoted for the first time. At approximately the same time, between 851 and 853, Archbishop Theutgaud of Trier claimed the primacy of Gallia Belgica, the ecclesiastical provinces of Trier and Reims, a thing he could have done only on the basis of forgeries. Pseudo-Isidorean ideas appear in some documents from Le Mans, that is, in a bull falsely attributed to Gregory IV, in the *Gesta Aldrici*, and in the *Actus pontificum,* but these last were already completed in 841 and 836–38 respectively. Benedictus Levita was first quoted in West Frankish capitularies in 857, and from then on the examples become more frequent. Pseudo-Isidore played a big role in the processes of Rothad of Soissons (861–64) and especially of Hincmar of Laon (869–72). The immediate occasion for the making of the forgeries was probably provided by the royal assembly of Épernay in 846, at which the West Frankish episcopate and its reform program suffered a serious defeat at the hands of the imperial aristocracy. According to the oldest witnesses the forgers' *atelier* is to be sought in the ecclesiastical province of Reims. The setback at Épernay affected primarily Hincmar of Reims, and it may have given a temporary advantage to Ebbo's adherents. The curious office of primate, which the forgers inserted between Rome and the metropolitan as a "passive court of appeals", to use Fuhrmann's expression, seems to have been expressly invented in the interests of Ebbo's faction, who sought to find in the Archbishop of Trier support against their own metropolitan. It should be borne in mind that Theutgaud of Trier was the first and for a long time the only Archbishop who laid claim to a primacy in the meaning of pseudo-Isidore.

The effects of the False Capitularies and False Decretals were limited in the ninth century. The forgeries provided Nicholas I with important tools but they did not give his pontificate its special character. It has been rightly stressed that the forgeries, far from establishing papal power, presupposed it. But they did give to Rome's authority a juridical form and in the eleventh century they became an essential instrument in the papal government of the Church, a basis of the Roman primacy of jurisdiction.

The great controversies of the Carolingian Age died out in the 860's, while the growth of canon law came to a standstill in the 880's and 890's. Pseudo-Isidore was admitted into the *Collectio Anselmo dedicata,* an Italian canonical collection of 882–96, and into the acts of the East Frankish Synod of Tribur in 895. The forgeries also played a role in the Formosan troubles, but then they withdrew entirely into the background. Synodal legislation ceased in West Frankland at Fîmes and Ver in 881–84, in Italy at Pavia in 891, in Burgundy at Vienne in 892, and in East Frankland at Tribur in 895.

At Rome intellectual life reached its peak in the pontificates of Nicholas I, Hadrian II, and John VIII. The outstanding scholar was Anastasius the

Librarian, who was on friendly terms with the Emperor Louis II[1] and in 855 even came forward as the imperial antipope, but afterwards again had *entrée* to the Lateran. He wrote the *vita* of Nicholas I in the *Liber pontificalis* and, "as a sort of private secretary from 861 or 862", acquired great influence over papal policy. Hadrian II entrusted him with the direction of the chancery by making him librarian. Anastasius became famous not least of all for his translations from Greek — lives of saints, acts of the general councils of 787 and 869–70, documents of the ecclesiastical history of the seventh century, pseudo-Dionysius, and Theophanes. His interest in Church history was shared by John the Deacon, who, it is true, did not complete a church history that he had planned in cooperation with Anastasius, but composed a *vita* of Gregory the Great and began a *Vita Clementis,* important for the history of the Apostle of the Slavs, Constantine-Cyril, which was completed before 882 by the one who commissioned it, Bishop Gauderic of Velletri. The quarter-century of cultural flowering at Rome also became significant for the development of the medieval idea of the Eternal City. It was ended by the collapse of the Carolingian papacy, made visible in the discontinuance of the traditional papal *vitae* in the *Liber pontificalis.* Already there were in the *Liber pontificalis* no *vitae* of the murdered John VIII and his short-lived successors, Marinus I and Hadrian III. The last Bishop of Rome to receive a biography of the old type was Stephen V (885–91), predecessor of Formosus.

Ravenna, which belonged in law to the Papal State but was in fact more closely connected with the Carolingians, produced in Agnellus (d. after 846), author of the *Liber pontificalis ecclesiae Ravennatensis,* an historian of the first rank. In South Italy the court of Benevento under Arichis had become a centre of culture at the height of the Carolingian Age, but after the mid-century it lost its importance with the disintegration of the principality. The archabbey of Montecassino was connected not only with the Lombard Princes of Benevento but also with the Carolingians and the Byzantine Emperors. The monastery's historiography, which began with a monastic chronicle in 867, was resumed at Capua after the destruction of the abbey by the Muslims in 882. At Capua the monk Erchempert (d. after 904) wrote his continuation of the *History of the Lombards* by Paul the Deacon. Brought down to 889, it is characterized by anti-Frankish sentiment. In the later ninth century Benevento and Capua were eclipsed by Naples, which, like Venice, was politically a part of the Byzantine Empire but in reality was independent and maintained close relations with Rome. The historiography of the bishopric began in Naples around the middle of the ninth century

---

[1] Anastasius composed the famous letter of Louis II to Basil I of 871, which based the "genuine" imperial office on Rome and the coronation by the Pope and thereby marked an epoch in the development of the Carolingian imperial idea. Anastasius was perhaps also the teacher of the Imperial Princess Irmingard; cf. (also for what follows) H. Loewe in *Wattenbach-Levison* IV, 394 ff., 460 ff., 465 ff., 472.

and developed in the following period. Here too there arose in the last decades of the ninth century a literature of translations from Greek, which made the city a focus of Graeco-Latin culture. Eugenius Vulgarius and Auxilius, writers at Naples at the turn of the century, were the spokesmen of the Formosans and, as such, testify to a connection with Rome.

Following the deaths of the Emperor Louis II in 875, Louis the German in 876, and Charles the Bald in 877, the Carolingian courts gradually lost their cultural importance. However, the *artes* and law were still cultivated at Pavia, which had a great tradition as the "capital" of Lombard-Frankish Italy and was one of the great school centres organized by Lothar I. At Milan, which in the Carolingian Age became a powerful rival of Pavia, a group of Irish monks, from whose circle came an encomium of Lothar I, even pursued Greek studies. In 877 Andrew of Bergamo, following Paul the Deacon, wrote a history of Carolingian Italy, which was not entirely free from reservations with regard to the Franks. From Verona, next to Pavia the most important educational centre of North Italy, where law was also taught, came the *Carmen de Adelardo episcopo* (c. 900), containing a lament for Louis II, Charles the Bald, and John VIII. In the circle around the Emperors of the Spoletan house was composed the *Libellus de imperatoria potestate in urbe Roma,* a sharp protest against the alienation of imperial rights by the last Carolingians. The *Gesta Berengarii* glorified the deeds of the Friuli antiking. The last mirrors for princes were from the West Frankish Kingdom: Hincmar wrote them for Louis the Stammerer (877–79) and his sons, Louis III and Carloman. As *laudator temporis acti,* the great Archbishop of Reims, shortly before his death (882), composed the treatise *De ordine palatii* for the young King Carloman and his magnates. In this he was following the example set by Adalard of Corbie. In a different manner Notker of Sankt Gallen in 884 with his *Vita Karoli* held up to Charles the Fat the image of his great ancestor. Abbo of Saint-Germain-des-Prés in his epic, *De bello Parisiaco,* celebrated the resistance of Paris to the Vikings. Imperial historiography ceased in West Frankland in 882, in East Frankland in 891.

The Viking invasion of 879–91 had also seriously affected the very heart of Carolingian *Francia*. In Champagne, however, the continuity of the schools of Laon was undisturbed. From Laon came Manno, the last teacher of the court of Charles the Bald; assuming office in 864, he survived his lord until 893. A group of Irish grammarians worked toward the close of the century in the strong city, whose walls defied every assault. In 893 Archbishop Fulk commissioned Remigius of Auxerre and Hucbald of Saint-Amand to restore the intellectual life in his diocese of Reims. Remigius, a relative of Abbot Lupus of Ferrières, was the last in the series of the great "humanists" of Auxerre. As successor of his master Heiric, he taught at Auxerre from 876 until his call to Reims. After the assassination of Archbishop Fulk in 900 he went to Paris, where he died in 908. Hucbald (c. 840–930) had studied under

171

his uncle Milo and under Heiric. His literary connections reached from Soissons to Utrecht and Mainz. The abbey of Saint-Amand in Hainaut had maintained its position in the midst of destruction and collapse. It was famed not only for its scriptorium but also as a refuge of the *artes:* from here proceeded the sequences, so significant for poetry and music. The abbey's central location between Champagne and the lower Rhine is revealed in its surviving manuscripts. From Saint-Amand came not only the Eulalia Sequence, the oldest poem in French, but also the Old High German song in praise of the West Frankish King Louis III, the victor of Saucourt (891).

In the likewise severely tried province of Cologne the most important late Carolingian culture centre was the abbey of Werden, which had not been affected by the devastation and maintained close connections with Hainaut. It was the place of origin of the *Musica enchiriadis* of Abbot Hoger (d. 902). The schools of Liège experienced a new development under Bishop Stephen (901–20), who, like Radbod of Utrecht, had studied at the West Frankish court under Manno of Laon.

Abbot Regino (892–99) undertook the reorganization of the abbey of Prüm, frequently sacked by the Vikings. When, because of struggles with the nobility, Regino finally had to leave the monastery in the Eifel mountains, Archbishop Radbod of Trier (883–915) gave him the monastery of Saint Martin at Trier, which had also been destroyed, and there the scholarly Abbot died in 915. The ecclesiastical restoration at Trier was aided by a textbook of harmony, with which Regino took his place beside Hoger of Werden and Hucbald of Saint-Amand, and by the manual of canon law, *De synodalibus causis,* which was completed in 906 and dedicated to Archbishop Hatto of Mainz. Regino lived on among posterity especially as the author of a world chronicle, finished in 908, which represented an uncommon achievement for this period.

In the East Frankish Kingdom Saxony first came into the light in the closing phase of the Carolingian Renaissance. Literary production, it is true, was limited to the missionary bishopric of Bremen-Hamburg, with the *Vita Anscharii* and the *Vita Rimberti,* and to the imperial abbey of Corvey, where Abbot Bovo I (879–90) was himself a writer. In the monastery on the Weser the "Poeta Saxo" composed around 890 an epic to glorify Charles the Great, and the monk Agius wrote a *vita* of Hathumod of Gandersheim, a daughter of the ancestor of the Liudolfings.

The real centres of intellectual life in the East Frankish Kingdom lay thereafter in Franconia, Swabia, and Bavaria. Under Charles the Fat there existed a close relationship between the royal chapel and the monasteries of Sankt Gallen and Reichenau on Lake Constance. Under Arnulf the imperial annals were continued at Regensburg and Niederaltaich. Sankt Gallen then experienced its first flowering with three luminaries, Ratpert (d. 890), Tutilo, and Notker (c. 840–912). In *Casus sancti Galli* Ratpert wrote the history of his monastery. Tutilo was an important artist and musician, noted for his tropes. But both were eclipsed by Notker Balbulus, who, despite a defect in speech, was a gifted poet. He determined the liturgical function and poetical laws of the sequence and showed himself to be a master of narration in his *vita* of Charles the Great, composed around 884. Sankt Gallen and Reichenau also appear at this time as centres of religious poetry in the Old High German dialect, which was carried to Freising by a pupil of Sankt Gallen, Waldo, brother of Solomon III of Constance. Thus the monasteries on Lake Constance then replaced Fulda and Weissenburg in their function in connection with East Frankish education and German literature, for which the "more deeply historical" designation of *teutonica lingua* (in place of *theodisca lingua*) became customary at Sankt Gallen and Mainz around 880. Apparently from a Rheno-Franconian or upper Rhine family came Gerald, an epic poet of equal stature with the lyric poet Notker. Gerald, probably in the last years of the ninth century, dedicated his Latin poem *Waltharius* to Ercanbald, Bishop of Eichstätt (c. 882–912).[2] The heroes of the epic — the Visigoth Waltharius and the Frank Hagano — appear in Gerald's work not only as skilled in the use of weapons but also as men educated in the *artes*, like the ninth-century Carolingian magnates from the families of William of Toulouse and Eric of Friuli.

Seen as a whole, the accomplishment of the fourth Carolingian generation was not inconsiderable, even though it was confined to the *artes*. Especially in poetry works of high merit appeared. No less important than the individual achievements were the continuity of the schools in several old educational centres, the work of reconstruction that soon began in the great metropolitan sees, and the springing up of new educational centres in Saxony. Thus it came about that even under the most severe trials intellectual life did not die out, and the legacy of the Carolingian reform and renaissance was substantially preserved for a new age.

[2] Schaller disagrees. He goes back to the older view of the Waltharius epic.

The Byzantine Church in the Age of Photius

CHAPTER 24

The Byzantine Church from 843 to 867

Despite the ending of the quarrel over images, the Church in the Byzantine Empire knew no peace in the succeeding decades. Whether the iconoclast faction was still so strong that it was able to contribute to the unrest may be disputed. But the opposition between the monks, or, more correctly, between the monastic "zealots" and a moderate Church policy represented especially by the imperial court and the higher, non-monastic clergy — an opposition incarnate shortly before in the two outstanding figures of Theodore of Studion and the Patriarch Nicephorus — continued to smoulder and flared up again and again. The new Patriarch Methodius (d. 847) was obliged as early as 845–46 to excommunicate the Studites.[1] In recent years these monks had formulated their own notion of the role of monasteries in the Church. They regarded themselves as the tribunal with authority to control the Patriarch and the guardians of the canons; they were especially the sworn enemies of any policy of adjustment, of any *oikonomia*.

From the outset Methodius could not be a patriarch of the Studites; he saw himself faced with a difficult situation. He was concerned to purge the episcopate of iconoclast elements and of any type of compromised clerics. This course was followed more strictly than had been the case under Tarasius. Whoever had weakened during the second period of Iconoclasm was deposed, as was also everyone who had received orders from such a bishop.[2] But how were the resulting great gaps to be filled up? As a moderate churchman, Methodius could not be interested in filling all episcopal sees with Studites. On the other hand, there was a lack of candidates who now fulfilled all the canonical requirements. To Methodius it seemed a lesser evil to let *epikeia* operate in regard to irregularities, but this evoked the strongest opposition from the Studites. Methodius did not put up with it for long, but demanded of them the condemnation of everything that had been written against the recourse to *epikeia* on the part of the Patriarchs Tarasius and

---

[1] *Grumel Reg,* no. 434.   [2] Ibid., no. 435.

Nicephorus.[3] This amounted to no less than the censuring of quite a number of pieces written by the Studites' hero, Theodore. Schism resulted, and Methodius died before the quarrel could be ended.[4]

It was now important for the monks to obtain as Patriarch a person belonging to their faction and to direct him according to their views. The choice of the Empress Theodora fell on the monk Ignatius, son of the former Emperor Michael I Rhangabe. The adherents of the dead Methodius, especially Gregory Asbestas, Archbishop of Syracuse, who had escaped from the Muslims to Constantinople and under Methodius had been prominent in Church government, opposed this choice. But the Empress had her way, apparently by not allowing any election by the synod. Asbestas and his friends bowed to the imperial will. But Ignatius insulted the Archbishop during the very rite of his consecration, and shortly afterwards deposed and excommunicated him, the pretext probably being some sort of irregularities in regard to ordinations that Gregory had performed on orders of the Patriarch Methodius. This deposition produced Ignatius's first quarrel with Rome, for the Curia reserved the case of Asbestas to itself, since he had had recourse to the Holy See.[5]

The case would probably have been forgotten, had not Ignatius especially excelled in making enemies, even at court. The Empress Theodora was not capable of governing independently. She gave all her confidence to the Logothete Theoctistus, who succeeded in removing dangerous rivals from the regency council, notably the Empress's brother, Bardas. The proclamation of the attainment of his majority by the Emperor Michael III was again and again postponed and his preparation for assuming the administration was criminally neglected. Bardas exploited all this to acquire a decisive influence. Ignatius was hardly concerned about the Emperor; in fact, he was all the more favourably disposed to the Empress. Then in 856 there occurred a *coup d'état:* Theoctistus was assassinated, Michael was declared by the Senate to have reached his majority, Theodora was deprived of influence, and Bardas assumed the direction of affairs. It goes without saying that Ignatius thereby lost his influence at court — a situation that he did not intend to put up with. When the rumour suddenly made the rounds that Bardas was

[3] Ibid., no. 432.

[4] In regard to the Studite schism the article by E. von Dobschütz, "Methodios und die Studiten" in *ByZ* 18 (1908), 41–105, and the critical notes by V. Grumel in the supplement to *Reg,* no. 436, should be compared.

[5] The case of Asbestas has to a great extent remained unclarified. Cf. V. Grumel, "Le schisme de Grégoire de Syracuse" in *ÉO* 39 (1941 f.), 257–67. It does not seem to me to be certain that Gregory was rehabilitated by the synod in the interval between Ignatius and Photius nor is this to be deduced from the words of Pope Nicholas I (*MGEp* VI, 498 f.), for, to the Pope's question, "Quibus documentis?" Byzantium would have been able to reply with the protocol of the synodal discussion. More probable to me seems to be an informal but striking rehabilitation by Photius when he appointed him to officiate at his consecration.

living in incest with his widowed daughter-in-law, the Patriarch believed it without any proof and refused Bardas communion.[6] Bardas soon discovered an opportunity for retaliating. The ex-Empress, unhappy with her enforced inactivity, seems to have hatched a conspiracy, and the Patriarch was perhaps not entirely ignorant of it. Bardas compelled Theodora to enter a convent, and Ignatius himself was to give her the veil. But Ignatius refused, and in this Bardas saw an admission of his complicity. Shortly after, when a conspiracy against the government was discovered, the leaders of which were again sought for in the highest circles, Ignatius tried to protect the plotters. To Bardas this amounted to treason and he had the Patriarch deported to the island of Terebinthos in October 858.

What happened in the succeeding months continues to be rather obscure, despite all the research thus far undertaken.[7] With some probability the course of events can be summarized somewhat as follows. Ignatius was prepared to resign under certain conditions. He declared that he agreed to a new election, with the provision that the Patriarch-elect should bind himself to recognize the legitimacy of Ignatius's patriarchate, maintain communion with him, and respect his measures as Patriarch. In other words, he was prepared to recognize a successor who belonged more or less openly to the monastic party. The search for a candidate was not a simple matter, but finally a compromise was reached and the choice fell on Photius.

Photius was recommended in several respects. His parents had acquired the aura of confessors by enduring persecution for their devotion to images. The Patriarch Tarasius had been his uncle. A daughter of the Empress was his sister-in-law. He had enjoyed the confidence of the minister Theoctistus and was regarded as the greatest scholar of his day. At the moment of his election, he was head of the imperial chancery, nominated not by Bardas but by Theoctistus, and thus he was in an exposed position in the administration, but apparently not yet involved in ecclesiastical politics. He was prepared to agree to Ignatius's conditions, and so he could be consecrated *per saltum* — he was a layman when elected — and enthroned before Christmas of 858.

Everything seemed to be in order, but it took only a couple of months for strife to break out openly again in the Church. That Archbishop Gregory Asbestas had consecrated Photius may have been a determining factor. In any event it was an indiscretion, if not in regard to Ignatius, certainly in regard to the Holy See, where, unfortunately, Gregory's case was still

[6] However one may evaluate the rumours, we hear nothing of any process of purgation or the like which Ignatius would first have had to demand.
[7] Cf. V. Grumel, "La génèse du schisme photien" in *StudiBiz* 5 (1939), I, 177–85; P. Stéphanou, "Les débuts de la querelle photienne vus de Rome et de Byzance" in *OrChrP* 18 (1952), 270–80; id., "La violation du compromis entre Photius et les Ignatiens", ibid. 21 (1955), 291–307; F. Dvornik, "Le premier schisme de Photius" in *Izvestija Bulgar. Archaeol. Inst.* 9 (1935), 301–25.

pending. But the fundamental cause of the difficulties was probably the basically different interpretation of the election agreement, that is, of the concessions to the resigning Patriarch. Photius probably saw in them a respecting of the honour due to his predecessor, a protecting of Ignatius against further measures. But the Ignatians apparently regarded Photius as little more than the executor of their policy, whose being or non-being depended on to what extent he proved to be an "Ignatian". Photius would in no event now condescend to this. Very soon the Ignatians saw the compromise as having been broken, and so, in February 859, they met in Hagia Eirene, deposed Photius, and declared Ignatius to be the sole legitimate Patriarch. Photius replied to this open declaration of war with a synod of at least 170 bishops in the church of the Holy Apostles, probably in March 859.[8] He regarded himself as no longer bound by the compromise. Reference was made to the particular circumstances under which Ignatius had become Patriarch, especially the dispensing with an election, and he was formally deposed.

The circumstance that on the occasion of his resignation Ignatius had so emphatically insisted on the acknowledgment of the legitimacy of his patriarchate shows that the sore spot had already been detected here quite early. But if this argument was so clearly pressed now, years later, this fact alone proves that Photius was not prepared to give in, for, in general, irregularities of this sort in a patriarchal election were not taken too seriously at Byzantium. Against the will of Photius Bardas's government supported the synodal measures against the Ignatians with brute force.

The schism was now public, and so Photius was ready to send his formal notice of enthronement to his colleagues in the patriarchate and to the Roman See. In this there was mention, apparently in pretty general terms, of the "retirement" (ὑπεξελθόντος) of Ignatius.[9] The embassy which carried this letter to Rome also presented to Pope Nicholas I a letter from the Emperor Michael III,[10] in which he asked for the dispatch of papal legates to a council being planned in Constantinople for the liquidation of the remnants of Iconoclasm.[11] The Pope[12] acknowledged the orthodoxy of Photius's synodical, but found the case of Ignatius a bit unclear and sent his legates, Radoald of Porto and Zachary of Anagni, not only to take part in the council but also with the duty of investigating the case of Ignatius. The Pope reserved the decision to himself personally, but he gave Photius

---

[8] *Grumel Reg,* no. 459.

[9] Text in *PG* 102, 585–93. Cf. *Grumel Reg,* no. 464. The letter to the oriental patriarchates in *PG* 102, 1017–24.

[10] *Dölger Reg,* no. 457.

[11] On Iconoclasm in the time of Photius see F. Dvornik, "The Patriarch Photius and Iconoclasm" in *DOP* 7 (1953), 67–97; also G. Ladner in *Tr* 10 (1954), 591.

[12] *MGEp* VI, 433, 439.

to understand that, despite the lack of interstices in his ordinations, he could still obtain recognition.

The synod met in the church of the Holy Apostles at Constantinople in April 861 in the presence of the papal legates.[13] The *acta* are lost but we have a Latin extract in the collection of Deusdedit. We do not know what was decided in regard to the iconoclasts, but the case of Ignatius was again opened. The legates let themselves be convinced that he had become Patriarch contrary to canon law and declared his deposition. Thereby they doubtless exceeded their instructions, but just the same the Holy See became through their agency the deciding factor in the schism within the Byzantine Church, and it was probably this success which induced Nicholas I not to punish them particularly at first. The legates also brought forward the papal demand for the return of Illyricum to the Pope. But in this matter they were unsuccessful, and it may be suspected that this failure, linked with the problem of the Bulgar mission, unnecessarily complicated matters.

Photius did not yet cease his exertions at Rome. He wrote to the Pope in the summer of 861.[14] It was of course easy for him to justify his elevation from the lay state to the episcopacy by means of historical examples. If the Pope's demands in regard to Illyricum had not been fulfilled, this was not his fault, he said, but due to the Emperor's refusal; he, for his part, would have acquiesced without more ado. Finally, he asked the Pope, in conformity with the canons, not to receive any self-styled "pilgrims" from Constantinople without letters of recommendation from the appropriate bishop. The Pope's reply was evasive.[15] It demanded new evidence of the guilt of Ignatius and a new process. Byzantium circumvented these demands by silence; it would perhaps have been difficult to state what was to be regarded as new matter. But because of this the request of Photius that no pilgrims from Constantinople be received without credentials was made in vain. Agents of the Ignatians, headed by the Abbot Theognostus, gave the Pope a version of the events which was certainly no closer to the truth than that which he had heard from the mouth of his legates.[16]

---

[13] On the state of the sources, see the general bibliography for this chapter. See also *Hefele-Leclercq* IV, 1, 225–77; *Grumel Reg,* nos. 466–68. For the canons of the synod see footnote 14.

[14] *PG* 102, 593–617. The references to local canons which rejected the consecration of a layman *per saltum* but were not accepted in Constantinople were probably to the Council of Sardica, canon 10, a synod whose decree in this question was adopted in canon 17 of the synod of 861 but whose general validity was not undisputed in Byzantium, even if Photius failed to mention canon 2 of the Trullan Council. The passage in regard to the letter of recommendation can refer to the Council of Antioch, canon 7, but also to Sardica, canon 9.

[15] *MGEp* VI, 443, 447.

[16] There is a report by Theognostus in *Mansi* XVI, 296–301, and *PG* 105, 856–61. To what extent this report was authorized by Ignatius or can even be regarded as his work must remain undecided. The fact is that even as late as 861 Ignatius refused any appeal to Rome and would not permit Rome to intervene.

Now, suddenly, there was no further mention of an objective examination of the records of Ignatius. Probably in August 863 the Pope held at the Lateran a synod which deposed both Asbestas and Photius, declared the deposition of Ignatius null and void, and, after a delay of two years, punished the papal legates.[17] This new attitude of the Pope brought to the stage the Emperor Michael III, who in a haughty letter treated the Pope as a subject and declared that his request for the presence of papal legates at the Council of 861 and the renewed examination of the records of Ignatius at that synod were due merely to a desire to be accommodating.[18] Equally haughty was the reply of the Pope;[19] it is easy, due to its words on the question of the primacy, to overlook the incompatibility of its other expressions. All the more surprising, then, was the conclusion that fully accredited agents of the two Byzantine parties and of the Emperor should again reopen the whole complex of questions in Rome, a conclusion understandable only if one reflects that the question of the Bulgar mission urged the Pope not to burn all his bridges. And yet it was exactly this question that brought about the decisive break.

The Pope was interested in the Bulgar mission, not least of all, because he incorrectly regarded the Bulgarian principality as belonging apparently in its entirety to Illyricum. The Greek mission in Bulgaria in 864–66 could not be to his liking. Then the change of heart in Prince Boris, who was concerned for the autonomy of his young Church, which Photius was not prepared to grant — nor was the Pope for that matter — gave new hope to Nicholas I. Here was the prospect of coming closer to the possession of Illyricum in a roundabout way. The masterly character of the *Responsa ad consulta Bulgarorum* has been extolled from the missionary and pastoral point of view. At the same time it is easy to forget the grave fact that it was Pope Nicholas I who, without any regard for the duties of his office, was here attacking the rites of the Greek Church, even exposing them to ridicule.[20] Nevertheless, he was so happy over his success that in a new letter to Constantinople of 28 September 865 he made a further offer of negotiations, but on the basis of the decrees of the Lateran Synod of 863 — that is, with the understanding that Photius had become Patriarch unlawfully and that Ignatius, now as before, was the sole legitimate Patriarch.

But neither Photius nor his Emperor Michael III was prepared to negotiate

---

[17] The events can best be reconstructed from the *Narrationis ordo de Photii repulsione* (*MGEp* VI, 556–61).

[18] *Dölger Reg,* no. 464. This can be reconstructed only in fragments from the Pope's letter (*MGEp* VI, 454–87). It cannot be proved that Photius composed the Emperor's letter.

[19] See the previous note. If now the Emperor was denied the right to convoke the synod of 861, this was hardly compatible with the fact that the Pope was represented at it.

[20] On the *Consulta* see now G. T. Dennis, "The 'anti-Greek' Character of the Responsa ad Bulgaros of Nicholas I" in *OrChrP* 24 (1958), 165–74. I do not think that the *responsa* can be exculpated so simply. In any event, Photius and his Church saw in them a general attack on their rite.

again. Quite the contrary. Photius decided on the strongest — perhaps it should be termed desperate — counterstroke, unprecedented in history since Dioscorus of Alexandria had suppressed the statement of Leo I at the Rubber Synod of 449, only for this very reason to be deposed by an ecumenical council two years later. The first and quite understandable countermove[21] was the defence of the Byzantine rites with a view to the attitude of the Roman missionaries in Bulgaria. In this Photius was standing on a not unjustified defensive. But, unwilling to let it go at that and in spite of the convictions that he had earlier expressed, he now himself made a question of faith and orthodoxy out of a question of rites. Above all, there now emerged the charge of heresy in the matter of the *Filioque* — that is, Photius condemned, not only the addition to the creed, but the content of the addition.

All this was brought to the knowledge of the oriental Patriarchs in the spring or summer of 867 in the solemn form of an encyclical. Out of the quarrel in matters of mere ecclesiastical discipline and canon law there proceeded, now *ex professo,* a secular question of faith. Even this was not enough. In August or September of the same year Photius convoked a synod, concerning which we are informed very inadequately and only tendentiously. But in any event it deposed the Pope and decreed anathema against him.[22] Photius must have been sure of the consent of his Emperor or otherwise he would not have dared to turn to Louis II and Engelberga with the request that they risk everything in order to topple Nicholas from his throne. The circumstance that at this time the Western imperial pair were hailed at Byzantium as βασιλεῖς fits into the details of this coalition policy.[23] Photius's procedure proves that he was not a great politician but allowed himself to be carried away by his ill humour. Apparently he had no idea of the development of the doctrine of the primacy in the West, just as he also apparently had only an inadequate notion of the independent life of the Western Church. But he likewise overestimated his own position at Constantinople and did not know how to read the signs of the times. His most powerful protector, the Caesar Bardas, had already been assassinated on 21 April 865. The Emperor Michael III had thus escaped from a tutelage on the part of his minister that was perhaps too self-assured but was nevertheless purposeful, only to fall into the hands of an unscrupulous adventurer, Basil the Macedonian, who for his part had the Emperor killed a few weeks after the deposition of the Pope and himself mounted the throne. This change of sovereign, for which Basil had to seek legitimation and propaganda support from those who had hitherto formed the opposition, meant the overthrow of Photius and the reinstatement of Ignatius in his former rights on 23 November 867.

[21] *Grumel Reg,* no. 481; *PG* 102, 721–41.

[22] *Grumel Reg,* no. 482.

[23] On this see F. Dölger, *Byzanz und die europäische Staatenwelt* (Ettal 1953), 312–15.

CHAPTER 25

The Byzantine Church from 867 to 886

The unscrupulous adventurer Basil changed very quickly into the outstanding and diplomatically skilled Byzantine Emperor of the old school. The change from Photius back to Ignatius was a first necessity in domestic politics, but it could not suffice. To rely on the Ignatians alone would have amounted to ruling without an adequate majority in the clergy, or actually with a minority. Hence it was important to reassure the Photians also and, in addition, to come to terms with the papacy, without whose cooperation a genuine pacification of the Byzantine Church was unthinkable. As a conclusion to all the negotiations Basil from the start envisaged a great council, which alone could supply the authority necessary in view of the complicated problems.

At first the Emperor briefly informed the Pope about events.[1] The Pope who replied, however, was no longer Nicholas I but Hadrian II (867–72). He immediately addressed the Emperor and the new Patriarch.[2] He declared his intention to adhere to his predecessor's policy, recommended the Ignatian Theognostus, who had been staying in Rome till then, and was surprised merely that Ignatius had not yet sent him his synodical. Since the arrival of the papal embassy at Constantinople was delayed and the Emperor was greatly concerned to expedite matters, the latter[3] and now also the Patriarch[4] wrote to Rome a second time. The Emperor's course can easily be determined from the extant letter. He referred to the last offer of Pope Nicholas — who of course had known nothing of his deposition by Photius — that the two ecclesiastical factions should again explain their case to the Pope. In such a procedure it was unthinkable that the overthrow of Photius might eventually be annulled. It was a question rather of the supporters of Photius, of the fate of those ordained by him and of those who had signed the acts of the Council of 867. Here the Emperor urgently recommended the exercise of moderation. All protestations of leaving the affair to the Pope's judgment were in effect connected with a sort of preliminary investigation by the Pope, for, in the final analysis, the question was to be discussed at the council in Constantinople. This interpretation may not have been immediately clear from the tone of the imperial letter, but the events that followed abundantly confirm it. In order really to enable the Roman preliminary inquiry to arrive

[1] The letter is not extant. In *Dölger Reg* it is not mentioned or else it is confused with the second letter of the Emperor in its date.

[2] *MGEp* VI, 747–50.

[3] *Dölger Reg,* n. 474.

[4] *Grumel Reg,* n. 489; resume in *Mansi* XVI, 325–28. Complete text in the Latin translation by Anastasius in *Mansi* XVI, 47–49.

at a judgment, representatives of both the Patriarch Ignatius and the deposed Photius went to Rome by the Emperor's command. Photius was represented by Peter of Sardis, who was, however, shipwrecked and drowned *en route*. A monk in his suite named Methodius, who managed to be saved, refused, on arriving in Rome, to defend Photius's case.

Thus in the summer of 869 there met at Saint Peter's a synod which strove less for the pacification of the Byzantine Church, as desired by the Emperor, than for retaliation against the Synod of 867.[5] There was no longer any question of a hearing of both parties. Photius was solemnly condemned and deposed. If repentant, he could at most be admitted to communion as a layman. Anyone who had signed the synodal acts of 867 could only be absolved by the Pope personally. Persons ordained by Photius were to be regarded as deposed. Bishops who had been consecrated by Ignatius but had later, understandably, recognized Photius were to be reinstated only when they had signed a *libellus satisfactionis* that was being drawn up in Rome. The synod ended with a solemn burning of the *acta* of 867; it was regarded as miraculous, since the documents burned despite a downpour.

Pope Hadrian sent to Constantinople the Bishops Donatus and Stephen and the Deacon Marinus, later Pope. The legates were instructed to preside over the Council of Constantinople and to direct its course in such a way that the questions would not be opened again but the Roman decrees would be unconditionally implemented. This, however, was not how Basil had conceived of the synod. His aim was certainly that a preliminary inquiry should take place in Rome and perhaps even a preliminary decision should be reached, but the real solution should be realized by the ecumenical council. It may safely be assumed that Ignatius also was little inclined to let the case be decided definitively by Rome.

The legates arrived in Constantinople and the synod was opened on 5 October 869.[6] But the atmosphere was tense. Twelve Ignatians constituted the episcopal representation at the opening session. The presidency was assumed, not by the papal legates, but by a deputy, the Patrician Baanes, representing the Emperor in accord with the ancient synodal law. The number of participants was only sixty-six bishops at the ninth session and had reached 103 only by the final session. This meant that the signing of the *libellus* encountered the greatest resistance. But whereas the legates Radoald and Zachary had gone wrong through tractability in 861, the present legates made up for this weakness by an extremely rude inflexibility. Without any *discretio spirituum* they demanded the signing of the *libellus,* whose basic component, the *formula Hormisdae,* had once been composed in order to administer an orthodox profession of faith to heretics. The demand became embarrassing

---

[5] Session VII of the Council of 869–70 summarized the acts of this synod; see *Mansi* XVI, 121–31, 372–80.

[6] *Hefele-Leclercq* IV, 481–546; *DThC* III, 1273–1307 (M. Jugie).

when Byzantine bishops declared that in 860 — hence, long after the change in the patriarchate — Pope Nicholas I had been in communion with them and appealed to the legate Marinus as a witness to this. He apparently tried to make the best of a bad job by a subtle distinction. In order to salvage at least a remnant of genuine conciliar activity, the Emperor finally declared that he would not sign the *acta* unless Photius was heard. The ex-Patriarch was summoned but wrapped himself in contemptuous silence. When a bishop undertook to discuss the case for the ex-Patriarch, the legates stopped him short. At length their obstinacy carried the day entirely, though their success was in no sense gratifying. Canon 21, for example, which again put Constantinople in the second place, behind Rome, and condemned the attempt of Photius to depose the Pope, and then at the same moment provided the other Patriarchs with immunity in a similar manner, can hardly have been conceived in the Roman meaning, as the notion of the pentarchy clearly comes out of the *acta* of the council.

But the legates had to endure their real failure shortly after the close of the council (28 February 870). A Bulgar delegation had taken part in the last session. It had come to ask the council for a decision as to which patriarchate, Rome or Constantinople, the young Bulgarian Church really belonged, now that Rome too had denied the Bulgar Prince an archbishop of his choice. The Byzantines saw to it that this question should be decided outside the council, under the Emperor's presidency and in consultation with the representatives of the oriental patriarchates alone. The legates protested vigorously but in vain. The conference decided without them that Bulgaria belonged to the Patriarchate of Constantinople. Only now did the papal legates produce a letter in which Pope Hadrian forbade Ignatius to intervene in Bulgaria in any manner. Now that the council was ended, Ignatius declined to take any notice of this letter,[7] and Bulgaria was long lost to the Roman Church. Despite everything, Photius could be content. Naturally, Pope Hadrian protested to the Emperor and to Ignatius against the proceedings in Bulgaria, where the Roman mission now had to take its departure. Ignatius, however, was able to point out that Rome had begun this procedure, and Hadrian had to admit it.[8] It is not certain whether he broke off communion with Ignatius over this matter, but in any event it is probable that he never anathematized his adversary at Constantinople publicly and solemnly, as he had anathematized Photius.

But even in unimportant matters Ignatius could not now count on any Roman effort to be accommodating;[9] in fact, it often seemed that in Rome

---

[7] *Liber pontificalis* II, 182–85.

[8] *Grumel Reg,* n. 505. The letter of the Patriarch can be inferred from the Pope's reply (*MGEp* VI, 762).

[9] Thus Rome did not even accede to his request that lectors ordained by Photius might be ordained priests nor to the request of others for the rehabilitation of Bishop Paul of Caesarea,

people had become convinced that the stubbornness of Photius had been a degree less. Still, Ignatius must have urgently needed Rome's aid. The vacancies in the lower and the higher clergy, put there by Rome's inconsiderate measures — how were they to be filled? Rome did not allow even a lector ordained by Photius to become a priest. The old bishops who had been consecrated by Ignatius but in 858 had sworn fidelity to Photius in good faith had a hard time forgetting that they had been forced to sign the *libellus satisfactionis* and certainly blamed Ignatius for allowing things to proceed so far. But those bishops who had now been entirely disqualified for having signed the *acta* of the Council of 867 must have powerfully excited opinion against Ignatius. A great part of the Byzantine higher clergy regarded the Council of 869–70 not as an ecumenical synod but as a case of humiliation of the Byzantine Church and of a betrayal of its freedom to Rome.

And the fortunes of Photius were again on the rise. For, as Emperor, Basil had to be careful, now as before, not to cause the Photian opposition to harden, quite apart from the fact that Photius was much too shrewd a tactician not to gradually supplant Ignatius in the Emperor's favour. Ignatius seems to have recognized the signs of the time and to have become reconciled with Photius toward the end of his life.[10] Meanwhile, Photius had returned from exile and had risen to be tutor of the imperial princes. He may also have resumed his position as a professor.

When Ignatius died on 23 October 877, Photius was able to reoccupy the patriarchal throne without difficulty. Apparently Ignatius had never doubted the validity of Photius's episcopal consecration and, once his relations with Rome had become chilled, saw no further reason to regard the laicization of the ex-Patriarch by Hadrian II as relevant. Even before the death of Ignatius the Emperor had begun new negotiations with Rome[11] in order to have the differences between Ignatians and Photians settled by means of a review of the trial of Photius. Pope John VIII was not unfavourable. Byzantine aid against the Muslim peril in Italy was desired, and no practical experience compelled the Pope to share with conviction the views of the intransigent Ignatians, unhappy with their master's attitude toward Photius, especially since John had no more satisfactory experiences with Ignatius than Nicholas I had had with Photius. And so the Pope sent the Bishops Paul and Eugene to Constantinople with letters to the Emperor and Ignatius and the commission to establish peace.[12]

---

who had indeed been consecrated by Photius but very soon had gone over to the party of Ignatius (*MGEp* VI, 760f.).

[10] It is very uncertain whether Ignatius asked absolution for Photius at Rome, as Bishop Stylian of Neocaesarea later wrote to Pope Stephen V (*Mansi* XVI, 432). Stylian lets it be understood that the letter was composed by Photius himself in Ignatius's name (cf. *Grumel Reg,* n. 506).

[11] *Dölger Reg,* n. 496.   [12] *MGEp* VII, 64.

The envoys, however, found not Ignatius but Photius. For this eventuality they had no instructions, and it was left to their resourcefulness how to deal with this complicated situation. And first they decided not to act at all but to get the Emperor to apply again to the Pope. He requested the recognition of Photius and the convoking of a new synod.[13] A letter from the clergy of Constantinople informed the Pope of the unanimous acceptance of the new Patriarch in his episcopal city. The Pope consulted his closest collaborators and then wrote to the Emperor that he was disposed to recognize Photius in spite of everything, if he would apologize for his earlier deeds in the presence of the future synod. He said that he absolved Photius and his episcopate by virtue of the supreme apostolic authority, but he still demanded as a condition that Photius should refrain from any pastoral activity in Bulgaria. If these conditions should be met, the Pope would excommunicate anyone who did not recognize Photius as Patriarch.[14]

The Pope's legates received from Rome a *commonitorium* which made them conversant with the new situation and which was read at the synod and signed by the participants. The *commonitorium* was brought by Cardinal Peter, who was to reinforce the papal embassy. Under these circumstances the great synod could finally be opened at the beginning of November 879 under the presidency of the Patriarch Photius.[15] There were seven sessions. Almost 400 bishops took part — an impressive testimony to the number of Photius's adherents when compared with the 103 bishops who, after much delay, could be mustered for the final session of the anti-Photian Synod in 870. There was basically not much to discuss. For Photius it was of the greatest importance to be able to appear before the Fathers of the Council not as Patriarch by virtue of Rome's indulgence but as Bishop of Constantinople again installed and never legitimately deposed. It is possible that even before the session the papal legates had learned that for this reason Photius would hardly preside over the synod as a repentant sinner. And if the Pope had demanded as a *conditio sine qua non* of a rehabilitation of the Patriarch a full renunciation of the Bulgarian Church, it was not difficult for Photius to point to his accommodating attitude to Nicholas I in this question and to transfer the responsibility to imperial policy. Whether or not the *commonitorium* was corrected in this regard even before the beginning of the synod, in any event the Fathers listened to a text in which there was no

---

[13] *Dölger Reg*, n. 497.

[14] *MGEp* VII, 166–87, together with the letters written at the same time to Photius, to the clergy of Constantinople, and especially to the Ignatians.

[15] *Hefele-Leclercq* IV, 585–606. On the question of the authenticity and integrity of the acts, see V. Laurent, "Le cas de Photius dans l'apologétique du patriarche Jean XI Bekkos" in *ÉO* 29 (1930), 396–415; M. Jugie, "Les actes du synode photien de Sainte Sophie" in *ÉO* 37 (1938), 88–99; also, F. Dvornik, *Le schisme de Photius*, 543–53; id., "Les actes du synode photien et Georges le Métochite" in *ÉO* 37 (1938), 99–106.

mention of apologies by the Patriarch, and the Pope's commands in the matter of Bulgaria seemed to have been altered to requests and recommendations. The other Roman documents also were read rather in "stylized" paraphrases than in a translation that reproduced the original.[16] Either the legates did not notice or they kept quiet from tactical considerations. For without a doubt they desired peace in conformity with the mind of the Pope, even a peace with concessions to the mentality of the Byzantines, provided that the Bulgarian question was not again decided to the detriment of Rome and that the anticipated imperial aid against the Muslims in Italy was not jeopardized. They were in no way equal to the extraordinarily clever management displayed by Photius.

But the conduct of the legates was not undignified. Under all circumstances they upheld the doctrine of the papal primacy and emphasized, despite all the contrary assertions of the Photianist bishops, that it was Pope John VIII, who, by virtue of his supreme authority, again installed Photius in the office of Patriarch. They did not fail to stress that they regarded the assumption of the patriarchate by Photius before the arrival of the papal decision as an illegitimate procedure. As regards Bulgaria, Photius stressed his good will at the synod and declared that he had not undertaken any official actions in Bulgaria. Thus was this condition of papal absolution satisfied. The annulling of the Synod of 869–70 by the legates may perhaps have been prescribed in the Latin original of the *Commonitorium,* although this point must remain controverted. The decrees of the Synod — it passed a series of canons, including one against the elevation of laymen to the episcopate, and declared the Synod of 787 to be ecumenical — were signed by all the participants in the fifth session on 26 January 880.

There were two further sessions, the authenticity of which has been incorrectly doubted. The first, in a small group in the imperial palace, promulgated the *horos* of the Synod, a profession of faith with an appendix which anathematized any addition to the Creed of Nicaea-Constantinople, without discussing the dogmatic question of the *Filioque*.[17] The protocol of this session was promulgated at a solemn gathering of the Council Fathers at Hagia Sophia in mid-March and with this the Synod ended. Still unresolved at the Council was the question of Bulgaria, for which the Fathers had declared themselves to be incompetent. But outside the Synod it seems that a compromise was prepared in the sense that Bulgaria should be subject to the Roman jurisdiction but no difficulties should be caused to the Greek mis-

---

[16] V. Grumel, "Les lettres de Jean VIII pour le rétablissement de Photius" in *ÉO* 39 (1940), 138–56.

[17] Cf. V. Grumel, "Le filioque au concile photien de 879–80 et le témoignage de Michel d'Anchialos" in *ÉO* 29 (1930), 257–63; id., "Le décret du synode photien de 879 à 880 sur le symbole de la foi" in *ÉO* 37 (1938), 357–72; also, M. Jugie, *Le schisme byzantin,* 127f., and F. Dvornik, *Le schisme de Photius,* 537–39.

sionaries there. The compromise, it is true, did not take effect, but the fault lay with the Bulgars themselves, who, in their striving for an autonomous Church, opposed any interference by Rome.

Pope John VIII ratified the decrees of the Council of Constantinople, but with the somewhat two-edged postscript that he rejected everything which the legates might have done contrary to the apostolic prescriptions.[18] He no longer insisted on the demand that Photius should apologize and limited himself to expressing amazement that so much had happened otherwise than he had intended. The Pope cannot have been satisfied with the course of the discussions. His accepting of them may have been facilitated by the circumstance that meanwhile a Byzantine fleet had freed the Papal State for some time from the Muslim peril. But it seems to me that the Pope's real greatness lies beyond anything political and consists in the fact that, despite opposition from his own officials, especially from Marinus, legate in 869–70, he disregarded any concern for mere prestige in order to guarantee peace to the Byzantine Church. He understood that Photius could not be managed, and once Photius showed himself inclined to recognize the authority of the Holy See — and he often did so during the Synod — he saw no compelling reason to reject him. Furthermore, he apparently realized that not a few of the *gravamina* of the former Ignatians were mere faction squabbles. The fact that Ignatius had become reconciled with Photius likewise favoured the latter.

Basically, John VIII recognized what Nicholas I was not prepared to admit, namely, that Rome was confronting not so much as an individual adversary at Constantinople as the spirit of a Church, which jealously guarded its old rights, genuine and imaginary, which was always basically prepared at any time, in spite of any discord, to make common cause against Rome — compare the attitude of the two Patriarchs in the Bulgarian question — and that the *summum bonum* of Church unity could only be assured if the problems were solved in the spirit of Christian charity and less in the spirit of authoritative thought.

How little this sympathetic attitude of the Pope was esteemed in Rome appears in the fact that his recent adversary, Marinus, was elected his successor. The new Pope certainly did not regard Photius as a legitimate Patriarch. But it is not demonstrable and not very likely that he officially excluded him from his communion. There seems to have been no "second Photian Schism".[19] Pope Stephen V also,[20] who was perhaps less receptive to the Orthodox

---

[18] *MGEp* VII, 227f.

[19] V. Grumel, "Y eut-il un second schisme de Photius?" in *RSPhTh* 32 (1933), 432–57, and, independent of it, F. Dvornik, "Le second schisme de Photius — une mystification historique" in *Byz (B)* 8 (1933), 425–74; V. Grumel, "La liquidation de la querelle photienne" in *ÉO* 33 (1934), 257–88.

[20] V. Grumel, "La lettre du pape Étienne V à l'empereur Basile Ier" in *RÉB* 11 (1953), 129–55.

world, certainly did not officially break off relations with Photius, but rather left things alone. Not much time would have been available to him for such a step, for Photius suffered a second overthrow in 886. Apparently no ecclesiastical politics are to be looked for behind this event. Instead, it may be accepted that entirely personal reasons induced the new Emperor Leo VI to remove Photius, his former and perhaps somewhat too pedantic teacher, and replace him with the younger imperial brother, Stephen (886–93). The date of death of Photius, who probably retired to a monastery, is uncertain. Perhaps the year was 891.

CHAPTER 26

Photius: Work and Character

Whereas Ignatius found a secure place in the Byzantine calendar of saints and, in addition, a hagiographer,[1] prejudiced though he was, Photius was denied the latter altogether and the former to a great extent. Traces of his cult are sparse, even if not insignificant. It can easily be shown that the fathers of the great break of 1054 hardly based their claims on Photius and that his council, the Synod of 879–80, for a long time had no prospect of being recognized as ecumenical, and, in fact, has never completely obtained such recognition. He became a chief Byzantine witness to the doctrinal differences between East and West relatively late, probably in the twelfth century, and even then partly because of cheap pseudepigrapha, as represented by the *Opusculum contra Francos*.[2]

The most recent age has gone a step further: it has demonstrated the absence of any grounds for postulating a second Photian Schism, if not absolutely, at least so as to offer an extremely probable case. Some have gone farther and have set as their goal a complete rehabilitation of the Patriarch, but because of the state of the sources it has not been possible to follow them blindly in this. That Photius cannot be called the one solely responsible for the Schism is certain. The way in which Rome tried to deal with his case was not distinguished in the final analysis by the amalgamating of the circumstances — the question of the Patriarch's legitimacy on the one hand, the Bulgar mission on the other — which were placed in a relation to each other which did not befit them. But Photius, with his encyclical of 867 and the synod of the same year, at which he excommunicated and deposed the Pope, risked a step which no apologetic has yet been able to cope with. And he never condescended to utter a public word of regret for this serious wrong. The

---

[1] See the sources, p. 515.

[2] For the whole complex of his posthumous life one should consult the excellent chapter which Dvornik has included in *The Photian Schism*, 383 ff.

sense of innocence, which he expressed in regard to it, can only with difficulty have convinced even his adherents. Considered from the angle of historical developments, the Schism can be understood as the colliding of two concepts of the nature of the Church, which had long developed separately without persons becoming aware of this on the one side or the other: the "Constantinian" Byzantine idea, carried along by the idea of the "pentarchy" of patriarchates[3] and intimately bound up with imperial supremacy in ecclesiastical questions, and the new Roman idea, characterized by a strongly emphasized consciousness of the primacy of the *Sedes Romana*. The proponents of these ideas were two personalities, Photius and Nicholas I, neither of whom measured up to the high demands of his pastoral office, since neither felt himself to be nor acted as the *servus servorum Dei*.

In regard to Photius there is, in addition, a further question, which is more important than that of the reality of the "second" Schism: whether he made peace with Rome merely from the standpoint of *oikonomia,* that is, from considerations of expediency, or whether he actually disavowed his encyclical and did not see in the dogmatic and disciplinary accusations only something that could be manipulated. The celebrated question of the *Filioque,* in so far as it concerned an addition to the Creed, was a purely disciplinary matter, but it was capable of being posed dogmatically, that is, with regard to the content of the article. Photius discussed both problems in his encyclical. He rejected any addition to the Creed. But he also repudiated the doctrine of the *Filioque,* seeing in it a destruction of the Father's role as sole principle in the Trinity and hence a heresy. This was not especially an attack on the Roman Church, which did not at that time admit the *Filioque* into its own liturgical use. Nor was the "false doctrine" laid at the door of the Roman Church. Photius was attacking the Latin missionaries in Bulgaria, but no one knew better than Photius where they came from. Hence the charge made in this regard offered the opportunity for a subtle diplomatic game. It is remarkable that the anti-Photian Synod of 869–70 did not take up this point at all.[4] But even the great Photian propaganda Synod of 879–80 completely excluded the dogmatic question and contented itself with prohibiting additions to the Creed. Even so, there were two qualifications here which have usually been too little noticed. The prohibition did not apply if there was a question of disposing of a heresy; and the prohibition spoke of the adding of "false words". In this connection it did not expressly mention *Filioque,* but it thereby created an opportunity which could be seized upon at the proper time. In a purely formal sense there was no need for the papal legates to

---

[3] The theory of five more or less autonomous patriarchates, whose teamwork constitutes the unity of the Church. Dvornik, *op. cit.,* 220, shows how strong the idea of the pentarchy already was at the Council of 869–70.

[4] Although Pope Nicholas was fully aware of its import.

refuse their assent, since the faith of the Roman Church was not directly concerned and the Roman discipline was not touched.

The controversy was again taken up by Photius around the mid-880's in a letter to the Archbishop of Aquileia.[5] In this also it was not only the addition but the doctrine of the *Filioque* which was rejected. Again the accusation of error was not directed against Rome; instead, it was raised precisely by having recourse to the Roman version of the Creed. Rome became Photius's oath-helper. The *Mystagogia*[6] is probably also to be interpreted in this sense. Accordingly, the dogmatic question remained in abeyance. From the viewpoint of the history of dogma it may be said that the burden of proof for the *Filioque* fell upon those who had introduced it into the Creed. Earlier than the Latin synonyms, the terms "from", "to proceed", and so forth in Byzantine theology had received a restricted, specifically Trinitarian meaning, in the light of which the somewhat confused linguistic usage of Latin theology, when viewed by Byzantium, could not but appear suspicious. It required roughly 300 years and more for people to begin to have a mutual understanding. To be sure, Photius's grasp of the theology of the Trinity was not up to date. His recourse to the teaching of the Greek Fathers was, whether consciously or unconsciously, insufficient; it must be called into question even in the case of so dedicated a student of patristics as he was. Documents such as the Creed of the Synod of 787 with the formula *per filium* carried no weight with him. Thus his theology was not a happy point of departure for any evaluation of the Byzantine viewpoint.

There remains the question of the relationship of Photius to the papal primacy. The contention that the doctrine of the papal primacy had been unknown in Byzantium and was first introduced when Nicholas threatened Photius has often been repeated, but it is a foolish legend. The accents of Pope Nicholas were stronger, the extent of his demands was greater, but the substance of the demands was known to Byzantium and in properly spaced intervals, when the Byzantine Church found itself in an embarrassing situation, it was acknowledged and exploited. The fact that Photius deposed a Pope and thereby despised the basic rights of the primacy cannot be explained away by any good will toward the Patriarch, cannot even be passed off as a political *faux pas*. Even though good will may be appealed to in order to dismiss this episode as something transitory, the question remains as to whether Photius did not persist in his standpoint in this particular matter and create an arsenal that he himself indeed never used but that was nevertheless more representative of his deepest convictions than were the official utterances in regard to Rome from his second patriarchate. But here philological clarity is still somewhat lacking. Involved is a work entitled *Against those who assert that*

---

[5] *PG* 102, 793–821. Cf. *Grumel Reg*, n. 529.
[6] *PG* 102, 263–391.

Rome is the Primatial See.[7] The arguments of Gordillo[8] and Dvornik[9] against its authenticity are no stronger than those of Hergenröther,[10] Dölger,[11] and Jugie[12] for it. A comprehensive analysis is still unavailable. *In dubiis pro reo.*

More interesting is a work that is undoubtedly by Photius, *Collectanea on the Episcopal and Metropolitan Office and Related Questions from Synods and Historical Works.*[13] Here there seems to be involved, not a polemic, but a collection of historical notes. These notes, however, contain, carefully arranged, whatever in the opinion of the collector the history of the papacy displays in the way of mistakes and errors. Such a collection would be planned only by one who felt a need of using it. In other words, the impression is unavoidable that, in the conviction of the Patriarch, both the Trinitarian teaching of the West, of that West whose leader was Rome, and also the doctrine of Rome's primacy offered sensitive areas which it was important to determine in order to be able to go into action with a wealth of historical arguments in case of need. So long as Rome recognized him, he saw no reason to dip into his arsenal; but he tended it and occasionally opened the gates in order to allow his adversary of tomorrow to see his riches. Basic questions in regard to the Church and theology thereby obtained the character of something to be manipulated. Politics triumphed.

Whether Photius thought also of a universal primacy of the Church of Constantinople seems to me to be another question.[14] We know nothing about his dreams. It probably cannot be proved that he had favoured the primacy *expressis verbis,* if one does not fail to note that a strict interpretation of the term "first see" must first reckon with the primacy within the Eastern Church, while its extension to the Universal Church would have to be formulated separately. In my opinion, no such notion of the primacy can be sifted especially from the *Epanagoge,* the introduction and first part of which are certainly from Photius; in this connection it is of no particular importance for the Patriarch's views whether the *Epanagoge* was ever published as a law code or not. Not even the Constantinian ecclesiastical system was destroyed

---

[7] *Rhallis* IV, 409–15, and M. Gordillo, "Photius et primatus Romanus" in *OrChrP* 6 (1940), 1–39.

[8] See the preceding footnote.

[9] *The Photian Schism,* and id., *The Idea of Apostolicity in Byzantium and the Legend of the Apostle Andrew* (Cambridge, Mass., 1958), 253.

[10] *Photius* I, 622ff.; III, 171.

[11] *ByZ* 40 1940), 522–25.

[12] "L'opuscule contre la primauté romaine attribué à Photius" in *Mélanges L. Vaganay,* II (Lyons 1938), 43–66.

[13] *PG* 104, 1219–32.

[14] Dölger, *Byzanz und die europäische Staatenwelt* (Ettal 1953), 101–5, especially stresses this tendency of Photius. The passage from the *Quaestiones Amphil.* cited by him speaks of κοινὸν κράτος which was transmitted to Byzantium; but this means the universal Empire, not the ecclesiastical primacy.

by the treatise on the patriarchal power, and no authentic papalism can be deduced from it. The insistence on the full authority of the Patriarch is stronger than one is accustomed to in Byzantine Church history, but the principle of the old imperial authority continues.[15] In the ups and downs of the fundamentally still obscure constitutional relationship between Emperor and Patriarch, the *Epanagoge* represents only one phase, during which an imposing Patriarch sought to establish in writing the influence that he actually exercised. In this work there is no reference to the universal primacy. Not even in the encyclical of 867 — and where would it have been more appropriate? — did Photius raise such claims. As regards the Latin polemics of a Ratramnus and his associates, these are without difficulty explained by the reproaches of Pope Nicholas, for whom the obstinacy of Photius sufficed in order to accuse him of such attempts.

Thus the portrait of the Patriarch remains unclear. In pure hypothesis one may conclude that Photius was principally concerned for the recognition of his position as Patriarch. In order to achieve this, the recognition of the Roman primacy served just as well as its denial and limitation. But he thereby proved that he would always remain a controversial figure in Church history. Even the Byzantines have recognized, or at least sensed, this. The case of Photius has become a model in Byzantine Church history. Meagre as were the effects of his schism on the events of 1054, if direct connections are sought, still the precedent of his schism was, as such, an example.

What is amazing in this personality is that one cannot do justice to it with an evaluation of his policy in regard to the internal schism and in regard to Rome. This is true of the history of the Greek Schism as a whole. An ecumenical writing of Church history cannot be satisfied to let fall on the Byzantine Church and her prelates only one cone of light that illuminates the relations of East and West. Photius was the most universal *savant* of his age, and this erudition was not only an apanage of classical philology. His famous *Library* deals for more than fifty per cent with authors of Christian antiquity and has thereby preserved an enormous amount of material for patrology, material that would have been lost without him. In his *Quaestiones disputatae,* the so-called *Amphilochiana,*[16] he pours before us a treasure of excerpts, which shows him to have been a theologian of the broadest interests and especially a "theologian of taste". His real forte seems to have been exegesis. The "Antiochene" method of his biblical interpretation combined philological precision and theological insight and so stood in the most favourable contrast to the involved allegorizing of his contemporaries and successors in East and West. He deliberately tackled not a few problems which were not taken up again until modern times by theologians, who then

---

[15] Cf. A. Esser, "Die Lehre der Epanagoge und eine oströmische Reichstheologie" in *FZThPh* 10 (1963), 63 ff.

[16] *PG* 101, 45–1172.

boasted of their own discoveries.[17] But one of the most pleasant surprises is provided by Photius as preacher. It goes without saying that he too sacrificed to the genius of Byzantine rhetoric, but this never concealed the basic concern for exhortation and edification. He found tones which could touch directly and which revealed a solicitous shepherd far from politics.[18]

It is in this context that the Byzantine mission work in the time of Photius should be placed. His initiative may be inferred in the mission to the Chazars as well as in those to the Bulgars and Moravians, and we know of his exertions to gain the Armenians back to Orthodoxy. And finally his numerous letters and patriarchal *acta* must be mentioned.[19] Care for the moral purity of the clergy induced him time and again to take up his pen. Just as often he sought to protect the people against the caprice of officials: he sharply censured the encroachments of these latter, not only in the case of lesser revenue officers or distant governors but also in regard to high officials, such as the heads of the urban administration of Constantinople. But from his writings always emerges his striving to give peace to the Church and to come to an understanding even with those who were not inclined to become "Photians". Apart from the Schism, Photius could have entered into history not only as a great scholar but also as an important Patriarch. One is almost tempted to close a basically imperfect circle and say: Photius is simply the Byzantine. In any event, he authentically represents the Byzantine Church of his day, its doings and its dreams, its glory and its danger.

[17] Cf. K. Staab, *Die Pauluskommentare der griechischen Kirche* (Münster 1933), and J. Reuss, *Matthäus-Kommentare aus der griechischen Kirche* (Berlin 1957).
[18] Edited by S. Aristarches, 2 vols. (Constantinople 1900f.); some in *PG* 102, 548–76. Important is C. Mango, *The Homilies of Photius, Patriarch of Constantinople, English Translation, Introduction and Commentary* (Cambridge, Mass. 1958).
[19] Summary in *Grumel Reg,* n. 508–89.

The Church and the Western Kingdoms from 900 to 1046

CHAPTER 27

The New Kingdoms

The Church and the Carolingian *Imperium* had come together because of an inner affinity. Because both institutions strove for a supranational unity resting on their Christian character, the universality of the Church had contributed to the consolidation of the Empire, and, conversely, the wide expanse of the Empire had made possible a uniform organization of the ecclesiastical situation, oriented to the Roman tradition. The disintegration of the Empire, accompanied in France and Italy by the collapse of the royal authority, could not but hurt the Church especially seriously. The victory of the private powers caused her to fall more strongly than before under the influence of German-Roman juridical notions. Forced to adjust herself to the varying regional ways of life, she lost much of her own intrinsic energy, based on her unity and universality. And since scholarship needed supra-provincial cooperation, the theological studies that had been happily initiated decayed.

For that very reason the Church historian is not wrong when he calls the tenth century a *saeculum obscurum* or *ferreum*. But he should connect with it not so much the idea of decay as of transformation and reorientation, and be aware that much of what at first acted destructively helped to rebuild the new West and the new Church.

France

The West Frankish Kingdom had relatively little to suffer from outside enemies in the tenth century. The Magyar raids, beginning toward the close of the ninth century, seldom got farther west than Lotharingia.[1] The Muslims, established at Freinet from about 888, chiefly harassed the neighbouring lands. And it was possible gradually to master the various groups of Northmen

---

[1] Cf. R. Lüttich, *Ungarnzüge in Europa im 10. Jahrhundert* (Berlin 1919); G. Fasoli, *Le incursioni ungare in Europa nel secolo X* (Florence 1945) and *CCivMéd* 2 (1959), 17–35; on the Magyars see also Chapter 31.

from the time when the Seine Vikings, under Rollo, had received land in fief from King Charles the Simple, and, giving up their way of life, their language, and their religion, began to settle down.[2] But West *Francia* had to endure internal warfare, for there was no longer a strong crown which would have been able to curb the anarchy. The process of dissolution of the royal power, which had already started under Charles the Bald (840–77), went on all the more unchecked in the tenth century when the West Carolingian family could maintain its claim to legitimacy only with the greatest difficulty against the far more powerful Robertians, who were seeking the crown. A change occurred only after the death of the childless Louis V in 987. The Robertian who was then elected his successor, Hugh Capet, founded a dynasty which was to reign in the direct line until 1328 and in collateral lines until 1848. Hugh Capet did, it is true, take over a kingdom that was already smashed to pieces. While the independent principalities had already reached the considerable number of twenty-nine at the beginning of the century, this had grown to fifty by 987.

The result for the Church was a very ticklish situation. Since the feudal princes — counts, marquises, or dukes — gradually usurped all rights of sovereignty, a considerable portion of the French bishoprics fell under their control. At the time of the Investiture Controversy the Capetians disposed of only twenty-five of the total of seventy-seven bishoprics. The princes' ecclesiastical sovereignty assumed to some extent the legal character of the proprietary church system and led, especially in the Midi, to serious abuses. Like any other object of value, bishoprics there could be given, in whole or in part, to members of the family, including wives and daughters, or sold to outsiders. Furthermore, they were useful to the princes who controlled episcopal elections as means of providing for their sons, with the result that in some dioceses there was an invariable dynastic succession for a long time.

Not rarely the churches became the playthings of political power struggles. The archbishopric of Reims, which was, strictly speaking, directly under the King, had a particularly difficult time.[3] Allied to the Robertian antiking, Raoul, the powerful Count Herbert of Vermandois was able in 925 to have his five-year-old son Hugh elected Archbishop and himself entrusted with the administration of the church property. A quarrel that soon broke out induced King Raoul in 931 to promote the monk Artaud to the see; he maintained himself also under the Carolingian Louis IV until 940, when Count

---

[2] W. Vogel, *Die Normannen und das fränkische Reich* (Heidelberg 1906); H. Prentou, *Essai sur les origines et la fondation du duché de Normandie* (Paris 1911); D. Douglas, "Rollo of Normandie" in *EHR* 57 (1942), 417–36.

[3] Cf. A. Dumas, "L'église de Reims au temps des luttes entre Carolingiens et Robertiens" in *RHÉF* 30 (1944), 5–38; H. Zimmermann, "Frankreich und Reims in der Politik der Ottonen" in *MIÖG, ErgBd,* 20 (1962f.), 122–46.

Herbert of Vermandois and Count Hugh of Neustria, enemies of the King, took Reims and enthroned Hugh of Vermandois as Archbishop. But the German King Otto I, who was protecting Louis IV of France from his vassals, restored Artaud to Reims by armed force in 948. The attempt of the sons of Herbert of Vermandois to recover the first French see for their brother at least after Artaud's death in 961 failed.

There was further chaos under King Hugh Capet. In 988 he entrusted the see of Reims to Arnulf, a bastard of the second last Carolingian, but in 991 had him deposed by a synod for having betrayed the city to his uncle, Duke Charles of Lotharingia. The Reims *scholasticus,* Gerbert of Aurillac, later Pope Silvester II, was elected as Arnulf's successor. The canonical quarrel that then ensued ended only with Arnulf's reinstatement. Because of the participation of the papacy and of the Emperor Otto III it acquired an importance that extended beyond France and hence will be treated in another context. In any event, Hugh Capet's conduct corresponded throughout to the views of the time. By virtue of the tie of vassalage linking the bishops to their princes, felony was regarded as a valid ground for deposition.

Nevertheless, the situation of the churches of France was better than one might think at first glance. The victory of particularism had as a consequence that the bishops and abbots did not, as in Germany, come into possession of important new rights of sovereignty. Hence they were less engrossed with the new forms of government. On the contrary, the arbitrary actions of so many lords of churches strengthened the forces of resistance of which the French churches disposed on the basis of a long tradition. Thus the old canon law did not fall into oblivion. Just as the French crown at the period by no means renounced its claim to supreme authority despite its actual powerlessness, churchmen also held firmly to certain basic principles, for example, to the right to free canonical election. Since they were not linked, for better or for worse, with a system of government, they were also able much more easily to develop a religious and ecclesiastical initiative of their own, and in this they not infrequently had the backing of pious princes. Here one need only recall the reform work of Cluny or the peace movements. And so when in the eleventh century the papacy had recourse to forces within the Church for the great reform, no country was so open to its exertions as France. It was not only the religious and ecclesiastical sense that had grown up among clerics and lay persons that contributed to this, but also the sovereignty over the Church as divided among King and princes. The princes were not powerful enough to maintain their rights against pressure from the reformed papacy, and the King could decide upon renunciation more easily than the German monarch could, because the political rights of the French ecclesiastical princes had a less pretentious range.

Italy

Italy's political and ecclesiastical situation provides an especially bewildering picture. The Lombard Kingdom, once again in the possession of Berengar of Friuli since the death of the Emperor Lambert in 898, was so weak that Berengar could defend it only with difficulty from occupation, first by King Louis of Provence, who went back to his homeland, blinded, in 905, and then, from 921, by King Rudolf II of Transjurane Burgundy. The assassination of Berengar in 924 smoothed the way for Rudolf, but he had to make way for Hugh of Vienne. Hugh firmly maintained his authority for about twenty years, until the opposition of the Margrave Berengar of Ivrea and his followers compelled him to flee. When Hugh's son and successor Lothar died in 950, a native prince, Berengar of Ivrea, finally gained the crown again. But a year later the German King Otto I seized the Lombard Kingdom and thereby determined the fate of mediaeval Italy. In addition to the kingship there also arose great dynastic principalities in North and Central Italy, such as those of the Margraves of Tuscany, Ivrea, Friuli, and that of the Aledramids of Piedmont. Farther south, the independent remnants of the Lombard Kingdom — the Duchies of Spoleto and Benevento, the Principality of Salerno, the County of Capua — maintained themselves. After the death of the Emperor Louis II (875) the Byzantines had again established themselves in an energetic struggle with the Muslims and were again able to combine their themes of Calabria and Langobardia. Gaetà, Naples, and Amalfi were under nominal Byzantine suzerainty.

The political chaos invited enemies in. The Magyars invaded from 899 and soon extended their frequent plundering expeditions to the south also. From Freinet the Spanish Muslims infested the northwest, while the Sicilian and African Muslims attacked South and Central Italy. Freinet could have been taken in 942 by King Hugh of Italy and the allied Byzantines, if Hugh had seriously desired this; it did not fall until 983. In the south the North African Aghlabid Dynasty was able to complete in 902 the conquest of Sicily, begun in 827, but its push into South Italy, undertaken in 900–02, was unsuccessful. The Muslim bands which had established a stronghold on Monte Argento at the mouth of the Garigliano, not far from Gaetà, were in no dependence on Sicily or North Africa. From this camp they collected blackmail until the combined forces of the Byzantines, the Princes of Capua, Salerno, and Spoleto, and Pope John X and the Romans put an end to their operations in 915.[4]

In the devastated and fragmented country the Church found conditions

[4] For the Magyars, see *supra,* footnote 1. For the Muslims of South Italy in the ninth and tenth centuries, see N. Cilento in *Archivio della storia della provincia Napoletana* 77 (1959), 109–22; M. Amari, *Storia dei musulmani di Sicilia,* revised by C. A. Vallino, II–III (Catania 1933–39). For the Battle on the Garigliano, see P. Fedele in *AS Romana* 22 (1899), 181–211; O. Vehse in *QFIAB* 19 (1927), 181–204.

that differed from one territory to the next. This was true even of the Byzantine holdings: the churches in the theme of Langobardia were, apart from the Terra d'Otranto, for the most part Latin and did not belong to the patriarchate of Constantinople, whereas those of the theme of Calabria belonged to the Byzantine sphere of liturgy and law.[5] Of course all of them were strictly dependent on the imperial government. Entirely different conditions prevailed in the north. Since inner feuds as well as the incursions of the Magyars forced the cities to self-defence, the Lombard bishops gained a preeminent position through the expanding of the power of *missi,* which in 876 Charles the Bald had granted to all Italian bishops for the territory of their cities. By incorporating important parts of the rural area into the urban territory, soon also gaining comital rights over the city or even over whole districts, and forcing the secular nobility into vassalage, they developed real city-state territories. The city rights of the bishops of Central Italy were less extensive. In the great maritime cities, such as Venice, dominion was acquired by a secular patriciate.

In Rome there was in preparation a development similar to that in the territories of Benevento, Capua, and Naples, where the rulers of the moment disposed of the bishoprics. The anarchy getting under way from 882 had constantly increased the influence of the Roman aristocracy and of the neighbouring princes. The crowning of powerless Emperors, Louis of Provence in 901 and Berengar of Friuli in 915, amde no difference; Rome had to take care of itself.

The first step toward a greater concentration of strength was taken in 904. In that year there returned to the Eternal City Sergius III, elected in 897 but forced to yield to the Formosan John IX. His return was effected by the aid of the Frankish upstart, Duke Alberic of Spoleto, and of a faction of the Roman nobility led by Theophylact. The intruder Christopher, who in 903 had overthrown the recently installed Pope Leo V, experienced the fate of his predecessor. He was imprisoned and probably killed together with Leo.

The pontificate of Sergius III meant the final victory of the anti-Formosans. They compelled the Roman clergy, all assembled in synod, to declare invalid the ordinations conferred by Formosus. This measure, which took effect far beyond Rome and even in South Italy, evoked sharp protests and malicious charges on the one hand, while on the other it posed the theologically important question of the validity of the ordinations, which was discussed with real competence especially by the Formosan Auxilius, a Frank living in Naples.[6] But Sergius III was too firmly in control to have to worry about his

[5] Thus W. Holtzmann, "Papsttum, Normannen und griechische Kirche", 71f., cited *infra,* 538, with the other literature.

[6] E. Dümmler, *Auxilius und Vulgarius, Quellen und Forschungen zur Geschichte des Papsttums im Anfang des 10. Jahrhunderts* (Leipzig 1866).

opponents, who lived outside Rome. Belonging to the Roman nobility, he relied on Theophylact, since 904 financial director *(vestararius)* of the Holy See and at the same time commander of the Roman militia *(magister militum)*. Theophylact's preeminence, which is difficult to define but was expressed in titles such as *dux, senator Romanorum, consul et dux,* was reinforced by the marriage of his daughter Marozia to Alberic of Spoleto and assured peace in Rome for some time.

The papacy's position at first still depended on the ability of the Roman Bishop of the moment.[7] The energetic Sergius III was followed by Anastasius III (911–13) and Lando (913–14), of whom we know virtually nothing. The next Pope, John X (914–28), transferred to Rome from the archiepiscopal see of Ravenna, was without doubt a strong personality. The accusation that John had previously lived in an illicit union with Theophylact's wife, Theodora, comes from Liutprand of Cremona, whose obsession was with discovering love affairs, and may be believed as little as the liaison, also reported by him, between Sergius III and Marozia. John X, who, with Theophylact and Alberic of Spoleto, was one of the chief promoters of the league against the Muslims and took part personally in the battle on the Garigliano in 915, was not subservient to the Roman nobility. After the deaths of Theophylact and Alberic (c. 924), he even began to pursue an independent policy, allying with King Hugh of Italy, to whom he promised the imperial crown, and seeking to assure the greatest possible power to his own brother, Peter. But here he ran afoul of Marozia, now head of the house of Theophylact and, since 926, wife of the Margrave Guy of Tuscany. Peter was killed in 927; in 928 John X was shut up in prison, where he died, probably strangled. His successors, Leo VI (928–29), Stephen VII (929–31), and finally Marozia's own son, John XI (931–36), were of no importance: the papacy had lost its freedom.

Marozia's fall brought no change. Free to marry again because of the death of Guy of Tuscany, she offered her hand and, with it, rule of Rome to Hugh of Italy, who was then at the height of his power. The ambitious plan, to which Hugh consented, was incompatible with the Romans' consciousness of their freedom. Incited by Alberic, son of Marozia and Alberic of Spoleto, they stormed the Castel Sant'Angelo, where the wedding was being celebrated. Hugh fled ignominiously, Marozia landed in prison, and Alberic assumed power, which, outdoing the achievement of his grandfather, he brought to its peak (932–54). Merely the titles used by him — *senator omnium Romanorum, patricius,* perhaps granted by the Byzantine Emperor,

---

[7] Cf. G. Buzzi, "Per la cronologia di alcuni pontefici dei secoli X–XI" in *AS Romana* 35 (1912), 611–22; P. Fedele, "Ricerche per la storia di Roma e del papato", ibid. 33 (1910), 174–247; 34 (1911), 75–115, 393–423 (important for the destruction of the "pornocracy" legend); L. Duchesne, "Serge III et Jean XI" in *MAH* 33 (1913), 25–64; T. Venni, "Giovanni X" in *AD Romana* 59 (1936), 1–136.

and finally *princeps* — and then his coinage, bearing his own name and that of the Pope, reveal the enhanced and now undisguised claim to princely authority. Thanks to a shrewd policy, which was not oriented to expansion or to recovery of territory, except for the Sabine country, but to the security and order of the existing territorial possessions, Alberic's position remained unshaken. Even the condition of the Church was improved. Personally pious, the *princeps* called upon no less than Odo of Cluny to reform the monasteries in and around Rome and on his family property built the monastery of Santa Maria all'Aventino. Naturally, he kept the Popes in strict dependence.[8] But it was clear to Alberic that this situation could not continue forever, because of the uncontestable right of the papacy to rule Rome and the *Patrimonium*. In an effort to assure his family the rule in the future also, shortly before his death he had the Romans swear to select his son Octavian as the next Pope. This was agreed to, and, after the death of Agapitus II (946–55), Octavian mounted the throne of Peter, putting aside his original name[9] and styling himself John XII (955–64). In this union of *princeps* and *pontifex* Alberic's goal seemed to have been realized.

And yet his calculations included an error. Oriented to the dimensions of a city-state, they caused the universal element, and hence the real essence of the Eternal City, to come out the loser. The Christian West still looked upon Rome as its capital, as the seat of the *vicarius Petri,* who was entrusted with the care of the Universal Church, and at the same time as the place where an Emperor, to be anointed by the Pope, had to assume the protectorate of Christianity. Since the imperial office was vacant and the papacy had fallen prey to the Roman nobility, the call for a *renovatio imperii* gained momentum. As soon as a strong ruler answered it, Alberic's system was done for. That ruler appeared in the King of Germany, Otto I.

Germany

When the East Carolingian Dynasty expired in the person of Louis the Child, and Conrad I (911–18) was raised to the throne, the royal authority was in the process of dissolution in Germany. The East Frankish tribal nobility, all along not particularly devoted to the crown, set about the intensive cultivation of its immune districts by means of colonization and the founding of churches and monasteries, which it endowed with its patrimonial

[8] W. Sickel, "Alberich II. und der Kirchenstaat" in *MIÖG* 23 (1902), 50–126; O. Vehse, "Die päpstliche Herrschaft in der Sabina bis zur Mitte des 12. Jahrhunderts" in *QFIAB* 21 (1929f.), 120–75; A. Rota, "La riforma monastica del 'princeps' Alberico" in *AD Romana* 79 (1956), 11–22 (this probably overstresses the political motives).
[9] Before him Mercurius had taken the name of John II (533–35); John XII's gesture, imitated by John XIV, became the rule from Gregory V; cf. F. Krämer, "Über die Anfänge und Beweggründe der Papstnamenänderungen im Mittelalter" in *RQ* 51 (1956), 148–88.

goods. The ancient way of life peculiar to the German tribes had developed further and found its support in the "later" tribal dukedom, which had risen to power through the wars with Vikings, Slavs, and Magyars. If the crown intended to enforce its authority, it had to have recourse to the Carolingian legacy of the unity of the state and so to the Frankish State Church. This attempt did not succeed at once. The struggle waged by Conrad I with the aid of the Church[10] against the tribal dukedom was a failure.

His successor, Henry I (919–36), founder of the Saxon Dynasty, at first followed a different course[11] because of Conrad's failure. Henry avoided the alliance with the Church and sought a federal union of the tribes under Saxon leadership. But he slowly came around again to the Carolingian policy, especially after the recovery in 926 of Lotharingia, which in 911 had gone over to France. It was important to the Church that Henry again instituted the politically important palace chapel and regained the disposal of all the bishoprics, except those of Bavaria, whose duke did not have to renounce his ecclesiastical sovereignty until the reign of Otto I. The Carolingian tradition came to life again in full force under this same Otto the Great, Henry's son. The severe struggles which Otto had to endure with the nobility and the tribal dukes may be passed over here. But they had an effect on the Church too. Motivated by the understanding that the crown would not master the inner political opposition without a complete domination of the Church, Otto, in the words of Mitteis, proceeded "to make the Church the central institution of the kingdom". What he began, the succeeding rulers of the Saxon and Salian Dynasties continued.

The King's will was regarded as virtually unlimited in the State Church that thus came to birth. The nomination of the bishops, who were mostly not connected with the tribes, was determined by political viewpoints. Usually they were men who had been brought up in the royal chapel and trained in the service of the chancery or in other functions. In order to be able to demand of the churches achievements of greater consequence for the state, the rulers were sparing neither in donations of crown property nor in privileges of immunity, which gave the bishops full jurisdiction, even over serious criminal cases, and hence made the ecclesiastical *advocatia* the equivalent of a countship. From the time of Otto III even whole counties with all their rights were bestowed upon episcopal sees or royal abbeys. Usually connected with jurisdiction were other profitable rights — tolls, market, ban — so that the Ottonian privileges laid the foundation on which an episcopal territorial power could be erected. The celibacy of the ecclesiasti-

---

[10] M. Hellmann, "Die Synode von Hohenaltheim (910). Bemerkungen über das Verhältnis von Königtum und Kirche im ostfränkischen Reich zu Beginn des 10. Jahrhunderts" in *HJ* 73 (1954), 127–42; also, H. Fuhrmann in *ZBLG* 20 (1954), 136–51.
[11] Cf. C. Erdmann, "Der ungesalbte König" in *DA* 2 (1938), 412–41; M. Linzel, *Heinrich I. und die fränkische Königssalbung* (Berlin 1955).

cal princes made it possible to regrant vacated offices freely, as the occasion arose.

So strict a dependence of the prelatial churches on the King was conceivable only in an age which did not yet know the essential distinction between state and Church, but merely the functional distinction between *Sacerdotium* and *Regnum*. Since both powers, as members of one superposed unity under the rule of Christ, regarded themselves as bound to the same religious and political goal, royal service, secular administration, and divine service could all be conceived as one and the same religious and moral accomplishment.[12] The ruler, from whose hand the bishops, at their investiture by ring and staff, received, not only the property and the secular rights of sovereignty, but also the ecclesiastical function, was in the view of that age not simply a layman. His anointing, which, given the state of contemporary theology, could be regarded as a Sacrament, raised him to the sphere of *vicarius Christi* and made him, according to the anointing formula in a Mainz *Ordo,* a participant in the episcopal office and an intermediary between clergy and people.[13] Thus the theocratic form of dominion, elaborated under the Carolingians, gained new force and validity. It reached its climax in the religious and political ideas of Otto III and motivated both Henry II and Henry III to serious reform efforts.

Since at the time there was no free Church, it was basically more advantageous for the bishops to be under the rule of a king rather than of a prince. The theocratic king pursued an objective religious and political general policy, whereas the princes were motivated by selfish interests. Hence the German episcopate in the tenth and eleventh centuries presented on the whole a really favourable picture; in fact, there were in it not a few exemplary and saintly ecclesiastical princes. Naturally, the Ottonian system could not last forever. As soon as the Western mind began to distinguish more carefully and hence to surmount the primitive phase of the relationship, the Church had to lay her hand again on the episcopal office and attack the theocratic form of investiture. The collapse of the Ottonian State Church that actually occurred weakened the crown considerably. For the German bishop continued to be a Prince of the Empire until 1803 and from the time of the Concordat of Worms (1122) was on the way to constructing his territorial power in competition with the secular princes and to the disadvantage of the imperial power.

[12] O. Köhler, *Das Bild des geistlichen Fürsten in den Viten des 10., 11. und 12. Jahrhunderts* (Berlin 1935); J. Fleckenstein, "Königshof und Bischofsschule unter Otto dem Grossen" in *AKG* 38 (1956), 32–62; H. W. Klewitz, "Cancellaria" in *DA* 1 (1937), 44–79; id., "Königtum, Hofkapelle und Domkapitel im 10. und 11. Jahrhundert" in *AUF* 16 (1939), 102–56.
[13] Texts in P. E. Schramm, "Die Krönung in Deutschland bis zum Beginn des salischen Hauses" in *ZSavRGkan* 55 (1935), 319f.; on the Mainz *ordo,* cf. also C. Erdmann, *Forschungen zur politischen Ideenwelt,* 54–91; on the theocracy, cf. 516, the bibliography to this section, and E. H. Kantorowicz, *The King's Two Bodies* (Princeton 1957), 42–86; also F. Kempf in *RQ* 54 (1959), 204–06.

The Ottonian-Salian State Church was never a real national or territorial Church. The presuppositions for the concept of a national state were then lacking, particularly in the Carolingian successor states, in which the awareness of the earlier unity disappeared only slowly.[14] Otto I intended to be, not so much a German King, as successor of Charles the Great. For this reason it was in the Aachen chapel, the burial place of the great Charles, that he had himself acclaimed and anointed as King and seated upon Charles's throne, with its many relics. It is true that Charles's *Imperium* could not be re-established, but the Western concept of unity, fed by the Carolingian and the Christian traditions, impelled Otto beyond the German area of his authority, as his position of hegemony expanded and consolidated itself. It was more than a national deed when, outdoing his father's victory near Riate in 933, he so decisively defeated the Magyars on the Lechfeld near Augsburg in 955 that their raids ceased. Widukind's report that the victorious German army thereupon proclaimed Otto Emperor[15] may have been invented, but all of Western Christendom looked upon him as its liberator.

The struggles in the north and east also and the related political expansion did not concern merely Germany. A new missionary movement, conducted by German and other priests, expanded the Church's territory, as will be described later. Otto apparently did not intend to attack the independence of the neighbouring Western states, but he occasionally intervened in their affairs. Thus he saved the crown for Conrad of Burgundy, the underage son of King Rudolf II, who had died in 937. Conrad was brought to Otto's court and kept there for a while; in this way was frustrated the plan to annex Burgundy that had been concocted by King Hugh of Italy. Hugh had married the widowed Queen of Burgundy and had arranged the engagement of his son Lothar to Rudolf's daughter Adelaide. And in France Otto supported the Carolingian, Louis IV, once the latter had renounced Lotharingia, against the Robertian, Hugh of Neustria, not only in several campaigns but also by his exertions to have the Reims schism settled at the Synod of Ingelheim in 948 in accord with Louis's desires.

The position of hegemony which elevated the German King above the Western monarchs hinted of itself at a final enhancement, at its sanction by the Pope in the imperial anointing and coronation. Since this presupposed

---

[14] A. Schulze, *Kaiserpolitik und Einheitsgedanke in den karolingischen Nachfolgestaaten 876–962* (dissertation, Berlin 1926); O. Ebding, *Der politische Zusammenhang zwischen den karolingischen Nachfolgestaaten* (typed dissertation, Freiburg im Breisgau 1950); G. Tellenbach, "Von der Tradition des fränkischen Reiches in der deutschen und französischen Geschichte" in *Der Vertrag von Verdun,* ed. by T. Mayer (Leipzig 1943); W. Kienast, *Deutschland und Frankreich in der Kaiserzeit 900–1270* (Leipzig 1943).

[15] Widukind, III, 49 (ed. Hirsch-Hohmann, 128f.); cf. also H. Beumann, *Widukind von Korvei. Untersuchungen zur Geschichtsschreibung und Ideengeschichte des 10. Jahrhunderts* (Weimar 1950), 228–65; C. Erdmann, *Forschungen zur politischen Ideenwelt,* 44–46; J. A. Brundage, "Widukind of Corvey and the 'Non-Roman' Imperial Idea" in *MS* 22 (1960), 15–26.

the possession of Italy, the politics of the Saxon Dynasty was oriented to the conquest of the Lombard Kingdom. Henry I had probably thought of an expedition to Italy and Rome in his last years. Perhaps it was for this reason that, probably in 935, he acquired at great cost from King Rudolf II of Burgundy the holy lance, a relic adorned with nails from the cross of Christ, which was thought to be Constantine's lance; it was therefore regarded as a symbol of imperial authority and could signify a claim to Italy.[16] In any event, Otto I was thereafter determined to acquire the Italian royal crown and the Roman imperial crown.

Nationalistic minded historians of the nineteenth century chalked this up to him as a serious mistake. The scholars' quarrel started by them seems strange to us, and yet its arguments, derived more from the modern than from the mediaeval viewpoint, are to some extent to be heard even today.[17] The Italian policy of the Dukes of Swabia and Bavaria, so runs the explanation which favours Otto, forced the German King to lay hands on Italy and then on Rome; furthermore, he had to control the Pope in order to keep the German Church dependent and to carry through his missionary plans in the east and north. These and other considerations, however, stress only more or less correct partial aspects. Otto's real motives originated in intellectual and spiritual strata which are scarcely accessible to us today. Aspirations for power, the Christian universalist idea of a *renovatio imperii Francorum,* and a magic and religious appreciation of the imperial anointing probably fused here, but in such a way that it is not possible to determine exactly the share of the individual elements.

[16] W. Holtzmann, *Heinrich I. und die heilige Lanze* (Bonn 1947); M. Lintzel in *HZ* 171 (1951), 303–10; H. E. Mayer in *DA* 17 (1961), 507–17; M. Uhlirz, "Zu den heiligen Lanzen der karolingischen Teilreiche" in *MIÖG* 68 (1960), 197–208; P. E. Schramm, *Herrschaftszeichen und Staatssymbolik,* II (Stuttgart 1955), 492–537.

[17] H. Hostenkamp, *Die mittelalterliche Kaiserpolitik der deutschen Historiographie seit von Sybel und Ficker* (Berlin 1934); F. Schneider, *Die neueren Anschauungen der deutschen Historiker über die deutsche Kaiserpolitik des Mittelalters und die mit ihr verbundene Ostpolitik* (Weimar, 5th ed. 1942); L. Hauptmann, "Universalismus und Nationalismus im Kaisertum der Ottonen" in *Festschr. K. G. Hugelmann,* I (Aalen 1959), 189–211; W. Smidt, *Deutsches Königtum und deutscher Staat des Hochmittelalters während und unter dem Einfluss der italienischen Heerfahrten. Ein 200jähriger Gelehrtenstreit* (Wiesbaden 1964); other literature, especially Litzel and Rörig, in the next chapter.

CHAPTER 28

Rome, the Papacy, and the Empire: 962 to 1002

The desire of Otto I, King of Germany, to gain the Lombard royal crown and the Roman imperial crown was entirely within the realm of the possible. It was important only to wait for the proper moment. This seemed to have arrived when, after the death of King Lothar of Italy in 950, his young widow, Queen Adelaide, daughter of Rudolf II of Burgundy, was unwilling to give way to Berengar of Ivrea, who had forced himself into power; she was therefore thrown into prison. Probably appealed to for aid, Otto entered Lombardy with a strong army, assumed the royal authority at Pavia, unelected and uncrowned, and married Adelaide (951). Envoys sent on to the Pope discussed the question of the imperial coronation with him, but the ruler of Rome, Prince Alberic, did not want a new Emperor, and so Pope Agapitus II had to refuse.

His attention claimed by difficulties within Germany, Otto soon relinquished even the Lombard Kingdom, assigning it to Berengar of Ivrea and his son Adalbert in exchange for vassalage, except for the northeastern part of Lombardy, which was placed under the Duke of Bavaria. Without knowing it, Otto had thereby smoothed his route to Rome. For Berengar, involved as early as 956, because of a violation of the territorial arrangements, in a war which was directed by Otto's son Liudolf and which was temporarily ended by Liudolf's death in 957, constantly extended his sphere of power. By conquering the Duchy of Spoleto in 959 and, in that connection, plundering or occupying small frontier districts belonging to the Papal State, Berengar became a threatening neighbour of Pope John XII. The youthful Pope had to fear Berengar's expansionist drive all the more, since his own position had been shaken by a foolish and miserably ruined attempt against Capua and by his religiously frivolous and even immoral life. In his distress, therefore, he sent two agents to Germany in 960 to ask Otto's help and to invite him to receive the imperial crown in Rome. Some Lombard princes and bishops also appeared at the German court and demanded war.

Otto made the most of the propitious hour. In a treaty concluded with the papal envoys he promised on oath, apparently in imitation of a formula submitted to Charles the Fat in 881, to protect the person of the Pope and the *Patrimonium Petri,* the territorial extent of which was to remain inviolate, without the advice of the Pope neither to sit in judgment nor to issue orders in Rome which would affect the Pope or the Romans, and to oblige the future regent of the Lombard Kingdom to defend the *Patrimonium.*[1] He then made

[1] Cf. K. Hampe, "Die Berufung Ottos des Grossen nach Rom durch Papst Johannes XII." in *Festschrift für K. Zeumer* (Weimar 1910), 153–67; on the oath, see E. Eichmann, *Kaiserkrönung,* II, 165–83.

ready his journey to Rome. To guarantee the succession he had his six-year-old son and namesake elected and crowned King. In the late summer of 961, accompanied by Queen Adelaide, he appeared in Lombardy with a strong force, restored his sovereignty there temporarily almost without striking a blow, and at the beginning of the new year set out for Rome. On 2 February 962, he and Adelaide received the imperial anointing and were crowned in Saint Peter's.[2]

This solemn act bound Church, Empire, and Christendom into a unity heavy with consequences for the future. In so far as the altered circumstances would allow, the *renovatio imperii Francorum* had become a reality. The extensive territory under his rule, comprising two kingdoms, his position of hegemony, and his victories over the neighbouring pagan peoples had pointed out Otto as the successor of Charles the Great and had led him to Rome to have his pre-eminence ratified sacramentally. Except for certain rights in Rome and in the Papal State, the imperial coronation could add nothing to his power of government, which remained fundamentally his power as King, even if, because of the possession of two kingdoms — to which in 1033 Conrad II would be able to add a third, that of Burgundy — it had a quasi-imperial character. Hence, Otto and his successors did not, by virtue of their imperial title, demand any subjection from the other Christian Kings of the West. The rights of suzerainty which they acquired from time to time over neighbouring rulers to the north or the east were the results of a policy independent in itself of the imperial office. But the anointing and coronation at Rome transmitted the imperial title and the imperial dignity.

The conferring of the imperial dignity, of course, would not have meant much unless it was destined for a ruler endowed with power. Here there was involved a fundamentally important double relationship. The quasi-imperial power of the German monarchs and its hegemonial radiation gave importance and esteem to the imperial dignity, while the imperial dignity surrounded what was basically a royal power with a mysterious glamour supported by a genuine symbolic force and made it appear as an imperial power. Surpassing all other rulers in dignity and authority, the German Emperor appeared to occupy the throne of the world and to be charged by God in the first place to espouse the cause of Christianity, just as he was entrusted in a special manner with the protection of the Pope, the father of Christendom. The universal characteristic, present in the Christian essence of the imperial office, would be consolidated by the fact that the German Empire would be more and

---

[2] According to H. Decker-Hauff, "Die 'Reichskrone'", P. E. Schramm, *Herrschaftszeichen und Staatssymbolik*, II (Stuttgart 1955), 560–637, the "Vienna Crown" had been made before 962 for the imperial coronation; this is denied by J. Deér, "Otto der Grosse und die Reichskrone" in *Beiträge zur Kunstgeschichte und Archäologie des Mittelalters*, Akten zum 7. internationalen Kongress für Frühmittelalterforschung (Graz–Cologne 1961), 261–77; on the coronation, see E. Eichmann, *Kaiserkrönung*, I, 129–49.

more regarded as the continuation of the world-wide Roman Empire. This development owed its origin to the rivalry, soon to begin, with the Byzantine Emperor as well as to the current ideas of renewal, harking back to antiquity and Rome, and to the theology of the four world-empires.[3]

On the juridical questions posed by the union of the German kingship and the Roman imperial office Otto I and his successors, except Otto III, seem to have had no misgivings. Things developed, so to speak, automatically. It is true that the anointing and coronation at Rome, since 850 the unique means of imparting the imperial dignity, continued to be reserved entirely to the Pope as his prerogative, but it lost its importance by virtue of the fact that the Popes could no longer, as John VIII once did, select an Emperor from among the Western Kings. In his own lifetime Otto I had his son and namesake crowned as Emperor in 967 and enhanced the imperial prestige of his house by the marriage of Otto II to the Greek Princess Theophano, probably a niece of the Byzantine Emperor John I Tzimisces.[4]

Although the elevation of the heir to the throne to the rank of coemperor did not take place after that, still the power substantially claimed by the German monarchs of the tenth and eleventh centuries guaranteed, even and especially in Imperial Italy, the claim to the imperial dignity and made it slowly into a *ius ad rem*, into a legal reversion. *Regnum* and *Imperium* became thereby so correlated that the election and anointing of the German King already implied the elevation of the future Emperor, and, conversely, the imperial anointing denoted the climax and finale of the progressive elevation of the German monarch. So long as the Saxon and early Salian theocracy endured, the imperial office was, for all practical purposes, not subject to the influence of Pope or Romans. If one disregards the ideas of Otto III, it was not the Romans but the Germans who appeared as the Imperial Nation. The German kingship and its power assumed an imperial character, and the Pope, in the imperial coronation that was his right, had only to ratify sacramentally what had already been decided and acted upon in ruling.

Of course there is question here merely of one of several possible views, but one that was favoured by the circumstances of the time. The imperial office was a much too ambiguous creation, subject to various interpretations, for its relationship to the *Regnum* to be unequivocally pinpointed. While the

[3] On the Roman content of the imperial idea, see especially P. E. Schramm, *Kaiser, Rom und Renovatio, passim,* and C. Erdmann, "Das Ottonische Reich als Imperium Romanum" in *DA* 6 (1943), 412–41. But there was also a non-Roman imperial idea; for it, see E. E. Stengel, "Kaisertitel und Souveränitätsidee" in *DA* 3 (1939), 1–56, 16 (1960), 15–72 (*Imperium* among the Anglo-Saxons); C. Erdmann, *Forsch. zur politischen Ideenwelt,* 1–16, 31–43; on the Ottonian imperial office, ibid., 43–51. On the relevant theology: E. Kocken, *De theorie van de vier wereldrijken en van de overdracht der wereldheerschappij tot op Innocentius III* (Nijmegen 1935); P. van den Baar, *Die kirchliche Lehre der Translatio Imperii Romani* (Rome 1956); W. Goez, *Translatio imperii* (Tübingen 1958).

[4] M. Uhlirz thinks otherwise: cf. here *JbbDG: Otto III.,* 1f. (with bibliography).

Germans, like the Franks before them, might have felt that their rulers owed the *Imperium,* next to God, to their own inherent strength,[5] the Romans and the Pope clung to the conviction that the *Imperium* was at their disposal. The Roman people were unable to carry their claim, but the Pope had a strong basis for his. It was he who conferred the imperial dignity by the anointing and coronation, and, according to Roman and ecclesiastical tradition, this meant, not an action to be undertaken, as it were, blindfolded, but an act somehow free and presupposing the examination of the one to be anointed — the doing of a favour. Thus supported, the papacy, once it had acquired its freedom in the Investiture Controversy and had assumed the leadership of Western Christendom, was to make demands which, because of the entanglement of the *Imperium* with the German *Regnum,* touched the foundations of German rule and contributed to the dramatic conflict with the Hohenstaufen.

Soon after his imperial coronation, Otto I, following the example of the preceding Emperors, issued a *privilegium* for the Roman Church in his own name and that of his son.[6] Despite the disappearance of almost all the earlier imperial *privilegia,* the regulations of the *Ottonianum* may safely be traced back to one text, which was slowly elaborated in the pacts of the ninth century and eventually reached its final form, probably in the pact of Charles the Bald of 876, from then on to pass, virtually unaltered, from one imperial *privilegium* to another, as, in the words of Stengel, "the pale shadow of the once living power notions of both parties". The producing of one or more such pacts may have induced Otto in the first part of his *privilegium* to confirm in favour of the Roman Church a downright fantastic territorial possession involving about two-thirds of Italy, although the poorly composed text contained obvious contradictions.[7]

The to a great extent utopian statements need not, of course, have troubled

---

[5] Widukind of Corvey is an especially important witness for the time of Otto I; see Chapter 27, footnote 15.

[6] *MGConst* I, no. 12. T. Sickel, *Das Privilegium Ottos I. für die römische Kirche* (Innsbruck 1883); E. E. Stengel, "Die Entwicklung des Kaiserprivilegs für die römische Kirche 817–962" in *HZ* 134 (1926), 216–41, revised in Stengel, *Abhandlungen und Untersuchungen zur mittelalterlichen Geschichte* (Cologne–Graz 1960), 218–48; H. Zimmermann in *MIÖG, ErgBd,* 20 (1962), 147–90 (on the history of the critical problem).

[7] The basis was the still extant privilege of 817, issued by Louis the Pious. To the possessions there described, comprising especially the Duchy of Rome, the Pentapolis, and the exarchate, were added in the course of time in more important grants: the territory of Naples, Gaetà, and Fondi, seven Spoletan cities, and then, probably by Charles the Bald, through the insertion of the promise of Quierzy, going back to Pepin and renewed by Charles the Great: Corsica, Venetia, Istria, the Duchies of Spoleto and Benevento, and a large area extending beyond Tuscany and into Lombardy with its frontier from Luni to Monselice. Opposed to the view given in the text and defended by Stengel is that of *Haller* II, 208–10, 551–53, who holds that the immense extent of the Papal State is proper to the *Ottonianum.* According to him, John XII, greedy for expansion, outwitted the naive Germans. Cf. also Stengel's reply in *Abhandlungen,* 243–45.

the Emperor. He was, however, bound to procure its property for the Roman Church only to the extent that he was able. It would take years for Otto to control Italy to some degree and to be able to think of restitution. The more he became conversant with the territorial situation in Italy, the more exactly he learned to distinguish, even in the *privilegium,* between appearance and reality, between the never realized wishful thinking and the genuine legal claims of the Roman Church in regard to territorial possessions. But even in the restitutions that were to be effected in justice, there was no question of an absolute alienation. The Emperor remained the sovereign lord even in the Papal State. The regulations of the second part of the charter, which, among other things, provided for an oath of loyalty to be taken before his consecration by the Pope, who was to be freely elected, and envisaged the Emperor as the final tribunal for complaints against papal officials, admit of no doubt. Most probably they belonged to the constant elements in imperial privileges, once they had been validly formulated in a *privilegium,* no longer extant but probably drawn up in 825 following the *Constitutio Romana* and other measures taken by Lothar I in 824.[8] John XII was quickly to learn what they meant for Otto I.

Back in Lombardy, Otto began the struggle against Berengar, who fell back upon a castle in the former exarchate. When, during the siege, the Emperor brought the neighbouring populations under his sovereignty, John XII regarded his rights as having been violated and, disregarding the oath of loyalty he had sworn to the Emperor, conspired with Berengar's son Adalbert. Otto thereupon returned to Rome in 963. The Romans had to swear for the future not to elect a Pope without the authorization of the Emperor. Then, contrary to the fundamental legal principle that the Pope can be judged by no one, Otto had John, now in flight, summoned before a synod and, on his non-appearance, deposed. Leo, *protoscriniarius* of the Roman Church, was then raised to the papacy as Leo VIII. This notorious violation of the law not only led to an uprising but, following Otto's departure, also enabled John XII to take hold of the reins again. A few months later he was carried off by a stroke, allegedly in a liaison. As his successor the Romans elected the blameless Benedict V. But once again might prevailed: Otto forced Leo VIII on the Romans and banished Benedict V to Hamburg. John's perfidy had cost the Roman Church dearly. The Emperor's new right to confirm the papal election reduced the Bishop of Rome to a momentous dependence.[9]

---

[8] The bold thesis of W. Ullmann, "The Origins of the Ottonianum" in *CambrHJ* 11 (1953), 114–28, that the entire second part was added in 963 in a new version interpolated by the imperial side, is probably wrong. Cf. also O. Bertolini, "Osservazioni sulla 'Constitutio Romana' e sul 'sacramentum cleri et populi Romani' dell' 824" in *Studi medievali in onore di A. De Stefano* (Palermo 1956), 43–78; K. Hampe, "Berufung Ottos des Grossen", *loc. cit.,* and Stengel, *Abhandlungen,* 222–25.

[9] H. Zimmermann, "Die Deposition Johanns XII., Leos VIII. und Benedikts V." in

In addition to the Emperor, the papacy had also from now on to reckon with the Roman nobles and their rivalries. A first revolt, of short duration, against John XIII (965–72) was severely punished by the Emperor (966). It was followed by a second, after Otto's death in 973, led by Crescentius de Theodora. Pope Benedict VI was overthrown in 974 and replaced by Boniface VII, who had Benedict strangled. Then, hard pressed by the imperial *missus,* the usurper fled to the Byzantines with the Church's treasury. His attack on Rome in 980–81, by which he intended to strip the reformer, Pope Benedict VII (974–83), of power, failed. But when the Emperor Otto II died at the end of 983, the adventurer emerged victorious against the unloved John XIV (983–84), who had been transferred from the see of Pavia at the Emperor's wish. John XIV was starved or poisoned in prison, while the hated and despised Boniface died in 985.[10] The next Pope, John XV (985–96), relied strictly on the nobles, to the dissatisfaction of the lower clergy. Under him the two sons of Crescentius de Theodora, John and Crescentius II, rose to high position. John was entrusted with the administration of the Church's property and bore the title *patricius.* The power-mad and avaricious Crescentius II did not hold any office but, especially after his brother's death, exerted a tyrannical pressure on the Roman Church.[11]

The tragic end of Benedict VI and John XIV indicated once again how badly the Popes, threatened by Roman factional strife, needed protection. But the German Emperors were certainly to be preferred as protectors to a Roman noble family that had gained power. The Ottos assisted the papacy out of its difficulties at Rome and brought it back into a larger context. And if the imperial protectorate also encroached upon the freedom of the papal election and of papal political activity, still, apart from the different course of Otto III, it did not attack the papacy's power of spiritual leadership in itself, quite in contrast to the rule of Charles the Great, who to a great extent had united the supreme direction of Church and Empire in his person and allowed the Pope hardly more than the position of a supreme Imperial Bishop. The German Imperial Church never attained to the compactness of the Carolingian territorial Church. More firmly even than before, it was to become a

MIÖG 68 (1960), 209–25, and "Papstabsetzungen" in *MIÖG* 69 (1961), 247–61; there, on page 254, footnote 42, the noteworthy view that in the deposition of John XII the attempt was made to neutralize the Pope's judicial immunity, which continued in force "nisi a fide devius", by accusing him of apostasy.

[10] On Boniface VII see M. Uhlirz, *JbbDG: Otto III.,* 58–60; Zimmermann, "Papstabsetzungen", *loc. cit.* 266–69.

[11] On the Crescentian family: the works of Kölmel and Gerstenberg (see the bibliography for Chapter 27); G. Bossi, *I Crescenzi. Contributo alla storia di Roma 900–1012* (Rome 1915); id., *AS Romana* 41 (1918), 111–70 (Crescentians in the Sabine district, 1012–1106); P. Brezzi, *Roma* (see bibliography for Chapter 27), disputes with Gerstenberg the origin of the Crescentians from the house of Theophylact (pp. 148–52); he also holds that the family of John XIII can no longer be determined, ibid. 142–44.

part of the Universal Church, once the Church's centre of gravity at Rome showed itself more markedly along with the renewed imperial office.

Otto I and his successors not infrequently had important questions affecting the German Church decided at papal synods, meeting in Rome or elsewhere in Italy, now and then even in a sense opposed to the wishes of the German prelates. And even the wishes of the Emperors did not have to be unconditionally complied with. Thus John XIII, in his *privilegium* of 967, seems to have restricted the jurisdictional sphere of the archbishopric of Magdeburg, about to be established, out of consideration for the Poles and contrary to the intentions of Otto I. Brought face to face with entirely new missionary problems by the German Emperor in his struggles with pagan frontier peoples, the papacy began to focus its gaze beyond the Empire on nations with which it had hardly concerned itself earlier. This matter will be taken up later. Now the Pope not infrequently had to deal with the spiritual affairs of France, because they were referred to him no longer only from France but also, in specific cases, by the German monarchs.

Italy naturally constituted an especially important topic of discussion between the two chiefs of Christendom. When in 964 Otto I captured and exiled Berengar, his authority in Italy was so little established that, after his return to Germany, a rising engineered by Berengar's son Adalbert had to be put down. Only his third Italian expedition (966–72), which put the Emperor in touch with the Lombard princes of South Italy and enabled the imperial frontier to be assured *vis-à-vis* the Byzantines, produced a somewhat orderly situation. This finally made it possible gradually to restore to the Roman Church, at least partially, the districts usurped by Italian nobles. The restitutions, begun in 967 and continued by Otto II, had to do with Ravenna and the counties of the old exarchate.[12] John XIII, to be sure, seems to have again turned over Ravenna and Comacchio to the Empress Adelaide, and later Gregory V had to cede the greatest part of his rights in the exarchate to the Archbishop of Ravenna.

The Roman Church lacked the means of administering a somewhat extensive territory with its own resources. In the tenth century things were in a bad way in general with regard to the landed property of the Italian churches. The German Emperors observed with great anxiety how everywhere great and petty lords were taking possession of ecclesiastical property in an increasing measure. So long as this involved monastic property, the bishops also helped themselves. Further losses occurred because of the widespread disregard of celibacy. Bishops, abbots, and priests provided for their illegitimate children as far as possible with clerical property. For political reasons alone the Ottos came out for the preservation and restitution

[12] The fundamental study by M. Uhlirz, cited in the bibliography, on the restitution includes, among other things, an important attempt to clarify the frontier line Luni—Monselice see footnote 7, *supra*).

of ecclesiastical property, especially in the strategically important zones and in the royal monasteries, which were bound to the imperial service. From 967 they treated of Church property at synods and diets. They issued laws, such as the *Capitulare de duello iudiciali* of 967, which introduced the duel as the method of proof in conflicts over property and excluded the sons of those obliged to celibacy from holding public offices, and the *Capitulare de praediis ecclesiasticis* of 998, which set a time-limit to the enfeoffing of property. They granted monasteries the right of inquisition, privileges of immunity, charters of protection, and confirmations of their property, and brought the complaints of plundered monasteries before their tribunal.[13] Meagre as this reform was in regard to depth, the problem of reform that was thereby thrown open was to have further effects in Italy.

Meanwhile, another danger loomed in the south. Provoked by a Byzantine raid on Messina, the Sicilian Muslims, under their Emir Abul Kasim, attacked Calabria and Apulia from 976. The Byzantine Emperor Basil II was too much preoccupied with the revolt of Bardas Sclerus to be able to help. Since Pandulf Iron-Head, the mightiest lord in the Lombard area, unfortunately died in 981, Otto II assumed charge of the defence against the infidel. From this time on he designated himself as Emperor of the Romans, in open rivalry with the *Basileus,* with whom he had been on bad terms ever since the death of John I Tzimisces. His campaign ended with defeat at Cape Colonna in Calabria in July 982, but the battle cost Abul Kasim his life and hence induced the leaderless Muslims to quit the mainland. Otto had already decided on a second military expedition, but in 983, at the age of twenty-eight, he was carried off by a sickness at Rome and was buried in the atrium of Saint Peter's. (Today he rests in the grottoes.) He left a son of the same name, not yet four years old but already crowned as King. The regency was conducted by Theophano and, after her death in 991, by Adelaide, until the young King was declared of age in 994.

In 996 Otto III set out on a journey to Rome. Pope John XV had come into conflict with Crescentius II and had been compelled to leave the city, but at the news of Otto's coming he had been called back, only to die soon after.[14] The Romans sent envoys to consult Otto about the imminent papal election. To their surprise he designated a German cleric, his relative Bruno, son of Otto of Carinthia, as Pope. He ascended the throne of Peter as Gregory V (996–99). Having received the imperial crown, the young ruler was ready with a second surprise. He declined to renew the *pactum* which Otto I had issued in his own name and that of his son, and would have nothing to do with the restitution of the Pentapolis, which Gregory V asked for.

[13] 967: *MGConst* I, no. 13; see M. Uhlirz, "Die italienische Kirchenpolitik der Ottonen" in *MIÖG* 48 (1934), 231 f. (with bibliography); 998: *MGConst* I, no. 23; see Uhlirz, *op. cit.* 288–92; *JbbDG: Otto III,* 276–9.

[14] F. Schneider, "Papst Johann XV. und Ottos III. Romfahrt" in *MIÖG* 39 (1923), 193–218.

But he did bring Crescentius II to trial for his acts of violence against John XV and the Romans and condemned him to exile. The Pope secured his pardon, a charity that Crescentius was to repay ill. Back in power after Otto's departure for Germany, he seems to have expelled the German Pope from Rome in the autumn of 996. It so happened that about the same time Otto III's former teacher, the Calabrian Greek John Philagathus, Bishop of Piacenza, who had gone to Byzantium to seek a bride for Otto, landed in Italy with the Byzantine envoy Leo. While Gregory V was living in Lombardy, where he held a synod at the end of January and the beginning of February 997, Crescentius, with the cooperation of the Byzantine Leo, who was staying in Rome, had Philagathus proclaimed Pope as John XVI.[15] This bold game called for fearful vengeance as soon as Otto III returned to Rome in 998. After the Castel Sant'Angelo had been taken by storm, Crescentius was beheaded there and, with twelve associates, suspended from the gallows, while John XVI, horribly mutilated by his enemies, had to endure, not only deposition by a synod, but a derisive parading through Rome, finally to be sentenced to life-long detention in a monastery.

Remaining in Rome, Otto III began in earnest the *renovatio imperii,* as he conceived it. The highly gifted ruler, just eighteen years of age, was in no sense a well rounded personality. His ascetical bent and almost fanatical piety made him welcome Odilo of Cluny as gladly as he sought out the great Italian hermits, Nilus and Romuald, and cultivate an intimate friendship with Adalbert of Prague. This friendship continued even when Adalbert, torn between the peace of the monastery and the apostolate, devoted himself to the mission to the east of Germany and in 997 suffered martyrdom in pagan Prussia. On the other hand, the young Emperor possessed an exalted consciousness of his position as ruler, aiming at universal recognition, political passion, and an enthusiasm for the *Imperium Romanum* that was nourished by his literary pursuits. Not the least influence on him was that exercised by Gerbert of Aurillac, his friend and the greatest scholar of the day.[16]

Educated in his monastery of Aurillac, then at Vich in mathematics and science, and finally at Reims, and appointed *scholasticus* of the Reims cathedral

---

[15] M. Uhlirz, *JbbDG: Otto III.,* 511–14; P. E. Schramm, *ByZ* 25 (1925), 89–105 (travel letters of the Byzantine envoy Leo), and "Kaiser, Basileus und Papst in der Zeit der Ottonen" in *HZ* 129 (1924), 424–75; on the execution of Crescentius, reported in what follows, see M. Uhlirz, *JbbDG: Otto III.,* 526–33.

[16] For Gerbert's letters, see the bibliography for this chapter (under "Sources") and P. E. Schramm, "Die Briefe Ottos III. und Gerberts aus dem Jahre 997" in *AUF* 9 (1926), 87–122; M. Uhlirz, *JbbGD: Otto III.,* 560–65 (letters and charters of Silvester II); H. Glaesener, "Les rapports du moine Gerbert avec les Ottonides et Notger de Liège" in *Revue du Nord* 31 (1949), 126–36; F. Eichengrün, *Gerbert (Silvester II.) als Persönlichkeit* (Berlin 1928); J. Leflon, *Gerbert. Humanisme et chrétienté au Xe siècle* (Saint-Wandrille 1946); O. G. Darlington, "Gerbert the Teacher" in *AHR* 52 (1947), 456–76.

school, Gerbert had made such a name for himself through an amazing mastery of all branches of the trivium and the quadrivium that in 980 he was asked by the intellectually curious Emperor Otto II to engage in a scholarly disputation at Ravenna with the learned German, Otric. In 982 he was appointed Abbot of Bobbio. Because of the impossible situation in his monastery he returned to Reims in 984 and acted as adviser of Archbishop Adalbero (969–89). When Adalbero's successor, Archbishop Arnulf, was deposed in 991, Gerbert was elected. The controversy thereby sparked, to be discussed later, brought him in 996 to Rome, where the Emperor Otto III got to know and admire him. This determined his future. When in 997 he fled from Reims, Otto III welcomed him at his court. In 998 he had him chosen as Archbishop of Ravenna and in 999, on the death of Gregory V, as Pope. Gerbert called himself Silvester II. He thereby fell in exactly with the renovation idea of his imperial friend. Set at the head of Christendom, Otto and Gerbert strove, as the new Constantine and the new Silvester, to lead the corrupt world back to its origin, to the idealized times of the first Christian Emperor and the contemporary Pope.

This cooperation occurred, it is true, in the form rather of a subordination than of an equality of the Pope. The mere fact that Otto III established his permanent abode in Rome[17] could not fail to encroach painfully on the freedom of the Roman Church. If the autonomy once aspired after by Stephen II and his successors, which had found expression in the *Constitutum Constantini,* had remained in force only to a limited degree since the imperial coronation of Charles the Great, the basic principle proclaimed in the *Constitutum,* that authority over Rome was abandoned to the Popes, and the Emperor had to reside elsewhere, had been recognized time and again in the imperial *privilegia* of the ninth and tenth centuries. But Otto III felt that he was bound neither by the *Constitutum* nor by the imperial *privilegia.* He even declared the *Constitutum* a forgery, appealing to the deceptive maneuvre of the Cardinal Deacon John, who had shown Otto I, at a time and for a purpose that can no longer be determined, a magnificent, especially prepared document of the donation as an allegedly genuine charter. And he did not hesitate to accuse the Roman Church of having bartered away the property of Saint Peter and then seeking to recoup her fortune with the Emperor's goods and rights. He bestowed not on her but on the Church of Ravenna the last three counties of the exarchate which had not so far been restored, and, spontaneously and with an express protest against any obligation of restitution, he bestowed on Saint Peter in the person of his successor, Silvester II, those eight counties which constituted the greatest part of the Pentapolis and which Gregory V

---

[17] P. E. Schramm, *Kaiser, Rom und Renovatio,* I, 105–15, II, 17–33; K. Hampe, "Otto III. und Rom" in *HZ* 140 (1929), 513–33; C. Erdmann, *Forschungen zur politischen Ideenwelt,* 92–111 (on the dignity of *patricius* and the Roman officialdom); C. Brühl, "Die Kaiserpfalz bei St. Peter und die Pfalz Ottos III. auf dem Palatin" in *QFIAB* 34 (1954), 1–30.

had demanded in vain on the basis of the *Ottonianum*. The constitutional sovereignty which Otto III vindicated in regard to the papacy, to a higher degree than had his predecessors, was not without consequences in the spiritual sphere. On occasion the Emperor participated in purely ecclesiastical discussions. On one occasion, for example, he signed, together with the *iudices* and the Pope, a judicial charter regarding the nomination to the see of Vich.[18] While he may have claimed no real jurisdiction in such cases, still there were also questions in which not only the papacy but also the *Imperium* had a substantial interest.

Thus Otto III had certainly played a decisive role in the establishing of contact with the Christian West by Poland and Hungary. Unfortunately, we are only inadequately informed about these important occurrences. In the winter of 999–1000 the Emperor undertook a pilgrimage to the tomb of his friend, the martyr Adalbert, who was buried in Gniezno. That the carefully discussed journey was intended to satisfy not merely personal devotion but at the same time expressly political and religious goals is clear especially from the devotional formula, "Servus Iesu Christi", which Otto attributed to himself in the charters issued during the journey. Assumed by the Apostles, it must probably be placed parallel to the Byzantine imperial attribute of *isapostolos*. Like the Byzantine Emperors, Otto III was claiming an apostolic mission. As a matter of fact, he brought along for the Polish Duke Boleslas a papal privilege which made Gniezno the metropolitan of a Polish territorial Church that was yet to be constituted, and thus drew Poland, in the first stages of its Christianization, into the sphere of the Roman Church. But Otto was also thinking of an expansion of his *Imperium*. Regardless whether he granted the Duke the dignity of *patricius* or intended to elevate him to royal rank but did not carry out his plan because Boleslas refused to give up Adalbert's remains, Boleslas was still presented by Otto with a replica of the holy lance, was accepted as *frater et cooperator imperii* into the rank of an ally and *feodalis imperii* and thereby was somehow incorporated into the Western *Imperium*.[19]

After Otto's return a similar decision was to be made for Hungary. In 1000 or 1001 Silvester II established the metropolitan see of Esztergom, with the right to found a Hungarian ecclesiastical province. Furthermore, the ruler, Vajk-Stephen, was honoured with the royal dignity, possibly along with the dispatch of a royal crown. To whom the last mentioned act is to be attributed from the juridical point of view — to Emperor or to Pope or to both — may continue to be controverted, but it is probably going too far to

---

[18] *Jaffé*, no. 3888; facsimile in *Pontificum Romanorum diplomata papyracea* (Rome 1929), plate X.
[19] P. E. Schramm, *Kaiser, Rom und Renovatio*, I, 135–46; M. Uhlirz, *JbbDG: Otto III.*, 310–26, 538–59 (with ample bibliography); against the thesis of Uhlirz, that Otto intended to confer the royal dignity on Boleslas see R. Wenskus in *ADipl* 1 (1955), 250–56; for Poland, see the bibliography for Chapter 31.

deny any share of the Emperor or even of the Pope.[20] And so a second country was definitely gained for the West.

Otto's plans went still farther. If the young Emperor visited the Doge of Venice, Peter II Orseolo, incognito in 1001, the real reason may probably be sought in the victorious naval expedition which had gained for Venice the rule of the Dalmatian coastal cities. Apparently Otto wanted somehow to add to his *Imperium* the growing area of Venetian domination, which pertained to Byzantium, but he did not find the Doge kindly disposed to the idea. The oldest Russian chronicle reports furthermore for 1001 about envoys of Otto who arrived in Kiev, while at the synod held at Todi at Christmas 1001 it was decided that Bruno of Querfurt should be consecrated as Archbishop in charge of the missions to the east. The consecration occurred at Rome in the autumn of 1002.

The exalted position occupied by Emperor and Pope in 1001 in the Christian West, which had now expanded eastward, reposed on a base that was much too weak. Neither the Germans nor the Romans were sympathetic with Otto's imperial ideas. In fact his eastern policy, which was supported by the imperial idea, differed considerably from his grandfather's course, which was directed to the interest of the German Kingdom, and encountered resistance in Germany, especially from the Archbishop of Magdeburg. Far more questionable, however, was the shifting of the centre of the *Imperium* to Rome. The decisive element in the *Imperium* being now the German royal power, this could be maintained only by a ruler moving about in the Empire, not by one residing in Rome. Quite as dissatisfied as the Germans were the Romans, for the presence of Otto III in Rome was incompatible with their right to relative autonomy. A conspiracy was hatched and in February 1001 Pope and Emperor were forced to leave the city. The revolt would probably have been crushed eventually, but the Emperor, calling for reinforcements, fell seriously ill and died on 24 January 1002, at the castle of Paterno near Città Castellana, at the age of twenty-two. Perhaps if he had lived longer he would have better adapted his imperial idea to the existing realities, but the *renovatio imperii* that he so eagerly pursued was a failure. The collapse of his system was also to hurt the Roman Church. The Crescentians immediately seized control again and made the Popes their creatures.

And yet the footprints of Otto III and Silvester II were not simply effaced. With the incorporation of Poland and Hungary the Roman Church had achieved a permanent gain. The prestige of the Holy See had increased, and its supranational task had been clearly stressed through the elevation of two non-Italian Popes. And even though the Emperor had sought, by exploiting the Roman Church's possibilities of universal radiation, to consolidate his

---

[20] M. Uhlirz, *JbbDG: Otto III.*, 374–76, and discussion of the problems with reference to the literature, 566–82; for Hungary cf. Chapter 31.

imperial position as "sanctarum ecclesiarum devotissimus et fidelissimus dilatator" and as "servus apostolorum", the pre-eminence of the Church was by the same token admitted by him in principle, however unintentionally. To the extent that the Christian West formed a unity at all, this rested on the *imperium spirituale et ecclesiasticum* of the Roman Church. As yet the Popes were in no position to do without an Emperor. However, as soon as they were able to use freely the power belonging to them and make it respected by the Christian peoples, the leadership of the Christian West would fall to them. Then the pontificate of Silvester II would appear in a new light: no less a person than Gregory VII reminded the Hungarians of the relationship of their first Christian King to this predecessor of his.

CHAPTER 29

The Church in Spain, Ireland, and England: 900 to 1046

So long as the states that emerged from the fragmented Carolingian *Imperium* had to fight for their existence, Spain, Ireland, and England were left, even more than before, to their own devices. Now and then, of course, there were contacts, but it was the ecclesiastical reform, only getting under way around 1050, that released the energies which were to affect also the churches on the periphery and incorporate them into Western Christendom, then in process of reconstruction.

Spain

From the time when the small Christian Kingdom of Asturias began to regard itself as the successor of the Visigothic Kingdom and the flourishing cult of Santiago at Compostela provided it with the conviction that it was under the heavenly protection of an Apostle, there had germinated the idea of the *Reconquista*. Conceived in the reign of Alfonso II (791–842) at a time of perpetual defensive against Muslim attacks, it was soon to produce its earliest fruits. The opportunity was provided by a dangerous political crisis into which the Emirate of Córdoba fell in the last quarter of the ninth century, the result of political, religious, and probably also social causes. Prominent families at Seville broke with the government at Córdoba and set up an oligarchy, which was, however, soon ruined by inner dissensions. They were not alone: revolt broke out everywhere, and as a consequence the power of the Emir Abd-Allah (888–912) was often confined to the limits of his capital. The revolt was the work especially of *Muwallad*, that is, of Spaniards who had adopted Islam. In the hill country between Roda and Málaga a purely Spanish state could be founded. Its ruler, the *Muwallad* Oma ibn Hafsun, deepened the opposition to the foreign rulers by returning to the Christian faith of his ancestors in 899.

The Asturian Christians did not let the favourable opportunity slip unexploited. Not content with sending aid to rebellious Toledo, they proceeded themselves to a frontal attack. Under the leadership of Alfonso III (866–910), they enlarged the kingdom in the west, in what became Portugal, to the Mondenego, in the centre to the Douro; in Castile, to the east, they gained so much ground that there too they reached the Douro under Alfonso's first son, García. Then King Ordoño II (914–22) was able to transfer the capital from Oviedo to León. It is probably in connection with these relatively great successes that, from this time, the imperial title appears occasionally in the historical sources for the Kings of León. But it is still disputed whether one may attribute any great significance at that period to a designation that is difficult to define, unofficial, and constitutionally irrelevant.[1]

Settlers poured into the conquered territory — Asturians and Basques and also Mozarabs, that is, Christians from al-Andalus who wished to exchange the Islamic yoke for Christian rule. Since freer economic methods could develop in the new area than in tradition-bound Galicia, it became the supporting pillar of the kingdom. Castile acquired special importance: here arose an individual and high-minded people, who were to play a decisive role in the future history of Spain.

The other districts of northern Spain that were under Christian rule also slowly acquired energy. In Navarre, already long independent, the Arista ruling family, that was related to the *Muwallad* family of the Banu Quasi, which ruled the middle Ebro valley independently and by which it was supported, was replaced in 905 by a new dynasty that was hostile to the neighbouring Muslims. And the counties of the Spanish March, rendered independent by the collapse of the Carolingian Empire, found their interest more and more in events within Spain.

The weakness of the Emirate did not continue. The government at Córdoba emerged victorious from a stubborn fight that did not end until the subjugation of Toledo in 932. Under the great ruler Abd-ar-Rahman III (912–61), who, imitating the Fatimids of Africa, even assumed the title of Caliph in 929, al-Andalus flourished and an amazing civilization developed.[2] Even though

---

[1] R. Menéndez Pidal, *El imperio hispánico y los cinco reinos* (Madrid 1950); P. E. Schramm, "Das kastilische Königtum und Kaisertum während der Reconquista (11. Jahrhundert bis 1252)" in *Festschrift für G. Ritter* (Tübingen 1950), 87–139; H. J. Hüffer, "Die mittelalterliche spanische Kaiseridee und ihre Probleme" in *Saeculum* 3 (1952), 425–43; A. Saitta, *RSIt* 66 (1954), 377–409; C. Erdmann, *Forschungen zur politischen Ideenwelt*, 31–37; H. Löwe in *HZ* 196 (1963), 552–55. In any event, for the earlier period there is hardly any question of a claim to hegemonic pre-eminence, such as later (from 1077) Alfonso VI of Castile would officially claim with the expanded title *imperator totius Hispaniae,* and Alfonso VII as *Hispaniae imperator* in 1135 would use for a short time in the sense of an imperial suzerainty.

[2] For political reasons relevant to the Fatimids and to Italy Abd ar-Rahman III in 951 offered an alliance of friendship to the German King Otto I. Impeded by expressions of religious hostility which first the Caliph and then Otto used in their letters, the negotiations seem to

the Caliph Hisham II (972–1009) was not very strong personally, there ruled in his stead the powerful viziers, Ibn Abi Amir (978–1002) and al-Musafar (1002–08). Once the Caliphate of Córdoba began to master the internal crisis, it resumed the struggle with the Christian North. In Ramiro II of León (931–50) it found a worthy opponent. But then civil wars disorganized the Kingdom of León and enabled the powerful Count of Castile, Fernán González, to gain autonomy. Hence the disunited Christian front could not stand firm when the Muslim commander of genius, the vizier Ibn Abi Amir, attacked. He quite rightly called himself al-Mansur, the victorious. León, Pamplona, Barcelona, the national shrine at Compostela itself fell into his hands and were destroyed. The Douro frontier was lost. What was left to the Christians was a ravaged territory.

This final display of Muslim power was followed by a sudden crash. After 1009 the Umayyad realm slowly broke up into numerous small principalities — the age of the wrens, the *reyes de taifas,* had arrived. The *Reconquista* received a new opportunity. As a matter of fact, Castile was able to gain back its part of the Douro frontier and even to advance a bit beyond it. But a grand-scale *Reconquista* was prevented by dissensions among the Christians. The fact that so powerful a monarch as Sancho III of Navarre proceeded to the annexation of Christian districts instead of moving against the Muslims might have made sense if his expanded dominion had remained intact, but he divided it up at his death in 1035. Besides León, whose King recovered the part that had been taken from him, and Navarre, there were now, as a consequence of the partition, two new kingdoms: the former Counties of Castile and Aragón, that had come into Sancho's possession. The balance of power was upset when Ferdinand I of Castile (1035–65) conquered León and united it with Castile in 1037. Rendered powerful by a wise administration of the two territories, Ferdinand slowly resumed the *Reconquista* from 1054, but he often preferred to accept tribute from the Muslim *taifas* instead of engaging in wars of conquest. His work was to be continued successfully by his second son, Alfonso VI (1065–1109), who, after an ill-starred division of the kingdom, managed to become sole ruler. Meanwhile, the Count of Barcelona had become the most powerful person in the Spanish March, without, however, having yet achieved the full political unification of Catalonia. He too now attacked the Muslims with a growing determination.

Entirely oriented to Spain, the idea of the *Reconquista* differed in more than one respect from the crusading idea that developed in the West in the eleventh century. Whereas the crusaders took the field against infidels of a different race, in order to expel them from the Christian lands of the East and to free

have been fruitless. The interesting but, unfortunately, incomplete report of the experiences of the monk, and later Abbot, of Gorze, John, whom Otto sent to Córdoba in 954, is in the *Vita Johannis Gorziensis,* cc. 115–136 (*MGSS* IV, 369–77); on the whole question see R. Holtzmann, *Geschichte der sächs. Kaiserzeit* (Munich, 4th ed. 1960), 969–74.

the Holy Land, the Spanish Christians and their Muslim opponents were racially distinct only in a slight degree. The *Reconquista* did not seek to expel or exterminate the Muslims; it sought rather to subjugate them and, without forcing conversion, make them serve the Christians. With reference to the Muslims Alfonso VI styled himself "Emperor of the two religions", and the crusaders, mostly French, and the Cluniac and eventually the Cistercian monks who came into the country were shocked at the liberties enjoyed by the subjected Muslims, or *Mudéjares,* in Christian Spain. On the other hand, of course, the religious motive of doctrinal conflict played a decisive role in the *Reconquista,* especially for propaganda. And yet in all this it was a question not so much of belief as such as of its concrete embodiment in Spain: by the subjugation of the Muslims people wanted to recover the Spanish mode of life as developed before the Islamic period; while entirely permeated by the Christian religion, it went beyond the sphere of the purely religious.

Wherever Christian rule was established, the Church flourished once more. Ancient extinct bishoprics were restored and new monasteries were founded. Attention was devoted to the continuity of the Church's inner life. The Spanish Church had its own, the so-called Mozarabic, liturgy, an important synodal legislation coming down from the Visigothic period, and a theological literature. The Muslim civilization, which developed so grandly in the tenth century, was transmitted especially by immigrant Mozarabs; it especially stimulated ecclesiastical learning in the branches of the quadrivium. The slow rise of the Spanish Christian civilization can be read, not least of all, in the Visigothic script, which came into use in the eighth and ninth centuries and reached its zenith in the next two centuries.

At first, of course, Christian Spain lived its own life. This isolation is the probable explanation of the fact that a synod meeting at Compostela in 959 decided to free the bishoprics of Catalonia from the archiepiscopal see of Narbonne, to which they had been subjected after the fall of the Visigothic Kingdom, and named Abbot Caesarius of Montserrat as Archbishop of Tarragona. It thus sought to restore the ancient Spanish ecclesiastical province of Tarragona, or at least the part of it that was under Christian rule; the city of Tarragona was still in Muslim hands. This measure, which in itself pertained to the Pope[3] and was in any event fruitless, was obviously to be guaranteed by the authority of the Apostle Santiago, at whose grave the synod met. Since Compostela belonged to the diocese of Iria, the Bishops of Iria bedecked themselves with the proud title: *episcopus sedis apostolicae.* In so doing they were probably thinking less of any competition with the Pope than of a pre-eminence among the bishops of Christian Spain.

Their hopes were to be destroyed when, in the eleventh century, Spain

---

[3] In 971 John XIII made Vich an archbishopric, but this measure ceased to be effective in the same year, following the murder of the new Archbishop; see P. Kehr in *AAB* 1926, no. 1, 13 ff.

emerged from its isolation. Compostela itself had contributed to this by attracting pilgrims from France, England, Germany, and Italy.[4] The influx seems to have been not inconsiderable around 950, and it grew beyond all limits in the eleventh and twelfth centuries. Furthermore, from the turn of the tenth century Cluniac monks crossed the Pyrenees and steadily gained influence in the Christian kingdoms,[5] especially in regard to Church reform, which had begun there and found expression at important reform synods.[6] Spanish Kings formed marriage alliances with princely dynasties of France, and the crusade notion, slowly awakening outside Spain, induced French knights to participate in the *Reconquista* in the second half of the eleventh century. Hence, Christian Spain was adequately prepared when Alexander II and the succeeding reform Popes sent legates to organize the Spanish Church according to Roman and Catholic principles and thereby to draw it into the great community of Western Christendom. This, of course, led to the re-establishment of the ecclesiastical provinces. Since Braga demanded its former metropolitan position, the Bishops of Iria-Compostela, to whom Pope Leo IX had refused the title of *episcopus sedis apostolicae* at the Synod of Reims in 1049, ran into difficulties: they had to be satisfied with being exempted from Braga and finally with becoming Archbishops.

Ireland

The situation of the Irish and the Anglo-Saxon Christians was fundamentally different from that of their Spanish coreligionists. Whereas, from 711 on, Islam conquered almost all of Spain in a rapid victorious march and in the following centuries yielded only a step at a time to the Christian *Reconquista,* the expansion of the Vikings, beginning in the ninth century, had a far less powerful military as well as intellectual impact. Wherever they obtained a foothold in the Christian West, the Northmen, confined to relatively small

---

[4] A. López Ferreiro, *Historia de la santa A. M. iglesia de Santiago de Compostela,* 3 vols. (Santiago 1898–1900); L. Vázquez de Parga – J. M. Lacarra – J. Uría Riu, *Las peregrinaciones a Santiago de Compostela,* 3 vols. (Madrid 1948f.); H. J. Hüffer, *Sant'Jago. Entwicklung und Bedeutung des Jakobuskultus in Spanien und dem röm.-deutschen Reich* (Munich 1957); T. O. Kendrick, *Saint James in Spain* (London 1960).

[5] G. de Valous, "Les monastères et la pénétration française en Espagne du XIe au XIIIe siècle" in *RMab* 30 (1940), 77–97; M. Defourneaux, *Les Français en Espagne aux XIe et XIIe siècles* (Paris 1949); for the earlier period, cf. C. J. Bishko, "Salvius of Albelda and Frontier Monasticism in Xth Century Navarre" in *Speculum* 23 (1948), 559–90.

[6] J. Zunzunegui, "Concilios y sínodos medievales españoles" in *HS* 1 (1948), 125–33; very important for the history of early mediaeval canon law in Spain is A. García Gallo, *El concilio de Coyanza* (Madrid 1951); J. Maldonado y Fernández del Torco, "Las relaciones entre el derecho canónico y el derecho secular en los concilios españoles del siglo XI" in *Anuario del derecho español* 14 (1942f.), 227–381.

areas, had to incorporate themselves slowly into the surrounding civilized world.

Of course, during the ninth century this was scarcely discernible in Ireland. At that time the island not only had to suffer from the general Viking danger, but also had to endure the establishing of a small kingdom at Dublin. But from 873 this caused no great concern. It was only at the beginning of the tenth century that matters became really critical. The Vikings launched new attacks and thereby inaugurated a hundred years' war (914–1014). On the entire coast extending from Liffey to Shannon there arose Norwegian colonies with the fortified towns of Dublin, Wexford, Waterford, Cork, and Limerick. Dublin was one of the busier ports of the worldwide northern trading area. Since the intruders came into closer relations with the Irish through marriages, political agreements, and cultural assimilation, the endless wars ceased to follow any clear lines. Finally two men broke the power of the foreigners: in the north the King of Meath, Mael Seachlainn, in the south the national hero, Brian Boru. The latter ruled all of Munster from 976, and in 1002 he acquired the High Kingship of Ireland, until then a monopoly of the Ui Néill family. In 1014 at the Battle of Clontarf he forever put an end to the Viking terror, but at the cost of his own life.

Although the Norwegians even after 1014 retained the small coastal Kingdom of Dublin and the cities of Waterford, Limerick, and Cork, and by no means completely gave up their national peculiarities, they still incorporated themselves into the Irish community in language, civilization, and politics. This naturally implied their total Christianization. Missionary efforts had long been made, particularly from England. The Irish Vikings were in closer connection with England from the time they conquered Cumberland, and the princely family dominant in Dublin had succeeded also in ruling the Danish Kingdom of York for a short time. King Sihtric died in 927. His son, Olaf Cuaran, was prevented by King Aethelstan of Wessex from succeeding in York. In 940 he left Dublin for England again and gained a footing there, but with varying success. During this time, in 943, he had himself baptized at the court of King Edmund of Wessex, who acted as his godfather. Although he had to seek out Dublin again the very next year, he remained true to the faith. Anglo-Saxon monks who came along with him preached the Gospel in the territory of Dublin with much success.

The contact thus established with the Anglo-Saxon Church led to closer ties, but just when is uncertain. In any event the first known Bishop of Dublin, Duncan, was consecrated and obliged to obedience by the Archbishop of Canterbury in 1028.[7] This connection of the young Church of Dublin with the see of Canterbury, first evident in 1028, fell in the reign of

---

[7] Cf. A. Gwynn, "The First Bishops of Dublin" in *Repertorium Novum*. Dublin Diocesan Historical Record 1 (1955), 1–26 (Dublin 1955 ff.).

Knut, whose extensive realm, embracing England, Denmark, and Norway, provided the English Church with unique possibilities for the evangelization of the North. Hence it was in accord with the existing situation that on the one hand the Archbishop of Canterbury should bestow his attention on the Dublin Viking state, and on the other hand the new Christians in Dublin, mindful of their Nordic origin, should prefer to have their Church established by an Anglo-Saxon metropolitan rather than by Irish abbots. What thus developed was, of course, different from that to which people in Ireland were accustomed. Organized according to the principles of Roman canon law, the Church of Dublin represented a genuine diocese, administered by diocesan priests and bishop and having clear territorial limits. An important assignment thus devolved upon it. The more the Dublin political creation expanded into an all-Irish kingdom, the more carefully was the Roman and Catholic form of its Church to be considered by the Irish reformers.

As a matter of fact, Church reform was urgent in Ireland. The Celtic monastic system had become antiquated. Many flourishing monasteries and monastic libraries had been reduced to ruins by the Vikings. The brutalization of spirits, a consequence of the ceaseless struggle, likewise fostered a movement of secularization, which had begun independently of the Viking peril. It was connected with the increasingly wealthy holdings of the monasteries, which must have enticed especially the founding families. For these possessed the right of having one of their members elected as abbot. In the event that they could not produce a qualified candidate, the law provided for the electing of another monk, but the founding families gradually expanded their privileged position into a real hereditary right. Unconcerned about the qualities required by the high office of abbot, they installed in their monasteries one of their members. He did not have to be a monk, and it actually came about that by far the greater number of monasteries were ruled by lay abbots. This development affected the very heart of the Irish Church, for the entire care of souls had become the province of the monasteries. Monks exercised priestly functions in a defined area belonging to the monastery; bishop-monks officiated at ordinations and consecrations; and ecclesiastical jurisdiction was in the hands of the abbots. Since the abbot did not necessarily have to be a bishop, and very often was not, all authority, including ecclesiastical jurisdiction, now belonged to numerous lay abbots, most of them probably married. Celtic family law had stifled canon law and created a situation that could hardly be tolerated any longer.[8]

The founding of the Church of Dublin must be seen against this background. The advantages which the diocesan and parochial organization there set up offered in comparison with the now problematic Celtic monastic

[8] Cf. the unprinted dissertation of J. G. Sheehy, *The Proprietary Church in Pre-Norman Ireland* (Rome, Univ. Greg. 1951).

system were not to be overlooked. Since the only too firmly consolidated right of the laity did not give hopes of a reform of the monastic constitution, the Church of Dublin seemed to point out the only possible remedy. Not merely receptive Irishmen, but also the Archbishops of Canterbury were interested in a reform; these last hoped in this way to be able to extend their metropolitan and primatial authority to all of Ireland. Once the Gregorian Reform was encouraged in England more powerfully than earlier by William the Conqueror, the Archbishops of Canterbury, Lanfranc and Anselm, sought to introduce it also on the neighbouring island. Though their exertions were ineffectual, a native Irish reform movement got under way. Making progress only laboriously, it was presented with a new situation by the Anglo-Norman invasion of 1172, which violently closed the "Celtic" period of Irish history. Unjustly as the conquerors at first dealt with the Irish Church, they forced it to incorporate itself definitively into the Universal Church.

Since the daughter Church of Scotland was organized according to the same Celtic monastic system, it knew the same portentous development. However, it had the good fortune to find a reform-minded Queen in the Anglo-Saxon Princess Margaret, who had fled to Scotland after the Battle of Hastings (1066) and there married King Malcolm III. It was due to her energetic efforts and those of her sons that Scotland exchanged the outdated Irish-Scottish ecclesiastical organization for the Roman.

England

Under the concentrated attacks of the Vikings in the second half of the ninth century, Anglo-Saxon England had far more to suffer than did Ireland. Without the heroic struggle of Alfred the Great, King of Wessex-Sussex-Kent (871–99), the whole country would probably have fallen to the conquerors, mostly Danes. But there continued to be a Viking Zone, known as the Danelaw because of the Danish law there prevailing, under Guthrum of East Anglia and Halfdan of Northumbria, and an Anglo-Saxon area claimed by Alfred; the frontier ran right through Essex and Mercia. But Alfred had not merely saved southern England; he had also united it more efficiently by strengthening the power of the state and by awakening a genuine national spirit. Sustained by these forces, his descendants in the tenth century were able to gain back what had been lost and to construct a strong single Anglo-Saxon Kingdom.[9]

The reconquest began under his son, Edward the Elder (899–924).

[9] On the Anglo-Saxon state, see R. H. Hodgkin, *A History of the Anglo-Saxons,* 2 vols. (Oxford, 3rd ed. 1952); F. M. Stenton, *Anglo-Saxon England* (Oxford, 2nd ed. 1947).

Danish rule was pushed back to the mouth of the Humber, and hence to Northumbria. In 927, on the death of Sihtric of Dublin, Alfred's grandson, Aethelstan (824–39), acquired the Kingdom of York. His authority, now expanding through Northumbria, was endangered when a nephew of Sihtric, Olaf Guthrithson, crossed over from Ireland and was supported by the Scots, the Britons of Strathclyde, and the Danes of Cumberland and North-umbria, but Aethelstan's victory at Brunanburh in 937 crushed the resistance. There were still other attempts to render all or part of Northumbria inde-pendent, but they had no lasting success and from 954 they ceased completely. Thus King Edgar (959–75) was able to complete in peace the work of his predecessors — the inner organization of the Anglo-Saxon state.

We must pass over what had been accomplished since Alfred for the government, the administration of justice, and the constitution. Growing consistently stronger, the kingdom, even in the first half of the tenth century, gained a position of hegemony *vis-à-vis* the other peoples living on the island. This found significant expression in the title *imperator totius Britanniae,* which the royal chancery not infrequently used in this or a variant form for the charters of its rulers from the time of Aethelstan.[10] The Dynasty of Wessex was so highly esteemed on the continent that politically important family ties were formed. Count Baldwin II of Flanders married a daughter of Alfred the Great; King Charles the Simple of France, a daughter of Edward the Elder. Aethelstan gave one of his sisters in marriage to Duke Hugh of Neustria, another to King Otto the Great. The son of Charles the Simple, Louis IV d'Outremer, lived at the English court from early childhood until his elevation to the French throne.

The Vikings who attacked England were pagans. If they preferred to direct their attacks against churches and monasteries, this was not merely for the sake of the treasures accumulated there, but also because of a hatred for Christianity. King Edmund of East Anglia had to pay for his loyalty to his faith by a cruel martyrdom in 870. But the blessing which, from the days of Alfred the Great, obviously rested on the military and political enterprises of the Anglo-Saxons made the Vikings reflect that the God of the Christians proved to be the greater bringer of prosperity and peace. Guthrum of East Anglia, whom Alfred forced to make peace, became a Christian, but just how many of his fellow Danes imitated him in this cannot be determined. But during the tenth century Christianity made progress irresistibly in the Danelaw; it merely needed time. As already mentioned, Olaf Cuaran, who had been baptized in England, was accompanied back to Dublin by Anglo-Saxon missionaries, who began to preach there. When Haakon the Good or Olaf Tryggvason crossed from England to Norway to assume the throne they

---

[10] See E. E. Stengel, "Imperator und Imperium bei den Angelsachsen" in *DA* 16 (1960), 15–72; also H. Löwe in *HZ* 196 (1963), 548–52.

took English priests along. This missionary activity in Scandinavia, originating in the initiative of Nordic rulers, will be treated in the next chapter.

The rise of the Anglo-Saxon Kingdom would hardly have prospered without the cooperation of the Church. It was for this very reason that the Kings took an interest in the reform of religious and ecclesiastical life. Mention has already been made of the exertions of Alfred the Great, which went beyond the purely religious sphere to include education in general and hence even provided for the translating of Latin works into Old English. However, the time was not yet ripe for such a grand-scale undertaking. Hence Alfred's successors sought more accessible goals: they continued the ecclesiastical legislation, had extinct dioceses restored, and made gifts to the churches.

With the betterment of ecclesiastical conditions the inner forces also began, of course, to move and to press for a reform of both monasticism and the diocesan clergy and of the care of souls. The desolate state of the monasteries — most of them had been abandoned or destroyed or had passed to the possession of more or less easy going canons — affected the Anglo-Saxon Church all the more unfavourably since it had previously been a monastic Church to a great extent. Receptive prelates, such as the Dane Oda, Archbishop of Canterbury (942–60), and Aelfheah, Bishop of Winchester (934–51), thus had high hopes of a revival of the monastic spirit. What they dreamed of was carried out by younger men whom they inspired — Aelfeah's pupils, Dunstan and Aethelwold, and Oda's nephew, Oswald. All three became monks. Dunstan ruled the monastery of Glastonbury from 942; Aethelwold, that of Abingdon from around 954; Oswald, probably in the early 950's, a monastic house of his own at Winchester, which he soon gave up. In their serious efforts for a renewal of the Benedictine way of life they encountered difficulties. The venerable Anglo-Saxon monastic tradition, which had meanwhile decayed, was in some respects out of date, and so the three young reformers obtained inspiration from the new monastic movements in France and Lotharingia. The sources of this inspiration were, on the one hand, Fleury-sur-Loire, reformed by Odo of Cluny in the 930's, and, on the other hand, Ghent, with the two monasteries of Saint Peter and Saint Bavo, which from 954 bore the clear stamp of Gorze with a strong admixture of the customs of Brogne. Dunstan eagerly studied the Lotharingian reform when he spent a period of exile lasting until 956 with the Ghent Benedictines. Oswald and Aethelwold sought a more exact knowledge of the customs introduced at Fleury, Aethelwold by sending his pupil Oscar there, whereas Oswald himself spent several years at Fleury.

Hardly had Anglo-Saxon monasticism in this way resumed contact with the monastic reform movements on the continent when its great hour struck. King Edgar, a zealous reformer, assumed the government and placed the three monks in leading positions. Dunstan first became Bishop of Worcester, then of London, and finally Archbishop of Canterbury (960–88) and chief adviser of the King. Oswald received the see of Worcester in 961 and from 971 to 992 was Archbishop of York. Aethelwold was Bishop of Winchester from 963 to 984. Monastic renewal, already begun and chiefly promoted by Glastonbury and Abingdon, now moved at full speed. Existing monasteries were reformed, new ones were founded. In an effort to provide a more secure orientation for the now flourishing monastic life, a council meeting at Winchester between 965 and 975 drew up the celebrated *Regularis Concordia,* probably at Oswald's urging. This was an *ordo monasticus,* probably formulated by Aethelwold and going into minute details. In it Dunstan and his two friends, after long consultation with bishops, abbots, and monks, took up the Lotharingian and the Cluny-Fleury reform initiatives and adapted them to Anglo-Saxon monasticism.[11]

The reform was by no means confined to the monasteries. Since originally the majority of the Anglo-Saxon sees had been connected with monasteries, it seemed natural to restore the old situation. Overzealous monk-bishops, such as Aethelwold, abruptly expelled from their cathedrals the canons who had established themselves there, while Dunstan and other Benedictine bishops sought to bring them back to a monastic mode of life or introduced monks among them, but avoided the use of force. In any event the monastic element was systematically strengthened in the English episcopate by King Edgar and Dunstan in an effort to get on with the urgently necessary reform of clergy and people. What had been prepared by Archbishop Oda of Canterbury and others was continued by Dunstan, who did all he could to put an end to clerical marriage, which had become almost the rule, and to remedy the defective education of priests and the abuses in the care of souls. Edgar seconded him by means of an extensive legislative activity that regulated both ecclesiastical and religious life, even in details. His cooperation was of course indispensable. A wholesome influence on clergy and people could, it is true, be expected from the monasteries and their schools — a hope which Aelfric, monk of Cerne, for example, sought to satisfy toward the close of the century by his masterly Anglo-Saxon version of homilies and of parts of Scripture[12] — but the King and the episcopate continued to be the real leaders of reform.

Hence it was profoundly significant that Dunstan composed his celebrated coronation *ordo* for the unusually long delayed coronation of King Edgar in 973, a rite that was to be used again and again in England, and thereby stressed the religious functions of kingship in a rich symbolism,

---

[11] *Regularis Concordiae Anglicae nationis monachorum sanctimonialiumque,* ed. T. Symons (London 1953); on the reform influences from Lotharingia and France, see K. Hallinger, *Gorze-Kluny,* II (Rome 1951), 874–91, 959–83; H. Dauphin in *RBén* 70 (1960), 177–96; E. John, *ibid.* 197–203 (denies any real influence from Lotharingia).

[12] M. M. Du Bois, *Aelfric: sermonaire, docteur et grammairien* (Paris 1943).

borrowed from Anglo-Saxon and continental customs.[13] Edgar's death two years later and the subsequent collapse of the Anglo-Saxon Dynasty could only have shaken him all the more. The family of Alfred the Great had more and more lost its vitality since the death of Aethelstan, a fact that it was only too easy to conceal during Edgar's prosperous reign. The doom now approaching did not come without warning. The egoism of the magnates, the incompetence of Aethelred II, who in 978 had taken the place of his murdered half-brother Edward, and the new Viking invasions beginning in 991 — all these so weakened the kingdom that in 1013 Aethelred fled to his brother-in-law, Duke Richard II of Normandy, while the Danish King Svein Forkbeard, who had undertaken the conquest of England, took possession of the throne (1013–14). Aethelred and his son Edmund Ironside both died in 1016, whereupon Svein's son, Knut, was able definitely to secure the throne for himself (1016–35). This mighty monarch, who also ruled Denmark from 1018 and Norway too from 1028, did not regard himself as the conqueror of England but as its lawful ruler, bound by the laws of his predecessors. Neither the magnates nor the people nor the Church — Knut was loyally attached to her — could complain.

Shrewd as it was to rule England according to its own laws, the forces which since Edgar's death were effectively undermining the state would have had to be fought more energetically. Knut's failure to do so would soon take its toll. His sons, Harold I (1035–40) and Harthacnut (1040–42), had a difficult time with the magnates. Their stern rule led on the death of Harthacnut to separation from Denmark. The English recalled Aethelred's son, Edward the Confessor, who was living in Normandy, and made him King (1042–66). The pious but scarcely qualified monarch was pretty much helpless against the higher nobility, which had become independent. The opposition grew when, following continental models, he sought to establish a central administration and as far as possible filled offices at court and in the Church with Normans or other Frenchmen. It was not very helpful that he succeeded in banishing his chief opponent, Earl Godwin of Wessex, for a short time, for the victory of the Norman faction that was thereby achieved gave a new impulse to the national opposition. Behind the national faction stood Godwin's son, Earl Harold; behind the Norman party, Duke William of Normandy. Since Edward was childless, both of these princes sought the crown. Following the King's death on 5 January 1066, Harold took it in a *coup d'état* and so brought on a war with Duke William, which was to bring England henceforth under Norman rule and thus into closer contact with the continent.

---

[13] P. E. Schramm, *Geschichte des englischen Königtums im Lichte der Krönung* (Weimar 1937), E. T.: *History of the English Coronation,* trans. by L. G. Wickham Legg (Oxford 1937); P. E. Schramm, "Die Krönung in England" in *AUF* 15 (1938), 305–91; H. G. Richardson, "The Coronation in Medieval England" in *Tr* 16 (1960), 111–202.

Edgar's death in 975 hurt the English Church even more than the state. The opponents of the monastic reform immediately raised their heads. Magnates took possession of monasteries, canons demanded the restoration of the position they had previously occupied in the cathedrals. Under Aethelred II Dunstan and his friends lost their influence at court. And so the reform that was in progress stopped half-way. While here and there it may have continued to operate quietly, as a whole it was wrecked, and the English Church to a great extent dropped back to the earlier level. Its strong dependence on the Kings and the earls led after Knut's death to serious abuses. Bishops were arbitrarily installed and deposed. Pluralism in high ecclesiastical offices and brazen simony were not rare. The state of stagnation made itself all the more conspicuous when the reform movements on the continent accelerated their rhythm from the beginning of the eleventh century and in 1049 the papacy assumed the leadership of the great reform. The English Church had fallen into a state of isolation.

Edward the Confessor had apparently sensed this and perhaps that is why he filled high Church offices with Normans and other Frenchmen. But he merely succeeded in enkindling a national English opposition to the foreign prelates. The most hated among them, Archbishop Robert of Canterbury, had to flee the country in 1052 and helplessly allow Bishop Stigand of Winchester to take his place. Naturally, the reform papacy, to which Robert appealed, could not tolerate such a violation of the law. Leo IX probably and his successors certainly sent legates to England to suspend Stigand. This disciplinary action was not without its impact on the English bishops, but Stigand himself remained defiant and even accepted the pallium from the antipope, Benedict X. The importance of this conflict is clear only if, disregarding Stigand's personal interests, the larger context is kept in mind. The closer the life of the childless Edward drew to its end, the more pressing became the choice between the two claimants to the throne, Earl Harold, chief of the national English party, and Duke William of Normandy. Stigand clearly belonged to Harold's faction. His defiant attitude could only confirm the view of the reform papacy that nothing could be expected from Harold and his adherents with regard to the renewal of the English Church. And so the future decision was prepared. In 1066 the Roman Church supported William's invasion in order to enable the continental reform to penetrate the Church in England.

CHAPTER 30

*The Spread of Christianity among the Scandinavians
in the Tenth and Eleventh Centuries*

The more the Christian West achieved inner consolidation in the course of the tenth century, the more powerfully was it able to act again on the pagan peoples living to the north and the east. It is true that missionary activity was now less systematic than it had been at the time of Charles the Great. Apart from the Ottonian mission policy, which affected the approaches to the Empire, the initiative lay to a great extent with those princes who wanted to elevate to a higher cultural, social, and political level their people, still clinging to their old gods and in general to the traditional primitive way of life. They could hardly achieve this goal without the Church's orderly structure and educational accomplishment. Moreover, their position within and without their own country was strengthened when they were accepted on equal terms into the great family of Christian rulers. In what follows, then, attention will have to be directed time and again to the political elements and their varying effects according to peoples and times.

It was probably overpopulation especially that caused the Northmen to take to their vessels in order to seek their fortune in the outside world by means of pillaging, trading, or territorial annexation. Occasionally, special causes also intervened. Thus, for example, the extension of the royal authority over all of Norway by Harold Fairhair (d. 933) and its definitive establishment in 872 motivated many of the dissatisfied to emigrate. Most of them went to Iceland, only recently discovered, others to their countrymen who had meanwhile settled the Faroes, the Hebrides, the Orkneys, and the Shetlands. Besides the migrations to foreign lands that slowly absorbed the intruders, the groups that returned should probably be regarded as connecting links in the Viking movement between the North and Christian Europe: merchants, pirates for a time, and kings' sons returning home from exile and reaching out for power.

In general, the Scandinavian expansion moved westward and eastward at the same time. What the Vikings, especially the Danes and the Norwegians, accomplished in the western sector has already been explained. A brief account of what was accomplished in the east, in particular by the Swedes, remains to be told. Gotlanders and East Swedes had established themselves in the southeast corner of the Baltic Sea as early as the seventh and eighth centuries. At the beginning of the Viking Age they penetrated into the interior of Russia, established colonies on important waterways that bound them together through routes for their ships, and opened up a regular eastern trade with the lands of the Chazar Kingdom, the Caliphate of Baghdad, and the Byzantine Empire. The Viking Rurik built up from Novgorod a state, which, after his death, probably in 873, his relative Oleg extended as far as Kiev. Despite immigration from Scandinavia, the Principality of Kiev was basically not a Swedish but an East Slavonic political creation, whose population gradually absorbed the foreigners. This process, together with the political turmoil in the Chazar and Muslim states, caused the eastern trade slowly to stagnate. For this reason, from the turn of the millennium the Swedes more and more concentrated their energies on the Baltic area.

The political development of the three Scandinavian countries can be learned only partially from the meagre sources. In the second half of the ninth century East Sweden at least must have constituted a political unity with the larger islands on its periphery. Whenever the other parts of the country were incorporated, the Swedish Kingdom was probably more or less completed by the beginning of the eleventh century. Norway had already been constructed in the ninth century by King Harold Fairhair, already mentioned, but after his death it suffered from struggles over the throne, which pitted Harold's descendants among themselves and at times also against the princely house of the Jarls of Trondheim. Denmark was in a state of weakness around 900. Thus the Swedes were able to conquer the important port of Haithabu (Schleswig) and establish a small state in South Jutland, which was extended at the expense of Germany. Connecting the Schlei with the Eider by means of a trade route, they gained an easy transit route for their North Sea trade. In 934 King Henry I restored the German March, recovered Haithabu, and forced King Gnupa to accept baptism.

But soon the Dane Gorm (d. c. 945), who ruled North Jutland, swept away the Swedish state in South Jutland.[1] The political unification of Denmark that he began was continued by his son, Harold Blue Tooth, who even succeeded in subjecting South Norway for a short time. He also took part in a Swedish civil war. His expansionist policy inaugurated a difficult period of struggle. King Eric of Sweden defeated and conquered Denmark around 988 and compelled Harold's son, Svein Forkbeard, to take up the life of a Viking. After Eric's death around 995, Svein returned home to resume his father's expansionist policy on a grand scale. Norway, defended by King Olaf Tryggvason at the cost of his own life (d. 1000), was partitioned between Svein and his ally, the Swedish King, and perhaps also the Norwegian Eric Jarl, while England was conquered by Svein on his own. His son, Knut, reached the summit of power when, to the possession of England and Denmark, he added also in 1028 the rule of Norway, which had become free in 1015.[2] But at his death in 1035 the unorganic structure fell apart. England

---

[1] H. Jankuhn, *Die Frühgeschichte Schleswig-Holsteins vom Ausgang der Völkerwanderung bis zum Ende der Wikingerzeit* (Neumünster 1955); O. Scheel, "Haithabu in der Kirchengeschichte" in *ZKG* 50 (1931), 271–314.

[2] L. M. Larson, *Canute the Great and the Rise of Danish Imperialism during the Viking Age* (New York 1912).

withdrew in 1042. In Norway Magnus, son of that King Olaf the Saint who had been expelled by Knut and had then fallen in the struggle that he resumed in 1030, seized the government in 1035 and in 1042 was even able to succeed Harthacnut in Denmark. The union of the two kingdoms induced the Swedish King Anund Jakob to support Knut's nephew, Svein Estrithson, in Denmark and Harold Hardrada, half-brother of Saint Olaf, in Norway against Magnus. After Magnus's death in 1047 both men succeeded to the royal power in their homeland. But Harold did not stay at home. Having set out for the conquest of England in 1066, he lost battle and life, and with him ended the Viking Age, characterized by so much waste. The political consolidation of Europe now forced the Scandinavians finally to complete the inner construction of their world, begun long before, and their incorporation into the great community of the Christian West.

One of the most essential presuppositions for this was the acceptance of Christianity. The missionary activity had already begun again in the tenth century; it was conducted on the one hand by German and on the other by English priests. Henry I's victorious campaign against King Gnupa of South Jutland had opened the gate to German preachers in 934. Archbishop Unni of Hamburg–Bremen went to Denmark and then, following in Anschar's footsteps, to the Swedish city of Birka, where he died in 936, but the real reconstruction only began under his successor, Archbishop Adaltag (937–88). It was at first restricted to Jutland. In the port cities of Haithabu (Schleswig), Riba, and Aarhus arose the first suffragan sees of Hamburg–Bremen around 948, the first permanent congregations in the country. The young Church, which soon numbered Danes among its priests, sent apostles to the Danish islands, to southern Scandinavia in the wake of Harold Blue Tooth's expansion, and finally to the Wagrians living in Holstein. These successes would scarcely have been possible without the protection of the Danish and the German rulers. In contrast to his decidedly pagan-minded father, Gorm, Harold Blue Tooth behaved at first in a friendly though reserved manner in regard to the mission and finally, around 960, was himself converted. To what extent his change of religion was determined by regard for Otto the Great can no longer be determined.

Otto the Great certainly favoured the spread of Christianity to Denmark for political reasons and in particular kept his protecting hand over the rising Church of Jutland, but his greater interest was centred on the broad area just outside the Empire that was inhabited by the Wends, which he aimed to open up to the Church through the two mission centres, Magdeburg and Hamburg–Bremen. It soon appeared fortunate that the Danish mission was less intimately connected with the Ottonian imperial policy. The Wendish Revolt broke out in 983, triggering a pagan reaction in Denmark also. They were promoted by Svein Forkbeard, who raised revolt against his father — Harold Blue Tooth died in flight in 985–86. But the young Danish

Church survived the blow, and when King Svein, who had been banished by Eric of Sweden, returned, he became a friend of Christianity. Under his protection and that of his son Knut the Christian religion permeated Denmark. But both monarchs had recourse chiefly to the English Church for aid. Avoiding the German mission centre, the bishops for the new sees established on the Danish islands were consecrated in England, until finally Archbishop Unwan of Hamburg–Bremen obtained the recognition of his metropolitan rights, not only from a travelling Danish bishop, but also from King Knut.

The evangelization of Norway followed a somewhat different course. There Christianity owed its victory to the Kings, and chiefly to those descendants of Harold Fairhair who lived in foreign countries, accepted Christianity there, and then, on their return home, acquired power. The first Christian King was the son of Harold Fairhair, Haakon the Good, who had been educated at the English royal court; when, following his father's death in 933, he landed in Norway to expel his half-brother, Eric Blood Axe, he brought English priests along. But neither he nor his successor, Harold Grey Fur (960–75), Eric Blood Axe's son, who came from York and had been baptized there, had any substantial missionary successes to record. The spell was first broken, with ruthlessness, by Olaf Tryggvason (995–1000), from a third branch of the royal house. His work was completed, at least to a degree, by Saint Olaf (1015–28; d. 1030).[3] The compulsion resorted to by the two Olafs was in great part politically oriented. When the rising kingship wiped out the cult of Asen and Vanen, it struck at the deepest roots of the resistance of the leagues of kinships and *things,* which clung to their old laws. Of course, merely an external change had been achieved by compulsory baptism. The real acceptance of the Christian faith, as this had been realized, at least partially, in the peaceful Danish and German missionary work in the southern districts of Norway, did not yet take place in the greatest part of the country. Though the miraculous phenomena occurring at the grave of Saint Olaf deeply impressed the Norwegians, the cult of Olaf, zealously fostered by King Magnus, promoted the magical belief in the King's healing power rather than the Christian religion. In both Norway itself and in Iceland, where the conversion had taken place in 1000, not without concessions to paganism,[4] there was needed an activity that would deepen the understanding

[3] A. Wolf, *Olav Tryggvason und die Christianisierung des Nordens* (Innsbruck 1959); C. Riederer, *Saint Olaf* (Avignon 1930); O. Kolsrud, "Nidaros og Stiklestad" in *Norwegia Sacra,* X (Oslo 1937).

[4] On the Christianization of Iceland, cf. E. Krenn in *NZM* 4 (1948), 241–51; on the concept of power in the reports of conversions, E. Krenn in *ZRGG* 7 (1955), 127–42; Saint Olaf did away with concessions to paganism. Christianity from the time of Olaf Tryggvason was also able to penetrate the islands around Scotland that were occupied by Norwegians. It was brought by Icelanders to Greenland, which was colonized from the end of the tenth century, and from there it probably reached the Viking colonies which must have existed in North

of the new religion while organizing it. Such a work was actually undertaken, chiefly by English priests. Immigration from England increased even in the second half of the eleventh century, since the Norman ecclesiastical policy of William the Conqueror disenchanted many Anglo-Saxon clerics with their homeland. English canon law, English architecture and manners came to Norway with them. Still, since the days of Saint Olaf there persisted a loose connection with the archbishopric of Hamburg–Bremen.

Paganism held out the longest in Sweden. Archbishop Unni's visit to Birka was a mere episode. Only the Christianization of Denmark and Norway, along with that of Russia and Poland, and Sweden's more active participation in the power struggles in the Baltic area created a more favourable situation. Danish, German, English, and probably even Russian apostles followed different routes. Under Olaf the Tax King (995–c. 1022), who was baptized around 1008, Christianity spread especially in West and East Gotland, and around 1014 the first Swedish bishopric was established at Skara. Olaf's son, Anund Jakob (d. 1050), worked in the same spirit. Although not a few of the succeeding Kings favoured Christianity, still a pagan resistance flared up again and again and could not be broken until toward the end of the eleventh century.

The more the Danish Church flourished in the eleventh century — it counted nine bishoprics around 1060 — the more urgent became the desire for an archbishopric of its own. Archbishop Adalbert of Hamburg–Bremen (1043–72), important and highly meritorious for his missionary work, received from Pope Leo IX in 1053 the title of Papal Legate and Vicar for the North. He did not actually reject the plans of the Danish King Svein Estrithson in regard to a Danish archbishop, but wanted to secure for his church the higher position of a primatial or patriarchal see. In the march of romantic and nationalistic interpretations of history the importance of this plan is often overestimated and, in addition, it is probably not presented entirely to the point.[5] Adalbert took it along to his grave. The future belonged to fully autonomous Scandinavian provinces. Denmark began with the archbishopric of Lund in 1104; Norway followed with that of Nidaros–Trondheim in 1152; Sweden obtained that of Uppsala in 1164.

America from the first decades of the eleventh into the fourteenth century. On the discovery of Greenland, cf. R. Hennig, *Terrae incognitae*, II (Leiden 1937), 253–8; on the discovery of America, *ibid.*, 262–67, 277–95. See R. A. Skelton, Thomas E. Marston, and George D. Painter, *The Vinland Map and the Tartar Relation* (New Haven–London 1965).

[5] H. Fuhrmann, "Studien zur Geschichte mittelalterlicher Patriarchate III" in *ZSavRGkan* 72 (1955), 120–70, 177f. (with more bibliography), shows that Adalbert probably held the pseudo-Isidorean view of Patriarch-primate. His intention of gaining twelve bishoprics by dividing the diocese probably had a connection with the plan for a patriarchate only in so far as he intended to create for the archiepiscopal see of Hamburg–Bremen a system of suffragans, "which, after the withdrawal of the Danish territories, would do justice to the strict requirements of canon law" (ibid. 177).

CHAPTER 31

Evangelization of the Slavs and the Magyars
in the Tenth and Eleventh Centuries

The extensive area settled by the Slavs, extending from the Dnieper to the
Elbe and the Saale and comprising Bohemia, Moravia, parts of the Danube
basin and the Balkan peninsula, had been affected by missionary work in the
ninth century only in the southeast and as far as Moravia and Bohemia.
Just as among the Scandinavians, so here too the much reviled *saeculum
obscurum* brought the decisive turning point. Broad sections of the Slavonic
East opened themselves up to Christianity and from then on grew into the
European cultural community of the Latin West or of the Byzantine-Slavonic
East. The by no means uniform process requires a separate treatment accord-
ing to countries and peoples.

The Wends

As the immediate neighbour of the Slavs, Germany acquired a special
political and religious task, to be fulfilled in its own interest as well as in that
of the West. The first Kings of the Saxon Dynasty were of course concerned
to provide better protection especially for their Saxon homeland from the
nearby Wends. To this end Charles the Great had already created a zone of
tributary dependence beyond the Elbe. Since it had disappeared in the ninth
century, Henry I restored it by means of several campaigns. Otto the Great
had a more ambitious aim: all the Wends living between the Elbe, the Saale,
and the Oder were to be subjugated. He succeeded somewhat in the case of
the Hevellians, Sprevanes, and Lebusans and in that of the Sorbs, while he
did not really touch the Liutizians (or Wilzi) in the Peene district and merely
exacted tribute from the Obodrites bordering them to the west.

Otto sought to permeate the subjugated areas not only politically by means
of establishing marches and burgwards but also ecclesiastically. Thus as early
as 948 the sees of Brandenburg and Havelberg were founded, while in 968
there followed in the Sorb territory those of Meissen, Merseburg, and Zeitz, the
last named being transferred to Naumburg in 1030. For the Wagrians and
the Obodrites it was possible to establish the see of Oldenburg, probably
in 968; from that date, in any event, it was subject to the archbishopric of
Hamburg–Bremen, whose sphere of activity accordingly embraced not only
the Scandinavians but also the Wends living farthest to the west. The other
dioceses just mentioned were subject to the archbishopric of Magdeburg.
Pope Agapitus II had already around 955 agreed to Otto's plan of transforming
the monastery of Saint Maurice that he had founded at Magdeburg in 937 into
a metropolitan see in charge of the mission to the Slavs; John XII had done

likewise in a charter drawn up soon after the imperial coronation. But the plan encountered sharp resistance, first of all from Otto's son, Archbishop William of Mainz, with whom the Emperor must have come to terms to some extent in 962, and then from Bishop Bernard of Halberstadt. But in 967 John XIII at the Synod of Ravenna definitively ordered the establishing of the metropolitan see; the death of both adversaries made it possible to carry out the decree in 968. On this occasion the new archbishopric was provided with rich honorary privileges for its clerics and with the primatial rank of honour among all churches to the right of the Rhine. Just how far the area of its jurisdiction was to extend to the northeast was apparently not determined precisely. In any event bulls of John XIII and Benedict VII (981), in enumerating the suffragan sees, do not mention the diocese of Poznań, founded around 968 in what was then the capital of the Duke of the Poles. It is true that Magdeburg then made good its claims to Poznań, but lost the see forever after the death of the second Bishop of Poznań, Unger, a German.[1]

The missionary work was too closely connected with political goals to be able to win the approval of the Wends. Hence when the Liutizians set in motion the great revolt of 983, the ecclesiastical work accomplished beyond the Elbe entirely collapsed along with the dioceses of Havelberg, Brandenburg, and Oldenburg. It held out in the Sorb territory and could be continued. The mission also continued among the Obodrites, who had taken part in the revolt, but in 1018 it was interrupted for a year and in 1066 for the most part wiped out by the still existing pagan reaction. The Liutizians remained unrelenting opponents; their league had included the tribes on the Havel and in Prignitz, probably loosely, during the revolt.[2] Since the Liutizians had no tribal prince of their own, they could long cling to their pluralistic organization in a league and to their polytheistic religion. Into the twelfth century this area was as good as closed to the mission.

Quite different was the course of events in Bohemia, Poland, and the Kievan state, for there large-scale political creations came into existence, whose rulers, for reasons of domestic and foreign politics, favoured Christianity either from the outset or at least in the course of time.

---

[1] Latest critical summary in W. Schlesinger, *Kirchengeschichte Sachsens*, I, 21–32; K. Uhlirz, *Geschichte des Erzbistums Magdeburg* (Magdeburg 1887); P. Kehr, "Das Erzbistum Magdeburg und die erste Organisation der christlichen Kirche in Polen" in *AAB* (1920), no. 1; G. Sappok, *Die Anfänge des Bistums Posen und die Reihe seiner Bischöfe 968–1498* (Leipzig 1937); A. Brackmann, *Magdeburg als Hauptstadt des Ostens im frühen Mittelalter* (Leipzig 1937); cf. also id., *Gesammelte Aufsätze* (Weimar 1941), 140–53, 154–87, 188–210; on the older papal charters for Magdeburg and the question of Poznań, cf. H. Beumann – W. Schlesinger in *ADipl* 1 (1955), 163–207; good bibliography on the beginnings of German-Polish relations in M. Uhlirz, *JbbDG: Otto III.*, 549f.

[2] W. Brüske, *Untersuchungen zur Geschichte des Lutizenbundes* (Cologne–Graz 1955); W. H. Fritze, "Beobachtungen zu Entstehung und Wesen des Lutizenbundes" in *Jb. für Geschichte Mittel- und Ost-Deutschlands* 7 (1958), 1–38.

Thanks to the work done in the ninth century, Bohemia and Moravia were no longer mission lands in the strict sense, but the tenth century brought a new situation in so far as the destruction of Greater Moravia by the Magyars shifted the initiative in both Church and state to Bohemia. Solely because of the Magyar peril, the Bohemian princes, of whom the Přemyslids exercised the ducal power in the western,[3] the Slavnikings in the eastern part of the country, regarded it as advisable to rely on Germany and in this way to achieve full incorporation into the Western Christian civilization. Though they were first in contact with Bavaria, their Dukes were bound to the German crown by Henry I and Otto the Great, a dependence that in no sense prevented their extending their rule over Moravia and Slovakia, over Silesia and the remnant of Chrobatia around Cracow and hence re-establishing in a sense the destroyed Greater Moravian state. The large and to a great extent already Christian territory, hitherto cared for chiefly by the Bishops of Regensburg, now needed a Church organization.

The ninth-century missionary work, carried on by the Bavarian Church and by the Apostles of the Slavs, Cyril and Methodius, has already been discussed. Here and there pagan resistance may still have been encountered in Bohemia at the beginning of the tenth century. This resistance or a broader dissatisfaction, not connected merely with pagan opposition, but aroused by the all too friendly attitude toward the Church displayed by the young Přemyslid Duke Wenceslas, who was under the influence of his grandmother Ludmilla, perhaps contributed to the assassination, first of Ludmilla in 921, then of Wenceslas in 929. Both were very soon honoured as martyrs and saints by the Czechs. But the real reasons for these acts of violence are to be sought in personal and political tensions existing between Wenceslas and an opposition rallying around his mother Drahomira and his brother Boleslas.[4] In any case, the next Přemyslid Dukes, Boleslas I (d. 972) and his son, Boleslas II (d. 999), adhered firmly to Christianity and even contributed to its consolidation.

The Church could be all the more intimately connected with the country since the two liturgies that had been introduced there lived side by side in peace instead of in their earlier rivalry, even though the Latin rite did firmly push back the Slavonic rite, especially in Bohemia. Instead there were other problems to solve. The Bohemian Dukes entertained the understandable desire for a diocese of their own, directly dependent on Rome. If Pope John XIII actually was asked in 966 for the establishment of autonomous churches

---

[3] W. Wostry, "Die Ursprünge der Primisliden" in *Prager Festschrift für Th. Mayer* (Feilassing–Salzburg 1953), 156–253.

[4] F. Dvornik, *S. Wenceslas, Duke of Bohemia* (Prague 1929); J. Pekař, *Die Wenzels- und Ludmilla-legenden und die Echtheit Christians* (Prague 1906); also *Wattenbach-Holtzmann* I, 321f.

by the Bohemians as well as by the Polish Duke, Otto the Great would have effectively frustrated at least the Bohemian plans. To him, the political overlord, it was obvious from the start that the Bohemian sees that were to be founded should be incorporated into a German ecclesiastical province, either Magdeburg or Mainz. Salzburg was not considered, since the Ottos wanted as far as possible to eliminate any Bavarian influence on Bohemia, which had been cared for ecclesiastically by Regensburg up to now and unchallenged. And so the see of Prague, definitively established in 976, was placed under the archbishopric of Mainz;[5] in this way probably Mainz was to be indemnified for its exclusion from the Wend mission territory. Moravia also obtained a bishop at that time, but probably he had no fixed see as yet, and his position was soon abolished at the request of the second Bishop of Prague, the Slavniking Voytech-Adalbert.

Among the Bishops of Prague this Adalbert deserves special consideration.[6] Political tensions, originating in Poland's expansionist policy, between his brother, the Slavniking Duke Sobleslas and the Přemyslid Boleslas II forced him to leave Prague. Following his pious inclinations, he entered the Roman monastery of Sant' Alessio. Recalled to Prague in 992, he encountered failure again after three years, for the same political reasons. While his family was almost wiped out by Boleslas II and forever deprived of authority, he worked as a missionary, first at the court of young Stephan of Hungary and then, after rather long journeying and a brief stay with the Polish Duke, among the pagan Prussians, only to suffer martyrdom there in 997. Adalbert was by no means the only one who carried the Christian religion from Bohemia to the neighbouring peoples. Before and after him Czech or German and other missionaries who had reached Bohemia went to the surrounding pagan lands. Their work was especially fruitful in Poland.

Poland

In the time of Otto the Great Poland, under the Piast Prince Mieszko I (d. 992), emerged from a past that eludes our grasp into the light of history. Mieszko's considerable power, based on cavalry and castles, quickly spread.[7] It is true that the Duke was forced to pay Otto the Great an annual tribute for his territory as far as the Warthe and to promise personal fealty, but he remained

---

[5] On Henry IV's charter (*MGDD* VI, 2, no. 390), H. Beumann – W. Schlesinger in *ADipl* 1 (1955), 236–50.

[6] H. G. Voigt, *Adalbert von Prag* (Berlin 1898); J. Loserth, "Der Sturz des Hauses Slavnik" in *Abhandlungen für österreichische Geschichte* 65 (1895).

[7] H. Ludat, *Die Anfänge des polnischen Staates* (Cracow 1942); A. Gieysztor, *Die Entstehung des polnischen Staates im Lichte neuer Forschungen* (Marburg 1956); Z. Wojciechowski, *Mieszko and the Rise of the Polish State* (London 1936); M. Hellmann, *Slavisches Herrschertum*, 260–62. There are no convincing proofs for Mieszko's descent from a Viking family.

essentially independent. After the death of Otto II he extended his rule over Pomerania as far as the mouth of the Oder, where the important commercial city of Wollin fell into his hands, subjugated the tribes living in old Chrobatia, and took from Bohemia Silesia and the area around Cracow. His son and successor, Boleslas Chrobry (992–1025), obtained Lower and Upper Lusatia in fief from Henry II, and, appealed to by the Bohemians against their brutal Duke Boleslas III, had himself proclaimed Duke at Prague in 1003. Since he refused to perform the feudal homage that he owed the German King for Bohemia, there broke out a war which lasted, with frequent interruptions, till 1018, and in which Henry II even made use of pagan allies, the Liutizians. Boleslas Chrobry had to relinquish Bohemia, but he retained the two Lusatias, Moravia, and Slovakia. Proceeding to Kiev in 1018, he was able to annex Red Russia also. Having reached the height of his fame, he had himself crowned King shortly before his death in 1025.

Under his son, Mieszko II (1025–34), there ensued a sudden collapse. Red Russia was recovered by Kiev, Moravia by Bohemia, the Lusatias by Germany, while the Hungarians took possession of Slovakia, which they retained until 1918. After the death of Mieszko II Pomerania detached itself from Poland. Bretislas I of Bohemia (1034–55) occupied Silesia and devastated Poland as far as Gniezno (1038), but he had to abandon his plan of conquest, since the Germans restored Duke Casimir, son of Mieszko II, to his country; in 1052 Bretislas was forced to cede Silesia to Poland, which, it is true, had to pay an annual tribute. Casimir transferred his residence from Gniezno, destroyed in 1038, to Cracow; as a consequence Poland acquired an orientation that was rather toward Kiev and Hungary.

The amazingly fast rise of the Polish state was accompanied by an equally spectacular series of baptisms. The impressive missionary success is in great measure to be attributed to the circumstance that, following the marriage in 965 of Duke Mieszko I with Dobrawa, daughter of the Přemyslid Duke Boleslas I, preachers came especially from neighbouring Slavonic Bohemia. What an important influence the Czechs actually exerted on the Polish Church then coming into existence appears on the one hand from linguistic studies and on the other from the Slavonic rite, which, alongside the Latin rite, came from Moravia and Bohemia especially into southern Poland.[8] Mieszko had himself baptized as early as 966. Soon, in 968 at the earliest, the first Polish bishopric was established in what was then his residence, Poznań, probably without any direct participation by the archiepiscopal see of Magdeburg and perhaps at first even without any dependence on it as a suffragan. In any event, Mieszko I entered into such close contact with the papacy that around 990 he presented his realm to Saint Peter for better protection against Ger-

---

[8] B. Stasiewski, "Zur Verbreitung des slavischen Ritus in Südpolen während des 10. Jahrhunderts" in *Forschungen zur osteuropäischen Geschichte* 7 (1959), 7–25.

many and Bohemia.[9] Behind this gesture was, of course, the aim of gaining Rome to the idea of a Polish ecclesiastical province. We know virtually nothing of the negotiations. But Mieszko's son, Boleslas Chrobry, must have pushed them more energetically just before the turn of the millennium.

He had reasons for his hurry. Archbishop Giseler of Magdeburg was exerting himself to extend his province throughout Poland, by claiming Poznań as a suffragan see and having the Silesian district as far as the Oder, that was under Polish rule, included in his suffragan see of Meissen by Otto III in 995. Boleslas Chrobry seems to have been successful with Gregory V in frustrating Magdeburg's plans at Rome and in carrying his own desire.[10] Since Otto III was also eventually won over, the actual decrees were probably drawn up in 999. By virtue of the papal charter of 1000, which Otto brought along on his pilgrimage to Gniezno, already described, Poland obtained its own ecclesiastical organization, with the metropolitan see of Gniezno, then the ducal residence, and the suffragan sees of Cracow, Wroclaw, and Kolberg, founded at the same time. Before long the diocese of Poznań would also be added. As remote as Otto III's imperial idea was from reality in many respects, as little as its universal characteristic was in accord with the purely Polish oriented efforts of Boleslas Chrobry, at Gniezno it displayed a surpassing farsightedness. The powerful push eastward, to be observed from the time of Mieszko, could have induced a Poland, disillusioned with the Christian West, to seek ecclesiastical and cultural incorporation into Eastern Christianity, which was under the guidance of Byzantium. Pope and Emperor met this danger just in time. Not too much, of course, was accomplished by the founding of bishoprics. Christianity still needed a long time to affect the peoples united in the Polish state not merely by the act of baptism but also inwardly. Unfortunately, we know little about this process. However, in the chaotic years 1034–40 the Polish Church was to experience painfully that paganism was still holding out stubbornly. And even in the second half of the eleventh century much still had to be done to complete its organization.

Russia

The Principality of Kiev or of the "Ros" (in Greek *Rhosia*)[11] owed its origin to the Vikings, or Varangians, and more precisely to the Varangian family of

---

[9] The charter, handed down in Deusdedit, *Collectio canonum*, III, 199 (ed. Wolf von Glanvell, p. 359), is very much controverted; cf. W. Leitsch, "Deusdedit und die Urkunde 'Dagone iudex'" in *Studien für ältere Geschichte Osteuropas* 2 (Graz 1959), 166–85 (with further bibliography).

[10] See W. Schlesinger, *Kirchengeschichte Sachsens*, I, 71–73; for Otto III at Gniezno, see *supra*, Chapter 28, footnote 19.

[11] The origin of the name "Ros" is disputed. It is derived from: 1) the Iranian Ruxs, who very early migrated to South Russia (this is still maintained by Vernadsky); 2) a Slavonic

Rurik. Centring, north to south, on the trade route from the Gulf of Finland and Lake Ladoga to the Black Sea, the principality embraced, with its two political centres, Novgorod and Kiev, an area which extended westward, except for the Baltic coast, as far as the western Bug, the San, and the Carpathians, and was bounded on the east by the Volga Bulgars, while in the steppe to the southeast and the south, especially exposed to nomads' attacks, the expansion differed, depending on the time. The Prince of Kiev, Sviatoslav (964–72), already had extraordinarily great power at his disposal. He destroyed the Chazar Kingdom in 969, attacked the Volga Bulgars and plundered their capital, and then, at first in an understanding with Byzantium, fell upon the Danube Bulgars. He even transferred his capital to Bulgaria until he was expelled by the Byzantines.

Under his son and grandson, Vladimir I (978–1015) and Jaroslav the Wise (1036–54), both of whom succeeded only after many struggles in becoming sole ruler, the state was consolidated by means of better defence against the Patzinaks, who were definitively routed in 1036, and by inner political measures. Vladimir introduced Christianity; Jaroslav promoted artistic and literary endeavours and displayed an important legislative activity. After his death the state disintegrated into individual principalities ruled by his sons and made progressively smaller by further divisions among heirs. But the house of Rurik somehow managed, despite ceaseless provocations, to hold together under its head, the Grand Prince of Kiev. When in 1139 Kiev lost its special position for good, a new phase of Russian history began.

At the time when the Russian state was founded, the East Slavonic subjects, like their Scandinavian rulers, were still pagans, even though the Gospel had already been announced to them here and there. A first concrete report of missionary successes comes from the Byzantine Patriarch Photius in 867, but we are not informed about the outcome.[12] Certainly there was a Christian church in Kiev in 944, but it does not have to be traced back absolutely, or at least not exclusively, to Byzantine priests. When Prince Igor died a year

---

form of the Finnish "Ruotsi", which is said to contain an Old Swedish linguistic root and to have denoted the immigrating Vikings (held by many scholars outside the Soviet Union); 3) the word "rod", originating in the common Slavonic language, meaning family, kinship, descent, and not correctly understood because of its manifold sense. This last is the view of the Soviet historian, B. D. Grekov, *Kievskaja Rus'* (Moscow 1949), cited by M. Hellmann, *Slavisches Herrschertum*, 248, footnote 15. Hellmann, for his part, would prefer to understand the word in the sense of "rule of the princes, as a body, of the house of the Scandinavian Varangians" (ibid. 264). This philological controversy is only one question in the discussion, now 200 years old, on the role of the Varangians in the forming of the Kievan state. See the bibliographical data in Hellmann, *op. cit.* 264, footnote 40.

[12] M. de Taube, *Rome et la Russie avant l'invasion des Tartares, I: Le prince Askold, les origines de l'état de Kiev et la première concession des Russes 856–882* (Paris 1947); G. von Rauch, "Frühe christliche Spuren in Russland" in *Saeculum* 7 (1956), 40–67.

later, the Princess Olga took over the government for her son Sviatoslav, still a minor. She was baptized either at Constantinople in 957 or at Kiev earlier. In any event there is reason to believe that after her return from Byzantium she asked Otto the Great for missionaries in 959–60. Apart from purely political reasons, this step was due to the fact that there were already long existing relations between the West and the Christian community of Kiev. Otto, of course, did not let slip the promising opportunity, but the bishop whom he sent, Adalbert, a monk of Sankt Maximin at Trier, consecrated at Mainz, had to leave Kiev after a brief stay (961–62); in 968 he became the first Archbishop of Magdeburg. Olga's influence had not sufficed to overcome the pagan opposition; furthermore, her son, who was devoted to paganism, now took charge of the government. For a while yet the Russian Christians had to get along without the aid of the ruling dynasty. However, the political relations of the Grand Princes with Christian rulers of the West and the East may have provided them with a certain support.[13] Jaropolk I, who in 973 sent envoys to Otto I, even received messengers of Pope Benedict VII in 977.

As the Russian state assumed a more stable shape after the adventurous conquering expeditions of Sviatoslav, the more clearly appeared the advantages connected with admission into the Christian community of nations. The decision was actually forced upon the Grand Prince Vladimir, when, as payment for military aid, he demanded from the Byzantine Emperors Basil II and Constantine VIII their sister, the Porphyrogenneta Anna, as his wife. After some difficulties he got his way, but in return he had to be baptized (988–89). Now, for his part, he was solicitous for the baptism of his people.[14]

So began the Russian Church. Who actually constructed it is still a matter of controversy.[15] Probably both Western and Byzantine and Slavonic missionaries took part. In fact, certain characteristics, such as the law of the tithe and a knowledge of the Bohemian Saints Ludmilla and Wenceslas and of Saint Vitus, the patron of Prague, clearly point to the West.[16] But the Byzantine-Slavonic element prevailed from the start. Since the Russians did not know Greek, the Greek Christian intellectual heritage reached them on the one hand by means of the Slavonic liturgy, going back to Cyril and Methodius, which was still in use, in Bohemia and Moravia to some extent, and especially in Bulgaria, where it had been elaborated, and on the other

---

[13] F. Dvornik, "The Kiev State and its Relation with Western Europe" in *Transactions of the Royal Historical Society,* series IV, 29 (1947), 27–46.

[14] N. de Baumgarten, *S. Vladimir et la conversion de la Russie* (Rome 1932); N. Zernov, "Vladimir and the Origin of the Russian Church" in *Slavon. and East Europ. Rev.* 28 (1949f.), 123–38, 425–28.

[15] On the much discussed question cf. G. Stökl, *Slavenmission,* E 85, with copious and critically classified bibliography in footnotes 8–16 on pp. 86f.

[16] H. F. Schmid, "Byzantinisches Zehntwesen" in *JÖByzG* 6 (1957), 45–110; F. Dvornik, "Die Benediktiner und die Christianisierung Russlands" in *BM* 35 (1959), 292–310.

hand by means of Slavonic translations of Greek works, made in Bulgaria and before long in Russia itself.

The beginnings of the ecclesiastical organization are obscure and disputed.[17] Although the few attested priests and bishops, occasionally called archbishops, must have been more closely connected with the Byzantine Church, relations with the Roman Western Church were not lacking. Vladimir and Popes John XV and Silvester II, for example, exchanged envoys. For the ecclesiastical hierarchy then coming into existence there was as yet no question of whether it should attach itself to Constantinople or to Rome. And even though the first certain Metropolitan of Kiev, the Greek Theotemptos, attended a synod at Constantinople in 1040 and thereby acknowledged himself to be a member of the Byzantine Church, some of his immediate successors time and again displayed a certain openness toward Rome and Western Christendom, especially since at that time the Grand Princes of Kiev, related by marriage with western ruling houses, were not inaccessible to Latin and Western influences.[18] Nevertheless, the ecclesiastical dependence on the Patriarch of Constantinople, already existing under Theotemptos, could hardly have been annulled now. The Schism beginning in 1054, but made final only after decades, excluded any further rivalry between East and West: with no formal break, but irresistibly, the Russian Church separated itself from Rome.

The Yugoslavs

The South Slavs of the Balkan peninsula became Christians without any official evangelization. Situated between the Eastern and the Western Churches, the Serbs, after a rather long wavering, decided for the Byzantine Slavonic sphere.[19] What especially attracted them there was the form of the Slavonic national Church, as it had been found in Bulgaria, due to the efforts of the disciples of Methodius, expelled from Moravia in 885, and further developed during the brilliant reign of the Tsar Simeon (893–927). The Croats of Dalmatia, on the other hand, whose Prince Branimir had made himself politically independent with the aid of the papacy around 880, belonged to the sphere of the Latin Church. The conversion of the Slovenes has already been treated. This work, which had made pretty good progress, collapsed under the Magyar storm, only to start over again after about a century, and not merely in the districts reconquered by Bavaria and protected by marches and colonization, but in Hungarian territory too. In the German

[17] Cf. G. Stökl, *Slavenmission*, E 86f., footnotes 10–12.
[18] N. de Baumgarten, *Généalogies et mariages occidentaux des Rurikides russes du X\u1d49 au XIII\u1d49 siècle*, 2 numbers (Rome 1927, 1934).
[19] A. Schmaus, "Zur Frage der Kultorientierung der Serben im Mittelalter" in *Südostforschungen* 15 (1956), 149–201.

part the archbishopric of Salzburg and the bishoprics of Freising and Passau interested themselves in the building of the Church.

The Magyars

When in 895–6 the Magyar tribes, under the leadership of Prince Arpad, crossed the Carpathians in order to occupy the Danube-Theiss plain and the entire Carpathian valley, what had taken place under the Huns and the Avars seemed to be repeating itself: a people from the steppe of eastern Europe moved into the most vulnerable spot in Central Europe. The foreigners came from the area between the Volga and the Don, where they had earlier been under Chazar and before that under Onugur Bulgar rule and where they had developed the unique Magyar character. Belonging to the Ugrian tribes, to the then southernmost branch of the great Finno-Ugric family of peoples, they had entered into relationships of blood and at the same time of way of life with their masters, so that they constituted a people of Finno-Ugric speech but of Bulgar-Turkish culture. Under pressure from the Patzinaks, they had slowly moved westward until they found a new home on the middle Danube. One can speak only with qualification of real settlement, however. Their nomadic way of life impelled them to plundering raids on neighbouring lands.[20]

Only after more than a half-century was a stop put to their frightfully destructive hordes from two sides. The growing strength of the German Kingdom, demonstrated by Otto the Great in the overwhelming victory on the Lechfeld in 955, barred them from the West. And in the East, where the Magyars directed their attacks against Constantinople, the Russian state altered the situation. It cut off the connection which the Magyars had maintained with their former home, especially with the Magyar tribes that had moved eastward. When, in addition, Sviatoslav of Kiev annihilated the Chazar Kingdom in 969, he deprived the Magyars of the Chazar market, on which they had unloaded their booty. Hence they had only the alternative of sharing the fate of earlier mounted pastoral peoples and perishing or of finding a way of life that allowed them, while approximating the surrounding civilization, to retain their identity. That they succeeded in choosing the second alternative was due to the Arpad Geza (d. 997) and to his great son, Vajk-Stephen (d. 1038).

Following Arpad's death in 907, political power had devolved upon many individual princes. Geza paved the way for undivided rule when, as Attila once did, he almost wiped out the clan of Arpad and accumulated so considerable a power that Vajk-Stephen was able to complete the work by

[20] R. Lüttich, *Ungarnzüge in Europa im 10. Jahrhundert* (Berlin 1910); G. Fasoli, *Le incursioni ungare in Europa nel secolo X* (Florence 1945).

definitively subjugating South Hungary and Transylvania. Stephen's political creation, which organically combined the Magyar individuality with German, Latin, and Slavonic elements, cannot be treated here, but the process of Christianization, now begun, does concern us. That Geza fostered it and Vajk-Stephen systematically pursued it was a necessity, for only thus could the Hungarian rulers free their people from their isolation.

Overtures for evangelization came from the Bulgar-Byzantine as well as from the Latin side. As early as about 950 the "Gyula" of Transylvania had been baptized,[21] but Geza's and Stephen's area of authority had its centre of gravity in Pannonia and hence was oriented to the Latin West. Thus Geza and Vajk-Stephen got German knights, colonists, and missionaries to pour into the country.[22] The marriage of Vajk-Stephen with Gisela, daughter of the Duke of Bavaria, perhaps the direct occasion of his baptism,[23] further strengthened the tie with the West. Under Geza Bishop Pilgrim of Passau (d. 991) had devoted himself with special zeal to the Hungarian mission, and with it he had connected a plan to gain for his see metropolitan authority over Hungary and Moravia. Although he even forged papal documents, which made Passau appear as the legitimate heir of the Roman bishopric of Lorch an der Enns, falsely turned into an archbishopric by Pilgrim, he could not carry his private designs.[24] Stephen, who made the Christianization of Hungary his life's work, naturally desired his own ecclesiastical province. He had the good fortune to find full sympathy in the Emperor Otto III and Pope Silvester II. The decision was made in 1000 or 1001: Stephen himself was honoured by Pope and Emperor with the royal dignity, and Esztergom was established as the ecclesiastical metropolis,[25] to which Stephen added a group of suffragan sees in 1009. But already around 1006 he had the archbishopric of Kalocza set up beside it for the eastern part of Hungary. And he probably handed over his country to Saint Peter, as Mieszko of Poland had done.

In this way the Magyars had made contact with the Christian community

[21] F. Dölger, *Ungarn in der byzantinischen Reichspolitik* (Leipzig 1942); G. Moravcsik, "Die byzantinische Kultur und das mittelalterliche Ungarn" in *SAB* (1955), no. 4; id., "The Role of the Byzantine Church in Medieval Hungary" in *The American Slavic and East European Review* 6 (1947), 134–51; E. von Ivánka, "Griechische Kirche und griechisches Mönchtum im mittelalterlichen Ungarn" in *OrChrP* 8 (1942), 183–94; B. Fehér, *Bulgarisch-ungarische Beziehungen in den 5.–11. Jahrhunderten* (Budapest 1921).

[22] K. Schünemann, *Die Deutschen in Ungarn bis zum 12. Jahrhundert* (Berlin–Leipzig 1923).

[23] On the question of Stephen's baptism, with sources and literature, cf. M. Uhlirz, *JbbDG: Otto III.*, 503–10.

[24] On the Passau charters of Otto III, cf. M. Uhlirz, *op. cit.* 471–7; footnotes 11 f. on page 477 for the bibliography on the forgeries; also H. Fichtenau, "Zu den Fälschungen Pilgrims von Passau" in *Festgabe A. Hoffmann* (Graz 1964), 8–100.

[25] M. Uhlirz, "Die Weihe des Aschericus zum Erzbischof ad Sobottin" in *JbbDG: Otto III.*, 566–71.

of peoples of the West. Stephen, venerated as a saint since the last decades of the eleventh century, energetically accomplished the Christianization of Hungary. His laws enjoined the building of churches, the sanctification of Sundays and holy days, and fasting and regulated ecclesiastical jurisdiction. There is question here, to be sure, of an initiative which was at first still rejected by large groups of the Hungarian people. The pent up bitterness against the Christian religion, against the foreigners brought into the country, and against the new form of government in general, was to break out in fearful uprisings after Stephen's death in 1038. Since his only son, Emmeric, had died in 1031, Stephen had designated as his successor the son of the banished Doge of Venice, Peter Orseolo, but he soon had to flee to Henry III of Germany. After a victorious struggle with the rebels, Henry put him back on the throne, but the feudal homage that Peter had to do to the German King so provoked the Hungarians that they not only overthrew the King in 1046 and eventually cruelly murdered him but in general they turned violently on everything that had been constructed since the days of Geza and Stephen. The Church was severely hurt by this frenzied outbreak of resentment; among the victims was Stephen's important assistant, Bishop Gerard.[26] Just the same, Stephen's work did not disappear. Andrew I (1046–61), scion of the line going back to Geza's brother, had fled from Stephen to Kiev and had become the son-in-law of Jaroslav the Great. He now gained the Hungarian crown and continued Stephen's policies, even forbidding the exercise of the pagan religion on pain of death. Bela I (1061–63) so thoroughly put down the last manifestation of the pagan reaction that thereafter the danger was non-existent. The Hungarian Church flourished under King Saint Ladislas (1077–95) and King Koloman (1095–1116) and at the beginning of the twelfth century came into contact with the Gregorian Reform.

The bewilderingly varied picture afforded by the Christianization of the individual countries in the North and the East acquires unity as soon as one observes the relations of these peoples to one another. To a great extent these came about by means of the northeast trade, which not merely connected Scandinavia and the Baltic area with the Chazar Kingdom and with the Muslim and Byzantine lands, but also extended to Bohemia, with Prague as the international market, to Moravia, to Poland, and to Hungary. The economic progress thus facilitated, the establishing of personal relations

---

[26] *Vitae S. Gerardi ep. Chanadensis* in *SS rerum Hung.*, II, 461–506; on the dating of the "Legenda maior" (ibid. 480–506), cf. E. Pásztor in *BIStIAM* 73 (1962), 113–40. Perhaps Gerard, a Venetian and tutor of Stephen's son Emmeric, was the author of the *Libellus de institutione morum* in *SS rerum Hung.*, II, 611 ff., a sort of mirror for princes. The hagiographical literature, which originated toward the close of the eleventh century, is connected with Gregory VII's instruction (c. 1083) to venerate the relics of all who took part in the conversion of Pannonia; cf. E. Pásztor, *loc. cit.* 113f.

transcending commerce, and other circumstances caused the peoples to advance beyond their old primitive cultural level and enabled their princes to seek new roads. Also important were ties of blood. Scandinavian princes expelled from their homeland could stay in Kiev, just as, conversely, Vladimir had found refuge from his brother Jaropolk in Sweden. And when Jaroslav of Kiev placed troops at the disposal of his son-in-law Andrew, who was returning to Hungary, he was acting from a sentiment of kinship, which was taken for granted by the young Eastern peoples and was often enough effective politically.

All these connections substantially promoted the missionary work. Bruno of Querfurt went as a preacher of the faith to Hungary, then after a short stay in Kiev to the Patzinaks, next stayed with Boleslas Chrobry in Poland, sent missionaries from there to Sweden, and died as a martyr in Prussia.[27] His life must have indicated to what extent the missionary movement was fundamentally a whole. Wherever the messengers of the Gospel worked and from whatever lands they came, they somehow worked hand in hand, even without knowing it. Of course, the favourable situation, as such, would have meant little, if it had not been made use of in the heroic efforts of so many apostles of the faith and in the far-seeing policy of the papacy and of Otto III. Western Christendom now spread beyond its Carolingian frontiers to that varied community of peoples which was to determine its future history.

CHAPTER 32

The Papacy and the Empire from 1002 to 1046

After the death of Otto III the situation both at Rome and in the Lombard Kingdom gradually reverted to what it had been before the days of the Ottos: domination by the nobles at Rome, and an Italian kingship handed over to the Margrave Arduin of Ivrea. In Germany too there were not lacking efforts to transfer the government to other hands, but the last scion of the Saxon Dynasty, going back in the direct male line to Henry I, Duke Henry of Bavaria, was able to enforce his claim and, as King Henry II (1002–24), to strengthen the Empire again by recourse to the sound principles of Otto I. Not Rome and the universal *Imperium* were regarded by him as the foundation of his throne, but rather the royal authority in Germany, in Italy, and

---

[27] H. G. Voigt, *Bruno von Querfurt* (Stuttgart 1907); R. Wenskus, *Studien zur historisch-politischen Gedankenwelt Bruns von Querfurt* (Münster–Cologne 1956); H. D. Kahl, "Compellere intrare. Die Wendenpolitik Brunos von Querfurt im Lichte hochmittelalterlichen Missions- und Völkerrechts" in *Zeitschrift für Ostforschungen*, 4 (1955), 161–93, interprets Bruno's celebrated encouragement to the war, not as a war against pagans in the sense of forced conversion, but as a war against apostate Christians.

eventually in Burgundy. The crown of Burgundy was only to devolve upon his successor, Conrad II, in 1033, but this was prepared for the German kingship by Henry II through an agreement on the inheritance with his uncle, King Rudolf III of Burgundy, and by the assumption of feudal suzerainty. Since the royal power in Italy was really quite limited, as the elevation of Arduin showed, and the Burgundian kingship promised little increase of real power, though it did assure the Alpine passes, Germany remained the essential basis. Henry II built it up solidly, especially by having recourse to the Church.

The Ottonian State Church, as the essential prop of the kingship, has already been discussed, but until the reign of Henry II there were really only rudimentary stages in constructing it. He was the first to develop it logically and to connect it to a system. As none of his blood relatives before him, he monopolized the nomination to episcopal sees and forced upon the electors candidates he designated, chosen mostly from the royal chapel, so that there was very little of that free assent which constitutes the essence of the *electio canonica*. On several occasions he convoked synods or intervened in ecclesiastical matters. Episcopal sees were subjected to the additional burden of hospitality, which Henry claimed to a greater degree than had been the earlier practice, for himself and his court on his ceaseless journeys.

The royal monasteries had to put up with more serious interference, for in their regard the King was acting as the lord of proprietary churches. Abbots were deposed or installed without regard for the right of election of the communities concerned, and Henry disposed of the monastic property as of any other goods of the Empire. He assigned abbeys or parts of their property to other churches, usually to cathedrals; all monasteries had to pay fixed dues, the *servitium regale,* and even the enfeoffment of secular vassals with monastic property was at times ordered. In these measures the personally pious monarch was motivated not solely by the material interest of the Empire but by a genuine desire for reform. A monastic reform movement had begun long before in Lotharingia and had radiated into the interior of Germany. Influenced by it, Henry II sent at first South German and Bavarian and later Lotharingian reform monks, of the Gorze and Saint-Vannes schools, as abbots to not a few royal monasteries. The friendship which the Ottos had cultivated with the great monastic personages of their day became under Henry II a co-operation in the top echelon in Germany. Behind this religious and political activity there stood, of course, the early mediaeval theocratic idea of kingship. Under Henry II and then under Henry III it experienced an exaltation that was to have a decisive effect on the reform of the Church.

His attention claimed by inner and outside struggles, Henry II left it to Duke Otto of Carinthia to go to Italy and attack Arduin of Ivrea. Only Otto's ill luck caused him to cross the Alps himself and to proclaim his taking possession of the Lombard Kingdom by being solemnly crowned at Pavia.

Since Arduin had retired without fighting to a powerful castle, he was undefeated but his rival kingship was based on such a weak foundation that it posed no serious danger for Henry. At the moment Henry was not yet in a position to think of a journey to Rome and the obtaining of the imperial crown. The son of Crescentius, John, who conducted the city government under the proud title of *patricius,* must have heartily welcomed this temporary waiver. His rule was so well established that after the death of Otto III he could allow Pope Silvester II to return to Rome and quietly await his death. The succeeding Popes, John XVII (1003), John XVIII (1003–09), and Sergius IV (1009–12), were, understandably, once again Romans by birth. They lacked the time for displaying an activity of any importance, and also the basis which the bond with the imperial office had afforded.[1]

The restored rule of the nobility at Rome led of necessity to rivalries among the families. As a matter of fact, power was wrested from the Crescentians by the comital house of Tusculum, which went back in the female line, through the sister of Marozia, to the house of Theophylact. The occasion was provided by the virtually simultaneous deaths of Sergius IV and the *Patricius* John on 12 and 18 May 1012. The Counts of Tusculum thereupon had their brother Theophylact acclaimed as Pope Benedict VIII, whereas the Crescentians chose a certain Gregory.[2] Defeated in the ensuing struggle, Gregory went to Germany. Henry II promised to make an investigation as soon as he should go to Rome, but then he recognized Benedict VIII. Whether or not Gregory experienced this decision, we hear nothing further of him. The victory of the Tusculans was complete. For decades now they ruled Rome and the *Patrimonium* as a sort of hereditary principality. Unlike Alberic they based their power, not on that of a *princeps,* but on that of the Pope; a member of the family assumed it each time and then assigned the most important secular functions to his brothers. Since other noble families, including the Crescentians, were given a share in the administration, there were no disturbances.

The Tusculans were smart enough not to oppose in principle the *Imperium* that had been restored in 962. And so, after preliminary negotiations, Henry II was able to receive the imperial anointing and coronation at Saint Peter's on 14 February 1014. Just how he and Benedict VIII then defined their respective competence is not known. It is probably to be attributed chiefly to the Pope that the imperial *privilegium* of Otto I was not renewed at that

---

[1] Of some significance is an encyclical of Sergius IV in *Jaffé* 3972 (regarded as spurious), *PL* 139, 1498; in it knights are invited to travel to Syria on Italian vessels in order to avenge in blood the destruction of the Holy Sepulchre at Jerusalem by the Caliph Hakim as well as to re-establish the Church there. P. Kehr, *Ital. Pont.,* VI, 2, p. 322, no. 1, and C. Erdmann, in *QFIAB* 23 (1931f.), regard the letter as authentic; A. Gieysztor, "The Encyclica of Sergius IV" in *Mediaevalia et Humanistica* 5 (1948), 3–23; 6 (1950), 3–34, would seem to have shown that it is a forgery which appeared at the monastery of Saint-Pierre de Moissac, not far from Toulouse, in 1096, a year after Urban II's call for the crusade.

[2] H. Zimmermann, "Papstabsetzungen des Mittelalters" in *MIÖG* 59 (1961), 280–84.

time. The rights of sovereignty there assigned to the Emperor may have been annoying to Benedict VIII. But on the other hand, Henry II did not renounce every right in Rome. The judicial sessions which he held during his brief stay show this, and it is probably not an accident that the title *patricius,* usurped by the Crescentian John, no longer appeared officially among the Tusculans. Basically, however, Henry II, Conrad II, and Henry III allowed a completely free hand to the Tusculans, who ruled until 1045. And the right of approval, which Otto I had acquired for papal elections and which his successors had augmented to a right of designation, apparently played no role in the elevation of John XIX and in that of Benedict IX, both of them falling in the time of Conrad II. The spirit of a really independent Rome was expressed in the *Graphia aureae urbis Romae,* the archeological and political work, written around 1030, of an unknown adherent of the Tusculans, probably a layman but in any event a scholar, who sought to recall to memory the glory of the ancient Roman Empire and, in Schramm's words, "to take the government of the city out of the hands of the Emperor and transfer it to those of a deputy, of a Roman *patricius*".[3]

Without disturbing each other, Henry II and Benedict VIII pursued their goals. Both on his journey to Rome and later Henry sought to tighten his control of the Lombard Kingdom. Since in Lombardy and in Central Italy he had especially favoured ecclesiastics, after his return to Germany there occurred a revolt of the secular princes, which drew Arduin of Ivrea from his lair and had him assume leadership. But Boniface of Canossa, in alliance with the loyal bishops, so thoroughly defeated the rebels that Arduin finally renounced his shadowy kingship for good in 1014 and entered the monastery of Fruttuaria, dying in 1015. But Henry had little power in Italy. He strengthened it by beginning systematically to fill the episcopal sees with Germans, first of all in the metropolitan provinces of Aquileia and Ravenna.

It cannot be determined whether Benedict VIII came to the papacy from the clerical or the lay state. But no matter: his ability quickly brought him prestige and influence. It is true that his interests were chiefly in politics and administration. After he had crushed the early opposition of the Crescentians and other families with the aid of his brothers, things in the *Patrimonium* could be put in some kind of order. But his glance went beyond the *Patrimonium.* The Muslims were causing anxiety in the Tyrrhenian Sea. Pisa was plundered in 1004 and 1011, and in 1015 Spanish Muslims under the Emir Mogehid conquered Sardinia. When in 1016 they destroyed the old maritime city of Luni from there, Benedict VIII intervened. Pisan, Genoese, and papal troops boarded ships, defeated the Muslims in a sea battle, and freed Sardinia. The Pope, moreover, paid close attention to the revolts which broke out against Byzantine rule in 1009 at Bari and elsewhere. Put to flight in 1011,

[3] P. E. Schramm, *Kaiser, Rom und Renovatio,* I, 193–217, II, 34–44, 68–111 (text edition).

the leaders of the revolt, Melo and his brother-in-law Dattus, not only obtained support from Benedict, who put Norman knights at their disposal,[4] but also from the South Italian Lombard princes, and hence in 1017 Melo was able to conquer northern Apulia. The victory of the Catapan Basil Bojoannes near Cannae in 1018 brought a turning point: the Byzantines advanced into Lombard territory and threatened Rome. Melo and, soon after, Benedict himself thus went to see Henry II in order to ask help. At Easter of 1020 Pope and Emperor took counsel at Bamberg in regard to their common tasks. On this occasion the Pope received from Henry an imperial *privilegium*,[5] which reproduced the *Ottonianum* word for word and added a few gifts, and also the promise to go to Italy. Melo was enfeoffed with Apulia, but he died at Bamberg. His brother-in-law, who had stayed in Italy, was captured and killed by the Byzantines.

Henry II finally set out for Italy in the autumn of 1021, and in the following year moved directly south in three army columns. He managed to take the Byzantine frontier fortress of Troia, though it was soon lost again, captured Pandulf of Capua, who had gone over to the Byzantines, and again attached Waimar of Salerno to the Empire, but in comparison with the cost this was a meagre success. The Pope had to be content that at least the progress of the Byzantines came to a stop.

Of greater importance was the reform synod which the Pope and the Emperor held at Pavia in March 1022 before the campaign. The Ottos had earlier exerted themselves to protect ecclesiastical and monastic property from expropriation, and in 1014 Henry II had returned to the subject at the Synod of Ravenna, arranged by him together with Benedict, by commanding the churches to draw up an inventory of their property. A Roman Synod immediately after the imperial coronation, whose decrees are unknown, may have discussed similar questions. But at Pavia in 1022 more radical decrees were prepared, at the urging of the Pope. They insisted strictly on the ancient requirement of celibacy for the subdiaconate and higher orders, a law that had to a great extent fallen into oblivion, and decreed that the sons of unfree ecclesiastics should remain in the father's condition. Involved here was not the inner reform of the Church but the preservation of Church property, which all too easily devolved by means of clerical marriage on the children. But, once formulated, the decrees were to gain momentum as the desire for inner reform grew strong.

Neither Pope nor Emperor was permitted to do much more. Benedict VIII died in April 1024, Henry II three months later. The good memory which people in Germany retained in regard to the Emperor, notwithstanding isolated reproaches, for example because of his alliance with the pagan

---

[4] See E. Joranson, "The Inception of the Career of the Normans in Italy" in *Speculum* 23 (1948), 353–96.

[5] *MGDD*, III, *Dipl. Heinrichs II.*, 427 (*MGConst* I, 65, no. 33).

Liutizians against the Poles, was enhanced into a cult by the zealous cooperation of the episcopal see of Bamberg, founded by him and charged with tending his grave, so that in 1146 Eugene III undertook his canonization. While this exaltation was based less on authentic historical than on idealizing and legendary tradition, it concerned a man who had taken seriously the Christian ideal of a king of his day.[6]

Benedict VIII was succeeded by his brother, the Tusculan John XIX (1024–32); the childless Henry II, by the founder of the Salian Dynasty, Conrad II (1024–39). There is little enough to say about John. Coming directly from the lay state, made Pope for the sake of his family's position of power, he apparently never achieved an inner relationship to his high office. Conrad II, on the other hand, showed himself to be equal to the task entrusted to him. Henry II's constructive work was now to produce its real fruits. In 1027 Conrad received the imperial crown at Rome in the presence of King Knut of England and Denmark and of King Rudolf III of Burgundy. It acquired greater importance through the gaining of the Burgundian Kingdom in 1033 and the consolidation of the imperial power in Italy. While the Emperor contented himself in South Italy with the homage of the Lombard princes and only perforce, during a second journey to Italy, deprived the rebel Pandulf of the rule of Capua, transferring it to Waimar of Salerno, he acted more vigorously in both Lombardy and Tuscany. But, differing from Henry II, he did not chiefly favour the spiritual princes at the expense of the secular. In fact in 1037 he especially singled out the lesser vassals among the secular nobles, the so-called *vavassores,* and because of them came into conflict with the Lombard bishops, above all with Archbishop Aribert of Milan.

In accord with some unfavourable sources from the eleventh century, some writers like to represent Conrad as a merely worldly-minded power-politician, without any feeling for the spiritual tasks of the Church. This picture probably needs correcting. Though less devout than Henry II, the first Salian substantially maintained the ecclesiastical policy of his predecessor, on the one hand promoting the Lotharingian monastic reform, on the other hand bringing to a completion the constructing of a German State Church. His effort to place the Church as much as possible at the service of the Empire caused him, as Henry II earlier, to require a money payment in the filling of wealthy episcopal sees. This was not a sale-purchase of the churches concerned and hence it was not really simony. Rather it was an effort, legally possible in the feudal structure, to connect the investiture with the paying of a *servitium regale.* To be sure, the more the religious conscience became refined in the course of the reform movement, the more sharply it reacted against this practice, so that soon Conrad II was listed among the simonists. The

[6] R. Klauser, *Der Heinrichs- und Kunigundenkult im mittelalterlichen Bamberg* (Bamberg 1957); P. Pfaff, *Kaiser Heinrich II. Sein Nachleben und sein Kult in Basel* (Basel–Stuttgart 1963).

change becoming evident in the standard of values was the expression of a deep-seated turning point: the West was preparing to enter upon a new phase in its development. The Church reform movements were among the most important progressive forces. If the German monarch intended to maintain his leading position, he had to remain in vital contact with them. Conrad II probably lacked the true instinct for this, but such was not the case with his young son and successor, Henry III. Taking up the reform on his own, Henry was to release a movement heavy with consequences.

Few early mediaeval rulers were so convinced of the sublimity of the theocratic kingship and of the heavy burdens connected with it as was Henry III (1039–56). His very exertions in the first years of his reign for a general peace in the Empire revealed this. While in France the Church rather than the then quite feeble crown fought against private warfare and developed the idea of the Peace of God, Henry III made use of the religious demands for peace in complete consistency. Guided by a correct understanding that justice must be united with mercy and pardon if genuine Christian peace is to prevail, he did not rest content with a mere peace edict. At the Synod of Constance of 1043 he proclaimed pardon to all his enemies from the ambo or the altar of the cathedral and urged those present to do the same. He made a like declaration at Trier. In 1044 he won a victory over Hungarian rebels, adherents of the usurper Aba, thereby enabling Stephen's lawful successor, Peter Orseolo, to recover the throne for a short time. Henry caused this triumph to end up, on the very battlefield of Menfö, as an impressive celebration, combining thanksgiving, penance, and general pardon. All this had nothing to do with weakness. Secular princes sensed the aim of a ruler intent on the constant extension of the royal power. And when Henry did not approve the canonically controvertible deposition of Archbishop Aribert of Milan, as decreed by his father, and made peace with Aribert, he stood forth in the sight of the bishops with all the authority of the theocratic ruler. In fact, he invested them no longer with the staff alone but also with the ring, the symbol of the spiritual marriage between the bishop and his church.

His monastic policy was his own. Whereas Henry II liked to subject abbeys to bishops, Henry III was so favourable to monastic efforts for liberty that he withdrew a group of monasteries from the power of their episcopal or noble proprietors and took them under his direct protection. Of course, this protection also meant domination, but the domination of the supreme religious and political power, which was to assure the monasteries of freedom, for to mediaeval man freedom meant also the state of subjection and service, ultimately to God, and so Henry could designate the subjection of the abbeys under his obedience as their freedom.[7] Much as this protectorate aimed at

[7] On Henry III's concept of liberty, see G. Ladner, *Theologie und Politik*, 63–70; on the mediaeval idea of liberty as such, see G. Tellenbach, *Libertas*, 2–33, 48–76 *(passim)*. H. Grundmann, "Freiheit als religiöses, politisches und persönliches Postulat im Mittelalter" in *HZ*

making financial sources of aid accessible to the imperial authority, its real and more fundamental goal consisted for Henry III in the maintaining and furthering of monastic discipline. Not in vain were Henry and his second wife, Agnes of Poitou, who as the daughter of William V of Aquitaine came from a house closely linked with Cluny, in intimate contact with the leaders of the monastic reform, the Cluniacs, the Lotharingians, and the hermits of Central Italy; Abbot Hugh of Cluny was even the godfather at the baptism of the heir to the throne, the future Henry IV, in 1051. The deep effect produced on the King by the reform ideas of the time appears especially in his renunciation of the fees which not a few kings or princes of his day did not hesitate to demand of bishops or abbots who were to be invested. He regarded them as simony. Certain happenings in Rome soon gave him the opportunity to enforce even outside Germany his strict views, fashioned in the spirit of the reformers.

John XIX was succeeded by his nephew Theophylact, who became Benedict IX (1032–45). Although the reports concerning his having assumed the papacy at the quite uncanonical age of twelve and concerning his wicked life must have been at least greatly exaggerated, still Benedict did not measure up to the papacy as Christendom in its restless religious state was expecting. But his spiritual inadequacies had less to do with his downfall than did movements within Rome against the Tusculan domination. An uprising in September 1044 compelled the Pope to flee. He was replaced, but probably not until January 1045, by the Bishop of Sabina, Silvester III, who was supported by a collateral branch of the Crescentians. After a few months Benedict was able to drive him out again, but he found in Rome so dangerous a situation that he was prepared to abdicate in the event that someone would reimburse him for the money that he had distributed to make sure his own election. What ensued is, unfortunately, very obscure. Probably Benedict discussed the financial settlement with a rather small group of men who were on friendly terms with him and apparently respectable, including his godfather, the pious Archpriest John Gratian of San Giovanni a Porta Latina, and, before or after his official abdication, received the hard cash from the hands of the Jewish Christian Baruch, called Benedict after his conversion.[8] Then John Gratian was made Pope under the name of Gregory VI (1045–6). He encountered no resistance in reform circles, if Peter Damiani, Prior of Fonte Avellana, may act as an example. On the contrary, he found

---

183 (1957), 23–53, attacks a specifically mediaeval idea of liberty, but his polemic is not wholly convincing.

[8] On the question of the relationship of Baruch-Benedict with Gregory VI on the one hand and with Gregory VII on the other, cf. G. B. Picotti, *AstIt* 100 (1942), 2–44 (with bibliography); id., *ADRomana* 69 (1946), 117–130, with the subsequent reply of R. Morghen; *Haller* II, 573f., 578–80; G. Marchetti-Longhi in *StudGreg* II, 287–333; good critical summary in P. E. Schramm, *GGA* 207 (1953), 67–70.

enthusiastic assent, which, it is true, cooled off or, as in the case of Peter Damiani, became the very opposite, once the story of the money transaction leaked out.

At first Henry III also recognized Gregory VI. When he crossed the Alps in the autumn of 1046, he was probably motivated only by the intention of visiting the pacified Lombard Kingdom and of receiving the imperial crown at Rome. Regardless whether he learned the details of Gregory's elevation before or during his journey, they led him to decide upon a radical intervention. The Synod of Pavia, held in the autumn under his presidency, must already have prepared for what was to come by a general prohibition of simony.[9] Subsequently, Henry met Gregory VI at Piacenza, but we are not informed about the discussions that took place there. In any event, on 20 December a synod met at Sutri, near Rome, to sit in judgment on the three claimants, notwithstanding the fact that Benedict IX and Silvester III had long before retired. Silvester III and Gregory VI were deposed at Sutri; three days later Benedict IX was deposed at a Roman Synod. At Henry's suggestion Bishop Suitger of Bamberg was then elected. Enthroned on Christmas 1046 under the name Clement II, the new Pope conferred the imperial anointing and coronation on Henry III and Queen Agnes.

These happenings have occupied scholars to our own day. A chief subject of controversy is the deposition of Gregory VI. That Gregory or his friends paid money would seem to have been established, despite Fliche,[10] and even the important reasons that are adduced, for example by Borino and Poole, to exclude a sale-purchase or similar simoniacal intrigues do not solve the problem: much as they may exonerate Gregory VI personally, they do not therefore put his judges in the wrong. Aversion to simony had now so increased that in the filling of an ecclesiastical office any mention of money was interpreted simoniacally, as has been noted in regard to Conrad II. As a matter of fact, all the reports, even the virtually contemporary sources, accept the fact of simony in the case of Gregory VI. Wherever criticism was expressed, it was aimed at the deposition by the unqualified Henry III — thus the unknown, probably French author of *De ordinando pontifice* — or it insisted on the Pope's immunity from judgment — thus Bishop Wazo of Liège.[11] Perhaps Gregory VI even acknowledged his own guilt and resigned his office, but in regard to the latter the renunciation was probably not made without pressure and hence it must have hardly differed from a deposition.

[9] See G. Tellenbach, *Libertas,* 210–12.

[10] A. Fliche, *La réforme grégorienne,* I (Louvain–Paris 1924), 107f.; refutation of this thesis by D. Freymans in *Revue belge de phil. et hist.* 11 (1932), 130–37; Amann in *Fliche-Martin* VII, 92–95, is also influenced by the highly unfavourable picture which Fliche draws of Henry III in *op. cit.,* I, 104–113, despite the allowances he makes.

[11] *De ordinando pontifice* in *MGLiblit* I, 8–14; for Wazo, see *Gesta episcoporum Leodiensium* II, 65, *MGSS,* VII, 228f; on both authors cf. also *infra,* Chapter 41.

But what may Henry III, the real actor in all this, have aimed at by the deposition? It would make little sense to present individually the various interpretations,[12] which are not always free from indignation, but it would be good from the outset to take note of the entanglement of the religious and political goals, without which the typically theocratic intervention here under consideration is unintelligible. The Emperor was concerned — there can be no doubt about it — with the reform of the Roman Church, of the spiritual pivot of Christendom. But, as the quasi-priestly ruler, he did not merely want to protect a movement of renewal radiating from Rome to the Universal Church; he wanted to guide and lead it, so far as he could.

The preliminary condition was that the papacy should be freed from domination by the Roman nobility. Hence Henry again had recourse to the old right of participating in the papal election, established by Otto I. It is true that from 1046 on he was careful to discuss the appointment of a new successor of Peter with Roman envoys, but it was he who made the designation and accordingly determined the subsequent election by the clergy and people of Rome. In order legally to establish this practice, which had not been made use of since Otto III, in 1046 he had the Romans confer upon him the patriciate, which the earlier masters of Rome had exercised at least *de facto,* occasionally while bearing the title of *patricius.*[13] The second innovation was that the Emperor was not to designate a single Roman, not even an Italian, as Pope. In this he resumed the policy of Otto III, but even more pointedly, in that he nominated only German bishops. He had no intention of incorporating the papacy into the German State Church, despite the theory of P. Kehr.[14] Henry III fully recognized the unique primatial position of the Pope, once he had been installed, and did not meddle in the administration. However, the provenience of the new Bishops of Rome from the German episcopate was intended not only to assure the reform better; it was also to bind the papacy as closely as possible to the *Imperium.* At the same time the Emperor must have expected from the German Popes a furthering of his imperial policy in Italy, although this viewpoint was probably not to the fore in 1046, because of the then prevailing peaceful situation.

Henry III's reform initiative has been harshly condemned at times. Church historians spoke of a tyrannical assault on the Church's liberty; profane historians, of an inexcusable myopia in unleashing a reform that would soon inflict the most serious damage on the power of the state. One witness from that period may verify on what unhistorical presuppositions such verdicts are based. He followed the events at Sutri and Rome as an unassuming

[12] Thus especially Fliche and Borino; the latter is rightly criticized by C. Violante, *La pataria;* in regard to the problem of Sutri as such, besides the work of Zimmermann cited in the literature, still valuable are the critical remarks of G. Tellenbach, *Libertas,* 212–17.

[13] On Henry III's patriciate, cf. P. E. Schramm, *Kaiser, Rom und Renovatio,* I, 229–238.

[14] Thesis of P. Kehr, *Vier Kapitel;* criticism by Tellenbach in *Libertas,* 206–10.

and scarcely noticed Roman cleric and then accompanied to Cologne the deposed Pope Gregory VI, whom Henry sent into exile for safety's sake. This was Hildebrand, who later was to mount the throne of Peter as Gregory VII and take up the conflict between *Regnum* and *Sacerdotium*.[15] From a man who was on principle an opponent of theocratic rule, who even bore the pain of banishment with Gregory VI, one really ought to expect a violent repudiation of Henry III. In actuality, however, he preserved a kind memory of the Emperor throughout his life and in this he was in agreement with almost all the leading reformers of his generation. Hence Henry III's reform initiative must have been regarded by these circles as an action that favoured the Church, and Henry's theocracy, despite criticism expressed here and there, must have corresponded so well with the views of his time that the future radical development, furthered by his all too early death and other adverse circumstances, could not be foreseen. During the Investiture Controversy itself William the Conqueror could govern theocratically in Normandy and England, just like Henry III, without coming into conflict with Gregory VII, a proof of how slowly the intellectual change beginning in the second half of the eleventh century was completed.

[15] Cf. G. B. Borino, "Invitus ultra montes cum domno papa Gregorio abii" in *StudGreg* I (1947), 3–46.

Constitution of the Church, Worship, Pastoral Care, and Piety: 700 to 1050

CHAPTER 33

Diocesan Organization

The more Germanic, Roman, and, to a degree, even Celtic ways of life in the Christian West blended into one distinct early mediaeval culture, the more powerfully did new institutions, based on Germanic and Roman juridical ideas, have to be developed in the Church. These relaxed the strictly hierarchical structure of the ancient Christian Roman episcopal constitution, and partly even dissolved it or covered it over. Prepared as early as the Merovingian period, this process got fully under way from about the eighth century. Accordingly, a new period of Church history, characterized *par excellence* by Germanic law, began. It lasted until about the end of the Salian Dynasty. It is true that even in the age of the Gregorian Reform there appeared a reaction, based on Roman constitutional principles, but it required serious work before a synthesis could be discovered in the rising canon law, in the *Decretum Gratiani* that was completed around 1140. This gave preference to the Roman element, so that in the future the Germanic influence was pushed back, even though it was never eliminated.

Rural Churches

The creative juridical initiative of the Germano-Roman nations had its roots essentially in a rural and feudal way of life that was different from the urban culture of antiquity. Even in late antiquity, the proprietary spheres of influence established by the senatorial nobility introduced a development unfavourable to the city, and this received a powerful stimulus from the wanderings of the peoples. Among other things, new churches arose everywhere in the country. The circumstance that they were built, endowed, and maintained by the owners of the property or by cooperative groups relieved the bishops of a duty which they would hardly have been able to satisfy, considering the means at their disposal, but at the same time it presented them with serious problems.

For since the founders of those churches asserted rights of ownership, there developed a new juridical form, opposed to the Roman constitution of the Church — the institution of the "proprietary church". It was probably not of specifically German origin. There had been more or less developed proprietary churches both in the West, for example in Gaul, and in the East of the Roman Empire — in the Byzantine Empire even with a centuries-long development culminating in the so-called *ktitoren* right — and finally, again in a special form, among the Slavs.[1] In the West, however, the Germanic peoples were undoubtedly the propelling element. Wherever they lived — in Spain, in Lombard Italy, in England, in Scandinavia, in Frankland — proprietary church types developed, whereas among the strata of the Romance populations the principles of the Roman ecclesiastical constitution became even stronger.[2] In Visigothic Spain, which, as is well known, to a great extent clung to continuity with Roman law, from the end of the sixth century up to the Islamic invasion the bishops carried on a constant fight against proprietary church usages. And while throughout the early Middle Ages the baptismal church organization, on a late Roman foundation which to a great extent preserved episcopal rights, maintained itself in Italy, nevertheless from the ninth century legal principles that may have been influenced by the proprietary church system made their way in.

In any event, the strongest influence proceeded from the Frankish proprietary church. In the Merovingian period there had been no lack of resistance in regard to the principle on the part of bishops. The little that had been accomplished by this means disappeared in the chaos that crept in from 639. When, at the turn of the seventh and eighth centuries, ecclesiastical property was secularized on a grand scale, even the baptismal churches that were still dependent on the bishop fell for the greatest part into lay hands. In order to guard against further losses, the bishops too now adopted

---

[1] The proprietary church was derived either from the Germanic family priesthood (Stutz) or from the lordship of the manor as such (A. Dopsch especially) or from both. *Feine RG,* paragraph 18, still holds to the Stutz thesis but in certain cases is prepared to accept an Indo-Germanic root; on it cf. also R. Höslinger, "Die 'alt-arische' Wurzel des Eigenkirchenrechts in ethnologischer Sicht" in *ÖAKR* 3 (1952), 267–73. The theory of the lordship of the manor, proposed by A. Dopsch, for example in *Wirtschaftliche und soziale Grundlagen der europäischen Kulturentwicklung aus der Zeit von Cäsar bis auf Karl den Grossen,* II (Vienna, 2nd ed. 1924), 230–49, is defended by many investigators within and especially outside the German-speaking world, each in his own way. The attempt of H. von Schubert to connect the proprietary church with the Arianism of the East Germans would probably no longer endure discussion.

[2] It is scholars of Romance lands especially, then, who have much to object to in the theory of U. Stutz. See the literature in *Feine RG,* paragraph 18, II, no. 4 (France), no. 6 (Italy), no. 7 (Spain). A good look at the difficulties is given by R. Bidagor, *La iglesia propia en España* (Rome 1933), and the exhaustive discussion by Wohlhaupter in *ZSavRGkan* 55 (1935), 367–77, and by Vincke in *AkathKR* 114 (1934), 308–18. A new attack on Stutz has been made by G. Martínez Díez, *El patrimonio eclesiástico en la España visigoda. Estudio histórico-jurídico* (Madrid 1959).

the proprietary church system for the churches still left to them. And since the monasteries did likewise, and in fact even tried to increase the number of proprietary churches as much as possible, soon there was no church in the Frankish Kingdom without a secular or a spiritual proprietor. The more or less successful exertions of the Carolingians, summarized in the ecclesiastical capitularies of Louis the Pious of 818–19, for a juridically acceptable form and the recognition of the proprietary church, both by the Carolingian episcopate, despite repeated protests, and by Popes Eugene II and Leo IV — these points have already been described. Here we are concerned merely to look at the legal institution as such and at its effects.

The proprietary church was a product of property law. It was reduced to juridical form by virtue of the stone altar firmly connected with the earth. For the church bulding and its equipment, rectory and cemetery, the landed property donated to the church with its peasants, the income from the tithe, offerings, and stole fees, in short whatever the altar attracted around itself belonged to it as its appurtenances and was, like the altar itself, the property of the landlord. From the time of Charles the Great this estate could no longer be taken from the Church. It was destined first of all to serve the Church and her function. But since the surplus revenues belonged to the proprietor, the proprietary church was exposed to the danger of exploitation. To be able to carry out its function, it needed a priest, just as the mill which the landlord set up on his property, usually with compulsory use by his peasants, needed a miller. Not the bishop but the proprietor of the church appointed this priest. If it so suited him, he took him, just like the miller, from the ranks of his serfs or slaves and in any event he laid down conditions which assured him the greatest possible usufruct and often even humiliated the priest. Proprietary rights over churches could be conveyed to other persons, both in the form of a loan (according to the law of benefice or libellar) and by means of inheritance or of sale, gift, mortgage, and the like. Although the church property was supposed to remain a whole and passed in its entirety to several heirs, greed brought it about that the proprietor reserved to himself, at least partially, especially lucrative revenues, in particular the tithe and the offerings, by either receiving them himself or selling the right to them, in whole or in part. Once this inclined plane had been set foot on, no stop was possible thereafter: during the eleventh and twelfth centuries the institution of the proprietary church clearly fell apart into a loose bundle of individual rights. The process was expedited, not least of all, by the reform movement in the Church.

In several respects the proprietary church was opposed to the ecclesiastical constitution, as this had earlier been developed with the aid of Roman law. To be sure, the power pertaining to the bishop of disposing of church property had earlier become less comprehensive in so far as donations were made to individual churches, but churches that had become holders of their own property had still been incorporated absolutely into the episcopal constitution. For, in accord with Roman law, the Church represented an institution of public law. Its virtually monarchical direction was in the hands of the bishop. He ordained his helpers — priests, deacons, and clerics — and appointed them to the ecclesiastical ministry with delegated power. Obliged to support them, he provided them with *stipendia* or with church property in the form of a loan.

So centralized an organization could not but appear strange to the Germanic peoples, who had different ideas and were on a more primitive level of culture. Since they knew neither the underlying Roman legal distinction between *ius publicum* and *ius privatum* nor the Roman form of the offcial positions and constructed both state and society less from above than from below, private and property law obtained preponderance in their proprietary churches. In order to carry out an economic enterprise the proprietor took a cleric into his service. The priesthood was for him a means to an end, whereas in the ancient Christian Roman constitution of the Church the opposite relationship prevailed: the property bestowed upon the church was supposed to serve the needs of the priesthood.

The proprietary church was too deeply rooted in early mediaeval culture to be extirpated; only its excesses could be curtailed. The reform laws of Charles the Great and his son solved this problem to a degree.[3] With the compromise then achieved between the interests of the laity and those of the clergy the Frankish proprietary church system was directed to a road which it was to cling to despite ceaseless violations of the law. Even though the church continued to belong to the proprietor, it was up to the bishop to supervise its maintenance. Furthermore, the priests of a proprietary church were expressly made subject to the bishop's jurisdiction. Not only did their appointment or removal require the bishop's assent, but the priests were obliged to make an annual report and to attend synods and court sessions. It was even more important to lessen the dependence of the clergy on the proprietors. And so, on the one hand, there was required for priests the condition of freedom and the consequent right of not being deposed except by the sentence of a court, and, on the other hand, the rent-free use of at least one hide of glebe, usually thirty acres, of the necessary structures with garden, of a portion of the tithe, and of the offerings. In return they had to carry out the ecclesiastical functions, while rights of use over and above this had to be reimbursed through payments of taxes, special services, and so forth.

This relationship between a loan and compulsory service basically amounted to the Frankish feudal system that had meanwhile come into existence.

---

[3] Especially important is the Capitulary of Louis the Pious of 819 in *MGCap* I, 276, cc. 6, 9–12, 29; cf. also ibid. 78, c. 54; 304, c. 5; *MGCap* II, 35, c. 18; 39, c. 32; *MGEp* IV, 203f.; the opinion of Hincmar of Reims, *De ecclesiis et capellis,* in *Mirbt* 126–28; the Roman Council of 826 in *MGConc* II, 576, c. 21.

Hence it was natural in the installing of the priests to have recourse to the current Frankish loan in benefice. Ordinarily, though this did not apply everywhere in France especially in the eleventh century, the proprietor thereby renounced the vassalage of commendation so that the priest, because he was not affected by the change of lord, acquired a right to a life-long usufruct. In the early Middle Ages the object of the loan was the proprietary church with all its appurtenances, so that a tax-free use should accrue to the priest for one portion of the undivided property in the sense of the capitulary of Louis the Pious. Accordingly, the Frankish proprietary church contributed in no small measure to the forming of the ecclesiastical benefice system, though the ecclesiastical benefice in the strict sense only grew out of the already mentioned decay of the unity of the proprietary church's property in the eleventh and twelfth centuries, for then the loan relationship to the benefice property, which was specified for the support of the priest, became obsolete.[4] In Frankish territory north of the Alps induction took place by word of mouth; to be more specific, by investiture with ecclesiastical symbols — book, staff, stole, bell rope, and the like. In return the priest had to make a gift *(exenium)* or pay a fee. The right to the offerings, the tithe, and the stole fees continued to be disputed, but often, especially in France, there was established the custom of dividing these into three parts, which usually yielded two-thirds to the proprietor. If the church fell vacant, the proprietor acquired the usufruct until there was a new appointment, a right which was transferred also to the higher ecclesiastical offices, in which connection it was termed *ius regaliae.* Despite the opposition of the clergy the proprietors were also able to secure the *ius spolii,* that is, the right to confiscate the movable property left by the deceased priest, either in whole or in part.

In Italy there also grew up a benefice system, but from other and older roots, while the Frankish type infiltrated only very slowly and incompletely. Already for a long time Italian bishops had endowed priests dependent on them, especially the rectors of the great baptismal churches *(plebes baptismales),* with the goods belonging to a rural church in the forms of loan customary there, but without any prejudice to the basic principle that the conferring of the office was performed by the bishop. But in Italy also in the ninth century the element of property law gained the upper hand. The appointment of the *plebanus* now took place by means of a contract of loan and lease, most often in the form of the libellar lease; indeed, even richly endowed churches were not infrequently granted to lay persons, who then, for their part, according to the circumstances, had to appoint a priest. In contrast to the Frankish priest of a proprietary church, the *plebani* of well-to-do churches had to pay a high tax. The contract, which was usually in writing, did not only regulate eco-

---

[4] Thus *Feine RG,* paragraph 20, I, no. 3; cf. there also the other theories on the origin of the Church benefice.

nomic matters; it often specified exactly the official rights and duties of the priest. The ecclesiastical authorities — bishop, archdeacon, dean — retained their claims to fees and their right of supervision and jurisdiction over the priests. Without doubt, the tradition of the Roman ecclesiastical organization was more influential here than it was on the Frankish benefice system.

Since the profit element in the proprietary church depended to a great extent on the tithe, the offerings, and the stole fees, their proprietors strove to acquire, as far as they could, the rights hitherto reserved to the baptismal churches: the right to the principal Sunday Mass, to burial, to baptism, and so forth. And they obtained them little by little. Of especially great consequence was the acquiring of the right to the tithe.[5] The demand for the tithe, appearing in the fifth century and thereafter often urged by the Church, gained general validity in the Frankish Kingdom when it was made into law by the Carolingians, first by Pepin the Short and then definitively by Charles the Great in the Capitulary of Herstal of 779. Regarded as compensation for the great secularization of Church property, the tithe at first benefitted only the baptismal churches and those built on royal land. But under Louis the Pious this important source of income was also unlocked to the proprietors of churches, so that now the old and already riddled system of baptismal churches was even further weakened. Now, however, the bishops had to define the new limits of tithing. They did so in the so-called determining by ban, that is, in charters which, by virtue of the episcopal ban, assured to the church concerned the rights and revenues belonging to it.

And so there arose, especially in France, more slowly in Germany, many rather small parish territories, comprising a few places or even only one village, with more or less defined rights. The parish territory was based on the parish ban, a productive right which bound the parishioners to their church in regard to the reception of the Sacraments, attendance at Mass, and the paying of the tithe, offerings, and stole fees, just as specified groups were bound by the mill, oven, and occupation *banalités*. Italy had not, or only slightly, taken part in the dissolution of the baptismal church system. The old mother churches in the south resisted the most tenaciously. But the bishops took care also of the growing population of Central and North Italy chiefly through new baptismal churches, in which there was not infrequently constituted a collegially organized clergy with *vita communis* and a department *(schola)* of its own for the administration of the total property. The proprietary churches appearing beside them could, it is true, gain many

[5] E. Perels, *Die kirchlichen Zehnten im karolingischen Reich* (Berlin 1904); E. Lesne, "La dîme des biens ecclésiastiques au IXe et Xe siècle" in *RHE* 13 (1912), 477–503, 659–73; 14 (1913), 97–112, 489–510; E. Widera, "Der Kirchenzehnt in Deutschland zur Zeit der sächsischen Kaiser" in *AkathKR* 110 (1930), 33–110; E. O. Kuujo, *Das Zehntwesen in der Erzdiözese Hamburg-Bremen* (Helsinki 1949); C. E. Boyd, *Tithes and Parishes in Medieval Italy* (New York 1952); other literature in *Feine RG,* para. 19, I, no. 3 d.

parochial rights, but ordinarily they had to leave the baptismal fonts to the old *plebes*.

The development taken by the rural parishes in the early Middle Ages has now probably become understandable in some degree. One must proceed from the ancient baptismal churches, which had been merged by means of territorial division, from the seventh century in Spain and Gaul, from the eighth century in Central and North Italy, into a system of large parishes. In tradition-oriented Italy they continued on, though of course not without modifications, into the high and late Middle Ages, whereas the Germanic peoples, while they retained the original form of the large parishes in many cases and even brought it to Scandinavia as late as the tenth and eleventh centuries, in the case of the old baptismal churches loosened the essential connection with the bishop to a far greater extent then was true of Italy. The churches belonging to larger or smaller associations constituted a special type, extending, apart from England, from the Lombard South to Scandinavia and varying in rights and customs. But the more the country was settled and included in pastoral activity, the less the large churches sufficed. Hence, strongly promoted by the proprietors of churches, there arose smaller parishes, mostly with defined rights, wrested from the baptismal and original churches. The result was a variety no longer clear: each church had its proper history, and represented an individual juridical creation that could be classified only imperfectly.

Urban Churches and Chapters

The urban churches were also in movement, but they had a different development. From time immemorial not only the cathedrals but also other rather large urban churches were served by several clerics, who from the close of the fourth century began here and there to lead a common life under the influence of monastic ideals. The notion of a community of clerics obtained a stable form from Augustine, but because of the meagre evidence supplied by the sources it cannot be determined how far its influence extended. The first organizations in Gaul go back to the sixth century. The term *clerici canonici* came into use in the West at that time to denote the bishop's clergy, and it was slowly applied to the members of the communities now arising, the so-called canons.[6] The *vita canonica* will be discussed later. Here we are concerned merely with the organizational merger into cathedral and collegiate chapters of canons. The terms *capitulum* and *capitularis* originated in the rule, which was read publicly, chapter by chapter, day after day. The origin of the early

---

[6] Originally all were termed canons who, as the bishop's clerics, were entered in the official list *(canon)* in contradistinction to the proprietary church priests who did not appear there. Later, the designation referred also to the canonical prescriptions followed by the "canons" or the *officium canonicum* discharged by them.

medieval chapters of canons is disputed. Probably one must assume several roots, for example, the households of bishops or of high ranking clerics, associations of priests under the bishop for administrative or liturgical purposes, and, above all, monastic communities established in the episcopal see, which enabled the bishop to call upon qualified members for assistance and thus gradually caused a cathedral chapter to take shape. In any event, by the eighth century there must have been a whole group of more or less clearly defined chapter-like communities. Clarity finally came out of the great reform legislation of Louis the Pious in 816–7: chapters and monasteries were clearly separated, and fixed rules were decided upon for both.[7]

The cathedral chapters occupied the first rank.[8] Their pertaining to the cathedral, the centre of all the churches of the diocese, procured for them an increasing influence in the government of the diocese, which, however, was only fully developed from the thirteenth century. Cathedral chapters were at first under the archdeacon, then the provost *(praepositus)*, and, for disciplinary matters, the dean, who was later virtually to assume the entire direction. As in every ordered community, there were special offices for specific functions. The *Primicerius* or *cantor* took care of the liturgy and the sacred rites; the *scholasticus* directed the cathedral school and sometimes the schools of the entire diocese; the church's treasure was confided to the *custos,* but his office could be divided between the *thesaurarius* and the *sacrista;* and the provost, responsible for the administration, was assisted by *camerarius* and *cellerarius.*

Along lines similar to those of the cathedral chapters, there were formed in the other larger churches both of the episcopal city and of other cities in the diocese collegiate chapters, as the collegial manner of life of diocesan priests flourished, especially during the eighth and ninth centuries in Lombardy, and spread even to the rural clergy. For all their monastic emphasis — common table, common property, choir service — the collegiate chapters had at the same time to see to the care of souls. This was the duty of the provost, who was later inclined to have the *custos* act in his place. The canons officiated at the liturgy by weekly turns; during his week a canon was known as *hebdomadarius.* At times the double function of care of souls and choir service led to the constructing of double churches. In the event that the cathedral chapters were obliged to the care of souls, cathedral parishes, often with their own churches, were established.

In certain regions — South and West Germany, France, here and there in

---

[7] For the monastic legislation, see *Corpus consuetudinum monasticarum,* ed. by Kassius Hallinger, I (Rome–Siegburg 1963): *Legislatio Aquisgranensis,* ed. by J. Semmler, 423–582; for the capitulary for the canons, see *infra,* Chapter 39 (sources).

[8] In addition to the works cited in the Literature for this Chapter, there are many studies of individual chapters; cf. also *Feine RG,* para. 19, II, 31, III, no. 2, and for Germany A. Werminghoff, *Verfassungsgeschichte der deutschen Kirche im Mittelalter* (Leipzig–Berlin 1913), 143–52.

North Italy — there arose not a few chapters of canonesses,[9] always attached to a chapter of canons. The proximity of chapters of canons to the monastic life had as a consequence that monasteries could be transformed into chapters and *vice versa*.

In the cities the bishops could better hold together the ecclesiastical property than was the case in the country until in the ninth century the process of dissolution set in. Since the considerable demands made by the secular rulers, and at times also arbitrariness on the part of the bishops, jeopardized the support of the canons, there occurred a division of the property between the episcopal table *(mensa episcopalis)* and that of the chapter; a third part was sometimes set aside for the obligations imposed by the royal service. But even the *mensa canonicorum* was in time divided between the chapter as a whole, for the common purposes, and the provost and canons. A new situation arose when, from about the tenth century, many canons gave up the *vita communis* and therefore had their share of the income from the common property delivered to their houses. This right to an individual usufruct of the still commonly administered capitular property led to the notion of the prebend: every chapter from then on possessed a fixed number of canonical prebends. As time went on they were more and more conferred, no longer by the bishop, but by the chapter, at times subject to the bishop's confirmation, and from the middle of the tenth century the one to be installed had to pay a *xenium* or *venditio*. Thus the chapters too entered into the benefice system. They would not have been able to take this road if private property had not been permitted to the canons. The reform movement of the canons regular in the second half of the eleventh century was to start with precisely this central point.

The nobility was especially interested in the chapters of canons. Although in the abstract every priest of a proprietary church was supposed to be in a condition of freedom, his social position remained depressed, and hence in that feudal-minded age it was all but impossible for a nobly born person to act as pastor of a lesser church. He entered either a monastery or a chapter. We do not know just how strong was the aristocratic element in the early mediaeval chapters. In any event, in the course of time prebends were very much sought by the nobility as means of support for younger sons, and there even began the tendency to exclude non-nobles here and there. As a matter of fact, from the late Middle Ages there were, in addition to those of common folk, some noble chapters and a somewhat larger number of mixed chapters.[10]

[9] K. H. Schäfer, *Die Kanonissenstifter im Mittelalter* (Stuttgart 1907); id., *RQ* 24 (1910), 49 ff.; J. Gampl, *Adelige Damenstifte* (Vienna 1960); new interpretations against those of Schäfer are defended by J. Siegwart, *Chorherren- und Chorfrauengemeinschaften* 42–48.

[10] Still basic is A. Schulte, *Der Adel und die deutsche Kirche im Mittelalter* (Stuttgart 1910); other literature in Werminghoff, *op. cit.* 111–18; L. Santifaller, *Reichskirchensystem*, 123–57, gives synopses of the social classes of bishops and cathedral canons.

Although the bishops no longer disposed of churches and clergy as absolutely as they once had and even had to have recourse to the forms of loan and lease pertaining to private law for the estate belonging to them and consisting in no small measure of proprietary churches and proprietary monasteries, still their authority over their dioceses remained substantially intact. In the Frankish Empire, of course, it had to be again enforced by the Carolingian reform. In the *capitula episcoporum,* as issued in the ninth century by Theodulf of Orléans, Haito of Basel, Hincmar of Reims, and others, one obtains a really vivid picture of the activity of a Frankish bishop.[11] By virtue of the *potestas ordinis* he ordained and confirmed and at Easter and Pentecost he also baptized; he prepared the holy oils and consecrated churches, altars, and sacred vessels. As *magister ecclesiae* he had to see to the education of the clergy, preach, and extirpate superstition and pagan customs. As possessor of the *potestas iurisdictionis,* he determined the holy days and imposed the attendance at Mass, the observance of fasting, the duty of tithing, and other commandments of the Church. Furthermore, he took care of the poor, widows, orphans, and the unfree, supervised the morals of clergy and laity, and officiated as ecclesiastical judge, if necessary by imposing penalties, which could include excommunication and, in the case of malfeasance on the part of clerics, even suspension and deposition. In the last case, however, appeal to the synod or to the King was allowed.

The bishop made a visitation journey annually and in this connection he held the ecclesiastical court. Furthermore, he gathered the clergy for diocesan synods, an institution attested since the sixth century; it was supposed to be held once or twice a year. Lay persons, especially the episcopal vassals and officials, also took part.[12] Although all possible questions of law, administration, and trials could be dealt with at the synod, the chief stress was on legislation. In the Carolingian period this consisted mainly in the application of the general capitularies, decreed by imperial and provincial synods, to the diocese in question.

This picture, drawn from Carolingian sources, of the rights and duties of the bishop remained standard for the succeeding period. It in no way implied a diminution of the episcopal power when from the middle of the ninth century it was understood in Frankish territory as *bannus episcopalis,* paralleling the royal and the comital ban. This meant the right to command and to forbid under penalty, so that, just as in secular law, a distinction may be made

---

[11] For the prescriptions of individual bishops cf. the lists by A. Werminghoff in *NA* 26 (1901), 665–70; 27 (1902), 576–90; see also E. Seckel in *NA* 29 (1904), 287–94.
[12] Benedict XIV, *De synodo dioecesana libri VIII* (Rome 1748); editio aucta libri XIII (Rome 1756); see also in the literature for this chapter H. Barion, C. de Clercq, and *Feine RG,* para. 21, II.

between the episcopal decree, court, peace, and administrative bans. The highest penalty, the great excommunication, is especially to be noted among the penalties of the ban, and in German it has retained the descriptive term "Kirchenbann". Since it could be threatened in connection with all instructions, it went beyond the sphere of the penitential system, of the penal and disciplinary law, became a clear parallel to the Germanic outlawry, and, by this extension, fell into the danger of being too much legalized and hence too formalized.

To be able to take care of his manifold duties, the bishop, in addition to the cooperation of all the clergy, needed special assistants as well as a division of the diocese into smaller areas. *Chorepiscopi* had only a brief importance. Appearing in isolated cases in the West before the eighth century, without it being possible to demonstrate a connection with the *chorepiscopi* that had appeared in the East in the fourth century and worked in the country *(chora)*, they increased in number in the Carolingian period. Their activity depended on the circumstances; they could help the bishops in ordaining and consecrating, in missionary work, or in administration, and in the large dioceses they could even receive their own special territory. Rivalries that could hardly be avoided induced the West Frankish episcopate to liquidate the institution entirely in the second half of the ninth century, whereas the German bishops let it continue into the tenth century.

Among the diocesan clergy the clerics active in the cathedral naturally stood closest to the bishop, at their head the archdeacon and the archpriest. Responsible for disciplinary matters, the administration of property, and the care of the poor, the archdeacon (of the more ancient form) accompanied his bishop on visitations. The archpriest, on the other hand, saw to the liturgy and care of souls at the cathedral and hence was more connected with the city.

The more the diocese grew in size as a consequence of more active colonization and of the permeation of the countryside by the Church, the more necessary it became to break up the diocesan territory into smaller districts. Thus was developed in the seventh and eighth centuries the system of territorially defined baptismal churches, whose direction was entrusted by the bishop to a rural archpriest. But as soon as many smaller parish territories appeared alongside the ancient baptismal churches — there has already been mention of this — they had to be combined in a new unity: hence the origin of the deaneries *(decaniae)*, often in connection with the boundaries of the old baptismal churches. Named by the bishop or the archdeacon, with the participation of the deanery clergy, the dean gathered his priests in the so-called "calendar chapters" to discuss pastoral and disciplinary questions, especially matters of penance. Wherever the old baptismal and original churches remained, a later form of the rural archpresbyterate developed. This was distinguished from the older form by the fact that it comprised a number of smaller parishes with limited rights. In Anglo-Saxon England and in Saxony there was no division into archpresbyterates or deaneries.

Above the deaneries, for matters of jurisdiction and later also of administration, were the archdeaconries, which were to limit the episcopal power of jurisdiction sharply. The more the zeal for reform lagged in the ninth century, the more oppressive the bishops felt the burden of their office to be — a burden they now had to bear on the part not only of the Church but also of the state. From the end of the ninth century they therefore proceeded to appoint archdeacons as ecclesiastical judges in several strictly defined territories and hence in specially created archdeaconries. The process began in the West and then moved slowly eastward until in the twelfth century it reached Salzburg in one direction and Saxony in the other and in the thirteenth century Poland. The new institution was introduced into England by William the Conqueror. The number and size of archdeaconries varied much. Cologne had four, Trier five, Constance ten, Mainz eventually twenty-two, Augsburg eight, but Münster thirty-four, Hildesheim forty, and Halberstadt thirty-eight, for in the Saxon bishoprics the original parishes were usually made archdeaconries. There might also be one single archdeaconry, as in Canterbury. There was an equal variety in regard to the appointing of the archdeacons. In the West German bishoprics, for example, the office was often attached to that of cathedral provost or cathedral dean and the provostship of the great collegiate chapters.

Archdeacons of the later type rose to considerable power. Because important revenues were connected with the judicial system, their office could be regarded as a profitable right and hence as a benefice that could be conferred and handed over by investiture; as a matter of fact investiture did take place in the eleventh century. Once established, the conferring of the office and the ban assured the archdeacon the autonomous position of a *iudex ordinarius*, who possessed his own proper archidiaconal ban and disposed of a staff of officials *(missi, officiales)*. In consequence of his right of visitation he gradually intervened in matters of administration, so that he became a real competitor to the episcopal jurisdiction. It was only from the fourteenth century that the power of archdeacons could be slowly undermined by the bishop with the aid of canon law and finally broken.

CHAPTER 34

Prelacies and the Secular Powers

The State Church which Constantine the Great and his successors had set up did not simply disappear in the Germanic kingdoms of the period of the migrations but was assimilated to the political and social conditions of the individual countries. In the strict sense, of course, this is true merely of the bishoprics and abbeys, for the papacy stood outside the Germanic political world until the alliance with the Carolingian monarchs and even after the imperial coronation of Charles the Great lost only a part of the autonomy that it had meanwhile acquired. Hence, its juridical position requires separate consideration.

Bishoprics and Abbeys

As with the lesser churches, so also in the case of the greater churches the development must be studied as it occurred in the area of Carolingian Frankish power. When the Carolingian *Imperium* collapsed, the essential had already been achieved: the elaboration of the forms which firmly enclosed bishops and abbots, with their churches, in the political organism. The occasions for this had been, and were to continue to be, on the one hand the state's claims to supremacy, and on the other hand the titles to proprietary churches. The last mentioned applied especially to monasteries, whereas bishoprics, because of their continuing position in public law, could only with difficulty become a part of the proprietary church system. Among the institutions that exerted influence on the incorporation of the greater churches into the political structure three were especially prominent: immunity, royal protection, and *advocatia*. They were all connected with the Church's real estate and manorial lordship.

As a Roman institution that freed the imperial domains from specific payments and public services, the immunity passed to the Frankish royal property and from there, once again in connection with late Roman forms, to other estates that were in the hands of the spiritual and temporal aristocracy and was extended without there having been any declaration as to the positive content of this extension. Privileges of immunity usually included merely the prohibition for state officials to enter the immune district *(introitus)*, to collect taxes there *(exactiones)*, and to employ the public authority against the inhabitants *(districtio)*. There naturally had to be a positive aspect, corresponding to this negative side — the immunist had to exercise certain rights of his own, especially judicial, within his territory. When there was a question of a secular lord, he probably enforced a protectorate which was based on autogenous Germanic law. Hence it was not derived from the crown and from the beginning bore within itself the tendency toward high justice, even though the Merovingian kingship succeeded in restricting it at first to low justice. On the other hand, the rights of lordship of ecclesiastical immunists had a less uniform origin. And even though the Merovingian and early Carolingian monarchs quite often confirmed the immunity of the prohibition of *introitus* in writing, they did not thereby grant any of the state's rights of sovereignty.

But a definitive change appeared under Louis the Pious. From his time immunity and royal protection were connected in charters of immunity. The royal protection elevated the freed churches to a juridical position which was equivalent to that of the secular immunity endowed with autogenous right, but at the same time fitted them into the system of the feudal state. Hitherto the greater number of bishoprics and monasteries that possessed immunity had not stood in the protection or proprietorship of the ruler. But now, by virtue of the connection of royal protection and immunity, they all fell under the dominion of the King, who could thereafter assert a supreme right of ownership, attenuated though it was. From the royal rights over the Church, thus prepared, was to emerge, at least in German territory, the greater churches' position as direct royal vassals and the spiritual principality.

This process began probably in the second half of the ninth century. It was stopped by the counts and princes in West *Francia* from the end of the century, but in Germany Otto the Great and his successors took it up again and continued it consistently. If the immunity of churches had hitherto been restricted to the scope of the lordship of property, thereafter ecclesiastical immunists obtained public rights of a judicial and financial nature, even in places (markets, episcopal cities) and in districts (forests, occasionally entire counties) which they did not possess as manorial lords or possessed only in part. Thus alongside the manorial immunity appeared the ban immunity, which was to contribute substantially to the building of the Church's territorial sovereignty. Furthermore, the immune jurisdiction was strengthened. Its powers were clothed in the forms of the royal ban and slowly led toward sovereign jurisdiction, at first for cases which were expiable by money payments, and probably only from the middle of the twelfth century in the full sense, including criminal justice.[1] Hence, to be an immunity judge became in time a really rewarding and, accordingly, coveted duty. Attended to by the Church's *advocati,* it had a development of its own, differing according to the country.

Already in Roman imperial law the churches had to be represented in court by *advocati,* who, with the decline of the *Imperium,* more and more became episcopal officials. But in the Frankish German world they increased in importance as soon as the protective function proper to the office — in the late Roman period it had been related to the concept of *patronus* — brought into effect the Germanic notion of the *mund* or protectorate. In order to furnish the full protection of rights, the *advocatus* had to be a man capable of bearing arms and fighting and hence a layman; the bearing of arms was forbidden to clerics. Hence in 802 Charles the Great prescribed to all bishops

---

[1] Thus T. Mayer, *Fürsten und Staat,* 169–84, against H. Hirsch, who had the possession of criminal justice begin with the eleventh century; in the case of poor criminals, who could not raise the considerable expiatory payments, the death penalty, according to Mayer, had indeed been exacted earlier.

271

and abbots the naming of *advocati*. As *advocati, agentes, defensores, causidici,* they represented the church in question and its real estate in matters of personal as well as of property rights before the public authority, protected it from without, and exercised the justice pertaining to the church over the peasants. Charles the Great had their activity, like that of the counts, supervised by his *missi*. Nevertheless, the Church's *advocati* functioned, not yet by virtue of the royal or of their own right, but at the order of the bishop or abbot. It was not until the mid-ninth century that the Carolingian *advocatia* of officials began slowly to change into the mediaeval *advocatia* of lords or nobles, for it was then that nobles, often powerful princes, assumed the function, partly asked to do so by churches that needed protection, partly motivated by the desire to extend their power in this way.

Their protection, of course, meant at the same time domination. It is true that this involved a territorially limited development. Italy, except for a few localities in the north under German influence, and West *Francia* south of the line Lyons–Bourges–Orléans–Chartres played no role in it; there the *advocati* remained restricted to their traditional task of representing their churches before the court. And in Normandy the greater power of the Dukes did not permit *advocati* to appear at all. But in the rest of West *Francia* and, from the end of the ninth century, in Germany noble *advocati* exercised various sovereign functions, not seldom to the detriment of the churches concerned. France took the lead but pretty soon found tolerable solutions. The more successfully the princes there constructed their territorial authority, the more willing were they from about the end of the eleventh century to let the *advocatia* of churches become a general grant of protection *(custodia, garde)*, in which they strictly bound the sub-*advocati* appointed by them to their rights and duties, with a curtailing of their jurisdiction, and supervised their activity. In Germany, on the other hand, especially in the south and west, economic feudalism reached such a peak that the peasant had almost nothing more to do with the state judge but rather with the *advocatus* of the manorial, spiritual, or temporal immune district and in this way the *advocatia*, both as protective and as judicial *advocatia*, became the dynamic element in the constitutional history of the tenth to the twelfth centuries. Hence, kings as well as spiritual and temporal princes showed an interest in the ecclesiastical *advocatia*, which was regarded as an hereditary fief from the middle of the eleventh century. The German Kings sought to make at least the judicial *advocatia* dependent on a grant by them. The ecclesiastical immunists had especially to come to an understanding with the immediate *advocati*. To a great extent the formation of the future territorial state depended on whether the Church's secular means of power, conferred with the *advocatia*, assisted the noble *advocatus* in the building up of his own political power or the spiritual immunist when the latter withdrew the *advocatia* and had the administration conducted by officials.

Monasteries especially had to suffer much from *advocati*. During the period of the Gregorian Reform, it is true, a quite large number of them succeeded in placing themselves under papal protection and in restricting the hereditary *advocatia* of the founding families, still continuing in practice, to judicial rights, but this by no means ended the struggle. This is attested by the numerous forged charters of the twelfth and thirteenth centuries, with which German monks sought to attack, first the *advocatia* system and the proprietary church, then the spiritual proprietors of churches. The new Orders had an easier time. The Cistercian abbeys, for example, were founded without *advocati* from the outset and were placed under the general protectorate, customary in France, of the King or territorial prince.

But the power struggle with the *advocati* had already recommended the appointing of nobles as bishops and abbots. Other circumstances also favoured this. The rising position of the prelates of the realm because of the granting of rights of sovereignty, the strongly graduated social sensitivity, the family policies of the dynasts, and the state policy of the kings — all these conspired to bring it about that in territories of German law the direction of the dioceses and of the important abbeys should regularly be entrusted to a noble.[2]

Nevertheless it is clear enough how different the juridical situation of the bishoprics and abbeys could be. The German royal bishoprics represented something quite different from those under the Capetians or the French princes, and these in turn were distinguished from the South French bishoprics, which were sold, given away, bequeathed, or granted in fief by the counts or viscounts as ordinary proprietary churches. There was a similar gradation among the monasteries, but the situation was the reverse for them. Whereas proprietary bishoprics in the strict sense were confined to the Midi, ordinarily every early mediaeval monastery, at least from around 700, had a proprietor, either from the lesser, middle, or higher nobility, all the way to the king, or from the ecclesiastical hierarchy — bishop or Pope. The higher the rank of the proprietor, the higher became the right, the so-called "liberty", of the churches subject to him.[3] Because of the slight power which the Kings of France possessed in the tenth and eleventh centuries, it made little difference at that time whether a bishopric or monastery depended on him or on a great magnate. In Germany, on the other hand, it really meant something to be directly under the King, to be a church subject to the crown only. For since, after the extinction of the East Carolingians, the entire Carolingian inheritance, regardless whether it was patrimonial or royal property, passed to the now emerging German Kingdom and was entrusted for its administration to the currently reigning King, the Carolingian East Frankish Church, embracing

---

[2] See Chapter 33, footnote 10; L. Santifaller, *Reichskirchensystem,* 123–33, gives a survey of the class relationships of the German bishops.

[3] On the notion of liberty, see *supra,* Chapter 32, footnote 7.

all the bishoprics and the immune abbeys that were under the royal protection, entered as a whole into the new German tribal federation, so that these churches were not property but a part, a member, of the realm and their chiefs later acquired the position of princes of the Empire. It is true that in the Saxon and Salian period, up to 1045, new monasteries were placed under the royal protection, but these royal monasteries, likewise direct royal vassals, did not completely attain the privileged position of the old royal abbeys coming from the Carolingian hereditary estate. Apart from the provost of Berchtesgaden, their abbots did not later become princes but prelates of the Empire.

The dependence of the greater churches is probably clearest in the election of the bishops and abbots, for it was precisely here that important sovereign rights had been elaborated in Frankish territory since Merovingian times. Ecclesiastical circles, of course, appealed time and again to the ancient canonical principle of the election of the bishop by clergy and people, *electio canonica,* which was occasionally expressly confirmed in writing for individual churches, especially abbeys, as free election, and in Germany had been granted to all bishoprics. But in early mediaeval society something quite specific had been made out of *electio canonica.* In the late Roman period an effort had been made to subject it to the control of the metropolitan and his suffragans. This in itself happy beginning of a guarantee by the authority of the hierarchy was, however, virtually lost in the Merovingian period and could not be revived under the Carolingians, despite some attempts by the West Frankish archbishops in the ninth century. And so the place of the higher ecclesiastical authority was taken by the King or, in West *Francia* from the end of the ninth century, often by a prince.

From the body of electors, clergy and people, which had become strongly differentiated both socially and juridically, there stood out prominently the cathedral canons and influential lay nobles and vassals of the see. If a real election took place at all, they made the decision, while people and clergy were restricted in practice to giving consent. The more select electoral group was in competition with the ruler who had an interest in the election. Since he belonged to the nobility, his fellow members represented not merely and not always the interests of the church in question but often also those of specific dynastic families and hence were, according to circumstances, more egoistically minded than a ruler concerned for the welfare of the state.

The absence of strict rules permitted a really varied practice, dependent on the concrete situation. Powerful princes virtually had full control of the election of a bishop. When the widowed church was to be again filled depended on their decision, and at times this took place by a mere act of nomination. But if there was an election, then the ruler could determine it by designation or by vindicating a right of confirmation after it had taken place; not infrequently the right of confirmation involved a rejection of the one elected and then, according to circumstances, an arbitrary naming of the bishop. Still, even for the princes there was an insurmountable legal barrier. Since the business of the election was still regarded as a full, active process in which clergy and people participated, an unwanted chief pastor could not be forced upon the diocesans. Regardless of the manner in which clergy and people assented, their assent had to be given somehow; otherwise, the election was uncanonical, invalid.[4]

The situation in regard to abbatial elections was similar and yet different. On the one hand, the real electors, the monks, represented a much more closed corporate body than did clergy and people in episcopal elections, even if the monastery's vassals also had a word to say. On the other hand, an abbey ordinarily depended not merely on the proprietor but also on the diocesan bishop. The abbatial election turned out according to the way in which the various interested parties made their influence prevail. Here the local bishop appointed the new abbot, there the proprietor of the monastery, while only a right of assent was left to the monks. But it also happened that both cooperated with the community or that the monks freely elected their abbot, eventually with the subsequent confirmation of bishop or proprietor, or that the abbot in office designated his successor. Naturally, from time immemorial the monks had exerted themselves for the two last mentioned forms, and they often carried their point wholly or in part, a tradition which the Cluniac reform movement energetically fostered.[5]

Election was followed by installation in office and consecration, two separate acts, which in themselves could be carried out by different representatives of the law. Naturally only bishops were taken into consideration as consecrators, whereas installation in office and in possession presupposed an authority which held rights of domination or of property in regard to the church concerned. In the case of bishoprics these were the kings or the princes who had taken their place; in regard to monasteries, in so far as they had no privileged position, they were the proprietors, that is, kings, princes, nobles, or bishops.

The fact that there was so strong a dependence in law on secular institutions was connected with the circumstances of the time. The more the feudal-vassalage institutions were elaborated and combined into the feudal system

[4] According to P. Schmid, *Begriff der kanonischen Wahl,* the early mediaeval idea of election must be distinguished from that appearing during the Investiture Controversy by the fact that it held an *electio ex ipsa ecclesia* as necessary. But this principle, coming down in tradition and again inserted into electoral privileges, had more and more lost importance from the end of the ninth century and hence could be infringed by the Ottonian and the early Salian Emperors without any great scruples.

[5] On the efforts of monks to free the election and investiture of the abbot from every outside influence as far as possible, cf. the important treatment, involving all the diplomatic material, by K. Hallinger, "Cluniacensis s. religionis ordinem elegimus. Zur Rechtsfrage der Anfänge des Klosters Hasungen" im *Jahrbuch für das Bistum Mainz* 8 (1958–1960), 244–60.

under the Carolingians, the more were the bishops and abbots drawn into this system. The important functions which they exercised even in the political field of themselves suggested the idea of binding them to the crown by means of vassalage. A welcome pretext could be found in the royal protection, which was granted to the immune churches from the time of Louis the Pious. As a matter of fact, from then on all bishops and the royal abbots had to commend themselves to the King and in the customary form of the giving of self — the placing of the clasped hands in the open clasping hands of the lord, — which was then followed by the oath of fealty.[6]

But the other propelling force of the feudal system, the *beneficium,* was also to be seen. Not merely Church property but also the office of bishop or abbot was drawn into the wake of the benefice system. Just as in the course of the ninth century, over and above the fiscal goods belonging to the endowment of an office, the very function of count was regarded as a *beneficium* to be conferred by the King and eventually hereditary and was by preference termed *honor,* so also in the ninth century the episcopal function became a profitable right, a domain, an *honor.* This materialization made it possible for the ruler thereafter to convey the *episcopatus,* that is, the office of bishop, with all its rights of ownership, administration, and usufruct, after the manner of a *beneficium* by delivering the symbol of the office, the pastoral staff — the ring was added under Henry III.[7] In the course of time, regularly from the end of the tenth century, this act was termed "investiture". It is true that its juridical character remained a problem, despite the existing undoubted parallel to investiture with a fief. The religious and ecclesiastical essence of the episcopal office was here overlaid by the Germanic law process of materialization, but it was not annulled, so that the Gregorian Reform was able to expose it again to view and limit the crown's right to a mere investiture with the *regalia.* The early mediaeval investiture of bishops and of royal abbots could the more easily appear in a feudal law sense when the vassalage acts of homage and oath of fealty were connected with it. Examined in detail, the causal connection was missing. The vassalage entered into by the higher prelates was not the juridical basis for the conferring of the *beneficium,* but in the tenth and eleventh centuries, when the concept of feudal law was more and more permeating the state and society, who would have distinguished these things carefully?

In a development similar to that of bishoprics, in the case of monasteries

[6] On this development, see, for example, F. L. Ganshof, *Feudalism* (New York, 2nd ed. 1961), 54ff.; there also the formula of an oath of fealty and a description of the attitude which Hincmar of Reims took to commendation; on the *beneficium* and *honor,* see ibid., 52–56.
[7] V. Habhart, *Zur Rechtssymbolik des Bischofsrings* (Cologne–Graz 1963); P. Salmon, *Mitra und Stab. Die Pontifikalinsignien im römischen Ritus* (Mainz 1960); id., *Études sur les insignes du pontife dans le rit romain. Histoire et liturgie* (Rome 1955); id., "Aux origines de la crosse des évêques" in *Mélanges Mgr. Andrieu* (Strasbourg 1956), 373–83.

the investiture of the abbot by the proprietor came into use, but not a few abbeys succeeded in avoiding an outside investiture. In the latter event, either one of the monks — *praepositus, prior, decanus* — presented the abbot's staff or the newly elected abbot himself took it from the altar.

Investiture would cost something. Secular vassals on succeeding to their hereditary fiefs ordinarily had to pay to their feudal lord an inheritance fee, the *relevium,* the amount of which was at first decided by an agreement, but later became a fixed charge. In the Germanic notion of law there was no reason to stop short with the investiture of bishops and abbots and to exempt them from the demand for payment. As a matter of fact, such payments were often made. However, canon law was opposed to them; it forbade any introduction of money in the conferring of ecclesiastical offices and denounced it as simony.

Whoever had the right of investiture could, at the death of bishop or abbot, easily claim special rights to the property of the widowed church or of the deceased prelate. In fact, it was often in the interests of the church in question that the use of its property during the vacancy should not be exposed to arbitrariness but should lie in the hands of the King in accord with a somewhat orderly procedure. Difficult as it is to lay hold of the exact juridical origin, still, appropriate rights were developed and took shape as the so-called *regalia* and *spolia.* Already exercised earlier, they were to play a not unimportant role in the twelfth century. Churchmen naturally felt the *ius spolii,* or right to the movable estate of a deceased prelate, to be particularly oppressive, but the *ius regaliae,* or right to the enjoyment of the church revenues during the vacancy, also contained dangers, in so far as the rulers were tempted to postpone the new appointment to the church for an excessively long time for the sake of the income. The Church thus tried to persuade rulers to renounce these claims and was successful to a great extent; Frederick II, for example, did so for the Empire in 1216, except for the revenues from the Empire's rights of sovereignty. But the rights as such were not annulled thereby. They were transferred to ecclesiastical offices and were to acquire a great importance for the papal financial system that was fully developed in the fourteenth century in the claim to *spolia,* to the income during a vacancy, and to annates.

The bonds created by homage on the one hand and investiture on the other gave rise to the performance of services, both personal and real. Just as secular vassals were, so too were the royal prelates bound to fealty to their lord and to provide him with *consilium* and *auxilium,* while the Church property that had been conferred upon them was regarded as belonging to the kingdom and hence as burdened with definite duties. We may summarize all these under the notion *servitium regis.* Bishops and royal abbots were bound to attend court and supply their military contingent, and they had to be prepared to act as envoys of the King, as his chancellor, and the like. Their churches had to bear the expenses of all this. In like manner the royal churches had to supply all the palace clerics who were occupied in chancery and chapel with benefices.[8] A record of 981, luckily preserved, shows how considerable were the army contingents to be supplied by the prelates. For the reinforcements of 2,090 mailed horsemen whom Otto II had requested from Germany twenty lay persons and thirty-one ecclesiastical institutions were enumerated; the lay vassals were to send only 586, the prelates 1,504 men.[9] Another example is also illuminating: When Bishop Wazo of Liège (d. 1048) was reproached for not having fulfilled his military duty in a specific case, he offered in atonement the payment of 300 pounds of silver. Of course, the royal churches were able to comply with their military obligations only by having vassals of their own. The King's right to be lodged by the royal churches on his travels could be very burdensome. Resorted to in Germany only from the time of Henry II but with increasing consistency, it led to the ruler's monopolizing all the rights of sovereignty — court, toll, coinage, customs — during his stay in an episcopal city. Such rights were first limited substantially by Frederick II in 1220. As other burdens could be added annual presents and, in the case of monasteries, precisely fixed annual payments.

So singular a development, running partly counter to the ancient Christian Roman episcopal organization, encountered certain opposition in its earliest phase, and hence in the Carolingian period. Thus in the reign of King Louis III (879–82) the West Frankish episcopate, Hincmar of Reims at its head, fought, not without success, for free episcopal elections. But on the other hand Hincmar fully recognized a royal right of consent, just as he regarded it as a duty of rulers in general to be concerned for the orderly elevation of qualified prelates. In 844–6 Frankish synods granted the King even the right to nominate the bishops to be elected.[10] A like vacillating attitude was taken in regard to the act of installation. It did not occur to Hincmar of Reims to reject commendation as such, but he must have opposed the *immixtio manuum* that was customary in it. And if he wanted the episcopal property to be maintained undiminished by the *oeconomus* during the vacancy, in his view it was still subject to the royal power, was to be handed over by the ruler to the newly elected bishop, and was regarded as a sort of royal *beneficium*. The Popes of that period also did not follow a uniform policy. To their not infrequent declarations in favour of the old electoral regulations, which in some few charters from the end of the ninth century, granting the right of

---

[8] S. Görlitz, *Beiträge zur Geschichte der königlichen Hofkapelle im Zeitalter der Ottonen und Salier bis zum Beginn des Investiturstreits* (Weimar 1936); H. W. Klewitz, "Königtum, Hofkapelle und Domkapitel im 10. und 11. Jahrhundert" in *AUF* 16 (1939), 102–56.

[9] *MGConst* I, 632.

[10] Synods of Yütz, Meaux, and Paris, *MGCap* II, 114, 399; on the whole question, cf. K. Voigt, *Staat und Kirche,* 369–78, 388–97.

election, among other things attacked the dominant share of Kings, there was opposed the recognition of positive royal rights, for example, the right to permit the election to take place or to permit the consecration — these were acknowledged by Hadrian II and John VIII. And so that John X could declare solemnly that, according to ancient custom, the conferring of a bishopric on a cleric pertained solely to the King and without his command the episcopal consecration might not take place.[11]

No doubt the papacy and the West Frankish episcopate were so compliant because in those difficult times, gradually becoming chaotic, the Church needed secular protection and as a matter of fact was always best provided for under a King. But the incorporation of the higher clergy, as it had begun in the ninth century and was thereafter steadily brought to completion, cannot be explained in this way alone. It would hardly have succeeded, had not the royal theocracy furnished the supporting foundation. The theocratic idea not only did not disappear with the dissolution of the Carolingian *Imperium,* but it was even consolidated in the coronation *ordines* which appeared in the ninth and tenth centuries, just as in the iconographic tradition and in general in the thought and feeling of contemporary men. Thietmar of Merseburg reproduced a very widespread sentiment in placing kings above bishops but protesting against any other dependence on the part of bishops, whom Christ has raised up as princes of this earth.[12]

The Papacy and Papal Institutions

The constitutional status of the Pope differed substantially from that of the bishops and abbots. But this does not mean that the Roman Church was entirely independent. We have already discussed the imperial confirmation of the papal election, a right that was originally Byzantine and then was found again under the Carolingians Lothar I and Louis II; likewise the right of the German Emperors to participate in the election discussions in an authoritative manner that was capable of becoming actual designation. However, it must not be forgotten that in the institution of a Roman Bishop the imperial rights did not go beyond the electoral act. No Emperor installed a Pope in his office by means of investiture, not to mention tried to bind him as a vassal by commendation. The views of sovereignty and proprietorship which in the Frankish world more and more fitted bishops and abbots into the political organization were not applied to the Roman Church. Since there was for the Emperors no adequate legal pretext for nullifying the juridical immunity pertaining to the Pope, the above mentioned depositions effected by Otto I and Henry III remained only episodes. Though the Popes

---

[11] *Jaffé* 3564, 3565, given in *PL* 132, 806–08, and Santifaller, *Reichskirchensystem,* 118–22.
[12] *Chron.* I, 26, *MGSS rer. Germ.,* ed. Holtzmann, 33 f.; on the theocracy, see the literature for Section VII and G. Tellenbach, *Libertas,* 70–76, 85–93.

may have fallen on occasion into serious dependence, they held to the principle that they stood not under but beside the Emperor. They even possessed an important right in the imperial anointing and coronation, and from 850 on there was no other act whereby the imperial dignity could be transmitted.

What enabled the Roman Church to maintain her political freedom was, most important of all, the Papal State, that Central Italian remnant of Byzantine rule, which let the papacy take the place there of the *basileus* and even claim imperial symbols of sovereignty, such as robes of state or tiara and imperial court ceremonial.[13] It is true there was a correlation involved: While the Papal State and the adoption of imperial characteristics greatly preserved the papacy from political subordination, the spiritual authority of the *vicarius Petri* protected the existence of the Papal State, for the motivation of the *Constitutum Constantini* — that the earthly Emperor must possess no power in that place where the heavenly Emperor had installed the head of the Christian religion — had an importance all its own.

Despite imperial protectorate and despotic control by the Roman nobility, the Roman Bishops and their co-workers never gave up the notion of autonomy. This is indicated, for example, by the expression *sacrum palatium Lateranense,* which appeared in the ninth century alongside the customary term *patriarchium* and in the second half of the tenth century even came to the fore. Behind it, of course, were the ideas of the *Constitutum Constantini.* They likewise lived on in the catalogues of judges, — the "older", composed probably between 867 and 877, and the "later", from the first half of the eleventh century, — two literary works which aimed to make the papal dignitaries equal to the officials of the Byzantine imperial court.[14] The clearest sign for the claim to quasi-imperial and hence to an autonomous position must probably have been the imperial symbol of the tiara, expressly mentioned in the *Constitutum.* Sergius III (904–11) is portrayed with it on a silver *denarius,*[15] and there is no basis for regarding the use of it by Sergius as an exception. It was precisely under Sergius III that the domination by the Roman nobility began, but the idea embodied in the tiara was to outlast it and overcome it. Liberated in the period of the Gregorian reform, the Roman Church set about elaborating a thoroughgoing claim to sovereignty over Rome and the Papal State.

Tenaciously as the Roman Church clung to the idea of the Papal State, the reality of the situation was pitiable for by far the greatest part of the period

---

[13] The inner connection between the programme of an autonomous ecclesiastical state, consisting of the remnant of Byzantine rule, and the claim to the symbols of imperial power clearly follows from the *Constitutum Constantini*. For the *Constitutum,* see *supra,* Chapter 10; the text quoted in what follows from the *Constitutum Constantini* in *Mirbt* p. 112, no. 18.

[14] Both lists in P. E. Schramm in *ZSavRGgerm* 49 (1929), 198–232; for the older list a possible dating as late as 962 is discussed by R. Elze in *StudGreg* IV (1952), 29–33.

[15] S. Déer in *ByZ* 50 (1957), 420–27, especially 425.

here under consideration. Of course, much may have been let go by default on the part of the Popes, but the chief cause of the failures lay in the existing circumstances. The struggle beginning in the late Roman Empire between the centralization of an imperial official bureaucracy and the decentralizing tendency of a new class of landowners rising through social restratification had led in the Eastern Empire to a predominance of the bureaucratic and in the West of the landowning element. In this a striking middle position had devolved upon the Roman Bishop: as the owner of many *patrimonia* scattered in and outside Italy, he properly belonged among the landlords, while his position of public law, early drawn into the service of the Empire, obliged him to assume specifically political functions for the city of Rome to an increasing extent. So long as Byzantine rule lasted, the extending of the papal rights caused no discord with the Italian landowners, particularly since these were aspiring likewise to lay hands on as many political rights as possible in the territories accessible to them. The change came with the Papal State, for then the hatred of the landed aristocracy was directed against the papal claims to sovereignty, which had replaced the imperial central power. In the struggle that began immediately and lasted until about the death of the Emperor Lambert (898) it was obvious that insufficient secular instruments of power were at the disposal of the Roman Church. Perhaps a firmly unified central government would have been able to solve the difficult problem, but such was simply non-existent.

We are unfortunately very poorly informed about the administrative organization at the Lateran. The *iudices de clero* or *iudices ordinarii* or *iudices palatini* are readily mentioned as the leading departmental heads — a slowly growing group, counting six officers at the beginning of the eighth century and seven in the ninth century, and unified as a college, consisting of the *primicerius, secundicerius, primus defensor, arcarius, saccellarius, nomenculator,* and *protoscriniarius.*[16] Originally these men took care of strictly circumscribed tasks, but in the course of the eighth century they must have become at times less interested in concrete administrative work and more in general policy. An exact dividing up of the work according to departments cannot be demonstrated. What the sources do mention are diplomatic mandates carried out in the name of the Pope and judicial activity in Rome in cases of contentious and voluntary jurisdiction. Furthermore, some palatine judges often played a leading role in Roman insurrections, now as opponents, now as assistants of the then reigning Pope. Likewise in regard to other high officials, such as the *vestararius,* who administered the wardrobe and the uncoined

---

[16] On the first six judges, see *supra,* Chapter 1; the original function of the last palatine judge, the *protoscriniarius,* is disputed. According to H. Breslau, I, 205–08, he was the chief of the urban *tabelliones;* according to Kehr in *AAB* (1926), no. 2, 21, and others, the technical director of the papal chancery. In any event in the tenth and early eleventh centuries he wrote personally a few papal charters. On the problem, see P. Rabishauskas, *Die römische Kuriale,* 69 f.

precious metals, or the *vicedominus,* the curator of the Lateran Palace, it must be asked whether their functions did not lose their original character somewhat as early as the eighth century. This in no way excludes the possibility of acquiring important power: in the ninth and tenth centuries the *vestararius* exercised important functions not connected with his office as such.

The constituting of a strong central administration encountered the further insurmountable difficulty that there was no reliable nobility of office. Of course young nobles were expressly trained for the higher administrative career in the *sacrum cubiculum* and enrolled among the clerics by receiving the tonsure or even the lower orders,[17] but this half-clericate remained in final analysis a mere form. It did not prevent the ones concerned from marrying or from pursuing a thoroughgoing family policy, which could very easily include the interests of their blood relatives in the territorial aristocracy. The most profound cause for the weakness of the Papal State is ultimately to be sought in the papacy itself. The Popes would not have been able to force the disintegrated Byzantine provinces into a unity without disavowing their priestly ideals and exalting the desire for power above everything else. The papal election saw to it that such purely worldly-minded men did not ordinarily ascend the throne of Peter; it was concerned chiefly with the Bishop of Rome and not with the secular prince. It goes without saying that political and economic interests also played a great role in it, again to the detriment of the Papal State. At almost every change of pontificate they altered the balance of power. The attendant internal discords undermined the power of the central government. A consistent policy in the Papal State was virtually impossible.

This is the background against which must be viewed the history of the Papal State as it has already been narrated according to the individual epochs up to the middle of the eleventh century. Already under Leo III inner discords led to the reestablishment of an imperial protectorate. Up to a certain point the ninth-century Emperors actually fulfilled the task intended for them, even though Louis II and then more crudely the Spoletan Dynasty more than once injured the interests of the Papal State. The catastrophe approaching from the death of Louis II in 875 set in completely with the death of the Emperor Lambert in 898. When Sergius III returned in 904 after a six-years' exile, the Roman landed aristocracy was definitely victorious. In all branches of the administration, so we may assume, the powers of government were, little by little, wrested from the hands of the Popes, while the manorial-feudal principle gained ground and was consolidated under Alberic. Thereafter the Roman Church was able to manage directly only a few fragments of the old patrimony, situated close to the city; almost

[17] On the *sacrum cubiculum* and the *schola cantorum (orphanotrophium),* see L. Duchesne, *L'état pontificale,* 103–05.

all other estates and territories passed in actuality under the control of the nobility. The German Emperors were unable to change this situation; in fact, they probably did not even understand what had recently happened. For they ruled the German Kingdom, a feudally organized political association of persons, on principles different from those which the Byzantine and then the papal bureaucracy sought to apply in the territory of the Papal State.

Thus the Roman Church saw herself faced with a new situation. So long as Roman noble families exercised the secular power — by no means always to the detriment of the Church — the papacy had to let things take their course; the interesting effort of Silvester II to introduce feudal bonds in law remained an isolated and ineffective attempt. But in the Pope's own house, the Lateran Palace, the collapse of the old order in the Papal State so hurt the prestige of the traditional offices that the Popes had to come to terms at least there with the exigencies of a changed age. This occurred most fully in the period of the Gregorian reform, but certain initial steps go back to the turn of the tenth and eleventh centuries. They concerned first of all the papal chancery.

As a matter of fact the history of the papal chancery reflects with special clarity the development of the early mediaeval administrative organization in the Lateran. There is no need to discuss here its origin, which perhaps goes back to the third century. The chancery staff was furnished by the ecclesiastical notaries, who had gradually merged into a *schola* under the direction of the *primicerius* and of his deputy, the *secundicerius*. The two chiefs of the *schola* and notaries who were probably expressly selected took care of the chancery business. In the first place were specifically ecclesiastical matters. But the more the patrimony grew and the Roman Church was entrusted with political functions for the city of Rome, the more frequently were questions of secular administration involved; not infrequently ecclesiastical notaries received the management of patrimonies. The notaries obtained their training in the *schola cantorum* or *orphanotrophium*. Although tonsured, they must ordinarily have led the life of married laymen.

The seventh and eighth centuries were an especially productive period for the chancery. The book of formularies, or *Liber diurnus,* must have been drawn up at the beginning of this period in its first version, later to be repeatedly expanded.[18] At the same time much effort was expended on a special official hand; the final form was achieved in the eighth century, hence at the time of the separation from Byzantium, in the so-called *littera Romana,* or "curial hand", a special calligraphic type of the Roman cursive minuscule, which in its solemnity in a sense competed with the Byzantine imperial chancery hand. Probably already well developed before Hadrian I in its essentials, it was

---

[18] Editions: of the Vatican codex by T. Sickel (Vienna 1889); of all three codices by H. Foerster (Bern 1958); the best guides to the many studies and the problems are L. Santifaller in *HZ* 161 (1940), 542–58, and, in *Wattenbach-Levison,* the supplement by R. Bucher, "Die Rechtsquellen", 55–57.

used exclusively for papal charters to the end of the tenth century, then in the next century alongside the triumphantly advancing Carolingian minuscule, until eventually it was given up.

Thanks to the *privilegia,* a form of charter introduced under Hadrian I and standing in contrast to the letters, the chancery personnel moved out of anonymity. For in them the writer named himself — *notarius, scriniarius, notarius et scriniarius sanctae romanae ecclesiae,* or, later, *sacri Lateranensis palatii* — and so did an official of higher rank, who with his own hand added the great final dating and thus affixed to the privilege a sort of official recognition. He was either one of the above mentioned palatine judges or the *bibliothecarius,* whose office began at the end of the eighth century. Ordinarily, the *bibliothecarius* was a bishop, though, by way of exception, the celebrated Anastasius, who was appointed by Hadrian II but had already participated in the composing of letters under Nicholas I, was an abbot. It is not possible that seven palatine judges and a librarian who was in competition with them could have directed the papal chancery in the strict sense. In order to understand their functions we must probably diminish the far too elevated ideas which are entertained even today about the operation of the papal chancery at that time. The *notarii et scriniarii* must have done the real work, while the high ranking *datores* added the final official touches to the engrossed charter and hence performed a formal act that was indeed honourable and finally profitable but required little knowledge. Such an organization quite easily proved to be inadequate as soon as the charters or letters to be formulated went beyond the sphere of the routine. This was true especially of difficult ecclesiastical matters. The chancery officials, who, except for the librarian, actually belonged to the laity, were certainly not sufficiently equipped to deal with them. But if the *dictatores* of charters and letters were most probably appointed according to circumstances, regardless whether they pertained to the chancery or not, then the chancery must to a great extent have lacked inner cohesion.

Patrimonial and political duties of administration had enabled the lay element in the chancery to rise. Hence the more the worldly property of the Roman Church declined, the greater the difficulties which the palatine judges and notaries must have encountered. Probably in decline as early as the ninth century, the palatine judges were entirely deprived of their position at the Lateran in consequence of the domination by the Roman nobility that was then beginning, so that toward the end of the tenth century they lost even the right to the dating of privileges, which they had hitherto maintained, though at times with difficulty, *vis-à-vis* the competing librarian. What they saved was, on the one hand, trivial honourary rights in the papal court ceremonial and, on the other hand, their judicial competence for Roman civil trials, which they exercised to the end of the twelfth century.

The process of decay affected the institution of chancery notaries in so far as there was at times less to do. Hence the officials began at the same time to compose Roman private documents and thus gradually to turn into the *schola tabellionum urbis*. Whenever this development began, in the tenth century or earlier, in any case it caused the end of the ecclesiastical and papal notariate, so that now the papal chancery definitely approximated the primitive situation then existing in the chanceries of secular rulers. Since thereafter it did not dispose of a completely organized staff, it all the more urgently needed a man who would concern himself with the current business and have sufficient authority to put his assistants in motion. At the royal court this person was the chancellor. Hence it should be noted that at the end of the tenth century a *cancellarius sacri palatii* likewise appeared in the Lateran Palace.

There have been many conjectures as to the origin and competence of this new official.[19] Like the chancellor functioning at secular courts, he is probably to be regarded as the actual director of the entire business of papal diplomatics, who left to the librarian little more than a sort of honourary presidency, so that in 1023 Benedict VIII could, without difficulty, grant the library to Archbishop Pilgrim of Cologne. Apparently, the chancellor saw to everything: the dictating; the fair copy, which at times he took care of personally, but ordinarily entrusted to a select urban *scriniarius,* who was perhaps in a loose relationship of employee, or, in cases where secrecy was to be maintained under certain circumstances, to a palatine cleric; and finally the official engrossment. Actually, the great dating, in itself the right of the librarian, was not infrequently added by the chancellor. The attempt of the Bishop of Silva Candida to secure the direction of the chancery for his see forever led in 1037, after Pilgrim's death, to a fusion of library and chancery, but the stipulated connection with Silva Candida fortunately was not permanent. Except for brief interruptions, the chancellor-librarians continued to be named by the reigning Pope; they were dedicated deacons or priests, who slowly built up a new chancery organization conducted by clerics and developed new types of charters. In this way the urban *scriniarii* were left completely behind. They were, it is true, still called upon for the engrossing of papal privileges issued in Rome, but this regard for a traditional right had to come to an end some day, and it did so when in April 1123 the Frenchman Aimeric assumed the chancellorship.

Chapter 35

Metropolitans, Primates and Papacy

The groupings of the ecclesiastical hierarchy above the diocesan level in the West fell victim to a great extent to the political chaos of the seventh and eighth centuries. The struggle with Slavs and Avars had dreadful conse-

[19] For what follows, R. Elze in *StudGreg* IV (1952), 38–40; P. Rabishauskas, *op. cit.* 89–100.

quences in Noricum, Pannonia, Illyricum, Thrace, and Greece, while in
Gaul under the last Merovingians the churches were so ruthlessly plundered
by the magnates that the metropolitan groupings crumbled and not a few
bishoprics remained unoccupied. Western Christendom suffered its cruellest
blows from Islam, whose domination produced in time the total ruin of the
episcopal organization in North Africa and later in Sicily and its partial
collapse in Spain. The withdrawal of Africa and Spain, with their self-
conscious churches governed by their respective primates, meant for the
Christian West the loss of a good bit of ancient Christian tradition. All the
more strongly then there moved into the field of vision the institution which
had held to its ancient right not merely in principle but had impressively
emphasized it in the Anglo-Saxon, Frisian, and Central German mission field
by the founding of bishoprics, and in England even of metropolitan sees:
the papacy. Of course it was unable to develop freely. More than ever before,
the crown drew the ecclesiastical hierarchy into the service of the state, and
even in the purely inner ecclesiastical sphere there was no lack of forces that
opposed the Roman claims. Hence, in the period to be discussed here, the
relations between the papacy and the episcopate were subject to a certain
amount of conflict. And yet substantial decisions were made at that time.
Whereas the passage of time greatly weakened the ancient rights of metropolitans and did not permit any genuine supermetropolitan organizations,
such as territorial primacies, to appear at all, it could do nothing that was
essentially detrimental to the papacy, based on divine right. And so there
was made ready the ecclesiastical development that was to begin with the
Gregorian reform.

Metropolitan Organization

The ancient Christian metropolitan organization emerged, as such, out of
the collegiality of the episcopate in the apostolic succession, without any
direct action on the part of the Holy See, even though it had to be in communion with the successor of Peter and to that extent the unifying function
of the Roman primacy was given recognition. Through this autogenous
origin the metropolitan organization differed essentially from the apostolic
vicariates of Thessalonica and Arles, which the papacy set up in the fifth
century as its deputy courts with delegated authority and which had virtually
ceased to operate in the sixth and seventh centuries. The metropolitan
organization was, at least in the West, preponderantly collegial. The highest
tribunal was the provincial synod, at which the metropolitan was not much
more than the chairman. He convoked it, directed it, and supervised the
implementation of its decrees. But his right of supervision could be extended
so that he visited the bishoprics and controlled the administration of a

286

widowed diocese. The Western provincial synods were competent for legislation as well as for administration and justice. For example, they erected new dioceses, played a decisive role in the instituting of new bishops, in exceptional cases permitted the transfer of a bishop to another see, brought accused *episcopi comprovinciales* before their court, and, according to circumstances, deposed them. However, their activity could be limited by higher tribunals. In Italy the Pope's position as territorial primate conferred preponderance on the Roman Synods; in North Africa the same was true of those convoked by the Bishop of Carthage. A supermetropolitan synodal practice had also developed powerfully in Visigothic Spain.[1] In addition to and above all these groupings there was, of course, the Holy See, bearer of the universal primacy and at the same time of the patriarchate of the West.

This juridical situation, now sporadic to a great extent, had to be put in motion again as soon as, in the Carolingian *Imperium,* the ecclesiastical provinces were restored in the heart of the Christian West or were established for the first time, as in Austrasia. The mere fact that Charles the Great carried out the hierarchical organization in agreement with the Holy See indicates how very much the situation had changed. Whereas in Christian antiquity dioceses and provinces were set up by the episcopate, in the future they resulted from the cooperation of the secular and of the papal authority, and in this the juridically decisive act, the canonical erection, pertained to the Holy See. The Carolingians probably saw the advantage of ecclesiastical provinces to lie chiefly in the fact that the episcopate was organized and hence could more easily be fitted into the unity of the Empire. To them what mattered most in the final analysis was an imperial episcopate as compact as possible. They summoned it to the great imperial synods to regulate there the more important ecclesiastical questions. The result was that provincial synods declined in importance; in fact the Western practice of meeting once a year was allowed more and more to fall into desuetude.

As has already been explained, the decay of the Carolingian Empire induced the rulers to an even greater degree to make the instituting of bishops dependent upon themselves. They thereby deprived the metropolitan group of an important right. As late as the time of Hincmar of Reims the Frankish metropolitans used to dispatch one of their suffragans to the widowed diocese as visitor, and the election took place under his supervision. There followed the examination of both the election and the elect by metropolitan and suffragans, confirmation by the metropolitan, and finally consecration. At that time the West Frankish episcopate even sought to establish a sort of right of devolution: in the event of a misuse of the right of election by clergy and people, metropolitan and suffragans were to be permitted to designate

---

[1] On Carthage and Toledo, cf. H. Fuhrmann, "Patriarchate" in *ZSavRGkan* 70 (1953), 139–47; on the above mentioned vicariates of Arles and Thessalonica, cf. ibid. 147–76.

the new bishop themselves.[2] This claim was aimed chiefly at the designation by the King, which had meanwhile made its appearance. Although on occasion it could be enforced by strong personalities of the type of Hincmar, all such efforts were rendered ineffectual by the constantly growing chaos. The naming of the bishops became of so much importance for the secular princes in their power struggle that it virtually passed into their hands, while the rights of the metropolitan group were restricted in practice to the consecration of the bishop-elect, who had already been invested, and to the related ceremony of the *scrutinium*.

Not only the secular rulers but also the bishops contributed to the weakening of the metropolitan constitution. The decline of the practice of holding synods on the one hand and, on the other, the enhanced prestige which the metropolitans possessed by virtue of the new title of archbishop and of the pallium, now pertaining to them, caused the West Frankish archbishops to try to consolidate their position in the sense of a superiority of jurisdiction with regard to the *episcopi comprovinciales,* for whom the significant expression *suffraganei,* or assistants, began to come into use from the close of the eighth century. The conflict erupting between Hincmar of Reims and his suffragans, some of whom appealed to the Pope, would have acquired no very special importance, had it not left its mark in the letters of the Popes, especially of Nicholas I, and above all in the pseudo-Isidorean decretals. The compilers of pseudo-Isidore were at pains to limit the powers of archbishops from below and at the same time from above: from below, by making the synodal procedure for the trials of suffragans as difficult as possible; from above, by enhancing the papal authority. Referring to the Council of Sardica, which had provided the Holy See as the court of final appeal for accused bishops, and to the demand of Innocent I that all *causae maiores* were to be sent to Rome, they had recourse to forged texts to make the right precise in the sense that the bishop could appeal to the Holy See at any stage of the process, and the Pope thus appealed to could at once summon the case before his tribunal, that synodal judgments handed down in regard to bishops needed to be approved by the Pope, and that, by *causae maiores,* for which Rome was to be competent, were to be understood especially matters affecting bishops. They installed a further guarantee by giving the widest possible interpretation of the claim long made by the papacy to the convoking and confirming of general councils and thereby subordinated much that had to do with synods

---

[2] Important texts from the works of Hincmar of Reims in *PL* 126, 190–97 (especially 194 C–D, 260 C–D), 311 D; on Hincmar, see H. G. J. Beck in *CHR* 45 (1959f.), 273–308; on the whole question, P. Imbart de la Tour, *Les élections épiscopales,* 195–209. Toward the end of the century individual archbishops tried to get full control of the elections of their suffragans; cf. also Dumas in *Fliche-Martin* VII, 212–15. The basic idea of creating a right of devolution was taken up by the Roman Synod of 1080; see the *Registrum* of Gregory VII, 14a, no. 6 (Caspar's edition, 182).

to the Holy See.[3] Nicholas I did not neglect to make use of the new principles, which approximated his own ideas. Neither he nor pseudo-Isidore had his own way, but their claims continued to be influential. They left more or less strong, direct or indirect traces in almost every pre-Gregorian canonical collection, outside South Italy, not to mention the Gregorian reform movement, which took up pseudo-Isidore and to some extent the letters of Nicholas I and gave them special prominence.

Finally, the metropolitan right was turned in a new direction by the stronger connection of the archbishops with Rome by means of the pallium. This liturgical mark of honour, probably originating in the Byzantine court ceremonial, in the West belonged properly to the Pope, but was given by him to other individual bishops as a special mark of favour.[4] Originally it possessed no juridical significance. It is true that the evangelization of the Anglo-Saxons led Gregory the Great, Boniface V, and Honorius I to grant the pallium to the archbishops designated as heads of the mission and, in connection with it, the right to consecrate their future suffragans. And Gregory III referred to this practice in connection with the appointing of Saint Boniface as missionary archbishop.[5] But these were special measures, which had nothing to do with the ordinary form of conferring the pallium. It was only the custom, appearing from the end of the eighth century, of honouring all metropolitans with both the archiepiscopal title and the pallium, on the Anglo-Saxon model, that led to changes. The papacy now transformed the bestowing of the pallium on archbishops into an act which was the equivalent of confirmation and afforded the possibility of deriving the metropolitan authority from that of the Pope.

The new norms drawn up by Rome obliged every newly elevated archbishop to ask for the pallium within three months and in that connection to submit his profession of faith. Before the reception of the pallium — and we here touch the decisive point — he was neither to officiate at the consecration of suffragans nor to occupy the throne. The juridical sense of the last mentioned requirement cannot be determined exactly from the extant ninth-century sources, but in the tenth century several pallium privileges make known that by this symbol the Pope intended to grant the right to

---

[3] On pseudo-Isidore and Nicholas I, see the bibliography in *Feine RG,* para. 17, II (end); the forgers probably intended to concede to the Pope in principle a right to convoke national synods but confined this, in regard to provincial synods, to specific cases, especially to synodal processes against bishops; thus H. Barion, *Synodalrecht,* 370–73; cf. also ibid., 377–82, and S. Kuttner, *StudGreg,* II (1947), 392, footnote 20.

[4] Indispensable for the pallium, even though not always to the point, is J. Braun, *Die liturgische Gewandung in Occident und Orient* (Freiburg 1907), 620–76; C. B. Graf von Hacke, *Die Palliumverleihungen bis 1143* (Göttingen 1898); on the origin in the Byzantine court ceremonial, see T. Klauser, *Der Ursprung der bischöflichen Insignien und Ehrenrechte* (Krefeld n. d.), 18–22.

[5] *Jaffé* 1829, 2006, 2020, 2239.

consecrate suffragans. In the same manner the right to the title of archbishop was also occasionally connected with the granting of the pallium, and in a privilege granted by John XIX rights typical of legates were appended for the first time: to have the cross borne ahead of one, to ride a horse caparisoned in red on feast days, to decide urgent cases that pertained of themselves to the Holy See.[6] Thus the pallium developed in time more clearly into a symbol of metropolitan authority. The conferring of the pallium made the archbishop seem ever more like the Pope's deputy with a delegated share in the universal primacy, a view which was in fact slowly to establish itself after the middle of the eleventh century. Before then it did not achieve general acceptance. John VIII complained about West Frankish archbishops who consecrated suffragans before obtaining the pallium,[7] and the chaos that followed him was certainly not the time for enforcing a better discipline. On the whole, this was of little importance. No movement of opposition in principle, based on ideas, resulted. The majority of the archbishops must have observed the Roman prescriptions. Even the idea, appearing with the conferring of the pallium, of a participation in the primacy seems to have been assimilated by them. It appears thus in a forged papal privilege, drawn up under Archbishop Frederick of Salzburg, probably in 974–77:[8] "Petri Apostoli successores per loca . . . constituerunt archiepiscopos qui eorum vices tenerent in ecclesiis." The identification, here realized, of archbishop and apostolic vicar must have shown that a characteristic feature of the ancient Christian metropolitan constitution, that is, its autogenous origin, based on the collegiality of the episcopate, had disappeared from the living consciousness of Western Christendom. The victory of the Roman idea was only a question of time.

Primates, Apostolic Vicars, Legates

The missionary activity of Willibrord and Boniface and the beginning of a Frankish Church reform induced the Popes in the eighth century to bestow on individual bishops the supermetropolitan dignity of archbishop and the authority of a vicar. These expedients became unnecessary when Charles the Great re-established the metropolitan organization: metropolitan function and archiepiscopal dignity were united. The creating of supermetropolitan tribunals was thereafter thwarted, even though two Carolingian Emperors and later several archbishops tried it. It was probably due to the initiative of the Emperor Lothar I that in 844 Sergius II entrusted Bishop Drogo of Metz with a vicariate over all the transalpine ecclesiastical provinces, and

[6] *Germania Pontificia,* I, no. 37; *Salzburger Urkundenbuch,* II, no. 74.
[7] *MGEE* V, no. 120, 110; no. 99, 93; Synod of Ravenna, c. 1, *Mansi* XVII, 337; P. Grierson, "Rostagnus of Arles and the Pallium" in *EHR* 49 (1934), 74–83.
[8] *Germania Pontificia,* I, no. 35, *PL* 135, 1081; on the forgery, see A. Brackmann in *Studien und Vorarbeiten zur Germania Pontificia,* I (Berlin 1912), 93–103.

Charles the Bald, after his imperial coronation, secured a similar privilege for Archbishop Ansegis of Sens from John VIII. Both arrangements at once collapsed on the resistance of the episcopate. In the very lifetime of Ansegis, Rostagnus of Arles requested and obtained the vicariate for Gaul. In the tenth century also other prelates received by papal charters the super-metropolitan authority of a primate, apostolic vicar, or legate, or claimed a primacy on their own. Thus the following claims were confirmed by the Holy See: that of Mainz to the vicariate and legateship for Germany and for Lotharingian Gaul; that of Trier for the same; that of Magdeburg for the primacy in the lands to the right of the Rhine and for equality with the other archbishops in the lands to the left of the Rhine. Sens is said to have claimed the primacy granted to Ansegis over Gaul and Germany to the end of the tenth century, but this is doubtful. And in 1049 the Archbishop of Reims came forward with the claim that he was the primate in Gaul. But the very opposition in which the charters or the claims stood to one another shows the unimportance in practice of the prerogatives contained in them. Besides, any clear juridical form was absent from the primatial rank that was sought at a given time.

Fundamentally, there was only a single consistently constructed doctrine in regard to primates, and it was based on the fabrication of the pseudo-Isidorean forgeries. The better to limit the power of metropolitans from above, it created from nothing a primate-patriarch as a supermetropolitan court of appeal with very few rights. Its fabricated examples were taken from the ancient Roman provincial divisions contained in the *Notitia Galliarum.* Since every province was divided into subdivisions, for example, Belgica Prima and Belgica Secunda, the bishop of the *sedes prima,* that is, the metropolitan of the first subdivision, was declared to be the primate-patriarch over the metropolitans of the other subdivisions. Theutgaud of Trier, whose see was indeed the metropolis of Belgica Prima, at once seized upon this idea. But he was outfoxed by Hincmar of Reims, who now, in a smooth reversal of the pseudo-Isidorean idea, had himself confirmed by the Popes as primate of Belgica Secunda, that is, of his own province. Not until 200 years later did the wish of the forgers seem to be fulfilled — their primatial construction was accepted and realized. But, of course, the churches so distinguished obtained nothing or very little more than an honourary rank.

The Papacy

The more the Eastern and the Western halves of the Church drew apart, politically and intellectually, in the eighth and ninth centuries, the more clearly was the Roman Church confined to the Germanic-Romance West. This implied a decisive turn in the development of the Roman Primacy. In the West there was no longer an Emperor nor was there a Patriarch who could have played the role of a rival ecclesiastical authority *vis-à-vis* Rome. Due to the patriarchate of the West and at the same time to the universal primacy, which eclipsed and, so to speak, absorbed the patriarchal authority, the Roman Bishop occupied, without challenge, the first place within the Western hierarchy. The Germanic peoples felt a special veneration for the successor of Peter. From the fifth century there had developed, inside and outside Rome and not least of all in Merovingian Gaul, a Peter cult, which centred around the Petrine power of binding and loosing and honoured the Prince of the Apostles as the gatekeeper of heaven; this cult was carried to the Anglo-Saxons by the Roman missionaries. Though not of specifically Germanic, not to mention Anglo-Saxon, origin,[9] it had an especially powerful appeal for the ingenuous Germans. Furthermore, it was of advantage to the Roman Church to be regarded as mother of all Western churches. The notion, already expressed by Innocent I[10] and quickly elaborated into legend in ecclesiastical Gaul, included many churches of Neustria and, in Austrasia, especially Trier and Cologne in the eighth and ninth centuries. All of them attributed their founding to men whom either Peter or his successor Clement had sent out or to disciples of Paul, until in the tenth century individual West Frankish sees proceeded to derive their origin, no longer from Rome, but from the group of the Lord's seventy-two disciples.[11]

The legends pointing to Rome were able to attest virtually nothing, and the cult of Peter very little that was definite, in regard to the prerogatives of the Holy See. Even the universal primacy, based on divine right and resolutely defended by West Frankish theologians against Photius,[12] needed a more exact formulation by the positive *ius ecclesiasticum* promulgated by man.[13]

[9] Thus T. Zwölfer, *Sankt Peter, Apostelfürst und Himmelspförtner. Seine Verehrung bei den Angelsachsen und Franken* (Stuttgart 1929), and, following him, *Haller* I, ixf., 467–71, with the thesis of the Germanic cult of Peter originating among the Anglo-Saxons, which was grafted like a strange shoot on to the idea of the primacy and thus revived it. Both authors were corrected by K. Hallinger, "Römische Voraussetzungen der bonifatianischen Wirksamkeit im Frankenreich" in *St. Bonifatius. Gedenkgabe* (Fulda 1954), 320–61; E. Ewig, "Der Petrus- und Apostelkult im spätrömischen und fränkischen Gallien" in *ZKG* 71 (1960), 215–51; id., "Die Kathedralpatrozinien im römischen und fränkischen Gallien" in *HJ* 79 (1960), 1–61; F. Susman, "Il culto di S. Pietro a Roma dalla morte di Leone M. a Vitaliano 461–672" in *AD Romana* 84 (1961), 1–192; cf. also J. Szöverffy, "St. Peter in Medieval Latin Hymns" in *Tr* 10 (1954), 275–322.

[10] *Jaffé* 311; *PL* 20, 551f.

[11] For France, Dumas in *Fliche-Martin* VII, 179–86; cf. also E. Ewig, "Kaiserliche und apostolische Tradition im mittelalterlichen Trier" in *Trierer Zeitschrift für Geschichte und Kunst* 24–26 (1956–58), 147–86; *Geschichte des Erzbistums Köln*, I, revised by W. Neuss and F. W. Oediger (Cologne 1964).

[12] Ratramnus, *Contra Graecorum opposita* in *PL* 121, 334–46; Aeneas of Paris, *Liber adversus Graecos,* cap. 187–209 in *PL* 121, 748–59.

[13] Whoever of the mediaeval authors had in view the primatial privileges of positive law did not at all have to deny the divine-law basic character of the Roman Primacy. The absolute antithesis of the two views in the form of a "Leonine" and of a "Cyprianic" type in the work

Here slight time-conditioned circumstances or even fundamental differences of opinion were influential. The papacy experienced this when, under Nicholas I, it not only took up the old tradition in its entirety but also tried energetically to carry it on. It aimed to assimilate the primatial claim to the new situation upon which it had entered at the beginning of the Carolingian period.

That this initiative was up-to-date is shown by the pseudo-Isidorean decretals, which, independently of Rome, were driving in the same direction. And still, insurmountable obstacles stood in the way. Even if the bishops did not presume to deny the basis in the divine law of the pre-eminence claimed by Nicholas, they were still aware that, as successors of the Apostles, they possessed a power which likewise went back to Christ. Thus was revived the ancient question, not clarified in early Christian times, of the relationship between the primatial and the episcopal power. The intellectual abilities then at hand were not in a position to solve it. The new claims of the Pope found all the less sympathy in that men of the early Middle Ages had a static juridical interpretation, which stubbornly defended the old law. Then, when, with the dissolution of the Carolingian Empire, political chaos set in, the successor states were established, and the papacy, humiliated under the domination of the Roman nobility, was deeply degraded, the initiative of Nicholas I became a thing of the past. But the past could continue to have influence. It certainly did in this case, even though to a degree that differed according to countries and personalities.

If we examine the canonical collections of that period,[14] two South Italian works, influenced by Greek notions of the Church, stand out as foreigners: the *Collectio IX librorum* (c. 920–930), and the *Collectio V librorum* (c. 1020). The typically Western compilations ordinarily hold fast to the Roman tradition; that is, they recognize in the Pope an ecclesiastical supremacy that was established by Christ. But with regard to the concrete rights of the papacy, they display considerable differences. Thus, for example, the *Collectio Anselmo dedicata,* compiled at Milan soon after 882, interprets the papal power as broadly as possible, following pseudo-Isidore, whereas Burchard of Worms in his decree (1025) observes definite limits determined by the claims of the episcopate; this in turn induced the probably South German compiler of the *Collectio XII partium* to stress the primacy more strongly. In the substantial treatises which Auxilius composed at the beginning of the tenth

of Klinkenberg cited in the Literature is therefore inadmissible in method, not to mention the scarcely convincing interpretations of individual passages; cf. also the criticism by H. Keller in *DA* 20 (1964), 354, footnote 134.

[14] On the mostly unpublished canonical collections, see *Fournier-LeBras* I (Paris 1931); Burchard's *Decretum* in *PL* 140, 537–1058; cf. A. M. Koeniger, *Burchard von Worms und die deutsche Kirche seiner Zeit* (Munich 1905); on the manuscript circulation of the *Decretum,* O. Meyer in *ZSavRGkan* 55 (1935), 141–83; F. Pelster, *MiscMercati,* 114–57; *StudGreg* I (1947), 321–51; on the acceptance of the *Decretum* in Italy, C. C. Mor, *ibid.* 197–206.

century in defence of the Formosan ordinations[15] there are even two views of the papal primacy to be met — an extremely papalist and a moderate.

In order to find a firm support in the confusing picture, the viewpoint of Burchard of Worms, and hence of the most successful author, should be briefly sketched. Despite a disputed passage[16] there can be no doubt that Burchard did not represent an episcopalist system but accepted a genuine Roman primatial power as founded by Christ. In his view the Pope was the highest tribunal for *causae maiores* and in particular in regard to controversies among bishops; his decretals occupied a special place among the sources of the law; he had the right to summon and confirm general councils; the tradition of the Roman Church was binding; canonical books were subject to her approval; synodal judgments on bishops were subject to the reservation, *salva in omnibus apostolica auctoritate;* bishops could appeal to the Holy See, and the Pope could depose or appoint bishops; transfers of bishops needed the consent of the provincial episcopate or of the Holy See. On the other hand, Burchard was unwilling to admit a direct papal power of jurisdiction over the individual faithful, except to a limited extent.

Other collections went further, teaching, for example, the infallibility of the Roman Church; the immunity of the Pope from judgment unless he was a heretic;[17] his right, in case of need, to modify old canons or to lay down new norms, to ordain the clerics of any church whatsoever, to absolve from all sins and from oaths, and so forth. Furthermore, the inherited sanctity of the *vicarius Petri* must have had defenders at the time of Auxilius, since he wrote against it.[18] What we are here listing concisely from sources of differing worth and of differing content must have shown at least that the stream of tradition relevant to the Roman Primacy divided to form a delta, but flowed on and, to a great extent, together with pseudo-Isidore and other more ancient sources, emptied directly into the Gregorian reform movement.

The canonical collections were the works of scholars, which did not by any means have to be in accord with juridical practice. Only the concrete

---

[15] Auxilius, *In defensionem sacrae ordinationis papae Formosi,* ed. E. Dümmler, *Auxilius und Vulgarius* (Leipzig 1866), 59–105; *De ordinationibus a Formoso papa factis* in *PL* 129, 1059–74; to be supplemented by E. Dümmler, *ibid.* 107–16; *Infensor et defensor* in *PL* 129, 1074–1102. At least the second work was known to both Peter Damiani and Humbert of Silva Candida; cf. J. Ryan, *Saint Peter Damian and his Canonical Sources* (Toronto 1956), 162–64.

[16] I, c. 3, *PL* 140, 549f.; better than the episcopalist interpretation of Koeniger (*supra,* footnote 14), 60, is that of P. Fournier, "Le Décret de Bourchard de Worms" in *RHE* 12 (1911), 470, footnote 1.

[17] The heresy stipulation was expressed clearly at the Roman Council of 869 and in Auxilius; cf. also J. Ryan in *MS* 20 (1958), 222–24, and S. Lindemanns, *La primauté du pape.* Nicholas I regarded the decrees of his predecessors as binding only in so far as they were orthodox at death; thus A. Greinacher, *Die Anschauungen des Papstes Nikolaus I.* (Berlin–Leipzig 1909), 15.

[18] Auxilius, *In defensionem sacrae ordinationis papae Formosi,* ed. Dümmler, 81–84; from the cited work of Lindemans, with his kind permission.

activity of the Holy See can give us an idea of what the primacy then actually meant. Mention has already been made of a powerful increase in Rome's authority. While the endeavour, beginning in the ninth century, to bind the archbishops more firmly to the Holy See by means of the pallium was not a complete success, the papacy became the ecclesiastical court which, together with the secular rulers, decided the founding of episcopal and metropolitan sees, not always to the satisfaction of the episcopate. Thus the Synod of Tribur in 895 referred harshly to the "iugum vix ferendum", which it said the Holy See imposed,[19] not least of all because the Roman decisions in regard to the archbishopric of Hamburg-Bremen were displeasing to the Archbishop of Cologne and his friends.

Growing prestige no doubt brought about the relationship which the Holy See gained with regard to the monks. Even in antiquity the incorporation of the monastic communities into the diocesan organization had brought on difficulties with the bishops. It was universally recognized that the Church's sacramental and disciplinary power in regard to monks pertained to the episcopate; until the turn of the tenth to the eleventh century there was probably not a single monastery, not excepting Bobbio and Fulda, that had been withdrawn by a papal privilege of exemption from the ecclesiastical jurisdiction of the *ordinarius loci*.[20] But from about the seventh century the Popes had issued charters of protection to individual monasteries in order to guarantee their property against alienation or pillage. Rulers did the same. It has already been explained how very much Louis the Pious strengthened his rule over bishoprics and monasteries by the combining of immunity and royal protection. The more the West Frankish royal power now declined, the more often did the monasteries of that kingdom seek papal protection; some of them, by commendation, even became the property of the Roman Church. This example was imitated. In the course of the tenth and especially of the eleventh century Italy, France, Germany, and the March of Spain were covered with a network of monasteries under papal protection or papal ownership. The initiative was taken, not by Rome, but by the monks, who especially looked for assistance against interference by bishops. Then, when around 1000 the papacy began to exempt individual favoured monasteries from the ecclesiastical jurisdiction of the diocesan bishop, Rome's primatial claim and monasteries' efforts for exemption coalesced into a real community of interests. In the monastic world, especially of France and to some extent of Italy, there now arose particularly zealous defenders of the Roman prerogatives. Abbot Abbo of Fleury (988–1004) is a typical example. Not only in his struggles for the privileges of his monastery, which he fought out with

---

[19] Tribur, c. 30, *Mansi* XVIII, 147; *MGCap* II, 230f.
[20] Thus Schwarz, *ZSavRGkan* 76 (1959), 34–98. It would not be surprising, then, that Burchard of Worms passed over in silence in his *Decretum* the exemptions that first appeared in his time.

the episcopate, but also in the troubles at Reims, to be discussed later, and in his writings, above all his *Compilatio canonum,* he again and again stressed the authority of the Holy See.

An innovation of the utmost importance appeared in the field of cult at the end of the tenth century. In 993 Bishop Ulric of Augsburg (d. 973) was canonized by Pope John XV at a Roman Synod. Soon after, John XVIII canonized Martial of Limoges, and then Benedict IX did the same for the Trier hermit, Simeon of Syracuse. Thereafter the Popes elevated saints in increasing numbers to the honours of the altar; bishops and synods continued to do the same until under Innocent III the Holy See reserved this right to itself and firmly established it in the decretals of Gregory IX (1234). This was the final result of a two-centuries' development, which belief in Peter, living on in the papacy, had prepared. How powerful this belief must have been, when it looked to the papacy, precisely at the period of its deepest humiliation, for the first time as the especially secure guarantor of the cult of new saints!

The veneration of Peter had long been active in the penitential discipline. Not a few Christians felt themselves drawn irresistibly to Rome to ask absolution of their sins from the vicar of the keeper of the keys and of the gate of heaven. If there was question of serious crimes, bishops were glad to send the guilty to the Pope, because they attributed to him a more certain judgment or even a greater authority. Basically they acknowledged thereby that the Holy See possessed a jurisdiction over all the faithful. Of course, strict legal norms were lacking; there were neither sins that were reserved to the Pope at that time nor a rule about cases already decided by the local bishop and then sent to Rome. This led to a sharp collision between Benedict VIII and Archbishop Aribo of Mainz.[21]

After the marriage of the Count of Hammerstein had been dissolved by a synodal decree on account of consanguinity, and excommunication had been decreed against the recalcitrant couple, the Countess Irmingardis appealed to the Pope in 1023. Thereupon Archbishop Aribo had the Synod of Seligenstadt issue a decree in 1023 to the effect that no penitent was allowed to seek absolution at Rome or to appeal there before he had performed the penance imposed at home; anyone who wished to appeal had to obtain the permission of his own bishop and get from him a document which would explain the facts to the Pope.[22] Although this decree strongly emphasized the disciplinary authority of the bishop concerned and made recourse to Rome difficult, in accord with pseudo-Isidore, it was probably directed neither against the Holy See's power to absolve nor against the right of the

---

[21] D. von Kessler, *Der Eheprozess Ottos und Irmingards von Hammerstein* (Berlin 1923).

[22] Synod of Seligenstadt, c. 18 in *MGConst* I, 633–39. Since Burchard of Worms took part in the synod and advocated a similar stand in his *Decretum,* the canon was probably formulated with his assistance. On the interpretation of the canon, see *Hauck* III, 536 (with footnote 1)–538.

faithful to appeal. The right adjudged to the local bishop involved a delicate limiting of the primatial power of the Pope, which embraced all the faithful. The relationship between papacy and episcopacy was so far from being clarified here that Benedict VIII now proceeded against Aribo, forbidding him the use of the pallium, while Aribo, energetically defended by his suffragans, persisted in his defiance. Benedict's death in 1024 ended the quarrel, and Aribo, under pressure from the new King Conrad II, was able to discontinue the process against the Countess Irmingardis without any substantial loss of prestige. But the problem persisted. John XIX had to annul the absolution of the Count of Auvergne, whom his bishop had excommunicated for adultery, and in a similar case a French synod confronted him with principles corresponding to the attitude taken at Seligenstadt.

Rome was not infrequently involved in difficulties occasioned by the deposition or installation of bishops. Ordinarily the initiative proceeded from one of the parties. Since almost always political interests were directly or indirectly involved, the secular rulers had an important and often a decisive word to say. In spite of this burdensome dependence in both the decisions and their execution, Rome turned her intervention to advantage. At the same time it was a further reminder of the primatial claims. Occasionally the Popes went quite far in this. Thus in 881 John VIII consecrated at Rome the Emperor's candidate for the see of Lausanne and seems eventually to have established him in preference to King Boso's adherent, whom the Archbishop of Vienne had consecrated. In the same way in 889 Stephen V thwarted the attempt of Archbishop Aurelian of Lyons, a partisan of King Eudes, to impose on the church of Langres a person agreeable to him in place of the bishop already elected, a sympathizer of Charles the Simple.[23] In cases of this sort the Popes were glad to send legates who took care to preside over the synods that were summoned and thereby secured greater respect for the claims made by Rome to summon and direct synods.[24]

Just how matters stood with regard to the Pope's competence in the trials of bishops was to appear toward the end of the tenth century. At issue was the tangled situation at Reims, brought about by the political treason committed by the Carolingian, Archbishop Arnulf of Reims, in 989 and his condemnation by the Synod of Senlis in 990 at the instigation of King Hugh Capet. According to pseudo-Isidore the synodal sentence required papal confirmation. The principle must have been clearly recognized at the time, for both synod and King wrote to ask the assent of John XV. It was only when the Pope neglected to reply that many French bishops and several abbots met in the monastery of Saint-Basle at Verzy in 991 and definitively

---

[23] T. Schieffer, *Legaten,* 28–30; on papal interventions from 900, see Dumas in *Fliche-Martin* VII, 215–17.

[24] On legates, see H. Barion, *Synodalrecht,* 386–91; on the Pope's right of convoking and directing, ibid., 370–86.

deposed Arnulf. Gerbert of Aurillac was chosen Archbishop of Reims in his stead.

The decision was preceded by a long discussion.[25] The abbots present, including Abbo of Fleury, protested because of the lack of papal approval. They were answered by Bishop Arnulf of Orléans with ideas very likely suggested by Gerbert. He did not rest satisfied merely with referring to the recourse to Rome that had taken place and to the emergency produced by the Pope's silence; he also posed the question of principle, of the value of the papal right. In his view a synod could judge bishops without Rome, if — here he took up an idea of Hincmar of Reims — the case were clear and its treatment were determined by law; he also referred to the African Church, which he said had never known a Roman judicial supremacy over bishops. Furthermore, in his decisions the Pope was bound by right and by Church law, and hence he could merely ratify the deposition of Arnulf. In the event that he intended to quash it, no one needed to obey him. Power alone did not make a judge; he had to dispose also of the requisite intellectual and moral qualities. It was just these presuppositions which were not present at that time in criminal and venal Rome — there followed a dreadful indictment of the tenth-century papacy. The arguments of the Bishop of Orléans were repeated by Gerbert at the Synods of Mouzon and Reims in part and more moderately and in some letters in detail and more pointedly.

The challenge laid down at Verzy naturally set Rome in motion. John XV sent Abbot Leo of Sant'Alessio all'Aventino as legate and finally summoned the two Capetian Kings, Hugh and Robert II, and the bishops to Rome. The only result was that a new synod, meeting at Chelles probably in 994, declared that Roman decrees which contradicted the decrees of the Fathers were null and void; for a Pope who should presume to act thus, the sentence of the Apostle applied: "haereticum hominem et ab ecclesia dissentientem penitus evita".[26] The Roman Church was equally unbending. In 995 Gerbert was suspended by the Legate Leo at the Synod of Mouzon. The same sentence overtook the participants of the Synod of Verzy, who had been summoned by Gregory V to the Synod of Pavia in 997 but had not presented themselves. Nevertheless, the papacy would have accomplished little, had not the Capetians, threatened in their already insecure position by the aligning of Rome alongside Otto III and the German episcopate, been ready to yield. Abbo of Fleury acted as their intermediary. Robert II, sole King since October 996, was even less able to fight longer because he was compromised by an unlawful marriage, and Gerbert encountered such serious difficulties

---

[25] A. Olleris, Œuvres de Gerbert (Paris 1867), 173–236; PL 139, 289–338.

[26] Richeri Historiarum libri IV, IV, 89, ed. R. Latouche, in ClassHist 17, 290–92; on chronological problems of the controversy, Gerbert's call to the service of Otto III, and the reinstatement of Arnulf, see M. Uhlirz, JbbDG: Otto III., 478–86, 487–93, 518–25.

in Reims that he fled to Otto III. And so in the summer of 997 the church of Reims was given back to Arnulf. As Pope Silvester II, Gerbert was to bring the matter to a definite end. In a charter he recognized Arnulf. The Archbishop, he said, had offended, but he could be reinstated "romanae pietatis munere", because his deposition had not obtained Rome's assent.[27] What Gerbert, as Arnulf's rival, had declared to be wicked and invalid, he had unhesitatingly done as Pope.

The importance of the controversy lay, not in Rome's actual victory, which depended essentially on political circumstances, but in the attitude adopted by the French episcopate. It throws a clear light on the forces of opposition which could be brought to bear in regard to Rome by the bishops of the time. The basic standpoint represented at Verzy and Chelles touched upon the worth of the good old law; set down in the canons of the past, it should bind the Pope too. Since there was here involved a general principle, applied to the secular authority in a similar manner, the position assumed by the bishops declared a limit which the old fashioned concept raised — the impossibility of conceiving of a monarch able to dispose of positive law as its sovereign. If it is added that the episcopal authority is of divine law and that the relationship between the college of bishops and the papacy was not sufficiently clear, the resistance that was offered becomes even more intelligible. It was not directed against the primatial power as such, at least not in the sense of a genuine episcopalism, not to mention a conciliarism. All involved, Gerbert included, were convinced that the vicar of Peter had received the universal primacy from Christ. And within the sphere of positive law in which even the primacy had to find its concrete elaboration, they fully recognized Rome's right to confirm synodal judgments on bishops, as demanded by pseudo-Isidore, and hence they conceded to the Holy See a very extensive supreme judicial sovereignty.

The anti-Roman reactions of particular groups of bishops are, then, not to be overestimated. If one examines the constitutional position taken by the hierarchy during the Carolingian and Ottonian periods, the picture favours the episcopate less than it does the papacy. Deep as was the papacy's humiliation, it still imperturbably kept the idea of its universal primacy before its gaze as its guiding idea. The concept of collegial unity, on the other hand, on which was based the canonical position of the bishops, had at that time been weakened to a considerable degree. It is true that under the Carolingians there was an imperial episcopate which, after the decay of the *Imperium*, survived energetically at least in Germany, but what mattered was not this old fashioned institution, mainly supported by imperial law. Far more important were the episcopal groupings fashioned by the ancient Church, and it was precisely these which, as has been seen, were unable to develop

[27] *Jaffé* 3908; *PL* 139, 273f.; J. Havet, *Lettres de Gerbert* (Paris 1889), 239f.

properly. And so the papacy was much better prepared for the coming development of the Church that was to be set in motion by the Gregorian reform.

CHAPTER 36

The Sacraments and the Mass

At the beginning of the Carolingian period liturgical life in the individual areas of the West displayed that wide diversity which had developed in the centuries of transition. In addition to the Roman liturgy, which was also used in England since the evangelization of the Anglo-Saxons as well as in the greater part of Italy, there were the Old Spanish, the not very uniform Gallican, the Ambrosian, and the Irish-Scottish or Celtic, consisting for the most part of borrowings. All of the preceding were in the Latin language. Frequently they were contrasted with the Roman liturgy under the collective name of Gallic liturgy.

The suppression of these liturgies started in Gaul, where bishops and abbots, in view of the chaos in their own liturgy since the seventh century, began to prefer texts from the orderly Roman liturgy. These texts circulated in the form of *libelli,* which contained particular formularies, and also in the form of the *Sacramentarium Gelasianum,* which obtained a new revision on Gallic soil around the middle of the eighth century: the so-called later *Gelasianum.* The general change took place under King Pepin, who around 754 prescribed the transition to the Roman liturgy, and definitively under Charles the Great, who obtained a Gregorian Sacramentary for himself from Rome around 785–6; it was imposed at Aachen as the obligatory model. Roman chant books, lists of pericopes, and *ordines* had long been eagerly copied in Frankish *scriptoria,* but the ritual directions of the Roman *ordines* experienced not unimportant adaptations to the established proper usages.

Since the Roman liturgy now prevailed in the Frankish Empire, it also advanced into Spain with the *Reconquista* that moved forward from the north. The recovery of Toledo in 1085 and, even earlier, the pressure exercised by Gregory VII brought about the decline of the Old Spanish liturgy, called "Mozarabic" ("arabicized") since the time of the Muslim conquest, which from now on survived only in vestiges.

In Scotland the Celtic liturgy yielded to the Roman at the instigation of Queen Margaret (d. 1093), in Ireland in consequence of a decree of the Synod of Cashel in 1172. Only the Ambrosian held its ground in the face of all threats by Peter Damiani and Gregory VII; it adopted only particular features of the Roman liturgy.

The development within the Frankish Empire became of decisive importance for the future. On the one hand, the texts contained in the liturgical books were taken over with great fidelity — all the feast days of local Roman saints were retained — and, on the other hand, consciously and unconsciously various additions from the local tradition and adaptations to local needs were made, which later passed on to the Universal Church. In particular, the Gregorian Sacramentary received from Alcuin a supplement which was gathered from Gelasian, Spanish, and local material and in the later manuscripts was at once blended with the Sacramentary itself. The tenth-century Fulda Sacramentary can be regarded as typical of the definitive amalgamation.

A significant work brought about the maturity of the German Church in the age of the Ottos for the Pontifical Mass. A monk of Sankt Alban at Mainz around 950 created the Roman-German *Pontificale*, which, among other things, included the renowned *Ordo Romanus Antiquus* as a part of it. This is the *Pontificale* which is the basis of the later *Pontificale Romanum*. Liturgical usage was put together in it from the West and the East Frankish Churches and expanded by special additions. Liturgical manuscripts from the northern lands then enjoyed a great reputation, even in their technical achievements. When in 998 Gregory V confirmed in writing various privileges of the abbey of Reichenau, he demanded in return on specified occasions the delivery of an *epistolarium*, an *evangeliarium*, and a *sacramentarium*.

The administration of baptism was only slightly affected by the changes. It should take place, as Charles emphasized in a decree of 789, "secundum morem Romanum". Making an inquiry among the bishops, he received from them around 811 a more or less clear and in part detailed explanation of the rite as carried out in their territories,[1] which in fact corresponded with the Roman tradition. Following the *exsufflatio,* the signing with the cross, and the proffering of the salt, the *scrutinia* occupied a good bit of space. Theoretically it was even prescribed that in this matter, as in the Roman *ordo scrutiniorum,* there had to be seven stages of preparation, distinct from one another in time, which, furthermore, consisted almost exclusively of exorcisms, even at Rome since the cessation of adult baptism, apart from the *traditio symboli et orationis dominicae.* The just mentioned *Ordo Romanus Antiquus* still gave the seven *scrutinia.* In the actual practice of the Carolingian Church, probably even at the time of that inquiry, as various signs indicate, apart from special occasions the bulk of the *scrutinia* were combined in a single preparatory act on the Wednesday of the fourth week of Lent, which was followed only by the concluding rites, with the baptism. In fact, Holy Saturday and the Vigil of Pentecost were now regarded as the only permissible days for the baptism of children, whereas these days had originally been set aside for the baptism of adults. Baptism itself was administered by immersion.

---

[1] Detailed reports are extant from Leidrad of Lyons (*PL* 99, 853), Theodulf of Orléans (*PL* 105, 223–40), and Amalarius (*PL* 99, 893–901).

The missionary work on the eastern frontier of the Frankish state brought it about that the baptism of adults continued to be a source of lively concern. After the unhappy experiences with forcible mass baptisms among the Saxons, people were ready to listen to Alcuin's voice, calling for an orderly procedure, without compulsion and with previous instruction. Augustine's *De catechizandis rudibus* was to serve as model for the instruction. The missionary conference on the Danube, arranged by Charles's son Pepin after the overthrow of the Avars in 796, accordingly required a preparation of forty, or at least of seven, days, with real instruction, and then seven days of direct ascetical and liturgical preparation. The preparatory instruction was to be concerned with the articles of faith. It was felt, with appeal to Matthew 28:20, that moral instruction could be left substantially to the time after baptism.[2] In such a manner and with a subsequent acclimating did the conversion of the Germans proceed.

Important changes occurred in this period in regard to the administration of the Sacrament of penance. For serious public offences, *causae criminales*, public ecclesiastical penance, directed by the bishop, remained in use throughout this time. It began with the inauguration of the penance on Ash Wednesday. The Roman tradition was made even stricter under the influence of oriental canons. On Ash Wednesday the penitents were not merely excluded from Mass; they were expelled from the Church, "as once Adam from paradise", — see the Adam door of the Bamberg cathedral — and the church was forbidden to them until Easter, or in serious cases for a longer period, as prescribed by the Synod of Worms in 868; only individual churches, which had received the privilege, remained accessible to them. Strict fasting was especially taken into consideration as a penance, and it was to be connected with specific exercises of prayer.

But commutations now played an important role. By this term was meant the possibility of "buying oneself off" from the severe penance imposed by substituting easier and shorter penitential works. In their beginnings the commutations accompanied the oldest Irish penitentials of the sixth century and only disappeared with the eventual suppression of these and the discontinuing of their "scale of penances" in the eleventh and twelfth centuries. Originally they were allowed only in justified cases, such as sickness or difficult work, but they soon became the general practice; often the possible substitutions were already given in the penitential itself. Most favoured was the converting of the strict fast into the praying of psalms; for example, three days of fasting could be represented by three times fifty psalms, which were usually connected with one genuflection each. According to Regino of

---

[2] Bishop Paulinus of Aquileia reported on the conference (*MGConst* II, 172–76). Even as to belief, in the collection of catechetical writings of Sankt Emmeran, belonging to this occasion, the mystery of Christ is treated in an extremely summary manner; J. M. Heer, *Ein karolingischer Missionskatechismus* (Freiburg 1911).

Prüm, one fast day could be commuted into 100 prostrations. Alms and pilgrimage were also taken into consideration. The pilgrimage to Rome was popular, but for it the consent of the bishop was required by the Synod of Seligenstadt in 1023. The far-reaching depersonalization of penance became clear when the *Poenitentiale Bedae* of the eighth century even allowed one to be represented by a substitute, who would perform the penance. While the Synod of Tribur in 895 even recognized money commutation, other synods fought with little success against commutations or particular forms of them.

In accord with Roman tradition, the public ecclesiastical penance was concluded on Holy Thursday by means of the reconciliation, the rite for which continued on at the cathedrals in an elaborate form throughout the whole of this period. The penitents were conducted before the bishop during the singing of *Venite, filii,* and he restored them to the community of the faithful with the imposition of hands and prayer.

For the rest of the faithful, confession once a year was now the general rule. A first testimony to this is provided by England around 670. Around the turn of the eighth century it was mentioned as a strict prescription for the Frankish realm by Theodulf (*Capitulare* I, 36). Confession was to be made before the beginning of Lent. In England the day preceding Ash Wednesday thus acquired the name Shrove Tuesday, from "to shrive", that is, "to hear confessions", because the penance imposed according to the penitentials and also the name of the penitent had to be "written". As the pattern for the examination of conscience were mentioned the seven or eight capital sins, "without which hardly anyone is able to live". If there were no serious offences, the penitent was at first dismissed with a blessing, an *absolutio,* whose sacramental character is not clear. In other cases, and in the ninth century even generally, after the corresponding penance one had to appear on Holy Thursday for reconciliation. In accord with the tendency to transfer forms of public penance to all, thereafter the ashes were also imposed on all on Ash Wednesday. From the end of the ninth century excuses were more and more sought that would permit the reconciling of individual penitents at once, before the performing of the penance. This practice became general around the turn of the tenth century, and thus confession was no longer connected with Lent.

In the period under consideration the Anointing of the Sick becomes clearer. In fact it appeared in connection with the penance of the sick, that is, with the forms of public ecclesiastical penance that were adapted for the sick, which everyone was careful to receive on his deathbed, but which, because of the heavy obligations connected with them, were postponed by the faithful as long as possible. The Anointing of the Sick was inserted into the penance of the sick between the assigning of the penance and the reconciliation; but from the tenth century it was frequently imparted only after the reconciliation, as the "last anointing". If possible, several priests should participate.

A considerable change took place also in the forms of ordination. Of the lesser orders, in the age of the Carolingian reform almost universally only the subdiaconate and the order of acolyte, or, instead of the latter, sometimes that of lector, continued in use, and these as real functions. But in books the old list of seven orders continued to be given, and they were now explained as developments of a general order. In the tenth century persons began to understand them as a ladder, on which the individual ascended to the higher orders. Leo VIII, chosen Pope as a layman in 963, hurried through them in a few days. The *traditio instrumentorum,* long customary for the lesser orders, was now adopted also for the higher orders. Ordination to the subdiaconate already approximated that to the diaconate in the Roman-German *Pontificale,* except that before the twelfth century the subdiaconate was not reckoned as a major order.

In matrimony, which, in accord with the forms of Germanic law, took place in such a way that the father or guardian of the bride handed her over to the bridegroom, there was no ecclesiastical rite in this period except in so far as the married couple then attended the nuptial Mass and received the priest's blessing. However, there first had to be an ecclesiastical investigation to determine whether there was any matrimonial impediment. Especially because of the degrees of relationship these constituted an important object of synodal decisions.

Despite complete fidelity to the text of the traditional Roman prayers, a grand-scale adaptation took place in the very heart of the liturgy, the celebration of Mass. Dramatic elements were added — incensations, changing position of the candlesticks, the giving of special prominence to the Gospel by means of a solemn procession and the place of its proclamation. The simple popular chants of the ordinary, now usually tended to by a choir of clerics, were musically enriched and provided with tropes, that is, with texts which corresponded, syllable for syllable, to the notes of the melody. The *jubilus* of the Alleluia was elaborated into the sequence, and there immediately occurred the springtime of sequence writing, especially with Notker Balbulus (d. 912). The praying of the Canon in silence, attested around 800, was also esteemed as a dramatic element: following the model of the Old Testament, only the priest was to enter into the sanctuary of the Canon. The Gallican pontifical blessing after the Lord's Prayer continued in use. And the kiss of peace was expressly encouraged. According to the prescriptions of Charles the Great, all present were to receive it. It was often regarded as a kind of substitute for communion. However, the custom soon developed that it was received only by the communicants and in such a way that it now proceeded from the altar and was passed on. Communion was still received under both species. As a rule the Host was only dipped into the Precious Blood *(intinctio);* or, only wine was administered, which was "sanctified" by contact with the sacred Host. Although in the Carolingian reform the effort was made to impose communion on Sundays, at least in Lent, for the majority of the faithful it was soon necessary to be satisfied with the number of times required for communion by the canon of Agde in 506 — on Christmas, Easter, and Pentecost. This canon was inculcated by many ninth-century synods. But even this norm was little observed, and still less when at the same period there was raised a demand for confession each time.

The national character of the northern peoples had a share in bringing about the changes just mentioned in the liturgy. Individual usages arose directly out of the Germanic language of symbols, such as praying with hands folded, or the related custom that the newly ordained priest placed his folded hands within the hands of the bishop at the promise of obedience, or the blow on the cheek at confirmation. But the greater prominence given to the sensible and the tangible in the adopting of the Roman liturgy was connected with the circumstance that the Latin of the liturgy was no longer comprehensible to even the Romance-speaking part of the population. To disturb the traditional liturgical tongue and change to one of the national languages, as Cyril and Methodius did farther to the east, was regarded in the West as unthinkable, for it was defended as a principle that in the liturgy it was permissible to use only the three languages of the inscription on the cross — Hebrew, Greek, and Latin; it had to be expressly stressed at the Synod of Frankfurt in 794 that one may at least pray in any language. And so people and altar drew farther apart, soon in the very church building itself. The altar was ordinarily situated near the back wall, in the place that had hitherto been allotted to the bishop's *cathedra* in cathedrals.

Nevertheless, in the Carolingian Renaissance it was still insisted, without lasting success, that the faithful should respond to the priest and sing the *Gloria Patri* of the Introit, the *Kyrie,* and the *Sanctus.* However, these chants soon passed everywhere to the clergy. In fact, there was regularly a group of priests to take care of Mass in the larger churches.

The distance from the daily life of the people was emphasized also by a change in the kind of bread. The pure white form of unleavened bread came more and more into vogue from the ninth century. It was soon brought to the altar in already prepared particles for the communion of the people. The sacred Host was then no longer handed to the recipient but placed in his mouth.

For all that, the Carolingian reform was not indifferent to the task of making the liturgy meaningful to the people. In a capitulary of 802 Charles the Great declared it to be a duty of the clergy to explain to the faithful "totius religionis studium et christianitatis cultum". It is characteristic that one of the explanations of the Mass appearing at this time, *Quotiens contra se,* obviously with an eye to the people, interpreted only those parts of Mass which were audible to the people, and hence it omitted the Canon. Certain of these explanations of the Mass, such as that of Walafrid Strabo, were characterized by a sober clarity. But only that type of liturgical exegesis which Amalarius of Metz methodically constructed, especially in his *Liber officialis,* appearing in various editions from 823 — the allegorical interpretation — became standard for the future. In this the Mass is explained as a synopsis and copy of the whole of salvation history, beginning with the call of the prophets of the Old Testament, who were heard in the Introit and *Kyrie,* and the *Gloria* of the angels, down to the last blessing of the Lord on his disciples at the Ascension, to which the conclusion of the Mass corresponded. The powerful attack which the Deacon Florus of Lyons opened on this manner of interpreting the Mass and even the formal condemnation by the Synod of Quierzy in 838 were unable to halt its victorious progress through the Middle Ages.

Thus in the details of its development did the Mass become exclusively the priest's business. Correspondingly, now also prayers were inserted into the Mass which were rather to foster his personal devotion and hence were to be said silently. A first sketch of this sort is attested by the ninth-century Amiens sacramentary, with its silent prayers on the way to the altar, at the incensation, at the offertory, at communion, at the end of Mass. Sketches with other texts followed. In particular there now appeared the so-called *apologiae,* wordy self-accusations, in which the priest at various places, but especially in the first part of the Mass, confessed his unworthiness and implored God's mercy. A moderate selection of silent prayers, with a limit to the *apologiae* and the addition of psalms — Psalm 42 at the beginning of the Mass appears here for the first time — was provided by the Rhine *ordo* of the Mass, which originated at Sankt Gallen around the mid-tenth century and from Mainz finally established itself everywhere as the basis of other forms.

Connected with the greater independence of the celebrant was the growth in frequency of the private Mass. The faithful wanted votive Masses for their special needs. In the monasteries, whose monks were now for the most part priests, the prayer brotherhoods, with the obligation of repeated Masses for a deceased member, operated in the same direction. Persons also celebrated Mass several times a day and frequently even without a server. This last point was censured by various synods as early as the ninth century as a serious abuse. Individual bishops as well as the reform Synod of Seligenstadt in 1023 finally specified three Masses a day as the absolute limit. Then Alexander II (1061–73) declared the single Mass as the rule. In the period under consideration the daily Conventual Mass at the hour of Terce was ordinarily, in most monasteries, the climax of the liturgy, while in other places Lauds in the early morning retained its preponderance and was attended by the faithful.

In this period the calendar of feasts also experienced a not unimportant enrichment. At the beginning of the ninth century in the Carolingian Empire the days of precept in addition to Sundays were, in accord with various synods, among others those of Aachen in 809 and Mainz in 813, and also the *Statuta Bonifatii,* the following: Christmas, the three following days, the octave day,

306

Epiphany, all the days of Easter week and Pentecost week, or at least the first three days, the Ascension, two feasts of Mary — that on 15 August and that on 2 Februar or 8 September — the feasts of John the Baptist, Peter and Paul, and Andrew. In addition, at times the anniversary of the dedication and the patronal feast might be included. Only a part of the lists of this period included Michael, Martin, Remigius, Lawrence, and All Saints. Alcuin is thought to have established the last named feast. In 799 it is in the list of the Synod of Reisbach, but it does not appear generally among the holy days until toward the middle of the ninth century. Two hundred years later, in the *Decretum* of Burchard of Worms, all the feasts mentioned, except Remigius, belonged to the general list of holy days. To them were added Silvester, the three Rogation days, and, in conformity with a decree of the Synod of Erfurt in 932, the feast day of each Apostle.

It is clear that in the details of liturgical life, even apart from the continuing influence of the earlier non-Roman liturgies in the various countries, there was no strict uniformity. Still, Burchard of Worms in the *Decretum* emphasized the principle that one should conform to one's metropolitan church. In addition, we find all the more frequently, for example, in Fulbert of Chartres (d. 1029), a saying that goes back to Gregory the Great[3]: If the faith is the same, differences of usage can do no harm.

All these developments in the practice of the liturgy and of the sacramental life occurred substantially in the eighth to the tenth centuries in the northern lands. Then they quickly gained acceptance by the whole Church. For after previously isolated liturgical usages had found the way southward, a double stream of powerful intellectual and institutional influence moved from the north toward Italy and the centre of Christianity in the tenth and eleventh centuries. The one was constituted by the Italian expeditions of the German Emperors from Otto the Great; in their retinue many clerics came south. The other proceeded from Cluny; as many manuscripts show, Montecassino was an important place of reshipment for the liturgical tradition from the north. And through the Normans also liturgical usages were transmitted from Normandy to the south.

CHAPTER 37

The Clergy and the Care of Souls

Once the development of the rural and urban churches and the subdividing of the diocese into smaller districts have been described, the question arises as to what concrete forms the life and work of the priest took in the early

---

[3] Gregory the Great, *Ep.,* I, 43 (*PL* 77, 497): "in una fide nil officit Ecclesiae consuetudo diversa".

mediaeval bishopric. One of the most urgent problems was decidedly that of bringing the rural clergy together as far as possible. The danger of isolation was especially present in the case of the priests of proprietary churches, and it was above all they who were in need of constant supervision and encouragement, because of their very deficient training and their dependent status, both for liturgical and pastoral functions and for their moral conduct. Even this problem was capable of solution only if the demands made were reduced to the most necessary.

At first the situation of the urban clergy was better. Certainly the above described association in collegiate chapters favoured the preservation of a religious spirit, though on the other hand, of course, it led to a distribution of offices, which withdrew the larger number of canons from real pastoral activity. Permitted by the authoritative Aachen rule of 816 to possess private property and, with few exceptions, not very much burdened with work, the canons not seldom lost the religious spirit and even partly gave up the common life and set up their own houses. Nevertheless, the basic idea proved to be so fruitful that it was taken up even outside the chapters. In the cities there were occasionally associations of clerics with a less strict organization than that of the chapters. Well known is a Paris confraternity of clerics of the ninth to the eleventh centuries, which was called the *societas duodecim apostolorum*. It met weekly for Mass, prayer, and a fraternal meal — a forerunner of those chapters of canons, newly founded or reformed in the eleventh and twelfth centuries, which were restricted to twelve members or to double or one-half of that number.

The principle of union also found application among the rural clergy. As a sort of makeshift, occasionally in the eighth and ninth centuries the *chorepiscopi* had arranged associations there and had exercised a certain supervision. Now, with the deaneries already described, a new order was established. The priests of each deanery now had to meet at the beginning of each month, *per Kalendas,* as specified in detail in a capitulary issued by Hincmar of Reims in 852. On this occasion, later referred to as a calend, Mass was first celebrated for the group; then followed the conference *(collatio)* under the presidency of the dean. Hincmar took the opportunity to admonish that the common meal which came next must not turn into a sumptuous banquet or a drinking bout. We learn from later prescriptions that the following subjects were treated at the conferences: the official duties of priests, parish activity, the Sacraments, questions of faith and of the spiritual life, correction of negligent colleagues. In particular, according to Hincmar, each time there should be a report on the public penitents of each congregation and their behaviour and the bishop should be notified. Common prayer, with intercession for the King, the ecclesiastical authorities, and the living and the dead, also pertained to the programme.

An important means of improving the care of souls, from which at the same time we learn details of its practice, were visitations. Great stress had been laid on them again since Carloman's capitulary of 742. Every year the bishop visited the places specified for this, usually the old parishes. This was, of course, every time a festival for the place in question, but it could also be a serious burden on the host, and for that reason various canons set limits to the expenses. The bishop administered confirmation, preached, and, assisted by the archdeacon or archpriest, who could also deputize for him, examined the state of the congregation. This examination became around 800 the synod or synodal tribunal, in which the assembled congregation or later selected synodal witnesses, were put under oath and invited to express themselves, even against the priest.

Toward the end of the ninth century the visitation of the priest was separated from it. For these visitations and synodal tribunals Abbot Regino of Prüm wrote his *De synodalibus causis* in two books. The first book is devoted to the visitation of the clergy. In the second are assembled legal regulations which were taken into consideration in regard to the laity and were of use in examining the moral and spiritual life of a congregation. We obtain abundant information on pastoral conditions, especially in the ninety-six visitation questions with which the first book begins and to a degree also in the parallel questions of the second book. The requirements expressed there coincide to a great extent with the *Admonitio synodalis,* originating around the mid-ninth century, also called the *Homilia Leonis* (Pope Leo IV), which from then on — and, incidentally, in an expanded form, still today in the *Pontificale Romanum* — was passed on as the bishop's closing address at synods. It contains material from Carolingian capitularies and synods and especially from Hincmar's regulations. Its content to a great extent reappears in the *Decretum* of Burchard of Worms.

Duties to which the priests were referred concerned the integrity of the parish property, the condition of the buildings, and the cleanliness of the church, which was not to be used as a granary, the neatness and care of vestments and vessels; the atrium of the church had to be inclosed, and women's dances were not to be permitted there. The pyx, with the Blessed Sacrament, lay on the table-shaped altar for the communion of the sick. Otherwise, only the four Gospels and, in contrast to the custom of previous centuries[1], relics of saints in a worthy setting were also on the altar.

Every day the priest had to rise for Lauds and during the day pray the canonical hours at the proper times, at each of which the bell was to be rung — Regino mentions Prime, Terce, Sext, and None. He was to have a cleric to sing the psalms with him and to read the Epistle and make the responses at Mass. He was to offer Mass daily at Terce, and then remain

---

[1] In the early Carolingian period in such cases a sort of sarcophagus was attached to the back of the altar; see *Braun* II, 548–55.

fasting until noon in order to be able to celebrate again for pilgrims who might arrive. The faithful were to attend Lauds, Mass, and Vespers on Sundays and holy days. In individual villages trusted men, called *decani*, were appointed to remind the others of this duty and of the obligation of ceasing from labour, which had to be observed *a vespera ad vesperam*. Even shepherds — *porcarii et alii pastores* — had to come to Mass on Sunday. Before Mass the pastor was to bless holy water and sprinkle the faithful. At the offertory the faithful were to present their offering; they gave candles and the like earlier. If there was no deacon or subdeacon present, the priest himself had to cleanse the vessels at the end of Mass. After Mass he was to distribute blessed bread *(eulogias)* from the offering of the people.

Books that the priest had to own were the sacramentary (or missal), lectionary, antiphonary (for the Mass chants), and homiliary, and also an orthodox explanation of the creed and the Lord's Prayer and a martyrology, in order to announce to the people the occurring feasts. Wherever possible, he should have the forty homilies of Gregory the Great. He had to know the psalms by heart and also the unchanging Mass prayers, the creed *Quicumque*, and the formula for blessing holy water. He should at least be able to read the other texts without making mistakes. He should also be capable of explaining to the people on Sundays and feasts something from the Gospel, the Epistle, or elsewhere in Scripture. He was to see to it that all knew the creed and the Lord's Prayer by heart. Children were to learn them from their godparents. The priest was to take care that no child died without baptism and communion; hence he should always take the holy oils and the Eucharist with him on excursions.[2]

The penitential system played a not insignificant role. The pastor had to summon the faithful to confession at the beginning of Lent. To avoid imposing penance arbitrarily, he should possess a penitential — a somewhat surprising demand in view of the decisive rejection of penitentials, with their inflexible and often inconsistent tariffs and their often frivolous commutations of penance, by various synods: "quorum errores certi, auctores sunt incerti", as Radulf of Bourges (d. 868), among others, described them.[3] The priest was warned not to let himself be bribed by public sinners whom

---

[2] This prescription relating to the Eucharist at least is found in the *capitula* of Ghaerbald of Leiden (*MGCap* I, 244) and in the *Statuta Bonifatii*, II, 4 (*Mansi* XII, 383f.).

[3] The oldest penitentials, as yet without any orderly arrangement, appeared among the Irish in the sixth century. Of Anglo-Saxon origin were new penitentials compiled in a systematic order, which go under the names of Cummean, Theodore, Bede, Egbert. Both types spread on the continent from the eighth century and were there combined with traditional penitential prescriptions; this made their inconsistency still more marked. When the elimination of the penitentials proved to be impossible, new penitentials were drawn up as a consequence of the Carolingian reform synods. Among them those of Halitgar and of Rhabanus Maurus were outstanding; c. 1010 appeared that of Burchard of Worms (*Decretum,* Book XIX). A clear arrangement was not realized even by them.

he ought to report for ecclesiastical penance. On the other hand, he must not invite public penitents to eat or drink without at the same time making amends by an alms.

It goes without saying that good example was especially impressed upon the priest. He was warned not to have a *mulier subintroducta* in his house. He must not bear weapons, a prescription that was certainly not insisted upon by many an episcopal lord. He must not find diversion with dogs and falcons or visit taverns. He was asked whether he had pawned the church vessels to the innkeeper or a dealer. He must not take part in weddings. At wakes he was not to let himself be induced to drink to the guests in honour of the saints and become intoxicated. He should always wear his clerical dress, even on journeys, at least the stole. If a priest without a stole was killed, only the customary *wergeld* had to be paid for him, not the triple *wergeld*. The priest should be especially concerned for the poor, and he should be hospitable to travellers passing through. He should visit the sick, absolve and anoint them, and bring them the viaticum personally, not through a lay person.

It is clear that with this mirror of duties, which was held up to the priests at diocesan synods and on parish visitations in the ninth and tenth centuries, at first only a programme was outlined that could leave the actuality far behind, but nevertheless a programme behind which stood the full authority, not only of the Church, but also of the contemporary state.

This much is certain: pastoral activity moved in primitive forms but it had firm outlines. The traditional forms of the Mass and the Sacraments constituted the supporting framework for the guidance of what was especially a liturgical care of souls. In order to guarantee to a degree at least this aspect of religious education, Carloman had already, in agreement with Saint Boniface, ordered at the *Concilium Germaniae* in 743 that every year each priest had to account to his bishop in a formal examination, especially in regard to the rite of baptism and Mass, a rule that, among others, was renewed by Hincmar in 852. A number of literary commissions that were produced for this examination, usually in the form of question and answer, have come down to us.[4]

There was no ecclesiastical catechism for children. The religious initiation and guidance of the young must have taken place substantially by way of custom. However, parents and godparents were directed to impress on the children the creed and the Lord's Prayer, and, according to Regino, at the annual confession the priest should begin by having each penitent recite them. Elsewhere the priest, according to the testimony of the confession *ordines,* asked at least the two questions about faith in the three Persons in the one God and in the resurrection of the body for judgment on good and evil. The sermon, which was required on all Sundays and holy days, could only

---

[4] Examples of this literature, which was termed *Ioca episcopi ad sacerdotes,* in A. Franz, *Die Messe im deutschen Mittelalter* (Freiburg 1902), 342f., 411f.

have been extremely jejune, if it was given at all, considering the level of education of the clergy. At the Synod of Aachen of 789 the following were mentioned as subjects which the sermon should especially deal with, in addition to the explanation of the scriptural pericopes: that there is one God, Father, Son, and Holy Spirit; that the Son become man; that the dead rise; and which sins bring one to hell.

The lack of an extensive preaching of the faith must have been all the more detrimental to the education of the people when the language of the liturgy was no longer understood. Nevertheless, the reform synods of 813 and the Synod of Mainz in 847 had expressly demanded that the priest must preach to the people "secundum proprietatem linguae" and translate the models of homilies "in rusticam Romanam linguam aut Theotiscam". For the intercessory prayers for the living and the dead, which in Regino were added after the sermon in several series, the use of the vernacular is probable at least in so far as the invitation to prayer each time was uttered in the vernacular, whereupon everyone was to recite the Lord's Prayer silently. The use of translations of the *Confiteor* as frankly acknowledged guilt in the same place at the public Mass cannot be proved before the twelfth century, whereas such texts for use in the confession of the individual *(Glaube und Beicht)* go back to the Carolingian period.[5]

But the people knew they were somehow included in the Mass. Bishop Herard of Tours presupposed in his *capitulare* of 858 that the people sang the *Sanctus* and only admonished the priest to sing it with them. The *Kyrie eleison,* as a repeated supplication, had then already become the starting point of the "Leise", from which later would grow the German liturgical song. If then, under Charles the Great and at his instigation, various explanations of the baptismal rites and especially of the Mass had appeared, this probably also found an echo in the instruction of the people. Finally, the celebration of the feasts of the liturgical year, emphasized by the cessation of work, must have deeply impressed the popular awareness. But with this we are already in the sphere of the spiritual life in the narrower sense.

CHAPTER 38

Forms of Devotion

A first task in the religious instruction of the people was constituted, even as late as the turn of the millennium, by the fight against the remains of paganism and against superstition. The penitentials down to that of Burchard of Worms are quite clear in this regard. Those remnants extended

[5] E. von Steinmeyer, *Die kleineren althochdeutschen Sprachdenkmäler* (Berlin 1916), 309–64.

from women who, while spinning and weaving, uttered secret sayings and from the wake at which "diabolical songs" were sung to real magic and to pagan sacrifices at wells, stones, and crossroads.

It was not to be expected, by reason of the condition of the preaching of the faith, that a religious life based on real spirituality was to be found in the broad masses of the people. The force of popular instruction lay in the institutional element. It had to be enough if what was indicated in law and prescription was observed. A religious impetus could be expected only gradually, through the example of monasteries and chapters, whose piety alone is in some degree accessible to us.

Like the cultural life in general, the devotional life of this period bore a monastic allure. This is true of the clergy, but even lay persons sought in associations of prayer, the forerunners of the later confraternities, contact with a monastery. The monastery was so much the model for the collegiate chapters of diocesan clerics that at that time it was not too unusual for a foundation of the canonical life to pass to the monastic life and conversely. The Synod of Cloveshoe in England in 747, brought about by Saint Boniface, was the first to require for all churches that everywhere the complete series of seven canonical hours, with psalmody and chant according to the usage of the Roman Church, that is, of the Roman basilical monasteries, had to be celebrated. This was something new. For in both East and West the diocesan clergy had been bound only to Lauds and Vespers, which were celebrated together with the people, and even in the bishoprics in the neighbourhood of Rome, as the *Cautio episcopi* of the *Liber diurnus* in the sixth and seventh centuries shows, the only other office required was the "Vigil" preceding Lauds, corresponding approximately to the present Matins. This requirement of the full monastic office, following the precedent of the Synod of Aachen of 816, was from now on repeated everywhere on the continent and, as we saw, was also applied to parish churches, but frequently private recitation by those who were impeded was not demanded.

The common choral office made available an important factor of religious formation — common spiritual reading. The readings were substantially longer than in the succeeding age of breviaries. In the Cluniac monasteries stress was laid on the importance of reading the entire Bible every year. In addition there came from the writings of the Fathers, from hagiography, and from the passions of the martyrs whatever the monastic or chapter library could offer. The reading in choir was frequently continued in the refectory. The spiritual reading of the individual was of secondary importance because of the cost of books. But it was cultivated and was especially recommended as *lectio divina,* reflective reading, which also contained the elements of contemplative prayer.

Alongside the reading in the choral office was the psalmody. The psalms occupied an important position even outside the choral prayer. Whoever learned to read learned it by means of the psalms, and this was so true that *psalmos discere* meant "to learn to read". Among the most important ascetical works of the ninth century was the *De psalmorum usu,* attributed to Alcuin, which, in a spirit of genuine enthusiasm for the subject, gives directions how one could have recourse to the praying of psalms for the most varied concerns and use them on the most varied occasions. The ancient practice of adding a collect or other kind of prayer to each psalm was, though no longer practised in choir, not forgotten, as, among other works, the commentary on the psalms by Bishop Bruno of Würzburg (d. 1045) shows. That persons were able to set the psalms in the light of their New Testament fulfillment and thus to make them something that could be prayed all the better by the Christian is apparent not only from this commentary but also from the many manuscripts of the psalter, extending into the high Middle Ages, which assign to every psalm a significant inscription as "vox Christi" or "vox Ecclesiae".[1] At least selected psalm verses and bits of psalms must have played a certain role in popular devotion also. In any case, collections of appropriate psalm verses were widespread. They had been early transmitted under the title of *capitella de psalmis.* In the *De psalmorum usu* they are called "post Dominicam orationem versus". They are the versicles, some of which survive in the *preces* of our breviary.

Around the turn of the millennium the psalms began to lose their popularity. The obligation of prayer that was imposed on a penitent was no longer expressed in psalms — 50 psalms, 150 psalms, with an equal number of genuflections. Instead of psalms there was assigned the same number of times the one psalm "Miserere" or even only one petition, such as "Miserere mei, Deus" or simply the Lord's Prayer. By means of the repetition of the Lord's Prayer 150 times there came about the "Pater noster psalter", which, after a certain popularity, was gradually supplanted by the Marian psalter, based on the Hail Mary, and by its definitive form, the rosary.

In this period there also began the history of the prayer book, which of course at that time could belong to few only. The Book of Cerne, of the eighth or ninth century, has come down in Ireland; it is a collection of the most varied types of prayers. Best known from the Carolingian world is the prayer book of Charles the Bald;[2] it is striking because of its effort to assist the royal suppliant to take part in the public liturgy. Two other collections of prayers of the ninth century, which go under Alcuin's name, also display strong dependence on the liturgy: the already mentioned *De psalmorum usu* and the *Officia per ferias,* as well as some other collections of the same time, which Wilmart has made known in detail. They borrow from the liturgy and from the Fathers, and the psalms are abundantly used. And then more

---

[1] P. Salmon, *Les "tituli psalmorum" des manuscrits latins* (Rome 1959).

[2] Charles the Bald's prayer book was edited by Felician Ninguarda, *Liber precationum* (Ingolstadt 1583). Cf. also *DACL* III, 865f.

personal viewpoints also came to the fore — *apologiae* and prayers for specific virtues occupy much space. Texts were provided in honour of the most holy Trinity and of the individual divine Persons. Of special fervour were the prayers in honour of the cross, which might be regarded as the most outstanding object of devotion of those centuries, next to the relics of the saints. A great wealth of texts was compiled, especially for the adoration of the cross on Good Friday, which even made their way into the liturgical books, just as in general a constant mutual exchange between those oldest prayer books and the contemporary liturgical books can be established.

In the piety of this rough epoch external exercises had a much greater importance than at other times. Instructors in this were the Irish monks. The genuflection, fifty times in connection with fifty psalms or repeated in a multiple of this number, praying for hours with outstretched arms, standing in cold water through entire nights, and in addition the ascetical roaming and the pilgrimage to holy spots were favourite exercises of great men of prayer and at the same time accomplishments prescribed for penitents.

If we would characterize the devotion of the epoch as it becomes evident in these and like forms, we may term it a piety of transition. On the one hand, strong forces of the tradition from Christian antiquity were still active. These revealed themselves perhaps most clearly in ecclesiastical art. Romanesque, and all the more the age preceding it, breathes the spirit of a firm, objective order with clear relationships. It is the art which, for all its autonomy, was in the most perfect harmony with the Roman liturgy. In the principal apse of many churches of this period the *maiestas Domini,* Christ royally enthroned, was represented. Even the representation of the Crucified, which appeared quite often now, was still far removed from a realistic reproduction of the event on Golgotha. The Crucified was still surrounded by angelic figures, as in Irish art, or by other symbolic attendant figures — Church and Synagogue, symbols of the evangelists, sun and moon — as in the manuscript illumination on the continent, and these pointed to the deeper meaning of the event. And then was elaborated the Romanesque crucifix, in victorious attitude, with the royal crown on the head, as at Gerokreuz around 976 and at Innichen in the eleventh century. The cross as a symbol of victory, already illuminated by the glory of Easter, was a favourite theme of Carolingian designers and versifiers,[3] just as it was a favourite subject of devout prayer.

With what force this manner of thinking was still effective is shown by a small feature, which, in the education of the people, was able to be of great importance: in the evangelization of the Slavonic and Baltic peoples and of the Magyars the interpretation of the Christian week culminating in Sunday as the day of the resurrection prevailed in the naming of the days of the week.

[3] Cf. the acrostic poetry and drawings of Rhabanus Maurus, *De laudibus s. Crucis* in *PL* 107, 133–294. Similar ideas in Alcuin; cf. H. B. Meyer, "Crux decus es mundi. Alkuins Kreuzfrömmigkeit" in *Paschatis Sollemnia* (Freiburg 1959), 96–107.

In place of the enumeration adopted from Judaism, which began with Sunday and hence designated Monday as the second day of the week and culminated in the Sabbath and which Christian antiquity had presumed to Christianize only by again counting Sunday as the eighth day, there appeared an enumeration in which Monday appeared as the first and Sunday as the last and crowning day of the week.[4]

But the transitional character of this epoch is seen, and very impressively, on the other hand, in the prominence of a new type of piety, one which came to maturity later in the Middle Ages and is still active in the popular piety of the present. In the interpretation of the Christian week Alcuin was already the representative of a change. In the series of weekly votive Masses that he drew up, Alcuin left undisturbed the traditional theme of the cross on Friday, but on Sunday, which he placed at the beginning of the week, the thought of the resurrection was now dislodged by its dedication to the most holy Trinity. The image of Christ which now came more and more to the fore was, as has been aptly said, no longer the "Christus passus et gloriosus" of early Christianity, but the "Christus patiens", in any event Christ on the borders of the Gospel reports.

It is amazing with what force the mystery of the Trinity began to dominate consciousness at this time. The Christian faith was termed with predilection *fides sanctae Trinitatis*. Alcuin composed his chief work under that title: *De fide sanctae Trinitatis*. In the abbey of Theodulf of Orléans (d. 821) the creed *Quicumque* formed part of the daily office. Not the mystery of Christ but the doctrine of the Three Divine Persons appeared now as the central object of faith.

This is in accord with the circumstance that at times Christ often stood simply for God and *vice versa*. Much as the human of the Gospels now came to the fore, and in this sense one could speak of a growing esteem of the Lord's humanity, his total figure was understood as a manifestation of divinity. In the Carolingian model catecheses, which have come down as sermons of Saint Boniface (*PL,* 89, 842–872), it is simply God who was born of the Virgin and was crucified for us. May he who created us, so ends one catechesis, lead us to everlasting joy, Christ our Lord. It is the same simplifying manner of thinking which we meet in the Old High German poetry, especially in the *Heliand,* where also the Germanic ideal of the hero determines the portrait. Christ is the God King, to whom one renders the service that one swore to him in baptism.

The force of this manner of thinking is to be recognized by this, that it even had a modifying effect on the Roman liturgy. The conclusion of the Roman oration, *Per Dominum nostrum,* emphasizing Christ's mediatorship based on

---

[4] Thus, for example, in Lithuanian Monday is called *pirmadienis* (that is, *prima dies*) and, correspondingly, the other days till Saturday; J. A. Jungmann, *Gewordene Liturgie* (Innsbruck 1941), 220f.

his humanity and extolling his glorified life with the Father and his reign, was not infrequently replaced by *Qui vivis,* which only left his divinity more in the field of vision. It was a necessary consequence of a presentation shortened in such a way that the obscuring of Christ's humanity also obscured the awareness of the nearness of God's grace, into which the Christian was admitted through the God-Man. The features of the family of God also faded in the picture of the Church, and the hierarchical lines became all the more prominent. The distance between priest and people was so magnified that if the reference in the canon of the Roman Mass to the faithful, "qui tibi offerunt hoc sacrificium laudis", was not expunged, it was still felt that it was necessary to supplement it by "pro quibus tibi offerimus". Church and Christian order now appeared above all as a matter of law, not unlike the political order, from which the Church was distinguished only by vague boundary lines, and behind the law stood the divine tribunal. The already mentioned progress of vehement self-accusations in the *apologiae,* which, for example in the so-called *Missa Illyrica* of the eleventh century, penetrated the entire Mass liturgy like a climbing plant, thus becomes understandable. Christianity acquired a moralizing feature and a melancholy mood.

On the other hand, if the one mediator Christ Jesus withdrew to some extent from sight in the glory of his divinity, afflicted man had all the more to look for other helpers. The early Middle Ages are the period of a greatly intensified cult of relics. Princes and prelates, among them even Charles the Great and Rhabanus Maurus, zealously exerted themselves to acquire relics from Rome and Italy and elsewhere, and in this persons were not always fastidious about the means. Transfers of the bodies of martyrs were now among the great feasts of Christianity. Countless are the forms in which precious reliquaries were produced and scarcely comprehensible the names by which they were known.[5] From the remains of saints persons expected protection and aid for body and soul.

In addition to and above the martyrs the cult of the Mother of God acquired an increasing importance. A great many of the new churches, including the palace chapel at Aachen, were dedicated in her honour. Pictures of the *Theotokos,* coming from the East, were now much copied. One day of the week, Saturday, first appears in Alcuin as Mary's day. In particular the Cluniac movement fostered the cult of Mary, the *mater misericordiae,* as she was now called with predilection. In every monastery at least one chapel was dedicated to her. It is reported of Saint Ulric of Augsburg by his biographer that, after the common office, he also prayed three shorter additional offices — one of the holy cross, one of all saints, and one of Mary. The daily *officium parvum beatae Mariae Virginis* was already widespread in the eleventh century. From this time also the *hymnus akathistus* from Byzantium, with its

---

[5] J. Braun, *Die Reliquiare des christlichen Kultes und ihre Entwicklung* (Freiburg 1940).

long series of honourary titles for Mary, exerted a growing influence, which manifested itself from then on in a springtime of Marian poetry and later, among other ways, was consolidated in the Marian litanies.[6]

How did this striking shifting of stress, or, to use the language of the Fathers, this different sort of illumination of the one world of faith, come about? For it is clear that no new content of belief is involved; in the same period the mere appearance of a deviation from the traditional statements of faith was able to produce the greatest excitement, as, for example, the events connected with Iconoclasm and the *Libri Carolini* or with the formulation of the Eucharistic presence by Radbert and Ratramnus show. Here we encounter the effects of that great agitation which had been evoked at the end of Christian antiquity by Western Arianism. The source of that tremor, whose vibrations continued through the centuries, must, in fact, be sought in Visigothic Spain in the sixth century. The conversion of the Visigothic nation to the Catholic Church, which was sealed at the national council of 589, had been preceded by repeated severe struggles and intellectual discussions, in which there was question of the correct Christology. To the Arian denial of the consubstantial divinity of the Son and its reference to the mediation formula, *Per Christum,* which had been used from time immemorial also in the Catholic liturgy and which was alleged to indicate a subordination of the Son in his divinity, the Catholic defence opposed the equally positive emphasizing of the oneness of essence of the Father with the Son, the unity of the divine being in the trinity of Persons, and this not only in the carefully sharpened definitions of the Trinitarian formula of faith but also in the formulation of liturgical prayer, and not least of all in the practical abandonment of the misunderstood mediation formula. The reaction on the Catholic way of thinking had to be all the more lasting, since the flexible Spanish liturgy was then undergoing a phase of active development and then definitively stabilized itself in this phase. Creedal struggles of a similar kind were, as we learn from Gregory of Tours, among others, also fought out on Gallic soil, but the decisive influence must have proceeded from Spain, whose Church experienced a period of flowering in the seventh century with Saint Isidore of Seville and others and thereby assumed the leadership in Christianity.

However, the Gallo-Frankish Church was not so much affected by the intellectual movement of the neighbouring country in direct transmission but rather in a roundabout way through the British Isles. "Spanish symptoms" have been detected more than once in the Irish-Scottish liturgy, and hence influences of Spain on Ireland in the seventh and eighth centuries, which must soon have been communicated to the Anglo-Saxon Church.[7] Boniface and Alcuin were then the great exponents of Anglo-Saxon influence on the

[6] G. G. Meersseman, *Der Hymnos akathistos im Abendland* (Fribourg 1958).
[7] Cf. the chapter "Spanish Symptoms" in E. Bishop, *Liturgica Historica* (Oxford 1918), 165–210.

continent and thereby on the religious culture of the Carolingian Renaissance, which became decisive for the remaining centuries of the Middle Ages. The way which the Creed of Nicaea-Constantinople travelled — from Spain, to which it had come from the oriental original homeland of the Christological controversies, to Ireland, from there to the Anglo-Saxons, through Alcuin from England to the palace chapel of Charles the Great, and, finally, on the occasion of the journey of Henry II to Rome in 1014, from Germany to the centre of Christendom — this is also the route on which the new mediaeval piety was formed and established.

If the religious life of the early Middle Ages lost, through the development just sketched, not a little of the freshness and confidence of earlier centuries, we can still identify signs of a new flowering on the new foundation. The more the Easter range of ideas with the glorified Christ was deemphasized, all the more did the devout soul turn to the manifestation of the earthly Christ. Christmas with its cycle of feasts gained in importance and popularity, and the earthly and visible element in the Easter mystery of redemption especially occupied the devout person. This last now became the favourite subject of imitative performances. Already in the Roman-German *Pontificale* of about 950 the Palm Sunday procession was a dramatic event. Around the same time it was reported of Saint Ulric that on Good Friday he laid the Eucharist in the "grave" and on Easter morning solemnly carried it back to its place. A similar rite, but with a crucifix, was also in use at the same time in the Frankish and English Churches, in accord with the *Regularis Concordia,* or collection of monastic rules of the tenth century. The *Quem quaeritis* of Easter Matins became at that time the point of departure of the Easter drama, which early found loving encouragement, especially at Sankt Gallen; traces of it are to be found as early as the eleventh century in the entire West, from Silos in Spain to Melk on the Danube.[8] Of a later date were the Passion play and the religious plays at Christmas and on other occasions, but they lay on the prolongation of the route adopted.

Even if the sacred representation and making present of salvation were no longer encountered fully understood, still, by means of such plays that looked back and reproduced and the celebrations corresponding to them during the Church's year, an intimate contact with the mysteries of faith was imparted in another way to the people's soul, and in the following centuries this would stabilize itself in a growing fervour.

[8] K. Young, *The Drama of the Medieval Church,* I (Oxford 1933), 577f.

SECTION NINE

Renewal and Reform from 900 to 1050

CHAPTER 39

The Renewal of Monastic and Canonical Life

Four principal causes had in the course of the ninth century led to an extensive decay of the monastic and the canonical life: secularizing usurpations by rulers, squandering of the property by lay abbots, lack of protection because of the growing weakness of the royal power, and the devastation wrought by Vikings, Muslims, and finally Magyars. But the vitality of Western Christianity was unbroken. There slowly arose monastic centres of strength whose effects soon reached beyond the cloister. The canons also were affected by the movement of renewal, though to a lesser degree.

Monastic Renewal

North of the Alps the impulse proceeded, on the one hand, from Lotharingia — Brogne, Gorze, Verdun, — and on the other hand, from France — Cluny in the Duchy of Burgundy and other abbeys, for the most part influenced by its spirit. While the Lotharingian centres influenced the German Empire particularly, Cluny and the other French reform centres spread to all the surrounding lands. A special initiative was displayed by Italian hermits. To about 1050 monasticism was so powerfully on the move that it began to go beyond its achievement to seek new forms and thus entered a new epoch of its history. At the beginning of the tenth century most monasteries were living on the intellectual legacy of Benedict of Aniane,[1] which of course had been modified here and there and was to be still further modified in the future, so that in the long run with regard to the constitution and the *consuetudines* various groups were formed. The differences that soon appeared were at first only nuances of one and the same striving for renewal; only later, especially after 1050, were they at times to cause conflicts among them.

---

[1] P. Schmitz, "L'influence de Saint Benoît d'Aniane dans l'histoire de l'ordre de Saint-Benoît" in *Il monachesimo nell'alto medio evo*, 401–15.

The Lotharingian and German Area

The first efforts for a monastic renewal in Lower Lotharingia are connected with the name of Gerard of Brogne (d. 959). A member of a not especially powerful noble family, Gerard, probably in 913 or 914, founded on property of his own a monastic community, for which he acquired the relics of Saint Eugene from the French monastic cell of Deuil. The history of the founding is as veiled in obscurity as is that of Gerard's monastic formation.[2] In any event, Brogne under Gerard's direction must have been of some consequence, for in 931/32 Duke Giselbert of Lotharingia presented the Abbot with the totally decayed monastery of Saint-Ghislain in Hainaut, perhaps inhabited by canons. The work of reconstruction accomplished there moved Marquis Arnulf of Flanders (918–65) to entrust Gerard with the revival of the Flemish abbeys, those of Saint-Bavo and Saint-Pierre de Mont-Blandin at Ghent and Saint-Bertin at their head. Thus in Flanders Gerard stepped into a position similar to that which had earlier fallen to Benedict of Aniane in the Carolingian Empire. And if Benedict's initiative weakened after his death, the same fate befell Gerard's life-work and for the same reason. Supported, not by a monastic reform centre, but by the personality of one ruler and one abbot, the renewal came to an end with the disappearance, first of Gerard, then of Arnulf.

The connection with specific persons is also to be observed in the monastic regeneration which began in Upper Lotharingia and soon operated in Lower Lotharingia and in Germany. Almost always it was produced, partly from religious, partly from economic reasons, by the proprietors of monasteries, laymen and bishops. The promoters in Upper Lotharingia can, for the most part, be reduced to a few families of the upper nobility. In Germany the royal monastery policy of the Ottos and the early Salians played a great role. And still there was a great difference from the above mentioned restoration endeavours of Arnulf of Flanders. While Arnulf depended essentially upon Gerard of Brogne, the Lotharingian and German proprietors could have recourse to a whole group of abbeys where the monastic life was flourishing. In 933 Bishop Adalbero of Metz had been able to establish at Gorze a real centre, full of ascetical seriousness. In like manner, in 934 Bishop Gauzelin of Toul founded one in the Toul monastery of Saint-Evre. Monks of both houses, especially of Gorze, were requested for the renewal of other monasteries. The radiation of Gorze extended beyond the dioceses of Metz, Toul,

<hr/>

[2] Gerard's *vita* in *MGSS* XV, 2, 654–73; fundamental study by J. M. De Smet, "Recherches critiques sur la Vita Gerardi abbatis Broniensis" in *RBén* 70 (1960), 5–61; earlier works, to the extent that they make use of the *vita,* are to be checked with De Smet, e.g., E. Sabbe, "Étude critique sur la biographie et la réforme de Gérard de Brogne" in *Mélanges F. Rousseau* (Brussels 1958), 497–524; J. Wollasch in *RBén* 70 (1960), 62–82 (on Gerard's founding of the monastery), 224–31 (on Gerard's place in the reform monasticism of his day).

and Verdun to Trier, Liège, and beyond. Ideas of Gorze were even carried from the Ghent monastery of Saint-Pierre de Mont-Blandin by Dunstan, who stayed there in 956, to England and used in the Anglo-Saxon *Regularis Concordia*.

Closely connected with Gorze was the monastery of Sankt Maximin at Trier, founded in 934 by Duke Giselbert. Otto the Great made use of the Trier monks. He made one of them Abbot of Sankt Moritz in Magdeburg; another, Adalbert, to whom he had earlier given the abbey of Weissenburg, was made first Archbishop of Magdeburg; and he had several royal monasteries reformed by Sandrad. When Bishop Wolfgang of Regensburg separated the collegiate church and the monastery of Sankt Emmeran, from Sankt Maximin he got Ramwold as Abbot of Sankt Emmeran. Because of his friendship with Duke Henry, the later Emperor Henry II, Ramwold became the centre of a Bavarian movement of monastic renovation. On reaching the throne, Henry II had a whole group of royal monasteries reformed: the abbeys of Prüm and Reichenau by Abbot Immo of Gorze; Lorch, Fulda, and Corvey by Poppo, who was probably from Sankt Emmeran; Hersfeld by Ramwold's friend, Abbot Godehard, whom Henry when Duke had appointed to Niederaltaich and Tegernsee and had learned to esteem because of the great successes he had had there. It was probably Conrad II who appointed the Niederaltaich monk Richer (d. 1055) as Abbot of Leno near Brescia, and he certainly gave him Montecassino in 1038, so that the Benedictine mother house under Richer's direction was given the stamp of Niederaltaich.[3]

The happily inaugurated movement of renewal stimulated greater achievements at the beginning of the eleventh century. Thus the Bishops Adalbero II of Metz and Berthold of Toul gave some of the monasteries subject to them, including Gorze, to the great reformer, William of Dijon, even though the abbeys did not need a real reform. Thus a branch under strong Cluniac influence took root in Upper Lotharingia, though it was unable to make much progress. But there now arose in the monastery of Saint-Vanne de Verdun, under the strong leadership of Abbot Richard (1005–46), a new Lotharingian reform centre, which united the Cluniac and the Lotharingian monastic customs in its own way. Called upon for monastic reform in the dioceses of Metz, Verdun, Liège, and Cambrai and in the nearby French bishoprics, Saint-Vanne became the mother of a monastic congregation counting more than twenty houses.

Although Richard from time to time returned their independence to the monasteries confided to him, with a few exceptions, he still had the abbots and *praepositi* whom he had appointed come to Saint-Vanne annually in order to maintain the spirit of the order. Several of his pupils had as far-reaching

---

[3] W. Wühr, "Die Wiedergeburt Montecassinos unter seinem ersten Reformabt Richer von Niederaltaich" in *StudGreg* III (1948), 369–450.

an influence as he did, especially Poppo of Stavelot. Richard had brought him from Saint-Thierry to Saint-Vanne and then entrusted him successively with the direction of Saint-Vaast and Beaulieu. But in 1020 he had to relinquish him to Henry II, who confided to the experienced man the royal monasteries of Stavelot and Malmedy and in 1022 also Sankt Maximin at Trier. Conrad II went even further. He not only bestowed on the reform Abbot his dynastic monastery of Limburg on the Hardt, but had a whole group of royal abbeys directed or at least supervised by him: Echternach, Saint-Ghislain, Hersfeld, Weissenburg, and Sankt Gallen. Since not a few proprietors followed the royal example, Poppo became the most powerful Abbot in the Empire. With Richard's death in 1046 and Poppo's in 1048, the Lotharingian-Cluniac mixed observance lost its driving force. Other impulses took its place; they will be treated in Chapter 52.

The success of the Lotharingian and German waves of renewal must not be either overestimated or underrated. Monastic reform centres here were less influential in turning the scale than the proprietors, whose ideas were not always uniform. Among them eagerness for reform stood alongside indifference, religious motives could be compromised by strong economic interests and by state and family politics, and now this, now that reform tendency was preferred. Just the same, the serious, increasing rather than diminishing exertions for renewal on the part of so many proprietors demands respect. The radiating strength of individual reform centres, moreover, found its limit in the Benedictine constitutional principles that were preserved in Lotharingia and Germany. The great goal of binding all abbeys to a single rule and *consuetudo* and of controlling the spirit of the order had been what Benedict of Aniane had sought to effect by means of the unity of the Carolingian Empire. His premature death and the decay of the Empire prevented success. For the future the relations of the monasteries to one another were based on the principle of autonomy, which was to maintain itself in the East Carolingian Kingdom.

In contrast to Cluny, in Lotharingia and Germany there were no congregations during the Ottonian and early Salian periods, but at most rather loosely constructed monastic groups, based on the notion of observance and on the association of prayer, which could be reorganized or even dissolved. The lack of any institutional stability had its drawbacks, of course; but in a movement of renewal it was not the organization that was ultimately decisive but the spirit, and many Lotharingians and Germans were affected by it.[4] A further distinction from Cluny and other French reform monasteries lay in the relationship to the diocesan bishop. The lack of protection on the part of the public authority in France aroused among the monks there the desire

---

[4] Irish and Scottish monks who came to the continent during the tenth century also took part in the renewal; cf. Sackur, *Cluniacenser,* I, 181–86, II, 124 f.; B. Bischoff in *Il monachesimo nell'alto medio evo,* 137 f.

to escape episcopal jurisdiction as far as possible and be directly subordinate to the papacy. Such a striving for exemption, proceeding from an unpropitious situation, was virtually non-existent in the Lotharingian and German monasteries, which were legally better guaranteed. This circumstance had little to do with the reform; of itself alone, exemption was in no sense able to preserve from decadence.

France

From unassuming beginnings the abbey of Cluny in French Burgundy developed into the most important reform centre. It owed its establishment in 910 to William the Good, Duke of Aquitaine and Count of Auvergne. In the very foundation charter the monastery's property was removed from the clutches of every power, secular and spiritual, the abbey was placed under the protection of the Holy See, and the free election of its abbot was granted. William gave it to Berno, Abbot of Gigny and Beaume, well known as a father of monks because of his monastic austerity. Other lords did likewise; Berno received three other monasteries — Déols and Massay in the County of Berry and Ethice in Burgundy. Shortly before his death in 927 he divided the six houses between his nephew Guy, who obtained Gigny, Beaume, and Ethice, and his disciple Odo, who received Cluny, Déols, and Massay, with the obligation of preserving the same observance.

Under Odo (927–42) Cluny's still rather small monastic community quickly gained influence. Not a few proprietors of monasteries called upon its Abbot for the renewal of old and the direction of newly founded monastic houses, especially in Aquitaine.[5] When Odo made personal contact with the Popes, he was even entrusted by Prince Alberic with the reform of Roman and nearby monasteries. The seventeen houses which were subject to him in 937 were, it is true, united only very loosely by the abbatial function *(abbatia)* which he exercised, even though one or the other house, such as Romainmoutier, was given to Cluny forever. Odo probably did not even seek the formation of a real union. Administered in Odo's spirit by the capable Aymard (942–54), Cluny was prepared for the prosperity which it was to experience, due to the superb qualifications and the extraordinarily long tenures of the next three Abbots. Mayeul (954–93), Odilo (993–1048), and Hugh (1049 to 1109) brought their monastery world-wide fame. Directly or indirectly, the Cluniac observance not only affected a large part of the French abbeys, but obtained entrance into Italy, with the beginning of the eleventh century into Spain, and from around 1050 into Lotharingia, Germany, and England.

Actually Cluny held to the same tradition that had been established by

---

[5] J. Wollasch, "Königtum, Adel und Klöster im Berry während des 11. Jahrhunderts" in *Neue Forschungen*, 17–165.

Benedict of Aniane and was followed by the Lotharingian centres of renewal. It did not add new intellectual or ascetical ideas, but continued certain basic tendencies of Benedict of Aniane, such as stricter observance of silence and lengthening of the choral office. The liturgy, elaborated in the direction of solemnity, became the dominant element. Precious vestments and vessels and splendid architecture heightened the brilliance. The piling on of additional prayers brought it about that, according to Odo's biographer, more than 138 psalms were prayed every day. The ritualistic excess left the monks little time for study, and manual labour all but disappeared. Because of the last mentioned circumstance even a highly born lord could be comfortable at Cluny, especially since clothing, food, cleanliness, and sanitation were suitably provided. The extraordinarily careful attention devoted to the remembrance of the dead must have attracted well-to-do families to make gifts and to show their good will in other ways.[6] Two elements in the constitution especially prevented a relaxation of monastic discipline: the right of the Abbot to designate his successor, and thus to assure continuity, and the forming of a monastic order.

The beginnings of the Cluniac Order have not yet been cleared up. However, Cluny succeeded in bringing a great part of the monastic houses that were committed to renewal into a more or less strong dependence. The principal element contributing to this was the priory system. For the most part the priories resulted from small monastic communities situated on estates of the motherhouse and called *cellae*. Even when they grew up to the size of a monastery or even founded priories of their own — la Charité-sur-Loire owned fifty, as far away as England — Cluny let them remain as far as possible in their subordinate position under a prior, whom the Abbot appointed and replaced at will. Besides the priories, there were subject to the motherhouse a group of abbeys, some almost entirely so, others to a certain degree. The dependent superiors had to make an oath of loyalty into the hands of the Abbot, like a vassal to his feudal lord. For all members of the order the ordination of monks, not their profession, was arranged at Cluny from the end of the eleventh century.

All in all there was question here of an imperfect type, soon outmoded by the Cistercians; its unifying bond consisted of the person of the Abbot. In a sense it recalls the manner in which a noble combined far scattered properties or rights, amassed in juridically different ways, into one estate in his person. And as a matter of fact the Cluniac union was constituted to a great extent for economic reasons. Without centralization it was impossible to avoid the fragmentation of property which began in France and Italy at the end of the tenth century. Of course, beside economic interests stood reform concerns:

---

[6] Around 1030 Abbot Odilo required all dependent houses to introduce the Commemoration of All Souls; cf. Sackur, *op. cit.* II, 245.

incorporated into the order, the monasteries of monks could be kept under discipline by the Abbot by means of visitation and other measures.

It is still a subject of controversy whether Cluny strove for a comprehensive reform of the Church over and above the monastic world and hence was at least one of the causes of the great movement that got under way around 1050. In the complex problem a distinction must be made between the non-ecclesiastical and the ecclesiastical spheres. Cluny probably did not aim at a transformation in principle of the early mediaeval world. Great as were the liberties granted it by the founder, Duke William, there is little reason for interpreting them as a demonstration against the existing juridical order. And if Cluny had no *advocatus,* it must be borne in mind that the *advocatia* of the nobility was not customary in all of southern France up to where Cluny lay, whereas in northern France even Cluniac houses could have *advocati,* and here and there even wanted them. With all their exertions for guaranteeing the monastic spirit of the houses entrusted to them, the Abbots of Cluny were able on occasion to accommodate themselves to the legal claims of proprietors. They understood their concerns. Since they did not have their many estates worked by their monks and only later, from around 1100, as far as possible by lay brothers, their economic system in the period here under consideration differed in no way from that of the feudal lords. A very special connection was signified by the proprietary churches which the Cluniacs acquired, even from lay persons, in an increasing degree during the tenth and eleventh centuries. For rounding out their possessions they even had no difficulty in buying up entire churches or partial rights to them. The contradiction to the principles appearing in the Gregorian reform was plain here. It showed how much Cluny was bound up with the Carolingian and Ottonian epochs. The occasional criticism of the then prevailing situation by isolated monks even in the tenth or eleventh century does not yet prove an opposition in principle to feudalism or theocracy; besides, such expressions, uttered, for example, by Abbo of Fleury or William of Dijon, came mostly from circles not directly belonging to Cluny. However, the indirect influence of the Cluniacs on the coming great reform of the Church is to be highly rated. In addition to monastic renewal as such, especially effective was the educational activity which the Cluniacs exercised, thanks to their friendly relations with the leading elements in society.

Within the Church, on the other hand, Cluny directly prepared for the Gregorian reform in one particular aspect: by its connection with Rome. From the first contact made by Abbot Odo, the papal protection envisaged in the foundation charter was again and again confirmed by the Holy See and as far as possible acted upon. Gregory V went beyond this by granting what became typical rights of exemption:[7] only bishops invited by the Abbot

---

[7] *Jaffé* 3896 (undated); M. Uhlirz, *JbbDG: Otto III.,* 287, dates it 999.

were to be qualified to consecrate, ordain, or celebrate Mass at Cluny, and the monks could receive orders wherever it pleased the Abbot. When, for this very reason, a controversy erupted in 1025 with the Bishop of Mâcon, to continue with interruptions, until the pontificate of Calixtus II a century later, John XIX not only confirmed the decree of Gregory V, but also exempted the monks of Cluny from episcopal excommunication and inter-dict.[8] Thus the motherhouse achieved full exemption. Other Cluniac houses sought to copy this, but only realized various successes or even none at all. Hence, the Cluniac Order did not form a closed exemption block, which cut vertically through the horizontally arranged diocesan system and, with its pyramid culminating in the Abbot and subject to the Pope, establish on the one hand the strength of the union in an order and on the other the papal supremacy over the orders. Nevertheless, the striving for exemption was of great significance: the hopes in this regard that were centred on the Holy See made the Cluniacs the promoters and defenders of the idea of the primacy before and during the Gregorian reform.

Cluny's radiation was by no means restricted to houses belonging to the order. Monasteries that were directed by Cluny's Abbots only for a short time and then given their autonomy also retained to a great extent a Cluniac stamp with the addition of their own special characteristics and transmitted this spirit to other monastic communities. Thus the monastery of Saint Benedict at Fleury-sur-Loire, renewed by Abbot Odo in 930, became a separate reform centre, to which recourse was even had for the monastic renewal in England by Dunstan's friends, Aethelwold and Oswald. Even farther extended the influence of Saint-Bénigne de Dijon, since the introduction there of Cluniac asceticism in an even stricter form by Mayeul's pupil, William of Volpiano, a Lombard noble, who became Abbot in 990. William's reform movement reached beyond its principal field of activity in France into North Italy, where his foundation of Fruttuaria was to be especially prominent, and into Normandy. The Norman monasteries, closely bound to the Duke, were also in some degree accessible to the influence of Richard of Saint-Vanne. Other groups were established by the monasteries of Aurillac, Marmou-tier, and Molesme, which had been reformed by Cluny. There were also monastic centres which were not directly affected by Cluny. Of these the most prominent was Saint-Victor de Marseille. From the time the first monastery became subject to it in 1034, Saint-Victor in quick succession attracted a whole group of monasteries of the Midi and then of Catalonia

---

[8] *Jaffé* 4079; re-edited text in L. Santifaller in *Römische Historische Mitteilungen* 1 (1956f.), 55f., with historical introduction; cf. also *Jaffé* 4083, 4080–81. On Cluny's exemption see, besides the works mentioned in the Literature by Lemarignier, who probably overestimates the importance of Cluny's exemption, and by C. Violante, also A. Hessel, "Cluny und Macon" in *ZGK* 22 (1901), 516–24; G. Tellenbach, "Der Sturz des Abtes Pontius von Cluny und seine geschichtliche Bedeutung" in *QFIAB* 42/43 (1964), 13–55.

and Spain, where it vied with Cluny,[9] and extended its influence as far as Sardinia.

Italy

The Cluniac movement first gained a firm footing in Italy with Mayeul of Cluny and William of Saint-Bénigne de Dijon. The dependent houses that both centres then established were for the most part in the North. Abbot Odilo, probably on the urging of Otto III, was able to take up again Odo's reform work in Rome. At the same time the important royal monastery of Farfa, on its own initiative and with the reserving of its liberty, accepted the Cluniac usages.[10] And when around 1011 Odilo's pupil Alferio returned to his homeland in order to found the abbey of Cava dei Tirreni with the aassistance of Waimar of Salerno, Cluny's spirit was finally operative in the South also, for Montecassino was never really touched by it. Independently of Cluny, Cava was to form from 1050 a large congregation reaching to Sicily.[11]

Meanwhile, there grew up in Italy a special, eremitically oriented form, which was to release new impulses. Itself the origin of Christian monachism in general and heroic realization of the *fuga mundi,* the eremitical life always and everywhere attracted high-minded persons, such as the little group in Lotharingia who in 933 revived Gorze and later Richard of Saint-Vanne. Although the Benedictines permitted individual members, with the consent of the abbot, to live as recluses or hermits,[12] they were on the whole dominated by the cenobitical idea. Wherever the latter was renewed and realized with strict discipline, eremitical inclinations went into eclipse; at Cluny, for example, they are only demonstrable after the death of Abbot Hugh at a time of inner crisis. On the other hand, Eastern monachism gave the eremitical element a much greater scope. Hence it was no accident that the attraction to eremitism was especially alive in Italy, where the Latin and Byzantine cultures were in direct contact. Two great personalities gave it a special stamp: the Calabrian Nilus and Romuald of Ravenna.

Nilus was the embodiment of the Italo-Greek type.[13] South Italy was full

---

[9] For the penetration of Spain by the two monastic centres, cf. the Literature to Chapter 29, footnote 5.

[10] G. Antonelli, "L'opera di Odone di Cluny in Italia" in *Benedictina* 4 (1950), 19–40; for the Roman monasteries (fifth to tenth century), G. Ferrari, *Early Roman Monasteries* (Vatican City 1957), must always be consulted; cf. also J. Schuster, *L'imperiale abbazia di Farfa* (Rome 1921) and *RBén* 24 (1907), 17–35, 374–402 (on Farfa's renewal).

[11] On Cava dei Tirreni, cf. L. Mattei-Cerasoli in *L'Italia benedittina,* ed. by P. Lugano (Rome 1929), 155–227; G. Colavolpe, *La congregazione Cavense* (Badia di Cava 1923).

[12] L. Gougaud, *Ermites et reclus* (Ligugé 1928); O. Doerr, *Das Institut der Inclusen in Süddeutschland* (Münster 1934).

[13] Bartholomew of Grottaferrata, *Vita S. Nili* in *PG* 120, 15–165; Italian translation by G. Giovanelli (Grottaferrata 1942).

of numerous monastic communities that for the most part lived according to Saint Basil's rule. Their number was increased in the ninth and tenth centuries by Sicilian monks, fleeing from the Muslims. An especially important centre, itself influencing the East, was constituted by the monastic heptarchy of Mercurion, a district between Orsomarso, Aieta, the river Lao, and the sea.[14] Nilus, born at Rossano around 905, had stayed there twice for his formation. In 950 he founded a settlement near Rossano, but then, in consequence of the Muslim invasions, he went to Campania, where he established Valleluce on Cassinese soil. Striving for greater solitude, he went to the territory of Gaetà, where the monastery of Serperi arose. Personal contacts with Otto III induced him first to accept the Roman abbey of Tre Fontane and finally to found that of Grottaferrata, still existing. He died there in 1004. Despite his surpassing personality and a fine ascetical as well as intellectual and cultural formation, such as was typical of Greek monachism, Nilus did not greatly influence the Latin world. Even his special preference for the eremitical life at most contributed to strengthen tendencies which had long been present in Central and North Italy and took shape in Romuald.

If one accepts the more probable chronology, Romuald, son of the Duke of Ravenna, entered the monastery of Sant'Apollinare in Classe around 972, when about twenty years of age, in order to atone for a murder committed by his father.[15] Dissatisfaction with the spirit prevailing there drove him into solitude. He spent the first years under the care of a hermit in the swampy district near Venice, then went with his teacher and a couple of Venetians to the Catalonian monastery of Cuxá, in the vicinity of which he lived for about ten years with his friends as a hermit. Having returned to Italy around 988, his unusual and charismatic personality excited amazement and the desire to follow him. Otto III, his enthusiastic admirer, had little success when in 998 he had him elected Abbot of Classe; a year later Romuald literally laid the crozier at his feet. Even later he could not bear to remain anywhere for long. Wandering restlessly through Central Italy, he reformed existing monasteries or founded new colonies of hermits, among them the at first still unimportant Camaldoli. At his death in the solitude of Val di Castro in 1027, he left neither a written rule nor an organizational summary of the eremitical communities that he had founded, several of which quickly disintegrated. If, in spite of this, his work continued, this was in great measure due to Peter Damiani, who in 1034 entered Fonte Avellana and in 1043 became its prior; he died in 1072. Peter gave the Italian hermit movement both a theological and a firmer organizational and economic basis, even though the congregation he constructed included not many more than ten settlements. Under

---

[14] B. Cappelli, "Il Mercurion" in *Archivio storico per la Calabria e Lucania* 25 (1956), 43–62.
[15] Bruno of Querfurt, *Vita quinque fratrum* in *MGSS* XV, 709–738, is more trustworthy in his reports of Romuald, whose pupil he was, than is Peter Damiani, *Vita B. Romualdi* in *FontiStIt* 94, ed. G. Tabacco (1957).

Prior Rudolf (1074–89) began the rise of Camaldoli; there the tradition going back to Romuald was defined in the *Eremiticae Regulae*.

Basically, Romuald strove for nothing more than a monastic way of life, intensified to extreme austerity but somehow continuing in the framework of the Benedictine rule. Hence he was interested in Benedictine reform centres and their *consuetudines,* especially those of Cluny, which he highly esteemed. There could be no question of an opposition in principle: Benedictines in the old tradition did not exclude the eremitical life, and Romuald and his disciples did not exclude the cenobitical life. In addition to the *eremus,* an isolated district with separate hut-like dwellings and a church in their midst, there was a monastery in Romuald's foundations. From the viewpoint of worth, of course, to Romuald's followers the eremitical life was incomparably higher than the cenobitical; the superior in charge of both communities had to be a hermit. Neither Romuald nor Peter Damiani regarded the monastery as the preparation for the *eremus* — both allowed fit disciples to be hermits from the outset — but rather they assigned it the function of intercepting the noise of the world and managing the economic affairs.

No doubt this shift of stress contained new and even revolutionary elements. Here the demands present in cenobitism, of fitting oneself into the whole, were less important than the personal striving of the hermit to find God in an heroic struggle against his own nature and the demons, in an excess of fasting, mortification, and prayer. From so subjectively oriented a training of the spirit issued fearless men who severely flayed the failings of the age. Their criticism struck at the monasteries with their great wealth as well as at the life of the laity and of the clergy, high and low, wherever it gave scandal. Small though the number of hermits was, the excitement which they caused was great. Basically, they were both driving and driven — driven, in so far as Western Christendom with increasing uneasiness was going to meet the great change that was becoming visible with the Gregorian reform. Thereby the hermits became a dynamic element. What they had been making ready in Italy since before 1050 was to be frequently repeated elsewhere, especially in France, and to lead to new monastic communities, both within and without the Benedictine family.

The Canons

By means of the reform legislation of Louis the Pious the *vita canonica* was separated once for all from the *vita monastica* and in the Aachen *Institutio canonicorum* of 816 it was defined even in regard to details. In all this there were adopted the essential points which were contained in the rule for canons composed earlier by Bishop Chrodegang of Metz (d. 766). As with the monks, the chief duty of canons was to consist of the choral liturgy, and their life was to be bound up with cloister, including common dormitory and refectory, and with the prescriptions of the rule. They were distinguished from monks by better clothing (linen), by the differentiation of the community according to orders received, and by the right to private property; furthermore, under certain circumstances they were permitted to live in individual dwellings within the cloister.

The concession of private ownership did not please all who took part in the Synod of Aachen; perhaps it must be ascribed to their dissatisfaction that the Aachen rule carries a text from Augustine which forbids private ownership.[16] But the ideal of poverty did not for that reason simply fall into oblivion. It could be taken seriously especially in those cathedrals, German mostly, where cathedral chapter and cathedral monastery were not yet separated and hence the possibility remained of urging a poverty relating to monasticism. Of course, if canonical elements insisting on the Aachen rule carried the day, the cathedral monastery incurred the danger of losing its monastic character with the dissolution of the principle of poverty or even of degenerating. Which tendency gained the victory depended on the local conditions, which can for the most part no longer be pinpointed. The far greater number of chapters did, in any event, permit private ownership by the canons.

Generally speaking, the Aachen canonical rule proved to be a centennial achievement. Not it but the circumstances of the time are the reason why many chapters fell into decay in the course of the ninth century. Once the West set about a reconstruction, the *vita canonica* flourished again. The renewal of the chapters ran parallel to that of the monasteries in the tenth and early eleventh centuries. Previous research did not recognize this fact clearly enough, since it accepted too uncritically the disparaging judgments which overtook the secular canons in the world of monks and later also in that of canons regular, and on the other hand failed to collect carefully the few positive testimonies scattered here and there. Although many monographs are still needed, a really favourable picture is now available.[17] In France, Lotharingia, Germany, and North and Central Italy — in the last mentioned especially from the beginning of the eleventh century — many cathedral and collegiate chapters can be identified, where both choral liturgy and common life in fidelity to the rule were carefully cultivated. The canons rendered inestimable service in the cathedral schools. And if from about 920 new foundations of chapters constantly occurred, the *vita canonica* must have been displayed in many places in a form worthy of credence, though it was often economic interests that settled matters.

Chapter reforms ordinarily originated with bishops or even rulers, such as the Emperor Henry II. As has already been shown, this was also the case with not a few monastic reforms, but there the renewed spirit was assured

---

[16] C. 112 (*MGConc* II, 386); cf. also c. 113 (ibid. 389).
[17] Many individual data in C. Dereine, *DHGE* 12, 366–75; for Germany in Siegwart, *Chorherren- und Chorfrauengemeinschaften*, 95–230.

more easily through the monarchical position of the abbot or even because of the formation of a congregation than it could be among the canons. The collegial organization among the canons limited the power of the provost, and unions similar to congregations were made virtually impossible by the juridical structure of the chapters. To this extent the great continuous progress was missing from the canonical movement of renewal. The deterioration of a chapter took place almost of necessity when it was no longer in a position to see to the adequate support of its members. And since from the end of the tenth century an extensive fragmentation of property and rights began in France and Italy, not a few smaller chapters, for the most part foundations of the lower nobility, fell into economic distress, which undermined discipline, whereas monastic congregations, such as the Cluniac and others, overcame the economic crisis; in fact they were even able to absorb rural collegiate chapters that faced ruin. The wretched condition of many communities of canons of the Midi and Italy is certainly one of the reasons why the reform movement of the canons regular began precisely there and not, for example, in German territory. Wherever the chapters lived in secure conditions, there was little occasion to depart from the Aachen rule, and it would be unfair to view this clinging to a tried tradition through the eyes of canons regular, striving for something higher, as an apostasy from the authentic spirit.

CHAPTER 40

Education and Learning

When persons set to work in the tenth century to restore monasteries and chapters or to found new ones, studies, which had also fallen into decay, were stimulated. Great achievements, however, were not to be expected. The time when scholars from all parts of the Carolingian *Imperium* made their way to the imperial court to work on greater themes in common belonged to the past. More than ever, scholarly effort withdrew into monastic and cathedral schools. It was they that, in a silent work of reconstruction, were preparing the future development of Western scholarship.

Every monastery possessed a school, at least for its own recruits. At the same time, however, not a few abbeys maintained a school for externs, in which pupils who were entrusted to them, but were not destined for the monastic life, were instructed. The teaching continued the Carolingian tradition. Among the masters who handed it on, three were outstanding at the turn of the ninth century: Remigius of Auxerre (d. 908), Notker the Stammerer of Sankt Gallen (d. 912), and Hucbald of Saint-Amand (d. 930). The greatest was Notker. Sankt Gallen owed it especially to him that it remained an important intellectual centre for the next century. Revived or new monasteries had to start from the beginning. Their attitude to studies varied. Cluny, for example, brought to scholarship a less comprehensive interest that did Fleury-sur-Loire or Lotharingian and German monasteries.

Less numerous but not of less quality were the cathedral schools operated by the canons. The cathedral school of Reims reached its climax under Gerbert of Aurillac.[1] His pupil Fulbert (d. 1029) established the fame of Chartres;[2] what he began as teacher and fostered as bishop was to outlive him, and as late as the twelfth century the school of Chartres still had its own special character. The German cathedral schools owed their flowering to the exertions of Archbishop Bruno of Cologne and his brother, Otto the Great. By preference it was in the cathedral schools that the Ottos and the Salians trained their future chaplains, chancery notaries, and bishops.[3] Italy was a country of too ancient a culture for studies to be able to die out. In the tenth century they lived on especially in the Lombard Kingdom. Cathedral and urban schools, like those of Pavia, Milan, Vercelli, Parma, Verona, and also Ravenna, maintained a high level.

The details of scholarship were set into the traditional framework of the seven *artes liberales*. The *trivium,* consisting of grammar, dialectic, and rhetoric, was followed by the *quadrivium* — arithmetic, geometry, music, astronomy. Concentration was on the *trivium* and, more specifically, on grammar. By hard work persons advanced from the *Ars minor* to the *Ars maior* of Donatus and eventually to Priscian's *Ars grammatica*. Manuals for dialectics, which followed, were Porphyry's *Isagoge* in the translations of Victorinus and Boethius, Aristotle's *Categories* and *Peri ermeneias* according to Boethius, Cicero's *Topics,* the *Logic* of Boethius, and so forth. An introduction to rhetoric was provided by various works of Boethius, the reading of ancient poets and prose authors, and then Cicero's *De inventione* and other systematic works. Ancient authors who were read included: Virgil, the *Ilias latina* (a crude, abbreviated translation of the first century after Christ), Martianus Capella, Horace, Persius, Juvenal, Boethius, Statius, Terence, Lucan; of the ancient historians Sallust was preferred.

Far less happy was the situation of the mathematical disciplines of the *quadrivium*. Apart from the relevant sections of Martianus Capella, the works of Boethius on arithmetic and geometry were especially used. Gerbert of Aurillac, who once visited Catalonia and made his own the relatively advanced mathematical knowledge imparted by Muslim Spain, was the first to go beyond this. He was even able to rediscover and use pertinent works of antiquity. Music offered a particular difficulty. It was studied as *musica*

---

[1] J. Leflon, *Gerbert, humanisme et chrétienté au Xe siècle* (Paris 1946); O. G. Darlington, "Gerbert the Teacher" in *AHR* 52 (1947), 456–76.

[2] L. C. MacKinney, *Bishop Fulbert and Education at the School of Chartres* (Notre Dame 1957).

[3] J. Fleckenstein, "Königshof und Bischofsschule unter Otto dem Grossen" in *AKG* 38 (1956), 38–62.

speculativa, theoretica, practica.[4] Gerbert, the Reichenau school, and others still took into account the mathematical elements, but in the eleventh century the theory of music more and more gave way to practical instruction in singing and composing. One of the great didactic achievements of the time was the new system of lines attributed to Guido of Arezzo.

All these studies, for which, in addition to pagan authors, the Church Fathers, especially Augustine, Jerome, Gregory the Great, then Isidore of Seville, Bede, and the Carolingian authors were called into service, found expression in a series of treatises. They were too much the product of their age to require discussion here.[5] Only very rarely did the mind move on from dialectics to authentic philosophical problems. Thus Gerbert, by means of a disputation which he had held at Ravenna in 980 with the Saxon Otric in the presence of Otto II, was motivated to compose the not uninteresting *Libellus de rationali et ratione uti,* dedicated to Otto III.[6] Reflecting on the logical connection between subject and predicate, he there touched upon the Aristotelian speculation on act and potency in analyzing the use of reason, but without venturing beyond the logical sphere into the rarer atmosphere of metaphysics.

Theology was in a pretty sorry state.[7] It lived on the store laid up in the Carolingian age. What Gregory of Tortona wrote on the Eucharist, with Christological digressions, toward the end of the tenth century, he took for the most part from Paschasius Radbertus, adding passages from a few reports of miracles. The Eucharistic treatise of Abbot Heriger of Lobbes is to be more highly esteemed. The scarcely original work of Abbot Adso of Montiérender (d. 999), *De adventu antichristi,* did not really deserve the influence which it was actually to exercise on the eschatological works of the following period. The few biblical commentaries composed at this time were also in the nature of compilations: Atto of Vercelli (d. 961) on Paul's Epistles, Bruno of Würzburg (d. 1045) on the Psalms, Theodoric of Fleury on the Catholic Epistles (c. 1000). Gerard of Czanád's *Deliberatio supra hymnum trium puerorum* does not fit into this category because of its prolixity and is more like a sermon. Basically, theological efforts were geared to the practical. Abbot Bern of Reichenau (d. 1048) discussed the Ember Days, the four Sundays of Advent, questions of music and singing, and the liturgy of the Mass. Odo of Cluny (d. 942) assembled from the opinions of the Fathers a meditation on the evil in the world, the so-called *Collationes,* which is dominated by monastic thought.

[4] In the work *Artes liberales* cf. K. G. Fellerer, "Die Musica in den Artes liberales" (33–49), and H. M. Klinkenberg, "Der Verfall des Quadriviums im frühen Mittelalter" (1–32); on the latter, K. Reindel, "Vom Beginn des Quadriviums" in *DA* 15 (1959), 516–22.

[5] On them see *Manitius* II, 638–725 (trivium) and 726–87 (quadrivium).

[6] *PL* 139, 159–68.

[7] The individual authors and their works in *Manitius* II, 18–81 (with copious bibliography).

Three theologians must be given special prominence. Bishop Atto of Vercelli (924–61) has left an account of a very extensive pastoral activity in his writings.[8] Besides his letters, including a pastoral letter to his people and clergy, sermons, and a collection of canons, entitled *Capitulare,* for the clergy of his diocese, he wrote an original work, *De pressuris ecclesiasticis.* Vividly and dramatically he described the encroachments of the mighty, especially in appointments to churches and sees and during the vacancies of bishoprics, and, with abundant citation of canons, contrasted all this with the rights of churches. Even more realistic is his *Polipticum quod appellatur perpendiculum,* a pitiless presentation of political abuses and their fateful consequences, leading to imposed outside rule.

The work of Rathier of Verona falls in about the same period.[9] Born at Liège around 887, he was educated in the famed school of the monastery of Lobbes (Laubach in Hainaut) and became a monk there. In 926 he went to Italy with Abbot Hilduin and in 931 succeeded him as Bishop of Verona. The foreign monk, lacking in inner balance, was not equal to a task that would have been difficult in any event. Imprisonment at the hands of King Hugh of Italy, banishment, return to Germany, brief interlude in Verona (946–8), Bishop of Liège (952–5), Abbot in Lower Lotharingia, Bishop of Verona for the third time (961–8), return home and death (974) — such were the chief stages in his agitated life.

Highly gifted as a writer and unusually conversant with the literature of pagan antiquity and the patristic theological works, Rathier unfortunately composed most of his writings either to justify himself or to accuse himself in tormenting self-reflection. His letters, sermons, and treatises are a real mine for a knowledge of the time. His most outstanding works are the *Praeloquia*[10], which could be called a great moral and sociological discussion. The entire citizen body of an Italian city there passes before us: artist, merchant, lawyer, judge, official, noble, lord and slave, teacher and pupil, rich man and beggar. There follows a mirror for kings, then one for bishops, while the last book is again directed to the generality, in order to give comfort and to awaken men spiritually. Rathier's *Excerptum ex dialogo confessionali* is of value for pastoral theology, as is also his *Synodica,* in which he gave the quite inferior clergy of Verona an elementary instruction in their official

[8] Works in *PL* 134, 27–894; *Polipticum,* ed. G. Goetz in *AAL* 37, 2 (1922); on the work cf. P. E. Schramm in *ZSavRGgerm* 49 (1929), 180–98. Biographies: J. Schultz (dissertation, Göttingen 1885); E. Pasteris (Milan 1925); R. Ordano (Vercelli 1948).

[9] *PL* 136, 9–758; the letters, edited by F. Weigle, in *MG Briefe der deutschen Kaiserzeit* 1 (1949). A. Vogel, *Ratherius von Verona und das 10. Jahrhundert,* 2 vols. (Jena 1854), is still indispensable; G. Monticelli, *Raterio di Verona* (Milan 1938); G. Misch, *Geschichte der Autobiographie,* II, 2 Frankfurt 1955), 519–650; on the deposition process at Verona, cf. F. Weigle, *Studi storici Veronesi* 4 (1953), 29–44, C. G. Mor, ibid. 45–56, and V. Cavallari, *Studi giuridici in onore di M. Cavallieri* (Padua 1960), 41–99.

[10] *PL* 136, 143–344.

duties. His *De nuptu illicito* deals with celibacy and especially with marriages between priests and priests' daughters, while *De contemptu canonum* explains to the refractory clergy of Verona the rights of the Bishop.[11]

The third author who came to grips with the abuses of his day as theologian and canonist, Abbot Abbo of Fleury (988–1004), wrote from the standpoint of monasticism. In fact, his two most important works, dedicated to Kings Hugh and Robert II of France, the *Apologeticus* and the *Collectio canonum,* were substantially geared to the struggles then getting under way between episcopate and monasteries.[12] Despite this one-sided tendency they provide a wealth of interesting ideas coloured by the desire for reform. The necessity of a strong royal power and the duty of rulers to protect the faith are as prominent as the ecclesiastical law on matrimony, the classes within the Church, social groups, simonical abuses, encroachments of bishops on monasteries, and so forth.

The predominantly practical interest called forth in the tenth century a relatively large number of works on canon law. The best of these appeared at the beginning and the end of the century. Thus Auxilius and Vulgarius defended the validity of the Formosan ordinations against Pope Sergius III with a profound knowledge of canon law and theology.[13] Even more highly to be esteemed is Regino of Prüm's work, appearing around 908, on the practice of the synodal tribunal; it was a successful attempt to explain in writing the actual procedure corresponding to Germanic law.[14]

We may skip over the canonical compilations that followed these works. All were surpassed by the *Decretum* of Bishop Burchard of Worms (1000–25), composed in 1008–12.[15] Geared to the requirements of practice, this canonical collection, divided into twenty books, instructed bishops on all questions of spiritual jurisdiction. It was no mere chance that the time of its origin fell during the reign of Henry II. The ecclesiastical juridical situation had stabilized itself and posed quite special reform problems; there was question here of a reform, which despite certain tensions to be noticed at times even in Burchard, still regarded *Regnum* and *Sacerdotium* as a unity. Inner balance

[11] *Excerptum ex dialogo confessionali* in *PL* 136, 391–444; *Synodica,* ibid. 551–68; *De nuptu illicito,* ibid. 567–74; *De contemptu canonum,* ibid. 485–522.
[12] Works in *PL* 139, 418–578; *Apologeticus,* ibid. 461–72; *Collectio canonum,* ibid. 472–508; P. Cousin, *Abbon de Fleury-sur-Loire* (Paris 1954).
[13] Partly edited by E. Dümmler, *Auxilius und Vulgarius* (Leipzig 1866); otherwise in *PL* 129, 1059–1112. O. Pop, *La défense du pape Formose* (Paris 1933).
[14] Regino of Prüm, *Libri duo de synodalibus causis,* ed. by Wasserschleben (Leipzig 1840); *PL* 132, 185–370; on the synodal court, see *supra,* Chapter 37.
[15] Burchard's *Decretum* in *PL* 140, 537–1058; the Worms *Hofrecht* in *MGConst* I, 640–44. A. M. Koeniger, *Burchard von Worms und die deutsche Kirche seiner Zeit* (Munich 1905); on the spread of the *Decretum,* cf. O. Meyer in *ZSavRGkan* 60 (1940), 141–83; F. Pelster in *MiscMercati* II, 114–57; id., *StudGreg* I (1947), 321–51; C. G. Mor, ibid. 197–206, on the *Decretum* in Italy before the Gregorian reform.

and usefulness assured the work a circulation previously unprecedented in the entire Christian West. Burchard's practical sense becomes further evident in his *Lex familiae Wormatiensis,* concerned with a manorial law composed around 1020, which sought to protect the peasants of the see of Worms from oppression and at the same time guard the financial interests of the Church.

The rise in the quality of studies stands out especially clearly in the field of historical writing.[16] Not until more than a century after the death of Regino of Prüm did an unknown monk of Reichenau again venture upon a chronicle of the world and of Germany (1040 or 1044); [17] it is known to us today only through those authors who copied it. On it is based, for example, the widely circulated brief world chronicle (to 1054) of Hermann of Reichenau. The history of the Saxon dynasty, produced in the reign of Otto I by Widukind of Corvey (to 957–8, with appendices to 973), found in Thietmar of Merseburg a new reviser, who made use of Widukind and other sources and carried the account to 1018, while Wipo's *Gesta Chuonradi imperatoris* describes the history of the Empire from 1024 to 1039. All the authors mentioned maintain a respectable level.

Among the numerous biographical works of the Ottonian and early Salian period the following are outstanding for their content: the work of Ruodger on Bruno of Cologne (d. 968–9), of Gerard on Ulric of Augsburg (d. 973), of Abbot John of Saint-Arnulf de Metz on John of Gorze (d. 974).[18] Adalbert of Prague (d. 997) found as biographers the Roman Abbot John Canaparius and Bruno of Querfurt;[19] Bishop Bernward of Hildesheim (d. 1022), his former teacher Tangmar.[20] The series was continued in the next period. In addition to the excellent *Historia Remensis ecclesiae* (to 948) by Flodoard (d. 966), there appeared in the first half of the eleventh century the precious histories of the sees of Cambrai and Liège, the former by an unknown writer, the latter by the canon Anselm (d. 1056).[21] In France the *Historiarum libri IV* of Gerbert's pupil, Richer of Saint-Remi at Reims, merits notice, despite its inaccuracy and subjectivism; Richer tried, while abandoning the annalistic form, to write a synthetically organized history of the French Kingdom from 862 to 995. In the French monastic world especially deserving of mention are two monks who worked at Fleury-sur-Loire, Aimoin and Andrew. Among other works, the first of these left a life of Abbo of Fleury (d. 1004);

---

[16] In what follows only those historical works are cited which are not mentioned in the sources for Chapters 27, 28, and 32.

[17] According to R. Buchner in *DA* 16 (1960), 389–96, Hermann of Reichenau was the author, and the work was the first version of his world chronicle.

[18] *MGSS* IV, 337–77 (incomplete, to 956).

[19] The *vitae* of Adalbert are mentioned in the sources for Chapter 31.

[20] *MGSS* IV, 757–82. F. J. Tschan, *St. Bernward of Hildesheim,* I–III (Notre Dame 1942–52).

[21] *Gesta Pontificum Cameracensium* in *MGSS* VII, 402–25; on the author's patron, Bishop Gerard I, cf. T. Schieffer in *DA* 1 (1937), 323–60. On Anselm's history, cf. the sources for Chapter 32.

the other, a life of Abbo's successor as Abbot and later Archbishop of Bourges (d. 1040–41).[22] Odo of Cluny (d. 942) found a qualified biographer in his pupil John. [23] A remarkable work, sober in the spirit of Cluny but not very reliable in details, is the *Historiarum libri V,* which the unstable monk Raoul Glaber began at Cluny and completed at Saint-Germain d'Auxerre in 1045. Earlier a monk at Saint-Bénigne, he is also the author of a biography of William of Dijon.[24] Italy, represented in the reign of Otto the Great by the excessively partisan but still important Liutprand of Cremona, was not particularly noted for historical works until the period of the Investiture Controversy.[25]

Scholarly interchange and practical activity induced several learned men to engage in a brisk correspondence. Gerbert of Aurillac seems to have been the first to have his many letters — 220 for the years 983–997 — collected in a private registrum.[26] A collection of those of his pupil, Fulbert of Chartres, has also been preserved. In Germany Froumund of Tegernsee kept a consecutive letter book (993–c. 1008), which was continued by his pupil, Abbot Ellinger of Tegernsee. Abbot Bern of Reichenau (1008–48) likewise left a collection of letters. The older Worms collection of letters was a product of the school but it includes political letters; those that are dated belong to the 1030's. In the next period letter-writing slowly became a special art, cultivated by special schools, and in the intellectual and political struggles from the period of the Gregorian reform people at times made greater use of it than of weapons. In the period under consideration there is no trace as yet of such a tendency, but the fact that people began at all to make collections of letters is important. It shows a growing awareness of the value of a literary influence and of intellectual interchange.

The peaceful picture presented by education and scholarship is not entirely

---

[22] Aimoin, *Vita Abbonis* in *PL* 139, 387–414; Andrew, *Vita Gauzlini,* ed. P. Ewald in *NA* 3 (1878), 349–83; on the other works of both men, see *Manitius* II, 239–246.

[23] Cf. the sources for the preceding chapter; among the *vitae* of Mayeul there cited, that by Odilo is the better; on the *vitae* of the Abbots of Cluny, see *Manitius* II, 130–55.

[24] Glaber's historical work is cited *supra* in the sources for Chapter 27; the *Vita Wilhelmi* in *ActaSS Ianuarii,* I, 57–67. P. Rousset in *RHÉF* 36 (1950), 5–24 (Glaber as interpreter of the contemporary outlook); A. Michel in *HJ* 70 (1951), 53–64 (division of world empires and churches); M. Vogelsang in *SM* 67 (1956), 24–38, 277–94 (Glaber as historian of Cluny); cf. also P. Lamma, *Momenti di storiografia cluniacense* (Rome 1961).

[25] For Italy see *Manitius* II, 166–75 (Liutprand); 179–81 (Benedict of Sant'Andrea); 197–203 (Chronicle of Salerno); 246–53 (Venetian sources); 294–99 *(Chronicon Novaliense);* also *Wattenbach-Holtzmann* I, 313–44.

[26] Editions of Gerbert's letters in the sources for Chapter 28; cf. the studies of F. Weigle in *DA* 10 (1953), 19–70; 11 (1955), 393–421; 14 (1958), 149–220; on the content and date, M. Uhlirz, *Schriften der Historischen Kommission der Bayerischen Akademie* 2 (Göttingen 1957). On the collections mentioned in what follows and the publications as such, cf. *Wattenbach-Holtzmann* I, 415–26 (with bibliography); on Bern of Reichenau, F. J. Schmale, *Edition der Briefe* (Stuttgart (1961) and the work in *ZKG* 68 (1957), 69–95.

in accord with the reality. In the first half of the eleventh century a certain uneasiness proceeded from the *artes liberales*. If around 1000 the grammarian Vilgardus at Ravenna preferred the pagan views of the ancient authors to Christian dogma, he was probably pretty much alone in doing so. The real danger threatened from the dialecticians. Thus, a sophistical attempt to show the doctrine of the *Verbum caro factum* as a logical contradiction had to be refuted by Bishop Wolfgang of Regensburg (d. 994). Similar dialectical attacks on Christian dogmas followed in increasing numbers in the course of the eleventh century; they presented Christian scholarship with the problem of the relations between faith and reason, theology and philosophy, and prepared the way for the new scholastic dialectic method.

CHAPTER 41

Heretical and Reform Movements Among
Clergy and Laity (1000 to 1050)

There is an unmistakable sign that, with the eleventh century, the Christian West was slowly entering upon a new phase of development. For the first time in its history heretical groups cropped up in various places: at Mainz in 1012, six and ten years later in Aquitaine, at Orléans in 1022, at Arras in 1025, soon after at Monteforte near Turin and in Burgundy, in the diocese of Châlons-sur-Marne in 1042–48, at Goslar in 1051. They probably had no connection with one another. And if one regards as their real source the lowest strata of the population, as does R. Morghen, or Italian merchants who are supposed to have taken up heretical ideas coming from the East and then to have borne them to French trade centres, as does E. Werner, these are unprovable hypotheses. Still, though, we find the carefully attested communities in Arras to have consisted of *rustici,* those of Orléans of clerics, and those at Monteforte of lay nobles. The contemporary chroniclers include them mostly under the term "Manichaeans", but nowhere is the properly ontological Manichaean dualism to be found. Instead, there is present an ascetical and moral dualism, which in individuals could go as far as the rejection of marriage, of the eating of fleshmeat, or even of killing animals.

The heretics took their religious and moral requirements to a great extent from the New Testament and did not hesitate to attribute their scriptural interpretation to the inspiration of the Holy Spirit. The essential point of the Gospels — faith in Christ, Son of God and Saviour — definitely took second place to the personal striving to lead a pious life, and could even disappear entirely from one's mental horizon. With such an outlook, any appreciation of the Church's sacramental life was of necessity lost. In the intellectually noteworthy centres of Orléans and Monteforte, as a matter of fact, the religious dynamism, with the abandonment of the Trinitarian and Christo-logical dogmas, was directed merely toward God the Father as creator, and in almost all groups baptism, the Eucharist, confession and penance, holy orders, consecration of churches and altars, and the cult of saints, the cross, and relics were regarded as useless; here and there the imposition of hands, whereby the Spirit was imparted, was retained.

The intellectual source of these movements, difficult to grasp, differing among themselves in individual points, yet containing much that was common, is controverted. One who holds to the road taken by Flacius Illyricus will see the basic tendency as a spontaneous Western striving for evangelical and apostolic ideals of life; this is the stand of R. Morghen. Others, with Baronius and like-minded scholars, incline rather to pay attention to the doctrinal content and to derive it, in this case, from the Bulgarian Bogomiles, so far as possible; this is the view of P. Dondaine.[1] The truth probably lies in be-tween. Any influences of the Old Bogomiles, who likewise represented a predominantly ethical and religious moralism[2] in opposition to the radical dualistic tendency, appearing in the eleventh century, of the "Dragovisian" Church, must have penetrated *via* Italy into the West; without them the many similarities of the heretical groups, which of themselves were not connected, are probably inexplicable. On the other hand, the heretics proceeded from a situation proper to the West. Since the development of the West had progressed to a definite maturity, gradually in all aspects of life new efforts to continue

---

[1] A. Borst, *Die Katharer* (Stuttgart 1953), 27–58, provides a good survey of research in the history of heresy since the Reformation.

[2] The Bogomiles, appearing from around the mid-tenth century, get their name from the Bulgarian (or Macedonian?) village priest Bogomil, who lived around that time. He represented a dualism in so far as he attributed dominion over the world to the devil, whom he regarded as son of God and brother of Christ, and hence he demanded separation from the world. At least the more intimate circle of his adherents, the so-called theorists, were to lead a pure "apostolic" life, avoid marriage, manual labour, and the use of flesh-meat and wine, pray, fast, and go on pilgrimage. The Bogomiles attacked ecclesiastical pomp and worldly possessions and power. They spread in the Balkan peninsula, especially in Bulgaria, and, after the subjugation of Bulgaria by the Emperor Basil II in 1018, also in Constantinople, and obtained a stable organization. In time their doctrines became differentiated. When the specifically Manichaean distinction between a God of heaven and an evil creator of this world entered their teaching and to what extent the Paulicians, transported from Armenia to Thrace, had an influence on this can no longer be precisely determined. In any event, in the eleventh century there were two main tendencies: alongside the older and more moderate dualism of the "Bulgarian Church" stood the radically dualistic "Dragovisian Church" — Dragowitsa was a Thracian country district. D. Obolensky, *The Bogomils* (Cambridge 1948); D. Angelov, "Der Bogomilismus auf dem Gebiete des byzantinischen Reiches" in *Annuaire Univ. Sofia,* Fac. hist.- phil., 44, 46 (1947, 1950), and, in Bulgarian, with a strong social and political emphasis, the second edition of id., *Das Bogomilentum in Bulgarien* (Sofia 1961); a good summary in: H. Grundmann, *Ketzergeschichte des Mittelalters,* II, G 24 f., A. Schmaus, "Der Neumanichäismus auf dem Balkan" in *Saeculum* 2 (1951), 271–99; E. Werner, "Die Bogomilen in Bulgarien, Forschungen und Fortschritte" in *StudMed,* third series, 3 (1962), 249–78.

the progress of early mediaeval culture began. Hence, one must not be surprised if religiously oriented natures found the official Church unsatisfying and set about preparing a spirituality of their own. In certain respects, many men did the same even within the Church; especially in the monastic world the inclination to stricter asceticism increased, not to mention the hermit individualists, whose numbers now grew constantly. The heretical movement was only one, in a sense the negative side of a religiosity inclining to radicalism, which at that time took hold of Western Christianity.

The more men were attracted by religious and ascetical ideals, the more clearly did certain moral abuses of the early mediaeval Church enter into the reflexive awareness. Criticism was directed especially against clerical marriage and against simoniacal or quasi-simoniacal practices.

In actuality, celibacy, to which the Western Church had bound major clerics since the fourth and fifth centuries, had to a great extent fallen into oblivion. In almost all countries the rural priests cohabited with women, either in concubinage or in a real marriage. Not a few clerics or canons attached to urban churches followed their example. There were even isolated cases of bishops or, in decayed monasteries, monks, who had wife and children. Concubinage on the part of a bishop, monk, or canon was pretty generally held to be intolerable, whereas in regard to the rural clergy it was to a great extent tolerated. Their lower origin, inadequate theological and spiritual formation, a very limited supervision by the ecclesiastical superiors, the fact that rural life was extremely difficult without a woman's aid — all these circumstances had contributed to alienate the rustic priests from the idea of celibacy; it was too lofty to be understood by them and by a great many of their parishioners. If isolated bishops, such as Atto of Vercelli, Rathier of Verona, and Dunstan of Canterbury, or even synods, and finally the Council of Bourges (1031) again enjoined the obligation of celibacy, they were to a great extent speaking to the wind. The solicitude of the official Church was concerned in this regard not least of all for Church property, for as far as possible it was made use of to provide for priests' children. To meet this danger most of all the Synod of Pavia in 1022 issued strict decrees at the instigation of Pope Benedict VIII. Economic motives were, of course, powerless in the face of so elementary an impulse as lay behind clerical marriage. Celibacy had to be sincerely approved by more extensive strata of Christendom; its violation had to be abhorred. And this is exactly what gradually took place. Though the movement at first may have found only a few followers, it slowly grew to such strength that it could be applied by the reformed papacy in the second half of the century. At the same time "Nicolaitism", meaning "lechery", appeared as the shibboleth for clerical marriage.[3]

Simony constituted a very complex problem. From Simon Magus, who

---

[3] On the origin of the word, cf. *LThK* VII, 975 ("Nikolaiten").

wanted to obtain from the Apostles by money the power to impart the Spirit (Acts 8:18–24), simony was and still is understood as the buying or selling of spiritual goods. If in Roman times and the early Middle Ages fees were not infrequently required for consecrations, the sacraments, burials, the taking possession of office, and so forth, this was to a great extent connected with legal customs. There was, to be sure, the danger of slipping in this way into real simony. Hence, from the fourth century synods and councils issued strict prohibitions; they even condemned payments connected with temporal goods that belonged to the Church. Gregory the Great went a step farther. He distinguished three rather than merely one form of simony: the *munus a manu* (money or gift), *munus ab obsequio* (services, favours), *munus a lingua* (intercession). He likewise energetically took up the notion, already developed, of *haeresis simoniaca*: whoever sinned against the Holy Spirit by simony should be regarded as a heretic.

Despite so universal a condemnation, the real situation could be controlled all the less when the young Germanic nations developed for Church administration forms that corresponded to their agrarian culture and were expressed in the institutions already described: proprietary church, investiture, and the rest. They slowly reversed the original relationship between function and ecclesiastical property. Whereas, according to the Roman and the ecclesiastical idea the function was in the centre and the Church property constituted an appendage specified for the support of the minister and for other tasks, in the canon law as stamped by Germanic notions the property law aspect moved into first place, the priest necessary for the function of the Church into second place. As a consequence, churches could be sold or otherwise alienated in whole or in part and payments could be demanded in making an appointment to a church. Since investiture at the same time handed over the function, the payments connected with it had at least the appearance of simony.

How far the materialistic feature could lead is shown especially clearly by the taking possession of the archbishopric of Narbonne in 1016. The Count of Cerdagne laid 100,000 gold shillings on the table on behalf of his ten-year-old son, in order to outbid the other competitor, the Abbot of Conques, who had become financially powerful through the sale of the monastery's goods; the lords who had the decision, a count and a viscount, agreed to this and divided the money. So shameless an example of jobbery was the exception, but more or less fixed fees must have existed ordinarily for the investiture of the more important churches.[4]

With each investiture was involved the acceptance of specified services. According to circumstances additional obligations were also required, and often enough the candidates made use of the intercession of influential persons. Accordingly, the three varieties of simony as defined by Gregory

---

[4] On the entire practice, cf. *Haller* II, 269f., *Fliche-Martin* VII, 466–71.

the Great were everywhere in use. Since those invested cherished the understandable desire to recover their expenses from church and office, not a few demanded money for purely spiritual official acts and hence fell into real simony. Whoever applied the strict standards of Gregory the Great and of the ancient synodal laws could not but regard the simoniacal heresy as one of the worst ills of the time.

Hence, there was no lack of warning voices. Atto of Vercelli and Rathier of Verona called for correction. Abbo of Fleury even more decisively took up the ancient ecclesiastical legislation and Gregory the Great's statements against simony; he was actually the first to enter into the juridical problem. To the distinction, complete in his day, between the altar as the sphere of the bishop and the proprietary church as the sphere of the proprietor and the resulting conclusion that the financial operations had nothing to do with the grace of the Holy Spirit but with the ecclesiastical property, Abbo opposed the inseparable unity of altar and church; any commercial activity within this entire holy field was, in his view, simony.[5] The more the conscience became refined, the more sharp was the reaction against the juridical forms of the age.

When William of Volpiano, the later Abbot of Saint-Bénigne de Dijon, was supposed to take the customary oath of loyalty to the officiating bishop before his ordination as a deacon at Locedia, he rejected it as a simoniacal demand. An ordination, he said, must not be purchased by anything, not even by an oath of loyalty. His disciple and successor, Abbot Halinard of Saint-Bénigne, at his elevation to the archbishopric of Lyons refused the oath of loyalty which he had to take to King Henry III. If he appealed to the prohibition of an oath in the Gospel and in the rule of Saint Benedict, and in the latter also to the duty of keeping oneself from worldly actions, fear of the taint of simony was probably included. In any case, William of Volpiano, from the time he ruled Saint-Bénigne and made it the centre of a reform group, propagated his own special hatred of simony not only among his monks but on the outside.[6] And he was not alone. Monastic circles, hermits, heretical communities — all contributed to the forming of an antisimoniacal movement. Their criticism found an increasing response in areas which were especially susceptible in regard to abuses, above all in Italy. Not by chance did whole groups of people rise up against simonists in Tuscany, Romagna, and Lombardy from around 1050. Earlier, around 1035, the Florentine John Gualbert sounded a first alarm. Since he was preaching to still deaf ears, he left the city, formed a monastic community at Vallombrosa, founded in 1036, and in other monasteries, and in the reform period, especially from 1062, used them as weapons against the simoniacal heresy. Vallombrosa's fighting spirit,

---

[5] *Apologeticus* in *PL* 139, 464f.; cf. also A. Fliche, *La réforme grégorienne*, I (Louvain–Paris 1924), 48–59.

[6] On William and Halinard, see H. Hoffmann, "Von Cluny zum Investiturstreit" in *AKG* 45 (1963), 174–81; in the work as such the question is probably treated somewhat onesidedly.

bordering on fanaticism, was to eclipse even such determined antisimonists as the Italian hermits and to fill Peter Damiani with a not unjustified anxiety.[7]

The danger from simony did not come merely from lay persons; clerics, high and low, even monastic circles contributed to it. Still, there was a distinction: clerics or monks could more easily be subjected to the ecclesiastical norms than could laymen. Hence a thorough reform could not escape a confrontation in principle with the rights of domination which the nobility, headed by the kingship, had acquired over many churches. Here basic principles of the Roman ecclesiastical constitution had been covered over with institutions of the Germanic type of canon law. Once persons became more keenly aware of this, the religious and political world of the early Middle Ages began to totter. Deep realization of the sort tends to mature slowly, and so in the period under consideration only isolated voices were heard in criticism. Hence Henry III and the German bishops could only feel that Halinard's refusal of the oath of loyalty was virtually an attack on the royal theocracy and the Imperial Church. It is to Henry's honour that, at the request of Lotharingian bishops, he dispensed Halinard from the oath.

Wazo of Liège also had ideas of his own.[8] At the deposition of Archbishop Witger of Ravenna, which Henry carried out at a synod of German bishops in 1044, Wazo remonstrated with him that such a measure pertained, not to the King, but to the Pope. When the Emperor, after the death of Clement II, questioned the episcopate in regard to a new Pope, Wazo came out for the still living Gregory VI; his deposition at Sutri, he held, was invalid, since a Pope can be judged by no one. And when Henry III insisted on the royal anointing, Wazo, in the spirit of political Augustinianism, observed that the episcopal anointing was higher: a bishop has to impart life, whereas to the King belongs the lesser function of fighting evil with the death-dealing sword.

Shortly after the Synod of Sutri the unknown author of *De ordinando pontifice*[9] began the most radical attack on the royal theocracy in general, especially that of Henry III. No lay person, according to him, might appoint clerics and dispose of Church goods — not even the Emperor; the election of Clement II, occurring at Henry's instigation, was invalid; moreover, the power of the sword belonging to kings pertained to the sphere of the devil rather than of God; in any event, Emperors were subject to the bishops and, like all the laity, to Church discipline. Even if this treatise were not of French but of Lotharingian provenance, it would be difficult to include it in the

---

[7] R. Davidsohn, *Geschichte von Florenz*, I (Berlin 1896), 163–70, 178–81, 226–51; id., *Forschungen zur älteren Geschichte von Florenz* (Berlin 1896), 41, 47–60; other literature on Gualbert and Vallombrosa *infra*, Chapter 52.

[8] *Gesta episcoporum Leodiensium*, II, 65, 58 in *MGSS* VII, 228–30, 224.

[9] *De ordinando pontifice* in *MGLiblit* I, 8–14; in regard to F. Pelster, "Der Traktat 'De ordinando pontifice' und sein Verfasser Humbert von Moyenmoutier" in *HJ* 61 (1941), 88–115, cf. the probably justified criticism of A. Michel in *StudGreg* I (1947), 87 f.

intellectual *milieu* constituted by Wazo, for it goes far beyond Wazo's attitude, which, despite everything, was loyal to the crown. A Lotharingian school of law that was making ready the struggle for the freedom of the Church, as postulated by Fliche, or other opposition groups cannot be demonstrated, at least for that time. There was probably none as yet, but here and there a mentality was coming to birth which was to become deeper, to spread, and finally, under papal leadership, to overcome the early mediaeval theocracy.[10]

How much the Church was able to display of the new initiative from the turn of the millennium was apparent in the movement of the Peace of God and of the Truce of God. The Midi was their place of origin. The process of political decomposition, which was especially active there, which fragmented the counties into power districts of viscounts, *châtelains,* and lords and furthered club-law, caused the bishops to intervene. The first to undertake self-help was the Bishop of Le Puy. At a synod in 975 he compelled the nobility by force to promise under oath not to attack the goods of the Church and of the *pauperes* and to give back what they had taken. We hear nothing more about similar efforts until the Council of Charroux in 989, representing the ecclesiastical province of Bordeaux. With it began the long series of synods which were to exert themselves for peace throughout the entire eleventh century and into the twelfth and partly even into the thirteenth. Although the goal was sought in various ways, certain basic trends can be isolated. The eleventh century efforts were welcomed, on the one hand, by the great princes and the King and, on the other hand, by the lesser folk; the middle and lower nobility, on the contrary, from whose ranks proceeded to a great extent the brigandage and violence complained about, held back and, according to circumstances, offered resistance. Occasionally, such peace synods were convoked, not directly by the bishops, but by secular magnates.

The powerful popular participation gave to not a few councils the character of a mass demonstration. Monks or clerics took care to bring along the relics of the titular saints of their churches in solemn procession, miraculous cures took place, a religious enthusiasm seized hold of the crowd and broke out into the cry, "Pax, pax, pax", while the bishops, in confirming the peace decrees, raised their croziers to heaven. This has been correctly called the first popular religious movement.

The masses went along, because the proclaimed peace was to protect not

---

[10] Fliche, *La réforme grégorienne,* I, 113–128; the explanation given by G. Tellenbach, *Libertas, Kirche und Weltordnung im Zeitalter des Investiturstreites* (Stuttgart 1936), 123–27, with the bibliography for Wazo and for the author of *De ordinando pontifice* in footnotes 16 and 15, is probably more correct. C. Dereine, "L'école canonique liégeoise et la réforme grégorienne" in *Annales du congrès archéologique et historique de Tournai* (1949), 1–16, accepts a Lower Lotharingian school of law but sees its special character in a moderate attitude, differing from that of the author of the above mentioned treatise and similar to that of Burchard of Worms before the reform and to that of Ivo of Chartres toward its end.

merely the churches and their ministers but also the bodies and property of the peasants and at times also of tradesmen. The Church brought her spiritual penal authority to bear against violators of the peace. The interdict, laid on the territory ruled by the guilty person, proved to be an effective collective penalty. Entirely new was the peace oath, which many synods required of the nobility. Furthermore, there was taken up at various times the obvious idea of having legal proceedings take the place of the feud. People did not even shrink from recourse to compulsion by war. This measure was not merely decided on here and there, as, for example, at the Synod of Poitiers, convoked by William V of Aquitaine between 1000 and 1014; there also arose peace militias prepared for war. Probably no one exerted himself so much for them, at least until 1050, as did Archbishop Aimo of Bourges, and with their aid he put a stop to the activities of many a robber knight. It is true that in 1038 his territorial militia, despite numerical superiority, suffered a frightful defeat at the hands of Eudes of Déols, but the institution of a diocesan army continued to exist. The slogan "war on war" was successfully taken up in many places in the second half of the century.

The Truce of God constituted a special form of the general peace movement. It consisted of the prohibition of feuds on specified days of the week. In most cases the suspension of hostilities was to last from Wednesday evening till early on Monday, but there were also briefer periods of respite. Attempts to extend it to longer periods, for example from Advent to the octave day of the Epiphany of from the beginning of Lent to Low Sunday, as well as to special feasts had little success. In themselves the decrees issued for the protection of clerics and peasants remained in force, but the old and frequently recalled duty of carrying conflicts over property before the judge steadily declined.

The origin of the Truce of God is obscure. We first meet it in 1027 in the acts of the Council of Toulouges (Roussillon). The idea spread quickly in the 1030's, first in Burgundy and Aquitaine and from there throughout France. It entered Spain, chiefly by way of Catalonia, while in 1037 and 1042 appeals made by the French episcopate and the propaganda of Odilo of Cluny propagated it in northwest Italy; Germany accepted it only toward the end of the century. However one prefers to interpret the Truce — as a giving way, in the guise of a compromise, vis-à-vis the all too tense earlier efforts, or simply as a new initiative alongside the other exertions — in any event it gave the peace movement fresh stimulation, especially since recourse was had both to the commitment under oath and to warlike compulsion.

Although the movement of the Peace and Truce of God attained its real goal only very imperfectly and even then only for a limited time, it was of importance as a pioneer. The fact that the French episcopate not only, as earlier, supported the crown in its care for the public order, but also worked for peace on its own authority gained it a new relationship to the Christian world. In itself this had long been based on the religious and political cultural unity of the early Middle Ages and the resulting cooperation of *Regnum* and *Sacerdotium,* but up till now the *Sacerdotium* had had to leave the constructing of a Christian world first of all to the crown, for only a hard fist could create order. Meanwhile, however, the ratio of forces had shifted: in France the *Regnum* had become weak, while the *Sacerdotium* had increased in authority as a consequence of the continually growing Christianization of the West. Its endeavours for peace found all the more assent in that, for mediaeval men, standing under Augustine's intellectual influence, *pax* and *iustitia* were rooted ultimately in the religious and supernatural and so directly concerned the *Sacerdotium.* And since, on the one hand, at that time the awareness of natural law began to lose its force in connection with the land and the people and, on the other hand, the secular, rational law that could be effectively enforced by a sovereign was still to be created[11], people and princes were especially amenable to the religious guarantee provided for the peace. Thus in the question of peace the French episcopate was able to stress a law fundamental for the Church's future position of leadership: the competence of the *Sacerdotium* for the spiritual and political goals of Western Christendom. Also pointing to the future was the practice now appearing whereby the Church summoned high and low alike to arms against violators of the peace and set in motion small or large armies. Thus the idea of the holy war was already present basically and with it the legal claim of the *Sacerdotium* to be allowed to exercise armed compulsion by means of laymen when essential interests of Christianity were threatened.

The idea of the holy war was to find powerful expression in the crusades. These, it is true, especially concerned knights, but the Church began even in the tenth century to assume a new attitude toward this social class. If previously the liturgical prayers had envisaged the King as the defender of the Christian religion, and even occasionally the army which he led, they were slowly applied also to the knight and to his vocation to war and found expression above all in the blessing of the sword with which the young knight was girded at his investiture. Formulas appearing in the second half of the tenth century assigned to the individual knight the protection of churches, widows, and orphans, as well as the defence of Christendom against pagans — hence specific royal duties — and in direct imitation of the texts of the anointing of a King. Soon after, at the latest in the eleventh century, there was a transition from the blessing of the sword as a thing to a dedication of the person of the knight; then regular liturgical *ordines* were composed, in which the knight was solemnly inducted into his armed vocation. This development, completed in various countries, and especially in Germany, could not but

---

[11] Cf. the stimulating brief study by V. Achter, *Über den Ursprung des Gottesfriedens* (Krefeld 1954); in this, among other things, the fact that the Peace of God appeared so late in Germany and that the old secular penalties were retained in all their severity alongside it is traced to the stubbornness of the old German Christian legal and political order.

acquire an up-to-dateness of its own by means of the initiative of the French episcopate in the Peace of God. However, the Church in France more and more disregarded the hesitations which opposed the notion of war by recourse to the oldest Christian tradition, despite the protests of individuals, such as Fulbert of Chartres. In the emerging idea of the holy war ideals lay at hand which were able to inspire knighthood so long as it was directed to the great aim — the defence of Christendom from Islam. The crusade idea was in the making.

If one surveys the exertions for reform and renewal in the Ottonian and early Salian period, there becomes clear a decided upward movement, which quickened its tempo from the turn of the millennium and engendered a growing uneasiness. What was then being concentrated was to burst forth in the coming great reform age. There is no doubt that the reform was brought about by abuses that had crept in, but its real motivating power was to be sought at a deeper level. Simony, clerical concubinage, a piety that was too external and too much oriented to a legalistic view of achievements, and other maladies had long been connected with Western Christendom. That there occurred a sharper reaction against them in the eleventh century was the consequence of a process of maturation: the West was slowly moving from the early into the high Middle Ages.[12]

Until around 1000 the Roman-Germanic community of nations was in the stage of coherence typical of early cultures. It was permeated with spiritual and secular forms of life: *Regnum* and *Sacerdotium,* law, morality, religion. Man felt himself to be hidden in this world, all-integrating, sacral-sacramental, even interspersed with magical notions, so long as it corresponded to his own inner condition and he accepted it without discussion as objective reality handed down by the ancestors. But as soon as he began to become intellectually more awake, he entered into a new historical stage: into that of diastase. This occurred from the turn of the millennium.[13] The old unity of culture was not destroyed, but the eye now took in its individual components. In a constantly growing process of differentiation they became more clearly distinct, were contrasted with one another, were slowly completed as special spheres. Naturally, this did not occur without tensions and struggles. The first voices of the dissatisfaction with the *status quo* have been recorded earlier in this section. The more powerful they grew, the more urgent became a reform which would seriously confront the problems of the day.

[12] On what follows, cf. A. Mayer-Pfannholz, "Phasen des Mittelalters" in *Hochland* 36, 1 (1938f.), 180–94.

[13] That the approach of the year 1000 put Western Christendom into a state of anxiety in regard to the end of the world, Antichrist, and the Last Judgment cannot be maintained in this general form. There were eschatological frames of mind here and there, both before and after the turn of the millennium; to some extent they could have been an accompanying phenomenon of the transition which became ever more noticeable in the West, but they probably had no far-reaching effect. Cf. F. Duval, *Les terreurs de l'an mille* (Paris, 3rd ed. 1908); E. Sackur, *Die Cluniacenser,* II, 223–26; E. Pognon, *L'an mille* (Paris 1947).

PART TWO

The Struggle for the Freedom of the Church

SECTION ONE

The Gregorian Reform

CHAPTER 42

Beginning of the Reform: the German Popes (1046 to 1057)

There can be no doubt that the Gregorian reform began with the German Popes. Even the unusual names assumed by Clement II, Damasus II, and Victor II revealed the desire to return to the old, pure Church, but this wish was directed merely to a moral renewal which attacked simony and Nicolaitism. It never entered the mind of these Popes, designated by the Emperor and loyally devoted to him, to undermine the foundation of the Carolingian-Ottonian cultural unity. And yet, once the reform got under way, it was to produce something like an avalanche. The future development was already in preparation under Leo IX.

The first two German Popes did not really get into action. A reform synod arranged by Clement II and Henry III did actually come out against simony on 5 January 1047, threatening the sale of ecclesiastical offices and consecrations with anathema and imposing the moderate penalty of a forty-days' penance on priests who knowingly let themselves be ordained by simonists,[1] but for the time being its decrees remained merely a programme. The Pope accompanied the Emperor on his expedition through South Italy, then returned to Rome, and in the summer heat caught malaria. As a consequence, on a journey into the Romagna and the Marches of Ancona he died at the monastery of San Tommaso in the province of Pesaro on 9 October. The Tusculans and Boniface of Tuscany were delighted, and Benedict IX returned to Rome, but the Romans sent envoys to Henry III. The nomination of Poppo of Brixen at Christmas 1047 proved to be another disappointment. Poppo, who styled himself Damasus II, succumbed to Roman fever on 9 August 1048, twenty-three days after his enthronement.

The new negotiations, at first probably centring on Halinard of Lyons,[2] ended at Christmas 1048 with the designation of Bruno of Toul. A more fortunate choice could hardly have been made. The nominee was highly

[1] *MGConst* I, 95, no. 49; cf. *Hauck KD* III, 594.
[2] Despite Haller's doubt, *Papsttum,* II, 578, he was perhaps suggested after the death of Clement II; see the chronicle of Dijon in *MGSS* VII, 237.

351

gifted and only forty-six years old. Born of the Alsatian family of the Counts of Egisheim, that was related to the Salian Dynasty, he was educated at Toul, of which he was made Bishop in 1026. He had been tested and proved in the service of both the Empire and Church reform. On 12 February 1049, he entered the Eternal City in the dress of a pilgrim, and, having been elected by clergy and people, ascended the throne of Peter as Leo IX; the reform thereby finally got under way.

The very election somehow indicated this, for Bruno had declared to the Emperor that he could enter upon the new post only if the Romans unanimously accepted him as Bishop. As little as this demand actually involved anything new — no contemporary doubted that a designation without an election following was contrary to canon law — it was still unusual to say as much to the Emperor. Bruno probably did not thereby intend to come out against the right of nomination but rather, in an authentic Lotharingian awareness of the freedom of the Church, to express that the election was an essential institution of canon law, binding in conscience, and not a mere formality.[3] In the same spirit he caused the necessity of canonical election to be insisted upon universally at the Council of Reims in 1049. Neither here nor in his much discussed monastic policy did he display any taking of a stand against the laity or even a project of a Papal Church as opposed to the Imperial Church.[4] Leo did not strive for any overthrow of the constitution but he was well aware of the independence of the ecclesiastical juridical order and hence of his own position.

The new Pope immediately collected around him a group of capable co-workers, whom he got mostly from Lotharingia and neighbouring areas. Apart from Halinard, who remained Archbishop of Lyons but was always at the disposal of the friendly Pope, these men were incardinated into the diocese of Rome and assigned functions. It was they who, even after Leo's early death, energetically pushed the reform work. It must suffice to name only the most important: Humbert, from the monastery of Moyenmoutier, in the diocese of Toul, Cardinal Bishop of Silva Candida from 1050; Frederick, son of the Duke of Lotharingia and Archdeacon of Liège, Chancellor of the Roman Church from 1051 to 1055, and eventually Pope as Stephen IX; Hugh the White, from the monastery of Rémiremont in the diocese of Toul, later Cardinal Priest; and Hildebrand, whom Bruno had brought with him to Rome,[5] perhaps as the contact with the Roman reform circles, and there

---

[3] Cf. Tritz in *StudGreg* IV (1952), 257–59; the interpretation does not absolutely depend on the question of who composed the *vita* (see the sources for this chapter).

[4] Cf. *Haller* II, 581–83, with the probably justified criticism of the views of Fliche and P. Kehr; also, R. Bloch, "Die Klosterpolitik Leos IX. in Deutschland, Burgund und Italien" in *AUF* 11 (1930), 176–257; A. Waas, "Leo IX. und das Kloster Muri" in *AUF* 5 (1913f.), 241–68.

[5] Sources in Steindorff, *JbbDG: Heinrich III.*, II, 72–75; on Hildebrand's entry into Cluny cf. G. B. Borino in *StudGreg* IV (1952), 441–56; the credibility of Bonizo, *Liber ad amicum*

ordained a subdeacon and entrusted with the administration of the property of the monastery of San Paolo *fuori le mura*. Without knowing it, Leo IX thereby made ready a fateful development. While he and his successors involved outstanding officials of the Roman clergy ever more actively in the reform of the Universal Church over and above their liturgical duties, there slowly developed the stable institution of the College of Cardinals, as the liturgical functions connected with the titular churches and the papal Masses were de-emphasized.

Another innovation also appeared more clearly. Unlike his predecessors, Leo IX did not reside in Rome. Restless, like the secular rulers of the day, he travelled from country to country. From 1050 South Italy saw him every year, and his three long journeys across the Alps took him not only in all directions through imperial territory but as far as Reims and in 1052, in order to mediate peace, even to the Emperor's camp before Bratislava. Reform synods interrupted his movements. Apart from Rome, where he held synods in 1049, 1050, 1051, and 1053, he deliberated with bishops at Pavia, Reims, and Mainz in 1049, at Siponto, Salerno, and Vercelli in 1050, and at Mantua and Bari in 1053; the date of the Bari synod is uncertain and may have been 1050. Since the Pope was everywhere approached for privileges but the chancery was localized in Rome, new methods of documentary authentication had to be found, which gradually detached the chancery from the city of Rome and allowed it to become an independent administrative organ of the papacy. And finally Leo's journeys meant incalculable gain for papal authority. While people had already always regarded the Bishop of Rome as head of the Universal Church, now this idea took on flesh and blood; a great part of Christendom looked at the Pope with its own eyes and let itself be captivated by the spell of his very being.

Three heavy tasks were imposed upon Leo IX: the reform of the Church, the struggle with the Normans of South Italy, and the confrontation with the Byzantine Church, which was to end in schism. Only the first two will be discussed here; the Schism will be dealt with later.

Reform centred on simony and Nicolaitism. Because the disregard of celibacy was so widespread, especially among the lower clergy, whom the Pope could reach only with difficulty, Leo took rather strong action only in Rome and its environs, forbidding the faithful by means of Roman Synods to have anything to do with incontinent priests and having the concubines of Roman priests reduced to slavery for the service of the Lateran Palace. Otherwise he was content, as, for example, at the Synods of Rome and Mainz in 1049, with general prohibitions of clerical marriage. His real fight was with simony. Simoniacal bishops of France and,

in *MGLiblit* I, 587, according to which Hildebrand bluntly condemned the method of designation in a conversation with Leo IX, is doubtful.

to some extent, also of Italy — in Germany Leo evidently relied upon the Emperor's opposition to simony — learned by experience the total seriousness of the synodal decrees of Rome, Reims, and Mainz (1049). The investigations, punishments, and depositions that now began were not to stop for decades.

The struggle was by no means always successful. That it did not flag but was waged with increasing exasperation was due to a special reason. Leo IX and his friends were concerned with something much deeper than the extirpation of a vice: the substance of the faith and the sacramental life seemed to them to be in jeopardy. Their refined religious conscience was dead serious about the denunciation, familiar since the fourth century, of simony as heresy, regardless whether, with Humbert, they believed that the divinity of the Holy Spirit was directly denied in the selling of holy orders and offices or, with Peter Damiani, assumed only an indirect attack on the faith.[6] Moreover, they saw the mystery of the Church betrayed. The simonists, they complained, obstructed the free operation of the Spirit, falsified the correct relationship of Christ to the Church, and degraded the *sponsa Christi* to a prostitute, while the Nicolaites dishonoured the spiritual marriage of the priest and the bishop with his church. Leo IX was especially distressed for the pastoral care of the souls of the faithful. Convinced, with Humbert of Silva Candida, that a simoniacal bishop could not confer valid orders, he wondered whether in the Church, so infected with simony, there were still enough priests who were able to dispense to the faithful the Sacraments that were necessary for their salvation. His attempt in 1049 to have all simoniacal ordinations declared invalid collapsed on the opposition of the Roman Synod, but, to be on the safe side, he not infrequently had simoniacally ordained bishops and priests "reordained".[7] However exaggerated or incorrect the theological motives of the reformers in their struggle were to some extent, they did not spring from blind fanaticism but from an honestly endured anxiety, which was justified to this extent that a whole network of economic and political interests had fallen upon the great and the lesser churches.

Leo's reordinations called theologians into the arena. Peter Damiani wrote his *Liber gratissimus,* in which he developed the theologically correct view of the validity of simoniacal ordinations, while Humbert of Silva Can-

---

[6] On the position of both theologians, cf. G. Miccoli in *StudGreg* V (1956), 77–81; theological motives in the struggle against simony and Nicolaitism in G. Tellenbach, *Libertas,* 152–59; in the *Liber Gomorrhianus* (*PL* 145, 159–90), composed in 1049, Peter Damian sketches a fearful picture of the low sexual morality in wide circles of the Italian clergy.

[7] Thus, probably correct is the view of L. Saltet, *Les réordinations* (Paris 1907), 183–86; A. Schebler, *Die Reordinationen* (Bonn 1936), 219–23; A. Michel in *RQ* 46 (1938), 46, 41 f.; id., *StudGreg* I (1947), 20, footnote 73; but a different opinion is held by A. Fliche, *La réforme grégorienne,* I, 133, footnote 2, and F. Pelster in *Gr* 23 (1942), 73, footnote 19.

dida maintained their nullity in the first two books of his *Adversus simoniacos*.[8] Thus sacramental theology fell again into a state of flux; it complicated the problem of simony and was complicated by it. It was no accident that shortly before this Berengarius of Tours had precipitated the Eucharistic controversy, in which Leo intervened in 1050 against Berengarius at the Synods of Rome and Vercelli. The problem of simony was only one facet of a complete revolution: the forms of the life of the early mediaeval religious and political world had become questionable, so that from various sides the duty was imposed on the Church of exploring more exactly her proper activity in the world by virtue of the Sacraments and of their ministers.

In another matter also the reform of itself led beyond the purely moral sphere. Forced by the struggle against simony to use the papal rights more energetically, Leo IX opened a new period in the history of the primacy. Other circumstances intervened favourably. The decree of the Council of Reims reserving to the Bishop of Rome the designation "universalis ecclesiae primas et apostolicus" concerned only a title,[9] but the conflict with the Byzantine Church gave to Leo's adviser, Humbert of Silva Candida, the opportunity to expound vigorously to Michael Cerularius the greatness of the Roman Church in two works of which only fragments are extant and in a long doctrinal treatise. The canonical collection in seventy-four titles, *Diversorum sententiae patrum,* composed in Leo's lifetime or soon after, perhaps also goes back to Humbert. It took up the reform ideas in their entirety, reorganized them, and elaborated the leading position of the papacy.[10]

The reform so happily introduced was soon overshadowed by the anxiety caused to the Pope by the Normans of South Italy. Ever since Benedict VIII had introduced Norman warriors to the South Italian Melo, in revolt against Byzantine rule, more and more knights had come from Normandy across the

---

[8] *Liber gratissimus* in *MGLiblit* I, 15–75; *Libri tres adversus simoniacos,* ibid. 95–253. The opponent in the first book of Humbert's work is not Peter Damiani but Auxilius, *De ordinationibus a Formoso papa factis;* Peter Damiani had earlier made use of the same author; cf. J. Ryan, *Saint Peter Damiani* (Toronto 1956), 162–64, with further literature. Also important is the letter on simoniacal ordinations in *MGLiblit* I, 1–7, which in the manuscripts is often ascribed to a Pope Pascasius or Paschalis, but by scholars usually to Guido of Arezzo, though A. Michel in *RQ* 46 (1938), 25–41, decides for Humbert of Silva Candida.

[9] The Reims decree (*Mansi* XIX, 738) was probably directed against the Bishop of Compostela, whom the Council even excommunicated because of his use of the title *apostolicus;* whether it was intended also to strike at the primatial ideas which were current in France, as Amann holds (*Fliche-Martin* VII, 102), is questionable.

[10] A. Michel, *Die Sentenzen des Kard. Humbert, das erste Rechtsbuch der päpstlichen Reform* (Stuttgart 1943); the above mentioned fragments, *De s. Romana Ecclesia,* transmitted in Deusdedit, *Collectio canonum,* I, 306, have been re-edited by A. Michel in P. E. Schramm, *Kaiser, Rom und Renovatio,* II (Berlin 1929), 120–36; also now the important study of J. Ryan in *MS* 20 (1958), 206–38; on the letters and acts relevant to the Schism, see A. Michel, *Humbert und Kerullarios,* 2 vols. (Paderborn 1924–30).

Alps to seek their fortune in the service now of one, now of another lord. They slowly established themselves, first Rainulf in Aversa, then William Iron Arm, son of Tancred of Hauteville. With his band William conquered the northern part of the Byzantine theme on the Adriatic and from 1042 styled himself Count of Apulia; his dependence on the Lombard Prince Waimar of Salerno was probably a mere formality. When in 1047 Henry III ceded the territory of the rebel Prince of Benevento to the Normans, whom he probably confirmed in their holdings, they attacked and by 1059 brought the greater part of the principality under their power.

At first Leo IX was not hostile to them, and in 1050 he had even accepted their homage in his own name and that of the Emperor. In the justified hope of recovering by their aid the jurisdiction over South Italy and Sicily that had been lost to the Roman Church since the Emperor Leo III, he then named Humbert as Archbishop of Sicily. But in the long run he could not remain deaf to the complaints of the population about the injustices of the Norman lords. He succeeded in gaining, at least for the Beneventans, the protection of Waimar of Salerno and of Count Drogo of Apulia, brother and successor of William Iron Arm. But when both of these died violent deaths, Drogo in 1051 and Waimar in 1052, he saw no other possibility than an effort to drive out the Normans forever, preferably in union with the Byzantines. Their governor, a South Italian and son of Melo, who had failed tragically, had offered an alliance.[11]

And so in 1052 Leo sought out the Emperor in Germany. Henry fell in with his plans and, in exchange for the cession of his rights of proprietorship to the see of Bamberg and to Fulda and other monasteries, gave him the Principality of Benevento and other imperial holdings in Italy, either as his own or at least for the exercise of the imperial authority. He even wanted to send an imperial army against the Normans, but let himself be dissuaded from this project by the objections of his chancellor, Bishop Gebehard of Eichstätt. Since Leo thought that he could not wait any longer, he recruited a small army of German knights at his own expense, combined it with Italian troops, and led his men south.[12] Before his army could join the Byzantines,

---

11 On the South Italian policy and Leo's war against the Normans, see the special study by O. Vehse, "Benevent als Territorium des Kirchenstaates" in *QFIAB* 22 (1930f.), 87–99; P. Kehr's thesis that Leo wanted to free himself from the Empire and the Imperial Church, in *AAB* (1930, no. 3), 56, is contradicted, probably correctly, by Haller, *Papstgeschichte*, II, 582f. The fact that Leo in his letter to Michael Cerularius, c. 12–14, in *PL* 143, 752–55 (the whole letter, ibid. 744–69, and in C. Will, *Acta et scripta de controversiis eccl. graecae et latinae s. XI*, 65–85), made use of the *Constitutum Constantini* was not intended to demonstrate his territorial power, much less his claims to South Italy, but rather his primatial position. See E. Petrucci, "I rapporti tra le redazioni latine e greche del Costituto" in *BIStIAM* 74 (1962), 68–76.

12 Leo IX gave his campaign the character of a holy war; see C. Erdmann, *Kreuzzugsgedanke*, 109–12, 107–09; see also *infra*, Chapter 51.

it was overwhelmed near Civitate, south of the Frento, on 16 June 1053, and the Pope became the Normans' prisoner.

The miserable failure of the campaign, anxiety about reform, and the conflict with the Patriarch of Constantinople, which, with the departure of the papal legates, was now moving toward misfortune, broke the Pope's spirit. Escorted back to Rome, Leo IX died on 19 April 1054.

After long negotiations Henry III definitely designated as Pope his chancellor, Gebehard of Eichstätt, in March 1055. Styling himself Victor II, he took possession of the Roman Church on 13 April. Although he was more directly involved in imperial politics than his predecessor, Victor energetically championed the reform. Together with the Emperor he held a reform synod at Florence in 1055 and on other occasions also took energetic action with authoritative measures. In France in 1056 important reform councils were organized by the Archbishops of Arles and Aix, in their capacity as legates, at Toulouse, and by the Roman legate Hildebrand, probably at Chalon-sur-Saône. Hildebrand's appointment shows that the new Pope did not disregard the co-workers of Leo IX who were still in Rome; Humbert's influence even grew constantly. But the chancellor, Frederick of Lotharingia, had to escape the clutches of Henry III, because of the political tensions between his brother Godfrey and the Emperor, by entering Montecassino. Godfrey the Bearded, for years at loggerheads with the Emperor, had married Beatrice of Tuscany, widow of the assassinated Marquis Boniface, and thereby provoked the Emperor to make an Italian expedition. Godfrey fled to safety.

His intimate relationship with the Emperor enabled Victor to gain the administration of the duchy of Spoleto and of the marquisate of Fermo. While the vested rights of the Roman Church to specific territories there may have played a role, the Emperor was especially influenced by the motive of enlarging the area under the rule of the German Pope in the interests of the Empire *vis-à-vis* Tuscany and the Normans. The death of Henry III on 5 October 1056 was to involve Victor still more powerfully in imperial politics. Entrusted by the dying Emperor with the care of the Empire and of his son, not yet six years old but already elected King, Victor managed through his diplomatic skill to assure the succession of Henry IV and the appointment of the boy's mother as regent; for the Empress he also gained the right to designate a successor in the event of the death of her son, a service which Gregory VII was later to make use of.[13] That he furthermore made peace between the imperial house and Godfrey the Bearded, by having Lower Lotharingia and Tuscany restored to Godfrey, gained the Duke's friendship for him and for the Roman Church. It was soon to be of the greatest use to the reformers.

[13] W. Berges, "Gregor VII. und das deutsche Designationsrecht" in *StudGreg* II (1947), 189–209.

When Victor returned to Italy in February 1057 his days were numbered. Visiting Central Italy after a Roman reform synod, he died at Arezzo on 28 July. With him ended the series of German reform Popes. His successor belonged also to the Empire, it is true, but his election took place under other conditions.

CHAPTER 43

Progress of the Reform: the Lotharingian and Tuscan Popes (1057 to 1073)

The unexpected death of Victor II confronted the reformers with the question of how they could preserve the papacy from a new Tusculan domination. The only one who was able to assure them of effective help — Henry IV and his weak mother, the Empress-Regent, were not considered — was Godfrey the Bearded, Duke of Upper Lotharingia and Marquis of Tuscany. The reformers knew how to gain his support. They chose his own brother as Pope and then selected the next two Popes from the Tuscan episcopate.

Nothing so clearly reflects the insecure situation of the Roman Church as does the elevation of the three Lotharingian and Tuscan Popes. The first election was the smoothest. The reformers forestalled any manoeuvre on the part of the nobility by quick action. Three days after receiving the news of Victor's death they elected Frederick of Lotharingia, who happened to be in Rome, and then had him consecrated and enthroned as Stephen IX on the next day, 3 August 1057. Time did not allow a consultation with the German court; apart from the emergency, the King's minority may have been a further excuse. In any event this unauthorized procedure was probably not based on the intention of excluding for the future any participation by the German ruler in the election. In the autumn Stephen IX sent Hildebrand to Germany; it may with good reason be assumed that he was supposed to justify the unusual papal election before the royal court and obtain its belated approval.

With Stephen IX there came to power a man from the school of Leo IX. After Henry III's death Victor II had brought him out of obscurity again, forced his election as Abbot of Montecassino, and made him Cardinal-Priest of San Crisogono. In accord with his most recent past, the new Pope strengthened the monastic element among the reformers. For decades thereafter Montecassino rendered valuable services to the Roman Church, and the hermit movement, especially at home in Central Italy and so important for the reform, now acquired an official influence in the sense that Stephen made its most important representative, the Prior of Fonte Avellana, Peter Damiani, Cardinal-Bishop of Ostia. But the pontificate was too brief for anything decisive to have taken place. Of a Roman Synod arranged in 1057 only strict decrees against clerical marriage are known today. The Pope entertained great plans for South Italy: resuming the policy of Leo IX, he thought of expelling the Normans. An embassy headed by Desiderius of Montecassino was to leave for Constantinople when, during a journey through Tuscany, Stephen died at Florence on 29 March 1058.

Having a foreboding of his death, Stephen, before leaving Rome, had had the clergy and people swear not to proceed to the election of his successor until Hildebrand had returned from Germany. This, however, did not prevent the Tusculans, right after receipt of the news of Stephen's death, from tumultuously elevating Bishop John of Velletri as Benedict X and, because Peter Damiani refused, having him enthroned by the Archpriest of Ostia. The reformers did not recognize the election. After Hildebrand's return they agreed, with the support of Godfrey of Lotharingia, on Bishop Gerard of Florence, a Burgundian by birth, and obtained the assent of the German court. The official election took place at Siena, but it is disputed whether it occurred before or after the royal consent. Finally, the Pope-elect, who styled himself Nicholas II, escorted by the Tuscan army under Godfrey's command, set out for Rome with the cardinal-bishops and with Guibert, imperial chancellor of Italy, who was probably sent by the German government. He excommunicated the Antipope at a synod held at Sutri, and, because Benedict X fled, was able to enter the Eternal City, where he was enthroned on 24 January 1059.

With Nicholas II a new trend in the reform began to show itself. Five cardinal-bishops had dared, contrary to custom, to elect a Pope outside Rome in alliance with a few friends of reform and with the German ruler. In the third book of *Adversus simoniacos,*[1] probably composed in 1058, Humbert of Silva Candida shows that this was more than an exceptional case, that among the reformers the realization was then gaining ground that, for the sake of the freedom of the Church, they must be prepared to eliminate traditional juridical rights. If in the earlier books he had sought to demonstrate the invalidity of simoniacal ordinations and the absolutely heretical character of simony, he now investigated the causes of this evil.

What actually made it impossible to eradicate simony was its involvement with the contemporary world. The simoniacal gift, *munus a manu,* as well as the services and the interventions connected with the attaining of an office, which since Gregory I had been reckoned as simony, *munus ab obsequio* and *munus a lingua,* were not based really on a simoniacal intention but on juridical and lifelong habits, conditioned by the times and bound up with the proprietary church system. Selecting the chief cause, then, Humbert condemned lay investiture as an unlawful abuse and as a perversion of the proper relationship between priests and laity. He stressed the perversion especially in regard to episcopal elections: Whereas, according to the ancient rules, first the clergy, in agreement with the view of the metropolitan, then the people with

---

[1] *MGLiblit* I, 198–253; the literature on simony will be found in that for Chapter 41.

the subsequent assent of the prince, were to elect, now the decision of the prince came first, and the rest of the electors, with the metropolitan in the last place, had to conform blindly. Humbert thereby indicated the aims of the reform, which were directed not merely at moral and religious abuses but against the religious and political world of the early Middle Ages in general. Despite specific differences, his attitude was also shared by other reformers. It led to a greater freedom of the Roman Church and to a more radical fight for moral reform.

The freedom of the Roman Church was arranged by the papal election decree, which Nicholas II issued at the Roman Synod of 1059 in order to legalize his own election and to guarantee future papal elections.[2] It provided for a threefold act of election: the cardinal bishops deliberated and then brought in the cardinal clerics; the rest of the clergy and the Roman people assented to the decision reached by them. Just as Humbert assigned to the metropolitan the first place in the carrying out of an episcopal election, the papal election decree put the cardinal bishops in the leading place, calling them, significantly, quasi-metropolitans. Their right was so extensive that, in the event of a substantial encroachment on the freedom of the election by the Romans, they could arrange the papal election outside Rome, having recourse to a few religious clerics and lay persons; the Pope thus elected, even if he had not yet entered Rome and been enthroned there, possessed the full governing authority. With the new law, which again conceived of the Church as a hierarchically arranged authority, running from the top down, the papacy broke away in principle from its connection with the people of the city of Rome. During the vacancy, the real representatives of the Roman Church were the quasi-metropolitan cardinal-bishops. Wherever they and the Pope then elected stayed, whether in or outside Rome, there was the Roman Church. Although the decree was not always observed in the future, still the basic idea expressed in it was established and led in the twelfth century to the exclusive right of the College of Cardinals to take part in the papal election.

By this decree Nicholas II obviously intended only to regulate the specifically Roman situation; he spoke only incidentally of a right belonging to Henry IV and his successors, which he conceded to Henry IV through the

[2] The substantially genuine (or "papal") and the forged (or "imperial") versions in *MGConst* I, 537–46; cf. also the critical remarks of A. Michel and H. G. Krause in their works cited in the Literature for this chapter. Michel's assumption of a pact formally concluded with the German court probably goes too far, but the opposing widespread view that the reformers had all along intended to exclude any participation of the German ruler in the papal election and hence kept the paragraphs dealing with the King in the decree intentionally obscure is probably wrong; cf. also the excellent study by Krause, which, however, insists too much on the political importance of the decree and disregards its basic intention that depends on the hierarchical notion; the study by F. Kempf, cited in the Literature, deals with this very point.

intervention of Guibert, Chancellor of Lombardy, and which succeeding rulers were on occasion to secure for themselves. The content of the right was taken for granted. It certainly involved the imperial right of assent. We do not know whether it had to do with the candidate to be elected or with the already elected Pope; perhaps this point played no particular role in the then universal form of an elevation proceeding by stages, which was juridically not very clear. In any event, the claim in the decree that the Pope had to grant specially to each succeeding German ruler such a right as a sort of privilege was new. There was here no thought of any arbitrary grant but rather of a confirmation of an old traditional prerogative, which it was not easy to annul. But since privileges could be forfeited, at least by misuse, the hierarchical feature of the decree again came to light in the papal grant of an imperial right: ecclesiastical authority was to be ultimately responsible for everything that concerned the papal election.

Naturally, the law alone was not enough. Benedict X, protected by the Count of Galeria, maintained himself in the vicinity of Rome. Since Godfrey of Lotharingia supplied no help, the Roman Church had to look elsewhere. Her distress induced her, probably at the urging of Abbot Desiderius of Montecassino and of Hildebrand, to make a decision of great portent. Visiting South Italy in the summer of 1059, Nicholas II received feudal homage and the oath of fealty from the Normans, Richard of Aversa, since 1058 Prince of Capua, and Robert Guiscard, Duke of Apulia and Calabria, and in return invested them with the territories they had conquered. The new vassals turned over to the Pope the churches of their lands together with the estates and bound themselves to loyal aid and, in the event of a disputed papal election, to the support of the "better cardinals". They paid feudal *census* merely for the parts of the *terra sancti Petri* that they occupied, and Robert Guiscard also for his own property.[3] Richard of Capua immediately took his duties seriously; he destroyed castles and strongholds of Roman nobles, including Galeria, and delivered Benedict X as a prisoner to the Pope.

Hence at one stroke the Roman Church had gained feudal suzerainty over much of Italy. German historiography is accustomed to chalk this up to her as a serious wrong. As a matter of fact, the Pope granted in fief lands which before the Norman conquest had belonged in part to the Emperor's sphere of authority,[4] but it is by no means established that Nicholas intended simply

---

[3] Robert Guiscard's oath of vassalage in Deusdedit, *Collectio canonum*, III, 285 (ed. Glanvell, I, 394); that of Richard of Capua, ibid. III, 288 (ed. Glanvell, I, 395); the latter of these is from the time of Alexander II but is probably essentially the same as that of 1059; see especially Kehr, *Belehnungen*, 22–26, 20 f.

[4] In 1059 there was question of imperial possession merely in the case of the Principality of Capua; at that time Salerno was not yet in Norman hands, and Henry III had turned over Benevento to the Roman Church (cf. Chapter 42). It is true that the Empire had long claimed all of South Italy.

to exclude an imperial suzerainty of the former Lombard principalities. In 1073, for example, Gregory VII obliged Richard of Capua to swear fealty also to the German King. The idea of a condominium was not unfamiliar; already in 1050 Leo IX had accepted the homage of the Normans in his own name and in that of the Emperor. For almost a decade the Roman Church had been exposed to the pressure of the Norman conquest, without having obtained sufficient support from the German rulers. Hence it can at least be understood that she accepted the voluntarily proposed feudal suzerainty and thus turned Norman hostility into a legitimate bond of vassalage.[5]

The royal German court, it is true, could from its standpoint have regarded the unauthorized Norman policy of the Pope as a violation of the law and reacted accordingly. Perhaps this was the deeper reason — the papal election decree probably played no role — why in 1061 (probably not in 1060) serious tension arose, but perhaps the reason is to be sought merely in a difference between Rome and Anno of Cologne. In any case, a synod at court condemned Nicholas and declared his decisions null. Cardinal Stephen, whom the Pope then sent to the Empress, was not received.[6] The break thus effected brought about a rather dangerous schism after the death of Nicholas II on 7 July 1061.

This time the Roman opposition acted more sensibly, sending to Henry IV the insignia of the dignity of *patricius* and asking for a new Pope. On the other hand, the reformers, led by Hildebrand — Humbert was now dead — on 30 September elected Anselm of Lucca, a Milanese by birth, who called himself Alexander II, and on the next day enthroned him with the aid of the troops of Richard of Capua. Then, at the end of October 1061, Bishop Cadalus of Parma was chosen Pope at the German court, in association with the Roman envoys and with Lombard bishops, at the instigation of the Chancellor of Lombardy, Guibert. He called himself Honorius II. The struggle between the two rivals for possession of Rome led to no decision, so that Godfrey of Lotharingia was able to intervene and induce both to retire to their dioceses until a definite decision should be rendered by the King.

Contrary to expectations, the decision favoured Alexander, for the *coup d'état* of Kaiserswerth, which removed Henry IV from his mother and made the reform-inclined Archbishop Anno of Cologne the real power, meant a change of policy. The Synod of Augsburg of October 1062, for which Peter Damiani composed his *Disceptatio synodalis,*[7] sent to Italy an investigating

---

[5] The assertion often made, that for the acquisition of feudal suzerainty the *Constitutum Constantini* served the Roman Church as her legal title, remains pure conjecture, demonstrable neither from the sources nor from inner necessity. In general, the territorial and political aspect, which later played so great a role in the relations between the papacy and South Italy, should be abandoned for 1059; the reformed papacy was concerned not so much for territorial possession as for vassals who could be called upon for military aid.

[6] Cf. H. G. Krause, "Das Papstwahldekret von 1059 und seine Rolle im Investiturstreit" in *StudGreg* VII (1960), 126–41.

[7] *MGLiblit* I, 76–94; also Kempf in *ArchHP* 2 (1964), 82–85.

commission that was well disposed to Alexander. Hence in 1063 Alexander II was able to enter Rome with Godfrey's aid. Cadalus's desperate attack on Rome was shattered on the weapons of Tuscan and Norman warriors. A synod meeting at Mantua at Pentecost of 1064, in which Anno of Cologne and other German bishops took part, definitively recognized Alexander. Till his death in 1072 Cadalus continued to regard himself as the legitimate Pope, but he was of no further importance.

Having emerged victorious from the struggle for her freedom, the Roman Church was able to dedicate herself to reform with redoubled zeal. The pontificate of Nicholas II had prepared for this with important decrees. Thus at the Roman Synod of 1059 clerics and priests were forbidden to acquire a church from lay persons, no matter whether with or without the payment of money. This first attack, undertaken in Humbert's spirit, against lay investiture — it is disputed whether is was supposed to affect merely the lesser churches or also bishoprics — was, it is true, only in the nature of a programme: the decree lacked any sanctions.[8] And so the Cardinal Legate Stephen, sent to France in 1060, did not try to apply it. Alexander II also, who renewed the prohibition in 1063, did not venture upon an open struggle. All the more sternly did the Synod of 1059 proceed against Nicolaitism. Its prohibition of attending the Mass of a married priest must have been all the more effective since already some of the faithful in Lombardy had risen up against Nicolaitism. Another decree suspended those clerics bound to celibacy who had retained a concubine since the regulations of Leo IX. A third law, issued at Hildebrand's urging, commanded the *vita communis et apostolica* for the clerics of one and the same church, thereby fostering the movement of the canons regular, that was destined to be so important.

Simony especially was to be the concern of the two following synods.[9] The decree probably issued in 1060 distinguished among simonists: between those ordained simoniacally by simonists, those ordained simoniacally by non-simonists, and those ordained non-simoniacally by simonists. One who belonged to the first two classes was to lose his office, but clerics of the third class, considering the difficulties of the time, might continue in office. Certain obscurities probably moved the Roman Synod of 1061 to explain this decree more precisely and especially to insist that the concession granted to the third class was valid only for persons already ordained and would not hold for the future. Hence, despite Humbert's radical position, the synod left open the theological question of the validity or invalidity of simoniacal ordinations.

---

[8] The 1059 synodal decrees in *MGConst* I, 546–48. Despite G. B. Borino, "L'investitura laica dal decreto di Nicolò II al decreto di Gregorio VII" in *StudGreg* V (1956), 345–59, one must hold to a prohibition of investiture.

[9] The decrees dated 1060 in *MGConst* I, 549–51, must be assigned to two synods: c. 1–3 probably belong to 1061, c. 5 to 1060; see. G. Miccoli, "Il problema delle ordinazioni simoniache e le sinodi Lateranensi del 1060 e 1061" in *StudGreg* V (1956), 33–81.

Nicholas II reigned too briefly to apply the decrees fully, but a relatively long pontificate (1061–73) was granted to Alexander II, the first reform Pope of whom this is so. Under him the reform reached an unprecedented intensity and expansion. In France, since Leo IX the favourite battle field, papal legates proceeded with synods and processes from 1063 on in almost uninterrupted succession. But even the proud German bishops, who were also vulnerable in consequence of the reintroduction of simoniacal practices by Henry IV, now learned to feel the Pope's heavy hand. Even the young, immature King considered it advisable to abandon the planned repudiation of his wife, Bertha of Turin, when Peter Damiani, sent specifically for this purpose, opposed him and was supported by a German synod.

England too was affected by the reform. The political and ecclesiastical situation at the close of the reign of King Edward the Confessor has already been described. There were two rivals for the succession: Earl Harold of Wessex and Duke William of Normandy. William thought that he could support his claim on an express promise made by Edward. After Edward's death on 5 January 1066, Harold at once had himself raised to the throne, whereupon William invoked the Pope's judgment, accusing Harold of perjury. The difficult legal question was probably less decisive for the Roman Church than the consideration of which of the two claimants supported her in her reform exertions and to that extent was the more fit. From this point of view the choice had to be for William and against Harold, for William had distinguished himself by his zealous promotion of reform in Normandy, without in any way relaxing his control, whereas Harold, in consequence of the earlier related usurpation of the archiepiscopal see of Canterbury, carried out by his partisan, Bishop Stigand of Winchester, and maintained in defiance of specially dispatched papal legates, gave the Roman reformers little or no reason for confidence. Advised by Hildebrand, then, Alexander II decided for the Norman and even sent him a specially blessed banner of Saint Peter for the expedition. Under this banner William and with him the Roman Church were victorious in the Battle of Hastings in 1066.

Alexander's expectation that William would now give England to the Roman Church in fief was not realized, but the King paid Peter's Pence, which had fallen into oblivion, and laid the foundation for a new development of the English Church. That three legates came to England at his request in 1070, held synods, and gave the Anglo-Saxon sees to Norman clerics, and the archbishopric of Canterbury to Abbot Lanfranc of Caen, was, it is true, only an initial success, for William and his immediate successors allowed Rome no great influence, but the closer contact then gained with the Church of the continent remained a fact that was not lost and was capable of being further developed.

The papacy realized still another success in Spain. The monastic reform movement of Cluny and Marseilles had been able to penetrate slowly from the beginning of the century, and now Rome followed. From 1065 to 1067 the Cardinal Legate Hugh the White held reform synods in Castile, Navarre, and Aragón. King Sancho of Aragón went a step further; he commended his country to the Pope in 1068 and introduced the Roman liturgy in 1071, whereas the other Christian kingdoms clung for the time being to the traditional Mozarabic liturgy, despite the zealous efforts of Roman legates. At the moment Christian Spain was in the process of gaining ground at Islam's expense. Rome accompanied this *Reconquista* with all the more active interest when French knights began to cross the Pyrenees and in 1064, together with the Spaniards, occupied the important fortress of Barbastro, which was, however, soon lost again. An expedition, prepared in 1072 by the French Count of Roucy, was discussed in Rome. Alexander blessed the undertaking and granted to every participant who confessed his sins a remission of penance. The anticipated conquests were to become fiefs of the Roman Church. But the expedition seems not to have been a success.

Portentous decisions occurred in South Italy too. With the capitulation of Bari in 1071 the Byzantines lost their last foothold. Robert Guiscard had already ventured the crossing to Sicily and had taken Messina in 1061; Palermo followed in 1072. Robert's brother Roger, to whom Alexander had sent a banner of Saint Peter in 1063, was to subjugate the island bit by bit and thereby open up to the Roman Church a new sphere of jurisdiction.

Meanwhile, struggles of a different sort were occurring in Lombardy. The upward development of this blessed land had produced a general ferment that affected the religious sphere also, especially in the cities, flourishing by virtue of their trade and industry. Instead of seizing upon the religious currents and leading them into the correct course, the urban clergy, belonging to the nobility and mostly married, persisted in their worldly manner of life and hence provoked the criticism of many of the faithful. This was a criticism supported by a genuine desire for reform, which of itself had nothing to do with tendencies related to class struggles, anticlericalism, or even heresy. In Milan it produced the revolutionary movement of the *Pataria*.[10] Under the leadership of the priest, Ariald of Varese, and of the Milanese noble, Landulf Cotta, a revolt broke out there on 10 May 1057, in which priests were forcibly obliged to celibacy. Stephen IX, approached by both sides, directed Hildebrand, who went to Germany as legate in the autumn of 1057, to go to Milan and gather information. The Pope waited for this, while the opposing groups at Milan consolidated their positions. A synod of bishops at Fontaneto

---

[10] In addition to the studies cited in the Literature for this chapter, cf. also Miccoli, "Il problema delle ordinazioni" (preceding footnote), and F. J. Schmale in *HZ* 187 (1959), 376–85. The name *Pataria,* appearing later and disputed in regard to its meaning, is probably connected with the Milan rag-fair. The important question whether Anselm I of Lucca (Pope Alexander II), of the Milanese family of the Baggio, took part in the formation of the *Pataria* or was even its intellectual author, is still unsolved.

condemned Ariald and Landulf *in absentia,* while the *Patarini* swore not to recognize any married or simoniacal priest. They could feel that they were confirmed in their opposition when in 1059 the Roman Synod issued severe decrees against Nicolaitism.

Nicholas II was well aware of the dangers connected with the *Pataria,* and so toward the end of 1059 he sent to Milan Peter Damiani and Anselm of Lucca; the latter at least sympathized with the *Pataria.* Peter Damiani, by a brilliant exposition of the Roman primacy, succeeded in overcoming the initial resistance of the citizens, who insisted on the special position of the Ambrosian Church, and in establishing order. The clergy swore to give up simoniacal and incontinent ways and obediently accepted the mild penalties imposed for their simoniacal procedures. But Peter had ventured too much. In a clear correction of his too gentle method the Roman Synod of 1060 issued the above mentioned decrees against simony, but it ratified the peace that had been gained by favouring Archbishop Guido, who was present, and rejecting Ariald's complaints.

This submission of the Archbishop was not merely a valuable victory of the idea of the primacy but the best solution of Milan's reform problem. The hierarchically minded reformers could only regard a revolution rising from below as an emergency measure. But since the weak Archbishop Guido let things return to the old groove, the *Pataria,* under the impassioned leadership of Erlembald, a brother of the now dead Landulf, let loose bloody struggles in the summer of 1066 and gained its first martyr in Ariald, who was killed during them. Other cities were also agitated. The people of Cremona drove out married and simoniacal priests; those of Piacenza, their bishop. The peace proclaimed by papal legates in 1067 did not last long. When in 1070 Guido, weary of his office, sent his ring and staff to Henry IV, the King at once invested the distinguished priest Godfrey. This notorious disregard of their right of election induced the Milanese to war against Godfrey, in which Erlembald displayed the banner of Saint Peter that the Pope had sent him. After Guido's death the priest Atto was elected Archbishop of Milan in 1072 under the presidency of a cardinal legate. Schism was the result. Since Henry IV clung to Godfrey, the Pope at the Roman Synod of 1073 excommunicated five royal councillors on a charge of simony.

This conflict between the Pope and the German King, in which the Investiture Controversy was already intimated, showed clearly the development that had occurred between 1057 and 1073: the struggle against simony and Nicolaitism had brought on the more serious struggle over the principle of the freedom of the Church. The signs pointed to the storm when Alexander II died on 21 April 1073, for now there mounted the throne of Peter the man who had guided Alexander's policy — the Archdeacon Hildebrand.

CHAPTER 44

Pope Gregory VII (1073 to 1085)

The reform entered its critical stage with Gregory VII, who, on 22 April 1073, during the very burial of the deceased Alexander II, was acclaimed as Pope by the Romans in the Lateran basilica and only then was elected at San Pietro in Vincoli by the cardinals and urban clergy and enthroned. For now one of the greatest of Peter's successors took charge of it and breathed his own spirit into it, without altering its substance or goal.

Gregory's age and provenance cannot be precisely determined. Born in Roman Tuscany, possibly at Soana, between 1019 and 1030, the son of Bonizo, who was probably not poverty-stricken but was likewise not of the nobility, Hildebrand went while still young to Rome, where he was educated in the monastery of Santa Maria all'Aventino, ruled by his uncle, and in the *palatium Romanum,* which cannot be more precisely defined. Having received the lower orders, he served Gregory VI, who was on friendly terms with him, as a cleric and accompanied him into exile in Germany. Set at liberty by the death of the deposed Pope in the autumn of 1047, he probably entered Cluny or a Cluniac monastery, but after a few months was summoned by Leo IX, brought back to Rome, and entrusted with the administration of San Paolo *fuori le mura.* The rise of his prestige among the reformers is attested by legations to France in 1054 and 1056 and Germany in 1057 and by his appointment as archdeacon in the autumn of 1059. Under Nicholas II he was regarded as one of the chief advisers, under Alexander II as the most powerful man in the Lateran.[1]

It is not entirely correct to speak of Gregory VII as the monk on the papal throne. Reluctant though he may have been to abandon the monastery — he continued to wear the monastic habit — and willingly as he made use of monks for the work of reform, he devoted himself resolutely to the apostolic activity imposed upon him; in fact he placed it above the purely monastic ideal in frank criticism of the excessively monastic concept of, for example, Peter Damiani or Hugh of Cluny. For Gregory was profoundly convinced that, ultimately, the great concern in the world was with the struggle between God's Kingdom and that of the devil, with the warlike efforts of God's children that peace, justice, and the love of God might fill as many men as possible. All Christians were summoned to this struggle, but especially the spiritual and secular rulers. Gregory clung to the old view of the world throughout: God's Kingdom was the *ecclesia universalis* with the powers of the *Regnum* and *Sacerdotium* instituted by the

[1] On his family, cf. the critical survey of the bibliography in Schramm in *GGA* 207 (1953), 67–70; on his entry into Cluny, G. B. Borino, "Ildebrando non si fece monaco a Roma" in *StudGreg* IV (1952), 441–56 (with the other literature).

Lord; but he intended that God should be again able to act freely in his Kingdom.

Since priests were primarily responsible for divine things, for him the two powers were not simply side by side; the *Sacerdotium* possessed the higher rank, and Gregory did everything to free it again for God's work and to guarantee the authority belonging to it, but one alone could, in his view, claim to be the proper interpreter of the divine will — Peter's vicar in Rome. For Christ, who gave Peter supreme authority and bade him establish the Roman Church, prayed for Peter's faith so that the Roman Church cannot err, and Peter lives on by entering, as Gregory firmly believed, into a sort of personal union with every successor and elevating him, by virtue of his own merits, to a better and holier being.[2] Hence all Christians must obey the Pope, who is responsible for their salvation, and under his leadership fight for the Kingdom of God, not only priests and monks who are subject to his superepiscopal authority, but also secular rulers.

With this claim, oriented to the spiritual sphere, Gregory did not intend to strip the *Regnum* of power or to expel it from the *ecclesia universalis;* he only demanded that the ruler really belong to the *corpus Christi.* If by his evil deeds the ruler revealed himself as a member of Satan's Kingdom, then basically he was depriving himself of power; for then he was commanding, no longer in God's name, but in that of the devil, and this contradicted the nature of the *ecclesia universalis.* From this Gregory deduced the radical and then even unheard of conclusion: by virtue of the papal right to decide ultimately who is of God and who is of the devil, he claimed that he could depose an unworthy ruler and free his subjects from their oath of allegiance.[3]

Persons have sought, incorrectly, to trace Gregory's thought directly to Augustine. The great Pope knew little of Augustine and, except for Gregory the Great, had likewise no relationship with the other Fathers. All the more directly did Scripture interest him, especially the New Testament and there, by preference, Saint Paul, a kindred spirit. In addition, he was naturally committed to the ideas which the ecclesiastical *milieu,* with its Augustinian colouring, and the contemporary reform movement brought him, but, apart from the claim to deposition, he neither enriched them with new ideas nor

---

[2] *Reg.,* II, 55a (no. 23), VIII, 21; in Caspar ed., 207, 561; W. Ullmann, "Dictatus Papae 23 in Retrospect and Prospect" in *StudGreg* VI (1959–61), 229–64, would like to have it that the sanctity refers merely to the office and not to the person of the Pope, but he does not bear in mind that a personally inherited holiness was championed in the Formosus controversy and was rejected at that time by Auxilius (cf. *supra,* Chapter 35, footnote 18). Perhaps Gregory VII was familiar with the relevant passage of Auxilius, in which the citation of Ennodius is missing; it is demonstrable that other writings of Auxilius were used by the reformers; cf. J. Ryan, *Saint Peter Damiani,* 162–65, 200. Further, despite Ullmann's objection, Gregory's *mystique* of Saint Peter probably entered here.

[3] *Reg.,* II, 55a (no. 12, 27), IV, 2, VIII, 21; in Caspar ed., 204, 208, 293–97, 544–63; for Gregory's political doctrine and that of his friends, see Chapter 50.

articulated them into a consistent reform programme, let alone into a new world-view in anticipation of the future. Withal, Gregory's greatness is to be sought, not in his ideas, but in his religious, perhaps mystically gifted, personality, in the abundance of the divine experience given to him, taken up by his genius, and converted into action.

It would be going too far to say that the measure of his thought and activity could be deduced merely from his personal, religious experience. That Gregory intended to follow ecclesiastical tradition appears in his calling for the drawing up of new compilations of the law, which were to work out the authentic and venerable statements of ecclesiastical tradition that were inspired by the Holy Spirit. Before this wish could be more or less satisfactorily fulfilled by his friends, headed by Anselm of Lucca, he had himself collected canonical material dealing with the Roman primacy, mostly taken from pseudo-Isidore, arranged it in sections, and for each section composed a concise sentence, suggesting the chapter headings of a canonical collection. Thus originated the famed *Dictatus papae,* which was put into Gregory's *registrum* of letters.[4] There in twenty-seven sentences were summarized the most important primatial rights, with no systematization but with the already mentioned prerogatives of the Roman Church — her foundation by Christ and infallibility — and of the papacy — the inherited personal sanctity of the Pope and his right of deposition: the honorary privileges, including that of having his foot kissed and the exclusive right to use the imperial insignia, this last probably directed against the Byzantine Patriarch; the supreme legislative and judicial power and its effects; superepiscopal authority with regard to the deposition and institution of bishops, ordaining of clerics, determining of diocesan boundaries, and so forth; and excommunication and absolution from oaths as a consequence of the papal coercive power. The listing was not oriented to a concrete goal, connected with the reform or with negotiations for union. It was supposed merely to provide a synopsis of the primatial rights as they could be identified in tradition. Its use depended on the situation of the moment, that is, on the question, to be constantly investigated anew in the concrete case, whether and to what extent the interests of God's Kingdom required an intervention.

Gregory's election was charged with the tensions in regard to Henry IV

---

[4] *Reg.,* II, 55a; in Caspar ed., 201–08; basic is K. Hofmann, *Der "Dictatus Papae" Gregors VII. Eine rechtsgeschichtliche Erklärung* (Paderborn 1933). The various theories on the origin and aim of the *Dictatus* in K. Hofmann, "Der 'Dictatus Papae' als eine Indexsammlung?" in *StudGreg* I (1947), 531–37; the theory of an index of a collection was advanced by G. B. Borino, "Un'ipotesi sul 'Dictatus Papae' di Gregorio VII" in *AD Romana* 67 (1944), 237–52; its utility with regard to form is demonstrated by S. Kuttner, "Liber canonicus. A Note on 'Dictatus Papae' c. 17" in *StudGreg* II (1947), 387–401. Borino's assumption of a mere index of a collection that had nothing at all to do with Gregory's ideas is as little correct as is Haller's view in *Papsttum,* II, 382f., that it was a revolutionary reform program going far beyond the assembled sources.

which, because of the Milanese question, had clouded the last days of Alexander II. They probably did not permit an application to the young King for his approval of the election. Since Henry continued to associate with the excommunicated advisers and hence fell under the ban himself, no notice of the election was probably sent to him.[5] It remained to be seen whether the King would react, but he did not. And, when the Saxon revolt broke out, he threw himself, so to speak, at the Pope's feet in an extravagantly humble letter in which he acknowledged his failings. Gregory could breathe freely and turn to the great concern of his heart, the reform.

The Reform

The first Roman Reform Synod, that of 1074, renewed the old rules, decreeing exclusion from the ministry for simony, suspension for Nicolaitism. The synod of the following year drew the reins tighter: for simonists it now decreed permanent deposition, while in regard to incontinent priests it referred to the regulation of 1059, calling for a boycott by the people. Resistance was not lacking; in particular the requirement of celibacy encountered widespread rejection.[6] Polemical writings appeared, and there were scenes of violence at Rouen and in several places in Germany. But Gregory was unmoved. The Roman Synod in the autumn of 1078 obliged every bishop, under pain of suspension, not to tolerate any *fornicatio* among his clergy. Furthermore, priests who sold their official functions were suspended. The most decisive blow had to do with ordinations. The spring Synod of 1078 declared all ordinations performed by the excommunicated to be legally invalid *(irritas);* the autumn synod of that year decreed the same thing for ordinations which were imparted for money or as a result of petition or services or without the consent of clergy and people and without the approval of the proper ecclesiastical superiors.[7] Although both decrees most probably did not intend to decide the dogmatic question of the sacramental validity or invalidity of such orders, their obscure wording increased the existing uncertainty. This is to be observed in Gregory VII himself. On the one hand, he avoided taking a stand on the dogmatic question; on the other hand, he allowed his legate, Amatus of Oléron, to have his own way when at the Synod of Gerona in 1078 he declared the absolute nullity of simoniacal ordinations. Hence it should cause no surprise that the question came up in the polemics and in general caused much unrest.

But the question of investiture made the conflict more bitter. Here Gregory

---

[5] Thus G. B. Borino in *StudGreg* V (1956), 313–43; less convincing is A. Michel, *Papstwahl und Königsdekret*, 211–16.

[6] For the council's decrees see C. Erdmann, *Studien zur Briefliteratur*, 227, footnote 3.

[7] *Reg.*, V, 14a, VI, 5b; in Caspar ed., 372, 403f.; on the dogmatic question, see A. Schebler, *Die Reordination*, 235–45; A. Nitschke in *StudGreg* V (1956), 153–55; G.B.Borino, ibid., 411–15.

was probably led into a quarrel that he had not sought. At first he entirely disregarded the decree promulgated by Nicholas II and renewed by Alexander II but never enforced. He did not have recourse to it until the Lenten Synod of 1075.[8] Even if he is supposed to have then duly published the decree,[9] this was probably done at first without great emphasis. The reasons for this caution are unknown to us, but there is reason to believe that about the same time he had the above mentioned *Dictatus papae* entered into the *registrum* of his letters. Just as he intended to use the rights there summarized only to the extent that it seemed necessary to him, he probably planned to apply the investiture prohibition according to the circumstances. Perhaps it would have played no great role in Gregory's reform work, had not something unforeseen intervened — Henry IV's extravagant counterattack in 1076, to be discussed below. For then Gregory became inexorable. He not only insisted on the prohibition for Germany. He had it promulgated in France by his legates in 1077 and more precisely formulated at the Roman autumn Synod of 1078: it was forbidden to clerics, under penalty of excommunication and annulment of the completed action, to accept from a layman the investiture of bishoprics, abbeys, and churches. The Lenten Synod of 1080 decreed the same but expressly extended the prohibition to lesser ecclesiastical functions and now also visited excommunication on the investing layman.[10] The Investiture Controversy that thereby erupted but by no means affected all countries was not to be settled for decades.

Gregory was here concerned, not for a question of power, and far less for economic interests, but for reform, which, in his view, could only be achieved when the appointing of priests and bishops, freed from the smothering influence of kings and proprietors of churches, again took place according to the canonical rules, which gave scope to the divine activity. The free election envisaged by the old canon law required, of course, a further guarantee, and Gregory did not hesitate to set it up. A decree of the Lenten Synod of 1080 not only enjoined the control of elections provided by the old law, which was now to be exercised by a bishop named as visitor, and the confirmation of the election by the metropolitan or the Pope. It also laid the foundation for the hitherto unknown right of devolution: in the event of an uncanonical election the electors' right to fill the office was to

[8] C. Erdmann, *Studien zur Briefliteratur,* 254, footnote 2, doubts whether the synod was at all concerned with the decree.

[9] Actual publication is defended by G. B. Borino, "Il decreto di Gregorio VII contro le investiture fu promulgato nel 1075" in *StudGreg* VI (1959–61), 329–48; cf. there the opposing opinions, rejected by Borino with noteworthy but not always sound reasons, which either deny publication outright or restrict it to a definite circle of persons. In an earlier study of the problem, *StudGreg* V (1956), 345–59, Borino went farther: Nicholas II, he claimed, issued no prohibition of investiture and consequently Alexander II did not renew it; its author was Gregory VII.

[10] 1078 (*Reg.,* VI, 5b); 1080 (*Reg.,* VII, 14a); in Caspar ed., 403, 480f.

pass to the metropolitan or to the Pope.[11] What the papal election decree of 1059 had imperfectly attempted, by empowering the quasi-metropolitan cardinal-bishops to choose the new Pope outside Rome in an emergency, was in 1080 perfectly achieved for the instituting of bishops. The final decision no longer lay with the electors, among whom the secular ruler had spoken the decisive word, but with the ecclesiastical authority: the hierarchical principle, already applied in 1059, had gained a new and portentous victory.

The autumn Synod of 1078 also risked a first attack on the right of the proprietors of churches by desiring to enlighten the laity as to how much danger for the salvation of souls was involved in the possession of churches and tithes. In the same year the reform Synod of Gerona stated that lay persons must not really possess churches; wherever this could not be avoided, at least the taking of the offerings was forbidden. The moderate attitude of the reformers could count all the more on partial successes, since already for some time there had been in progress a movement that was seeking to transfer proprietary churches from the lay to the ecclesiastical hand.[12]

Gregory VII did everything to translate his reforming laws into fact. Like his predecessors he made use of legates for this purpose but introduced an important innovation. While he entrusted hitherto customary legates, dispatched only for a specified time, merely with particular tasks or visitations of remote lands, he had the real reform activity attended to by standing legates, usually taken from the country in question. Thus in 1075 he named Hugh of Die for France and Amatus of Oléron for the Midi and Spain; in 1079 Cardinal Richard of Saint-Victor de Marseille for Spain; in 1080 Bishop Altmann of Passau for Germany; and in 1081 Anselm of Lucca for Lombardy. In this group, all of whom were bishops except Richard of Saint-Victor, a great activity was especially displayed by Hugh and Amatus. Many provincial synods convoked by them imposed Gregory's reform decrees. There was a shower of penalties on simoniacal bishops or those failing otherwise, and even the proud Archbishop Manasses of Reims had to accept his own deposition. Since Gregory reserved the final decision to himself, there were frequent appeals to Rome. The Pope had many important cases decided by the Roman reform synods, which annually proclaimed a series of excommunications, suspensions, and depositions. The final struggle with Henry IV naturally took the personal direction of the reform work more and more out of Gregory's hand.

There is no doubt that Gregory's pontificate was a turning point in the

---

[11] *Reg.,* VII, 14a; in Caspar ed., 482.

[12] *Reg.,* VI, 5b, no. XXXII; ibid., the prohibition of possessing tithes (no. XVI and c. 7); in Caspar ed., 402, 401, 404f.; Synod of Gerona, c. 3–5, *Mansi* XX, 519; also H. E. Feine, "Kirchenreform und Niederkirchenwesen" in *StudGreg* II (1947), 505–24 (with the other literature); T. Mayer, "Gregor VII. und das Eigenkirchenrecht. Die ältesten Urkunden von Hirsau und Muri" in *Zeitschrift für Schweizerische Geschichte* 28 (1948), 145–76.

history of the Roman primacy. It is not to no purpose that people speak of the "Hildebrandine Church" that was now beginning. But if the individual activities are looked at, they show little that was fundamentally new. The widespread view that Gregory sought to undermine the position of bishops and metropolitans is not borne out by the sources. The often cited right of devolution, prepared in 1080, in no way excluded the right of the metropolitan. And the further argument, that the primacy of Lyons was set up in 1079 in order, on the one hand, to replace the earlier form of the vicariate with a virtually meaningless primacy, and, on the other hand, to strike at Archbishop Manasses of Reims or the champions of lay investiture, has been shown to be untenable. When Gregory complied with the request of Gebuin of Lyons, he honestly believed he was restoring an ancient institution, without realizing that he was actually converting an invention of pseudo-Isidore into reality for the first time.[13] If he were concerned merely for centralization, he would have ignored Gebuin's request and thus spared himself the intermediate tribunal.

Actually, Gregory sought no constitutional changes for the benefit of the Roman primacy. What he contributed of his own was his *mystique* of Saint Peter, already mentioned. Profoundly convinced that no Christian could be saved who was not bound to Peter's vicar in unity, harmony, and obedience, he used all the rights assembled in the *Dictatus papae* to the extent that he regarded as necessary. Such a religious dynamism, entirely oriented to the personal responsibility of the Pope, brought about the definitive turning point. While Gregory's own personal charism may have been extinguished with his death, the monarchical form of government of the Roman Church had become a reality. There remained merely the task of justifying it more precisely and guaranteeing and perfecting it.

Gregory's *mystique* of Saint Peter affected not only priests but also the laity. He expected the princes especially to be loyal adherents of Saint Peter and his vicar. Words such as *fidelitas, fidelis, miles Sancti Petri* or *sanctae romanae ecclesiae* or *sanctae apostolicae sedis* constantly recur in his letters. As early as the time of Alexander II Counts William of Burgundy, Raymond of Saint-Gilles, Amadeus of Savoy, and others had bound themselves by a solemn oath to defend the *res Sancti Petri*. Gregory did not fail to make use of Christian princes for the interests of religion and of the Church. Thus he authorized some of them to proceed with force against unworthy bishops who defied ecclesiastical penalties or he asked for their help when the Roman Church or specific areas of the Christian world were threatened. Convinced that genuine love demanded that the machinations of the *corpus diaboli* be obstructed by force of arms and that life be risked for the brothers, he had no hesitation

---

[13] H. Fuhrmann, "Studien zur Geschichte der mittelalterlichen Patriarchate" in *ZSavRGkan* 71 (1954), 61–84 (especially 79f.); see *supra,* Chapter 35.

about summoning the laity to a holy war. In fact, he even established a troop of his own, the *militia Sancti Petri,* and sought to turn it into a real army in times of crisis, by voluntary enlistments, by military aid which he claimed from bishops or vassals, or by mercenaries.

Hence it was very important to him to augment the loyalty of the *fideles Sancti Petri.* Since *fidelitas* was based on the religious connection with Peter and hence lacked a clear juridical form, he strove to strengthen it further in the most varied ways — simple promises of obedience, payment of *census,* pledge of military aid, vassalage. All possibilities were used by him, often with appeal to genuine rights or rights so regarded.[14] This very lack of any systematization and of juridical clarity should indicate how little Gregory was concerned for a secular system of government. It is true that his effort to make use of the princes somehow as co-workers led to a real entanglement of reform and politics. Hence, in what follows the two spheres, which in his view were not to be separated, will be discussed together.

Reform Policy in the Various Countries

Characteristic of Gregory VII's broad view, embracing all Christendom, was his alert interest in the northern missionary area, where at last the definitive decision was made in favour of Christianity in Sweden also. How carefully he followed the development appears from his pastoral letters of 1080–81 to Olaf III of Norway and to the Swedish Kings Inge and Alsten, which, in addition to instruction on the faith and on the royal office, contained the suggestion that clerics be sent to Rome for study. Already Christianized Denmark, which counted nine sees around 1060, had secured closer ties with the Roman Church under Alexander II. King Svein Estrithson had at that time expressed the desire for an archbishopric of his own and for the *patrocinium Petri* and had begun to pay Peter's Pence. Like Alexander, Gregory too was entirely favourable to the idea of a Danish archbishopric, without presuming a decision; in addition, he sought to strengthen the friendly relations thus inaugurated. If he gladly clarified the *patrocinium Petri* suggested by Svein, he further proposed that one of the King's sons should come to Rome with a military force in order to be set over a rich province on the sea — Dalmatia was probably meant — and there to undertake the defence of Christendom. The letter, sent in 1075, did not find Svein alive. The discord then ensuing in Denmark among his sons induced the Pope to urge neutrality on the Norwegian King.[15]

---

[14] C. Erdmann, *Kreuzzugsgedanke,* 185–211, 134–65; P. Zerbi, "Il termine fidelitas nelle lettere di Gregorio VII" in *StudGreg* III (1948), 129–48. W. Wühr, *Studien zu Gregor VII.,* 52–66, discusses succinctly the political and juridical dependence of particular countries as demanded by Gregory.

[15] *Reg.,* II, 51, 75; in Caspar ed., 192–94, 237 f.; other letters to the King of Denmark in *Reg.,*

There was also no dearth of connections with the countries to the east of Germany. Boleslas II of Poland paid voluntary tribute, Vratislav of Bohemia continued to pay the *census* which Nicholas II had stipulated when he allowed Duke Spitignev to wear the mitre. Gregory VII was concerned with Bohemia chiefly because of the controversy between the Bishops of Prague and Olomouc. But his essentially good relationship with Vratislav cooled because of the loyalty which Vratislav observed toward Henry IV, whom the Pope had excommunicated and deposed. Boleslas II of Poland recommended himself to Gregory by his receptiveness to the papal reform wishes. In 1075 the Pope sent legates who were especially to improve the organization of the Polish Church. The Roman influence declined when Boleslas lost his crown because of the assassination of Bishop Stanislas of Cracow in 1079.

Relations with Hungary were overshadowed by the struggle for the throne between Solomon and Geza. For the sake of better protection, Solomon became Henry IV's vassal. Gregory regarded this as an injustice to the Roman Church, to which King Stephen had once given the kingdom as her own. Hungary, he said, must continue in the liberty proper to it and must not be subjected to any ruler of another realm, but only to the Roman Mother, the church which treats her subjects, not as servants, but as sons.[16] But the opportunity for deducing concrete rights from this claim was lacking, for Geza, favoured by the Pope but also relying on Byzantium, was, after his victory over Solomon, not interested in any further protection by the Pope, as was true also of his successor, Ladislas. All the greater was the success achieved in the Kingdom of Croatia-Dalmatia. The new ruler, Demetrius-Zwonimir, Geza's brother-in-law and zealous for reform, had himself crowned King at a reform synod presided over by papal legates in 1076 and presented with the banner of Saint Peter; in this connection he took an oath of loyalty to the Pope, which was modelled on the formula of an oath of vassalage.[17] The relationship thus established, which, at least in the Roman interpretation, must have been one of feudal law, was used by Gregory to prepare for an improvement of the state of the Church.

Contact with Kiev was established in a curious way. Demetrius-Izjaslav, brother-in-law of Boleslas of Poland, was forced in 1073 to flee to Poland for the second time. Since Boleslas not only did not aid him, but even robbed him of a part of his treasures, he turned for help to Henry IV and then, when this was of no avail, to the Pope, to whom he offered his kingdom through his son, Peter Jaropolk. After some waiting, Gregory bestowed the kingdom on Jaropolk, sent him back to his parents with legates, and got Boleslas to return the treasures. The hopes which he set on this bond, probably understood

---

I, 4, V, 10, VII, 5, 21; to the King of Sweden in *Reg.,* VII, 5, 21; to the King of Norway in *Reg.,* VI, 13. For earlier developments in the North see Chapter 30.

[16] *Reg.,* II, 13, 63; in Caspar ed., 144–46, 218f.

[17] Deusdedit, *Collectio canonum,* III, 278, ed. Wolf von Glanvell, 383.

by him as one of vassalage but not clearly defined, were not fulfilled, when in 1076 Izjaslav recovered his kingdom with Polish aid. Although Izjaslav and his successor Jaropolk continued to be friendly toward the Roman Church, Greek influence, which had never yielded and grew constantly stronger, definitely became preponderant after Jaropolk's death in 1086.

Gregory consciously included the Byzantine Church in his care for Christendom. Despite the Schism the Popes had been in direct relations with the Emperor until the investiture of the Normans with South Italy. Under Alexander II concrete negotiations for union must have been begun. Probably connected with them was the Byzantine embassy which Gregory received a few months after his election and which he reciprocated in Byzantium through the Patriarch Dominic of Grado. Before Dominic's return, Gregory, probably on his own initiative, decided in the spring of 1074 to send a Western army to the East to free the Christians of Asia Minor from the Seljuk threat. By means of this assistance he hoped to realize the reunion of the Church. Toward the end of the year letters again went out to summon the *fideles* of Saint Peter to the holy war in Asia Minor, which the Pope would direct personally.[18] But the tension with the French King and soon with Henry IV caused the Pope to drop the as yet premature plan. He remained in friendly contact with the Emperor Michael VII; this was all the more possible, since Robert Guiscard, whom the Greeks hated, had been excommunicated.

But Michael had to yield in 1078 to Nicephorus III, and the latter in 1081 to Alexius I Comnenus. The first of these changes on the throne gave Robert Guiscard the notion of crossing over to the Balkan peninsula and attacking the Byzantines, as the alleged avenger of Michael VII. Gregory VII, who in the meantime had become reconciled with Robert, supported the undertaking, while the new Emperor Alexius, continuing the war with Robert, still regarded the Pope as an opponent of the Norman and sought to gain him to his side. Gregory, who seems to have even excommunicated Alexius, had profoundly miscalculated. Robert's Balkan adventure, happily inaugurated by the victory of Durazzo, ended in a complete fiasco. The Antipope Clement III, set up meanwhile by Henry IV, did not fail to establish good relations with the Byzantine world. Only the need of Alexius I and the surpassing diplomacy of Urban II led again to a *rapprochement* between the reform papacy and Byzantium.

In a class by itself was Gregory's attitude to the English Church and its master, William the Conqueror. The new King rejected the homage of vassalage which Gregory seems to have once demanded through legates, but he paid Peter's Pence and promoted the politically necessary reform of the Church, supported by Archbishop Lanfranc of Canterbury. Numerous

---

[18] *Reg.,* I, 46, 49, II, 31, 37; in Caspar ed., 69f., 75f., 166f., 172f.

reform synods saw to improved conditions. To what extent it was possible to combine serious efforts with sensible moderation appears, for example, from the Synod of Winchester of 1076, which left married priests in office but forbade any future marriage. Furthermore, the English Church prepared to move into Ireland. As early as about 1028 the Bishop of Dublin had been consecrated at Canterbury and had obliged himself to obedience. Lanfranc of Canterbury and his successor Anselm considered the Irish Church as under their jurisdiction. Gregory VII's attention must have been called by Lanfranc to the reform tasks at hand in Ireland and under the circumstances he must have been motivated to send a pastoral letter to King Toirdelbach and the Irish. It was a small token but full of future promise. Under Paschal II papal legates were to attend a first Irish reform synod.

Since Gregory saw that what was essential was being achieved in England, he came to terms with William's outlook, which was that of a State Church now coming clearly into the light. The King named the bishops, invested them — there was no Investiture Controversy in England and Normandy during the entire eleventh century — confirmed synodal decrees, and decided the limits of ecclesiastical jurisdiction. The reform ideal of William and Lanfranc obviously continued in the old conservative notions, as these had inspired the Emperor Henry III and the German bishops. Only on one point did the Pope remonstrate: William did not permit the English bishops to go to Rome or to have any contact with the Pope without his knowledge. In this matter a serious conflict might have occurred. To the King it may have been only proper that Lanfranc was intent on maintaining his ecclesiastical rights against Rome and did not love the troublesome Pope.[19] After the capture of Rome by Henry IV in 1084, Lanfranc even made contact with the Clementists. Without a real break actually occurring, the English Church for years maintained a neutral attitude in regard to the schism.

Spain had become accessible to the Roman reform under Alexander II. Gregory energetically carried the happy beginnings further by means of standing legates. Reform councils, such as that of Gerona in 1078 and that of Burgos in 1080, especially attacked simony and Nicolaitism. Gregory achieved his greatest enduring success when the Mozarabic rite was now replaced by the Roman even outside Aragón. Rome's reforming and liturgical initiative awakened among the Spanish Cluniacs the fear that they would lose their influence. Hence Robert, Abbot of Sahagún, their most important monastery, began to intrigue against the legate and to gain King Alfonso VI. Gregory VII became so exasperated that he threatened the King, not only with excommunication, but with war. The conflict, which cost Robert of

---

[19] Literature on Lanfranc in Chapter 53, footnote 11; for Lanfranc's relationship to the forgeries which were produced to prove the primatial position of Canterbury with regard to York, cf. R. W. Southern, "The Canterbury Forgeries" in *EHR* 73 (1958), 193–226.

Sahagún his office, ended at once, and the Council of Burgos in 1080 became a complete triumph for the legate.

Spain was in the very thick of a phase of the *Reconquista*. As in the days of Alexander II, knights, full of crusading ardour or of mere lust for booty, were still hurrying from France to render assistance. Thus two princes who were zealous for reform, Hugh I of Burgundy and William VI of Aquitaine, supported the enterprises of the King of Aragón. In the battles, fought with varying fortune and varying alignments — Muslims could take the field along with Spanish Christians and vice versa — Alfonso VI succeeded in capturing Toledo in 1085. If the hope of now subjugating all of Andalusia was frustrated by the invasion of the Almoravids, still a decisive victory had been gained.

At the beginning of his pontificate Gregory VII took special pains with regard to the French knights. He was at the same time pursuing a material goal. Just as Ebolus of Roucy had done, they were to recognize the lands to be conquered as the property of the Roman Church; according to very ancient law, he said, Spain belonged to Saint Peter. Some years later he communicated the same view to the Spanish kings and magnates in a pastoral letter: "ex antiquis constitutionibus" the realm had been given to the Roman Church as her own.[20] The papal admonition had only one success: Count Bernard of Besalú acknowledged himself to be *miles sancti Petri* and agreed to a feudal *census*.

In no country was the reform so energetically pushed as in France, but even here its successes were modest. The Midi proved to be relatively willing; several of the South French princes had earlier sworn special fealty to Saint Peter, and now Count Bertrand of Provence entrusted his territory in 1081 and Count Peter de Melgueil the country of Substantion in 1085 to the Roman Church as fiefs. Not a few feudal lords and their clerical relatives renounced their proprietary rights over churches, for the sake of their salvation or out of fear of excommunication.[21] Things were more difficult in the area ruled by King Philip I. The anarchic situation as such, and the blackmail extorted from merchants and pilgrims going to Rome in particular, induced Gregory in 1074 to threaten him not merely with excommunication and interdict but with deprivation of his authority. Despite these and other tensions a break never occurred. The unflagging energy of the standing legates, on

[20] *Reg.*, I, 7, IV, 28; in Caspar ed., 11f., 343–47. What Gregory meant by the "antiquae constitutiones" is not clear. For his claim the following have been mentioned: arrangements made by Recared with Gregory I but no longer known; the *Constitutum Constantini;* documents now lost, which can no longer be specified as to time; legal claims to the land taken from the Muslims; an idea of Gregory's concerning universal leadership and having as its aim religious dependence. No interpretation is convincing. For the literature see especially B. Llorca, cited in the Literature for this chapter.

[21] L. de Lacger, "Aperçu de la réforme grégorienne dans l'Albigeoise" in *StudGreg* II (1947), 211–34.

occasion mitigated by the Pope, and the resistance, now stronger, now weaker, but always moderate, of the King and of some of the bishops and nobles produced a general ferment, though as yet the end of the reform struggle could not be predicted. Even the prohibition of investiture, urged in 1077, did not lead to any struggle over principle.[22]

Italy caused the Pope great anxiety. When he went south in 1073 he was able to take possession of Benevento and to renew his feudal relationship with Richard of Capua, but Robert Guiscard held aloof. He and Richard intended to bring the few remaining territories under their rule. Robert conquered Amalfi in 1073 and Salerno in 1076. In 1077 he besieged Benevento, while Richard tried in vain to take Naples. The attack on Benevento was not the sole act which violated the territorial rights of the Roman Church. The two princes had during this whole time taken possession of papal property within and without the Papal State. The Pope had to look on helpless. Excommunication, several times pronounced, had no effect on Robert, and the war planned against him in 1074, in alliance with Gisulf of Salerno, Beatrice and Matilda of Tuscany, and Godfrey of Lotharingia, to which Gregory summoned the South French *fideles* of Saint Peter, without finding any response, got no farther than wretched beginnings. Only the Treaty of Ceprano in 1080 prepared the way for peace. Not only did Gregory have to accept the conquests tacitly; Robert guaranteed the *terra sancti Petri* only in so far as the Roman Church could prove her rights. The *census* was regulated as in 1059 and 1062.[23]

Beyond the continent Gregory's attention was directed to Sardinia and Corsica. Since he regarded both islands as the property of the Roman Church by virtue of the *privilegium* of Louis the Pious, he sought to vindicate this claim in cautious letters and through his legates.[24]

His chief supports were the Marchionesses of Tuscany, Beatrice (d. 1076) and especially Matilda, wife of Godfrey of Lower Lotharingia. Between

---

[22] Hard pressed by Henry IV, Gregory, probably in 1081, had Peter's Pence collected in France by specially dispatched legates, relying on a forged charter of Charles the Great, which he regarded as genuine; see the instruction for the legates in *Reg.*, VIII, 23, in Caspar ed., 565–67. The tradition for a Gallic Peter's Pence has long been demonstrable; see C. Erdmann, *Kreuzzugsgedanke*, 203. Furthermore, Gregory claimed rights to Brittany; cf. A. A. Pocquet du Haut-Jussé in *StudGreg* I (1947), 189–96; Erdmann, *op. cit.* 359–61; mentioned in a privilege granted by Gregory to a monastery, the claim was based on Breton testimonies; whether there is here an allusion to the *Constitutum Constantini* and, if so, to whom it should be ascribed, the Bretons or Gregory, is not certain.

[23] *Reg.*, VIII, 1a–c; in Caspar ed., 514–17.

[24] E. E. Stengel, "Untersuchungen über die Entwicklung des Kaiserprivilegs", in his *Abhandlungen und Untersuchungen zur mittelalterlichen Geschichte* (Cologne - Graz 1960), 234f., 246, footnote t, doubts that the passage of the *Pactum Ludovicianum* referring to Sardinia, Corsica, and Sicily was interpolated later, at the time of Gregory VII; he regards the passage as probably authentic. Cf. also A. Dove, "Corsica und Sardinien in den Schenkungen an die Päpste" in *SAM* (1894), 223ff.; Wühr, *Studien zu Gregor VII.*, 54; Erdmann, *op. cit.* 201.

1077 and 1080 Matilda even made over her considerable property to the Roman Church and received it back for her free disposal and lifelong enjoyment. Her life became the mirror of the reform struggle. Put under the ban by Henry IV in 1081, she lost a good part of her dominions for more than a decade.

The difficult situation in Italy obstructed Gregory VII in any effective reform activity. If the south had to be counted out almost entirely, because of the political chaos, in Central and North Italy the opposition of the clergy hostile to reform stiffened as the tension with Henry IV increased. The head of the opposition was Archbishop Guibert of Ravenna, who was excommunicated in 1076 and ineffectively deposed in 1078. On the other hand, the protagonist of reform, the Lombard popular movement of the *Pataria,* noticeably lost strength from 1075 when Erlembald perished in a fight in Milan; with Henry IV's Italian expedition in 1081 it moved entirely into the background. Not the opposition of Robert Guiscard but that of Henry IV ultimately determined Gregory's reform policy in Italy. The first dramatic conflict of 1076, which forever estranged the Pope and the King, blazed forth on questions affecting the Church in North and Central Italy.

The relations of Gregory VII to Germany and the German King were objectively weighed down by the Ottonian-Salian Imperial Church system. The Church, gathered around the theocratic monarch, had thus far withstood every intervention of any importance by the reform papacy. Even Alexander II had not achieved more than individual successes and in the Milan conflict he had experienced how little he could enforce his wishes. Henry IV's yielding in the autumn of 1073, motivated by the Saxon revolt, caused Gregory to hope for a change in principle, and so in 1074 he sent two legates to Germany to hold a reform council. The project failed, not because of Henry IV, whom the legates restored to the Christian community, but because of the juridical standpoint of the German episcopate. If the head of the opposition, Archbishop Liemar of Bremen, had not possessed the courage to go to Rome and appease the enraged Pope, there would have been a collision. Henry IV restrained himself, although at the Lenten Synod of 1075 five of his councillors were again excommunicated and the prohibition of lay investiture was made known to him; in fact he even entered into negotiations as suggested by Gregory on the investiture question and in the autumn of 1075 abandoned the simoniacal Bishop of Bamberg.

In reality he did not intend to comply with the Pope's reform wishes. This was to be revealed by the Italian policy that he inaugurated after his victory over the Saxons on 9 June 1075. One of the excommunicated councillors, Count Eberhard, crossed the Alps, intervened in Lombardy against the *Patarini,* and negotiated with Robert Guiscard, unsuccessfully, about a bond of vassalage to the German King. Then Henry assumed a more severe tone. Contrary to the promises made in 1073, he invested as Archbishop of Milan, not Godfrey, who had been first appointed but had not made any progress, but another Milanese cleric, Tedald, and designated for the sees of Fermo and Spoleto, disregarding Rome's metropolitan rights, men whom the Pope did not even know. Gregory quite rightly felt that he had been deceived and challenged. He sent Henry a letter of admonition which, in addition to the uncanonical appointment of the three Italian bishops, referred also to the unlawful association with the excommunicated councillors; by word of mouth the King was threatened with excommunication.

Neither Henry IV nor the German episcopate showed themselves equal to the strained but in no sense inextricable situation. Incited by the disgusting slanders of the disloyal Cardinal Hugh the White and labouring under the delusion that Gregory's position was not only undermined in Christendom and in Italy but even in Rome, where on Christmas of 1075 Cencius de Prefecto had perpetrated an assault on him, the German bishops at the Diet of Worms of 24 January 1076 sent the Pope a formal letter of defiance, while Henry IV, in a letter of his own, by virtue of his office of *patricius* declared that Gregory had forfeited his authority and called upon him to renounce his dignity. A recast manifesto proceeded from the royal chancery to the German clergy. At Piacenza the Lombard bishops joined with the German episcopate.

Gregory answered the extravagant attack when, at the Roman Lenten Synod, in a solemn prayer to Saint Peter, he suspended Henry from governing, annulled oaths of loyalty made to him, and excommunicated him.[25] The condemning of the King, something unprecedented, was not to fail in producing its effect. It mattered little that Henry, for his part, had Gregory excommunicated. His political opponents, the princes of Saxony and South Germany, now met for common action. Their meeting at Tribur in October involved the King, who had come with an army and was encamped at Oppenheim, in even greater difficulties as a consequence of a growing defection, when a radical group of princes worked for an immediate new election.[26] Gregory, who wanted to force Henry to obedience but not to sacrifice him, had sent two legates, whose mediation produced a compromise. A new election was prevented, and Henry even seems to have succeeded in evading the delicate question of investiture, but he had to dismiss the excommunicated councillors and in writing promise the Pope obedience and penance. For their own safety, the princes agreed not to recognize Henry as King if he

[25] *Reg.*, III, 10 a; in Caspar ed., 270; the writings connected with the Worms meeting in *MGConst* I, 106–13, now better in Erdmann, *Die Briefe Heinrichs IV.*, no. 11–12 and Appendix A. The critical problems in K. Jordan, *Gebhardt-Grundmann* I, para. 86, footnote 3. On the disloyal cardinal see F. Lerner, *Kardinal Hugo Candidus* (Munich - Berlin 1931).

[26] On Tribur and the scholarly controversy concerning it, cf. K. Jordan, *Gebhardt-Grundmann* I, para. 87.

had not been released from the censure by the anniversary of the excommunication and invited the Pope to the Diet of Augsburg, called for February 1077, where he should settle their quarrel with Henry.

Gregory accepted and set out. Henry, who wanted at any price to prevent a coalition between Pope and princes, now hurried boldly across the Alps in order to obtain absolution from Gregory. On three days he appeared in penitential garb before the castle of Canossa, to which Gregory had withdrawn as a precaution, while inside the castle Matilda of Tuscany and Henry's godfather, Abbot Hugh of Cluny, implored the Pope for clemency. Despite justified misgivings and the great prospect of the court of arbitration, Gregory eventually decided to discharge his priestly office. On condition that Henry should give satisfaction to the princes and grant the Pope a safe conduct for his visit to Germany, Henry was received back into the Christian community. Whether he was thereby also to be restored to the royal dignity and the oaths of loyalty were again to apply was apparently an incidental question to the Pope, who thought along spiritual rather than juridical lines.[27] In any event he employed the royal title for Henry thereafter. Henry could, then, be satisfied with what he had achieved, but the act of submission, the complete reversal at Canossa of the early mediaeval relationship of *Regnum* and *Sacerdotium,* cannot properly be measured against this success of his. With the turning point at Canossa there was announced a new epoch in Western history, whose problems were to be thrashed out in the succeeding period, extending to Boniface VIII.

From the political viewpoint, Gregory had acted unwisely. His opponent, for so the King, struggling for his rights, remained, was free of his fetters; the King's adversaries, the princes, who had intended to make use of the Pope merely for their own ends, now went their own way. Having abruptly decided on a new election, at Forchheim in March 1077 they chose Duke Rudolf of Swabia as King, making him renounce hereditary right and the nomination of bishops to be elected, but probably not their investiture.[28] As early as the autumn of 1076, when a new election was being considered, Gregory had reminded the princes of the right of designation which in 1056, at the suggestion of Victor II, they had granted on oath to the Empress Agnes in the event of an election of a successor to Henry IV and which Gregory, as successor of Victor II, intended to exercise together with the Empress if a new election were to take place.[29] Since at Forchheim the princes had silently ignored this right and since Gregory was not interested

[27] Bibliography and critical evalution in Schramm in *GGA* 207 (1953), 93–95; also, G. Miccoli, "Il valore dell'assoluzione di Canossa" in *Annali di Scuola Norm. di Pisa* 27 (1958), 150–57; K. F. Morrison, "Canossa. A Revision" in *Tr* 18 (1962), 121–48.

[28] H. Hoffmann in *DA* 15 (1959), 398 f.

[29] W. Berges, "Gregor VII. und das deutsche Designationsrecht" in *StudGreg* II (1947), 189–209.

in the elevation of an Antiking, he did not recognize Rudolf's election, although the legates he had sent to Forchheim took part in it and Rudolf offered all assurances.

The neutrality that he now maintained for years, connected with his claim to act as arbiter, gained him, then as now, much blame. Gregory did not let himself be guided by strictly political views. In his judgment, that one should be king on whose side was *iustitia,* and hence God himself. This religiously determined attitude alienated both factions. The princes, pursuing their selfish aims, feared that Gregory might decide for Henry; Henry would have had to make ecclesiastical concessions which he regarded as irreconcilable with the rights of the crown, if the Pope should act as arbiter.

And so the arbitration court did not materialize. Henry especially was able to prevent it time and again, and the time thus gained worked in his favour. The Antiking, virtually confined to Saxony, constantly lost ground. The stronger Henry grew, the more emphatically did he maintain his ecclesiastical rights. Gregory had to come to a decision; the adherents of reform in Germany no longer understood his hesitation, and both claimants to the throne pressed him for a judgment. The envoys sent by Henry in 1080 must have settled the question. If Bonizo's report can be trusted, they held out the threat of an Antipope if Rudolf were not excommunicated. Gregory finally gave his verdict at the March Synod of 1080. In a solemn prayer to the Princes of the Apostles he again excommunicated Henry and deposed him.[30] Firmly convinced that he had carried out the judgment of God and of the Princes of the Apostles, at Easter he even prophesied that Henry's ruin was to be expected by the feast of Saint Peter in Chains. Matters were to turn out quite differently.

Henry, behind whom stood the greatest part of the German and Lombard episcopates, caused the Synods of Bamberg and Mainz to renounce obedience to the Pope and then at Brixen in June 1080 had Guibert of Ravenna elected as Antipope.[31] When in the autumn his rival Rudolf remained on the battlefield after an encounter, Henry could make ready for armed conflict with Gregory. The phantom King, Count Hermann of Salm, who was not elevated until August 1081, presented no danger.[32] As early as the spring of 1081 Henry went to Italy and at once marched on Rome, his Lombard friends having opened the way by their victory at Mantua the previous fall over the troops of Countess Matilda. His efforts to take Rome, made only for brief periods,

---

[30] *Reg.,* VII, 14 a; in Caspar ed., 483–87; Bonizo's account in *Liber ad amicum,* l. 9, in *MG Liblit* I, 612–20; cf. Meyer von Knonau in *Jbb DG* III, 242 f.

[31] Synod of Brixen, *MG Const* I, 117–20; Henry IV's letter in Erdmann, *Die Briefe Heinrichs IV.,* Appendix C.

[32] While Gregory probably did not demand a vassal status from Rudolf, he went very far in regard to Hermann of Salm; cf. *Reg.,* IX, 3; in Caspar ed., 575 f. On the whole question and Fliche's theory of interpolation, see Wühr, *Studien zu Gregor VII.,* 62–66.

failed in this and the next year, but in 1083 at least the Leonine City fell to him.

Gregory's situation became increasingly hopeless. Matilda of Tuscany could not help, Robert Guiscard was carrying out his Balkan campaign, and Jordan of Capua had submitted to the German King in 1082. Henry IV, scattering Byzantine coins among the Romans, began negotiations. A synod held in Rome with his approval led to no result, since, having become suspicious, he not only sent no representative but even obstructed it. In any event, he was prepared to sacrifice the Antipope, if Gregory would give him the imperial crown. His moderate offer captivated all who thought along political lines, but for Gregory it was not a political question but a question of conscience. Henry in his view remained an enemy to the divine order so long as he did not do penance and did not thus disavow his acts. This unyielding attitude, heedless of danger, drove thirteen cardinals and other prelates as well as warriors into the enemy's camp in the spring of 1084 and induced the Romans to open the gates to Henry. While Gregory remained in the impregnable Castel Sant'Angelo, the Roman clergy and people on Henry's motion elected Guibert as Pope; he called himself Clement III and at Easter gave Henry the imperial crown.

Still, Gregory was not lost. Robert Guiscard approached with a powerful army. Henry abandoned the city, which Robert took at his first assault. But a new misfortune now occurred: as a result of the looting a great part of Rome went up in flames. Gregory could not stay. To the curses of the population he left the city with the Normans and, accompanied by a few loyal persons, went to Salerno, where he died on 25 May 1085. His well attested last words were: "I have loved justice and hated iniquity; therefore I die in exile."[33]

Gregory VII, whom the Church canonized in 1606, rises up for all times as a sign of veneration and of contradiction. Even a scholarship intent on the utmost objectivity probably cannot settle the controversy. This undying figure requires more than historical understanding, important as it is to free its real nature from the outmoded wrappings of mediaeval thought, which is so alien to us; it demands faith in the possibility that God's care can, at specific times, summon men, who, discharging the prophetical office, are to tear down and to build up, and that Gregory was sent for this purpose. But even then there remains the question, for the most part exceeding our reasoning power, to what extent Gregory was the pure or the humanly tarnished instrument of the divine will. Gregory himself probably suffered from this uncertainty. One thing, however, is not to be doubted: the Pope felt himself to be one seized upon by God and acted accordingly. If, even in the

---

[33] See G. B. Borino, "Storicità delle ultime parole di Gregorio VII" in *StudGreg* V (1956), 403–11.

most extreme distress, he made no dishonourable compromise with Henry IV, it was not obstinacy that guided him but his faith, able to move mountains, in his mission. He assisted the reform in its critical hour to a definitive break-through; the opposition, driven to extremes, had to be worn out. Gregory's heroic example called forth the religious forces of resistance and animated them for the struggle. The defeated Pope conquered in his successors, fashioned the face of the West for more than two centuries, and determined the figure of the Church into our own day.

CHAPTER 45

Stubborn Fight and Victory:
From Victor III to Calixtus II

Victor III

For the reform party Gregory VII's death was a severe blow. It was only after a year that it was able seriously to consider the succession at Rome, now abandoned by Clement III, and to elect Desiderius of Montecassino on 24 May 1086. Desiderius, who came from the house of the Lombard Princes of Benevento, was certainly an important personality. To him Montecassino owed a flowering never again attained, and, made a cardinal by Stephen IX, he had rendered a number of services to the reform Popes, especially in their dealings with the Normans. But even he seemed doubtful that his nature, more inclined to diplomacy than to struggle, and also sickly, was equal to his new tasks. Threatening struggles in Rome and perhaps even a dissatisfaction with his election in his own camp induced him to return to Montecassino without having been consecrated. Eventually meeting again with the reformers at Capua, he decided on 21 March 1087, after excited scenes caused especially by Hugh of Lyons, to accept his election and to call himself Victor III.[1] The consecration could take place at Saint Peter's tomb under the protection of the Normans, but Victor soon had to leave the Eternal City. A second attempt, undertaken with the aid of Tuscan troops, to establish himself in Rome failed. What plans the new Pope may have had in mind — his name, probably connected with Victor II, points to a readiness for reconciliation, despite the perhaps renewed excommunication of Henry IV — there was no time to realize them. Scarcely had a first synod, held at Benevento, ended, after excommunicating not merely the Antipope but also the dissatisfied Gregorians, Hugh of Lyons and Richard of Saint-Victor de Marseille, and probably renewing the earlier prohibitions of

---

[1] On the difficulties connected with Victor's elevation, cf. Becker, *Papst Urban II.*, 78–90.

simony and investiture, than Victor III was carried off by death on 16 September 1087.

Urban II

Half a year elapsed before the reformers elected the Cardinal-Bishop Eudes of Ostia as Pope under the name of Urban II on 12 March 1088, at Terracina, where they immediately enthroned him. Born about 1035 at Châtillon, the son of a noble, he was educated for the clergy in the school of Saint Bruno at Reims and there he was appointed archdeacon between 1055 and 1060. Probably between 1067 and 1070 he entered Cluny and rose to be prior. Abbot Hugh, from whom Gregory VII had asked for some monks in 1078, had to give him up in 1079–80.[2] The Pope made him Cardinal-Bishop of Ostia and in 1084 sent him as legate to Germany. His election to the papacy, recommended by Gregory VII as well as by Victor III, was to prove fortunate. Fully assenting to Gregory's principles, but elastically adapting their implementation to the present situation, Urban II led the reform papacy out of the narrow pass and toward victory.

Nothing reflects the situation facing the new Pope better than the relatively well transmitted polemical literature of the day. If in 1074–75 the prescribing of celibacy and of a boycott of married priests had stirred intellects,[3] since the decisions of 1076 and 1080 there were other themes for debate: Gregory VII's integrity, his right to depose and excommunicate Henry IV and to absolve from oaths of loyalty to him, his recourse to armed force, the strict prohibition of associating with the excommunicated, the juridical immunity of the anointed King, Henry's patriciate, the raising up of the Antipope, and so forth. Most deserving of mention of the German defenders of the kingship were: Wenrich of Trier, Wido of Osnabrück, and an anonymous monk of Hersfeld, author of *De unitate ecclesiae conservanda,* which probably appeared in 1092–93. Outstanding among the Gregorians were: Gebhard of Salzburg, Bernold of Sankt Blasien, and Manegold of Lauterbach, the last mentioned famous for his so-called doctrine of "popular sovereignty", which interpreted the kingship as an office transmitted by the people and hence terminable in the case of a defaulting ruler.[4]

But more decisive were the accomplishments of the Italian authors. In the Antipope's own city of Ravenna appeared the work of the jurist Peter Crassus, which traced the irremovability of the King to the Roman law of

---

[2] The dates, differing somewhat from those of earlier studies, are in Becker, *op cit.,* 24–53.
[3] For the polemics cf. the bibliographical citations in the sources for this section. Celibacy was especially condemned by the so-called pseudo-Ulric, probably composed in Germany, and by Sigebert of Gembloux, and was defended by Bernold of Sankt Blasien; see *Wattenbach-Holtzmann* I, 395f.
[4] Sources and literature in *Wattenbach-Holtzmann* I, 396–409; H. Weisweiler, "Die päpstliche Gewalt in den Schriften Bernolds von St. Blasien" in *StudGreg* V (1956), 129–47.

inheritance. Here too another jurist fabricated false papal privileges, allegedly for Charles the Great and Otto the Great, and had Ulpian's *lex regia* worked in, in the sense of an irrevocable transmission of the authority of the Roman people to the Emperor, in favour of Henry IV. From the discussion of the schism, revived with the death of Gregory VII, proceeded the work of the Clementist Guido of Ferrara, which, gratifying by its moderate judgment of Gregory and its positive exertions in regard to the investiture question, was in great contrast to the approximately contemporary hate-productions of Cardinal Beno and of Bishop Benzo of Alba. Of the Gregorians no less than Anselm of Lucca, Cardinal Deusdedit, and Bonizo of Sutri intervened in the last part of the controversy, but their real achievement, which gave their party the intellectual superiority, was in canon law. Anselm's highly significant canonical collection, compiled under Gregory VII, was now followed by the important collections of Deusdedit and Bonizo, undisturbed by the bleak situation.[5]

Urban II had no need to despair. So profound an intellectual movement as the reform could not be suppressed by armed force; in fact, the opposing camp itself was accessible to it. It was really only a relative opposition. Clement III fought simony and Nicolaitism straightforwardly. But since he approved of the old, ever more outdated, Imperial Church system and was burdened by the flaw of an uncanonical elevation, he maintained a position which was basically a lost cause. Some Clementists, not to speak of bishops who were labouring under the censures of the reformed Church outside the territory under German control, hence cherished the tacit wish to be united with the successor of Gregory VII.

Urban knew this and sought to accommodate them. Thus, in his announcement of his election he professed the goals of Gregory VII and had the prohibitions of simony, clerical marriage, and lay investiture renewed at the Synod of Melfi in 1089, but as early as March 1089 he instructed his legate in Germany, Bishop Gebhard of Constance, to be generous. Relying on his power of dispensation, he himself went to the limits of what was then possible. In individual cases he recognized bishops who had been invested by their king, including Archbishop Anselm of Milan, who had been canonically elected but invested by Henry IV. Milanese whom Archbishop Tedald, never recognized by Rome, had ordained could retain their function if their ordination had not been simoniacal and if Tedald's simony was not known to them, and the Masses of priests ordained in the Catholic Church who had gone over to the schism were not to be molested. The old zealots, Hugh of Lyons,

---

[5] On the Italian authors, see *Manitius* III, *passim;* K. Jordan, "Ravennater Fälschungen aus den Anfängen des Investiturstreites" in *AUF* 15 (1938), 426–48; id., "Der Kaisergedanke in Ravenna zur Zeit Heinrichs IV." in *DA* 2 (1938), 85–128; G. A. Krause, *Papstwahldekret,* 234–54. The relatively late and not very abundant polemical literature from France in *Wattenbach-Holtzmann* I, 772–74.

Amatus of Oléron, and Richard of Saint-Victor, lost their function of legate and no new standing legates were named to replace them. And recourse to armed force met with little sympathy from Urban. Residing on the Tiber island at Rome from the autumn of 1088, he had in the succeeding summer taken the city by storm and, following the coronation Mass, was solemnly conducted through the streets, but the meagre successes which the victory brought him caused him to renounce further struggles with the Roman Clementists. Money gained him entrance to the Lateran Palace in 1094 and it was probably the same means that won him Castel Sant'Angelo in 1098.

The first years of the pontificate were lived under the pressure of the imperial predominance. Urban sought to impair this by arranging in 1089 the marriage of his loyal comrade in arms, the forty-three-year-old Matilda of Tuscany, with the seventeen-year-old Welf V, son of the deposed Duke Welf IV of Bavaria, thereby producing an almost unbroken stretch of territory from South Germany to Tuscany, but this outcome only induced Henry IV to go to Italy and seek a definitive solution. Urban experienced the King's successfully conducted campaigns against Matilda's troops in 1090–92 to the extent that he had to flee to the Normans from Clement III, who now again took possession of Rome.[6] But then catastrophe overtook Henry. It came about after a defeat suffered near Canossa in 1092 and the formation of a league of hostile cities — Milan, Cremona, Lodi, Piacenza — with the defection in 1093 of his own son, Conrad, who had himself crowned King of the Lombards at Milan. Betrayed by almost all, even by his wife Praxedis, and cut off from Germany, Henry remained locked up in the territories of Padua and Verona until he was reconciled with Welf IV in 1096 — the unnatural marriage between Welf V and Matilda had broken up — and could go to Germany in 1097.

Urban II, who definitively returned to Rome at the end of 1093 and in 1094 again appointed the inexorable Hugh of Lyons as standing legate in France, now took hold of the reins resolutely. As early as 1094 he set out on a two-year journey via Tuscany and Lombardy to France. As a matter of fact the reform needed thoroughgoing consultation. Urban's mildness had especially caused a revival of the tiresome question of the validity of simoniacal and schismatic ordinations. Bonizo of Sutri, Deusdedit, Bruno of Segni, Bernold of Sankt Blasien — all wrestled with it in that decade, but only Bernold succeeded in solving the difficult theological problem to some extent. It was all the more urgent to establish binding norms, at least for practical action. This was done at the well attended Council of Piacenza, meeting under Urban's presidency in March 1095. With regard to schismatics it decreed the nullity of all orders conferred by Guibert of Ravenna since his condemnation and of the orders conferred by his adherents who had been excommunicated by

[6] According to Klewitz in *QFIAB* 25 (1934f.), 120f., Urban stayed in Rome from the end of October 1088 to July 1089 and from the end of 1089 to around the end of July 1090, the rest of the time in South Italy.

name and by all bishops who had usurped the see of a Catholic bishop, unless
the cleric ordained knew nothing about the condemnation of the ordaining
prelate; on the other hand, orders obtained from originally Catholic bishops
who had later gone over to the schism retained their validity. The Council
proceeded more strictly against simoniacal ordinations. It declared them all to
be invalid, except the orders of those clerics to whom the simony of the ordaining bishop was not known.[7] It is obvious that the decrees, which were open
to varying theological interpretations and were lacking in consistency, left
the dogmatic problem unsolved.

As early as 1089 Urban had renewed the prohibition of investiture at
Melfi. He returned to it at Clermont, where on 28 November 1095 he opened
another brilliant synod. Not only were the appropriate decrees of Gregory VII
repeated; the synod now forbade bishops and clerics to become the vassals
of the King or of any other layman, thereby advancing the demand of the
Sacerdotium for freedom to a point which not even Gregory VII's legislation had ventured to take up.[8] This new prohibition was renewed by several
French synods — Rouen in 1096, Poitiers in 1100, Troyes in 1107, and so
forth. Urban had it recalled to mind in a somewhat modified form in his
last Roman Synod in 1099. The same synod also made stricter the prohibition
of investiture, by threatening with excommunication, not only the one
investing and the one invested, but also the one ordaining a person who had
received lay investiture. Thus the reform struggle centred more and more on
the problem of investiture.

The Cluniac Pope's special love and gratitude belonged to monasticism, as
numerous privileges attest. Although Urban seldom granted full exemption,
he was happy to lessen the authority of the local bishop and in addition placed
many monasteries under papal protection. With a sure instinct for the spiritual
forces of his age, he also assured the canons regular their due place in the
Church by placing their ideal of the *vita apostolica* on par with the monastic
ideal of perfection and forbidding the canon regular from entering a monastery without the permission of his community and his provost.[9]

Urban intended to be more than a mere reformer working inside the

---

[7] Cc. 8–10, 3–4, in *MGConst* I, 561 f.; for the theological problem see Chapter 53.

[8] C. 17, in *Mansi* XX, 817; on the other hand, cf. Gregory VII's *Reg.*, V, 5, in Caspar ed.,
353: "quod ad servitium et debitam fidelitatem regis attinet, nequaquam contradicere aut
impedire volumus". Also important are cc. 29–30, in *Mansi* XX, 818, which forbid lay persons
to retain tithes, altars, or churches.

[9] C. Dereine, "L'élaboration du statut canonique des chanoines réguliers, spécialement sous
Urbain II" in *RHE* 46 (1951), 534–65; for the canons regular see Chapter 52. Fliche's opinion,
Fliche-Martin VIII, 292, that Urban permitted monks to engage in the care of souls is connected with the question whether cc. 2–3 of the Council of Nîmes (*Mansi* XX, 932) are
genuine, which Dereine denies in *Studia Gratiana*, II (Bologna 1954), 317f. On the whole
question of the relations between monachism and the episcopate in Urban's day, cf. C. Violante, *Il monachesimo cluniacense*, 206–18.

Church. And so he did not shrink from proclaiming the Peace of God, which had been instituted in France and promoted by the Cluniacs, for South Italy at the Synods of Melfi in 1089 and Troia in 1093 and universally at Clermont in 1095. Likewise at Clermont he covered with the Peace of God not only clerics, monks, and women, but the person and goods of crusaders, even on days when it was lawful to fight. The Council of Clermont is especially famed for a creative initiative of the Pope, incalculable in its effect on the immediate and later times — the summons to the First Crusade.[10] While the Emperor, shut up in a corner of Italy, was in a sense forgotten, the Pope, spontaneously acknowledged by the faithful as the true leader of the Christian West, with no participation by kings, set in motion a supranational army for the defence of the Christian East and for the conquest of the Holy Land. From then on the final victory of the reform papacy was only a question of time, and this victory was permanent. For two centuries the Vicar of Christ, eclipsing the power of the Emperor and of kings with his spiritual authority, was to preside over Western Christendom.

The causes and the course of the Crusade will be discussed later, as will also the relations which the Pope instituted right after his elevation with the Emperor Alexius I and the Byzantine Church for the liquidation of the Schism. But it is time to examine his relations with the Western monarchs. The reform policy encountered little difficulty in Spain, especially since the Pope did not prevent the Spanish Cluniacs from recovering their old influence and sent Roman cardinals in place of the former standing legate, Richard of Saint-Victor. He elevated the new Archbishop of Toledo, a monk of the Cluniac monastery of Sahagún, to the dignity of primate, but at the same time he encouraged, with the Count of Barcelona, the reconstruction of the city and metropolitan see of Tarragona. Thus began the new ecclesiastical division of Spain.

The Pope had to deal with no slight difficulties in England. On the death of King William I in 1087 his lands were divided between two sons — Robert acquired Normandy, while William II became King of England. Normandy recognized Urban II, but William II maintained neutrality and gave such free rein to his lust for money and power at the expense of the English Church that the fruits of reform achieved under his father were imperilled. Lanfranc's death in 1089 suited him very much. Only a serious illness moved the King in 1093 to fill the archbishopric of Canterbury again with Abbot Anselm of Bec. This great theologian, trained in Lanfranc's school, had no intention of simply accepting William's acts of caprice. After some lesser clashes he forced the King to a decision in the question of the schism by demanding to be allowed to receive the pallium from Urban II. When an attempt to have Anselm

---

[10] There is no official version of the summons; the sources are summarized in A. Waas, *Kreuzzüge*, I, 71, footnote 241.

deposed failed, William dealt directly with the Pope, who sent the Cardinal Legate Walter of Albano to England. Walter obtained the definitive recognition of Urban but in return had to make all sorts of concessions, in particular to acknowledge the special law that papal legates could come to England only at King William's desire. Anselm took no part at all in the negotiations. He was summoned to court only after their conclusion to receive the pallium which the legate had brought along. It was suggested by some of the courtiers that he should take it from William's hand, but this manner of receiving it would have made the King seem to be a papal vicar, and so Anselm courageously refused. He carried the point that he should take the pallium from the altar and put it upon himself.

Urban seems not to have entirely approved the all too elastic proceedings of Walter of Albano. In 1096 a new legate tried with no success to gain better conditions for the Church.[11] William is said to have obtained a postponement of the controversial questions in Rome by a part-payment of Peter's Pence. Soon Anselm came into a greater conflict. Indicted by the King for having supplied unfit troops, he reproached him for the secularization of ecclesiastical property and for his lack of a will to reform and intended to appeal to the Pope. Since he refused to take the oath demanded of him, that he would never appeal to the Pope, he had to leave England, while William confiscated the goods of his church. Anselm went first to Lyons and then to Rome. Urban did not permit him to resign and even had the quarrel discussed at the Synods of Bari in 1098 and Rome in 1099, but could not bring himself to take serious action until death relieved him of the decision he had finally promised.

Urban also displayed the greatest prudence in regard to Philip I of France when in 1092 the King repudiated his wife and presumed to marry Bertha of Montfort, wife of the Count of Anjou. The scandal of this double adultery was punished by Hugh of Lyons at the Synod of Autun in 1094 with anathema, to which personal interdict was added in 1097. Urban only confirmed the excommunication in 1095 at the Council of Clermont and thereafter allowed himself to be gained to mildness time and again by Philip's empty promises, but without yielding in principle. When Urban died, the King had again incurred excommunication. His marriage affair allowed Philip no intensive struggle against the demands for reform. From this point of view the Pope could be satisfied with France in general; in no other country, despite rather frequent interventions, did he find so much obedience.

In South Italy, the refuge that he sought time and again till 1093, Urban interested himself in the Church organization so far as the fluid political situation following the death of Robert Guiscard in 1085 allowed. Robert's son, Duke Roger of Apulia, who in 1089 became Urban's vassal, was too

---

[11] Besides Becker, *Papst Urban II.,* 210–12, cf. also J. Deér, "Der Anspruch der Herrscher des 12. Jahrhunderts auf die apostolische Legation" in *ArchHP* 2 (1964), 171–76.

young and insignificant to keep the rebellious barons in check. And the rule of Richard II of Capua — Jordan had died in 1090 — was on so fragile a foundation that in 1098 he had to call for the help of Roger of Apulia and in return place his principality under the latter's feudal suzerainty. Thus the political centre of gravity shifted to Sicily, where Robert Guiscard's brother, Roger I, captured the last pocket of Muslim resistance in 1091 and set out to construct a firmly consolidated state. Hence Urban established especially close relations with Roger I, which led to a fruitful cooperation in rebuilding the Sicilian Church. It is true that Roger tolerated no independent action by Rome, and the nomination of Bishop Roger of Troina as legate without his consent even caused a conflict. It was settled by the portentous privilege of 5 July 1098, in which Urban renounced, during the reigns of Roger and Roger's successor, any appointment of legates without an understanding with the rulers, granted them legatine delegation, and left it to Roger's discretion whether to be represented at Roman synods.[12]

Relations with Henry IV remained unsettled. Urban considered peace even less when in 1095 he had met Henry's rebellious son Conrad at Cremona, received from him an oath of safety, held out the prospect of the imperial crown, and arranged the engagement of the young King with a daughter of Roger of Sicily. Henry's return to Germany in 1097 hardly affected the ecclesiastical situation. The Emperor did, indeed, succeed in re-establishing his political authority, but he was unable to prevent the dissolution of the Clementist unified front in the episcopate and the defection of individual bishops to the Gregorians. Urban's policy of the open door bore its fruits. To this was added the propaganda directed by the German Gregorians at the masses of the population, carried to them especially by the preachers sent out from around 1080 by Hirsau and the monasteries under its influence. Thus also in Germany the reform party was slowly making progress when, on 29 July 1099, two weeks after the taking of Jerusalem by the crusaders, Urban II departed this life.

Paschal II

Sixteen days later Cardinal Rainerio, born at Bieda in Romagna, became Pope under the name of Paschal II. He had been a monk of an Italian monastery, which cannot now be identified but was probably not Cluniac,[13] before

---

[12] *Jaffé* 5706; *ItalPont* VIII, Regnum Norman., no. 81; to the Literature cited for the chapter add: J. Deér, *loc. cit.* 125–33. Urban's privilege led to the celebrated controversy over the *Monarchia Sicula,* extending from the beginning of the sixteenth century until the time of Pius IX, that is, the royal claim to legatine rights and to absolute authority over the Church.
[13] On the Pope's home and family: March, *Liber Pontificalis Dertusensis,* 91–95; on his monastery, ibid. 154, footnote 3; the opinion there defended, that it was a monastery in the Abruzzi, is not convincing, since the authority, Ordericus Vitalis, by the monastery of "Vallis Brutiorum", ordinarily would seem to mean Vallombrosa.

being made Cardinal-Priest of San Clemente by Gregory VII. The new Pope was basically different from his worldly-wise predecessor in his simpler nature, partly inflexible, partly timid. Inclined to intransigence, he was rather to stress than to reconcile the antitheses in the problems of the age, but actually in that way to prepare for their later solution.

It was the question of investiture that was especially at stake. It had been pretty generally established as a principle that simony and Nicolaitism were to be fought against. And the death of the aged Guibert of Ravenna on 8 September 1100 settled the difficulties inherent in the schism, for the two Antipopes set up by the Roman Clementists in 1100, the schismatic Bishops Dietrich of Santa Rufina and Albert of Sabina, were captured in turn and confined in South Italian monasteries, while the Archpriest Maginulf, proclaimed as Silvester IV in 1105, had to flee Rome after a few days, despite the armed assistance of the Marquis Werner of Ancona; but he did not renounce the dignity until 1111. Thus at the Synod of Guastalla in 1106 Paschal II was able to declare the restoration of unity and let all schismatic ecclesiastics retain their office, provided that there were no simoniacal or other offences involved. There remained only the prohibition of investiture as a still unresolved problem; in fact, since the tightening of the regulations by Urban II it had acquired an actuality which it had not had under Gregory VII or under Urban. A settlement could no longer be avoided; the Investiture Controversy in the strict sense was now just beginning.

It is distinctive of the new state of affairs that now a real Investiture Controversy even broke out in England, occasioned by the change on the throne following the death of William II in August 1100. In order to secure his own succession, which was not beyond question, the new King Henry I, himself also a son of William the Conqueror, called Archbishop Anselm back from banishment, only to experience the surprise that Anselm refused to do the customary vassal's homage, appealing to the Roman Synod of 1099 that he had himself attended. Anselm, it is true, was concerned less for the question of investiture than for obedience to the laws of the Roman Church. Hence he supported the King's effort to obtain for England a papal dispensation from the prohibition of investiture and went to Rome for this purpose. Paschal, who had just renewed the prohibition in 1102, denied the request. Henry then refused to readmit Anselm, returning from Rome, into England (1104) until the excommunication of English ecclesiastics who had accepted investiture and of the royal councillors, announced by Paschal in 1105, moved him to come to terms with Anselm. The settlement, approved by Paschal, between the two men, who held each other in esteem, was ratified at a meeting of the Great Council in London in August 1107: Henry renounced investiture with ring and crosier but retained the right to receive homage from the bishops before their consecration. Furthermore, he maintained his influence on the elections of bishops by being present in person.

In France too, meanwhile, a practical solution had been prepared, without there having been open conflict or an official concordat, as in England. In France, however, there ceased not only investiture with ring and crosier, but, differing from England, also the homage of vassalage; the French King was satisfied with an oath of loyalty. Just the same, he renounced neither his power to dispose of the temporalities of sees, with the legal consequences — usufruct during vacancies, possible seizure of the adminis-trative authority, and so forth — nor the customary services, and hence he conveyed the temporalities by means of an informal act, termed a *concessio,* to the bishop elected with his permission.[14]

Thus in both France and England there was first made a distinction be-tween ecclesiastical office and possession of temporalities. In itself the idea was not new,[15] but the merit of having first pondered deeply over the investi-ture question and of having led to a solution belongs to the great canonist, Ivo of Chartres. The handing over of the episcopal office, so he explained, was certainly to be refused to the laity, since it implied a sacramental act; on the other hand, the *concessio* of the temporalities could be granted to the King without difficulty, for it was a purely secular act, to be performed in any desired manner, to which the King could make a certain claim in so far as, according to Augustine, property is based on constitutional law and hence the churches owed their goods to distribution made by the King. Ivo's ideas, expounded as early as 1097 in a letter to Hugh of Lyons, had an in-fluence in France on the new arrangement that was in preparation, but they also won importance for the English Investiture Controversy, since at that time Ivo's pupil, Hugh of Fleury, made use of them in his impor-tant *Tractatus de regia potestate et sacerdotali dignitate,* dedicated to the English King.[16]

Paschal was wise enough to tolerate the two compromises that had been reached without his direct participation. They did not actually mean a genuine juridical solution. In England the real problem, investiture with the tempo-ralities, had been evaded, and the *concessio* of the French King was open to

---

[14] The new practice can probably not be ascribed to 1098, the opinion of Haller and Schwarz; it was not prepared until the first decades after 1100, according to Becker, *Studien zum In-vestiturproblem,* 104–22 (with bibliography).

[15] Development of the notion up to Ivo of Chartres in Hoffmann in *DA* 15 (1959), 394–405.

[16] Ivo's letter in *MGLiblit* II, 642–47; Hugh of Fleury, *Tractatus de regia potestate et sacerdotali dignitate,* ibid., 472–94. For the ideas see Becker, *Studien zum Investiturproblem,* 143–53; Hoff-mann, *loc. cit.* 405–18, with valuable special literature. Hoffmann rightly denies the existence of a strictly organized or even definitive "théorie chartraine"; however he must have under-estimated Ivo's teaching to some extent, at times missing its meaning; thus, Ivo hardly displayed a real contradiction when on the one hand he quoted Augustine (Hoffmann, 107 f.) and on the other hand made use of a passage from Justinian's *Institutes* (Hoffmann, 108 f.), for the latter refers to a special question which did not concern Augustine — the inalienability of ecclesiastical property.

various interpretations. But the essential thing, the renunciation of investiture with the office, was achieved, and the rights conceded to the kings to the customary services of the bishops could be entirely reconciled with the inner union of ecclesiastical office and property as demanded by the reformers. But for Germany the compromises thus far reached, and tolerated rather than accepted by the reformers, did not suffice. Considering the great damage that the royal authority had suffered at the hands of the secular princes since the death of Henry III, the German ruler not only could not renounce the rights of sovereignty which the more important churches had received in the greatest abundance since the days of the Ottos; he had to insist, with regard to the reform, on a clear regulation of his relations to the churches and their goods. For the reform principle of the inseparable unity of office and ecclesiastical property could not be applied here without a careful distinction. If it were a question only of the goods donated by private persons and of purely ecclesiastical income, such as offerings, stole fees, and tithes, then the principle could probably have been carried. But what had counties, margraviates, and even duchies, what had important political rights of usufruct to do with the churches? No king with a sense of responsibility could admit that they simply became inviolable church property in the sense of irrevocable gifts.

These difficult questions were to be presented to Paschal as soon as he was confronted, no longer by Henry IV, who had been again excommunicated at the Roman Synod of 1102, but by his son, Henry V. (The rebel, King Conrad, had died in 1101.) Henry V's revolt in 1104, the perfidious imprisonment and forced abdication of his father at the end of 1105, the Diet of Mainz with its recognition of Henry V at the beginning of 1106, the struggle that then flared up and only ended with the father's death in the summer of 1106 — this tragedy of the Salian Dynasty concerns us here in so far as Paschal II espoused the cause of the young King, who posed as a protagonist of reform, by absolving him from his oath not to intervene in the government without his father's consent and sending legates to the Diet of Mainz. He himself departed for the north in the spring of 1106 in order at last to establish peace between papacy and *Imperium*. He was to be disillusioned: Henry V's envoy, who found him during the Synod of Guastalla in 1106, insisted on the right of the Empire. Thereupon, the Pope did not go to Germany, as people were expecting, but to France, where in fact he could anticipate only the best reception. In 1104 Philip I had finally yielded on the marriage question and had adequately met the desires of the reformers by the renunciation in practice of investiture with ring and crosier. He and his son, Louis VI, now concluded an alliance with the Pope at Saint-Denis in 1107. France and the papacy had come together in a friendship that was to endure for centuries. All the more obstinate, then, was Paschal's attitude in his conference at Châlons-sur-Marne with Henry V's embassy. To the German demand for the royal right of investiture he replied with a blunt refusal, which he then had ratified at the subsequent Synod of Troyes, just as he had done a year earlier at Guastalla, by a repetition of the prohibition of investiture.

Nevertheless, the cleavage was not completely irreconcilable. Thus in 1109 a perhaps semiofficial memorandum, composed in the Empire, probably under the direct influence of Ivo's ideas, distinguished between the spiritual function and the secular property and, while adhering to the right of investiture, declared that the form of investiture was unessential.[17] This already more differentiated outlook was to influence the negotiations which Henry V undertook when in the summer of 1110 he began his journey to Rome. Paschal indeed again rejected investiture but recognized a royal claim to the *regalia,* that is, to the goods and rights of the Empire which had been transferred to the bishops, and hence he proposed the radical solution of leaving to the churches as their property only the purely ecclesiastical revenues, such as tithes and so forth, and goods originating in private gifts, while all *regalia* were to be given back in accord with a papal command; in return, Henry was to renounce investiture.

Well meant as the proposal was, it was a stranger to reality. As though a peremptory order from the Pope, opposed to the will, not only of the bishops who had an interest in the *regalia,* but also of the secular princes, who feared the overgrowth of the royal power that would accompany such a restitution, could have annulled so deeply rooted a political order! Henry V must have clearly seen through it; but since he wanted the imperial crown, he declared his acceptance and had the secret treaty that had been agreed to, the content of which was to be published before the imperial coronation, ratified at Sutri on 9 February 1111. When on February 12 Paschal began the coronation rite in Saint Peter's and had the reciprocal charters read, a real tumult broke out. Bishops and princes indignantly rejected the papal command, whereupon Henry V demanded the imperial crown and the right of investiture. Since Paschal refused both, Henry denounced the treaty, arrested Pope and cardinals, and led them prisoners out of Rome, which was in a state of wild excitement and filled with the clash of weapons. After two months he succeeded in the Treaty of Mammolo in extorting from the Pope investiture with ring and crosier, to take place after the canonical election and before consecration. In addition, Paschal had to promise never to excommunicate Henry and to put the concession of investiture in the form of a written *privilegium* and crown Henry as Emperor on 13 April.[18] On the way back to Germany Henry won a further prize. Meeting Matilda of Tuscany, he had himself appointed heir of her patrimonial goods, which had been enfeoffed to the Roman Church, though in this a recognition of the papal right of proprietorship could hardly have been avoided.

[17] *Tractatus de investitura episcoporum* in *MGLiblit* II, 501–04; *Wattenbach-Holtzmann* I, 411f.
[18] The *acta* for 1111 in *MGConst* I, 134–52; Paschal's privilege was valid for Henry V, not for his successors.

With his brutally gained victory over Paschal Henry had won nothing. The Pope might have been weak, but the reformed Church, growing into a supranational power structure, tolerated no exception for the *Imperium*. Besides, the Emperor had committed the serious psychological error of clinging to ring and crosier as symbols of investiture, though he related investiture merely to the *regalia*.[19] It was this that produced the greatest commotion among the reform circles of Italy and France. Even in the College of Cardinals harsh things were said about Paschal. There was a demand for the repudiation of the "pravilegium" and the excommunication of the "heretical" Emperor. The Pope, mindful of his oath, could not assent to the excommunication, and he was unwilling either to approve expressly or to reject the anathema which a synod meeting at Vienne under Archbishop Guy in 1112 and two cardinal legates in Germany in 1115 hurled at the Emperor, but he probably agreed to the annulling of the privilege by the Roman Synod of 1112. Having become more firm with the passage of time, he himself condemned the concession at the Roman Synod of 1116 and renewed the prohibition of investiture and the threats of excommunication included in it.

And yet an important decision had been made in 1111. The Roman Church could no longer revoke the recognition, given at Sutri, of the royal right of *regalia,* the idea of which was then more exactly defined for the first time. Thus a certain readiness for an understanding became evident in the Gregorian polemical writings that soon appeared. Even the intransigent Placid of Nonantula, who, like Guy of Vienne in 1112, condemned the royal investiture with the temporalities and clung firmly to the churches' free right of ownership, was willing to concede to the Emperor not only the due services of the bishops but also investiture with the special political rights, using of course other symbols than ring and staff, and the possibility of confirming by charter their possession by a bishop already consecrated. Even more clearly did the *Disputatio vel defensio Paschalis papae,* originating at the Curia, distinguish between *temporalia* and *spiritualia,* proposing for the investiture with the temporalities the symbol of the sceptre, which was actually used later. And if Godfrey of Vendôme at first raged fiercely against lay investiture as being heretical and simoniacal, even in him there grew at least the recognition that an investiture with the temporalities made after consecration could be accepted.[20]

---

[19] Cf. the papal report in *MGConst* I, 149: ". . . quamvis ille (Henry) per investituras illas non ecclesias, non officia quelibet, sed sola regalia se dare assereret"; T. Schieffer, "Nochmals die Verhandlungen von Mouzon" in *Festschrift für E. E. Stengel* (Münster–Cologne 1952), 336.
[20] Placid of Nonantula, *Liber de honore ecclesiae,* especially Chapters 37, 93, 82, 118, in *MGLiblit* II, 575–639, especially 585, 615, 605, 625. *Disputatio vel defensio Paschalis papae* in *MGLiblit* II, 659–66, especially 666. Godfrey of Vendôme in *MGLiblit* II, 680–700, especially 691f. Rangerius of Lucca was quite intransigent in his polemical poem, *De anulo et baculo,* especially verses 879f., 891ff., 901ff., in *MGLiblit* II, 508–33. The imperial viewpoint was energetically

The adjustment thus prepared in learned discussion could not be translated into reality under Paschal. The Pope insisted ever more strongly on the disavowal of the privilege. Neither the threatening proximity of the Emperor, who came to Italy in 1116 to enter into the inheritance of the Countess Matilda — she had died in 1115 — nor Henry's efforts at negotiations were able to divert him from that. Then a revolt had broken out in Rome because of the growing power of the Pierleoni, who supported the papacy. Paschal regarded it as advisable to leave the city in the spring of 1117, whereupon, summoned by the opposing faction, the Emperor came to the city for a few months. It was only at the beginning of 1118 that Paschal could dare to fight his way back. Scarcely had he done so when he died in the stronghold of the Pierleoni on 21 January 1118.

Gelasius II

The election of Paschal's successor, occurring on 24 January, fell on the chancellor John,[21] of a distinguished family from Gaetà, a former monk of Montecassino, who had directed the papal chancery since the time of Urban II and was on friendly terms with Paschal. Gelasius II, as he styled himself, was to learn sadly how powerless he was in Rome. Ill treated and imprisoned, immediately after his election, by Cencius Frangipane for personal reasons that elude us, but soon set free by the Romans, he had to flee on 1 March to Gaetà from the Emperor, who had occupied the Leonine City and was searching for him. In his absence the opposing party, in an understanding with the Emperor, set up an Antipope. Archbishop Maurice of Braga accepted the nomination as Gregory VIII, a figure scarcely to be taken seriously, to whom the Romans gave the nickname "Burdinus", stupid ass. Gelasius, it is true, was able to return to the Lateran after Henry V's departure, but his situation remained extremely precarious, all the more as now the whole family of the Frangipani was against him. Their attempt to seize him misfired, but it induced him to leave the city. Accompanied by a few cardinals, Gelasius sailed to France, fell ill, and died at Cluny on 29 January 1119.

Calixtus II

It was providential that the Bishop of Rome had left his church a widow while he was abroad, for in the hopeless situation the reform papacy needed outside help. The cardinals surrounding the death bed of Gelasius were therefore well advised when they at once proceeded to the new election at Cluny and selected as Pope on 2 February, not a Roman cardinal, but Archbishop Guy of Vienne. Since the curialists who had remained behind in Rome with

defended in the Farfa *Orthodoxa defensio imperialis* in *MGLiblit* II, 535–42. See Schieffer, *loc. cit.* 336–38.

[21] On his family see March, *Liber Pontificalis Dertusensis,* 181, footnote 2.

their staffs approved the election, the new Pope, who took the name Calixtus II, was universally recognized. Son of the Count of Burgundy, whose family was related to the Salians and other royal houses, a zealous bishop for thirty years, filled with the reform ideas, far-sighted and energetic, Calixtus was the right man both to settle the Roman situation and to solve the German question.

Even before his journey to Rome he extended the hand of peace to the Emperor, whom Gelasius had excommunicated together with the Antipope. Henry V had too great difficulties in the Empire not to accept it. The negotiations begun at Strasbourg between him and the papal envoys, William of Champeaux and Pons of Cluny, reached a preliminary conclusion in the charter of a treaty which two cardinals drew up with the Emperor; it lacked only ratification. For this purpose Calixtus proceeded, during the Council of Reims, which he had just opened, to Mouzon, where the Emperor awaited him. Since there had been a failure in the preliminary negotiations, apparently on both sides, to expound the controverted points with the necessary clarity, Calixtus demanded of Henry the express renunciation of investiture with the temporalities and of the right to take possession of church property. Hence at the last moment he gave him to understand that he intended to allow him merely the French practice, that is, the continuation of the services owed to the King, but the abolition of any investiture, even with the temporalities. Henry V, on the other hand, sought at least the vassalage of the bishops as tolerated for England and, in addition, an investiture with the *regalia*. Hence he did not agree to the newly formulated papal demand, but called for a postponing of the decision. Thereupon the deeply disillusioned Pope rode back to the council, where he was to find another surprise. While the participants, convinced of the Emperor's guilt, decreed anathema on Henry and his adherents, they could not make up their minds to extend the prohibition of investiture, demanded by Calixtus, also to church property. Merely investiture with bishoprics and abbeys was forbidden, while the disposal of tithes that happened to be in lay possession and of ecclesiastical fiefs was left an open question. Calixtus did not become soured. He now knew the controverted points and was willing to consider them in new negotiations for peace.

Meanwhile, he was carefully preparing for his journey to Rome. After a really triumphal progress through Lombardy and Tuscany, he was joyfully welcomed by the Romans in the summer of 1120. At last they again had a ruler, under whose authority the factional quarrels would become silent. Not until April 1121 did Calixtus, who had visited South Italy, dispatch troops to Sutri to capture the Antipope, who was entrenched there. Stripped of his episcopal dignity, Burdinus vanished into a South Italian monastery. Now peace with the Emperor was not long in coming. Unnerved by civil strife, Henry decided in the autumn of 1121 to entrust the starting of the negotiations with Rome to the German princes. Calixtus agreed to this and sent three cardinals, including the future Pope, Lambert of Ostia, to Germany. After two weeks of complicated deliberations the Investiture Controversy was brought to an end by the Concordat of Worms on 23 September 1122.

In it Henry renounced investiture with ring and staff but retained the right to investiture with the *regalia* by means of the sceptre, to be performed in Germany immediately after the election, but in the case of the Burgundian and of the Italian sees within six months after consecration. He also granted canonical election and free consecration. However, in German territory he retained a substantial influence on the election — it was to take place in his presence or in that of his authorized representative and in the event of a dissenting outcome it was to be decided by him, with the cooperation of the metropolitan and the suffragans, in favour of the *sanior pars*. The Roman Church's sphere of influence, the *Patrimonium Petri*, was excepted from the regulations of the concordat.[22]

The concordat, which despite certain shortcomings ranks with the best negotiated settlements of Western history, consisted of two documents: the one contained the concessions made by the Emperor to Calixtus and the Roman Church; the other, those made by the Pope to Henry V. It should be noted that the papal concessions were made to Henry alone, a circumstance which in ecclesiastical circles favoured the opinion that the papal privilege would cease with Henry's death. This thesis, entirely defensible under the formal aspect, and even maintained by a few modern historians, could not, however, prevail against the more deeply based nature of the treaty now concluded. In the *Calixtinum* there was involved not the granting of papal favours but an old imperial right, which the Pope, once harmony had been achieved, had to acknowledge along with the Church's juridical claims. Though later the representatives of the Church as well as the Emperors, according to the status of the power situation, might try to alter the arrangements in their favour, the substance of the concordat proved to be a stable juridical basis.

Measured by the compromises reached in England and France, Calixtus granted the Emperor more for Germany and less for Burgundy and Italy. Henry could accept the last point: in Burgundy the King played no great role, and in Italy the bishops were being more and more eclipsed by the growing power of the cities. But in Germany too the royal power had been essentially impaired. Basically the Ottonian imperial constitution fell to pieces with the concordat. The dependence of the bishops and of the royal abbots, assured not merely by the rights conceded in the *Calixtinum*, but also by homage, not mentioned there but actually performed, was weakened by the fact that the prelates, in the process of German constitutional development,

22 *MGConst* I, 159–61. The deciding of contested elections by the King should take place "metropolitani et conprovincialium consilio vel iudicio". On the obscure formulation, D. Schäfer, "Consilio vel iudicio" = "mit minne oder mit rehte" in *SAB* 37 (1913), 719 ff.

were changed from royal officials into vassals of the crown, into spiritual princes of the Empire, who aspired to strengthen their secular power, based on law and something that could no longer be arbitrarily taken away, and thus they came together with the secular princes in a community of interests. As holders of an ecclesiastical office, whose juridical identity Henry V had to recognize by renouncing investiture with the office, they also belonged to the supranational body of the ecclesiastical hierarchy. And since the papacy was ever more strongly making the Church into a genuine monarchy, they had two lords to serve for the future. Thus an entirely new relationship, founded on the principle of the distinction in the two public-law spheres of the state and the Church, was being prepared, and its difficulties were to become clear in the following 180 years.

Both contracting parties had the treaty ratified within their juridical spheres — the Emperor by the secular princes at the Diet of Bamberg in 1122, the Pope by the Lateran Council of March 1123. Calixtus overcame the resistance which he found there among the strict Gregorians by declaring that the concessions made to Henry were not to be approved but tolerated for the sake of peace. Everything depended on how persons acted in the future in regard to the problems inherent in the treaty, problems that as yet could not be mastered by ideas. From the old fighters for reform, who thought in now bogged down categories, there was not to be expected the elasticity which the new age, announced in the concordat, required. The Roman Church needed younger energies that would push forward. Calixtus seems to have at least suspected as much, for shortly before the council he elevated, among others, the Frenchman Aimeric to the rank of cardinal-deacon and around the same time, before 8 May, entrusted to him the weightiest curial post, that of chancellor. This important man, friend of Saint Bernard and of the Carthusian Prior Guigo, was to lead the Roman Church into a new stage of the reform and, to achieve this goal, even to accept the responsibility for the Schism of 1130.

The Lateran Council of 1123 brought to an end the numerous general synods which the Popes since Leo IX had arranged, in order to issue, in union with the bishops of the various countries, decrees universally binding. Without being essentially different from them, it alone has been recognized as ecumenical, and as the ninth ecumenical, First Lateran Council, inaugurated a new period in this sense, that thereafter the Popes decided the more important ecclesiastical questions in consistory, with the cardinals and bishops who happened to be present, and only rarely convoked general councils. The definitive character of this Council also appears clearly in the decrees. What the reform had decreed earlier against clerical marriage, against simony and lay domination of churches and church goods, what it had decreed in regard to the Peace of God or the rights and duties of crusaders — all was here summarized impressively. In the decrees relevant

401

to the care of souls and the administration of the Sacraments, what is striking is how much the power of the diocesan bishop was taken into account both in regard to his own clergy and in regard to monks, to whom pastoral work was forbidden. The age of the emergency, which had required so much intervention by the reform Popes against the rights of the local bishop and the granting of privileges to the monks who were fighting for the reform, was past. If the reform was to continue, it needed the cooperation of the bishops and of new forces emerging from the clergy and from monasticism.[23]

In reality there was still much to do. Nowhere, not even in France, had a definitive result been obtained. Germany and, with it, Italy only opened themselves up completely to the reform from 1122. The Church in Spain was in the process of reconstruction. In England the State Church system had by no means been overcome: Henry I clung more firmly than ever to his remaining rights and after the death of Anselm of Canterbury in 1109 cut off the bishops from communication with Rome, regardless of the protests of Paschal II. Ireland found itself in a first irresolute change, after the Synods of Cashel in 1101 and Rath Breasail in 1111 had begun to free the Church from its entanglement with the lay powers; the second of these synods had even provided for a definite hierarchy with twenty-six bishoprics and two metropolitan sees, one of the metropolitans to be also the primate.[24] Of the Scandinavian Kings, Eric of Denmark succeeded in obtaining in principle from Urban II, against Liemar of Bremen, the right to a Danish archbishopric, and hence a legate sent by Paschal II was able to elevate the see of Lund to metropolitan status in 1104. This arrangement actually continued in force, even when Archbishop Adalbero II of Bremen again obtained from Calixtus II and from Innocent II the confirmation of his metropolitan rights in the North. It was now only a question of time till Norway and Sweden received their own archbishoprics. The Christianization of the North could only direct missionary interest to the still pagan Baltic peoples. The evangelization of the Wends was resumed: Adalbero of Bremen set about advancing toward Mecklenburg, Boleslas III of Poland had Bishop Otto of Bamberg go with German priests to Pomerania. Poland again made contact with the reform in 1103, when Paschal II sent a legate who held a reform synod at Gniezno. In Hungary too, whose King Koloman had made his renunciation of investiture at the Synod of Guastalla (1106), a connection was also made, especially through the important reform councils of Esztergom in 1104 and 1112.[25]

---

[23] F. J. Schmale, *Studien zum Schisma des Jahres 1130* (Cologne - Graz 1961), 43–48 and *passim*.
[24] A. Gwynn, "The First Synod of Cashel" in *IER* 66 (1945), 81–92; 67 (1946), 109–22; MacErlean, "The Synod of Rath Breasail" in *Archiv. Hibernic.* 3 (1914), 1–33.
[25] On King Koloman and his ecclesiastico-political ideas, see J. Deér, "Der Anspruch der Herrscher des 12. Jahrhunderts auf die apostolische Legation", *ArchHP* 2 (1964), 156–62; on the reform, E. Pásztor, "Sulle origini della vita comune del clero in Ungheria" in *La vita comune del clero*, II, 71–78.

Hence the spirit of the reform had found entry everywhere; with it had arrived a new way of considering and moulding the world. For the reform struggle that has just been described must be understood as the expression of a much more profound change affecting all facets of life, which the Christian West was then experiencing. A later section will explain this to the extent that it affected the Church.

The Byzantine Church from 886 to 1054

CHAPTER 46

The Byzantine Church from Photius to the Tetragamy

The forced abdication of the Patriarch Photius in 886 still did not give a hint that the confusion within the Byzantine Imperial Church would end. The new Patriarch Stephen I (886–93), brother of the Emperor Leo VI, was unable to obtain recognition by the intransigent Ignatians, led by the Metropolitan Stylian Mapas, because he had received the diaconate from Photius. Again and again Stylian tried to win Rome to his side, but we are unable to say in each case what position the Pope took, since the papal letters in the famous collection of documents of the anti-Photians, in so far as they are authentic, probably did not keep that form in which they had left the Roman Chancery. Pope Formosus seems to have made an effort toward union by sending legates to Constantinople in 892, making a distinction between the invalidity of the ordinations of Photius's first patriarchate and the validity of those of the second patriarchate. The attempt failed, but it had no further consequences.

Reconciliation finally occurred under Pope John IX. It was probably the Patriarch Anthony Cauleas (893–901) who was able to convince Stylian of the senselessness of his opposition. Furthermore, the new Patriarch had been enrolled in the clergy, if not under Methodius, then at the latest under Ignatius, and hence he was not vulnerable in the way that Stephen was. We do not know whether a papal letter[1] prepared or only ratified the reconciliation of the factions, nor can we say for certain whether it took place in the presence of papal legates.[2] In any event, Rome and Constantinople now recognized "Ignatius, Photius, Stephen, and Anthony" as lawful Patriarchs, that is, at least the second patriarchate of Photius was no longer under attack.[3] Stylian accepted the formula, and only a few of his former adherents persisted in schism.

Anthony Cauleas died not long after the conclusion of peace in 899. There

[1] *Mansi* XVI, 457 AB.
[2] Cf. F. Dvornik, *Le schisme de Photius,* 364 ff.
[3] *Grumel Reg,* no. 596.

now occured what seemed to be a belated recognition of Photius, when, as a result of the Emperor's initiative, there mounted the patriarchal throne a relative of Photius, though possibly only by spiritual ties, in the person of Nicholas I Mysticus (901–7, 912–25).[4] Nicholas was unquestionably one of the great Patriarchs of Constantinople, and much in his character and activity is reminiscent of Photius. He too had first followed an administrative career in the service of the state. The fall of Photius made him dread disgrace at the hands of the friend of his youth, Leo VI, and so he withdrew to a monastery. But eventually the Emperor recalled him to court, where he became *mystikos,* or private secretary.

As Patriarch he displayed an uncommon zeal, and the dossier of his correspondence is among the most bulky in the patriarchal chancery.[5] In his patriarchate the Byzantine Church extended its frontiers far to the East. Abasgia and Alania, in the Kuban region, accepted Christianity, and Byzantium sent an archbishop to this mission territory. Far from the centre of Byzantine civilization and in perpetual confrontation with the surviving remains of barbarian paganism in his jurisdictional area, he needed constant encouragement from the Patriarch.[6] In several circles in Armenia there was discernible a turning from Monophysitism to Byzantine Orthodoxy, which the Patriarch followed with interest.[7] The Christianizing of the Chazars is said to have been furthered from Cherson.[8] The Patriarch even directly contacted the Muslim Emir of Crete to obtain relief for the Christians of the southern Aegean;[9] he finally turned also to the Caliph of Baghdad and assured him of the protection of the mosque in Constantinople and of the free exercise of their religion by Muslim war prisoners in the capital.[10] Together with the Emperor he regulated the important relations of rank of the bishoprics of the Empire by including the ancient bishoprics of Illyricum and South Italy in the official *Notitiae episcopatuum*[11] and sought to control the ecclesiastical system of fees. He gradually became the convinced champion of *oikonomia,* of clemency, of yielding, of patient waiting in all fields. It has rightly been pointed out that earlier historiography has not done justice to this Patriarch, because to the observer it is always Nicholas the politician who is in the foreground.

There were three situations especially in which Nicholas had to show

---

[4] On Nicholas Mysticus, cf. *Beck* 550; *LThK* VII, 995 (Baus); C. de Boor, *Vita Euthymii,* 160–88. There is no really comprehensive evaluation of the Patriarch.

[5] The texts in *PG* 111, 9–392.

[6] *Grumel Reg,* nos. 599, 609, 610, 619, 715.

[7] Ibid., nos. 647, 648, 649, 716.

[8] Ibid., nos. 676, 680.

[9] Ibid., nos. 600, 646.

[10] Ibid., nos. 659.

[11] Ibid., nos. 598. The authentic text in H. Gelzer, "Ungedruckte und ungenügend veröffentlichte Texte der Notitiae episcopatuum" in *AAM* XXI, 3 (Munich 1900), 550–59.

himself as a politician. The first had to do with his role in the treason of Andronicus Ducas; the next with the revolt of the latter's son, Constantine Ducas. The reports on the Patriarch's connection with these events go back to sources in which great confidence has been reposed without subjecting them to criticism.[12] In addition, the political background of the first of these revolts is entirely unclear. A judgment in regard to the Patriarch's attitude is not possible in view of the present state of our knowledge.

More important was the famous Tetragamy Controversy.[13] In 901 Leo VI had lost his third wife by death, and he still had no son. But before long he was presented with a son and heir by his mistress, Zoe Carbonopsina; Leo was willing to legitimate this son, the future Constantine VII Porphyrogennetos, and designate him as his successor. The Patriarch Nicholas was prepared to administer solemn baptism, which he did on Epiphany of 906, and also to recognize the baby prince as legitimate, contrary to all state and ecclesiastical regulations, which of themselves were directed against a third marriage, not to mention a fourth. But the Patriarch laid down as a condition that Leo must separate from his leman. At first Leo agreed, but after a short time he broke his promise, married Zoe, and elevated her to the dignity of Augusta.[14] The Patriarch thereupon forbade the Emperor to enter a church.

Leo countered by consulting Rome and the oriental Patriarchs as to the permissibility of a fourth marriage. In view of such an infringement of his autonomy, Nicholas seems to have been inclined to offer the Emperor a dispensation *motu proprio,* but the Emperor was no longer disposed to bow to his Patriarch.[15] Rome sent legates — whether Nicholas held himself aloof from them or the Emperor kept them away from him is not known — who brought the papal reply that there were no canonical considerations contrary to a fourth marriage. The legates of the oriental Patriarchs delivered the same verdict. Nicholas had to go into exile and submit his resignation.[16]

---

[12] *Grumel Reg,* no. 733.

[13] Cf. *DThC* IX, 365–79; *LThK* IX, 1381f. The most important older presentation is undoubtedly that in the commentary by de Boor on the *Vita Euthymii.* There is a Russian commentary on the *Vita* by A. P. Každan in *Dve bizantijskie chroniki X veka* (Moscow 1959). Meanwhile, research has disclosed as the special theorist of the controversy the famed Metropolitan of Caesarea, Arethas, a theorist who also accomplished a decisive change of fronts. His many works on the theme have now been published to a considerable extent; cf. R. J. H. Jenkins - B. Laurdas, "Eight letters of Arethas on the Fourth Marriage of Leo the Wise" in Ἑλληνικά 14 (1956), 293–372; P. Karlin-Hayter, "New Arethas Texts" in *Byz(B)* 31 (1961), 273–307; 34 (1964), 49–57.

[14] A third marriage had already been forbidden by the Empress Irene *(Dölger Reg,* no. 359); the Emperor Basil I had expressly forbidden a fourth marriage *(Rhallis* V, 252) and Leo VI himself in his twenty-second novel had basically recognized only the first marriage as fully legitimate and in his ninetieth novel had given his judgment of a third marriage.

[15] Nicholas now sought to secure himself by a pact with his metropolitans, which threatened with anathema and perpetual deposition all who would yield in the question; *Grumel Reg,* no. 611.   [16] *Grumel Reg,* nos. 612–14.

Once again a "case" had been manufactured. It is easy to defend Rome's position by reference to the primatial idea, but more difficult to justify the absence of any regard for the development of canon law in the Byzantine Church. No adjustment and no understanding were attempted; each side exerted itself to carry its own viewpoint just as it was. The representatives of the oriental Patriarchs, heaven knows under what presuppositions, joined themselves to the Roman view.

Leo's confessor, the monk Euthymius, succeeded Nicholas as Patriarch, and the Byzantine Church split into the unyielding factions of Nicholaites and Euthymians, even though the position adopted by Euthymius differed little from that of his predecessor. He regarded the Roman decision as a dispensation in a particular case, which in no way bound him to recognize a fourth marriage in principle.[17] With his synod he rejected such a request and also declared that any third marriage was unlawful. He deposed the priest Thomas, who had blessed the Emperor's fourth marriage, and was unwilling to review this judgment even on the intervention of the Empress.[18] He refused to perform the religious coronation of the Empress.[19] Hence the schism within the Byzantine Church cannot be fastened onto the canonical outlook of Euthymius; it is connected rather with the fact that Nicholas was compelled to abdicate, contrary to the rules of the canons. And so Euthymius had to pay after the death of Leo VI in 912.

Leo's brother and successor, Alexander, restored Nicholas to his rights[20] and drove the disgraced Euthymius into exile. For his part, Nicholas decreed anathema and deposition for the adherents of his supplanter. This judgment quite needlessly affected all those whom Euthymius had ordained.[21] In a letter to Pope Anastasius III[22] Nicholas reproached the Latin Church with having encouraged unchastity by tolerating a fourth marriage, contrary to the Apostle Paul. He demanded that the Pope excommunicate the authors

[17] Ibid., no. 626.

[18] Ibid., nos. 625, 629.

[19] Ibid., nos. 627, 628.

[20] There is a text, alleged to come from Leo VI, in which he repents of his fourth marriage and designates Nicholas as his Patriarch, who is to be reinstated in all his rights. The text has stirred up a controversy, especially in regard to the question of whether it was Leo or only Alexander who restored the Patriarch. It would probably be difficult to label the text as a clever forgery by the Patriarch. It is quite possible that on his deathbed Leo wanted to make peace with the Nicholaite faction and that the present text is a formulation of the Emperor's ideas, put in writing by Nicholas. But everything indicates that its implementation, that is, the reinstatement of Nicholas, was only carried out by Alexander. Cf. N. Oikonomides, "La dernière volonté de Léon VI au sujet de la tétragamie" in *ByZ* 56 (1963), 46–52; also, P. Karlin-Hayter in *Byz(B)* 32 (1962, appeared 1963), 317–22; again, N. Oikonomides, "La 'préhistoire' de la dernière volonté de Léon VI au sujet de la tétragamie" in *ByZ* 56 (1963), 265–70; P. Karlin-Hayter in *Byz(B)* 33 (1963), 483–86.

[21] *Grumel Reg,* nos. 630, 631, 632.

[22] Ibid., no. 635.

of the Roman decision; not of course Pope Sergius III, who was already dead, and also not Leo VI, since, according to Nicholas, he had repented. As Rome did not go along with these demands, the Pope was deleted from the diptychs.

Meanwhile there fell to the Patriarch duties which deeply involved him in the most urgent questions of Byzantine foreign policy.[23] It is possible that after the death of the Emperor Alexander in 913 he wanted to place at the side of the little Constantine VII a vigorous guardian and coemperor in the person of Constantine Ducas, but in the meantime he found out that he had himself been appointed regent together with a few senators. In any event, he first had to deal with the insurrection of Constantine Ducas. He contrived to ruin it, but he thereby forfeited considerable public sympathy. And the mother of the child-emperor, the widowed Empress Zoe, challenged his political influence. But worst of all was his meeting with the victorious Tsar Simeon of the Bulgars, who was quite frankly reaching for the Byzantine imperial crown. This invasion of the Bulgars called for all of the Empire's defensive forces, including those of a united Church.

And so the call for peace and unity was heard throughout the second patriarchate of Nicholas Mysticus. But, as always in Byzantium, imperial pressure was finally required in order really to establish it. The pressure was due to Romanus Lecapenus, who had already made himself guardian and father-in-law of the Emperor.[24] In 920 there at length took place a Synod of Union. The document issued at its close[25] is of noteworthy good sense: the cause of the controversy, the fourth marriage of Leo VI, was entirely excluded. New regulations were issued only for the future: from the eighth indiction of the year of the world 6428, that is, from 1 September 920, a fourth marriage was forever forbidden, while a third was possible but only with reservations and subject to ecclesiastical penance.

Union was effected without Rome's participation. The question was: what would be Rome's attitude to it? Shortly after the synod Nicholas condescended to write again to Rome, this time to Pope John X.[26] He requested the sending of legates to condemn fourth marriages in accord with the common faith of all Christendom. But Rome would not agree to any stipulations. Again Nicholas had to give way: in a new letter he only proposed that at Rome the Roman permission for Leo VI to enter into a fourth marriage be regarded as pure *oikonomia*, for, according to him, thus did Pope Sergius III understand his position.[27] There was apparently no

---

[23] Cf. J. Gay, "Le patriarche Nicolas Mystique et son rôle politique" in *Mélanges C. Diehl*, I (Paris 1930), 91–100.

[24] This easily follows from the letter of the Patriarch to Lecapenus of 919–20 (*Grumel Reg*, no. 665) in *PG* 111, 273–77.

[25] *Grumel Reg*, no. 669; *Rhallis* V, 4–9.

[26] *Grumel Reg*, no. 671.   [27] Ibid., no. 675.

reply to this nor to a third letter.[28] Only a fourth letter, in which no conditions were laid down, was successful. Papal envoys arrived in Constantinople, probably in the spring of 923. What was discussed is known only from a letter of the Patriarch to the Tsar Simeon, according to which the Roman legates condemned the tetragamy and solemnly made peace with the Byzantine Church.[29] It is unlikely that Rome should have so suddenly changed its position or that once again its legates should have exceeded their mandate without there being some information to this effect in the Roman sources. To me it seems possible that the legates recognized the legislation of the synod of 920 as particular law binding the Byzantine Church.

Once again a serious quarrel had been eventually adjusted. Apparently Rome had not given way on any point, and in Byzantium it was clear that a genuine ecclesiastical peace was unthinkable without Rome's participation. Rome had won, and more clearly than in the Photian affair. But the triumph had been purchased at a price that was to become increasingly expensive in the succeeding decades, a lack of interest on the part of the Byzantine Church in crossing the path of the Roman Church. Each held itself aloof, the alienation grew, and the later break was nothing more than drawing the final line.

CHAPTER 47

The Road to Schism

In the further course of the history of the Byzantine patriarchate in the tenth century there appear historical figures who, on the one hand, amazingly resemble the contemporary Popes, and, on the other hand, once again make very clear the special characteristic of the "Constantinian" ecclesiastical system — the intimate connection between Church policy and the politics of a ruler who regarded himself as Emperor of the world. In other words: the history of these decades cannot be understood apart from the violent quarrels between East and West over questions of the "Roman" imperial office, and it is not going too far to state with M. Michel that "the schismatic tendencies in New Rome [acted as] a barometer for German influence in Old Rome".

The Emperor Romanus I Lecapenus (919–44) aspired by means of an unscrupulous family policy to supplant the Macedonian Dynasty represented by his ward, Constantine VII. He also intended to reserve the patriarchal throne for his house. So long as his son Theophylact was still a child, he appointed two successive Patriarchs, Stephen II (925–8) and Tryphon (928–31), who were regarded only as caretakers and, accordingly, remained

---

[28] Ibid., no. 711.   [29] Ibid., no. 712.

in total anonymity. When Theophylact was barely sixteen years old, his father appointed him Patriarch (933–56), and Pope John XI — according to Liutprand, under compulsion from Alberic — made himself a party to the farce, solemnly legalizing the grotesque canonical situation by the presence of his legates. It is not improbable that the same Pope by written explanations of the rank of the see of Constantinople furthered still more the striving for autonomy at Byzantium.[1]

What is related of the way of life of the young Patriarch corresponds pretty closely to what is reported of Pope John XII. It is amazing that his church enjoyed the confidence of the Bulgarian Tsar Peter, who consulted it on the treatment of the sect of the Bogomiles, which had only recently appeared. The detailed doctrinal explanation which thereupon left the Patriarch's chancery and is one of the most important documents for the history of the sect, originated, of course, not in the Patriarch's theological scholarship but in that of the *chartophylax* John.[2]

It is characteristic of the regenerative powers of the Byzantine Church that the pontificate of Theophylact was a mere interlude. In the person of the monk Polyeuctus (956–70) he obtained a successor of surpassing repute. Fearless in regard to all authorities, austere and unpolished, and concerned to maintain the purity of ecclesiastical discipline, he defended the notion of the charismatic character of the imperial office but at the same time opposed any "identification" of political with purely canonical and religious interests. He denied to the victorious Emperor Nicephorus II the satisfaction of venerating as martyrs Byzantine soldiers who had fallen in the struggle against Islam;[3] he prevented the marriage of this Emperor with the widow of the Emperor Romanus II, the notorious Theophano, so long as there remained the suspicion of a spiritual relationship between the two of them;[4] and after the assassination of Nicephorus he denied entry into the churches and imperial coronation to the new Emperor John I Tzimisces, who had inspired the crime, so long as Theophano remained at court and the murderers were unpunished.[5] He laid down another condition for Tzimisces: no coronation would take place until Tzimisces declared null the "Caesaropapist measures" of his predecessor, that is, a law which made any episcopal consecration dependent on the Emperor's permission.[6] And all the Emperors bowed to the man's harshness and determination.

---

[1] Liutprand of Cremona, *Legatio,* 62.

[2] New edition and commentary by I. Dujčev, "L'epistola sui Bogomili del patriarca costantinopolitano Teofilatto" in *Mélanges E. Tisserant,* II (Città del Vaticano 1964), 63–91.

[3] *Grumel Reg,* no. 790.

[4] Leo the Deacon, 50 (Bonn).

[5] Ibid. 98.

[6] *Grumel Reg,* no. 793: the Patriarch demanded the restoration to the synod of a *nomos* of the Emperor Nicephorus II of *ca.* 964 (*Dölger Reg,* no. 703), in which it was enacted that no episcopal election was valid without the Emperor's assent; cf. *Dölger Reg,* no. 726.

410

The tocsin in regard to the situation of the Empire and of the Church in foreign policy was rung with the imperial coronation of Otto the Great in 962,[7] that is, the recurrence of an event which had already led to severe shocks in 800, because it was at the same time the sign of the determining influence of a rival "non-Roman" imperial power on the papacy, which thereby abandoned the relatively independent, and for Byzantium tolerable, position between the two world powers. It is not surprising that the representatives of Rome's papal aristocracy, expelled and hamstrung by the Germans, turned to Byzantium. In view of the obscurity of the canonical situation at Rome, it would be presumptuous to label as schismatic every supporting of such an expellee by Byzantium. It could likewise be no more than a consequence of this same obscurity in the rapid succession of Popes if the mention of these Popes by name in the Byzantine liturgy — their admission to the diptychs — was gradually taken quite lightly. Byzantium's reaction was more sensitive when the new Emperor of the German nation reached out for the Byzantine possessions in South Italy, and the Roman Church in his train raised its ancient patriarchal claim to this territory. The most striking countermove of the Byzantine Church was the elevation of Otranto to metropolitan status with the right to consecrate the Bishops of Acerentila, Turcicum, Gravina, Macceria, and Tricarium.[8] The succeeding conflicts in South Italy, not very happily managed by either side, which eventually led to the marriage of the Emperor Otto II and the Byzantine Princess Theophano, somewhat relaxed the ecclesiastico-political situation, but mistrust remained the dominant attitude.

The circumstance that the usurper of the papacy, Boniface VII, escaped with the treasure of Saint Peter's from the German Count Sicco to Constantinople and acted from there as his headquarters could not but strengthen this outlook. Ten years later (984) Boniface succeeded in recovering Rome. The role of the Byzantine court and patriarchate in the following disturbances at Rome was probably of no great importance. And the Antipope John XVI (997–8), the celebrated John Philagathus of Rossano, pertained rather to the conflict between the Crescentians and the Saxon Dynasty than to the intrigues of the Byzantine court.

At this time the Patriarch of Constantinople was Sisinnius II (996–8), who is said to have sent the encyclical of the Patriarch Photius, with its serious charges against Rome's faith and discipline, to the oriental Patriarchs in a new edition.[9] To those who hold this thesis, the overthrow of the "Byzantine" Pope John XVI was a sufficient motive for such a step by the Patriarch, although it should be borne in mind that the encyclical as such

---

[7] On the problem, cf. W. Ohnsorge, *Das Zweikaiserproblem im früheren Mittelalter* (Hildesheim 1947), 62 ff., and A. Michel, *Humbert und Kerullarios,* I (Paderborn 1925), 9 ff.

[8] *Grumel Reg,* no. 792.

[9] Cf. A. Michel, *op. cit.* 16 f., and the contrary view in *Grumel Reg,* no. 814; Michel's reply in

was in no way concerned with the drastic events in Rome and must have appeared hopelessly out of date in regard to its principal content, the complaint about the Roman mission to Bulgaria. As regards the external evidence, if the arguments against authenticity are not entirely convincing, neither are those in favour of it. It is probably advisable, in the hypothetical state of the question, not to make any fuss about it. Be that as it may: peace with Rome was again a fact in the days of Pope John XVIII (1003–09). However, it was not lasting. There is a tradition, though not of unimpeachable testimony, according to which the Patriarch Sergius II (1101–19) again struck the Pope out of the diptychs.[10] The support given by Pope Benedict VIII to the Norman opposition to Byzantine rule in South Italy is more likely to have been the reason for this than a synodical of Pope Sergius IV, containing the *Filioque*. The combining of papal policy with the purely political interests of the Normans and of the German Emperor in South Italy produced in this area a new situation, which would continue to be decisive for the entire period of the crusades and would really only reach its climax under Charles of Anjou.[11] On the other hand, the reaction of the Byzantines confused ecclesiastical and secular just as perversely as did the policy of their papal opponents. And this is the basis from which the Byzantine Patriarch Michael Caerularius drew his strength.

Michael was the successor of a Patriarch, Alexius the Studite (1025–43), who brought to the patriarchal throne little of the old spirit of his monastery. His patriarchal *acta*[12] are full of canonistic notifications of a laudable reform zeal, but in fact he bowed, in the age of the decay of the last Macedonians on the imperial throne, to every public violation of the rights of the Church without protesting, so far as is known. And just as Theophylact was followed by a Polyeuctus, so now Alexius was followed by the masterful figure of Michael Caerularius (1043–58), who, characteristically, referred the *Constitutum Constantini* to his see[13] and from it deduced quasi-imperial rights. It is difficult to do him justice, for his headstrong, not to say revolutionary, personality

ByZ 38 (1938), 454 ff. Grumel's negative view is also that of M. Jugie, *Le schisme byzantin*, 158, footnote 1.

[10] A. Michel, *Humbert und Kerullarios*, I, 19 ff.; cf. *Grumel Reg,* nos. 818, 819.

[11] According to Raoul Glaber, *Historiae sui temporis,* IV, 1 (*PL* 142, 670–72), Pope John XIX had received an embassy from the Byzantine Patriarch Eustathius (1019–25), which asked him to declare the Church of Constantinople to be the primatial Church of the entire East, just as the Roman was the patriarchal Church of the whole world (cf. *Grumel Reg,* no. 828, and *Dölger Reg,* no. 817). Implied here was certainly no request for the Pope to sell the Roman primacy, as Michel in *ByZ* 54 (1952), 414, holds — quite the contrary. Jugie, *op. cit.* 168 f., made this clear. On the other hand Michel's arguments in "Weltreichs- und Kirchenteilung bei Rudolf Glaber" in *HJ* 70 (1951), 53–64, against Glaber's reliability are very noteworthy.

[12] *Grumel Reg,* nos. 829–55.

[13] But probably only later (cf. *Skylitzes* II, 643). The *Donatio,* as to its text, was probably not known at Byzantium until 1054. Cf. E. Petrucci in *BIStIAM* 74 (1962), 45–106.

represents an exception in the history of the Byzantine patriarchate. It is historically impossible to gauge him by the standards of the Church reform just getting under way in the West, for he summarized an ecclesiastical development which was not alien to the papacy of that day and for which the notion of reform, even in the West, was not the only sponsor.

As a young aristocrat, Michael had already been implicated in a revolt, and it was reported that he was seeking the crown. The enterprise was discovered, and, as so often, the monastery was his only salvation. But this was not the end. He became a cleric and under the Emperor Constantine IX Mono-machus (1042–55) soon rose to influence on policy. As *synkellos* of the Patriarch he acquired the expectation of the succession, which he actually obtained in 1043. The ecclesiastical situation between East and West which he encountered can hardly be described as one of formal schism, but as one of a growing ecclesiastical independence of the patriarchate of Constantinople *vis-à-vis* the unstable condition of Rome, as one of deliberate mutual with-drawal. It was more dangerous that the political estrangement had led also to a "ritual" estrangement, that people in Byzantium were more and more of the opinion that only in New Rome were religious customs, the religious life in its totality, and finally religious faith unimpaired or, to put it perhaps better, had been preserved unharmed. The idea of the primacy, which in Byzantium had never become a universal conviction equal to any trial of strength, was weaker than ever and had been so for some decades. Now, in addition, the papacy had linked itself with the competing imperial power in the West and, recently, even with the most dangerous foes of the Empire in South Italy, the Normans. It was precisely this question of the Normans that was to start the stone rolling.[14]

The good services rendered by these intruders to the papacy soon changed into the opposite, and the Popes themselves were interested in again getting rid of the spectre. Here, then, Byzantine and papal policy suddenly agreed again on something. But the resources of both were, by themselves, too little to deal with the danger, and so the idea of a great alliance of the two Empires and of the papacy began to stir. One of the strongest advocates of this idea was that very Byzantine who had to be the best informed about the situation, Argyros, *catepan* of the Byzantine Empire's Italian possessions. The Emperor Constantine IX could be gained for the plan without difficulty, but in Michael Caerularius it found an implacable opponent.

The reasons for this opposition were probably complex in nature. Argyros was the son of that Melo who in 1009 had fought against Byzantium in Apulia under papal and German protection. The son had been raised in Byzantium but belonged to the Latin rite and at the beginning of the 1040's

---

[14] See A. Michel, "Schisma und Kaiserhof im Jahre 1054" in *L'Église et les églises,* I (Cheve-togne 1954), 352–440.

played a highly ambiguous role as Byzantine commander in South Italy. If not by virtue of his rite, then because of his political background and past, Argyros could impress a convinced Byzantine as someone quite suspicious.[15] Michael hated him. And it was probably worth considering who would finally gather the fruits of a victory over the Normans — the Pope, the German Emperor, the Byzantine Emperor, or a *dux et princeps Italiae,* as Argyros had had himself proclaimed in 1041. Furthermore, it was to be suspected that a coalition with the Pope would again only give rise to a control by the Roman Church over the Byzantine. The self-willed Patriarch was in no way inclined to bow to such as that.

And so he began a campaign of discriminating against the Roman Church, of an acidity not attained even by that of Photius. Michael was not concerned about proceedings on the highest plane, such as an encyclical to the oriental Patriarchs, who did not have much to say, but with a tumult in the capital against the new direction of imperial policy. His propaganda had to do with ecclesiastical ritual, especially the use of unleavened bread in the Latin Church, its custom of fasting on Saturdays, and so forth. Thanks to his meagre theological culture he only discovered the *Filioque,* so to speak, at the eleventh hour.[16]

In any event, he began with drastic measures in his own episcopal city. On his orders the churches of the Latins were closed; the upshot was disorderly scenes, in which even the consecrated Hosts were not always spared. Propagandist for the Patriarch was Archbishop Leo of Ochrida, with his circular to the Bishop of Trani, a Latin. Fundamentally it was directed at the Pope and demanded no less than the removal from the Latin Church of all rites which were displeasing to Byzantium. It is noteworthy, however, that this letter expressed no anathema.[17] The Bishop of Trani sent it on to the Curia, and Cardinal Humbert of Silva Candida was commissioned to reply. Michael Caerularius thereby found an opponent who was his match and whose temperament vied with that of the Patriarch. The eventual elimination of Pope Leo IX by death left the field to two warriors, between whom no compromise was now possible. Humbert's reply[18] to the Greek circular contained all the claims of the reformed papacy, but distorted by historically questionable amplifications, by the incorporating of the *Constitutum Constantini,* and by the claims of the papacy to South Italy. The Cardinal charged the Greek Church with "more than ninety heresies". Willingness for an

---

[15] Ibid. 366f.

[16] At least substantially authentic, the so-called *Panoplia* of the Patriarch attests the violence of these struggles. Edited in A. Michel, *Humbert und Kerullarios,* II (Paderborn 1930).

[17] Text in Will, *Acta et scripta de controversiis ecclesiae graecae et latinae . . .* (Leipzig 1861), 52–64, and *PG* 120, 836–44.

[18] Will, *op. cit.,* 65–85, the so-called first letter of Pope Leo IX to Michael; it came from Humbert's pen. Cf. Michel, *Humbert und Kerullarios,* I, 44 ff.

understanding was, it is true, expressed formally, but the violence of the tone left little hope.

Meanwhile, the situation in South Italy had reached a crisis. Pope Leo managed to collect a contingent of troops, and at their head he marched against the Normans. Shortly before, Argyros had had to accept a reverse from these very Normans at Siponto, and he was unable to bring his troops to join those of the Pope. Leo IX suffered a severe defeat and became the Normans' prisoner in June 1053; from captivity he tried to take care of the Church's affairs as best he could. The Pope's defeat was by implication a defeat for Byzantine interests in South Italy. The alliance desired by Argyros was more urgent than ever, and the imperial court could only bow to this line of argument. The Emperor Constantine IX wrote to the Curia and expressed his desire for peace in the Church as the precondition of a political alliance,[19] and even Michael Caerularius had to yield to pressure and make known to the Pope in moderate tones his wish for an understanding.[20]

The Curia now decided to send an embassy to Constantinople to bring about peace. It was headed by Humbert, who was accompanied by the Roman Chancellor, Frederick of Lotharingia, and Archbishop Peter of Amalfi. Before the departure for Constantinople Humbert conferred at length with Argyros, who was probably not sparing with warnings against the Patriarch. In Constantinople the embassy was honourably received by the Emperor, whereas its visit with the Patriarch was more than chilly. The Romans felt that they were not properly honoured, the Patriarch that he was not greeted according to protocol. The scene ended, so to speak, with a silent handing over of the papal letter, which, again written by Humbert, was not capable of banishing the Patriarch's fears that the political alliance could impair his authority in the Byzantine Church. There was no conversation, and Humbert devoted himself all the more zealously to political propaganda. He had his polemic against the Greeks translated, plunged into further polemics, and finally attacked the aged monk, Nicetas Stethatos, who had dared to write against unleavened bread. Humbert's pressure on the Emperor led to a miserable disputation in Nicetas's monastery on 24 June 1054, after which Nicetas had to recant and his treatise was committed to the flames.[21]

In this situation the Patriarch, in a violent polemic which did not spare the court, succeeded in making propaganda in his own favour, and the legates decided to leave without having accomplished their purpose, but not without first, in a solemn act, having laid a bull of excommunication of the Patriarch and his accomplices on the altar of Hagia Sophia on 16 July 1054.

[19] *Dölger Reg,* no. 911.
[20] *Grumel Reg,* no. 864.
[21] For the literature, see *Beck* 535 f.

Its text[22] went much too far. It anathematized the "pseudo-Patriarch" Michael Caerularius, Archbishop Leo of Ochrida, and other adherents of the Patriarch as simonists, Arians, Nicolaites, Severans, Pneumatomachoi, Manichaeans, Nazarites, and so forth, and thereby subjected to anathema not merely the Greek doctrine of the procession of the Holy Spirit, for example, but also such things as the marriage of Greek priests and other legitimate Greek usages.

Pope Leo IX had been dead for three months; whether the legates knew this cannot be determined. The questionable nature of their proceedings is underscored by the unspeakable misuse of dogmatic deductions. After this act the legates took their departure of the Emperor in a very amicable fashion — as always, he was helpless — and set out on their return journey. It may be that at the time of their leaving the translation of the bull had not yet been laid before the Emperor or he had not yet reflected on its import. But this was quickly rectified, and Constantine IX was induced to call back the envoys, probably to discuss the complex of questions in a common meeting. This was not in the interest of the Patriarch. He rallied the people and proposed a session under circumstances in which the legates could have felt themselves to be in personal danger. The effort to calm spirits thus misfired, and now the Emperor suggested to the legates on his own that they leave, after the mob had even begun to besiege the imperial palace. The Emperor ceased to resist and bowed to the Patriarch's propaganda: Argyros was sacrificed, and the Emperor's closest advisers had to leave the palace.

What followed was only the epilogue. On Sunday, July 24, the Emperor convoked a synod, whose *semeioma* presented the events in its own fashion. The legates were disqualified as being legates of Argyros, the text of their bull of excommunication was incorporated into the *semeioma* as a horrible example, it was interpreted as an excommunication of the entire Orthodox Church. The excommunication was turned back on the legates and their supporters.[23]

This, then, was the celebrated Schism of 1054. The historical evaluation scarcely needs to be covered over with the juridical. Whether the excommunication was legal, now that the Pope was long dead and as yet had no successor, is controverted.[24] In regard to its content, it was to a great extent

---

[22] Latin text of the bull in *PL* 143, 1002–04. The Greek translation was incorporated into the synodal protocol to the Greek counteranathema, *PG* 120, 736–48; cf. Will, *op. cit.* 153–68. There can scarcely be any question of a falsification of the Latin text of the bull in this *semeioma* (*Grumel Reg*, no. 869), but the situation is different with regard to the reporting of events in Michael's letter to the oriental Patriarchs (*Grumel Reg*, no. 870–72); cf. A. Michel, "Die Fälschung der römischen Bannbulle durch Michael Kerullarios" in *ByzNGrJb* 9 (1932f.), 293–319.

[23] *Grumel Reg,* no. 869; cf. the preceding footnote.

[24] Its nullity is upheld by M. Jugie, "Le schisme byzantin" in *DThC* XIV, 1356, and to a degree by E. Herman in *OrChrP* 8 (1942), 209–18; its validity by A. Michel in *ByZ* 42 (1943–49), 193–205. On 7 December 1965, simultaneously at Rome and Istanbul, the mutual excom-

an unlawful amplification of Humbert's own personal resentments, even if the central question was included. But in form it did not, in any event, attack the Orthodox Church as such, and not its head, the Emperor, but only Michael and his abettors. Similarly, Michael did not excommunicate the Pope or the Roman Church, but only the legates and their backers, as Argyros and his circle were alleged to be. What was meant by both sides was, in any case, something different, and of this there can be scarcely any doubt. According to the formalities of law, no acts had been performed which would permit one to speak of a schism in the strict sense. But the vehemence in word and act was new and unprecedented, the repertory of mutual recriminations had been substantially enlarged in comparison with the Photian Schism, and the generalizations were grotesque. The cold war between the two hierarchies could only be substantially reinforced, whatever consequences were drawn from the occurrences, and rearming on both sides was energetically pushed again — a situation hardened, to which eventually no one would be able to say what name should be attached.

The term "schism" cannot be rejected out of hand, but it would be false to designate the situation as hopeless from then on. Even then the Emperor was still basically in control of the government of the Church, and there remained the question whether another Emperor than the weak Constantine IX would not have suddenly changed course again. Besides, in Byzantium the violent character of the Patriarch was well known, and the extent to which all the events were the result of his own vehement policy was hardly underrated. And, finally, it was not to be excluded that in time Rome might enter upon a path which would no longer adhere to the subjective line of a Humbert

The oriental Churches did not follow the policy of the Ecumenical Patriarch throughout with flying colours. Above all it was the Patriarch Peter III of Antioch, a former cleric of Constantinople, who pursued his own course and was not inclined to wheel around to Michael's direction.[25] For a long time churchmen almost universally took no more notice of this "Schism" than did Byzantine historiography.

munications were cancelled by Pope Paul VI and the Ecumenical Patriarch Athenagoras I (translator).
[25] On Peter III of Antioch and his letters, cf. Michel, *Humbert und Kerullarios,* II, 416 ff., and *Beck* 535.

CHAPTER 48

The Inner Life of the Byzantine Church
between Photius and Caerularius

It is becoming ever clearer that the charge of hostility to culture, which was raised in regard to the iconoclasts, sprang to a great extent from the polemics against the heretics and that, on the contrary, an Emperor like Theophilus, the last iconoclast, was one of the significant protagonists of a self-realization of the Greek mind after generations of stagnation. So too the Patriarch Photius, as the scholar of his age, must at the same time be considered as the first great representative of this self-realization, to which pertained love for the treasures of ancient civilization along with impartiality of thought, confidence in reason, and enthusiasm for form and its classical setting. In this regard, classicism for Photius referred to the pagan writings of antiquity as well as to those of the Church Fathers. This movement culminated in Photius but did not end with his downfall. Its tracks are found everywhere, and a generation after his death a circle of busy philologists and encyclopedic compilers formed around the Emperor Constantine VII Porphyrogennetos (912–59). It stored up much, even if in epitome, in the granary of tradition and perhaps even reduced to the form of a means of education what in Photius had served education more impartially and more freely. This movement also prevailed in theology.

A philologist of great importance, a philologist of ecclesiastical literature too, was especially Photius's pupil, Arethas, Metropolitan of Caesarea in Cappadocia, a scholarly glossator and scholiast, not only of classical literature but also of the Bible and of the earliest Christian literature — Justin, Tatian, Athenagoras, Clement, and so forth.[1] A younger contemporary of Photius, Nicetas Byzantios, opponent of the Armenian Monophysites, of Islam, and of the Latins, and, as such, scarcely original, still surprises by a scholastic method of argumentation, which for that epoch seems almost rationalistic.[2] His type is encountered a century later in the Metropolitan Stephen of Nicomedia, author of brief summaries on philosophical propaedeutics and on particular questions of theology. He is of interest most of all because the opposition of the pneumatics and enthusiasts, represented by the great

---

[1] Still available on Arethas is the monograph by S. Kugeas, ʻΟ Καισαρείας ʼΑρέθας καὶ τὸ ἔργον αὐτοῦ (Athens 1913). More recent bibliography in *Beck* 591–95, where are to be found also data on the widely scattered editions. More recent editions by Karlin–Hayter and others are mostly related to the struggles in the Tetragamy Controversy. Cf *Byz* 28–34 (1958–64).

[2] *PG* 105, 588–841; J. Hergenröther, *Monumenta graeca ad Photium eiusque historiam spectantia* (Regensburg 1869), 84–138; *Beck* 531f.

mystic, Simeon the New Theologian, caught fire on his works.[3] And here may be mentioned a special sort of work, the Χιλιόστιχος θεολογία, composed around the turn of the tenth century by Leo Choirosphactes, in whom Arethas saw an odious "Hellene". We are referring to an exposition of theology in verse, which seems to feed entirely on the Hellenistic mystery theology and neo-Platonic terminology.[4] Even the work of encyclopedic compilation that was going on around Constantine VII found expression in theological literature. Theodore Daphnopates, a high official under the Emperor Romanus II (959–63), produced the Chrysostom eclogues, extracts from the sermons of this Church Father, which, in the form of homilies on the most varied virtues and vices, like the excerpts of Constantine VII from profane literature, summarized the thought of John Chrysostom.[5] To this group also belonged Simeon Metaphrastes, with his eclogues from Basil, Chrysostom, and homilies of pseudo-Macarius.[6]

This Simeon owes his name Metaphrastes to his hagiographical activity. With this we reach a field of theological writing that was more intensively cultivated in this period than ever before. The sufferings endured in the age of Iconoclasm gave this *genre* an unexpected upsurge. Already in the period between the two iconoclast epochs a deacon, Stephen, had written the life of the most important martyr of the cult of images, Stephen the Younger, monk of Mount Auxentius.[7] Immediately after the death of Theodore the Studite in 826, his merits were celebrated by his successor, Naucratius, in a circular, which found entry into the saint's memorial liturgy.[8] A deacon, Ignatius, later Metropolitan of Nicaea, wrote, probably around the middle of the ninth century, the *vitae* of the confessors and Patriarchs, Tarasius and Nicephorus.[9] Probably the famous outlaw of the Photian Schism, Archbishop Gregory Asbestas, was the author of the life of the Patriarch Methodius.[10] But a whole group of other confessors, John Damascene,[11] Joannikios,[12] Peter of Atroa,[13] George of Mitylene,[14] and others, had their panegyrists. Patriarchal biography found revisers, who, abandoning the *genre* of real hagiography, became the chroniclers and pamphleteers of their age, so agitated in ecclesiastical politics: for example, Nicetas David, with a very biased biography of the Patriarch Ignatius, in which Photius does not have a redeeming feature,[15] and an anonymous monk, with a *vita* of the Patriarch Euthymius, in which the Patriarch Nicholas Mysticus suffers the same fate

---

[3] His works have not yet been critically edited. On him and his conflict with Simeon the New Theologian, cf. I. Hausherr, *Un grand mystique byzantin: Vie de Syméon le Nouveau Théologien* (Rome 1928), li ff.; *Beck* 531 f.

[4] The work is found in Vat. gr. 1257. Cf. *Beck* 594.

[5] *PG* 63, 567–902; *DHGE* XIV, 80–82 (J. Darrouzès).

[6] Some of them published in *PG* 32, 1115–1382, and *PG* 34, 861–965.

[7] *BHG* 1666, 1666a.   [8] Ibid. 2311.   [9] Ibid. 1698, 1335.   [10] Ibid. 1278.

[11] Ibid. 884.   [12] Ibid. 935.   [13] Ibid. 2364f.   [14] Ibid. 2163.

[15] *PG* 105, 488–574, and *Mansi* XVI, 209–92.

as Photius did at the hands of Nicetas David.[16] In addition the edifying hagiographical romance, without any historical background, is represented by, among other works, the *vita* of Saint Theoctiste of Lesbos by a Magister Nicetas,[17] or, under the auspices of the monastic interchange between East and West, by a Greek version of Saint Gregory the Great's account of Saint Benedict of Nursia,[18] or, as evidence of a national hagiography within the framework of the Empire, by the life of the Georgian Hilarion[19] — a variegated wealth, partly of undifferentiated encomia, partly of fanciful stories, partly of still naive reporting in the spirit of the hagiography of the early seventh century.

But it was exactly this last type which was to achieve its destiny in the period under consideration, and indeed in the name of classicism of rhetorical form, for which the scholars of the age, including the theologians, became ever more enthusiastic. And it is not unlikely that the plan of producing a complete *menologion* of this style originated with Constantine VII. The task was performed by a high imperial official, Simeon, who died around the close of the millennium and entered history as *metaphrastes,* the "translator" of the old *vitae* into the rhetorical style. As regards the external form the work is uneven: the summer months of the calendar of saints are dealt with substantially more briefly than the winter months, perhaps for liturgical reasons. The feasts of the Lord are omitted, probably with regard for the available "panegyrists". Metaphrastes adopted some ancient texts almost unaltered, and some he created entirely, but in most cases he produced a version in keeping with the taste of the age. Metaphrastes thereby created a standard Byzantine work, which, while not free from contamination and admixture, permanently dominated the aspect of hagiography. The tradition of the old, naive *vitae* thereafter often fell into oblivion. This may be regretted, but the appreciation of the achievement of Metaphrastes must start from what he intended and what accorded with the taste of his age.[20]

At least as important as the contribution of this period to hagiography was its contribution to the history of Byzantine mysticism. In Simeon the New

---

[16] Edited by C. de Boor (Berlin 1888) and P. Karlin-Hayter in *Byz(B)* 25–27 (1955–57), 8–152: Commentary with Russian translation, by A. P. Každan, *Dve bizantijskie chroniki X veka* (Moscow 1959).

[17] *BHG* 1723.

[18] Ibid. 273.

[19] Edited by P. Peeters in *AnBoll* 32 (1913), 236–69.

[20] The *Menologion* of Metaphrastes has still not been entirely published. Most of the texts, strongly mixed with non-Metaphrastean texts, in *PG* 114–16. On the sifting, cf. *Beck* 572–75. On the transmission, see especially *Überlieferung und Bestand der hagiographischen und homiletischen Literatur der griechischen Kirche,* especially I, 2 (Leipzig 1938); id., "Symeon Metaphrastes und die griechische Hagiographie" in *RQ* 11 (1897), 531–53; H. Zilliacus, "Zur stilistischen Umarbeitungstechnik des Symeon Metaphrastes" in *ByZ* 38 (1938), 333–50.

Theologian it acquired a prophet of a unique sort. Merely from the viewpoint of phenomenology, his importance is based on his having made the break-through from the mystical treatise to the entirely personal mystical confession or even hymn. As regards the sociology of his mysticism it should be noted that he always sought to prepare the way whereby it should move out of the monastery to the laity in the Church. But in regard to context he pursued a course which had probably never been unfamiliar in Byzantium but at first had difficulty in asserting itself *vis-à-vis* the strict line of Evagrian mysticism: the mysticism of the metaphysical feeling, of the αἴσθησις νοερά. That Messalian ideas stood as sponsors here can be disproved with difficulty, but in Diadochus of Photice the doctrine of the empirical nature of the mystical grace found an orthodox herald, and the introduction of the so-called Macarius homilies of Messalian origin into the treasure of the tradition of orthodox mysticism did more than was necessary.[21] The impetus of this mysticism, which wanted to "experience", and that as quickly as possible, united early with the method of the so-called "Prayer of Jesus", which was likewise not foreign to Simeon.[22] It culminated in light visions, which were so uniquely formulated in Simeon's language that one is induced and forced to seek their locale in an area midway between spiritual and corporal, which can scarcely be defined. Because Simeon was a hymnographer and ecstatic confessor and not a theorist, areas of the classical mysticism, such as the so-called "physical theory", the contemplative effort to penetrate, in patience and hope, into the divine *rationes* of creation and of history, certainly come off badly — something doubtless understandable in the case of the hymnographer, who only wants to express his last experience, but dangerous for the systematizers of the later period, who do not adequately take into consideration the literary character of Simeon's avowal.

In Simeon that enthusiasm of the old monachism again breaks out, which the hierarchy, probably incorrectly, thought had been expelled, the conviction of the special mediating role of the monk as the bearer of the Spirit between God and the sinner.[23] In this connection it is of only superficial interest to state that Simeon developed his own peculiarities fully after he had broken with the monastery of Studion, which, thanks to its strongly cenobitic outlook and hierarchical organization, apparently was remote from such trains of thought. For conflict with the hierarchy did not fail to occur: two interpretations of theology, an enthusiastic and irrational and a scholastic, opposed each other intransigently, because apparently neither Simeon nor his direct opposite, the above mentioned Stephen of Nicomedia, was willing

---

[21] Cf. I. Hausherr, "Les grands courants de la spiritualité hésychaste" in *OrChrP* 1 (1935), 114–38; F. Dörr, *Diadochus von Photike und die Messalianer* (Freiburg 1937).

[22] On the origin of this method, cf. I. Hausherr, *Noms du Christ et voies d'oraison* (Rome).

[23] He was the author of the little work on confession, falsely attributed to John Damascene, *PG* 95, 283–304; cf. K. Holl, *Enthusiasmus und Bussgewalt* (Leipzig 1898).

to admit the limitations of his own "method", and, correspondingly, two mutually exclusive interpretations of the nature and significance of the *charisma* in the Church. In the course of time the antitheses were smoothed away but their traces could not be entirely obliterated.[24]

If in Simeon's lifetime there was already evident the withdrawal from the Studites' cenobitic ideal, interested in ecclesiastical politics and living in an alternating relationship of friendship and hostility to the hierarchy, on the other hand this period meant "topographically" a shift of the centre of gravity of the Byzantine monastic world from Bithynia to Athos, the holy mountain of the future.[25] With the Muslim raids into Bithynia around the turn to the ninth century there apparently began a devastation of the monastic settlements on and around Olympus. And when as a consequence of the Byzantine offensive of the tenth century this danger could also be exorcised, the Seljuk invasion in the second half of the eleventh century again brought new and intensified dangers. The progress of monasticism on Athos is certainly connected with this.

The origins of the Athonian monastic colonization are covered with a darkness which is ever more transfigured by legend. Colonies of anchorites more or less entered the light of history in the ninth century. Rarely of any size, they eventually joined in a loosely organized community and discussed the most pressing community matters under a *protos*. A significant turning point in this development came with the founding of the so-called "Great Laura" on Athos by Saint Athanasius. Athanasius was born in Trebizond. Encouraged by his patron, the Emperor Nicephorus II Phocas, around 961 he built the first large monastery on Athos and gave it a rule, which conformed to that of the Studites but also borrowed from that of Saint Benedict. Athanasius not only succeeded, thanks to the imperial authority, in establishing his monastery devoted to the common life on the mountain, against the ill will of the anchorites already there, but in 971 or 972 he was able to induce Nicephorus's successor, the Emperor John I Tzimisces (969–76), to grant the whole monastic territory a *magna carta,* the so-called *Tragos,* extant in the

---

[24] *PG* 120, 321–687, contains the hymns only in Latin translation. The German translation by K. Kirchhoff. *Licht vom Licht* (Munich, 2nd ed. 1951), while a poetical work, does not reproduce much of the unique nature of Simeon's poetry. A collection of his works in the critical edition by V. Krivoshein, in the *Sources chrétiennes,* by now comprises three volumes (Paris 1963–65). Of the literature, besides Holl's book mentioned in the preceding footnote and Hausherr's in footnote 22, worthy of special mention are: H. M. Biedermann, *Das Menschenbild bei Symeon dem Jüngeren, dem Theologen* (Würzburg 1949), and D. L. Stathopulos, *Die Gottesliebe bei Symeon dem neuen Theologen* (dissertation, Bonn 1964); other data on the literature in *Beck* 583–87.

[25] An Athos bibliography of no less than 2634 titles is given by I. Doens, *Le millénaire du Mont Athos,* II (Venice–Chevetogne 1965), 336–495. Deserving of special mention are: F. Dölger (ed.), *Mönchsland Athos* (Munich 1943), R. M. Dawkins, *The Monks of Athos* (London 1936), and E. Amand de Mendieta, *La presqu'île des caloyers* (Bruges 1955).

original. In this the existence of a new large abbey in the overall structure of the administration of the mountain was duly taken into account.[26] Other foundations arose — of these the national monastery of the Georgians, the *Iberon,* should be mentioned — which also followed the cenobitic ideal, and a charter of the Emperor Constantine IX Monomachus of 1046 confirmed in general, despite all still existing opposition, the regulation of the community made by John I. Thus was the foundation laid for the amazing development of a monastic republic, which was soon to become the protagonist of Orthodoxy.

Besides these very promising beginnings of a new monastic territory, the monastic idea at this period also experienced the most serious injuries, which can be summarized under the juridical notion of charistikariate — the presenting of monasteries to lay persons by bishops or Patriarchs and Emperors. In some cases there may have been no doubt that the intention of the *charistikarioi* was, through the assumption of the monastery, to assure it a protection against oppression from all sides, especially from that of the *fiscus,* to correct evils that arose, and, with the best of intentions, to relieve the monks of the burden of secular business. But more frequently such a gift ministered only to greed. And in its origin the charistikariate must be seen as a secondary aspect of the attempt by the magnates, the *dynatoi,* to extend their possessions and also to invade the small holdings of the free peasant communities — an attempt with which imperial legislation had to contend again and again in the tenth century. The movement proceeded both from the top down and from the bottom up, that is, occasionally the peasants purchased the protection of a magnate from the pressure of taxation and the harshness of the state's impositions by a voluntary renunciation of their freedom and entry into a tenant relationship. And likewise in the case of the commendatory monasteries, at first the desire of the monasteries seems occasionally to have been directed to a protector. In any event, the movement established itself and led to serious harm to discipline in the monasteries and even to the monasteries' material substance.

The Abbot's power disappeared as the monks looked rather to the *charistikarios* than to their spiritual superior. The *charistikarios* now determined the number of monks in the monastery, the maximum provision for their material life, the necessities for the monastery's library and liturgy, ordinarily in the interest of his own income, which he intended to draw from the monastery. The invasion of the small farms of the peasants by the *dynatoi* could be achieved by some kind of legal fiction, such as adoption or bequest, but in the case of monastic property an ecclesiastical legal formality was needed, and

---

[26] Two *vitae* of Athanasius: a) ed. by L. Petit, in *AnBoll* 25 (1906), 5–89; b) ed. by M. J. Pomjalovskij (St. Petersburg 1895). Rules, last will, and charters can most conveniently be consulted in P. Meyer, *Die Haupturkunden für die Geschichte der Athos-Klöster* (Leipzig 1894).

this was supplied by the charistikariate. At first the grant was for a time, but it goes without saying that the *charistikarioi* sought to make the property hereditary. Thus were developed the intermediate forms, "for three lives", which only thinly concealed the yielding of the ecclesiastical authorities, whom one must probably regard as themselves allied to the *charistikarioi* by family ties. *De iure*, of course, there was never a transfer of ownership but only of authority. But since, despite some initial opposition, the right of the founders to the ownership of their churches was more and more firmly established even in the central Byzantine period, and the founder (*cf.* κτήτωρ = κτίστης) was more and more identified with the "benefactor" and "restorer" *(charistikarios)*, the rights of ownership of the founder, even when conditioned by the purpose of the foundation, were easily transferred to the *charistikarios*.[27] A Patriarch as energetic as Sisinnius II (996–8)[28] flatly forbade any such donation, but a successor, Sergius II (1009–19), had to annul this regulation and recognize the charistikariate with slight restrictions.[29] The Patriarch Alexius the Studite (1025–43) did indeed complain in great distress about the situation, but his regulations did not attack the roots of the evil and were content rather with quite general precautions.[30] And so the situation persisted and came to flower under the Comneni.

The power of the Patriarch grew, not with regard to the internal affairs of his Church, but in connection with the neighbouring churches and, in extent, through the gaining of new territories. The Byzantine advance against the Islamic East brought territorial gains of great importance. Ancient sees, which for centuries had figured only formally on the lists, could now be occupied again, and others, as new capitals of political provinces, were elevated also in ecclesiastical rank. In this process not even the frontiers of the ancient patriarchates were observed, but rather the primacy of the "Ecumenical Patriarch", who adopted this title even on his seal from the time of Caerularius, was powerfully stressed. Here imperial and patriarchal policy went hand in hand. If the Bulgarian archbishops had obtained autocephaly from Byzantium under their powerful Tsar Simeon (893–927), the victorious campaigns of the Byzantine Emperor Basil II (976–1025) put an end to it. Now the Archbishop of Ochrida was again subject to the Patriarch, and what autonomy he enjoyed was due to the Emperor's favour rather than to anything of his own. Any rights of Rome in ancient Illyricum were ignored

[27] The fundamental study of the institution is E. Herman, "Ricerche sulle istituzioni monastiche bizantine" in *OrChrP* 6 (1940), 293–375. Valuable as an introduction is R. Janin, "Le monachisme byzantin au moyen âge: Commende et typica" in *RÉB* 22 (1964), 5–44.

[28] *Grumel Reg,* no. 809; the text is lost.

[29] *Grumel Reg,* no. 821; cf. Balsamon, *Rhallis* II, 614.

[30] *Grumel Reg,* no. 833; text in *Rhallis* V, 20–24, and *PG* 119, 837–844.

by Byzantium now as before.[31] The Syrian Emperors seem to have removed Seleucia in Isauria from the patriarchate of Antioch, by exploiting the political situation, and even when Antioch itself was again a part of the Empire there seemed to be no necessity for making a change. Coloneia became the new metropolitan see of the Armenian upland between 1020 and 1035; it had previously belonged to the ancient metropolis of Sebaste, but was now the theme capital. Melitene also, the capital of old Armenia Secunda, the much contested Euphrates fortress, was again occupied by a metropolitan in the tenth century, but its connection with the Empire did not survive the Seljuk invasion. Other new metropolises were, for example, Kamachos in the Mesopotamian Theme, Keltzene, Taron, and Arsamosata, all in Armenia and all owing their ecclesiastical rank solely and briefly to their importance as frontier fortresses of the Empire. A consequence of the continuing rehellenization was also the establishing of metropolises in the Peloponnesus, such as Sparta in 1081–82 and, even earlier, Christianupolis.

As we have seen, it was Antioch especially that had to endure the encroachments of an Ecumenical Patriarch, thinking in terms of a primacy, on territories not his own. Following the reconquest of 969 the Emperors at first installed Patriarchs here at their discretion and had their candidates approved by the *Synodos endemusa* in Constantinople. The Patriarch John III (996–1020) even had himself consecrated at Constantinople, contrary to canon law, and then, as consecrated Patriarch, bestowed this right of consecration in principle on the see of Constantinople. Peter III (1052–56), who had made his career in the patriarchal service at Constantinople, protested against this spurious right, but unsuccessfully.[32] The jurisdictional primacy of the Ecumenical Patriarch was advancing under the shadow of the imperial authority.

---

[31] Cf., for example, J. Snegarov, *La fondation de l'église orthodoxe bulgare*, Εἰς μνήμην Σ. Λάμπρου (Athens 1935), 278–92; H. Gelzer in *ByZ* 2 (1893), 41 ff.
[32] Cf. V. Grumel, "Les patriarches grecs d'Antioche sous la seconde domination byzantine" in *ÉO* 33 (1934), 130–47.

SECTION THREE

Changes within the Christian West during the Gregorian Reform

CHAPTER 49

The New Shape of the Church:
Law and Organization Before Gratian

The struggle for the *libertas ecclesiae* aimed at something more comprehensive than a mere liberation from the power of the laity. The reformers wanted to find the way back to the ancient, pure Church, to the free play of the forces proper to her. For the sake of clarity it was especially necessary to investigate the juridical sources. Since the usual collections, especially that of Burchard of Worms, did not suffice for this purpose, they extracted from the papal *registra,* the *Ordines romani,* the *Liber diurnus,* from conciliar acts, from the writings of the Fathers and historical works, from imperial *privilegia* and the law of Justinian a wealth of hitherto unused texts, not to mention the pseudo-Isidorean forgeries, regarded as genuine, whose content was now for the first time entirely exploited. The material, combined into unsystematic collections, no longer extant — the *Collectio Britannica* is the nearest to them — seems to have been at the disposal of several canonists working from the time of Gregory VII; of itself it called for systematically arranged collections.

Thus, throughout the reform period new canonical compilations were coming into existence. They began, to mention only the more important, with the still unpublished Collection in Seventy-Four Titles, *Sententiae diversorum patrum,* which is probably to be ascribed to Humbert of Silva Candida and to the period before Gregory VII.[1] From the time of Gregory VII, Cardinal Atto composed the *Breviarium* or *Capitulare;* Anselm of Lucca, Gregory's friend and co-worker (d. 1086), in the last years of his life the much used and important *Collectio canonum;* Cardinal Deusdedit around 1087 a likewise noteworthy collection of canons, which was oriented rather to the Roman Church; a few years later Bonizo of Sutri, another strict Gregorian,

---

[1] For the bibliography on the collections, see the Sources and the Literature for this chapter. Michel's view as to the time of the "Collection in Seventy-Four Titles" finds support in the fact established by M. L. Levillain, "Saint-Denis à l'époque mérovingienne" in *BECh* 87 (1926), 299–324, that Saint-Denis possessed a manuscript of the collection even before 1065. Reference by C. Dereine, "L'école canonique liégeoise" in *Ann. du congrès arch. et hist. de Tournai* (1949), 2, footnote 2.

the *Liber de vita christiana;* and finally, between 1105 and 1113, Cardinal Gregory, the *Polycarpus.* In France the great canonist, Ivo of Chartres, published three collections between 1094 and 1096: the *Collectio trium partium,* the *Decretum,* based on it and on Burchard of Worms, and the shorter, more practical, and hence more widespread *Panormia.* In Spain there appeared between 1110 and 1120 the *Collectio Caesaraugustana,* which borrowed from Ivo and at the same time from the Gregorian collections and on which other compilations depended.

The authors of these private works were confronted with the difficult problem of separating the authentic from the false or from what was valid only locally. Although in the general view the norm lay with the papacy, it still needed a more precise definition. The demand of a few radicals, that only those laws which had been issued or approved by the Popes should be adopted, proved to be inadequate. Hence the more judicious recognized all texts which did not contradict the laws of the Roman Church; accordingly, they envisaged the idea of a *ius commune* as the totality of a somehow coherent legal system that culminated in the authority of the Holy See, without implying that every particular had to be positively decreed by the papacy.[2] Naturally in this abundantly unclear principle of choice there were some contradictions among individual canons. To solve them became at times the more urgent task. For this the canonists were not merely satisfied with a hierarchical gradation of individual texts; they also worked out important rules of textual criticism and eventually instituted the dialectical method in order to cancel the contradictions with distinctions and subdistinctions. Bernold of Sankt Blasien, Ivo of Chartres, and finally Alger of Liège were especially concerned with establishing a method of concordance. The science of canon law began slowly to pervade intellectually the source material at hand in the collections, but the sought for *concordantia discordantium canonum* was not achieved until around 1140 with the *Decretum* of Gratian.

The struggle for an ecclesiastical legal system, motivated by the understanding that for canon law the early mediaeval awareness, rooted in customary law, did not suffice, announced a new age. Its onward pressing *élan* assured the Church a wide lead over what was possible to the states. Gradually recognized by all Christian countries of the West, the canon law, always assuming more stable forms, fashioned the Church into a truly supranational power structure. This had as a consequence that the supreme guardian and interpreter of ecclesiastical law, the Pope, grew to overshadow the ruling position of the Emperor and the kings, a position which from the time of Alexander III

---

[2] Cf. S. Kuttner, "Liber canonicus. A note on 'Dictatus Papae' c. 17" in *StudGreg* II (1947), 389–97; J. M. Salgrado, "La méthode d'interprétation du droit en usage chez les canonistes d'origine à Urbain II" in *Revue d'Université d'Ottawa* 22 (1952), 23*–35*; R. Losada Cosme, "La unificación interna del derecho y las colecciones anteriores a Graziano" in *Rev. Españ. de derecho canón.* 10 (1955), 353–82.

was consolidated and extended by a steadily increasing decretal activity. Nevertheless, it would be ill-advised to see the development of ecclesiastical law as directed merely to the exaltation of the papal power. What the reformers stressed, not without sharp criticism of the early Middle Ages, was the fundamental hierarchical principle of the Church, in no sense restricted to the Pope. By making it the juridical form of the Church, they achieved a sharper separation between laity and priesthood and prepared for a more compact and, so to speak, corporative association of clerics as the real representatives of the Church.

Despite the clericalization now getting under way, the laity did not simply become hearers and flunkies. Besides their right to the administration of certain Sacraments, which was ever more elaborated by the canonists, they possessed not inconsiderable powers in questions of the clergy or of ecclesiastical administration. Thus, for example, it pertained to the so-called synodal witnesses, as spokesmen of the people, publicly to criticize the holders of ecclesiastical office and their activity to the visitor. Not a few parish congregations acquired an effective share in ecclesiastical life by certain locally different rights of control. And if the people in the long run lost their now meaningless right to elect the bishop, they still elected their pastor in many more places than earlier research admitted. In the flourishing cities, with their growing number of parishes, the citizens were able to gain not only the right of presentation or nomination but also influence on the administration of ecclesiastical property and control of the property of foundations.

Proprietorship of churches was, it is true, taken away from the laity, at least in principle, after the attempt, made occasionally in the reform period, to distinguish between the temporalities *(ecclesia)* and the spiritualities *(altare)* in regard to the lesser churches also had failed. The first two Lateran Councils thus held to the principle that lay persons must not possess any ecclesiastical property and that the lesser benefices were to be granted by the bishop. This claim was favoured by the decay of the right of proprietorship of churches, which had meanwhile got under way, its fragmentation, through supersaturation, into purely individual rights — into the *ius fundi,* the *ius regaliae* and *ius spolii* (that is, the right to the revenues during a vacancy and the right to the estate of the dead cleric), into rights to particular ecclesiastical revenues, such as tithes and offerings, into the right of nomination and conferring of benefices, into the right of bestowing ecclesiastical office. Thus Gratian and his sucessors down to Alexander III were able to bring about a solution in keeping with the hierarchical principle. They replaced the right of proprietorship with the *patronatus* subject to ecclesiastical legislation as *ius spirituali annexum* (Alexander III). On the one hand this maintained the Church's right of proprietorship; on the other hand, out of gratitude for the foundation, it conceded to the previous proprietor the right of presentation of the cleric to be instituted and specified honorary rights, but it likewise imposed obligations, such as a subsidiary construction burden. Actually the whole thing remained to a great extent mere theory; in practice the old right of proprietorship lived on everywhere, more or less energetically.

The history of the proprietary church system probably shows how laboriously the reform made its way to the lower levels of the ecclesiastical organization. Thus the lesser clergy remained essentially bound by the old relationships, despite their greater dependence on the ecclesiastical offices above them. The hierarchical principle had a graduated operation: whereas it produced its full effect in the case of the papacy, its force was already diminished in regard to the bishops. Free episcopal election was undoubtedly a lasting achievement of the reform. The amount of influence still allowed to rulers could be eliminated later in some countries — by Innocent III in England and Germany. The people's share became insignificant during the twelfth century, so that the election was carried out chiefly by the diocesan clergy and, from the end of the century, by the cathedral chapter alone. And yet the frequent disputed elections, often due not to oppositions within the church but to those springing from state and family politics, show how much the election still depended on secular factors.

And the bishop's own authority was strictly limited. Competing with it was the growing power of archdeacons, reaching its peak in the thirteenth century, not only in jurisdiction but also in important administrative tasks, such as visitation of and appointments to parishes, holding of synods, and so forth. Episcopal authority suffered a more painful, because enduring, loss at the hands of the cathedral chapter, which was able in the thirteenth century to secure a share in the government of the diocese. Bishops would certainly not have completely excluded these rivals of theirs, but perhaps they would have been better able to limit them if they had not been distracted, especially in Germany, by state and territorial political interests. Thus they found themselves in no position to keep pace adequately, through the systematic completion of their own proper hierarchical position, with the new development of the ecclesiastical organization, beginning about the time of Alexander III, which was powerfully to display the Pope's monarchical power.

In the early twelfth century, now under consideration, the relations between Pope and bishop were as yet no real problem. Although the reform Popes had often dealt sternly enough with individual bishops, these emergency measures must not be regarded as aimed at episcopal power as such. The more the Investiture Controversy neared its end, the more the Popes endeavoured to show regard for the rights of the bishops. Not only the First Lateran Council, already discussed, but the noteworthy prudence of Calixtus II and his immediate successors in regard to monastic exemption clearly indicate this. And is it not characteristic of the spirit of the age that the mightily flourishing new Orders of the Cistercians and the canons regular wanted to be subject to the local bishops, the canons regular because of their natural bond with the episcopate, the Cistercians because of the idealism of their period of foundation, and idealism that would quickly fade?[3] In any event there could be as yet no question of a tendency to bind the whole episcopate directly to Rome as far as possible. If the Pope occasionally decided the disputed election of a bishop not directly subject to him, if he officiated at the consecration and then required the customary oath of obedience, the initiative here lay usually with the bishop and his faction.

Much less favourable was the position of the metropolitans. From the Carolingian period it had become the custom that they requested the pallium from the Pope. Proceeding from this, the reform Popes began soon after the middle of the eleventh century to demand that new archbishops receive the pallium in person. With its solemn investiture was included gradually, more commonly from Paschal II, the taking of an oath of obedience, modelled on the oath of vassalage, that is, of an oath which earlier the suffragans of the Roman Church and a few other, mostly Italian, bishops had had to take according to an older formula. The new formula included also the obligation of the periodic *visitatio liminum apostolorum*.[4] The new development meant the triumph of the old Roman view, already to be discerned in the later Carolingian period, that the exercise of the metropolitan right of consecration depended on the possession of the pallium. The connection with Rome, secured symbolically and juridically, made it easy to regard the metropolitan authority as a participation in the universal authority of the Pope. This did not necessarily involve a diminution of archiepiscopal powers. As a matter of fact, at first most rights remained intact, and they were even extended by the right of devolution, established in 1080 for irregular episcopal elections. Just the same, metropolitans meant less in practice than they had meant in the early Middle Ages. The reason must be sought in the bishops rather than in the Popes. Out of the old opposition supported by the spirit of pseudo-Isidore, many bishops preferred, in juridical matters, to apply directly or by appeal to the Holy See.

The primates making their appearance from the time of Gregory VII possessed virtually no influence. Mention has already been made of this institution, which was conceived as a voluntary tribunal of appeals. Its origin was a scholarly pseudo-Isidorean invention, which, having recourse to the Roman provincial divisions in Gaul, ascribed to the metropolitans of the respective "first" provinces, such as *Lugdunensis Prima,* the position of primate or patriarch over the metropolitans of the subordinate provinces of the same name, for example, *Lugdunensis Secunda* and so forth. The idea

[3] G. Schreiber, *Kurie und Kloster im 12. Jahrhundert,* I (Stuttgart 1910), 100–08, 83–91; on the Pope's regard for episcopal rights, cf. ibid. 58–63, 65–74, 77f., 112f., 177–79; F. J. Schmale, *Studien zum Schisma des Jahres 1130* (Cologne–Graz 1961), *passim.*

[4] T. Gottlob, *Der kirchliche Amtseid der Bischöfe* (Bonn 1936); E. H. Kantorowicz, *The King's Two Bodies* (Princeton 1957), 348–50; J. B. Sägmüller, "Die Visitatio liminum bis Bonifaz VIII." in *ThQ* 82 (1900), 69–117. On the pallium, see Chapter 35, footnote 4.

did not acquire reality until the reform period. The initiative probably proceeded not from the papacy but from French archbishops of a *prima sedes,* who, on the basis of pseudo-Isidore, regarded as genuine, thought that they could reclaim an ancient right. Once Gebuin of Lyons had obtained the primacy for his see in 1079, the erecting of other primatial sees, at least in France, was only a question of time: they came into existence for Narbonne in 1097, for Bourges under Paschal II, for Vienne in 1119. Outside France the Popes elevated to the same position the churches of Toledo in 1088, Salerno in 1098, Pisa in 1138, Grado in 1155; Canterbury's claim foundered on York's opposition. It is true that honorary precedence was gained rather than real power. Little interest was displayed for the envisaged possibility of appeal. And if recourse was had to it, the metropolitans thus affected offered active or passive resistance.

Accordingly, since the bishops were not interested in a strong metropolitan authority nor the metropolitans in any kind of primatial authority, even only a weak one, the hierarchical principle, with its striving for a comprehensive juridical unity of the Church, especially benefited the summit — the papacy. The reform period brought the definitive change. In the struggle for the *libertas ecclesiae* the Roman Church had finally been able to realize the freedom proper to her, that is, her primatial claims based on genuine or what was regarded as genuine tradition. These comprised especially: free papal election, now sufficiently assured both in regard to the German ruler, who in the course of the Investiture Controversy lost the right of consent as recognized earlier by Nicholas II, and in regard to the Roman people and clergy, who still shared in the election but were restricted and slowly pushed aside by the prerogatives of the cardinals; then, the exclusive right to convoke general synods, which were arranged by the reform Popes at Rome or elsewhere in place of the earlier Roman provincial synods and constituted the preliminaries to the general councils of the Middle Ages — Innocent III was the first to identify the Fourth Lateran Council intentionally with the ancient ecumenical councils; and, finally, the principle of supreme legislative, judicial, and administrative authority, to the extent that it was possible to seize upon it in tradition.

In the present state of research it is not always easy to define the extent of this by no means unlimited fulness of power, further developed by the decretal law, for the period of the reform and the early twelfth century. If, for example, Gregory VII claimed to change ancient canons in cases of necessity, he was not claiming any properly legislative right;[5] only the development begun with Gratian created the presuppositions for this. And the right of granting privileges and dispensations, despite some initial starts, as with Ivo

---

[5] Cf. S. Kuttner, *op. cit.* 396, footnote 42; G. Ladner, "Two Gregorian Letters" in *StudGreg* V (1956), 225–42.

of Chartres for papal dispensation, was not yet adequately clarified. More or less the following rights were then valid for the supreme judicial power: the Pope's immunity from trial, except in the case of heresy,[6] his judicial competence both for exempt monasteries and for all bishops and, in general, for all *causae maiores,* and, finally, the position of the Roman Church as the supreme court of appeals. The primatial administrative rights comprised chiefly the basic supreme supervision, the establishing, defining, and suppressing of dioceses, the transfer of a religious community to another Order, the granting of exemption to monasteries, the exerting of influence on the filling of sees, made possible by a process instituted at the Holy See or by use of the right of devolution, which the Roman Synod of 1080 had granted to the Pope as well as to the metropolitan for the case of irregular episcopal elections. Further possibilities of intervention were added from the end of the twelfth century by the legal stabilization of episcopal elections. In like manner, the rights to the filling of lesser benefices and the constituting of a papal sovereignty over finance and the religious Orders belong to the later development beginning with the decretal law.

If the papal monarchy was completed only later, still the reform assisted it toward the break-through and brought to an end the extensive independence of the early mediaeval episcopate. All the more should it be observed how little resistance it encountered in this. To be sure, there was no lack of angry protests in regard to particular measures or even in regard to the basic attitude of Gregory VII, who, according to the repudiation of 1076, sought to wrest all power from the bishops so far as he could; particular rights of the Pope were questioned in principle; and even reformers like Ivo of Chartres occasionally wished for a careful defining of papal competence. But, on the whole, friends and foes were agreed, and strict anti-Gregorians recognized the Roman primacy as much as did its direct defenders.[7] Only one writer was bold enough to lay the axe to the roots: the Norman Anonymous.[8] According to him, the primacy was not a divine institution but one created by men because of Rome's being the capital of the world, and hence in no sense was it something necessary for salvation; all bishops were vicars of

[6] According to the clear demonstration by J. Ryan, "Cardinal Humbert: De s. Romana ecclesia. Relics of Roman-Byzantine Relations 1053–1054" in *MS* 20 (1958), 206–38 (especially 219–24), the heresy clause was not coined by Humbert, as W. Ullmann, "Cardinal Humbert and the Ecclesia Romana" in *StudGreg* IV (1954), 111–27, stated, but was taken by him from the ecclesiastical tradition of the late Carolingian period, without his having interpreted it in the strict sense. For the late Carolingian tradition, cf. Chapter 35, footnote 17.

[7] Cf. K. Mirbt, *Die Publizistik im Zeitalter Gregors VII.* (Leipzig 1894), 553.

[8] Especially in Treatises III, V–VI, in *MGLiblit* III, 656–62, 679–86; on the author, cf. H. Scherrinski, *Untersuchungen zum sogenannten Anonymus von York* (Würzburg 1940); P. de Lapparent, "Un précurseur de la réforme anglaise, l'Anonyme de York" in *AHD* 15 (1946), 149–68; G. H. Williams, *The Norman Anonymous of 1100 A.D. Towards the Identification and Evaluation of the so-called Anonymus of York* (Cambridge, Mass. 1951).

Christ and thus to be judged by no one. The real mother of all the churches was not Rome but Jerusalem. Whoever sought to create a higher authority split the one Church. This language was so unprecedented that it faded away into empty space.

It was not so much the principle of the primacy as such as its practical application that the reform established. That this occurred was to a great extent due to the papal legates. Already in the earliest periods the Roman Church had dispatched legates with particular commissions, and from the fifth to the eighth century it had even maintained permanent representatives, the *apocrisiarii,* at the imperial Byzantine court and at that of the Exarch in Ravenna. Furthermore, it had elevated Boniface and other heralds of the Gospel as missionary legates and as early as the fifth and sixth centuries had entrusted outstanding bishops of remote lands with an apostolic vicariate. This stream of tradition, almost choked off, was put to use from about 1056 by the reform Popes for the system of legates.

While it is true that the old principle remained in force — that legates should receive as much authority as their assignment required — still, since the comprehensive reform work demanded general powers, the legates appointed for this, usually cardinals or local bishops, were made vicars of the Pope and disposed of the full primatial authority to the extent that this was then claimed by Rome. Of course, there were also legates with special tasks; they were chosen preponderantly from lower clerics. The activity of reform legates consisted principally of visitations and the holding of synods, in connection with which the opposition was often broken by stern punishments, even deposition, and by interventions in the filling of sees. The Popes seem not yet to have reserved certain details of jurisdiction to themselves, as they did later, but they still did not feel bound by the decisions of their legates. The legates' activity, competing with episcopal and metropolitan functions, was restricted to the extent that the reform produced results and that the Popes could count on the co-operation of the bishops. Calixtus II's instruction to the legate in Germany, William of Palestrina, to proceed "inoffensa caritate", must have ranked as a guiding principle for the early twelfth century.

A real differentiation of classes of legates had not yet been made. It began only with Alexander III and amounted to the following groups: *legati a latere,* equipped with a wealth of special rights, which developed into a *iurisdictio ordinaria; legati missi,* with less authority; *nuntii apostolici* for particular assignments; *vicarii apostolici* or *legati nati,* who were local archbishops and bishops.

Still more decisive was to be the effect of another product of the reform — the College of Cardinals. Its origin is disputed.[9] From the fifth century the

---

[9] The following is based on the trail-blazing study by Klewitz and the work of Kuttner that continued it; see the Literature for this chapter.

priests of the Roman titular churches had to provide a weekly liturgical ministry for the cemeterial basilicas of San Pietro, San Paolo, and San Lorenzo, and then also for Santa Maria Maggiore and San Giovanni in Laterano. In the eighth century probably, this service was altered to the extent that thereafter it was attended to in the Lateran basilica by seven bishops of the nearby dioceses and in the other four basilicas by the priests of the titular churches which had been increased, in groups of seven, to the number of twenty-eight. Since from the time of Gregory the Great clerics who were employed in, or incardinated into, another church than that from which they came were called *cardinales,* this title was now used also for the bishops and priests who were made use of in the Roman weekly ministry. Their functions were purely liturgical, and so they made no claim to any special position of authority in the Roman Church.

There were now also "cardinals" in many churches inside and outside Italy; they must not be confused with the Roman cardinals. The most important group among them was made up of the so-called *presbyteri de cardine;* their precedence consisted in this, that their churches, as opposed to private oratories and proprietary churches, belonged to the bishopric or to the cathedral and hence were attached to the pivot *(cardo)* of the diocese.[10] Both ideas must be borne in mind in the formation of the College of Cardinals. Since the Popes had to provide the enthusiasts for reform whom they gathered around themselves with important Roman churches, they usually enrolled them among the cardinal bishops and cardinal priests. Occupied with reform duties, the new cardinals naturally dissociated themselves from the duties of the hebdomadal ministry, to which of itself the possession of their churches obliged them. As co-responsible representatives of the Roman Church, the pivot of the Universal Church, they thus became *episcopi* or *presbyteri cardinis romani.*

The beginning was made by the Cardinal-Bishops; the papal election decree of 1059 elevated them for the period of the vacancy to be the actual representatives of the Roman Church. The Cardinal-Priests, no less zealous assistants in the reform struggle, won their position in the time of the Anti-pope Clement III and of Pope Urban II. For virtually only the Gregorian Cardinal-Priests had gone over to Clement, with whom they acquired such influence that Urban II had to have the same consideration for the Cardinal-Priests who adhered to him. Finally, Cardinal-Deacons also made their appearance under both claimants, and in the time of Paschal II they numbered eighteen. How this came about is controverted. The deacons originally numbered seven but the suppression of the archdeacon reduced them to six.

---

[10] This idea was not entirely foreign to early mediaeval Roman and papal sources. Other "cardinals" were of liturgical origin. Thus the Popes granted to a few cathedrals, the first being Magdeburg in 968, a cardinal clergy with liturgical prerogatives, while something similar occurred in France by virtue of customary law. See S. Kuttner in *Tr* 3 (1945), 165–72.

They had long pertained to the Lateran basilica and performed both liturgical and administrative functions for the Pope. In the course of the general development they acquired the rank of cardinals. There is, however, less insight into why with them were associated the twelve so-called regionary deacons, all the more since we know nothing for certain about this group. The origin of this last mentioned body, which cannot be fixed as to time, was somehow connected with the new regionary division of the city, which probably occurred in the tenth century.

Under Paschal II the College of Cardinals reached its final complement with seven (later six) bishops, twenty-eight priests, and eighteen deacons. International in composition, it thereafter stood at the Pope's side as an advisory and assisting institution and was able to strengthen its influence in the succeeding period, especially during the Schism of 1130–38, but at the same time no clear regulation of its right as co-speaker with relation to the papacy was reached. The cardinals' advisory function became so important, at least in consistory, that the Popes felt they could dispense with more frequent general synods. The more stable organization that was slowly being prepared included a treasury belonging to the college and administered by the Cardinal *Camerlengo* and a more precise regulation of the revenues.

The centralizing exertions of the reform papacy necessarily had to transform the old administrative organs. The history of the papal chancery has already been discussed. Now it gradually freed itself from any connection with Rome's *scriniarii*. The frequent papal travels, beginning with Leo IX, of themselves brought it about that the documents to be issued *en route* were engrossed by the chaplains accompanying the Pope — the *scriniarii* concerned with Roman private documents naturally did not come along — or by scribes of the country in question. The next step quickly followed: the librarian-chancellor appointed one and later two and on occasion more clerics of the Lateran palace as permanent *scriptores* and thus laid the ground for an official college of clerical *scriptores,* which in the long run, and definitively from the assumption of office by the Chancellor Aimeric in April 1123, deprived the urban *scriniarii* of any possibility of participating and even of the engrossing of solemn *privilegia* issued in Rome, hitherto allowed them. The new development also revolutionized papal diplomatics. The curial hand employed by the *scriniarii* was replaced by the Carolingian minuscule, soon elaborated to meet the chancery's requirements. A new formal language, resuming the forgotten rhythmic rules of the *cursus latinus,* arose and new types were added to the old, remodelled charters. When in 1118 the Chancellor John of Gaetà ascended the papal throne as Gelasius II, the new chancery tradition was firmly established, thanks to his thirty-years' activity. Its membership drawn from the Catholic world, headed by a cardinal until toward the close of the twelfth century and from time to time more carefully organized, into the

fourteenth century the chancery represented the most important administrative office of the papacy.

Furthermore, the financial system was reorganized. Following the model
of Cluny, Urban II subordinated it to a *camerarius* and thereby founded the
Camera apostolica. The at first modest office acquired around 1140, in addition
to the administration of the treasury, that of the library and archives, and
Hadrian IV's *camerlengo,* Cardinal Boso, assumed the care of papal property
in the Papal State. From then on progress was continuous. The *camerlengo*
acquired the rank of highest papal court official, and in the thirteenth and
fourteenth centuries the *Camera* was at least to limit the importance of the
chancery, if it did not entirely surpass it.

There were perhaps papal chaplains even before the reform, but one may
probably speak of a papal *capella* in the strict sense only from the end of the
eleventh century. This institution, modelled on that of royal and episcopal
courts, affected the development of the Roman Curia to the extent that the
clerics associated in it could be employed in any service and in any newly
created office. Thus the Pope at last had a separate court of his own, detached
from the city of Rome, which he could organize at his discretion. Hence it
was not pure accident that, from the end of the eleventh century, in place of
the old terminology, *sacrum palatium Lateranense,* the term still current, *Curia
Romana,* established itself. It placed the papal court on a footing of equality
with the Germanic-Romance *Curia Regis.* The equality was so consistently
aspired after that the Popes from Urban II even introduced the court offices
of steward, cupbearer, and so forth, though these acquired no importance.
With the possibility of the free development of its administrative apparatus,
the reform papacy had taken a decisive step forward.

CHAPTER 50

The New Relationship of the Church to Western Christendom

The hierarchical principle of the reform had to do, not with the Church
such as we understand her today as an institution distinct from state and
society, but with the *ecclesia universalis* coming down from the early Middle
Ages and including state and society. The reformers clung throughout to
this religious and political structural unity, but in it they sought to bring
eventually to full prominence the aspect of religious value. And since priests
were responsible for religious matters, they demanded that the *Sacerdotium,*
through its hierarchical summit, the Pope, should lead the Christian world.

They thus established a new relationship to Christian kingship. The
theocracy exercised by secular rulers appeared to them to pervert the right

436

order; it contradicted the higher value and the higher function of the priestly office. As proofs were again brought forth the ancient notions stressing priestly pre-eminence: the comparison of gold with lead, of sun with moon, of soul with body, or the distinction between the life-giving priestly function and the royal function linked with the terror of the sword, or the directly divine origin of the priesthood *vis-à-vis* kingship, made necessary by original sin, established by men merely with God's assent, and often misused under the influence of original sin. But all of this would have profited little, had not the sacramental character of the anointed kingship, in the sense of a specific participation in the priesthood and the kingship of Christ, been denied by the reformers. For them, thinking in strictly hierarchical categories, the secular ruler was a layman, who, even though he was the holder of an important function in the *ecclesia universalis,* had to stand, not over, not beside, but below priests.

Just how this relation of dependence was to be explained concretely was not systematically worked out by Gregory VII and his friends — this was only done in the succeeding two centuries — but they claimed for the priesthood the right to decide on the qualifications of a ruler, especially if he proved to be intolerable because of a godless, tyrannical government. For this case Gregory VII demanded the judicial competence of the Pope, as the supreme shepherd of souls, endowed with the power to bind and loose, and also the right to excommunicate, to absolve from oaths of loyalty, and to depose. While his ideas were not unchallenged, they pretty generally prevailed, apart from the claim to depose, which encountered serious doubt even in ecclesiastical circles and was not again put into practice by a Pope until 1245. Nevertheless, rulers affected by the Church's coercive power again and again refused obedience.[1]

The incisive initiative of the reform could not but shake violently the structure of the Western world. The adherents of kingship naturally showed fight. To the extent that they were defending the old theocracy, as especially the Norman Anonymous at the beginning of the twelfth century sought to

---

[1] Gregory VII was not a systematic thinker. His undoubtedly Augustinian outlook lacked precision. Although he did not know a proper sphere of what belonged to the state, still he derived the political power of a Christian king from God; on the doctrine of the diabolical origin of secular rule, attributed to him, cf. A. Nitschke in *StudGreg* 5 (1950), 190 f. From such an attitude, hierocratically oriented but spiritualistic and not sufficiently differentiated, opposed conclusions can be drawn, and they were drawn as soon as one began, from the time of Gratian, to investigate the problem of the relations between *Regnum* and *Sacerdotium* more precisely. The two letters containing Gregory's claim to depose are in *Reg*, IV, 4, VIII, 21; in Caspar's ed., 293–97, 544–63. On Gregory's political doctrine, cf. the Literature for Chapter 44. On the doctrine of the reformers in general, cf. Voosen (in the Literature for this chapter), *passim* (with further bibliography); A. Fliche, *La réforme grégorienne,* 3 vols. (Louvain 1924–37), *passim;* C. Mirbt, *Die Publizistik im Zeitalter Gregors VII.* (Leipzig 1894); A. Fauser, *Die Publizisten des Investiturstreites* (Munich 1935).

do in far too bold dialectics,[2] they were, of course, fighting a lost battle. The theocracy had become antiquated. But the West was in the process of out-growing the early mediaeval stage of development of the coherence and of perfecting new, differentiated social forms.

This process had an effect on the reform. The West was not disposed merely to accept a papal hierocracy in exchange for the obsolete royal theocracy, and Gregory VII's radically religious impetus moved without any doubt in a hierocratic direction. Gregory himself released the counter-forces which now appeared. In his one-sided spiritual thought what mattered basically was merely the spiritual and political will of the *ecclesia universalis,* and for it the ecclesiastical authority should thereafter be responsible. He thereby unintentionally split the striving for a uniform goal on the part of the earlier *ecclesia universalis;* for, previously, spiritual-political and secular-political aims had been so intimately interwoven that even a secular ruler could see to the religious and political total goal. Gregory, to be sure, wanted to preserve unity by demanding that kings entirely subordinate their interests to the spiritual-political goal, but the rulers agreed to this only under conditions. For their part, they now took up the secular-political aim and developed it to relative autonomy.

The course of the Investiture Controversy, the at times clearer distinction achieved by rulers between spiritual office and *temporalia,* is an example of what the development amounted to. Despite their only too conservative clinging to outdated theocratic rights, the German and Italian defenders of Henry IV showed a good instinct for the difficulty of their time when to the claim of the reformers they opposed the traditional Gelasian principle, never given up even in the early Middle Ages, of the twofold division of power and stressed that not only the priest but also the king received his power directly from God. Their position, which was by no means irreconcilable with that of Gregory VII and his followers, was further strengthened from time to time in the future.

Good assistance in this connection was provided by Roman law; already made use of in the Investiture Controversy, it would be further exploited by the schools of legists soon to flourish. And so the *Regnum* slowly trans-formed its earlier rule, based on anointing and service to the *ecclesia universalis,*

---

[2] To the Norman Anonymous the Church is the bride, not of *Christus Sacerdos,* but of *Christus Rex.* Since both priests and kings are elevated by sacramental consecration above the natural person-being to a grace-bestowing person, they represent the God-Man Christ in the sense that the priest is associated with the human, suffering nature of Christ, but the king with the divine, glorified nature of the Redeemer. On the basis of these two premises the author assigns to the secular ruler the highest position in the Church: the king has to institute priests and transmit to them, by virtue of his sacramentally established right, both the administration of Church property and the power to govern God's people; he summons and directs councils; in general he presides over the Church as *pastor, magister, custos, defensor, ordinator, liberator.* Cf. the treatises IV–V in *MGLiblit* III, 662–79, 684–86.

into a kingship by divine right, into a rule over an autonomous sphere of law and action, to be governed by virtue of the *potestas* directly conferred by God, which it from time to time systematically built up during the twelfth and thirteenth centuries and began to lead toward sovereignty. Here it was competing basically with that striving of the papacy, becoming ever clearer in the post-Gratian period, to bring the juridical sphere subordinate to it together as firmly as possible into a *regnum ecclesiasticum* under its monarchical power. Rulers were unwilling simply to be inferior even in regard to the sacred. Their being degraded to the lay state within the Church caused them to elaborate a theory of divine right, which was no longer based on a specifically ecclesiastical foundation but was even partly fed by originally pagan forces, as these survived, on the one hand, in Roman imperial law with its sanctification of ruler, law, and Empire, and, on the other hand, in the Germanic magical ideas of the royal "healing power", attached to the royal family.[3]

The process of the separation of *Regnum* and *Sacerdotium* took its time. If the early mediaeval "two-in-oneness" of the two powers, only functionally distinct and understood as if they were professions, was now slowly replaced by the sharper antithesis between two powers directly from God and ruling autonomous spheres of public law, the West still had to travel a long stretch before being confronted at the beginning of modern times with the ontologically distinct communities of Church and state. Despite a progressive decay, the unity of the *ecclesia universalis,* or *christianitas,* overlapping and embracing both spheres of law, remained throughout the twelfth and thirteenth centuries a basic fact of social and political life.

Before the Investiture Controversy the German Emperors, in spite of the indifferent or even negative attitude generally assumed outside Germany, had somehow represented the unity of the West. Afterwards they continued to insist that they were the leaders of Christendom, at least within the secular sphere, but the change that had meanwhile come over the West made their claim ever more questionable. The *regna,* growing stronger from the twelfth century and concerned for their autonomy, allowed the Emperor merely an honorary precedence but no encroaching jurisdictional power. And his relationship to the Roman Church had been reversed in the Investiture Controversy: the Emperor thereafter possessed no further rights over the

---

[3] F. Kern, *Gottesgnadentum,* 94–120, 213–16; M. Bloch, *Les rois thaumaturges* (Strasbourg 1924); P. E. Schramm, *Der König von Frankreich,* I (Darmstadt, 2nd ed. 1960), 145–55; id., *Geschichte des englischen Königtums,* 122–26. It is no accident that the first evidence for cures of scrofula by French and English Kings and for oil from heaven are from the early twelfth century. On royal curing powers, cf. K. Hauck, "Geblütsheiligkeit" in *Liber Floridus, Festschrift für P. Lehmann* (St. Ottilien 1950), 187–240. On the "law-centred kingship" of the twelfth and thirteenth centuries, see the impressive treatment by H. E. Kantorowicz, *The King's Two Bodies* (Princeton 1957), 87–192.

Pope, but the Pope did over the Emperor, who stood in need of anointing and crowning and was obliged to protect the Roman Church. What the brilliance of the *Imperium* had hitherto eclipsed now emerged into full light: the unity of the West was based ultimately on the common faith and on membership in the same Church. This foundation gained from the time of the reform an entirely new solidity through the supranational unification of the ecclesiastical hierarchy and the constructing of a common canon law recognized in all Christian countries. Thus the Church became the real bearer, and the papacy at her head became the leader, of Western Christendom.

Not only the supranational extent of his jurisdiction but also the nature and manner of his exercise of power lifted the Pope far above Emperor and kings. While it took a long time in most kingdoms before the power of the state adequately permeated the feudal classes to reach every subject more or less directly, the papacy had it easier from the start. Its jurisdiction extended not merely to the bishops and through them to their diocesans, but also directly to each individual Christian. Priests, monks, and lay persons turned this to account from the beginning of the twelfth century by taking their legal cases to Rome, directly or by appeal.

And if there was a secular field of law, always acquiring greater independence, still pre-eminence belonged to the spiritual field of law. The always valid principle of the Catholic doctrine of the state, whereby state and society are bound by the divine and the moral law and the interpretation of this law pertains to the Church, could not but have a much more powerful impact in the twelfth and thirteenth centuries than would be possible today. The dependence of the secular sphere of law was then so extensive that royal decrees which contradicted canon law in important matters could be declared null by the Church. In this way the Church's influence extended far into what was earthly. The Church laid down the norms for fundamental problems of human social life, for example, for the lawfulness of interest, of commercial profit, or of levying taxes. Marriage cases were subject to her authority almost exclusively; likewise, the oath, then so important for public and private life, from which the Church alone could dispense in specific cases. The educational system and many institutions of charity were under her control. Sharing responsibility for the welfare of the Christian people, the Church had always taken an interest in peace among the faithful to the extent that she was able to compete with the secular authorities. The peace initiative which the French clergy had assumed since the beginning of the eleventh century was taken up by the reform papacy under Urban II; laws dealing with the Peace of God were proclaimed at general synods. In the succeeding period the Popes took a further step: they sought from time to time to make peace among warring princes and not rarely were even invited to do so by at least one of the parties.

Finally, the Church's penal and coercive power acquired an unusually great importance. Excommunication and interdict, now decreed even against kings, produced a considerable effect in the course of the legal situation that was being stabilized. It was all the greater in that since Frankish times excommunication also involved consequences in civil law.[4] Although these prescriptions were not always observed, especially if they concerned princes, they were still recognized in principle in the secular sphere of law and were applied in their entirety against the heretics who spread so alarmingly from the twelfth century; here ecclesiastical and secular penal authority united for a pitiless struggle. During the reform period the Church had also gained the right to defend the interests of Christendom with arms: in other words, she had decisively expanded the *potestas coactiva materialis,* which had earlier belonged to her only in the lesser degrees of corporal punishment, such as the imposition of fasting, chastisement, incarceration of clerics and monks. The highest forms of penal authority were at that time comprehended under the image of the sword. While, then, the Church had previously possessed only the *gladius spiritualis* — excommunication, anathema — she thereafter wielded also the *gladius materialis* in the sense of the right to compulsion by war, either by summoning the secular rulers to use the material sword proper to them or by virtue of her own authority, as it were by the handing over of the material sword that belonged to her, calling knights and other laymen to arms.[5] How this portentous extension of the Church's coercive power arose out of causes conditioned by the age will appear from the history of the origin of the First Crusade in the next chapter.

The papacy's spiritual and political power of leadership, based on the primacy and embracing all of Christendom, was reinforced by particular secular-political rights. Thus, with the formation of the Papal State in 756 was gained the political autonomy of the Roman Church, which, while it

---

[4] See E. Eichmann, *Acht und Bann im Reichsrecht des Mittelalters* (Paderborn 1909).

[5] See the fundamental studies of A. Stickler, "Il potere coattivo materiale della Chiesa nella riforma gregoriana secondo Anselmo di Lucca" in *StudGreg* II (1947), 235–85; id., "Il gladius negli atti dei concilii e dei Romani Pontefici sino a Graziano e Bernardo di Clairvaux" in *Salesianum* 13 (1951), 414–45; id., "Il gladius nel registro di Gregorio VII" in *StudGreg* III (1948), 89–103. That the Church here acquired a new right follows only from the vehement discussion which went on from Gregory VII and which C. Erdmann describes in *Kreuzzugs-gedanke,* 212–49. What H. Hoffmann, "Die beiden Schwerter im hohen Mittelalter" in *DA* 20 (1964), 78–114, adduces against Stickler cannot detract from the new right of the Church mentioned above in the text, for the problem which he discusses concerns the quite different question of whether and to what extent, according to the teaching of churchmen, the king received from the hands of the Church the material sword which he wielded. If Hoffmann again adduces the many texts based on the traditional political Augustinianism of the Middle Ages, he is completing in a way deserving of gratitude the chiefly juridical source material used by Stickler, but he probably paid too little heed to the fact that the Augustinian texts are preserved very ambiguously and hence have been quite variously interpreted by the industrious canonists who were interested in them in the second half of the twelfth century. Cf. Kempf, "Kanonistik und kuriale Politik im 12. Jahrhundert" in *AHPont* 1 (1963), 11–52.

was curtailed by the Frankish and German Emperors and by the Roman nobility, was never actually suppressed and in the reform period acquired a new importance in so far as the Roman Church's consciousness of freedom no longer tolerated any political dependence. Regardless of the complicated legal situation and of the resistance of the Roman Commune that originated in 1143 and of the Hohenstaufen Emperors, the papacy claimed full political sovereignty over Rome and the *Patrimonium* — the expression "regalia beati Petri", appearing in 1059, is most probably to be explained thus[6] — and realized it, at first slowly, then after centuries definitively. The seeking of autonomy had been expressed in the eighth century not merely in territorial demands but also in the assumption of imperial insignia and honorary rights; a justification, so to speak, had been found for both in the *Constitutum Constantini*. The reformers, headed by Gregory VII, hence acted quite logically when, for proof of the quasi-imperial, or politically independent, position of the Pope, and, in this regard, for his pre-eminence over all other bishops, they referred to the *Constitutum Constantini*. (In regard to territorial claims, however, its use in the reform period is disputed, except in the case of Urban II, who once appealed to it in regard to Corsica and Lipari.[7]) As a matter of fact, in papal ceremonial thereafter the imperial honorary rights mentioned in the forgery played a greater role than formerly, especially the tiara and the scarlet mantle. In the twelfth century the mantle became the most important symbol in the investiture of a newly elected Pope, while the tiara, adorned from time immemorial with a ring-like gold trimming, gained no new function but did acquire a greater symbolic value in the course of the growing spiritual-political authority of the Pope.[8]

[6] J. Ficker, *Forschungen zur Reichs- und Rechtsgeschichte Italiens,* II (1869), 303f. For the claim to sovereignty appeal was frequently made to the *Constitutum Constantini;* see H. Löwe, "Kaisertum und Abendland" in *HZ* 196 (1963), 542–44.

[7] *Jaffé* 5448, 5449; *ItalPont* III 320; on the problem as such, cf. L. Weckmann, *Las Bulas Alejandrinas de 1493 y la teoría política del Papado medieval. Estudio de la supremacía papal sobre islas 1091–1493* (Mexico 1949); against this island theory, cf. J. Vincke in *ZSavRGkan* 67 (1950), 462–65.

[8] The tiara, called *phrygium* in the *Constitutum Constantini,* was taken directly from the Byzantine imperial ceremonial and was used by the Popes as an extraliturgical symbol of authority to be worn in specified processions; thus J. Deér, "Byzanz und die Herrschaftszeichen des Abendlandes" in *ByZ* 50 (1957), 420–27, is probably correct in his contention against P. E. Schramm, *Herrschaftszeichen,* 51–98, who preferred to derive the tiara from the imperial *camelaucum.* A substantial break-through in the history of the papal tiara, which Klewitz, "Die Krönung des Papstes" in *ZSavRGkan* 61 (1941), 96–130, would like to fix for 1059, has probably not been made as yet. In the procession on *Laetare* Sunday the Popes from Leo IX bore a golden rose, which they then usually gave away; cf. A. H. Benna, "Zur kirchlichen Symbolik: Goldene Rose, Schwert und Hut" in *Mitteilungen des Österr. Staatsarchivs* 4 (1951), 54–64. Connected with the Pope's quasi-imperial position was his right to elevate to royal rank, which the Popes from Gregory VII occasionally exercised without the Emperor; cf. H. Hirsch, "Das Recht auf Königserhebung durch Kaiser und Papst im hohen Mittelalter" in *Festschrift für E. Heymann,* I (Weimar 1940), 209–49.

The new self-awareness was expressed concretely: the emperor-like Pope began to pursue an independent state policy. Mention has been made earlier of the gaining of feudal suzerainty over the Normans of South Italy and of Gregory VII's attempt from the outset to attach politically to the Holy See as many countries as possible. Motivated by religious and political aims, Gregory still observed certain limits: he derived his demands, not from the primatial power, but from old juridical claims regarded as authentic and in the event of resistance let the matter drop. Hence it basically depended on the willingness of the princes whether they would enter into a relation of dependence with Rome; often enough they did so because they promised themselves political advantages as a result. Since England and Denmark were prepared only to pay Peter's Pence, and the feudal suzerainty over Croatia-Dalmatia, established in 1076, came to an end as a consequence of the union of Croatia with Hungary in 1091, the rights of the Roman Church outside Italy were restricted, on the one hand, to a few smaller territories, — the possessions of the Count of Provence, the County of Substantion with the bishopric of Maguelone, and the County of Besalú, — and, on the other hand, to Aragón and Catalonia.[9] Apart from the high tribute of 500 *mancusas* paid by Aragón — Catalonia paid only 30 *morabitini* — these acquisitions were of no great importance.

The papacy's international policy obtained an incomparably greater success in Italy. Gregory VII's claims to Sardinia and Corsica and to the Marches of Fermo and the Duchy of Spoleto were rather ineffective, it is true, and the great donation made by Matilda of Tuscany could not be taken possession of after the death of the Countess until the investiture of the Emperor Lothar III in 1136, but the feudal suzerainty over Norman South Italy continued, despite all difficulties, and for centuries to come influenced papal policy decisively. Interested originally rather in the armed protection afforded by the Norman vassals, which was necessary for the reform, the papacy was led ever more powerfully to the territorial viewpoint. The three stages of the rise of Norman power — at first the absorption of all earlier areas of political rule, then the feudal dependence of Capua on Apulia and thereby the limiting of direct Roman feudal suzerainty to the Duke of Apulia (1098), and finally the Norman Sicilian state created by Roger II from 1127 — presented the Roman Church with what were at times delicate problems. Unavoidable as the Italian territorial policy may have been, the Roman Church had to pay

---

[9] K. Jordan, "Das Reformpapsttum und die abendländische Staatenwelt" in *WaG* 18 (1958), 132f. assumes in both cases a transition from a relationship of protection to one of vassalage: according to him Aragón in 1068 entered into the protection relationship and in 1089 into vassalage, while Tarragona, belonging to the territory of the Count of Barcelona, acknowledged protection under Urban II but under Paschal II this was further developed and led to the feudal dependence of all Catalonia. J. Sydow in *DA* 11 (1954f.), 61, thinks that even after its extension to all of Catalonia in 1116 it was still only a relationship of protection.

for it in the future with difficult struggles that would gnaw away at the religious substance.

The proper task, before which the feudal political and territorial policy retreated, continued to be the spiritual-political guidance of Western Christendom. Its difficulties were to preoccupy the papacy throughout the twelfth and thirteenth centuries. Their source lay in a situation that was in many respects unclarified. The Pope did not stand at the head of a universal state, despite what is still to be read in the history texts. The papacy never led the *ecclesia universalis,* or *christianitas,* to a tangible political unity, not even after the reform. The papacy's unifying power, which, besides, was more and more impeded by the establishing of the two legal spheres, rested on the ecclesiastical primatial power over the *populus christianus.* Since the *populus christianus,* because of the as yet unconsummated separation between Church and state, formed an ecclesiastical and at the same time an earthly social unity and hence sought to realize the specifically Christian values, not merely with spiritual forces that were rooted in the conscience and in ecclesiastical discipline, but also with secular-political measures, the Church's power streamed out into secular spheres also. Here, of course, it encountered limits. If at all times the ecclesiastical obedience which is based on the faith contains an element of the voluntary to the extent that faith cannot be forced, how much more, then, did the mediaeval papacy's power, taking effect in the secular sphere, depend on the good will of the faithful! Involved were rights which flowed only indirectly from ecclesiastical authority and for the most part were not even necessarily connected with the essence of the Church, and were therefore conditioned by the time. For example, the Pope could launch a crusade only if the laity answered his call. And hence, to the extent that the papal initiative embraced secular spheres, it was based, not on a real dominion, but on the living relationship, subject to the vicissitudes of the time, between the Pope as leader and the Christian people as his followers. The stronger the secular-political determination of kingship grew and the more it affected the people, the more was the spiritual-political will, attended to by the Pope, forced back to the relationship within the Church between *ecclesia congregans* and *ecclesia congregata.*

The papacy was again and again confronted with the question of how far to acknowledge the autonomy of the secular-political will and of its most important protagonist, the kingship. A decision was all the more difficult, since up to the late thirteenth century a justification of the state in natural law was lacking and the traditional teaching of political Augustinianism, which conceived the *regnum* only in its religious function, was not equal to the new uncertainty. Not a few investigators are even of the opinion that the Church of the twelfth and thirteenth centuries succumbed completely to the Augustinian ideas. According to them, she wanted Western Christendom oriented exclusively to the spiritual-political goal, conceded no autonomy whatsoever to the secular-political will, and hence, from Gregory VII to Boniface VIII, staunchly defended a hierocratic claim. Their thesis, however, does not square with the facts. A readiness to acknowledge the secular-political will of kingship, to the extent that it put forward genuine rights, was in no way lacking to the Church. Effective in the Concordat of Worms, it grew stronger in the succeeding period. From the time of the reform the relationship of the Church and of the papacy to Christendom was determined not merely by a hierocratic but also by a dualistic ingredient. The next volume will show how the cooperation and the opposition of the two elements proceeded in the uncommonly agitated twelfth and thirteenth centuries.

CHAPTER 51

The Papacy, the Holy Wars, and the First Crusade

The papacy may be said to have assumed the leadership of Western Christendom with the First Crusade, but this was only the result of a long and by no means uniform development. Even though in earlier periods Popes, bishops, or abbots had occasionally summoned to arms for resistance to Vikings, Magyars, or Muslims, still war as such was reserved to the King. Only with the turn of the tenth to the eleventh century did the Church acquire a new relationship to war, especially through the movement, originating in France, of the Peace and the Truce of God. Compelled to self-defence, spiritual lords not infrequently conducted "holy wars" against violators of the peace.

But there also took place a transformation in the military class, the knights. There appeared a Christian ethos of knighthood, which obliged to the armed protection of churches and of oppressed fellow-Christians and hence to tasks which had hitherto been allotted to the crown. That new forces were here in readiness was discovered when the *Reconquista* began again in Christian Spain soon after 1050, reached its climax with the taking of Toledo in 1085, and was then checked by the Almoravids, coming from Africa. For from 1064 French knights took part in these struggles, which they looked upon as holy wars. Their aid became greater after the defeat of Alfonso VI of Castile at Sagrajas in 1086 and thereby, so to speak, readied France for the idea of a crusade. The Normans of South Italy were motivated by similar ideas and not merely by desire of conquest when, under the leadership of Count Roger I, they set about wresting Sicily from Islam. And the attack successfully made in 1087 on the North African pirate city of Mahdiya by the Pisans in alliance with Genoa, Rome, and Amalfi, had a crusade-like character.[1]

---

[1] On the *Reconquista,* see Mayer, *Bibliographie zur Geschichte der Kreuzzüge* (Hanover 1960), 2606–20; for the share of the French, ibid., 1720–25; on the whole question, Erdmann, *Kreuzzugsgedanke,* 51–106.

These pregnant ideas that were spontaneously making their appearance here and there were taken up by the reform papacy, which bound them together and eventually directed them to the Orient. Leo IX established the first contact when he turned the holy war, already familiar to him from Toul, to the goals of the reform, unmistakably in the little noticed proceedings against the Tusculans in 1049 and then in the large-scale campaign against the Normans "for the liberation of Christendom".[2] The enterprise failed, but the idea triumphed, despite the opposition of Peter Damiani and other reformers, and under Alexander II it acquired radiating force. No holy war was then waged in which the papacy did not have some share. The French knights who in 1063 made ready for the Spanish war for Barbastro obtained from Alexander II the first known crusade indulgence. Count Ebolus of Roucy submitted his plans for the Spanish campaign, and Alexander sent the banner of Saint Peter, which had meanwhile made its appearance, to Count Roger for the struggle in Sicily, to Duke William of Normandy as he was preparing to cross over to England, and to Erlembald, the gallant leader of the Milanese *Pataria*.

It did not matter whether the war was against unbelievers or Catholics — its religious goal was decisive. In fact, under Gregory VII the holy wars within Christendom for the benefit of the reform came entirely into the foreground and received a specifically hierarchical stamp through the idea that he entertained of an international *militia sancti Petri*. Great successes were, of course, denied Gregory; in fact, his militant outlook aroused opposition, and there ensued a lively discussion as to whether the Church or the Pope may wage war at all. This caused Anselm of Lucca to ponder the problem more deeply. Following Augustine, he expounded the lawfulness of the defensive war and the moral and religious principles to be observed in connection with it, and from this position defended the Church's right to prosecute her faithless members. He thereby laid the ground for the future teaching, developed by Gratian and the decretists, on the Church's power of material coercion in the sense of the right to armed force.[3] The expansion here present of the ecclesiastical *potestas coactiva materialis* did not really take effect for the moment, since it was applied to the pursuit of opponents of reform, branded as heretics and schismatics, and was very quickly blended with Gregory's struggle against Henry IV. So complex an initiative, calling forth opposition even from the well-intentioned, was not capable of carrying away the masses of knights or of finding support in the entire clergy. But once the papacy turned the pent up energies of Christian knighthood from crusades within Christendom to one against the infidel, it could be sure of a response on a broad front.

[2] For the period from Leo IX to Gregory VII, see Erdmann, *op. cit.* 107–211.
[3] Erdmann, *op. cit.* 212–49, deals with the discussion as such; the juridical problem is pinpointed by A. Stickler (see footnote 5 of the preceding chapter).

It was precisely this change that was made by Urban II. While he did make use of weapons at the beginning of his pontificate, he soon renounced this means. On the other hand, he had no hesitation about promoting with all his energy the holy war against Islam. The crisis of the age induced him to this: Christians had been forced to the defensive in both the Orient and Spain. Urban regarded the western sector as so important that he forbade Spaniards to take part in the crusade in the Orient. His special concern was for the rebuilding of strategically important Tarragona; in 1089 he granted for this work the same remission of ecclesiastical penance that was attached to a pilgrimage to Jerusalem.

Gregory VII had already planned a crusade for the liberation of the Eastern Christians, which was to help in liquidating the Schism. As a matter of fact, the Christian East was in an extremely critical situation since the great victory of the Seljuk Turks over the Emperor Romanus IV at Manzikert in 1071. Little by little, virtually all of Asia Minor came under Seljuk rule. The capable Emperor Alexius I Comnenus (1081–1118) could not exert himself because the Patzinaks were threatening Constantinople. In his distress he tried to hire as many Western knights as possible. Thus in 1089–90 he induced Robert the Frisian, Count of Flanders, who was returning home from a pilgrimage to Jerusalem, to send him 500 knights.[4] Hence it suited him very much when Urban II, soon after his election, began negotiations for union. These were encouraged by Alexius, who for his part asked for troops. Urban promised them but at first was unable to send any. Although the Emperor contrived to exorcise the threat from the Patzinaks by a brilliant victory in 1091, in 1095 he again had his request submitted to the Pope at the Council of Piacenza, according to the trustworthy report of Bernold of Sankt Blasien. Confident of his enhanced prestige, Urban now proceeded to take action: at Piacenza he called upon Christian knights to defend the Eastern Church. But this was only the overture. Once in France, he took the real step after rather long preparation by issuing the summons to the First Crusade at the Council of Clermont on 27 November 1095.

Just how Urban II reached this portentous decision is disputed. While the invitation at Clermont certainly went beyond that of Piacenza, it cannot be shown that the Pope first conceived the idea of a crusade in France and thought at Piacenza only of sending mercenaries. In certain respects the idea of aid in the form of a crusade was already in his mind at the time of his first contact with Alexius I in 1089–91. As early as 1089 he had, at least for the reconstruction of Tarragona, connected defence against the Muslims and pilgrimage to Jerusalem, two elements of decisive importance for Clermont, and in the same year he declared his intention of going to France. Possibly, then, he went there in 1095 with intentions long under consideration. At

---

[4] F. L. Ganshof, "Robert le Frison et Alexis Comnène" in *Byz(B)* 31 (1961), 57–74.

first he sought out Bishop Adhémar of Le Puy and conferred with him, since this prelate knew the East from a journey he had recently made to Jerusalem. When the summons to Clermont proceeded from Le Puy, the decision had probably been taken. Urban then met Raymond de Saint-Gilles, Count of Toulouse and Marquis of Provence, in order to gain him for the enterprise. Apparently he was counting on a relatively small army of knights of the Midi. His expectations were to be greatly surpassed. The fire kindled in Clermont became a conflagration that blazed up and spread to all of France and elsewhere.[5]

So far as the motivating ideas are concerned, the secret of the success lay not only in the concept of Christian knighthood and struggle, developed during the previous century and already made use of in the war against pagans, but also in the taking up of the notion of pilgrimage. The journey to Jerusalem had been the tacit desire of many Christians from time immemorial; it freed one from all other penitential obligations. But penitents who were pilgrims were not allowed to bear arms. On the other hand, at the Council of Clermont Urban granted the same full remission of the canonical penalties that was gained by pilgrims to Jerusalem, and hence he proclaimed for the first time the idea of the armed pilgrimage. Its propaganda force would probably have remained limited if persons had adhered to the Clermont decree, whereby the armed pilgrimage was merely a commutation for the penitential exercises imposed by the Church, understood in the sense of the customary so-called "redemption". However, the preaching of the crusade, now getting under way and increasingly eluding the supervision of the Church, probably disregarded the moderate decree of the Council and held out to the crusaders the prospect of a plenary indulgence, that is, the remission of all penalties for sin that were to be expected from God either in this life or in the next, and in this connection there may well have been mention occasionally of forgiveness of sins in a quite crude way.

By means of the spontaneously germinating notion of the indulgence, which was to cost the theologians of the twelfth and thirteenth centuries much sweat until it found its speculative solution in the doctrine of the Church's treasury of merits, the crusade acquired an immeasurable religious worth in the eyes of the faithful.[6] Its danger lost its terrors all the more as

[5] For Urban's journey to France, see A. Becker, *Papst Urban II.* (Stuttgart 1964), 213–25, who assumes that Urban first conceived the idea of a crusade in France.

[6] This explanation follows H. E. Mayer, *Geschichte der Kreuzzüge* (Stuttgart 1965), 31–46. Mayer convincingly attacks the almost universally defended view that at Clermont a plenary indulgence was proclaimed (*Mansi* XX, 815, c. 2). He also rejects Erdmann's thesis that in Urban's mind the idea of war against infidels, waged by the Church and knighthood, was in the foreground, while the notion of the pilgrimage came in only by accident. On indulgences, cf. A. Gottlob, *Kreuzzugsablass und Almosenablass. Eine Studie über die Frühzeit des Ablasswesens* (Stuttgart 1906); N. Paulus, *Geschichte des Ablasses im Mittelalter,* 3 vols. (Paderborn 1922f.); B. Poschmann, *Der Ablass im Lichte der Bussgeschichte* (Bonn 1948).

persons began to look upon death occurring in it as a kind of martyrdom. The association of expedition and pilgrimage was at once expressed symbolically, especially in the cloth cross which the knights even at Clermont had sewn to their garb; this was the sign of the crusade vow, a religious obligation, and at the same time the military symbol of an army resolved to fight. There also appeared a common battle cry, "Deus le volt", and a new ritual blessing, which added the sword to the old pilgrimage symbols that were retained, the staff and wallet. Inherent in all these forms was a special publicity value.

If Urban, with a keen psychological instinct, strongly emphasized Jerusalem as the goal of the expedition, this by no means meant that he was concerned only for the holy city or the holy sepulchre. (At that time there was as yet no mention of the Holy Land.) Rather he clung steadfastly to the original purpose of liberating Eastern Christianity from the Turkish yoke. This referred not exclusively but to a great extent to the Byzantine world; the Pope intended to remain true to his promise of help to Alexius, although the nature and manner of the supplying of aid turned out quite differently from what the Emperor had desired. Selfish power projects envisaging the gaining of territories were probably remote from Urban's mind; in fact, at Clermont he specified that the churches of the conquered lands should be under the rule of the conquerors.[7] No one could deprive him of the essential success: when, disregarding the kings and relying only on his apostolic authority, he summoned the knights to the holy war and found so powerful a response that for the first time in Western history a supranational army set forth for the defence of Christendom, he became the spontaneously recognized leader of the Christian West. The contact that the reform papacy had made with the Christian knights took effect fully now for the first time and led necessarily to a special crusaders' law. Ecclesiastical legislation extended the Peace of God and the protection of the Church to the goods of crusaders; on the part of the Church encouragement was given to the effort to free the possessions of participants from taxes for the duration of the crusade; and even a moratorium on debts was provided for.

The leadership of the enterprise by Pope Urban should have been expressed visibly in the person of the Papal Legate, Adhémar of Le Puy, who was entrusted with the political direction, while the military command was originally intended for Raymond de Saint-Gilles, Count of Toulouse.[8] Both arrangements foundered in the swelling crusading movement. Since, besides Raymond, other great princes also took the cross and set out with their own troops, the single command failed to materialize of itself; Raymond was merely the commander of his own troops. The slack organization also caused

---

[7] Erdmann, *op. cit.* 322f.
[8] J. H. and L. L. Hill, *Raymond IV de Saint-Gilles 1041 (1042) – 1105* (Toulouse 1959); Mayer, *Bibliographie*, 1963–65.

Adhémar's eclipse. His function was restricted rather to the spiritual care of one contingent, for Urban had clearly provided a chaplain with spiritual jurisdiction for each of two other units and hence had in a sense made them legates also.[9]

Although the direction of the entire undertaking slipped from the Pope's hands, he continued to be the supreme authority for the crusaders. But Urban had no influence on the crusade movement of Peter the Hermit of Amiens.[10] One of those wandering preachers of penance who held up to the people the ideal of the *vita apostolica et evangelica,* Peter began right after Urban's appeal to arouse his followers in central and northwestern France for the armed pilgrimage. The time was more favourable than ever. Religious excitement of the masses, now probably enhanced by eschatological ideas,[11] and economic difficulties, especially among the peasantry, had built up the hope of a better life to a high degree of intensity. This tension was relaxed by Peter's summons to go to the holy city of Jerusalem with a force such as the West had never yet experienced. The mob that followed him, consisting overwhelmingly of the lower strata of the population, received so many reinforcements *en route* through Germany, from the Rhineland, Swabia, and elsewhere, that from April to June of 1096 there set out from 50,000 to 70,000 persons, including women, in five or six large batches successively. Religious fanaticism and rapacity in the uncontrolled masses led to frightful persecution of Jews in German Free Cities and in Prague.[12] Only the first two contingents, travelling via Hungary and Bulgaria, reached Constantinople. The crowds that followed, incurring hatred because of their plundering and other deeds of violence, were almost totally exterminated in Hungary. The Emperor Alexius at first received the new arrivals amicably but had so many unhappy experiences with them that he quickly transported the troublesome guests to Asia Minor. Instead of waiting for the knights, they attacked the Turks concentrated around Nicaea, against the advice of Peter of Amiens, Fulcher of Orléans, and some nobles, and as a consequence, with few exceptions, lost either life or freedom.

Urban II's appeal had been directed to knights of military experience; they were to make careful preparations for the expedition up to 15 August and then set out. Of the many noble lords who took the cross the princes were, of course, the most prominent. Each collected for himself a more or

---

[9] H. E. Mayer, "Zur Beurteilung Adhémars von Le Puy" in *DA* 16 (1960), 547–52; Mayer, *Bibliographie,* 1936–41; J. Richard, "La papauté et la direction de la première croisade" in *Journal des savants* (1960), 49–58.

[10] H. Hagenmeyer, *Peter der Eremit. Ein kritischer Beitrag zur Geschichte des 1. Kreuzzugs* (Leipzig 1879); Mayer, *Bibliographie,* 1924–35.

[11] The eschatological motives were pinpointed in the important work by P. Alphandéry – A. Dupront, *La chrétienté et l'idée de croisade,* I (Paris 1954); cf. also the restrictive remarks of Mayer, *Kreuzzüge,* 17–19.

[12] E. L. Dietrich, "Das Judentum im Zeitalter der Kreuzzüge" in *Saeculum* 3 (1952), 94–131.

less large fighting unit. Thus in the summer a whole series of army divisions set out by different routes: either via Hungary and Bulgaria or via Italy and the Balkan peninsula, reached by ship, to Constantinople. Large armies were led by Duke Godfrey of Lower Lotharingia, son of Count Eustace of Boulogne and nephew and heir of Godfrey the Hunchback of Lower Lotharingia,[13] and by Count Raymond of Toulouse, while the brother of the French King, Count Hugh of Vermandois, to whom Urban delivered a banner of Saint Peter at Rome, Bohemond of Taranto, a son of Robert Guiscard, and Duke Robert of Normandy, Count Stephen of Blois, and Count Robert of Flanders, who travelled together, disposed of smaller units.

Alexius found himself in the greatest perplexity. His situation had improved. Following his victory over the Patzinaks in 1091, he had succeeded in inflicting a decisive defeat on the Cumans in 1095 and would now have been able to attack the Turks in Asia Minor, since with the death of Malik Shah in 1092 their sultanate had begun to crumble. Hence he was interested in Western mercenaries, not in Western armies of knights under their own commanders. In an effort to secure himself adequately against his uninvited helpers, he forced the princes into political subordination, taking some of them, according to Byzantine custom, into the imperial family as sons and requiring of all the oath of vassalage customary in the West. As a matter of fact the princes, more or less reluctantly, did enter the vassalage bond, except for Raymond de Saint-Gilles, who agreed merely to an oath guaranteeing the life and possessions of the Emperor.[14]

A first success, achieved in association with the Greeks, was the conquest of Nicaea. The authority of the Turks, who had been called upon for relief and had been defeated, thereupon collapsed in that area. Accompanied by only a few Byzantine troops — the main Greek army now concentrated on the coastal lands — the crusaders moved through Anatolia, defeated the Turks at Dorylaeum on 1 July 1097, and later at Heraclea, and then broke into smaller units. The main army detoured via Caesarea in Cappadocia to Antioch, while Bohemond's nephew Tancred and Baldwin, brother of Godfrey of Lower Lotharingia, decided on conquests of their own. Baldwin acquired a wealthy lordship around Edessa. Antioch, the next tactical objective, cost the crusaders immense toil. Only after a seven months' siege were they able to occupy the city on 3 July 1098, and then they had to beat back a great Turkish relieving army. Since the princes regarded themselves as no longer bound by the oath sworn to the Emperor because of the meagre aid, and eventually no aid at all, rendered by the Greeks, each of them sought to gain territory for himself. Bohemond took Antioch. Byzantium had never

---

[13] J. C. Andressohn, *The Ancestry and Life of Godefroy of Bouillon* (Bloomington, Ind., 1947); Mayer, *Bibliographie*, 1942–62; the other leaders, ibid. 1966–76.
[14] On the juridical bonds, cf. F. L. Ganshof, *Mélanges M. Paul – E. Martin* (Geneva 1961), 49–63.

got over the loss of this important city, which the Turks had not taken until 1085. After a long delay Raymond finally managed to get the crusaders moving toward Jerusalem. An offer of help by Alexius was repulsed: the crusaders intended to keep the districts to be conquered in Syria and Palestine. Jerusalem, which the Fatimids of Egypt had lost to the Seljuks first in 1070–71 and then in 1078 and had recovered in 1098, fell to the crusaders on 15 July 1099. The victors engaged in a frightful blood bath among the local Muslims.

Raymond de Saint-Gilles was first chosen ruler, but he declined; then Godfrey of Lower Lotharingia was elected. He did not assume the title of king but that of Guardian of the Holy Sepulchre. His juridical position was weakened by the claims to an ecclesiastical state, put forward by the new Patriarch of Jerusalem, Archbishop Daimbert of Pisa, in favour, not of the Roman Church, but of the patriarchate.[15] Godfrey died in 1100 and was succeeded by his brother Baldwin (1100–18), who put an end to all vacillation. He had himself crowned King and was otherwise able to consolidate his authority. The Frankish conquest spread to the interior as well as along the coast. Almost all the coastal cities had been taken by 1111; but Tyre held out until 1124 and Ascalon till 1153. The territory that had been acquired was broken down into four rather large states, united loosely under the King of Jerusalem: the Kingdom of Jerusalem, the County of Tripolis, the Principality of Antioch, and the County of Edessa. Their preservation and defence were to cost the West more heavy sacrifices. The very first years brought great losses. During and immediately after the crusade Western pilgrims and crusaders kept setting out, but the poorly organized expeditions almost all ended miserably. In the one year 1101 three great enterprises, conducted by Lombards, Germans, and the French, were completely annihilated by the Turks in Anatolia.

Thereafter the papacy had to assume the chief responsibility for the crusader states. This brought it an enhanced prestige and, with the crusade tithe introduced under Innocent III, also financial power, but at the same time it made the limits of papal influence much clearer on occasion. The unsteady ground on which the Pope stood as leader of Christendom was perhaps never made so clear as in the history of the crusades. Momentous as was the effect of the First Crusade on the Christian West and on the papacy, its full importance in Church history can only be estimated if the reaction of the Byzantine world is understood. This will be treated in the next volume.

[15] J. G. Rowe, "Paschal II and the Relation between the Spiritual and Temporal Powers in the Kingdom of Jerusalem" in *Speculum* 32 (1957), 470–501.

CHAPTER 52

The "Vita Evangelica" Movement
and
The Appearance of New Orders

From about the middle of the eleventh century the religious state began to differentiate itself once for all. There is no doubt that the Gregorian reform contributed to this change, occasionally by direct intervention, but basically it was a spontaneous religious movement, which had its own prehistory and its own dynamics. It has already been noted how, from the beginning of the eleventh century, there gradually emerged a critical attitude *vis-à-vis* the wealthy monasteries and chapters that had been incorporated into the economic and political system of feudalism. In the final analysis this was really the same striving as that of the reform papacy, struggling for the freedom of the Church, namely, the determination to return to the original *ecclesia apostolica et evangelica,* and the consequent protest against early mediaeval forms of life, stamped to a great extent by Germanic law. In the world of monks and canons this impulse was based especially on the idea of poverty.

To high-minded men it was no longer enough that the individual monk must possess nothing, whereas the monastic community could dispose of a large income. To them poverty meant the fullest possible renunciation of earthly assurances. And so, alone or with companions, they betook themselves to remote forests in order to be entirely free for God. They earned their livelihood by the work of their hands, as occasion demanded, turning sections of forest into arable and meadow. Their radicalism could go to the extent of maintaining that the possession of proprietary churches, of rights to tithes and altars and the like, was incompatible with monasticism and even of refusing documentary authentication of the land given them. In conflicts over possession they preferred to accept injustice rather than to institute a suit. Finally, their protest was directed against the grand-scale building activity which monasteries of the old type not infrequently displayed, the lavish decoration of monastic churches and the costly vestments and vessels; their own dwellings, oratories, and churches were kept poor and bare.

This movement, spreading ever further in the second half of the eleventh century, was not represented by monks alone. The principle of poverty had already been related in patristic times to clerics, with reference to the primitive community at Jerusalem, and in particular cases had been put into practice, for example by Augustine. And even if the Aachen rule for canons of 816 allowed private ownership, the stricter interpretation was not forgotten and in the eleventh century acquired an arousing force. It is difficult to determine when and where individual canons began to institute a genuine *vita communis* with renunciation of private ownership; the meagre sources

453

point overwhelmingly to Central and North Italy. As early as the Roman Synod of 1059 Hildebrand became their spokesman and, sharply criticizing the Aachen rule, demanded personal poverty for all canons. So radical an attack, of course, had little effect; the reform had to come from below. And in fact from time to time more canons adopted the principle of poverty and thus appeared as a special group, called canons regular, in contradistinction to the older type of canons who clung to private property. But the striving for evangelical and apostolic poverty urged to still more resolute efforts. Even diocesan clerics now sought out the *eremus*.

If till then the ideal of the *vita evangelica et apostolica* had been oriented to the poverty of cenobites or hermits, toward the end of the century it acquired a broader meaning. As Christ, with the Apostles, went from place to place to proclaim the Kingdom of God and called no place his own where he could lay his head, this most extreme self-denial for the sake of the Gospel was now translated into action by isolated monks, clerics, and hermits.

The relations between monastic centres and the laity changed considerably in the eleventh century. Since the monasteries of the older type maintained a manorial economy, they were involved, with their servants and maids, their serfs, rent-paying peasants, and vassals, with the most varied strata of the population. A special position was occupied by the so-called half-*conversi*, pious folk who settled on the edge of the cloister, renounced parts of their rights of ownership, and led a quasi-monastic life. From them emerged the institute of lay brothers during the eleventh century, especially at the instigation of hermits of Saint Romuald's type and of the Vallombrosans.[1] The cause of this new form, which flourished powerfully in the twelfth century, is to be sought in the progress toward sterner asceticism, which, in addition to monks and clerics, also embraced lay persons and prepared them to undertake poverty, celibacy, and claustral discipline as serving brothers. As a favourable circumstance was added the striving of not a few of the new communities to work their own property themselves. Such a goal could scarcely have been achieved without lay helpers living the monastic life. Basically at stake here was a spiritual concern — the more effective isolation of the cloister from the world.

This world-fleeing characteristic, however, in no way impeded an influence on the lay persons living outside. On the contrary, the very hermits and the

[1] K. Hallinger, "Woher kommen die Laienbrüder?" in *Analecta S. O. Cist.* 12 (1956), 1–104; also printed separately as a book (Rome 1956). On p. 97 cf. the discussion of "conversus": It was used for two entirely different classes, namely, on the one hand, authenticated from the sixth to at least the fifteenth century, for those full-fledged monks who, in contradistinction to the *oblati* or *nutriti,* entered the monastery as mature men, and on the other hand for the rising number of lay brothers in the eleventh century. These latter were not monks in the proper sense. Even if they, for the most part, made the monastic renunciations, they did not make monastic vows until the fourteenth century.

cenobitic proponents of a stricter asceticism were in a much closer contact with the broad masses of the people than were the monasteries of the older order. To an ever greater degree their ideals appealed to the restless lay folk. Mention has already been made of the popular religious movements before and during the Gregorian reform. It will suffice here to single out the *Pataria* as an example. What it undertook against clerical incontinence and simony was done every bit as implacably, though without recourse to weapons, by the founder of Vallombrosa, John Gualbert; the *Pataria* knew this and hence requested the dispatch of Vallombrosan monks. In France and Lower Lotharingia there occurred a perhaps even closer *rapprochement* of ascetics and populace. The faithful penetrated even into the *eremus* to be edified and have their souls tended to or even to settle there. Conversely, protagonists of the *vita apostolica et evangelica* did not hesitate to leave the cloister and preach to the assembled people, sharply attacking abuses. Thus there appeared itinerant preachers toward the close of the century. How powerfully they influenced the masses was shown by the unfortunate crusade initiative of Peter the Hermit of Amiens.

Like many other itinerant preachers, Peter the Hermit acted without any ecclesiastical commission. No wonder that the bishops exerted themselves to correct the chaotic system of preaching. From the viewpoint of logic alone, the movement could only be neutralized by the founding of new preaching Orders, but apparently the time was not yet ripe for this, and so itinerant preaching more and more became an illicit activity, exercised by heretics. In general, within the orthodox Christian sphere the feverish search for new forms of the *vita apostolica et evangelica* slowly ceased. From time to time there emerged from the process of fermentation more clearly sketched, new religious communities, which adopted fixed customs, while other foundations did not cling to their original *élan* and reverted to the old monastic or canonical institutes. The situation was somewhat stabilized in the third decade of the twelfth century.

Differentiation in Monasticism

The search beginning in various places for new forms was not occasioned, apart from individual cases, by evil living on the part of the traditional monasticism, for this, thanks to the renewal in progress since the tenth century, was on the whole on a considerably high level.[2] Monastic centres such as Saint-Victor de Marseille and Cava dei Tirreni expanded especially after 1050. Similarly, the abbey of La Chaise-Dieu in the diocese of Clermont, founded in 1043 by the hermit, Robert de Tourlande, and to a great extent

[2] For what follows, see the Literature for Chapter 39; P. R. Gaussin, *L'abbaye de La Chaise de Dieu* (Paris 1962); J. Semmler, *Die Klosterreform von Siegburg* (Bonn 1959); H. Jakobs, *Die Hirsauer. Die Ausbreitung und Rechtsstellung im Zeitalter des Investiturstreites* (Cologne - Graz 1961).

already filled with the new spirit, flourished and quickly developed into a distinguished congregation. Cluny reached its zenith at the same time under Saint Hugh (1049–1109). Its usages found entry into England, Lotharingia, and Germany, partly by the direct, partly by the indirect route. Thus the Piedmontese monastery of Fruttuaria, belonging to Saint-Bénigne de Dijon, communicated its own Cluniac stamp to the German abbeys of Siegburg and Sankt Blasien in 1068–70, which in turn became monastic reform centres. Still greater importance was gained by the abbey of Hirsau, revived in 1065, as soon as it adopted under Abbot William (1069–91) the reform ideas of Gregory VII for questions of principle and the *consuetudines* of Cluny for monastic daily life. In its steep rise, which it is true lasted only a few decades, Hirsau, with its many monks, lay brothers, and other adherents of both sexes, loosely bound to it, became not merely a centre of monastic strength but a bulwark and refuge of the Gregorian reform, struggling against clerical incontinence, simony, lay investiture, and royal theocracy. Even itinerant preachers proceeded from Hirsau, though we can no longer determine precisely the content and extent of their propagandizing.

The movement of the *vita evangelica* had been prepared to a great extent by the followers of Romuald, who were gathered together into congregations, on the one hand by Peter Damiani, prior of Fonte Avellana, and on the other hand by the hermits at Camaldoli. The Florentine John Gualbert took a different route. Dissatisfaction with the lax spirit in the abbey of San Miniato, which he had entered in 1028, and opposition to the simony of his Abbot and of the Bishop of Florence drove John out of the monastery and the city and caused him to seek out hermits, including those of Camaldoli, until 1036 when he established himself at Vallombrosa. There he formed a cenobitic community with his companions. In his own lifetime, and hence up to 1073, there came into existence a group of daughter houses. A cenobitic manner of life, characterized, however, by eremitical austerity, the formation of lay brothers, a relentless antisimoniacal propaganda, which reached its peak in the ordeal by fire in 1068 of the Vallombrosan monk, later cardinal, Peter Igneus[3] — all this gave to John Gualbert's foundation a special actuality of its own.

The new ideas had an even stronger effect in France and Lotharingia toward the end of the century. Two examples will suffice to indicate how varied the initiatives could be and how hard it was for them to endure in the long run.[4] The group that gathered around Eudes, *scholasticus* of Tournai,

---

[3] In addition to G. Miccoli, *Pietro Igneo* (Rome 1960), see Chapter 41, footnote 7.

[4] C. Dereine, "Odon de Tournai et la crise du cénobitisme au XIe siècle" in *RAM* 3 (1947), 137–54; id., "La spiritualité 'apostolique' des premiers fondateurs d'Afflighem 1083–1100" in *RHE* 54 (1959), 41–65. The powerful influx of lay persons which Afflighem experienced is to be observed in many new eremitical foundations and occasionally even in new Benedictine monasteries, such as Hirsau; often the itinerant preachers were responsible for it. E. Werner, *Pauperes Christi* (Leipzig 1956), *passim,* would like to derive it from the economic

first adopted the life of canons, then that of Benedictines, in a later phase they subscribed to the radical ideal of poverty, and finally, rendered cautious by famine in 1095, they were content with the customs of Cluny; the whole development lasted from three to four years. Even more instructive is the story of the monastery of Afflighem in Brabant. Founded in 1083 as a hermitage by six penitent robber knights and attached to a hospice for travellers and those seeking safe escort, the colony developed quickly, under Abbot Fulgentius, appointed in 1088, into a large community, consisting not only of monks but of male and female lay *conversi*. Fulgentius (d. 1122) and the first generation followed the strict idea of poverty, including the rejection of the possession of churches or *villae,* but under the pressure of the younger recruits they had to revert slowly to the customs of traditional monasticism.

Only the more important of the new foundations can be singled out here from the complicated profusion. When Stephen of Thiers (d. 1124), founder of the Order of Grandmont,[5] sought the solitude of Muret near Limoges and gathered disciples around him, he was basically influenced, with regard to the community that came into existence in 1080–81, by the impressions gained when he had lived in the society of Calabrian hermits. To a great extent he rejected the forms of Western monasticism. He did not allow landed property, herds of cattle, rents, and proprietary churches, and the Gospel was for him the sole norm of monastic life; his sons were to be called neither canons nor monks nor hermits, and they were to seek their task in nothing but penance. Although Stephen did not dispense with a type of profession and choir service and hence with a certain organization of the community into monks and lay brothers, still the strongly lay characteristics of his rudimentary constitution brought it about that the lay brothers occupied a leading position, which eventually produced strife. Much as Stephen scrupulously avoided fixed constitutional forms, he must have created a living monastic spirit. Supported by it, the community, which moved to nearby Grandmont, was able to condense its unique character in a rule under the grand prior Stephen of Liciac (1139–63) and develop into an esteemed Order.

Quite different was the origin of the Order of Fontevrault.[6] Its founder, the diocesan priest, hermit, and itinerant preacher Robert of Arbrissel (d. *ca.*

and social situation and from class hostilities; he here touches a very important point, but the danger of perverting the picture through ideological prejudices is not always avoided; cf. the critical remarks of H. Jakobs, *op. cit.* 190–95, in regard to Hirsau.

[5] J. Becquet, "Étienne de Muret" in *DSAM* IV, 2 (1961), 1504–14; articles by the same author in *RMab* are important: 42 (1952), 31–42 (institutions); 43 (1953), 121–37 (the first reports); 46 (1956), 15–32 (the first customs); also in *Bull. de la Soc. archéol. et hist. du Limousin* 87 (1958), 9–36 (rule).

[6] R. Niderst, *Robert d'Arbrissel et les origines de l'ordre de Fontevrault* (Rodez 1952); cf. also J. Buhot, "L'abbaye normande de Savigny" in *MA,* third series, 7 (1936), 1–17; L. Raison – R. Niderst, "Le mouvement érémitique dans l'ouest de la France à la fin du XIe siècle et au début du XIIe siècle" in *Annales de Bretagne* 55 (1948), 1–46.

1117), had such an effect on the masses that many men and women, on fire for the evangelical life, constantly accompanied him. In order to lodge them, he established double monasteries, which, shortly before his death, he united into a congregation under the direction of the first foundation, Fontevrault (1100–01). He entrusted the supreme direction to the Abbess-General: as Christ on the cross had once committed his beloved disciple to the Mother of God, so the monks of the Order, as new beloved disciples, were to be in the maternal keeping of the Abbess. From a like union of eremitical and itinerant preacher motives, but without the female element, proceeded other Orders: that of Tiron, founded by Bernard of Abbeville (d. 1117), that of Savigny, founded by Vitalis (d. 1122), and that of Cadouin, founded by Gerald of Salles (d. 1120).

Whereas itinerant preaching exercised only a passing and isolated influence on the monastic movement, *eremus* and evangelical poverty had an enduring power of attraction. Even at the end of the period here under consideration, the two ideals led in Italy to the founding of the monastery of Pulsano in Apulia in 1120 by John of Matera (d. 1139) and of Montevergine (1124) and other South Italian and Sicilian monasteries by William of Vercelli (d. 1142). Pulsano and especially Montevergine became centres of Orders.[7] But to what extent the centre of the movement was then in France is apparent from the history of Chartreuse and Cîteaux.

La Grande Chartreuse owed its origin to the diocesan priest Bruno, originally from Cologne. Around 1056 he assumed the direction of the philosophical and theological studies at the cathedral school of Reims, but he ran foul of Archbishop Manasses of Reims and of his successor and was thereby strengthened in his desire to abandon the world. For a short time he stayed with Abbot Robert at Molesme, but he then went with some companions into the solitude of Lêche-Fontaine. He soon left here with six friends and around 1084 began to live again as a hermit in the valley of Chartreuse. The founding of an Order or the like was not envisaged, and the community might even have broken up entirely when in 1090 Bruno had to obey the call of Pope Urban II, his former pupil, and go to Rome. A year later the Pope allowed him to look again for a solitude in South Italy. In the wooded district of La Torre in the diocese of Squillace he established the hermitage of Santa Maria dell'Eremo, into which in 1097–99 he incorporated the cenobitic daughter house of Santo Stefano in Bosco for sick companions.

That every trace of Bruno's earthly work — he died in 1101 — was not lost was due less to the hermits of La Torre than to those of Chartreuse,

---

[7] Penco, *Monachesimo in Italia,* 248–58; L. Mattei Cerasoli, *La congregazione benedittina degli eremiti di Pulsano* (Badia di Cava 1938); G. Angelillis, "Pulsano e l'ordine monastico pulsanese" in *Arch. stor. Pugliese* 6 (1953), 421–66; G. Mongelli, *Abbazia di Montevergine, Regesto delle pergamene,* 5 vols. (Rome 1956f.); A. Tranfaglia, "Montevergine" in *L'Italia benedittina,* ed. by P. Lugano (Rome 1929), 379–439.

especially to the important Prior Guigues de Chastel (d. 1137), who in 1128 fixed by rule the way of life established by Bruno and probably further developed it. What characterized the Carthusian Order, which spread slowly and within a modest range, was the peculiar combination of the eremitical and the cenobitic form, an extreme austerity, which, however, was linked with a healthy instinct for what was endurable, and finally an organization corresponding to the goal, in which the two achievements of the age — the institute of lay brothers and the Cistercian constitution — were made use of. Here the spirit by which the poverty movement of the eleventh century was animated found a particular but so authentic expression that it has continued to the present in the Carthusians in its original strictness without any substantial mitigation and, a unique fact in the history of religious Orders, has never needed a reform.

Like Chartreuse, Cîteaux too proceeded from a love for solitude and for a stricter poverty but with a far closer adherence to the Benedictine cenobitic tradition. The founder, Robert of Molesme (ca. 1028–1112), had lived as a monk since his youth in several Benedictine monasteries without finding contentment. Even the abbey of Molesme, which he founded with some hermits in 1075, moved into the old feudal pattern as a consequence of increasing property, and so in 1098, with twenty like-minded companions, Robert left in order to build a new reform monastery in the wilderness of Cîteaux near Langres. He did not make much progress. In 1099, at the order of the papal legate, Hugh of Lyons, he returned to Molesme, but his disciples continued his work, within modest limits under Abbot Alberic (1099–1109), with growing success under Abbot Stephen Harding, an Englishman (1109–33). The individual stages of development can be determined more or less surely only when the research that has recently been in a state of flux has been concluded. That from the beginning Cîteaux opposed the traditional Benedictinism was nothing new. The renunciation of proprietary churches and of the letting out of monastic property, connected with an economy of dues and rents; the principle, supplanting the preceding, of economic operation conducted by oneself, which the adoption of the institute of lay brothers fostered; the necessity present in time-consuming manual labour of restricting the far too extended choral service of the Cluniacs and other branches; the principle of poverty, related to clothing, table, church, and its adornment — this programme linked the Cistercians to many other, in some cases older, communities. And yet they succeeded in outstripping all the monastic reform centres that were striving for the *vita evangelica* and in eclipsing the traditional monasticism headed by Cluny.

Cîteaux owed its rise especially to three circumstances: to its location in Burgundy, where a community representing the new ideas could establish itself *vis-à-vis* Cluny and the many other monasteries of the older type only with difficulty unless it had an aggressive spirit; to the entry, probably in

1112, of Bernard of Clairvaux, a charismatically gifted genius, who brought along thirty companions, the first fruits of his future impassioned recruitment; and to an elastic constitution, combining centralization with a relative autonomy of the monasteries. This constitution was based rather early on two main supports that were to be completed later: on the organic union between mother and daughter monasteries, with the duty of visitation by the abbot of the mother house, and on the annual general chapter at Cîteaux, the supreme authority for supervision and legislation. The growth of the Order will be treated in the next volume.

The Canons Regular

The spread of the canons regular — their origin has already been discussed — occurred in various ways. The most obvious idea was that of inducing the old communities, especially in the cathedral chapters, to renounce private ownership. Bishops or canons, especially in Italy and the Midi, and individuals elsewhere too, notably Archbishops Conrad of Salzburg and Norbert of Magdeburg, pushed this reform, but naturally with varying and often slight success. The situation was much more favourable if the canons who had opted for poverty withdrew and founded houses of their own. This happened everywhere. Existing houses not infrequently assisted houses that were being established to get over their first beginnings. Common customs, association of prayers, or even juridical dependence produced bonds that were sometimes loose, sometimes intimate. Additional recruits came from diocesan clerics, who sought out the desert and there formed communities. Some of them, it is true, went on to become monks, such as Bruno of Cologne, Vitalis of Savigny, and Gerald of Salles, already mentioned. But others, including Norbert, the founder of Prémontré, adhered to the *ordo canonicorum*. To enumerate all their many foundations would be tedious. But the powerful, even though overrated, flowering of the Premonstratensian Order showed how very much this initiative was in harmony with the time. A final group originated in lay communities, which in the course of time became chapters of canons regular as their lay element became more and more eclipsed. Their origin was often connected with the aim of lodging travellers on dangerous or deserted routes and, if necessary, of escorting them. The most celebrated example is the hospice on the Great Saint Bernard, the origin of which is still obscure.[8] Pilgrim routes became especially important, and canons regular acquired particular merit for their protecting of the pilgrimage to Santiago.

In contrast to Western monasticism, which possessed a Benedictine tradition that had applied to almost all monasteries since the eighth and ninth

---

[8] L. Quaglia, *La maison du Grand-Saint-Bernard des origines aux temps actuels* (Aosta 1955); A. Donnet, *Saint Bernard et les origines de l'hospice du Mont-Joux* (Saint-Maurice 1942).

centuries, the canons regular still had to define their way of life more exactly.[9] From the closing decades of the eleventh century the rule of Saint Augustine is repeatedly mentioned as its basis, but more recent research has shown that this must be understood relatively. In the first phase of their development, the canons regular appealed to a multilayered wealth of tradition: the Aachen rule of 816, which, referring to the Acts of the Apostles, they amended in favour of the principle of poverty; conciliar decrees and patristic writings, including Augustine, especially the so-called *Regula ad servos Dei* (often called *Regula tertia* in the literature[10]); his sermons on the life of clerics; and his own *vita* by Posidius. Thus arose between 1070 and 1130 those statutes of the canons regular that were soon known as the *ordo antiquus*. If we disregard the rule, formerly ascribed to Gregory VII, whose authenticity has recently been denied,[11] they are characterized by wise moderation. For the most part still unpublished, they need further investigation. Only some of their authors are known. Ivo of Chartres compiled an *ordo* for Saint-Quentin de Beauvais, as did Peter de Honestis, prior of Santa Maria Portuensis at Ravenna, for his house and its congregation. A far more popular *liber ordinis* originated at Saint-Ruf in 1100–10.

But these usages were not in accord with the ascetical severity which the eremitically inclined canons regular observed. Their efforts to draw up their own *consuetudines* found an Augustinian basis of tradition in the so-called *ordo monasterii* or *Regula secunda*. Since the ascetics there found confirmation of their ideas of manual labour, fasting, abstinence, and so forth, there appeared among them the notion that this was the original rule of Augustine. Probably first used at the beginning of the twelfth century at Springiersbach in the diocese of Trier, and from there transmitted to Prémontré, the text acquired great importance. Relying on it, the eremitically

---

[9] For what follows, see Dereine in *DHGE* XII, 386–91; C. Dereine, "Coutumiers et ordinaires des chanoines réguliers" in *Scriptorium* 5 (1951), 107–13; addenda, ibid. 13 (1959), 244–46; A. Carrier, *Coutumier du XIᵉ siècle de l'ordre de Saint-Ruf en usage à la cathédrale de Maguelone* (Sherbrooke near Quebec 1950); J. Leclercq, "Un témoignage sur l'influence de Grégoire VII dans la réforme canoniale" in *StudGreg* VI (1959–61), 173–227; P. Pauly, "Die Consuetudines von Springiersbach" in *TThZ* 67 (1958), 106–11; J. Siegwart, *Die Consuetudines des Augustiner-Chorherrenstiftes Marbach im Elsass* (Fribourg 1965).

[10] Editions of the *Regula ad servos Dei* and of the *Ordo monasterii* (mentioned in the next paragraph) in *PL* 32, 1377–84; *PL* 66, 995–98 (= *PL* 32, 1449–52); D. de Bruyne in *RBén* 42 (1930), 320–26, 318f.; J. C. Dickinson, *The Origins of the Austin Canons and their Introduction into England* (London 1950), 274–79, 273f.; Jordan of Saxony, *Liber Vitasfratrum,* ed. by R. Arbesmann – W. Hümpfner (New York 1943), LXXVI–LXXX, 485–504; concerning Augustine's authorship there has recently been a lively discussion, which has probably not yet been completed; on it cf. the critical report on the literature in J. C. Dickinson, *op. cit.* 255–72, in which Hümpfner's position (in the above mentioned edition of Jordan of Saxony) is not taken into consideration.

[11] C. Dereine, "La prétendue règle de Grégoire VII pour chanoines réguliers" in *RBén* 71 (1961), 108–18.

living canons regular opposed to the previous practice, or *ordo antiquus,* an *ordo novus* and thus started a controversy like that between Cistercians and Cluniacs. Then mixed forms were developed in the immediately following period.

A further tension-loaded element sprang from the problem of the care of souls.[12] If the Aachen rule was directed principally to the choral liturgy and claustral discipline, this basically monastic feature could not but be even stronger among the canons regular, especially since many of them sought solitude. On the other hand, the inner understanding between the heralds of the *vita apostolica* and the laity involved in the religious movement led to explicitly pastoral contacts and even to itinerant preaching. Furthermore, the new chapters not infrequently obtained proprietary churches, so that the question to be answered was whether the canons regular were themselves to assume the care of souls there or were to employ diocesan priests. Many older chapters, moreover, were attached to urban parishes, and the canons at the cathedral had to undertake specific tasks of the diocesan administration. Should not the idealistic fervour permeating the canons regular be used for the urgently necessary reform of the care of souls? Various answers were forthcoming. Among both the bishops and the canons regular there were voices that regarded the ascetical principle of flight from the world as irreconcilable with pastoral activity, while others maintained that no one was better qualified for pastoral labours than the canon regular, a view shared by the reform papacy. Both views were carried into practice. In Italy and France the contemplative principle was adhered to, though not exclusively, whereas on German soil it was without difficulty combined with pastoral work.

At least at the outset the types of canonical organization displayed a great diversity.[13] Reformed chapters of canons, for example, had an organization differing from that of new eremitical or hospital foundations. In these last the lay element, consisting of *conversi* or even of *conversae,* could play an important role. If women took part, double monasteries were formed, and the male

---

[12] C. Dereine, *DHGE* XII, 391–5; F. J. Schmale, "Kanonie, Seelsorge, Eigenkirche" in *HJ* 78 (1959), 38–63; C. Dereine, "Les chanoines réguliers dans l'ancienne province ecclésiastique de Salzbourg d'après les travaux récents" in *RHE* 43 (1948), 902–16; id., "Le problème de la cura animarum chez Gratien" in *Studia Gratiana,* II (Bologna 1954), 305–18. The problem of the care of souls was discussed at the time precisely in connection with monks; see P. Berlière, "L'exercice du ministère paroissial par les moines dans le haut moyen âge" in *RBén* 39 (1927), 227–50; P. Hofmeister, "Mönchtum und Seelsorge bis zum 13. Jahrhundert" in *SM* 65 (1953f.), 209–73; R. Foreville – J. Leclercq, "Un débat sur le sacerdoce des moines" in *SA* 41 (1957), 8–111; C. Violante, "Il monachesimo cluniacense di fronte al mondo politico ed ecclesiastico" in *Spiritualità cluniacense,* 197–227.

[13] Dereine in *DHGE* XII, 389–401; for the individual communities, cf. ibid., from column 379 on, *passim,* as well as Heimbucher and Cottineau; in addition, P. Pauly, *Springiersbach. Geschichte des Kanonikerstifts und seiner Tochtergründungen im Erzbistum Trier von den Anfängen bis zum Ende des 18. Jahrhunderts* (Trier 1962).

element, whose superior was usually called abbot in France, prior in Italy, and provost in the Empire, was ordinarily divided into canons and lay brothers. Here, then, were no essential differences from the Benedictine monasteries. The same was true of the forming of congregations.

Without entering into the juridical structure of the individual groupings, which in many cases still needs clarification, the most important centres of congregations for the period here dealt with were: in Italy, Santa Maria in Portu at Ravenna, whose founder, Peter de Honestis, died in 1119, the Lateran Canons Regular, Santa Maria del Reno at Bologna, and San Frediano at Lucca; in France, Saint-Ruf at Avignon, probably going back to 1038–39, Saint-Quentin de Beauvais, Saint-Victor de Paris, founded by William of Champeaux around 1110, and Arrouaise in the diocese of Arras (1090); in Germany, Rottenbuch in the diocese of Munich and Freising (1079), Marbach near Colmar (1087), and Springiersbach in the diocese of Trier (before 1107). All were to be eclipsed by the Premonstratensian Order, founded by Saint Norbert.

Norbert of Gennep (c. 1082–1134), scion of a noble family from the lower Rhineland, quite early became a canon at Xanten and soon after a royal chaplain at the court of Henry V. At a moment of extreme peril he underwent a complete change of life and, after receiving the priesthood in 1115, began to work as an itinerant preacher, in Germany until 1118, then in France, where he was authorized to preach by Pope Gelasius II. The claim that Calixtus II did not renew the permission in 1119 and obliged Norbert to join a congregation is at least unprovable. It is true that, at the request of the Bishop of Laon, Norbert undertook the reform of the local chapter of Saint-Martin and, when he failed, sought in 1120 a solitude not far away, where he founded Prémontré, but changes of this sort were by no means unusual for an itinerant preacher. It was only in 1121 that the eremitical life at Prémontré acquired a more stable form through the adoption of the canonical manner of life and was thereafter organized in the sense of the *ordo novus*. Though Norbert again and again went out as an itinerant preacher until his elevation to the archbishopric of Magdeburg in 1126, Prémontré, which became a double monastery because of the reception of *conversae,* retained its contemplative and ascetical character. In the daughter houses that soon appeared, however, the pastoral element frequently obtained greater recognition, especially in Germany. In any case, a preaching Order in the strict sense did not proceed from Prémontré, even though preaching was exercised in particular places, such as the Saxon "circaries".

The history of the Premonstratensians shows unmistakable parallels to that of the Cistercians. Both groups quickly spread, although the ideas they represented were not original with them. Prémontré was only one among many eremitically oriented canonicates, but in its founder, Norbert, it possessed an outstanding personality, as Cîteaux did in Bernard of Clairvaux.

An unconditioned devotion to religion, coupled with the charism of impassioned preaching, a will keenly intent on a goal, and intimate relations with nobles, princes, Emperors, and Popes provided Norbert with an uncommonly powerful influence. When he went to Magdeburg in 1126, the continuation of his work was assured. In the same year Honorius II confirmed the Order, which Norbert's pupil and friend, Hugh de Fosses, Abbot-General of Prémontré (1129–61), happily developed further, borrowing from the organizational form of the Cistercians but without adopting the notion of filiation.

The Military Orders

The above-mentioned communities, especially those composed of laymen, which were interested in conducting hospices and in caring for pilgrims, answered not merely an urgent need of the West. More than ever, Christians were seeking the Holy Land, ever since its recovery by the crusaders, and wanted to be taken care of there. From the effort to supply them with aid emerged the Templars and the Hospitallers.

Hugh of Payens (d. 1136), a knight from Champagne, joined with eight companions in 1119 in a religious community obliged to poverty, chastity, and obedience, with the added duty of providing armed protection to pilgrims *en route* from Jaffa to Jerusalem. Since Baldwin II of Jerusalem housed them in the royal palace, the so-called Temple of Solomon, the name "Templars" came to be applied to them. In their manner of life they conformed to the canons regular. The early difficulties were overcome when Hugh of Payens visited France and interested Bernard of Clairvaux. With the latter's help a religious rule was decided on at the Synod of Troyes in 1128 and the Patriarch Stephen of Jerusalem supplemented it in 1130. Bernard's propaganda — he composed for this purpose *De laude novae militiae ad milites Templi* — assured the Order a powerful growth.[14] Directed by a grand master, it was divided into three classes: knights, serving brothers, and chaplains. The more the crusade states had to maintain themselves against Muslim attacks, the more were the Templars, and soon also the Hospitallers, employed as an always available militia for their defence. This circumstance alone procured for the Templars rich gifts in all countries of the West and made them a powerful international society, conversant with finance, independent of the King of Jerusalem and of the ecclesiastical hierarchy, especially since the Holy See granted them important privileges of exemption.

Somewhat different was the history of the founding of the Hospitallers. Around 1070, and hence before the First Crusade, merchants from Amalfi,

---

[14] P. Cousin, "Les débuts de l'ordre des Templiers et Saint Bernard" in *Mélanges Saint-Bernard* (Dijon 1954), 41–52; Bernard's treatise is in *PL* 182, 921–40.

resuming earlier attempts, had founded a Christian hospital in Jerusalem and dedicated it to the Alexandrian Saint, John the Almoner, who was later unobtrusively supplanted by Saint John the Baptist. Intended for the care of the sick, the community acquired an enhanced contemporary significance after the First Crusade, under its masters, Gerard (d. c. 1120) and Raymond du Puy (1120–60). In East and West, and especially in France and the Italian port cities, arose foundations and excellently managed hospitals. Privileges of exemption granted by Popes and testimonies of favour on the part of lay persons gave the community a growing prestige. To the care of the sick was added from 1137 the duty of armed border patrol. This made the Hospitallers explicitly a military Order, divided, like the Templars, into three classes: knights, brothers, and chaplains. The hospital work was almost entirely turned over to the brothers. The new development was completed in the statutes, drawn up around 1155, and based on the life of canons regular.

The period treated here meant an epoch-making change in the history of religious Orders. The concept of *vita apostolica et evangelica,* which caused the older forms of monachism to withdraw into the background, which broke the monopoly of the monks and set up Augustinian canons and lay communities beside them, retained its dynamic force. It assured the new Orders, especially the Cistercians and Premonstratensians, a brilliant development but without being bound to them. When, toward the close of the twelfth century, their fervour cooled, the *vita apostolica* again became a problem. It found the long desired up-to-date expression in the mendicants.

CHAPTER 53

The Beginnings of Scholasticism

The difficulties already set forth in regard to canon law were true to an even greater degree in philosophy and theology. The more the scholars, attached to tradition, sought to appropriate the intellectual treasures that had come down to them, the more pressing became the question of how to reconcile the differences and contradictions that were brought to light there. Even in the Carolingian period the heterogeneous material in tradition had occasionally evoked violent discussions, but the problem of methodology became more and more familiar to Western scholars only from the eleventh century. It found its solution in scholasticism.

Among the dynamic forces of the time, dialectics played a decisive role. Some of its protagonists began to travel about in the eleventh century. Thus, the Milanese cleric, Anselm of Besata, after finishing his studies under the philosopher Drogo at Parma, went from Lombardy to Burgundy and from there to Germany, finally entering the chancery of Henry III. His *Rhetori-*

465

machia, a curious work on rhetoric and dialectics, composed around 1050 in an affected style, treats, among other things, the principle of contradiction in so inflated and inadequate a manner that it has a painful effect. Other dialecticians had even more self-confidence. They attacked theological questions with their meagre philosophical equipment; dogmas of faith, such as the virgin birth of Christ, his redemptive death, and his resurrection or the immortality of the soul were syllogistically destroyed. Their model may have been the objections raised by Marius Victorinus in his commentary on Cicero's *De inventione,* written before his conversion.[1] How widespread this skeptical and frivolous attitude was cannot be determined, but in any event it was strong enough to call forth an antidialectical opposition in the ecclesiastical camp.

One of the spokesmen of the opposition was the Benedictine, Otloh of Sankt Emmeram at Regensburg (d. 1070). Doubts about faith, which must have cost him a great deal during his studies before he entered the monastery, moved him to a radical return to the Bible, the Fathers, and hagiography. He did not absolutely repudiate secular knowledge but frankly regarded it as not permitted to monks and sharply rejected the tendency to prefer Plato, Aristotle, or Boethius to the teaching of the Church. The canon regular Manegold of Lautenbach (d. 1103) was even more severe with secular knowledge. In his *Opusculum contra Wolfelmum,* which is based on the commentary of the Neoplatonist Macrobius on the *Somnium Scipionis,* he sought to show that the teachings of Macrobius, Pythagoras, Plato, and of the Aristotelian logic were sophistry and error, irreconcilable with Christian doctrine and a danger to salvation. In his view the dogmas of faith destroyed the ancient philosophy.

To a great extent Manegold depended on Peter Damiani (d. 1072), and, as a matter of fact, the ardent superior of the hermits occasionally did make use of weighty arguments.[2] He cared nothing for dialectical skill in proofs, once called grammar a work of the devil, warned against the *artes liberales,* which should be termed *stultitiae* rather than *studia,* and preferred to regard all human efforts for wisdom as foolish in the final analysis. To him the absoluteness and transcendence of God were above everything. They tolerated no limitation on the part of human understanding. Even the law of contradiction — Peter pushed it as far as the question of whether God could undo something that had been done, such as the founding of Rome — could not be applied *vis-à-vis* God's unlimited omnipotence. The last mentioned postulate, untenable in itself and advanced even by Peter with obvious

---

[1] See J. de Ghellinck, "Réminiscences de la dialectique de Marius Victorinus dans les conflits théologiques du XI⁰ et XII⁰ siècles" in *RNPh* 18 (1911), 432–35.

[2] The evidence for what follows is in F. Dressler, *Petrus Damiani,* 175–85, 200–04; for the work on the principle of contradiction, see the Sources for this chapter; the passage on philosophy as the *ancilla theologiae, PL* 145, 603 C–D.

hesitation, must not be taken seriously. That there is here discerned the danger of a double truth, as Endres holds, is an only too logical deduction which is not in keeping with Peter's thought. The whole attitude of the so-called antidialecticians must be estimated with the same caution. It in no sense consisted of absolute negation. Otloh applied dialectics to theological problems, though quite clumsily; Manegold referred expressly to the harmony between philosophy and faith, especially in ethics and the doctrine of virtue; and the warnings of Peter Damiani were meant chiefly for his hermits, to a lesser degree for the laity, and not at all for the diocesan clergy, for whom he even required a solid scholarly formation. His real concern was for the right order between the secular and the spiritual, philosophy and theology; philosophy — and here he took up an old idea — was to exercise the serving function of handmaid to theology. However, it is correct that Peter, Otloh, and Manegold contributed little to a realization of this concern. As childish as the use of dialectics may often enough have been, it was not to be stopped. The course of the Eucharistic controversy provides a clear example.

The Eucharistic controversy did not come about by chance. The Western Church lacked a uniform Eucharistic doctrine summarizing the patristic tradition, such as John Damascene (d. c. 750) had worked out for the Eastern Church. It would have been all the more desirable in that the incompleted initial efforts of the Latin Fathers pointed in two directions. One group, going back to Ambrose, stressed rather the changing of bread and wine into the Lord's body and blood, while another group, with Augustine, gave special prominence to the dynamic symbolic power of the Sacrament, which incorporates the faithful into Christ and into the mystical body of the Church. The two viewpoints led in the Carolingian period to the doctrinal controversy, already mentioned, between the realistic and metabolistic outlook of Paschasius Radbertus and an Augustinian-oriented opposition, headed by Ratramnus. This theme engaged especially Rathier of Verona and Heriger of Lobbes in the tenth century. Though Heriger took pains with a synthesis of realism and symbolism, he basically followed Paschasius Radbertus, whose explanation pretty generally established itself in the course of time.[3] However, it was not entirely satisfactory. Since Paschasius had identified the Eucharistic and the historical body of the Lord without more precisely explaining the Eucharistic species, his teaching could and probably did promote a grossly materialistic "Capharnaitic" interpretation.

A reaction did not fail to show itself. A pupil of Fulbert of Chartres, Berengarius (d. 1088), since 1029 *scholasticus* at Tours and at the same time archdeacon of Angers, sought to restore the dynamic symbolic teaching of Augustine to prominence. The ensuing discussion differed from that of the

[3] In addition to J. Geiselmann, *Die Eucharistielehre der Vorscholastik* (Paderborn 1926), 267–81, cf. J. Lebon, "Sur la doctrine eucharistique d'Hériger de Lobbes" in *Studia mediaevalia in hon. R. J. Martin* (Bruges 1948), 61–84.

Carolingian period, on the one hand by the much greater use of dialectic thought, progressing at times even to metaphysics, and on the other hand by the broad and deep effect which it produced: the problem never set the theologians free until it had been essentially clarified. Even in the first phase of the struggle Berengarius had to contend with a whole group of equal or even superior opponents.[4] In addition, the official Church intervened. His doctrine was condemned by Leo IX at the Synods of Rome and Vercelli in 1050 and by the Synod of Paris in 1051. On the other hand the Council of Tours in 1054, presided over by the legate Hildebrand, accepted Berengarius's explanation that the body and blood of Christ are present after the consecration. In 1059, however, Berengarius was forced at the Roman Synod to sign a formula drawn up by Humbert of Silva Candida, in which the Lord's body contained in the consecrated bread was described crudely[5] as: "sensualiter manibus tractari vel frangi aut fidelium dentibus atteri".

This introduced the second phase of the controversy. Ten years later Berengarius submitted the formula and the doctrine on which it was based to a comprehensive dialectical criticism and moved into a radically spiritualistic symbolism. The consecrated bread is body in so far as it is image, sign, pledge of the real body; it awakens a remembrance of Christ's Incarnation and Passion and leads the mind that reposes in these mysteries to mystical union with the Lord. The bread remains bread even after the consecration; that is, the substance appears in the accidents, they are the coconstitutive principle of form. In the last mentioned argument Berengarius directed the debate to the metaphysical, but without having correctly understood the Aristotelian basic ideas that he used — *materia, forma, accidens, substantia.* Nor did his opponents yet know their real meaning. Hence their achievement is to be all the more highly esteemed in that, undertaking the speculative way on their own, they explained the process of change ever more clearly in the sense of a transubstantiation. Lanfranc (d. 1089) began the task, Guitmund of Aversa (d. c. 1095) completed the doctrine.[6] When in 1079 Berengarius was again summoned to Rome by Gregory VII, he had to swear to a formula of faith that was far better thought out: "[panem et vinum] substantialiter converti in veram et propriam et vivificatricem carnem et sanguinem Iesu Christi".[7] The post-Berengarian period brought nothing basically new, but only an assimilation of the individual aspects, which then found their first systematic recapitulation in the school of Anselm of Laon (d. 1117).

[4] For the individual authors cf. Geiselmann, *op. cit.* 299–331.

[5] Lanfranc, *De corpore et sanguine,* II, in *PL* 150, 410 D.

[6] Geiselmann, *op. cit.* 365–75 (Lanfranc), 375–96 (Guitmund), 397–444 (the other writers); add Bernold of Sankt Blasien, *De veritate corporis et sanguinis Domini,* ed. J. R. Geiselmann (Munich 1936); J. Weisweiler in *Scholastik* 12 (1937), 58–93.

[7] *Registrum* of Gregory VII, VI 17a, No. 1, *MGEp sel.* 2, ed. Caspar, 425–27.

The papacy's playing an important role in the Eucharistic controversy shows again the concentrated strength of the Gregorian reform movement. However, what was involved was rather an indirect relationship. The controversy as such was not caused by the reform, and it was the theologians who decided it, while Rome supervised its course. The situation was quite different in regard to the discussion of holy orders, which has already been frequently mentioned in connection with specific synodal decrees; this proceeded directly out of the struggle over reform. The severe measures in regard to simonists, who were branded as heretics, and the numerous excommunications, especially those hurled against antipopes and their adherents, of themselves raised the very old problem of whether heretics or schismatics could confer valid orders at all. Since Cyprian had bluntly denied that they could and Augustine had held the contrary and both views had entered into the tradition of the Church, a sure orientation was lacking. The controversy waged over the Formosan ordinations had produced excellent works at the beginning of the tenth century, especially the writings of Auxilius, who was influenced by Augustine. In the 1050's Auxilius was used by Peter Damiani and by Humbert of Silva Candida; Peter agreed with him, whereas Humbert roughly rejected him.[8] Much as Peter's *Liber gratissimus* surpassed Humbert's *Adversus simoniacos libri III* in theological depth, he too left many points unresolved. The reason lay in the unsatisfactory state of sacramental theology. Clarification would come only with the doctrine, appearing in the twelfth century, of *character sacramentalis* and the later distinction of *sacramentum, sacramentum et res,* and *res sacramenti.*

Another circumstance that impeded a solution was the fact that, in addition to the power of orders, promotion to the priesthood and the episcopate also imparted a function to which jurisdiction was attached and that at the time orders and jurisdiction had not yet been clearly enough distinguished. Through the union of the power of jurisdiction with ordination and vice versa there belonged to the Church a decisive importance in so far as incorporation into her constituted the prerequisite for the effectiveness of the priestly function. By "Church" at that time was in no sense meant, as Sohm assumed, a community of love and grace existing only in Christ, but also a corporate body, defined in regard to jurisdiction.[9] It was not merely accidental

---

[8] For Auxilius see Chapter 35, footnote 15; for the recourse to him by Peter Damian and Humbert, cf. Chapter 42, footnote 8.

[9] J. Fuchs, "Weihesakramentale Grundlegung kirchlicher Rechtsgewalt" in *Scholastik* 16 (1941), 496–520; H. Barion, "Ordo und regimen fidelium" in *ZSavRGkan* 77 (1960), 112–34; R. Sohm, *Kirchenrecht,* 2 vols. (Munich–Leipzig 1923); id., "Das altkatholische Kirchenrecht und das Dekret Gratians" in *Festschrift für A. Wach* (Munich–Leipzig 1918); see in this regard G. Ladner, *Theologie und Politik vor dem Investiturstreit* (Baden bei Wien 1936), 130–32 (footnote 234) and Barion *(supra); A.* Schebler, *Die Reordinationen in der "altkatholischen Kirche"* (Bonn 1936), 215–81, does not perhaps do full justice to the problem; the same may be said of the controversy between F. Pelster in *Gr* 46 (1938), 66–90, and A. Michel in *RQ*

that from about 1060 canonists especially were interested in the difficulty. They no longer presumed bluntly to declare simoniacal or schismatic orders invalid, but, by virtue of the distinction between the Sacrament, which ordination communicates, and the *virtus sacramenti,* the overwhelming number of them reached the view that, if a person no longer belonged to the unity of the Church, his ordinations would have to be regarded not merely as illicit but also as ineffectual, for he did not possess the Holy Spirit. They thus required for every simonist or schismatic who returned to the Church the traditional *impositio manuum,* which they regarded as a giving of the Spirit. Only a few, such as Bernold of Sankt Blasien, explained the primitive ceremony in the sense of a reconciliation.[10] For the moment matters remained in these modest and unsatisfactory initial doctrinal efforts.

While a whole group of talented men were going to great pains about specific timely questions, partly in harmony, partly in disagreement, what was really essential was being accomplished far away from daily strife by a lone worker: with the effortless ease proper to the nature of a genius Anselm was raising the problem of philosophy and theology to a speculative height never reached since the days of John Scotus Eriugena. Born not far from Aosta in Piedmont in 1033 and educated by Benedictines, he left his home and after three years sought the monastery of Bec in Normandy in order to study under the very famous Lanfranc of Pavia.[11] In 1060 Anselm entered Bec as a monk and soon assumed the office of teacher. He became prior in 1063 and Abbot in 1078. His promotion in 1093 to the archbishopric of Canterbury involved him in the already described conflicts with the English Kings William II and Henry I. He died in 1109.

Like all Western theologians, Anselm steeped himself in the writings of Augustine especially, but in his case there was a genuine intellectual encounter based on congeniality of soul. The celebrated guiding principles which Anselm carefully proposed for the relations between philosophy and theology, between reason and grace, are basically Augustinian. He frankly admitted his ardent wish somehow to understand the divine mysteries within the limits set for man, but he wanted to know that it was always directed only to truths which his soul already believed and loved; he did not wish to understand in order to believe, but he believed in order to understand — "neque enim quaero intelligere ut credam, sed credo ut intelligam".[12]

---

46 (1938), 29–39, *StudGreg* I (1947), 79–84, and of J. Gilchrist, "'Simoniaca haeresis' and the Problem of Orders from Leo IX to Gratian" in *Proceedings of the Second International Congress of Medieval Canon Law,* ed. S. Kuttner – J. Ryan (Vatican City 1965), 209–35.

[10] On the individual authors, cf. A. Schebler, *op. cit.* 235–98.

[11] Lanfranc, born *c.* 1010, prior at Bec in 1043, Abbot of Saint-Étienne de Caen in 1063, Archbishop of Canterbury from 1070 to his death in 1089. A. J. Macdonald, *Lanfranc. A Study of his Life, Work and Writing* (London 1926); D. Knowles, *The Monastic Constitutions of Lanfranc* (Edinburgh 1951); see also Chapter 44, footnote 42.

[12] *Proslogion,* I in *PL* 158, 227.

The idea urged inner understanding so that, according to circumstances, facts became clear to the thinking believer which were invisible in the merely accepted truth of faith, which at times could even make the faith itself clearer. The movement, summarized by Anselm in the brief formula, *Fides quaerens intellectum*,[13] thus went really beyond faith and, faith always presupposed, ended in reason. This is able at times to clarify in its existence a truth belonging to the divine sphere and hence to establish it on *rationes necessariae*, while the inner, inaccessible nature of the divine mysteries presents itself to the investigating human mind merely in image, parable, and relationship of suitability.

Anselm's speculation, proceeding from faith as a matter of principle, knew no real separation between philosophy and theology. This should be especially kept in mind in regard to his works composed at Bec. Except for *De casu diaboli*, they were all concerned with questions which would today be assigned to philosophy — *De grammatico, Monologion, Proslogion, De veritate, De libertate arbitrii*. Two of them especially stand out. In the *Monologion* Anselm tried to prove the existence of God by means of cosmology. In so doing he used the category of causality less than that of participation; however, he did not continue in a Platonic character but progressed to the sovereign divine nature, standing above all participation. All things are contained in the inner utterance of God which begot the Eternal Word, before, during, and after their created existence; everything that has become is a copy of the divine Word.

The *Proslogion* leads even more deeply into Anselm's specific thought. It contains the much admired, much attacked, so-called ontological proof. The argument presupposes an idea of God that is immanent to human thought and hence from the outset it contains an existential factor. In this idea God confronts us as the greatest that can be thought of at all. But, continues Anselm, the greatest cannot be merely in our intellect, for then another could be thought of which would be greater in so far as it really existed outside our intellect. Hence, the greatest, that is, God, must be in our mind and at the same time in external reality. Attacked on serious grounds by a contemporary, Gaunilo, monk of Marmoutier, and defended by Anselm in *Liber apologeticus*, the argument has been put to one side among the scholastics since Thomas Aquinas and, outside scholasticism, sharply rejected by Kant especially, but it has decidedly attracted some modern thinkers, such as Descartes, Leibniz, and Hegel, and is again taken seriously today.

Toward the end of his life Anselm treated specifically theological questions. In *De fide Trinitatis et de incarnatione Verbi* he stressed the distinction between the divine nature and the divine Persons against Roscelin, who, on the basis of his problematic doctrine of universals, assumed in the

---

[13] This was the original title of the *Proslogion*.

Trinity "tres res per se separatim". The *De processione Spiritus Sancti* was produced in connection with Urban II's efforts for union. *De conceptione virginali et originali peccato* and *Cur Deus homo* deal with the mystery of the Incarnation. The second of these not only displayed Anselm's method to perfection. It also made obsolete the patristic and early mediaeval theory of redemption — that of a buying back of fallen humanity by Christ from the dominion of the devil — by the deep idea that Christ became man in order to make satisfaction for all mankind to the divine honour, outraged by sin. Anselm's doctrine of satisfaction was further developed by the great scholastics of the thirteenth century and was thus firmly incorporated into Catholic theology.

Anselm has rightly been called the Father of Scholasticism. It was he who, boldly and undismayed, showed his contemporaries how dialectics and metaphysical speculation could be applied to theological questions without violating the reverence due to mysteries of faith by rationalistic arrogance. Others emulated him in this, such as Bruno of Segni (d. 1123) in his *De Trinitate* and *De incarnatione Domini* and Eudes of Cambrai (d. 1113) in *De peccato originali*.[14] And a younger generation was even then ready to extend the movement that had just experienced its break-through, to deepen it, divide it up, and arrange it systematically. With them really appeared Early Scholasticism. Anselm decisively contributed to making this possible.

Probably none of the many fruitful initiatives of the age of the Gregorian reform so definitely transformed the medieval world as did the intellectual development just sketched. Entering the stage of alert awareness, Western man began to reflect on basic questions of his essential Christian existence. While he still always looked with reverence to the tradition handed down to him, he now applied more strongly the critically distinguishing reason in order to take vital possession of the inherited intellectual property, to come to terms with it, and thereby to press on to new knowledge. The more absolutely he pursued this course, the more the minds separated. In a struggle that never again came to rest the West was thereafter to experience drastically the tensions implied in its form of existence.

---

[14] Bruno of Segni in *PL* 165, 973–84, 1079–84; on him see B. Gigalski, *Bruno, Bischof von Segni, Abt von Montecassino* (Münster 1898); R. Grégoire, *Bruno de Segni, exégète médiéval et théologien monastique* (Spoleto 1965). Eudes of Cambrai in *PL* 160, 1071–1102.

BIBLIOGRAPHY

GENERAL BIBLIOGRAPHY TO VOLUMES III AND IV

Section A contains various works, some of which also pertain to the history of the Eastern Church, e.g., works on the early councils, which are not repeated in Section B.

A. The Western Church

I. SOURCES FOR THE HISTORY OF THE WESTERN CHURCH

1. ANCILLARY SCIENCES

For aids to study (Chronology, Paleography, Libraries, Diplomatics, Archives, Heraldry, Geography, Cartography, and Statistics) see vol. I of this Handbook, 435–46.

2. SOURCES

A. Potthast, *Bibliotheca historica medii aevi, Wegweiser durch die Geschichtswerke des europäischen Mittelalters bis 1500,* 2 vols. (Berlin, 2nd ed. 1896; reprint Graz 1954); L. J. Paetow, *A Guide to the Study of Medieval History* (New York, 2nd ed. 1931); C. W. Previté-Orton, *The Study of Medieval History* (Cambridge 1938); *Guide to Historical Literature,* published by the American Historical Association (New York 1960), contains much on medieval Europe and the Byzantine Empire, esp. 169–232; *Repertorium fontium historiae medii aevi, primum ab A. Potthast digestum, nunc cura collegii historicorum e pluribus nationibus emendatum et auctum,* ed. by Istituto Storico Italiano and the Unione Internazionale degli Istituti di Archeologia, Storia et Storia dell'Arte in Roma (cit. *RepFont*); to date vol. I: *Series collectionum* (Rome 1962); U. Chevalier, *Répertoire des sources historiques du moyen-âge:* biographical, 2 vols. (Paris, 2nd ed. 1905–7); id., topographical, 2 vols. (Montbéliard 1894–1903).

The following national sources are important because of their treatment of other territories: A. Molinier, *Les sources de l'histoire de France,* 6 vols. (Paris 1902–06); Dahlmann-Waitz, *Quellenkunde der deutschen Geschichte,* ed. by H. Haering, 2 vols. (Leipzig, 9th ed. 1930–31), new printing in preparation; W. Wattenbach, *Deutschlands Geschichtsquellen im Mittelalter bis zur Mitte des 13. Jahrhunderts,* I (Stuttgart–Berlin, 7th ed. 1904), II (Berlin, 6th ed. 1894); Wattenbach-Levison, *Deutschlands Geschichtsquellen im Mittelalter.* Vorzeit und Karolinger, 4 fasc. prepared by W. Levison and H. Löwe, supplement by R. Buchner, *Die Rechtsquellen* (Weimar 1952–57); Wattenbach-Holtzmann, *Deutschlands Geschichtsquellen im Mittelalter, Deutsche Kaiserzeit,* I: (900–1125), previously in 4 fasc. (Tübingen, 2nd and 3rd editions 1948); K. Jacob – H. Hohenleutner, *Quellenkunde der deutschen Geschichte im Mittelalter,* 2 vols. (Berlin 1959–61), until 1250.

3. Collections of the More Important General Sources

J. P. Migne, *Patrologiae cursus completus. Series latina* (to 1216), vols. 1–217: Texts; 218–21: Indices (Paris 1841–64). *Suppl.* ed. by A. Hamman (Paris 1957 seqq.). Reference for new editions and catalogue of authors in *Rep Font* I, 434–54; accurate catalogue of the papal sources by *Santifaller NE*, 57–62.*Monumenta Germaniae Historica* (cit. *MG*), ed. by Deutsches Institut zur Erforschung des Mittelalters (various places of publication, 1826 seqq.). The chief series are: *Scriptores, Leges, Diplomata, Epistolae, Antiquitates.* A new small series contains political writings of the late Middle Ages, sources for the cultural history of the German Middle Ages and critical studies of texts, an index to all the works with a survey on the histories of the *MG*, bibliographical guide in *Rep Font* I, 466–78. *Die Geschichtsschreiber der deutschen Vorzeit* (German translations from the *MG*), 104 vols. (various places of publication, 1847 seqq.), indexed in the *Rep Font* I, 286–90; J. F. Böhmer, *Fontes rerum germanicarum,* 4 vols. (Stuttgart 1843–68), *Rep Font* I, 102; P. Jaffé, *Bibliotheca rerum germanicarum,* 6 vols. (Berlin 1864–73), *Rep Font* I, 349; M. Bouquet, *Recueil des historiens des Gaules et de la France. Rerum gallicarum et francicarum scriptores,* 24 vols. (Paris 1738–1904), new ed. by L. Delisle from vols. 1–19 (Paris 1868–80), *Rep Font* I, 7–9; *Académie des Inscriptions et Belles Lettres: Chartes et diplômes relatifs à l'histoire de France,* 16 vols. (Paris 1908 seqq.), *Rep Font* I, 3 seq.; *Recueil des historiens de France,* with the series: *Documents financiers, Obituaires, Pouillés, Rep Font* I, 9 seq.; *Documents relatifs à l'histoire des croisades* and *Recueil des historiens des croisades,* the last collection with several series, *Rep Font* I, 4–7; *Collection de textes pour servir à l'étude et l'enseignement de l'histoire,* 51 vols. (Paris 1886–1929), *Rep Font* I, 161–63; *Collection de documents inédits sur l'histoire de France,* 134 vols. (Paris 1835 seqq.), *Rep Font* I, 156–60; *Les classiques de l'histoire de France au moyen-âge* (with accompanying translations), 25 vols. (Paris 1923 seqq.), *Rep Font* I, 130 seq.; *Les classiques français du moyen âge,* 89 vols. (Paris 1910 seqq.), *Rep Font* I, 131–33; L. A. Muratori, *Rerum italicarum scriptores,* 25 vols. (Milan 1723–51), nuova ediz., iniziata da G. Carducci e V. Fiorini, continuata a cura dell'Istituto Storico Italiano, 34 vols. in 109 fasc. (Città di Castello, then Bologna 1900 seqq.), *Rep Font* I, 510–22; *Istituto Storico Italiano per il medio evo, Fonti per la storia d'Italia,* 94 vols. (Rome 1887 seqq.), *Rep Font* I, 272–74; *Regesta chartarum Italiae,* 34 vols. (Rome 1907 seqq.), *Rep Font* I, 606 seq.; *Rerum Britannicarum medii aevi scriptores,* ed. by the Master of the Rolls (cit. *Rolls Series*), 99 vols. (London 1858–96), *Rep Font* I, 612–9; *Royal Historical Society, Camden Third Series,* 90 vols. (London 1900 seqq.), *Rep Font* I, 629–31; *Medieval Classics,* since 1953 = *Medieval Texts* (with accompanying translations), 16 vols. (London 1949 seqq.), *Rep Font* I, 413; collected sources for other lands in *Rep Font* I.

4. Councils, Doctrinal and Canonical Decisions, Canon Law

J. Hardouin, *Acta conciliorum et epistolae decretales ac constitutiones summorum Pontificum,* 12 vols. (Paris 1714–15), *Rep Font* I, 317; J. D. Mansi, *Sacrorum conciliorum nova et amplissima collectio,* 31 vols. to 1440 (Florence, then Venice 1759–98); new printing with continuation to 1902 by J. B. Martin, L. Petit, 60 vols. (Paris 1899–1927), *Rep Font* I, 402–04; *Conciliorum oecumenicorum decreta,* ed. by Centro di Documentazione Bologna (Freiburg i. Br., 2nd ed. 1962); H. Denzinger, A. Schönmetzer, *Enchiridion symbolorum, definitionum et declarationum de rebus fidei et morum* (Barcelona–Freiburg, 33rd ed. 1965); C. Mirbt, *Quellen zur Geschichte des Papsttums und des römischen Katholizismus* (Tübingen, 4th ed. 1925 = 5th ed. 1934), somewhat one-sided but worthwhile. *Corpus Iuris Canonici,* most important editions: Editio Romana iussu Gregorii XIII (Rome 1582); Aem. Richter (Leipzig 1833–39); E. Friedberg, 2 vols. (Leipzig 1879–91); *Codicis Iuris Canonici Fontes,* ed. by Petrus Card. Gasparri, since vol. VII by Iustinianus Card. Serédi, I–VIII plus IX: *Tabellae* (Rome 1923–39).

476

Works on the history of the sources of canon law: A. van Hove, *Prolegomena.Commentarium Lovaniense in Codicem Juris Canonici* (Malines - Rome, 2nd ed. 1945); A. Stickler, *Historia iuris canonici*, I: *Historia fontium* (Turin 1950); P. Fournier – G. Le Bras, *Histoire des collections canoniques en Occident depuis les fausses décrétales jusqu'au décret de Gratien,* 2 vols. (Paris 1931–32).

5. The Papacy

Liber Pontificalis, ed. by L. Duchesne, I–II (Paris, 2nd ed. 1907–15, new printing 1955), Supplementary vol. III ed. by C. Vogel (Paris 1957), containing the original lives of the popes by Pandulf extending from Paschal II to Honorius II; previously edited by J. P. March, *Liber Pontificalis prout exstat in codice Dertusensi* (Barcelona 1925). On the origin of the entire 2 vols., cf. *LThK,* VI (2nd ed. 1961), 1016 seq.; J. M. Watterich, *Pontificum Romanorum qui fuerunt inde ab ex. saec. IX usque ad finem saec.* XIII Vitae, 2 vols. (Leipzig 1862), contains materials gathered from many sources; *Bullarium Romanum:* among the various editions, neither reliable nor complete, the most used is *Editio Taurinensis,* ed. by A. Tomassetti, 24 vols. (Turin 1857–72); P. Jaffé, *Regesta Pontificum Romanorum ab condita ecclesia ad a. 1198, 2ª* edit. cur. S. Loewenfeld, F. Kaltenbrunner, P. Ewald, 2 vols. (Berlin 1885–88; reprint Graz 1958). This indispensable work is now supplemented with a territorial arrangement of papal documents (to 1198) begun by P. Kehr, commissioned by the Göttinger Gesellschaft der Wissenschaften. It has since 1931 been continued by the "Pius Foundation for Papal Documents and Medieval Research". The following have thus far appeared: P. F. Kehr, *Regesta Pontificum Romanorum, Italia Pontificia,* I–VIII, cong. P. Kehr, IX, ed. by W. Holtzmann (Berlin 1906–35; 1962), X, for Calabria and the islands in preparation. *Germania Pontificia,* I–III, cong. A. Brackmann (Berlin 1910–35), cf. *Santifaller NE,* 69.
Studies on other areas are published by the Pius-Foundation for Papal Documents and Medieval Research in the *NGG* (since 1926 the *AGG*); survey by *Santifaller NE,* 66–68. Studies for Spain by P. Kehr, for Portugal by C. Erdmann, for Germany and Switzerland by A. Brackmann, for France by W. Wiederholt, H. Meinert, and J. Ramackers, for the Netherlands and Belgium by J. Ramackers, for England by W. Holtzmann.

6. Civil Law

Codex Theodosianus: — *cum perp. commentariis Jac. Gothfredi,* ed. by J. P. Ritter, 6 vols. (Leipzig 1739–43); — *cum constitutionibus Sirmondianis et leges novellae,* ed. by T. Mommsen, P. Meyer, 2 vols. (Berlin 1904–05); — recogn. P. Krueger (Berlin 1923); — Translation by Clyde Phan, 1 vol. (Princeton 1952).
Corpus Iuris Civilis: — ed. by Dion. Gothofredus, 6 vols. (Lyons 1589); ed. by P. Krueger, T. Mommsen and others, 3 vols. (Berlin 1912–20). The Celtic and Germanic collections are for the most part published in the above supplied collections in the *Rolls Series* and in the *MGLL* (see More Important General Sources); when necessary, they are cited below for particular chapters. The documents relating to secular rulers are edited in the sources on national history; cf. *Rep Font* I. Due to the close association between the papacy and the Empire the following are of special interest: *MG Diplomata Karolinorum; regum Germaniae ex stirpe Karolinorum; regum et imperatorum Germaniae;* cited individually in *Rep Font* I, 475; J. F. Böhmer, *Regesta Imperii,* new edition by the Wiener Institut für öster. Geschichtsforschung in the following sections: I, *Carolingian 751–918;* II, *Saxon 919–1024;* III, *Salian 1024–1125;* detailed citation in *Santifaller NE,* 14 seq.

477

7. HISTORICAL-STATISTICAL WORKS WITH OR WITHOUT SOURCE EDITIONS

P. B. Gams, *Series episcoporum ecclesiae catholicae* (Regensburg 1873; Suppl. 1879–86); L. H. Cottineau, *Répertoire topo-bibliographique des abbayes et prieurés,* 2 vols. (Mâcon 1935–39); *Gallia Christiana, in provincias ecclesiasticas distributa,* ed. by D. de Saint Marthe and by the monks of Saint-Maur, 16 vols. (Paris 1717–1865), *Rep Font* I, 279 seq.; *Gallia Christiana novissima. Histoire des archevêchés, évêchés et abbayes de France,* 7 vols. (Montbéliard, then Valence 1899 seqq.), *Rep Font* I, 280; F. Ughelli, *Italia Sacra,* 2nd ed. by N. Coleti, 10 vols. (Venice 1717–22), *Rep Font* I, 753–55; *España Sagrada,* by Henrique Flórez (and continuators), 56 vols. (Madrid 1747–1879; 1918; 1950 seqq.), *Rep Font* I, 252–55 with source texts; J. L. Villanueva, *Viage literario a las iglesias de España,* 20 vols. (Madrid 1803–51); W. Dugdale, *Monasticum Anglicanum,* 2nd ed. by J. Calley and others, 6 vols. (London 1817–30, 3rd ed. 1846), *Rep Font* I, 236; D. Farlati – J. Coleti, *Illyricum Sacrum,* 8 vols. (Venice 1751–1819), *Rep Font* I, 256 seq.; *Germania Sacra.* Historical-statistical material on German dioceses, cathedral chapters, collegiate and parish churches, monastic and other ecclesiastical institutions, ed. by the Kaiser-Wilhelm-Institut für Geschichte (now Max-Planck-Inst.); to date: *Diocese of Brandenburg* by Abb, Bünger, and Wentz (1929–41), *Diocese of Havelberg* by Wentz (1933), *Diocese of Bamberg* by Frhr. v. Guttenberg (1937), *Archdiaconate of Xanten* by Classen (1938), *Cistercian Abbey of Altenberg* by Mosler (1965), *Diocese of Würzburg,* 1 (line of bishops to 1254) by Wendehorst (1962).

The works of the "Pius Foundation" (v. supra Papacy) with important source material.

8. MONASTIC ORDERS

L. Holstenius and M. Brockie, *Codex regularum monasticarum et canonicarum,* 6 vols. (Augsburg 1759); B. Albers, *Consuetudines monasticae,* 5 vols. (Stuttgart–Vienna, then Montecassino 1900–12), *Rep Font* I, 181; K. Hallinger, *Corpus consuetudinum monasticarum, cura Pont. Athenaei S. Anselmi de Urbe editum;* of the 25 planned volumes to date vols. I and II (Siegburg 1963).

9. LITURGY

Cf. bibliography by H. Baus in vol. I of the Handbook 492 seqq. The following concern the medieval period: *Henry Bradshaw Society, founded in the year of our Lord 1890 for the editing of rare liturgical texts,* 92 vols. (London 1891 seqq.), *Rep Font* I, 322 f.; V.-M. Leroquais has collected the manuscripts on liturgical matters for France: *Les sacramentaires et missels,* 3 vols. (Paris 1924); *Les bréviaires,* 5 vols. (Paris 1934); *Les pontificaux,* 3 vols. (Paris 1937); *Les psautiers,* 2 vols. (Mâcon 1940–41); *Le Pontifical Romain au moyen âge,* ed. by M. Andrieu, *Studi e Testi,* 86, 87, 88, 99 (Vatican 1938–41); *Les ordines Romani du haut moyen âge,* ed. by M. Andrieu: *Spec. Sacr. Lovan. (infra* no. 11) 11, 23, 24, 28 (Louvain 1931–36); U. Chevalier, *Repertorium hymnologicum,* 6 vols. (Brussels 1892–1920); G. M. Dreves–C. Blume, *Analecta hymnica medii aevi,* 55 vols. (Leipzig 1886 seqq.), *Rep Font* I, 29 seq.; *Hymnologische Beiträge,* ed. by Dreves-Blume, 4 vols. (Leipzig 1897 seqq.), *Rep Font* I, 336.

10. HAGIOGRAPHY

Acta Sanctorum, ed. by J. Bolland and successors, the "Bollandists", 70 vols. (published in various places, 1643 seqq.); new printing vols. 1–43 (Venice 1734–40); vols. 1–60 with changes (Paris–Rome 1863–70); more detailed references and survey arranged according to monthly and liturgical calendar in *Rep Font* I, 16 seq.; *Bibliotheca hagiographica Latina antiquae et mediae aetatis,* 2 vols. (Brussels 1898–1901, Suppl. 1911, new imp. 1949) contains name-index of the *ActaSS* as well as codices and bibliography; *Martyrologium Romanum,* 3rd ed. (Rome 1949); *Martyrologium Romanum, ad formam editionis typicae scholiis historicis instructum,* ed. by H. Delehaye *et al.; ActaSS. Propylaeum ad Acta Sanctorum Decembris* (Brussels 1940); F. Doyé, *Heilige und Selige der röm.-kath. Kirche,* 2 vols. (Leipzig 1930–32); *Bibliotheca Sanctorum,* ed. by Istituto Giovanni XXIII, an extensive Encyclopedia, to date 6 vols. (Rome 1961 seqq.).

11. PHILOSOPHY AND THEOLOGY

Beiträge zur Geschichte der Philosophie (since 1930: *und Theologie) des Mittelalters, Texte und Untersuchungen,* 39 vols., first edited by C. Baeumker, now by M. Schmaus (Münster 1891 seqq.), *Rep Font* I, 59–61; *Florilegium patristicum,* since 1930: *tam veteris quam medii aevi auctores complectentes,* first edited by G. Rauschen, then by B. Geyer and J. Zellinger, 44 vols. (Bonn 1904–44), *Rep Font* I, 261 seq.; *Spicilegium sacrum Lovaniense. Études et documents pour servir* à l'histoire des doctrines chrétiennes depuis la fin de l'âge apostolique jusqu'à la clôture du concile de Trente: Université catholique et collèges O. P. et S. J. de Louvain, Paris, 28 vols. (Louvain 1922 seqq.), *Rep Font* I, 711.

Textes philosophiques du moyen âge, 7 vols. (Paris 1955 seqq.); *Rep Font* I, 740.

II. MATERIALS ON WESTERN HISTORY

1. UNIVERSAL HISTORY

a) GENERAL ACCOUNTS: *Peuples et Civilisations. Histoire générale,* ed. by L. Halphen and P. Sagnac (Paris 1926 seqq.), V. L. Halphen, *Les barbares, des grandes invasions aux conquêtes turques du XIe s.* (4th ed. 1940); VI, L. Halphen, *L'essor de l'Europe, XIe–XIIIe s.* (2nd ed. 1940); *Histoire Générale,* ed. by G. Glotz and others (Paris 1925 seqq.); vol. 14 begins the series "Le Moyen-Age": I, 1–2, F. Lot, C. Pfister, F. L. Ganshof, *Les destinées de l'Europe en Occident de 395 à 888* (2nd ed. 1940–41); II, A. Fliche, *L'Europe occidentale de 888 à 1125* (2nd ed. 1941); III, C. Diehl, G. Marçais, *Le monde oriental de 395 à 1081* (1944); VIII, H. Pirenne, G. Cohen, H. Focillon, *La civilisation occidentale du XIe au milieu du XVe s.;* IX, 1, C. Diehl and others, *L'Europe orientale de 1081 à 1453* (1945); *The Cambridge Medieval History,* planned by J. B. Bury (Cambridge 1911–36), II: *The Rise of the Saracens and the Foundation of the Western Empire* (1913); III: *Germany and the Western Empire* (1924); IV: *The Eastern Roman Empire 717–1453* (1927); V: *Contest of Empire and Papacy* (1929). Vol. II reaches to about 814, III until into the 11th cent., vol. V from about 1050–1200; *Historia Mundi,* ed. by F. Valjavec (Bern 1952 seqq.); V: *Frühes Mittelalter* (1956), with sections: Das frühe Germanentum — Die Reitervölker Eurasiens — Das frühe Slaventum — Die Araber und der Islam — Die Grundlegung des Abendlandes (Carolingian Period); VI: *Hohes und spätes Mittelalter* (1958), with sections: Das Abendland — Die byzantinische Welt — Die Welt des Islam — Ausklang und Übergang (Humanism and Renaissance); *Propyläen-Weltgeschichte,* Eine Universalgeschichte, ed. by G. Mann and A. Nitschke, V: *Islam. Die Entstehung Europas* (Berlin - Frankfurt - Vienna 1963), embracing also the high and the greater part of the later Middle Ages. Also worthwhile are: *Propyläen-Weltgeschichte,* ed. by W. Goetz, III–IV (Berlin 1932–33); *Neue Propyläen-Weltgeschichte,* ed. by W. Andreas, II (Berlin 1940); A. Cartellieri, *Weltgeschichte als Machtgeschichte, 381–911. Die Zeit der Reichsgründungen* (Munich - Berlin 1927); id., *Die Weltstellung des deutschen Reiches 911–1047* (1932); id., *Der Aufstieg des Papsttums im Rahmen der Weltgeschichte 1047–1095* (1936); id., *Der Vorrang des Papsttums zur Zeit der Kreuzzüge 1095–1150* (1941).

b) Shorter Summaries: J. Calmette, *Le monde féodal* in Clio, *Introduction aux études historiques* (Paris, 5th ed. 1951); J. Génicot, *Les lignes de faîte du moyen-âge* (Casterman, 3rd ed. 1961); R. W. Southern, *The Making of the Middle Ages* (London 1953); C. Dawson, *The Making of Europe 400–1000* (London, 2nd ed. 1951); W. von den Steinen, *Der Kosmos des Mittelalters. Von Karl dem Grossen zu Bernhard von Clairvaux* (Bern–Munich 1959); K. Hampe, *Das Hochmittelalter 900–1250* (Munich–Cologne, 4th ed. 1953); F. L. Ganshof, *Le Moyen-Âge: Histoire des relations internationales*, I (Paris 1953); N. F. Cantor, *Medieval History* (New York 1963); C. W. Previté-Orton, *The Shorter Cambridge Medieval History*, 2 vols. (Cambridge 1952); S. Painter, *The Feudal Monarchies* (Ithaca, New York, 1951).

c) Works on Cultural and Intellectual History: G. Schnürer, *Kirche und Kultur im Mittelalter*, 3 vols. (Paderborn 1924–29, I, 3rd ed. 1936); C. Dawson, *Religion and the Rise of Western Culture* (London 1950); *Histoire générale des Civilisations*, III, ed. by E. Perroy (Paris 1955); J. Bühler, *Die Kultur des Mittelalters* (Stuttgart, 3rd ed. 1941; new printing 1949); L. A. Veit, *Volksfrommes Brauchtum und Kirche im Mittelalter* (Freiburg 1936); Th. Steinbüchel, *Christliches Mittelalter* (Leipzig 1935); H. Meyer, *Geschichte der abendländischen Weltanschauung*, III: *Die Weltanschauung des Mittelalters* (Paderborn–Würzburg, 2nd ed. 1952); *The Medieval World 300–1300*, ed. by N. F. Cantor (New York 1962).

2. National Histories

England: *The Oxford History of England*, ed. by G. N. Clark (Oxford 1934 seqq.): II, F. M. Stenton, *Anglo-Saxon England* (2nd ed. 1947; often reprinted); III, A. L. Poole, *From Domesday Book to Magna Carta 1087–1216* (2nd ed. 1955); A. L. Poole, *Medieval England*, 2 vols. (Oxford, 2nd ed. 1960); C. Petit-Dutaillis, *The Feudal Monarchy in France and England from the 10th to the 13th Century* (London 1936); J. E. A. Jolliffe, *The Constitutional History of Medieval England from the English Settlement to 1485* (London, 2nd ed. 1947).

France: E. Lavisse, *Histoire de France depuis les origines jusqu'à la Révolution* (Paris 1900 seqq.): II, 1, C. Bayet, C. Pfister, A. Kleinclausz, *Le christianisme, les barbares, Mérovingiens et Carolingiens* (1903); II, 2, A. Luchaire, *Les premiers Capétiens 987 à 1137* (1901); G. Duby, R. Mandrou, *Histoire de la civilisation française. Moyen âge au XVIᵉ siècle* (Paris 1958).

Germany: G. Gebhardt, H. Grundmann, *Handbuch der deutschen Geschichte*, I: *Frühzeit und Mittelalter* (Stuttgart, 8th ed. 1954). O. Brandt, A. O. Meyer, *Handbuch der deutschen Geschichte*, I (Potsdam 1935–41), new ed. by L. Just (Constance 1952 seqq., incomplete); P. Rassow, *Deutsche Geschichte im Überblick* (Stuttgart, 2nd ed. 1962); *Jahrbücher der deutschen Geschichte*, ed. by Hist. Kommission der Bayerischen Akademie der Wissenschaften (1862 seqq.). An indispensable reference work arranged chronologically according to the reigns of the individual rulers (from the beginning of the Carolingians until 1158, 1190–1233, 1298–1308); presentations proceed chronologically upon the quotation of all sources. W. v. Giesebrecht, *Geschichte der deutschen Kaiserzeit* (until 1190), 6 vols., the last ed. by B. von Simson (Leipzig, I–III, 5th ed. 1881–90; IV, 2nd ed. 1877; V–VI, 1880–95); K. Hampe, F. Baethgen, *Deutsche Kaisergeschichte in der Zeit der Salier und Staufer* (Heidelberg, 10th ed. 1949).

Italy: L. M. Hartmann, *Geschichte Italiens im Mittelalter* (Gotha 1897 seqq.): II, 2, to IV, 1 (1903–15), unfinished, reaches from the Carolingian period until 1017. *Storia politica d'Italia*, dir. da A. Solmi, 3rd ed. (Milan 1937 seqq.): VI, G. Romano, *Le dominazioni barbariche in Italia 395–888* (1940); VII–VIII, C. G. Mor, *L'età feudale* (1952–3); *Storia d'Italia Illustrata* (Milan 1936 seqq.): III, L. Salvatorelli, *L'Italia medioevale dalle incursioni barbariche agli inizi del sec. XI* (n. d.); IV, L. Salvatorelli, *L'Italia comunale. Dagli inizi del sec. XI alla metà del sec. XIV* (n. d.); *Storia d'Italia*, ed. by N. Valeri, I: *Il medioevo* (Turin 1959).

Spain and Portugal: R. Konetzke, *Geschichte des spanischen und portugiesischen Volkes* (Leipzig–Berlin 1939); *Historia de España*, ed. by R. Menéndez Pidal (Madrid 1940 seqq.): III–IV,

E. Lévi-Provençal, *España musulmana hasta la caída del califato de Córdoba 711–1031,* Introduction by A. García Gómez (1950–57); VI, J. Pérez de Urbel, R. Arco y Garay, *España cristiana. Comienzo de la Reconquista 711–1038* (1956); R. Soldevilla, *Historia de España,* I–II (Barcelona 1952–53); L. García de Valdavellano, *Manual de la historia de España* (Madrid 1952); A. Ballesteros y Beretta, *Historia de España,* vol. II and the beginning of III (Madrid 1920, 1922), 2nd ed. from I–III in 5 vols. (Barcelona 1943–48); P. Peres, *Historia de Portugal,* I–II (Barcelos 1928–29).

For the other countries, national histories are cited in their respective sections.

3. General Church History

Histoire de l'Église depuis les origines jusqu'à nos jours, ed. by A. Fliche, V. Martin and others (Paris 1934 seqq.): VI, E. Amann, *L'époque carolingienne* (1947); VII, E. Amann, A. Dumas, *L'Église au pouvoir des laïques 888–1057* (1948); VIII, A. Fliche, *La réforme grégorienne et la reconquête chrétienne 1057–1125* (1946); XII: *Institutions ecclésiastiques de la chrétienté médiévale,* Livre I, G. Le Bras, *Préliminaires et Ière partie* (1959); XIII, A. Forest, F. van Steenberghen, M. de Gandillac, *Le mouvement doctrinal du IXe au XIVe s.* (1951); *Die Kirche in ihrer Geschichte. Ein Handbuch,* ed. by K. D. Schmidt and E. Wolf (Göttingen 1960 seqq.); for the Middle Ages (= vol. II) to date: fascicle E, G. Haendler, *Geschichte des Frühmittelalters und der Germanenmission;* G. Stökl, *Geschichte der Slavenmission* (1961); fascicle G, 1: H. Grundmann, *Ketzergeschichte des Mittelalters* (1963); B. Llorca, R. García Villoslada, F. J. Montalban, *Historia de la Iglesia católica* (Madrid 1950 seqq.), II, R. García Villoslada, *Edad media 800–1303* (2nd ed. 1958); K. Bihlmeyer, H. Tüchle, *Kirchengeschichte,* II: *Das Mittelalter* (Paderborn, 17th ed. 1962), E. T.: *Church History* (Westminster, Md., 1963); J. Lortz, *Geschichte der Kirche in ideengeschichtlicher Betrachtung,* I: *Altertum und Mittelalter* (Münster, 21st ed. 1962), numerous English translations; H. v. Schubert, *Geschichte der christlichen Kirche im Frühmittelalter* (Tübingen 1921), to the end of the ninth century.

4. Church History of Individual Lands

Austria: E. Tomek, *KG Österreichs,* 2 vols. (Innsbruck–Vienna–Munich 1935–48); J. Wodka, *KG Österreichs. Wegweiser durch ihre Geschichte* (Vienna 1959); A. Maier, *KG Kärntens,* Part 2: *Mittelalter* (Klagenfurt 1953).

Belgium: E. de Moreau, *Histoire de l'Église en Belgique,* 5 vols. and supplementary vols. (Brussels 1940 seqq.), I–II: *Histoire de l'Église en Belgique des origines au XIIe s.* (2nd ed. 1945).

Bohemia: A. Nägle, *KG Böhmens und Mährens* I, 1–2 (Vienna - Leipzig 1915–18), reaches only to 973.

Denmark and other northern lands: P. G. Lindhardt, *Den nordiske kirkeshistorie,* I (Copenhagen 1950); *Handbok i Svensk kirkohistoria,* I, Y. Brilioth, *Medeltiden* (Stockholm 1948); *Den Danske kirkeshistorie,* ed. by H. Koch and B. Kornerup; I, H. Koch, *Den aeldre middelalder indtil 1241* (Copenhagen 1950); G. Gustafson, *Svensk kirkehistoria* (Stockholm, 2nd ed. 1963).

England: *History of the English Church,* ed. by W. R. W. Stephens and W. Hunt, 8 vols. in 9 (London 1899–1910, later printings); II, W. Hunt, *History of the English Church from its Foundation to the Norman Conquest 597–1066* (1899); III, W. R. W. Stephens, *History of the English Church from the Norman Conquest to the Accession of Edward I 1066–1272* (1901); *Ecclesiastical History of England,* ed. by J. C. Dickinson: I, H. Deannesley, *The Pre-Conquest Church in England* (London 1961); J. Moorman, *A. History of the Church of England* (London 1953); S. C. Carpenter, *The Church in England 597–1688* (London 1954); J. Godfrey, *The Church in*

Anglo-Saxon England (Cambridge 1962); *The English Church and the Papacy in the Middle Ages,* ed. by C. H. Lawrence (London 1965).

FRANCE: C. Poulet, *Histoire de l'Église de France,* 3 vols. (Paris 1946–49); A. Latreille, E. Delaruelle, J. R. Palanque, *Histoire du catholicisme en France,* 2 vols. (Paris 1957–60); M. Bury, *Histoire de l'Église d'Alsace* (Colmar 1946).

GERMANY: K. Hauck, *Kirchengeschichte Deutschlands,* 5 vols. (Leipzig I–IV, 4th ed. 1904–13; V/1, 2nd ed. 1911; V/2, 1920, last printing 1950 seqq.), I: to 751; II: 751–911; III: 911–1122; extends beyond Germany.
Individual German territories:
KG Bayerns by R. Bauerreiss, 5 vols. (St Ottilien 1950–5); *KG Schwabens* by H. Tüchle, 2 vols. (Stuttgart 1950–54); *Württemberg KG,* I, by K. Weller (Stuttgart 1936); *Pfälzische KG* by E. Mayer (Kaiserslautern 1939); *KG der Pfalz* by L. Stamer, 4 parts (Speyer 1936–65); *Thüringische KG* by R. Herrmann, 2 vols. (Jena 1937–47); *KG Sachsens* by W. Schlesinger, 2 vols. (Cologne–Graz 1962); *KG Mecklenburgs,* I, by K. Schmaltz (Schwerin 1935); *KG Pommerns* by H. Heyden, 2 vols. (Cologne, 2nd ed. 1957); *KG Niedersachsens* (Göttingen 1939); *Mittelalterliche KG Ostfrieslands* by H. Kochs (Aurich 1934); *KG Schleswig-Holsteins,* I, by H. v. Schubert (Kiel 1907); II, by E. Feddersen (Kiel 1938).

IRELAND AND SCOTLAND: L. Gougaud, *Chrétientés celtiques* (Paris 1911), Eng. trans. *Christianity in Celtic Lands* (London 1932); A. Bellesheim, *Geschichte der Katholischen Kirche in Irland,* 3 vols. (Mainz 1890–91); W. Delius, *Geschichte der irischen Kirche von den Anfängen bis zum 12. Jahrhundert* (Munich–Basle 1954); A. Bellesheim, *Geschichte der katholischen Kirche in Schottland,* 2 vols. (Mainz 1883); W. O. Simpson, *The Celtic Church in Scotland* (Aberdeen 1935); J. H. S. Burleigh, *A Church History of Scotland* (Oxford 1960).

NETHERLANDS: R. R. Post, *Kerkgeschiedenis van Nederland in de middeleewen,* 2 parts (Utrecht 1957).

POLAND: K. Völker, *KG Polens* (Berlin 1930).

SWITZERLAND: Th. Schwegler, *Geschichte der katholischen Kirche in der Schweiz* (Stans, 2nd ed. 1945).

SPAIN: P. Gams, *Kirchengeschichte von Spanien,* 3 vols. (Regensburg 1862–79); Z. García Villada, *Historia eclesiástica de España,* 3 vols. in 5 (Madrid 1929–36), until 1085.

5. CONCILIAR AND PAPAL HISTORY

C. J. v. Hefele, H. Leclercq, *Histoire des Conciles,* III–V (Paris 1910–15); III, 560 seqq., 692–813; IV, 814–1073; V, 1073–1250; J. Haller, *Das Papsttum. Idee und Wirklichkeit,* new and completed edition by H. Dannenbauer in 5 vols. (Stuttgart 1950 seqq.); I: *Die Grundlagen* (1950), to the end of the 8th century; II: *Der Aufbau* (1952), to 1125; F. X. Seppelt, *Geschichte des Papsttums,* II: *Geschichte des Papsttums im Frühmittelalter. Von Gregor dem Grossen bis zur Mitte des 11. Jahrhunderts* (Munich, 2nd ed. 1955); III: *Die Vormachtstellung des Papsttums im Hochmittelalter von der Mitte des 11. Jahrhunderts bis zu Cölestin V.* (1956); E. Caspar, *Geschichte des Papsttums von den Anfängen bis zur Höhe der Weltherrschaft* (not completed), II: *Das Papsttum unter byzantinischer Herrschaft* (Tübingen 1933), reaches to about 750. Out of the papers selected by U. Gmelin: E. Caspar, *Das Papsttum unter fränkischer Herrschaft* (Darmstadt 1956 = reprint from *ZKG* 54 [1935], 132–264); W. Ullmann, *The Growth of Papal Government in the Middle Ages. A Study in the ideological relation of clerical to lay power* (London 1955), extends to about 1150; cf. F. Kempf, *Die päpstliche Gewalt in der mittelalterlichen Welt* in *Saggi storici intorno al Papato* (Rome 1959), 117–69.

Rome and the Papal State: *Storia di Roma,* ed. by Istituto di Studi Romani (Bologna 1938 seqq.), IX, O. Bertolini, *Roma di fronte a Bosanzio e ai Longobardi* (1941); X, P. Brezzi, *Roma e l'impero medioevale 774–1252* (1947); XII, *Topografia e urbanistica di Roma* (1958), 189–341; C. Cecchelli, *Roma medioevale;* F. Schneider, *Rom und Romgedanke im Mittelalter* (Munich 1926); L. Duchesne, *Les premiers temps de l'État Pontifical* (Paris, 3rd ed. 1911); L. Halphen, *Études sur l'administration de Rome au moyen âge 751 à 1252* (Paris 1907).

6. Ecclesiastical Legal and Constitutional History

Systematic Presentation with Historical References: G. Phillips, *Kirchenrecht,* 7 vols. (Regensburg 1845–72); VIII by F. Vering (1889); P. Hinschius, *Das Kirchenrecht der Katholiken und Protestanten,* I–VI, 1 (Berlin 1869–97); J. B. Sägmüller, *Lehrbuch des katholischen Kirchenrechts,* 2 vols. (Freiburg i. Br., 3rd ed. 1914; I, 1–4, 4th ed. 1925–34).

Works on Legal History: For sources see above, bibliography I, 4; H. E. Feine, *Kirchliche Rechtsgeschichte. Die katholische Kirche* (Cologne–Graz, 4th ed. 1964); W. Plöchl, *Geschichte des Kirchenrechts,* I: *Das Recht des ersten christlichen Jahrtausends. Von der Urkirche bis zum grossen Schisma* (Vienna, 2nd ed. 1960); II: *Das Kirchenrecht der abendländischen Christenheit 1055 bis 1517* (Vienna, 2nd ed. 1961); *Histoire du droit et des institutions de l'Église en Occident,* ed. by G. Le Bras (Paris 1955 seqq.), I, G. Le Bras, Prolégomènes (1955); see also *Fliche-Martin,* XII (Gen. Bib. II, 3); R. Sohm, *Kirchenrecht,* 2 vols. (Leipzig 1892–1923); B. Kurtscheid, *Historia iuris canonici. Historia institutionum,* I: *Ab ecclesiae fundatione usque ad Gratianum* (Rome 1941); C. Munier, *Les sources patristiques de droit de l'Église du VIIIe au XIIIe siècle* (Diss. Strasbourg 1957).

For individual countries the works are cited below in the proper section; especially important are the following: A. Werminghoff, *Verfassungsgeschichte der deutschen Kirche im Mittelalter* (Leipzig, 2nd ed. 1913); J. F. Lemarignier, J. Gaudemet, G. Mollat, *Institutions ecclésiastiques* in Lot-Fawtier, III (Paris 1962); J. B. LoGrasso, *Ecclesia et Status* (Rome, 2nd ed. 1952); S. Z. Ehler and J. B. Morall, *Church and State through the Centuries* (London 1954).

7. Secular Legal and Constitutional History

England: F. Pollock, F. W. Maitland, *History of English Law before the Time of Edward I,* 2 vols. (Cambridge, 2nd ed. 1911); J. E. A. Jollife, *Constitutional History of Medieval England from the English Settlement to 1485* (London, 2nd ed. 1947).

France: P. Viollet, *Histoire des institutions de France,* 3 vols. (Paris 1890–1903); E. Chénon, *Histoire générale du droit français public et privé* (Paris 1926–27); F. Lot, R. Fawtier and others, *Histoire des institutions françaises au moyen âge,* I: *Institutions seigneuriales* (Paris 1957); II: *Institutions royales* (1958); III: *Institutions ecclésiastiques;* R. Holtzmann, *Französische Verfassungsgeschichte* (Munich 1910).

Germany: R. Schröder and E. v. Künssberg, *Lehrbuch der deutschen Rechtsgeschichte* (Berlin, 7th ed. 1932); H. Conrad, *Deutsche Rechtsgeschichte,* I: *Frühzeit und Mittelalter* (Karlsruhe, 2nd ed. 1962). G. Waitz, *Deutsche Verfassungsgeschichte,* 8 vols. (Berlin I–II, 3rd ed. 1880–82; III–VI 2nd ed. 1883–96; VII–VIII, 1876–78), important because of their rich quotations of sources.

Italy: A. Pertile, *Storia del diritto Italiano,* 7 vols. (Turin, 2nd ed. 1928); P. S. Leicht, *Storia del diritto italiano, Diritto pubblico* (Milan, 2nd ed. 1940), *Le fonti* (1939), *Il diritto privato* (1941–44); G. de Vergottini, *Lezioni di storia del diritto italiano. Il diritto pubblico italiano nei sec. XII–XIV* (Milan, 2nd ed. 1960).

Spain: A. García Gallo, *Historia del derecho español,* 2 vols. (Madrid 1941–42; I, 3rd ed. 1945); E. Mayer, *Historia de las instituciones sociales y políticas de España y Portugal durante los siglos V a XIV,* 2 vols. (Madrid 1925–26).

For other lands literature is cited as needed.

8. Monographs on Ecclesiastical and Secular Legal History

a) State and Society: O. Gierke, *Das deutsche Genossenschaftsrecht,* 4 vols. (Berlin 1868–1912), English extracts by F. Maitland in *Political Theories of the Middle Ages* (Cambridge 1900); H. Mitteis, *Der Staat des hohen Mittelalters* (Weimar, 7th ed. 1962); F. Kern, *Gottesgnadentum und Widerstandsrecht im früheren Mittelalter* (Darmstadt, 2nd ed. 1954), Eng. trans., *Kingship and Law in the Middle Ages* (Oxford 1939); M. David, *La souveraineté et les limites juridiques du pouvoir monarchique du IXe au XVe siècle* (Paris 1954); T. Mayer, *Fürsten und Staat. Studien zur Verfassungsgeschichte des deutschen Mittelalters* (Weimar 1950); F. L. Ganshof, *Qu'est-ce que la féodalité?* (Brussels, 3rd ed. 1957), Eng. trans., *Feudalism* (New York 1961); H. Mitteis, *Lehnrecht und Staatsgewalt* (Weimar 1933); J. Calmette, *La société féodale* (Paris, 4th ed. 1938); M. Bloch, *La société féodale,* 2 vols. (Paris 1939–40), Engl. trans., *Feudal Society* (Chicago 1961); E. Lesne, *Histoire de la propriété ecclésiastique en France,* 6 vols. in 8 parts (Lille 1910–43); L. Santifaller, "Zur Geschichte des ottonisch-salischen Reichskirchensystems" in *SAW Phil.-Hist. Kl.* 229, 1 (Vienna, 2nd ed. 1964); L. White, *Medieval Technology and Social Change* (New York 1962).

b) History of Political Ideas: P. E. Schramm, *Herrschaftszeichen und Staatssymbolik,* 3 vols. (Stuttgart 1954–56); R. W.-A. J. Carlyle, *A History of Mediaeval Political Theory in the West,* 6 vols., the last from 1300 to 1600 (London, I, 3rd ed. 1930; II–III, 2nd ed. 1928; IV–VI, 1922–36); G. Tabacco, *La relazione fra i concetti di potere temporale e spirituale nella tradizione cristiana fino al sec. XVI* (Turin 1950); G. Pilati, *Chiesa e Stato nei primi quindici secoli. Profilo dello sviluppo della teoria attraverso le fonti e la bibliografia* (Rome 1961); M. Pacaut, *La théocratie. L'Église et le Pouvoir au moyen âge* (Paris 1957); H. X. Arquillière, *L'Augustinisme politique. Essai sur la formation des théories politiques du moyen-âge* (Paris, 2nd ed. 1955); E. H. Kantorowicz, *The King's Two Bodies. A Study in Mediaeval Political Theology* (Princeton 1957); A. Dempf, *Sacrum Imperium. Geschichts- und Staatsphilosophie des Mittelalters und der politischen Renaissance* (Darmstadt, 2nd ed. 1954); C. Erdmann, *Forschungen zur politischen Ideenwelt des Frühmittelalters,* ed. by F. Baethgen (Berlin 1951); C. H. McIlwain, *The Growth of Political Thought in the West from the Greeks to the End of the Middle Ages* (New York 1932); J. B. Morrall, *Political Thought in Medieval Times* (New York 1958).

c) Christian Kingship: *Das Königtum. Seine geistigen und rechtlichen Grundlagen, Vorträge und Forschungen,* ed. by T. Mayer 3 (Lindau–Constance 1956); *La regalità sacra. Contributi al tema del VIIIe congresso internaz. di Storia delle Religioni, Roma 1955* (Leiden 1959); A. Guinan, "The Christian Concept of Kingship" in *HThR* 49 (1956), 219–69; R. Folz, *L'idée de l'empire en Occident du Ve au XIVe siècle* (Paris 1953); E. Eichmann, *Die Kaiserkrönung im Abendland,* 2 vols. (Würzburg 1942); C. A. Bouman, *Sacring and Crowning. The development of the Latin ritual for the anointing of kings and the coronation of the emperor before the eleventh century* (Groningen 1957).

9. History of Monastic Orders

General: P. Hélyot, *Histoire des ordres monastiques, religieux et militaires,* 8 vols. (Paris 1714–19), from this: J. P. Migne, *Dictionnaire des ordres religieux,* 4 vols. (Paris 1847–59); H. Heimbucher, *Die Orden und Kongregationen der katholischen Kirche,* 2 vols. (Paderborn, 3rd ed. 1933–34); U. Berlière, *L'ordre monastique des origines au XIIe siècle* (Paris, 4th ed. 1928); *Il monachesimo nell'alto medioevo* in *Settimane di studio del Centro Ital. di Studi sull'alto medioevo* 4 (Spoleto 1957); G. G. Coulton, *Five Centuries of Religion,* 4 vols. (Cambridge 1923–50), begins at about 1000; P. Schmitz, *Histoire de l'ordre de Saint Benoît,* 6 vols. (Maredsous, 2nd ed. I–II; III–VI, 1948–49); S. Hilpisch, *Geschichte der Benediktinerinnen* (St Ottilien 1951).

FOR INDIVIDUAL COUNTRIES: D. Knowles, *The Monastic Order in England 943–1215* (Cambridge, 2nd ed. 1949); G. Penco, *Storia del monachesimo in Italia* (Rome 1961); J. Pérez de Urbel, *Los monjes españoles en la edad media,* 2 vols. (Madrid 1933–34).

10. LITURGY

L. Eisenhofer, *Handbuch der katholischen Liturgie,* 2 vols. (Freiburg i. Br., 2nd ed. 1941); M. Righetti, *Manuale di storia liturgica,* 4 vols. (Milan, I, 2nd ed. 1950; II, 2nd ed. 1955; III, 3rd ed. 1964; IV, 1955); A. G. Martimort and others, *L'Église en prière. Introduction à la liturgie* (Paris–Tournai–Rome, 3rd ed. 1965); J. A. Jungmann, *Missarum sollemnia* (Vienna, 4th ed. 1958), Eng. trans., *The Mass of the Roman Rite* (1950); T. Klauser, *Kleine abendländische Liturgiegeschichte, Bericht und Besinnung* (Bonn 1965); C. Vogel, *Introduction aux sources de l'histoire du culte chrétien au moyen âge* (Spoleto 1966).

11. LATIN LITERATURE AND GENERAL CULTURAL HISTORY

LITERATURE: M. Manitius, *Geschichte der lateinischen Literatur des Mittelalters,* 3 vols. (Munich 1911–31); I, from Justinian to the middle of the 10th century; II, to the investiture controversy; III, to the end of 12th century; C. Gröber, *Grundriss der romanischen Philologie,* II (Strasbourg 1902), 97–432; J. de Ghellinck, *Littérature latine au moyen âge,* 2 vols. (Paris 1939): I, to the end of the Carolingian Renaissance; II, to St Anselm; E. R. Curtius, *European Literature in the Latin Middle Ages* (New York 1953); E. Raby, *A History of Christian Latin Poetry in the Middle Ages* (Oxford, 3rd ed. 1953); id., *A History of Secular Latin Poetry in the Middle Ages* (Oxford, 2nd ed. 1957); A. Siegmund, *Die Überlieferung der griechischen christlichen Literatur in der lateinischen Kirche bis zum 12. Jahrhundert* (Munich–Pasing 1949).

LIBRARIES: F. Milkau, G. Leyh, *Handbuch der Bibliothekswissenschaft,* III: *Geschichte der Bibliotheken* (Wiesbaden 1955), contribution concerning the Middle Ages by K. Christ, pp. 243–498; J. W. Thompson, *The Medieval Library* (Chicago 1939); E. Lesne, *Hist. de la propriété* (see above: Gen. Bib., II, 8a), IV: *Les Livres, scriptoria et bibliothèques* (Lille 1938); reaches to the end of the 11th century.

EDUCATION: J. van den Driesch and J. Esterhues, *Geschichte der Erziehung und Bildung,* I: *Von den Griechen bis zum Ausgang des Zeitalters der Renaissance* (Paderborn 1951); W. Wühr, *Das abendländische Bildungswesen im Mittelalter* (Munich 1950); L. Maître, *Les écoles épiscopales et monastiques en Occident 768–1180* (Paris, 2nd ed. 1924); E. Lesne, *Hist. de la propriété* (see previous heading), V: *Les écoles de la fin du VIIIe siècle à la fin du XIIe* (Lille 1940); R. M. Martin, "Arts libéraux" in *DHGE* IV (1930), 827–43; H. Fuchs, "Enkyklios Paideia" in *RAC* V (1962), 365–98; *Artes liberales.* Von der antiken Bildung zur Wissenschaft des Mittelalters, ed. by J. Koch (Leiden–Cologne 1959).

12. PHILOSOPHY, THEOLOGY, SPIRITUALITY

GENERAL DEVELOPMENT OF LEARNING: *Fliche-Martin,* XIII (see above: Gen. Bib. II, 3); M. Grabmann, *Die Geschichte der scholastischen Methode,* 2 vols. (Freiburg i. Br. 1909–11); A. C. Crombie, *Augustine to Galileo. The History of Science 400–1560* (London, 2nd ed. 1957).

PHILOSOPHY: F. Ueberweg, *Grundriss der Geschichte der Philosophie*, vol. II by B. Geyer, *Die patristische und scholastische Philosophie* (Berlin, 11th ed. 1927); M. de Wulf, *Histoire de la philosophie médiévale*, 3 vols. (Paris, 6th ed. 1934–47); É. Bréhier, *La philosophie du moyen âge* (Paris 1937); É. Gilson, *La philosophie du moyen âge des origines patristiques à la fin du XIVe siècle* (Paris, 2nd ed. 1947); id., *History of Christian Philosophy in the Middle Ages* (New York 1954); id., *The Spirit of Medieval Philosophy* (London 1936); F. B. Artz, *The Mind of the Middle Ages* (New York, 2nd ed. 1954); F. Copleston, *A History of Philosophy*, II: *Augustine to Scotus* (London 1952).

THEOLOGY: H. Hurter, *Nomenclator literarius theologiae catholicae*, vol. I, until 1109; II, 1109–1563 (Innsbruck, I, 4th ed. 1926; II, 3rd ed. 1906); P. F. Cayré, *Patrologie et histoire de la théologie*, II (Paris–Tournai–Rome, 3rd ed. 1945); M. Grabmann, *Die Geschichte der katholischen Theologie seit dem Ausgang der Väterzeit* (Freiburg i. Br. 1933), Italian edition with supplements (Milan, 2nd ed. 1939). — Due to a lack of Catholic works on the history of Dogma, the following are relied upon: M. Schmaus, *Katholische Dogmatik*, 5 vols. (Munich, I–II, 5th ed. 1953–55; III, 1–2, 1940; 3rd ed. 1953; IV, 3rd ed. 1952–53; V, 1955); M. Schmaus, J. R. Geiselmann, A. Grillmeier, *Handbuch der Dogmengeschichte* (Freiburg i. Br. 1951 seqq.); A. von Harnack, *Lehrbuch der DG*, III, a reliable work on Protestant dogmatic history (Tübingen, 5th ed. 1932); R. Seeberg, *Lehrbuch der DG*, III (Leipzig, 4th ed. 1930), Eng. trans., *The History of Doctrines* (Grand Rapids, 6th ed. 1964); F. Loofs, *Leitfaden zum Studium der DG*, II (Tübingen, 5th ed. 1953).

BIBLE STUDY: F. Stegmüller, *Repertorium Biblicum Medii Aevi*, 7 vols. (Madrid 1950–61); H. Rost, *Die Bibel im Mittelalter* (Augsburg 1939); B. Smalley, *The Study of the Bible in the Middle Ages* (Oxford, 2nd ed. 1952); C. Spicq, *Esquisse d'une histoire de l'exégèse latine au moyen-âge* (Paris 1944); H. de Lubac, *Exégèse médiévale*, 2 vols. (Paris 1960–61); B. Bischoff, "Wendepunkte in der Geschichte der lateinischen Exegese im Frühmittelalter" in *SE* 6 (1954), 189–281; R. McNally, *The Bible in the Middle Ages* (Westminster, Md., 1959).

SPIRITUALITY: P. Pourrat, *La spiritualité chrétienne*, II (Paris, 4th ed. 1924); L. Génicot, *La spiritualité médiévale* (Paris 1958); J. Leclercq, F. Vandenbroucke, L. Bouyer, *La spiritualité du moyen âge* (Paris 1961) .

B. The Eastern Church

III. SOURCES FOR THE HISTORY OF THE EASTERN CHURCH

1. ANCILLARY SCIENCES

a) PALEOGRAPHY AND STUDIES IN HANDWRITING AND LIBRARIES: V. Gardthausen, *Griechische Paläographie*, 2 vols. (Leipzig, 2nd ed. 1913); W. Schubart, *Griechische Paläographie* (Munich 1925); E. M. Thompson, *Handbook of Greek and Latin Paleography* (2nd ed. 1913); R. Devreesse, *Introduction à l'étude des manuscrits grecs* (Paris 1954); R. Merkelbach, H. van Thiel, *Griechisches Leseheft zur Einführung in Paläographie und Textkritik* (Göttingen 1965); L. Polites, Ὁδηγὸς καταλόγου χειρογράφων (Athens 1961); A. Dain, *Les manuscrits* (Paris, 2nd ed. 1964); M. Richard, *Répertoire des bibliothèques et des catalogues des manuscrits grecs* (Paris, 2nd ed. 1958); id., Supplément, I (Paris 1965).

b) DIPLOMATICS: F. Dölger, *Byzantinische Diplomatik* (Ettal 1956); F. Dölger and J. Karayannopulos, *Einführung in die byzantinische Diplomatik* (Munich 1966).

c) SIGILLOGRAPHY: G. Schlumberger, *Sigillographie de l'empire byzantin* (Paris 1884); V. Laurent, *Documents de sigillographie byzantine* in *La collection C. Orghidan* (Paris 1952); id., *Les sceaux byzantins du médaillier Vatican* (Vatican 1962); id., *Le Corpus des sceaux de l'empire byzantin*, V seqq. (Paris 1963 seqq.).

d) NUMISMATICS: G. Schlumberger, *Numismatique de l'empire byzantin* (Paris 1884); W. Wroth, *Catalogue of the Imperial Byzantine Coins of the British Museum*, 2 vols. (London 1908); H. Goodacre, *A Handbook of the Coinage of the Byzantine Empire*, 3 vols. (London 1928–33); H. Longuet, *Introduction à la numismatique byzantine* (London 1962); A. Barozzi, "Byzantium and Numismatics. An Annotated Select Bibliography in *The Voice of the Turtle* 4 (1965), 229–42.

LEXICONS: C. du Fresne Ducange, *Glossarium ad scriptores mediae et infimae Graecitatis* (Paris 1688); E. A. Sophokles, *Greek Lexikon of the Roman and Byzantine Periods* (New York 1887); G. H. W. Lampe, *A Patristic Greek Lexikon* (Oxford 1961 seqq.); Ἱστορικὸν λεξικὸν τῆς Ἑλληνικῆς γλώσσης (Athens 1933 seqq.).

2. SOURCES

K. Krumbacher, *Geschichte der byzantinischen Litteratur von Justinian bis zum Ende des oströmischen Reiches* (Munich, 2nd ed. 1897); M. E. Colonna, *Gli storici bizantini dal IV al XV secolo*, I: *Storici profani* (Rome 1956); S. Impellizzeri, *La letteratura bizantina da Costantino agli iconoclasti* (Bari 1965); H.-G. Beck, *Kirche und theologische Literatur im byzantinischen Reich* (Munich 1959); G. Moravcsik, *Byzantinoturcica*, I: *Die byzantinischen Quellen der Geschichte der Turkvölker* (Berlin, 2nd ed. 1958). Since a great deal of Byzantine history involves the Turks this work complements Krumbacher's *Literaturgeschichte*; H. E. Mayer, *Bibliographie zur Geschichte der*

Kreuzzüge (Hanover 1960); W. Buchwald, A. Hohlweg, O. Prinz, *Tusculum-Lexikon grie-chischer und lateinischer Autoren des Altertums und des Mittelalters* (Munich 1963); E. Legrand, *Bibliographie hellénique ou description raisonnée des ouvrages publiés en grec par des Grecs aux XVe et XVIe siècles*, 3 vols. (Paris 1885–1903).

3. General Collections of Sources

J. P. Migne, *Patrologiae cursus completus. Series graeca* (Paris 1867–76), contents in *Rep Font* I, 420–29; R. Graffin, F. Nau, *Patrologia orientalis* (Paris 1903 seqq.), *Rep Font* I, 302–05; *Sources chrétiennes* (Paris 1942 seqq.), *Rep Font* I, 706–08; J. Pitra, *Spicilegium Solesmense,* 4 vols. (Paris 1852–58); id., *Analecta sacra Spicilegio Solesmensi parata,* 8 vols. (vol.6 did not appear) (Paris 1876–88); A. Mai, *Scriptorum veterum nova collectio,* 10 vols. (Rome 1825–38); A. Mai, J. Cozza-Luzi, *Nova Patrum bibliotheca,* 9 vols. (Rome 1852–88); A. Demetrakopulos,'Ἐκκλησιαστικὴ Βιβλιοθήκη, I (Leipzig 1866); A. Papadopulos-Kerameus, 'Ἀνάλεκτα 'Ιεροσολυμιτικῆς σταχυολογίας, 5 vols. (St Petersburg 1891); A. Vasiliev, *Analecta graeco-byzantina* I (Moscow 1893); W. Regel, *Fontes rerum byzantinarum,* 2 fasc. (St Petersburg 1892–1917); C. Will, *Acta et scripta quae de controversiis ecclesiae graecae et latinae saeculo undecimo composita extant* (Leipzig–Marburg 1861); *Corpus scriptorum historiae byzantinae,* 50 vols. (Bonn 1828–97), *Rep Font* I, 201–03; K. N. Sathas, Μεσαιωνικὴ βιβλιοθήκη, 7 vols. (Athens–Paris–Venice 1872–74); J. B. Bury, *Byzantine Texts,* 5 vols. (London 1898–1904); *Bibliothèque byzantine,* publiée sous la direction de P. Lemerle. Documents (Paris 1952 seqq.); *Collection byzantine,* publiée sous le patronage de l'Association Guillaume Budé (Paris 1926 seqq.); J. F. Boissonade, *Anecdota graeca e codicibus regiis,* 5 vols. (Paris 1829–33); id., *Anecdota nova* (Paris 1844); S. Lampros, Παλαιολόγεια καὶ Πελοποννησιακά, 4 vols. (Athens 1912–30); Μνημεῖα τῆς ἑλληνικῆς ἱστορίας (Athens 1932 seqq.); J. C. Wolf, *Anecdota graeca sacra et profana,* 4 vols. (Hamburg 1722–24); *Scriptores byzantini* (Bucharest 1958 seqq.); E. V. Ivánka, *Byzantinische Geschichts-schreiber* (Graz - Vienna - Cologne 1954 seqq.).

4. Synodal Decisions on Doctrine and Law

E. Schwartz, *Acta conciliorum oecumenicorum,* 9 vols. (Strasbourg–Berlin 1914–19), one vol. to be completed; G. Hofmann, *Concilium Florentinum,* 2 vols. (Rome 1929–30); id., *Documenta concilii Florentini de unione orientalium,* 3 vols. (Rome 1935–6); *Concilium Florentinum* (Rome 1940 seqq.); G. A. Rhallis, M. Potlis, Σύνταγμα τῶν Θείων καὶ ἱερῶν κανόνων, 6 vols. (Athens 1852–59), contains the great Byzantine commentaries on canon law: Zonaras, Balsamon, and Aristenos; A. Alibizatos, Οἱ ἱεροὶ κανόνες καὶ οἱ ἐκκλησιαστικοὶ νόμοι (Athens, 2nd ed. 1949); P. P. Joannou, *Discipline générale antique (IVe–IXe siècle),* 4 vols. (Grottaferrata 1962–64); V. Beneševič, *Joannis Scholastici synagoga L titulorum ceteraque eiusdem opera iuridica* I in *AAM* NF 14 (Munich 1937); J. Pitra, *Juris ecclesiastici Graecorum historia et monumenta,* 2 vols. (Rome 1864–68); J. B. Cotelier, *Monumenta ecclesiae graecae* I (Paris 1677); W. Voel, C. Justel, *Bibliotheca juris canonici vetus,* 2 vols. (Paris 1661); M. Gedeon, Κανονικαὶ διατάξεις, ἐπιστολαί, λύσεις, θεσπίσματα τῶν ἁγιωτάτων πατριαρχῶν Κωνσταντινουπόλεως, 2 vols. (Constantinople 1888–89); F. Miklosich, J. Müller, *Acta et diplomata graeca medii aevi,* 6 vols. (Vienna 1860–90), esp. vols. I and II; I. Croce, *Textus selecti ex operibus commentatorum byzantinorum iuris ecclesiastici* (Vatican 1939), with an important introduction by E. Herman; J. Oudot, *Patriarchatus Constantinopolitani acta selecta* I (Vatican 1944).

5. State Decrees Concerning Church Affairs

K. E. Zachariae von Lingenthal, *Ius graeco-romanum,* 7 vols. (Leipzig 1856–84); J. and P. Zepos, *Ius graecoromanum,* 8 vols. (Athens 1931); G. E. Heimbach, *Basilicorum libri LX* (Leipzig 1833–70); H. J. Scheltema, *Basilica* (Groningen–'s Gravenhage 1953 seqq.); P. Noailles, A. Dain, *Les nouvelles de Léon le Sage* (Paris 1944); G. E. Heimbach, *Constantini Harmenopuli Manuale legum sive Hexabiblos* (Leipzig 1851); C. Ferrini, J. Mercati, F. Dölger, St. Hörmann, E. Seidl, M. Κριτοῦ τοῦ Πατζῆ Τιπούκειτος. *Librorum LX Basilicorum summarium* (Vatican 1914–57).

6. Historical Statistical Works

M. Le Quien, *Oriens christianus,* 3 vols. (Paris 1740); O. Seeck, *Notitia dignitatum. Accedunt Notitia urbis Constantinopolitanae et Latercula provinciarum* (Berlin 1876); G. Parthey, *Hieroclis synecdemus et notitiae graecae episcopatuum* (Berlin 1886); E. Honigmann, *Le synecdèmos d'Hiéroclès et l'opuscule géographique de Georges de Chypres* (Brussels 1939); H. Gelzer, *Georgii Cyprii descriptio orbis Romani* (Leipzig 1890); id., "Ungedruckte und ungenügend veröffentlichte Texte der Notitiae episcopatuum" in *AAM* 21 (Munich 1901), 529–641; id., "Ungedruckte und wenig bekannte Bistümerverzeichnisse der orientalischen Kirche" in *ByZ* 1 (1892), 245–82, and *ByZ* 2 (1893), 22–72; H. Gerland, *Die Genesis der Notitiae episcopatuum* (Chalcedon 1931); H. Gelzer, H. Hilgenfeld, O. Cuntz, *Patrum Nicaenorum nomina latine graece coptice syriace arabice armenice* (Leipzig 1898); E. Schwartz, *Über die Bischofslisten der Synoden von Chalkedon, Nicaea und Konstantinopel* in *AAM* NF 13 (Munich 1937); A. Pertusi, *Costantino Porfirogenito De Thematibus* (Vatican 1952); G. Moravcsik and R. J. H. Jenkins, *Constantine Porphyrogenitus De administrando imperio* (Budapest 1949); F. Dölger, *Regesten der Kaiserurkunden des oströmischen Reiches von 565–1453,* 5 fasc. (Munich 1924–65); V. Grumel, *Les Regestes des actes du patriarcat de Constantinople,* fasc. 1–5 (Kadiköy 1932–47); R. Janin, *La géographie ecclésiastique de l'empire byzantin,* I: *Le siège de Constantinople;* III: *Les églises et les monastères* (Paris 1953); id., *Constantinople Byzantin* (Paris, 2nd ed. 1964).

7. Monasticism

E. Schwartz, *Kyrillos von Skythopolis* (Leipzig 1939); A. Dmitrievskij, *Opisanie liturgičeskich rukopisej,* I: Typika (Kiev 1895); P. Meyer, *Die Haupturkunden für die Geschichte der Athosklöster* (Leipzig 1894); *Actes de l'Athos* (= Vizantijskij Vremennik, Priloženie) 10–13, 17, 20 (St Petersburg 1903–13); *Archives de l'Athos* (Paris 1936 seqq.); F. Dölger, *Aus den Schatzkammern des Heiligen Berges* (Munich 1948); id., *Sechs byzantinische Praktika des 14. Jahrhunderts für das Athoskloster Iberon* in *AAM* NF 28 (1949).

8. Liturgy

E. Renaudot, *Liturgiarum orientalium collectio,* 2 vols. (Paris 1715–16); J. A. Assemani, *Codex liturgicus ecclesiae universae,* 13 vols. (Rome 1749–66); H. A. Daniel, *Codex liturgicus ecclesiae universae,* IV (Leipzig 1853); H. Denzinger, *Ritus orientalium,* 2 vols. (Würzburg 1863); F. E. Brightman, *Liturgies Eastern and Western,* I (Oxford 1896); A. Dmitrievskij, *Opisanie liturgičeskich rukopisej,* II: *Euchologia* (Kiev 1901); I. Mateos, *Le typicon de la Grande Église,* 2 vols. (Rome 1962–63). The most important and the most used of the Greek-Byzantine liturgical books *(Euchologion, Triodion, Pentekostarion, Parakletike, Menäen)* were published in Rome (1873–91) and Venice (1862–85); E. Follieri, *Initia hymnorum ecclesiae graecae,* 5 vols. in 6

(Rome 1960–66); W. Christ and M. Paranikas, *Anthologia graeca carminum christianorum* (Leipzig 1871); P. Maas and C. A. Trypanis, *Romani Melodi carmina genuina* (Oxford 1863); J. Grosdidier de Matons, *Romanos le Mélode: Hymnes* (Paris 1864 seqq.); L. Petit, *Bibliographie des accolouthies grecques* (Brussels 1926).

9. HAGIOGRAPHY

T. Joannu, Μνημεῖα ἁγιολογικά (Venice 1884); K. Dukakes, Μέγας συναξαριστὴς πάντων τῶν ἁγίων, 13 vols. (Athens 1889–97); H. Delehaye, *Synaxarium ecclesiae Constantinopolitanae* (Brussels 1902); Bibliography of printed works: F. Halkin, *Bibliotheca Hagiographica graeca,* 3 vols. (Brussels, 3rd ed. 1957); Bibliography of manuscripts: A. Ehrhard, *Überlieferung und Bestand der hagiographischen und homiletischen Literatur der griechischen Kirche,* 3 vols. in 4 parts (Leipzig 1936–52).

IV. MATERIALS ON EASTERN HISTORY

Extensive bibliographical materials concerning the relationships between Byzantium and the Slavic and Turkish peoples may be found in Moravcsik (Gen. Bib. III, 2).

1. POLITICAL HISTORY — GENERAL CULTURAL HISTORY

J. M. Hussey, ed., *The Cambridge Medieval History,* IV: *The Byzantine Empire and Its Neighbours* (Cambridge 1966); G. Ostrogorsky, *History of the Byzantine State* (Munich, 3rd ed. 1962; translated by J. Hussey; Oxford 1956); id., *Pour l'histoire de la féodalité byzantine* (French translation by H. Gregoire and P. Lemerle; Brussels 1954); id., "Agrarian Conditions in the Byzantine Empire" in *Cambridge Economic History of Europe,* I (Cambridge 1942); A. A. Vasiliev, *History of the Byzantine Empire* (Madison, 2nd ed. 1952; paperback, Madison 1958); id., *Byzantium and the Arabs* (in Russian), 2 vols. (St Petersburg 1900); Vol. I translated by H. Gregoire and E. M. Cunard as *Byzance et les Arabes* in *Corpus Bruxellense Historiae Byzantinae,* I (Brussels 1935); C. Diehl and G. Marçais, *Le monde oriental de 395 à 1081* and C. Diehl and R. Guilland, *L'Europe orientale de 1081 à 1453* (Paris 1936–45); L. Bréhier, *Vie et mort de Byzance* (Paris 1948); J. Lindsay, *Byzantium into Europe* (London 1952); N. H. Baynes and H. S. L. B. Moss, *Byzantium* (Oxford 1948; paperback, Oxford 1961); E. Stein, *Geschichte des spätrömischen Reiches 284–467* (Vienna 1928); id., *Histoire du Bas-Empire 476–565* (Paris - Brussels - Amsterdam, 2nd ed. 1957); A. H. M. Jones, *The Later Roman Empire,* 3 vols. (Oxford 1964); 2 vols. (Oklahoma 1964–66); J. B. Bury, *A History of the Later Roman Empire from Arcadius to Irene (395–800),* 2 vols. (London 1889); id., *A History of the Eastern Roman Empire, A.D. 802–867* (London 1912); C. Neumann, *Die Weltstellung des byzantinischen Reiches vor den Kreuzzügen* (Leipzig 1894); K. M. Setton and M. W. Baldwin, *A History of the Crusades* (Philadelphia 1955 seqq.); S. Runciman, *A History of the Crusades,* 3 vols. (Cambridge 1951–4; paperback, New York 1964–67); id., *Byzantine Civilization* (London 1933; paperback, New York 1961); id., *The Sicilian Vespers* (Cambridge 1958, paper covers, Harmondsworth, Middlesex, 1960); id., *The Fall of Constantinople 1453* (Cambridge 1965); F. Chalandon, *Les Comnène* (Paris 1900–12); P. Lamma, *Comneni e Staufer,* 2 vols. (Rome 1955); W. Miller, *The Latins in the Levant* (London 1908); id., *Essays on the Latin Orient* (Cambridge 1921); id., *Trebizond — the Last Greek Empire* (London 1926); J. Lognon, *L'empire latin de Constantinople et la principauté de Morée* (Paris 1949); A. Gardner, *The Lascarids of Nicaea* (London 1912); D. J. Geanakoplos, *Emperor Michael Palaeologus and the West* (Cambridge, Mass., 1959); id., *Byzantine East and Latin West: Two Worlds of Christendom in Middle Ages and Renaissance,* Studies in Ecclesiastical and Cultural History (New York 1966); id., "Graeco-Latin Relations on the Eve of the Byzantine Restoration; The Battle of Pelagonia 1259" in *Dumbarton Oaks Papers* 7 (1953); N. Baynes, *Byzantine Studies and Other Essays* (London 1955); D. Zakythinos, *Le despotat grec de Morée*, 2 vols. (Paris–Athens 1932–53); F. Babinger, *Mehmed der Eroberer und seine Zeit* (Munich 1953); J. P. Fallmerayer, *Geschichte des Kaisertums von Trapezunt* (Munich 1827); D. M. Nicol, *The Despote of Epiros* (Oxford 1957); H. Gelzer, *Byzantinische Kulturgeschichte* (Tübingen 1909); J. M. Hussey, *The Byzantine World* (London 1957, paperback 1961); N. Jorga, *Histoire de la vie byzantine*, 3 vols. (Bucharest 1934); W. Haussig, *Byzantinische Kulturgeschichte* (Stuttgart 1959); H. Hunger, *Reich der neuen Mitte* (Graz–Cologne 1965); L. Bréhier, *La civilisation byzantine* (Paris 1950); P. Kukules, Βυζαντινῶν βίος καὶ πολιτισμός (Athens 1954); C. Diehl, *Byzance. Grandeur et décadence* (Paris 1919; E. T., New Brunswick 1957); id., "Byzantine Civilization" in *Cambridge Medieval History,* IV (New York 1927); id., *Choses et gens de Byzance* (Paris 1926).

2. Church History

Due to the close relationship between Church and State in Byzantium, ecclesiastical and secular history are presented concurrently.

P. Bapheides, Ἐκκλησιαστικὴ ἱστορία, 3 vols. (Constantinople 1884–1928); B. Stephanides, Ἐκκλησιαστικὴ ἱστορία (Athens 1948); G. I. Konidares, Ἐκκλησιαστικὴ ἱστορία τῆς Ἑλλάδος (Athens 1954 seqq.); F. Haase, *Altchristliche Kirchengeschichte nach orientalischen Quellen* (Leipzig 1925); C. Lagier, *L'Orient Chrétien des apôtres jusqu'à Photius* (Paris 1935); id., *L'orient chrétien de Photius à l'empire latin de Constantinople* (Paris 1950); J. Pargoire, *L'église byzantine de 527 à 847* (Paris, 2nd ed. 1905); A. P. Stanley, *Lectures on the History of the Eastern Church* (London 1907); R. M. French, *The Eastern Orthodox Church* (London 1951); G. Zananiri, *Histoire de l'église byzantine* (Paris 1954); W. de Vries, *Rom und die Patriarchate des Ostens* (Freiburg–Munich 1963); F. Heiler, *Urkirche und Ostkirche* (Munich 1937); S. Bulgakov, *The Orthodox Church* (London 1935).

3. The History of the Church Councils — the Papacy and the Eastern Church

A. Grillmeier and H. Bacht, *Das Konzil von Chalkedon*, 3 vols. (Würzburg 1951–54); J. Haijar, *Le synode permanent* (σύνοδος ἐνδημοῦσα) *dans l'église Byzantine des origines au XIe siècle* (Rome 1962); F. Diekamp, *Die origenistischen Streitigkeiten im 6. Jahrhundert und das 5. allgemeine Concil* (Münster 1899); F. Dvornik, *The Idea of Apostolicity in Byzantium and the Legend of the Apostle Andrew* (Cambridge, Mass., 1958); id., *Byzance et la primauté Romaine* (Paris 1964; Eng. trans. by Edwin A. Quain, New York 1966); id., *The Photian Schism — History and Legend* (Cambridge 1948); id., *Les Slaves, Byzance et Rome* (Paris 1926); G. Ostrogorsky, *Studien zur Geschichte des byzantinischen Bilderstreits* (Breslau 1929); E. J. Martin, *A History of the Iconoclastic Controversy* (London, n. d.); *Cyrillo-Methodiana 863–1963* (Cologne–Graz 1964); A. Michel, *Humbert und Kerullarios,* 2 vols. (Paderborn 1925–30); *1054–1954: L'Église et les églises,* 2 vols. (Chevetogne 1954); S. Runciman, *The Eastern Schism* (Oxford 1955); M. Jugie, *Le schisme byzantin* (Paris 1941); W. Norden, *Das Papsttum und Byzanz* (Berlin 1903); W. de Vries, *Rom und die Patriarchate des Ostens* (Freiburg–Munich 1963); D. J. Geanakoplos, *Emperor Michael Palaeologus and the West* (Cambridge, Mass., 1959); B. Roberg, *Die Union zwischen der griechischen und der lateinischen Kirche auf dem II. Konzil von Lyon* (Bonn 1964); J. Gill, *The Council of Florence* (Oxford 1964); id., *Personalities of the Council of Florence and Other Essays* (Oxford 1964).

4. History of the Individual Eastern Churches

H. Grotz, *Die Hauptkirchen des Ostens von den Anfängen bis zum Konzil von Nikaia (325)* (Rome 1964); T. A. Kane, *The Jurisdiction of the Patriarchs of the Major Sees in Antiquity and in the Middle Ages* (Washington 1949); C. Lübeck, *Reichseinteilung und kirchliche Hierarchie des Orients bis zum Ausgang des 4. Jahrhunderts* (Münster 1901); T. E. Dowling, *The Orthodox Greek Patriarchate of Jerusalem* (London, 2nd ed. 1913); C. Papadopulos, Ἱστορία τῆς ἐκκλησίας Ἱεροσολύμων (Jerusalem 1910); W. Hotzelt, *Kirchengeschichte Palästinas im Zeitalter der Kreuzzüge* (Cologne 1914); C. Papadopulos, Ἱστορία τῆς ἐκκλησίας Ἀλεξανδρείας (Alexandria 1935); J.Maspéro, *Histoire des patriarches d'Alexandrie 518–616* (Paris 1923); C. Diehl, *L'Égypte chrétienne et byzantine* (Paris 1933); W.Riedel, *Die Kirchenrechtsquellen des Patriarchats von Alexandrien* (Leipzig 1900); P. Rohrbach, *Die alexandrinischen Patriarchen als Grossmacht in der kirchenpolitischen Entwicklung des Orients* (Berlin 1891); J. Charon, *Histoire des patriarcats melkites depuis le schisme monophysite du VIe siècle jusqu'à nos jours*, II¹ and III¹ (Paris 1909–10); C. Papadopulos, Ἱστορία τῆς ἐκκλησίας Ἀντιοχείας (Alexandria 1951); R. Devreesse, *Le patriarcat d'Antioche depuis la paix de l'église jusqu'à la conquête arabe* (Paris 1945); M. Gedeon, Πατριαρχικοὶ πίνακες (Constantinople 1890); G. Every, *The Byzantine Patriarchate (451–1204)* (London 1947); G. Arabazoglu, Ἱστορία τοῦ οἰκουμενικοῦ πατριαρχείου, I (Athens 1953); C. D. Cobham, *The Patriarchs of Constantinople* (Cambridge 1911); G. Zananiri, *Histoire de l'église byzantine* (Paris 1954); L. Bréhier, *Les institutions de l'empire byzantin 461–506* (Paris 1949); J. Hackett, *A History of the Orthodox Church of Cyprus* (London 1901); P. Kurites, Ἡ ὀρθόδοξος ἐκκλησία ἐν κόπρῳ ἐπὶ Φραγκοκρατίας (Leukosia 1907); M. Spinka, *A History of the Christianity in the Balkans* (Illinois 1933); S. Zankow, *Die Verfassung der bulgarischen orthodoxen Kirche* (Zürich 1918); I. Snegarov, *Istorija na Okridskata arkiepiskopija patriarchija* (Sofia 1935); F. Dvornik, *Les Slaves, Byzance et Rome au IXe siècle* (Paris 1926); A. Hudal, *Die serbisch-orthodoce Nationalkirche* (Graz 1902); L. K. Goetz, *Staat und Kirche in Altrussland* (Berlin 1908); E. E. Golubinskij, *Istorija russkoj cerkvi*, 2 vols. (Moscow 1900–01); A. M. Ammann, *Abriss der ostslawischen Kirchengeschichte* (Vienna 1950); L. Müller, *Zum Problem des hierarchischen Status und der jurisdiktionellen Abhängigkeit der russischen Kirche vor 1039* (Cologne 1959).

5. Legal and Constitutional History

N. Milaš, *Das Kirchenrecht der morgenländischen Kirche* (Mostar, 2nd ed. 1905); A. Pavlov, *Kursus des Kirchenrechts* (Russian) (Moscow 1902); A. Coussa, *Epitome praelectionum de iure ecclesiastico orientali*, 3 vols. (Grottaferro 1948–50); A. P. Christophilopulos, Ἑλληνικὸν ἐκκλησιαστικὸν δίκαιον (Athens, 2nd ed. 1965); N. P. Matses, Τὸ οἰκογενειακὸν δίκαιον κατὰ τὴν νομολογίαν τοῦ Πατριαχείρου Κωνσταντινουπόλεως τῶν ἐτῶν 1315–1401 (Athens 1962); S. N. Troianos, Ἡ ἐκκλησιαστικὴ δικονομία μεχρὶ τοῦ θανάτου τοῦ Ἰουστινιανοῦ (Athens 1964); K. E. Zachariä von Lingenthal, *Geschichte des griechisch-römischen Rechts* (Berlin, 3rd ed. 1892); A. Albertoni, *Per una esposizione di diritto bizantino con riguardo all'Italia* (Imola 1927); L. Wenger, *Die Quellen des römischen Rechts* (Vienna 1953); A. Knecht, *System des Justinianischen Kirchenvermögensrechtes* (Stuttgart 1905); M. Kaser, *Das römische Privatrecht*, II (Munich 1959); E. Seidl, *Römische Rechtsgeschichte und römisches Zivilprozessrecht* (Cologne 1962); E. Russos, Λεξικολόγιον ἐκκλησιαστικοῦ δικαίου, 2 vols. (Athens 1948).

6. Social and Economic History

J. B. Bury, *The Constitution of the Later Roman Empire* (Cambridge 1910); W. Ensslin, "The Emperor and the Imperial Administration" in N. H. Baynes and H. S. L. B. Moss, *Byzantium: An Introduction to East Roman Civilization* (Oxford 1948); J. Karayannopulos, *Das*

Finanzwesen des frühbyzantinischen Staates (Munich 1958); F. Dölger, *Beiträge zur Geschichte der byzantinischen Finanzverwaltung bes. des 10. und 11. Jahrhunderts* (Darmstadt, 2nd ed. 1960); D. A. Zakynthinos, *Crise monétaire et crise économique à Byzance du XIIIᵉ au XVᵉ siècle* (Athens 1948); E. Kirsten, *Die byzantinische Stadt. Acts of the XI International Byzantine Congress 1958*, no. V (Munich 1960); A. Stöckle, *Spätrömische und byzantinische Zünfte* (Leipzig 1911); G. Mickwitz, *Die Kartellfunktion der Zünfte* (Helsinki 1936); A. P. Každan, *Derevnja i gorod v Vizantii IX–X vv* (Moscow 1960); P. Lemerle, "Esquisse pour une histoire agraire de Byzance" in *RH* 219–20 (1958); G. Ostrogorsky, "Die ländliche Steuergemeinde des byzantinischen Reiches im X. Jahrhundert" in *Vjschr. Social- u. Wirtschaftsgesch.* 20 (1927); id., *Pour l'histoire de la féodalité byzantine* (Brussels 1954); id., *Quelques problèmes de la paysannerie byzantine* (Brussels 1956); R. S. Lopez and J. A. Raymond, *Medieval Trade in the Mediterranean* (New York 1955); A. S. Atiya, *Crusade, Commerce and Culture* (Bloomington 1962); A. R. Lewis, *Naval Power and Trade in the Mediterranean* (Princeton 1951).

7. POLITICAL THOUGHT — CHURCH AND STATE

J. Straub, *Vom Kaiserideal der Spätantike* (Stuttgart 1939); W. Ensslin, "Gottkaiser und Kaiser von Gottes Gnaden" in *SAM* (1943), 3 (Munich 1943); O. Treitinger, *Die oströmische Kaiser- und Reichsidee nach ihrer Gestaltung im höfischen Zeremoniell* (Jena 1938); A. Grabar, *L'empereur dans l'art byzantin* (Paris 1936); H. Hunger, *Prooimion. Elemente der byzantinischen Kaiseridee in den Arengen der Urkunden* (Vienna 1964); F. Dölger, *Byzanz und die europäische Staatenwelt* (Darmstadt 1964); W. Ohnsorge, *Das Zweikaiserproblem im frühen Mittelalter* (Hildesheim 1947); id., *Abendland und Byzanz* (Darmstadt 1958); P. E. Schramm, *Kaiser, Rom und Renovatio* (Darmstadt, 2nd ed. 1957); H. Schäder, *Moskau — das dritte Rom* (Darmstadt, 2nd ed. 1957); K. Voigt, *Staat und Kirche von Konstantin dem Grossen bis zum Ende der Karolingerzeit* (Stuttgart 1936); J. Westbury-Jones, *Roman and Christian Imperialism* (London 1939); A. Michel, *Die Kaisermacht in der Ostkirche* (Darmstadt 1959); K. M. Setton, *Christian Attitude towards the Emperor in the 4th Century* (New York 1941); H. Berkhof, *Kirche und Kaiser* (Zürich 1947); B. K. Stephanides, Ἔρευναι περὶ τῶν ἐν τῷ βυζαντινῷ κράτει σχέσεων ἐκκλησίας καὶ πολιτείας (Athens 1923).

8. MONASTICISM

Il monachesimo orientale (Rome 1958); S. Schiwietz, *Das morgenländische Mönchtum*, 3 vols. (Mainz 1904–38); R. Reitzenstein, *Historia monachorum und Historia Lausiaca* (Göttingen 1916); J. Brémond, *Les pères du désert*, 2 vols. (Paris 1927); K. Holl, *Enthusiasmus und Bussgewalt* (Leipzig 1898); A. J. Festugière, *Les moines d'orient* (Paris 1961 seqq.); U. Ranke-Heinemann, *Das frühe Mönchtum* (Essen 1964); A. v. Campenhausen, *Die aszetische Heimatlosigkeit im altchristlichen und frühmittelalterlichen Mönchtum* (Tübingen 1931); I. Hausherr, *Direction spirituelle en orient autrefois* (Rome 1955); O. Rousseau, *Monachisme et vie religieuse d'après l'ancienne tradition de l'église* (Chevetogne 1957); W. Nissen, *Die Regelung des Klosterwesens im Rhomäerreich bis zum Ende des 9. Jahrhunderts* (Hamburg 1897); P. de Meester, *De monachico statu juxta disciplinam byzantinam* (Vatican 1942); D. Savramis, *Zur Soziologie des byzantinischen Mönchtums* (Leiden–Cologne 1962).

9. LITURGY

J. M. Hanssens, *Institutiones liturgicae de ritibus orientalibus*, II, III, and Appendix (Rome 1930–32); S. Salaville, *Liturgies orientales, Le messe*, 2 vols. (Paris 1942); A. Raes, *Introductio in liturgiam orientalem* (Rome 1947); A. Baumstark, *Liturgie comparée* (Chevetogne, 3rd ed.

1953); id., *Die Messe im Morgenland* (Kempten–Munich, 4th ed. 1921); S. Antoniades, *Place de la liturgie dans la tradition des lettres grecques* (Leiden 1939); J. Tyciak, *Die Liturgie als Quelle östlicher Frömmigkeit* (Freiburg 1937); L. Clugnet, *Dictionnaire grec-français des noms liturgiques en usage dans l'église grecque* (Paris 1895); P. Oppenheim, *Introductio in literaturam liturgicam* (Turin 1937); J. M. Sauget, *Bibliographie de liturgies orientales, 1900–60* (Rome 1962).

10. GENERAL LITERARY AND EDUCATIONAL HISTORY

a) LITERATURE: K. Krumbacher, *Geschichte der byzantinischen Literatur* (Munich, 2nd ed. 1897); F. Dölger, *Die byzantinische Dichtung in der Reinsprache* (Berlin 1948); S. Impellizzeri, *La letteratura bizantina da Costantino agli iconoclasti* (Bari 1965); B. Knös, *Histoire de la littérature néogrecque. La période jusqu'en 1821* (Uppsala 1962); N. B. Tomadakes, Βυζαντινὴ ἐπιστολο-γραφία (Athens 1955); O. Bardenhewer, *Geschichte der altkirchlichen Literatur*, 5 vols. (Freiburg 1913–32); D. S. Balanos, Οἱ ἐκκλησιαστικοὶ βυζαντινοὶ συγγραφεῖς (Athens 1951); H.-G. Beck, *Kirche und theol. Literatur im byzantinischen Reich* (Munich 1959); G. Graf, *Geschichte der christlichen arabischen Literatur*, 5 vols. (Vatican 1944–53); A. Baumstark, *Geschichte der syrischen Literatur* (Bonn 1922); M. Tarchnišvili, *Geschichte der kirchlichen georgischen Literatur* (Vatican 1955).

b) LIBRARIES: V. Burr, "Der byzantinische Kulturkreis" in *Handbuch der Bibliothekswissenschaft*, III (Wiesbaden 1955), 146–87; O. Volk, *Die byzantinischen Klosterbibliotheken Griechenlands, Konstantinopels und Kleinasiens* (Diss., Munich 1955); V. Gardthausen, *Griechische Paläographie*, I (Leipzig, 2nd ed. 1911).

c) SCHOOLS AND EDUCATION: F. Fuchs, *Die höheren Schulen von Konstantinopel im Mittelalter* (Leipzig 1926); J. M. Hussey, *Church and Learning in the Byzantine Empire (867–1185)* (London 1937); G. C. Buckler, *Anna Comnena* (Oxford 1929); G. C. Buckler, "Byzantine Education" in N. H. Baynes and H. S. L. B. Moss, *Byzantium* (Oxford 1948); H. Zilliacus, *Zum Kampf der Weltsprachen im oströmischen Reich* (Helsinki 1935).

11. PHILOSOPHY — THEOLOGY — SPIRITUALITY

a) PHILOSOPHY: B. Tatakis, *La philosophie byzantine* (Paris 1949); C. Zervos, *Un Philosophe néoplatonicien du XIe siècle, Michel Psellos* (Paris 1920); P. P. Joannou, *Christliche Metaphysik in Byzanz* (Ettal 1956); P. E. Stéphanou, *Jean Italos, philosophe et humaniste* (Rome 1949); S. Salaville, "Philosophie et Théologie ou épisodes scolastiques à Byzance de 1059–1117 in *ÉO* 29 (1930), 142 ff.; J. Verpeaux, *Nicéphore Choumnos* (Paris 1959); H.-G. Beck, *Theodoros Metochites* (Munich 1952); I. Ševčenko, *Études sur la polémique entre Théodore Métochite et Nicéphore Choumnos* (Brussels 1962); F. Masai, *Pléthon et le platonisme de Mistra* (Paris 1956); L. Mohler, *Kardinal Bessarion als Theologe, Humanist und Staatsmann* (Paderborn 1923); K. M. Setton, "The Byzantine Background to the Italian Renaissance" in *Proceed. American Philos. Soc.* 100 (1956), 1–76. D. J. Geanakoplos, *Greek Scholars in Venice* (Cambridge, Mass., 1962).

b) THEOLOGY: H.-G. Beck, *Kirche und theol. Literatur im byzantinischen Reich* (Munich 1959); M. Jugie, *Theologia dogmatica christianorum orientalium ab ecclesia dissidentium*, 5 vols. (Paris 1926–35); M. Gordillo, *Compendium theologiae orientalis* (Rome, 3rd ed. 1950); id., *Theologia orientalium cum latinorum comparata*, I (Rome 1960); J. Tyciak, *Wege östlicher Theologie* (Bonn 1946); F. Heiler, *Urkirche und Ostkirche* (Munich 1937); H. Beck, *Vorsehung und Vorherbestimmung in der theologischen Literatur der Byzantiner* (Rome 1937); M. Jugie, *De processione spiritus sancti ex fontibus revelationis et secundum orientales dissidentes* (Rome 1936); U. Riedinger,

Die Heilige Schrift im Kampf der Griechischen Kirche gegen die Astrologie (Innsbruck 1956); S. Guichardan, *Le problème de la simplicité divine en orient et en occident aux XIVe et XVe siècles* (Lyons 1933); B. Studer, *Die theologische Arbeitsweise des Johannes von Damaskus* (Ettal 1956).

c) SPIRITUALITY: M. Viller and K. Rahner, *Aszese und Mystik in der Väterzeit* (Freiburg i. Br. 1938); I. Hausherr, "Les grands courants de la spiritualité orientale" in *OrChrP* 1 (1935), 114–38; id., *La méthode d'oraison hésychaste* (Rome 1927); id., *Direction spirituelle en Orient autrefois* (Rome 1955); id., *Noms du Christ et voies d'oraison* (Rome 1960); id., *Prière de vie et vie de prière* (Paris 1965); F. Dörr, *Diadochus von Photike und die Messalianer* (Freiburg i. Br. 1937); H. Urs von Balthasar, *Kosmische Liturgie* (Einsiedeln, 2nd ed. 1961); I. Hausherr, *Un grand mystique byzantin: Vie de Syméon le Nouveau Théologien* (Rome 1928); J. Meyendorff, *Introduction à l'étude de Grégoire Palamas* (Paris 1959); M. Lot-Borodine, *Un maître de la spiritualité byzantine au XIVe siècle: Nicolas Cabasilas* (Paris 1958); J. Gouillard, *Petite philocalie du cœur* (Paris 1953).

BIBLIOGRAPHY TO INDIVIDUAL CHAPTERS

Part One:
The Church under Lay Domination

SECTION ONE

The Papacy's Alienation from Byzantium and Rapprochement with the Franks

SOURCES

Wattenbach-Levison (General Bibliography I, 2); *Mansi* XII (Gen. Bib. I, 4); *Liber Pontificalis* (Gen. Bib. I, 5); Papal Documents (Gen. Bib. I, 5); *MGDD imperii*, I, ed. by Pertz (Merovingian sources and also material concerning the Mayors of the Palace); F. Böhmer and E. Mühlbacher, *Die Regesten des Kaiserreichs unter den Karolingern* (Innsbruck, 2nd ed. 1908); *MGDD Carolinorum* (sources from the earliest Carolingians to Charles the Great); *MGEp* III (Codex Carolinus: papal correspondence with the Carolingians); *MGLL Concilia* II (Frankish Synods) and *Capitularia* I; *MGSS rer. Langobardicarum et Italicarum* (Paul the Deacon and other Italian Sources); *MG Auct. ant.* XI 323 (Isidori Continuatio Hispana a. 754); *MGSS rer. mer.* II, 168–93 *(Cont. Fredegarii); MGSS* I and II (Carolingian Annals); *MGSS rer. Germ.* (single editions of sources including the Carolingian Royal Annals and Paul the Deacon); *MGSS* I and II (Carolingian Annals).

GENERAL HISTORY: Glotz, *Cambridge Medieval History,* Dawson, Génicot, Ganshof, see Gen. Bib. II, 1 a–c; Gebhard, Brandt-Meyer-Just, Rassow, Stenton, Hartmann, Solmi, Menéndez Pidal III, see Gen. Bib. II, 2; H. Dannenbauer, *Die Entstehung Europas* II (Stuttgart 1962); F. Lot, *La naissance de la France* (Paris 1948); G. Ostrogorsky, *Geschichte des byzantinischen Staates* (Munich, 3rd ed. 1963).

CONSTITUTIONAL AND POLITICAL HISTORY: Mitteis, David, Kern, Ganshof, Bloch, Lesne, Schramm, T. Mayer, Arquillière, Pacaut, Bouman, Folz: see Gen. Bib. II, 8 a–c; L. Knabe, *Die gelasianische Zweigewaltenlehre bis zum Ende des Investiturstreits* (Berlin 1936); W. Ulmann, *The Growth of Papal Government in the Middle Ages* (New York 1954); H. Steger, *David rex et propheta* (Nürnberg 1961); W. Mohr, *Die karolingische Reichsidee* (Münster 1962).

CHURCH HISTORY: Fliche-Martin VI, Biehlmeyer-Tüchle, Dietrich-Wolf, v. Schubert, Lortz, see Gen. Bib. II, 3; Hauck, de Moreau, Delius, Simpson, Deanesley, Godfrey, García Villada III, Rost, Bauerreiss, Tüchle, see Gen. Bib. II, 4; W. A. Philipps, *History of the Church of Ireland* (Oxford 1933); L. Biehler, *Ireland. Harbinger of the Middle Ages* (London 1963); id., *Irland, Wegbereiter des Abendlandes* (Olten–Lausanne 1961); J. Descola, *Histoire de l'Espagne chrétienne* (Paris 1951); *Le Chiese nei regni dell'Europa occidentale e i loro rapporti con Roma sino all'800,* 2 vols. (Spoleto 1960) [= *Settimane di studio del Centro Italiano di studi sull'alto Medioevo,* VII].

CONCILIAR AND PAPAL HISTORY: Hefele-Leclercq, Haller I, Seppelt II, Caspar, Ullmann, Kempf, see Gen. Bib. II, 5; Bertolini, Cecchelli, Duchesne, Halphen, see Gen. Bib. II, 5; P. Classen, "Karl der Grosse, das Papsttum und Byzanz" in *Karl der Grosse. Lebenswerk und Nachleben,* I (Düsseldorf 1965), 536–608.

CHURCH LAW AND LEGISLATION: Massen, Fournier – Le Bras, Stickler, see Gen. Bib. II, 4; Feine, Plöchl I, Le Bras, Werminghoff, Lot-Fawtier, see Gen. Bib. II, 6; C. de Clercq, *La législation religieuse franque de Clovis à Charlemagne* (Louvain–Paris 1936); H. Barion, *Das fränkisch-deutsche Synodalrecht des Frühmittelalters* (Bonn 1931); U. Stutz, *Geschichte des kirchlichen Benefizialwesens* (new imp. Aalen, 2nd ed. 1961); K. Vogt, *Staat und Kirche von Constantin dem Grossen bis zum Ende der Karolingerzeit* (Tübingen 1936).

MONASTICISM AND LITURGY: Schmitz-Räber, Hilpisch, Knowles, *Settimane di studio*, see Gen. Bib. II, 9; Eisenhofer, Righetti, Jungmann, Klauser, see Gen. Bib. II, 10.

LITERATURE AND EDUCATION: *Manitius* I, de Ghellinck I, Curtius, Raby, Siegmund, Lesne, Fuchs, see Gen. Bib. II, 11; D. Norberg, *Introduction à l'étude de la versification latine médiévale* (Stockholm 1958) [= Studia Latina Stockholmensia 5]; M. L. W. Laistner, *Thought and Letters in Western Europe 500–900* (London, 2nd ed. 1957); R. R. Bezzola, *Les origines et la formation de la littérature courtoise en Occident*, I (1944) [= *BÉH* 286]; R. Aigrain, *L'hagiographie. Ses sources, ses méthodes, son histoire* (Paris 1953).

PHILOSOPHY AND THEOLOGY: Fliche-Martin XIII, Grabmann, Crombie, Geyer *(Ueberweg)*, de Wulf I, Gilson, Schmaus-Geiselmann-Grillmeier, Harnack, Seeberg, de Lubac, Génicot, Copleston, see Gen. Bib. II, 12; J. Leclercq, *Aux sources de la spiritualité occidentale* (Paris 1964).

1. Christendom at the Beginning of the Eighth Century

LITERATURE

FOR AFRICA, SPAIN AND ITALY: C. Diehl, *L'Afrique byzantine* (Paris 1896); H. Leclercq, *L'Afrique chrétienne*, II (Paris, 2nd ed. 1904); España visigoda (Madrid 1940) [= R. Menéndez Pidal III, see Gen. Bibl. II, 2]; C. Diehl, *Études sur l'administration byzantine dans l'exarchat de Ravenne* (1888) [= Bibl. Écoles Françaises d'Athènes et de Rome 53]; L. M. Hartmann, *Untersuchungen zur Geschichte der byzantinischen Verwaltung in Italien* (1889).

ROME, BYZANTIUM AND THE ICONOCLASTIC STRUGGLE: H.-G. Beck, *Kirche und theologische Literatur im byzantinischen Reich* (Munich 1959) [= *Handbuch der Altertumswissensch. Byz. Abt.*, III]; J. Kollwitz, "Zur Frühgeschichte der Bilderverehrung" in *RQ* 48 (1953), 1–20; E. Caspar, "Gregor II. und der Bilderstreit" in *ZKG* 52 (1933), 29–89; O. Bertolini, see Gen. Bib. II, 5; V. Grumel, "L'annexion de l'Illyricum oriental, de la Sicile et de la Calabre au patriarcat de Constantinople" [= Mélanges Lebreton] in *RSR* 40 (1952), 191–200; L. R. Ménager, "La byzantinisation religieuse de l'Italie méridionale et la politique monastique des Normands" in *RHE* 53 (1958), 747–74; ibid., 54 (1959), 5–40; A. Michel, *Die Kaisermacht in der Ostkirche* (Darmstadt 1959).

GREEK LANGUAGE AND GREEK MONASTERIES IN ROME: H. Steinacker, "Die römische Kirche und die griechischen Sprachkenntnisse des Frühmittelalters" in *MIÖG* 62 (1954), 28–66; *Topografia e urbanistica di Roma* (Rome 1958) [= *Storia di Roma*, XXII]; F. Antonelli, "I primi monasteri di monaci orientali in Roma" in *RivAC* 5 (1928), 105–21; A. Michel, *Die griechische Klostersiedlung in Rom bis zur Mitte des 11. Jahrhunderts* (1953) [= *OstKSt* 1]; G. Ferrari, *Early Roman Monasteries* (1957).

EARLY HISTORY OF THE COLLEGE OF CARDINALS: J. Lestocquoy, "Administration de Rome et diaconies du 7e au 9c siècle" in *RivAC* 7 (1930), 261–98; J. Marrou, "L'origine orientale des diaconies romaines" in *MAH* 57 (1940), 95–142; O. Bertolini, "Per la storia delle diaconie romane nell'alto medioevo sino alla fine del secolo VIII in *ADRomana* 70 (1947), 1–145; H. W. Klewitz, "Die Entstehung des Kardinalkollegiums" in *ZSavRGkan* 26 (1936), 115–21; S. Kuttner, "Cardinalis: The History of a Canonical Concept" in *Tr* 3 (1945), 129–214.

GOVERNMENTAL ADMINISTRATION IN ROME: P. E. Schramm, "Studien zu frühmittelalterlichen Aufzeichnungen über Staat und Verfassung" in *ZSavRGgerm* 49 (1929), 167–232; T. Hirschfeld, "Das Gerichtswesen der Stadt Rom vom 8. bis 12. Jahrhundert" in *AUF* 4 (1912), 419–562.

2. The Revival of the Frankish Kingdom and the Crossing of the Anglo-Saxons to the Continent

FURTHER SOURCES

Venerabilis Bedae opera historica, ed. by C. Plummer (Oxford 1896); *Vita Willibrordi, MGSS rer. Mer.,* VII; H. A. Wilson, *The Calendar of St. Willibrord* (London 1918) [= Henry Bradshaw Society 45]; C. Wampach, *Geschichte der Grundherrschaft Echternach* I, 1 and 2 (Luxembourg 1929–30); *Vitae s. Bonifatii archiepiscopi Moguntini,* rec. W. Levison (1905), *MGSS rer. Germ.; Epistolae ss. Bonifatii et Lulli,* rec. Tangl, *MGEp* sel. I; lives of the companions and disciples of St. Boniface in *MGSS* XV.

FURTHER LITERATURE

H. E. Bonnell, *Die Anfänge des karolingischen Hauses* (Berlin 1866); T. Breysig, *Jbb. des fränkischen Reiches 714–741* (1869); H. Hahn, *Jbb. des fränkischen Reiches 741–752* (1863); H. Loewe, *Die karolingische Reichsgründung und der Südosten* (Stuttgart 1937); id., "Bonifatius und die bayrisch-fränkische Spannung" in *Jahrbuch für fränkische Landesforschung* 15 (1955), 85–127; W. Levison, *Aus rheinischer und fränkischer Frühzeit* (Düsseldorf 1948); id., *England and the Continent in the Eighth Century* (Oxford 1946); C. Wampach, *St. Willibrord. Sein Leben und Lebenswerk* (Luxembourg 1953); T. Schieffer, "Angelsachsen und Franken. Zwei Studien zur Kirchengeschichte des 8. Jahrhunderts in *AAMz* 1950, No. 20 (1951); id., *Winfrid-Bonifatius und die christliche Grundlegung Europas* (Freiburg 1954); *St. Bonifatius. Gedenkgabe zum 1200. Todestag,* published by the city of Fulda in conjunction with the Dioceses of Fulda and Mainz (Fulda 1954); H. Büttner, "Bonifatius und die Karolinger" in *Hessisches Jahrbuch für Landesgeschichte* 4 (1954), 21–36; W. Fritze, "Die Einbeziehung von Hessen und Thüringen in die Mainzer Diözese" in *Hessisches Jahrbuch für Landesgeschichte* 4 (1954) 37–63; id., "Slaven und Awaren im angelsächsischen Missionsprogramm I und II" in *Zeitschrift für slavische Philologie* 31 (1964), 316–38; *ibid.,* 32 (1965), 231–51; E. Wiemann, "Bonifatius und das Bistum Erfurt", *Herbergen der Christenheit* 2 (1957); H. Beumann, "Hersfelds Gründungsjahr" in *Hessisches Jahrbuch für Landesgeschichte* 6 (1956), 1–24; H. Appelt, "Die Anfänge des päpstlichen Schutzes" in *MIÖG* 62 (1954), 101–11; W. Schwarz, "Jurisdicio und Condicio. Eine Untersuchung zu den Privilegia libertatis der Klöster" in *ZSavRGkan* 45 (1959), 34–98.

REFORM: H. Barion, *Das fränkisch-deutsche Synodalrecht des Frühmittelalters* (Bonn 1931); H. Frank, *Die Klosterbischöfe des Frankenreichs* (Münster 1932) in *Beiträge zur Geschichte des alten Mönchtums* 17; T. Gottlob, *Der abendländische Chorepiskopat* (Bonn 1928); also F. Gescher, *ZSavRGkan* 19 (1930) 708–17; E. Lesne, *La hiérarchie épiscopale en Gaule et en Germanie 742–882* (Lille–Paris 1905); P. Fournier, *Le droit de propriété exercé par les laïques sur les biens de l'Église au haut moyen âge* (Lille 1943). See also the list of works given at the beginning of the section.

3. The Founding of the Carolingian Monarchy and the Progress of the Reform

FURTHER SOURCES

"Vita s. Pirminii" in *MGSS* XV, 17–31; *PL* 89, 1029–50 (Pirmin, Scarapsus); "De unctione Pippini regis nota monachi s. Dionysii" in *MGSS* XV, 1.

LITERATURE

FOR FRANKISH HISTORY: L. Oelsner, *Jahrbücher des fränkischen Reichs unter König Pippin* (1871).

FOR ROYAL CONSECRATION: E. Perels, "Pippins Erhebung zum König" in *ZKG* 53 (1934), 400–16; E. Müller, "Die Anfänge der Königssalbung im Mittelalter" in *HJ* 58 (1938),

317–60; A. Sprengler, *Gebete für den Herrscher im frühmittelalterlichen Abendland und die verwandten Anschauungen im gleichzeitigen Schrifttum* (typed dissertation, Göttingen 1950); H. Helbig, "Fideles Dei et regis" in *AKG* 33 (1951), 275–306; E. H. Kantorowicz, *Laudes regiae. A Study in liturgical acclamations and mediaeval ruler worship* (Berkeley and Los Angeles 1946) [University of California publ. 33]; B. Opfermann, *Die liturgischen Herrscherakklamationen im Sacrum Imperium des Mittelalters* (Weimar 1953); R. Elze, "Die Herrscherlaudes im Mittelalter" in *ZSavRGkan* 40 (1954), 201–23.

For Pirmin and South Germany: G. Jecker, "St. Pirmins Erden- und Ordensheimat" in *AMrhKG* 5 (1953), 9–41; A. Doll, "Das Pirminkloster Hornbach" in *AMrhKG* 5 (1953), 108–42; T. Mayer, "Die Anfänge der Reichenau" in *ZGObrh* NF 62 (1953), 305–52; H. Büttner, *Geschichte des Elsass* (Berlin 1939); id., "Christentum und fränkischer Staat in Alamannien und Rätien während des 8. Jahrhunderts" in *ZSKG* 43 (1949), 1–150; F. Zöpfl, *Das Bistum Augsburg und seine Bischöfe im Mittelalter* (Munich 1956); K. Reindel, "Die Bistumsorganisation im Alpen-Donauraum in der Spätantike und im Frühmittelalter" in *MIÖG* 72 (1964), 277–310; *Die Reichsabtei Lorsch. Festschrift zum Gedenken an ihre Stiftung* (Darmstadt 1964); J. Fleckenstein, "Über die Herkunft der Welfen und ihre Anfänge in Süddeutschland" in *Forschungen zur oberrheinischen Landesgeschichte*, ed. by G. Tellenbach, 4 (1957), 71–136; id., "Fulrad von St. Denis und der fränkische Ausgriff in den süddeutschen Raum" in *Forschungen zur oberrheinischen Landesgeschichte* 4 (1957), 9–39.

For the Reform of the Empire and Church: J. Fleckenstein, *Die Hofkapelle der deutschen Könige*, I: *Grundlegung. Die karolingische Hofkapelle* (Stuttgart 1959) [= Schriften der *MG* XII, 1]; U. Stutz, "Das karolingische Zehntgebot" in *ZSavRGgerm* 29 (1908), 180–224; E. Morhain, *Origine et histoire de la Regula canonicorum de St. Chrodegang* (1948) [= Misc. P. Paschini. Lateranum N. S. XIV]; C. Gindele, "Die gallikanischen Laus perennis-Klöster und ihre Ordo officii" in *RBén.* 69 (1959), 32–48; E. Bourque, *Études sur les sacramentaires romains,* II: *Les textes remaniés,* 1: *Le Gélasien du 8ᵉ siècle* (Quebec 1925); M. Andrieu, "La liturgie romaine en pays franc et les Ordines Romani" in *Les Ordines Romani,* II (Louvain 1948), XVII–XLIX; T. Klauser, "Die liturgischen Austauschbeziehungen zwischen der römischen und der fränkisch-deutschen Kirche vom 8. bis 11. Jahrhundert" in *HJ* 53 (1933), 169–89; C. Vogel, "Les échanges liturgiques entre Rome et les pays francs jusqu'à l'époque de Charlemagne" in *Le chiese nei regni dell' Europa occidentale . . .,* I, 185–295; id., *Introduction aux sources de l'histoire du culte chrétien au moyen âge,* I (Les sacramentaires), II (Les ordines, pontificaux et rituels) in *Studi medievali* 3 (1962), 1–99, *ibid.* 4 (1963) 435–569; id., "La réforme liturgique sous Charlemagne" in *Karl der Grosse. Lebenswerk und Nachleben,* II (Düsseldorf 1965), 217–32; H. Hucke, "Die Einführung des gregorianischen Gesanges im Frankenreich" in *RQ* 49 (1954), 172–87; H. Büttner, "Mission und Kirchenorganisation des Frankenreiches bis zum Tode Karls des Grossen" in *Karl der Grosse. Lebenswerk und Nachleben,* I (Düsseldorf 1965), 454–87.

4. *The Beginnings of the Papal State*

Collection of Sources

J. Haller, *Die Quellen zur Geschichte der Entstehung des Kirchenstaats* (Leipzig 1907).

Literature

The best new survey: P. Classen, "Karl der Grosse, das Papsttum und Byzanz" in *Karl der Grosse. Lebenswerk und Nachleben,* I (Düsseldorf 1965).

Individual Problems: P. Kehr, "Die sogenannte karolingische Schenkung von 774" in *HZ* 70 (1893), 335–441; E. Caspar, *Pippin und die römische Kirche* (Berlin 1914); id., "Das

Papsttum unter fränkischer Herrschaft" in *ZKG* 54 (1935), 132–264; R. Holtzmann, *Der Kaiser als Marschall des Papstes* (Berlin–Leipzig 1928); L. Wallach, "Amicus amicis, inimicus inimicis" in *ZKG* 52 (1933), 614–15; L. Levillain, "L'avènement de la dynastie carolingienne et les origines de l'État pontifical" in *BÉCh* 94 (1933), 225–95; P. E. Schramm, "Das Versprechen Pippins und Karls des Grossen für die römische Kirche" in *ZSavRGkan* (1938), 180–217; R. Holtzmann, "Die Italienpolitik der Merowinger und des Königs Pippin" in *Das Reich. Festschrift für J. Haller* (Stuttgart 1940), 95–132; M. Lintzel, "Der Codex Carolinus und die Motive für Pippins Italienpolitik" in *HZ* 161 (1940), 33–41; A. Brackmann, "Pippin und die römische Kirche" in *Gesammelte Aufsätze* (1941), 397–420; J. Haller, "Die Karolinger und das Papsttum" in *Abhandlungen zur Geschichte des MA* (1944), 1–40; O. Bertolini, "I papi e le relazioni politiche di Roma con i ducati longobardi di Spoleto e di Benevento III" in *RSTI* 9 (1955), 1–57; id., "I rapporti di Zaccaria con Costantino V e con Artavasdo..." in *AD Romana* 68 (1955), 1–21; id., "Il primo periurium di Aistolfo verso la Chiesa di Roma" in *Misc Mercati* 5 (1946) [= Studi e Testi 125], 160–205; id., "Il problema delle origini del potere temporale dei papi nei suoi presuppositi teoretici iniziali: il concetto di Restitutio nelle prime cessioni territoriali alla Chiesa di Roma" in *Misc. P. Paschini* (1948), 103–71; E. Griffe, "Aux origines de l'État pontifical" in *BLE* 53 (1952), 216–31, *ibid.*, 55 (1954), 65–89; J. Deér, "Zum Patricius Romanorum-Titel Karls des Grossen" in *AHPont* 3 (1965), 31–86 (with a survey of the literature concerning the Patriciate of the Carolingians); G. Tangl, "Die Entsendung des ehemaligen Hausmeiers Karlmann in das Frankenreich im Jahre 754 und der Konflikt der Brüder" in *QFIAB* 40 (1960), 1–42; id., "Die Passvorschrift des Königs Ratchis und ihre Beziehung zu dem Verhältnis zwischen Franken und Langobarden" in *QFIAB* 38 (1958), 1–67.

SECTION TWO

The Greek Church in the Epoch of Iconoclasm

SOURCES

1. CHRONICLES AND HISTORICAL WORKS: *Nicephori archiepiscopi Constantinopolitani opuscula historica,* ed. by C. de Boor (Lipsiae 1880); *Theophanis Chronographia,* ed. by C. de Boor (Lipsiae 1883); *Georgii monachi chronicon,* ed. by C. de Boor (Lipsiae 1904); *Symeon Magistros u. Logothetes, Chronik, ed. sub nomine Leo Grammaticus,* ed. by I. Bekker (Bonn 1842); *Genesius,* ed. by C. Lachmann (1834); *Theophanes Continuatus,* ed. by I. Bekker (Bonn 1838); *Scriptor incertus de Leone Armeno,* ed. by I. Bekker in the edition of *Leo Grammaticus* (Bonn 1842), 335–62; H. Grégoire, "Un nouveau fragment du Scriptor incertus de Leone Armenio" in *Byz(B)* 11 (1936), 417–27.

2. HAGIOGRAPHIC SOURCES: "Vita Stephani Junioris auct. Stephano diacono" in *PG* 100, 1069–1185; "Vita Nicetae Mediciensis auct. Theostericto" in *ActaSS* April 1 (1865), App. 18–27; "Vita Germani I Patriarchae", ed. by A. Papadopulos-Kerameus, Μαυρογορδάτειος Βιβλιοθήκη, Ἀνέκδοτα Ἑλληνικά (Constantinople 1884), 3–17; "Vita Nicephori Patriarchae auct. Ignatio diacono", ed. by C. de Boor in *Nicephori opuscula historica,* 139–217; "Vita s. Theodori Stud. aust. Michaele monacho" in *PG* 99, 233–328; "Vita s. Tarasii Patriarchae auct. Ignatio Diacono", ed. by I. A. Heikel, *Acta Soc. Sc. Fennicae* 17 (1891), 395–423; "Vita s. Methodii Patriarchae" in *PG* 100, 1244–61.

3. SYNODAL ACTS (cited according to location): Sources for Emperors and Patriarchs are listed by number in: *Dölger Reg* and *Grumel Reg*.

4. FURTHER SOURCES: Letters of the Patriarch Germanos in *PG* 98, 156 seqq.; Writings and Letters of Theodoros Studites in *PG* 99; The Works of the Patriarch Nicephorus in *PG* 100, 205–849; *Pitra S* I, 302–503; *ibid.* IV, 292–380.

LITERATURE

K. Schwarzlose, *Der Bilderstreit* (Gotha 1890); L. Bréhier, *La querelle des images* (Paris 1904); E. J. Martin, *A History of the Iconoclastic Controversy* (London 1930); V. Grumel, "Images" in *DThC* VII, 766–844; id., "Recherches récentes sur l'iconoclasme" in *ÉO* 29 (1930), 92–100; G. Ladner, "Origin and Significance of the Byzantine Iconoclastic Controversy" in *MS* 2 (1940), 127–49.

SECTION THREE
The Age of Charles the Great (768 to 814)

SOURCES

See bibliography for Section One. Also *MGEp* IV.

LITERATURE

Karl der Grosse. Lebenswerk und Nachleben with the assistance of H. Beumann, B. Bischoff, H. Schnitzler and P. E. Schramm, ed. by W. Braunfels (Düsseldorf 1965), vol. I: *Persönlichkeit und Geschichte,* vol. II: *Das Geistige Leben,* vol. III: *Karolingische Kunst* (hereafter cited as Karlswerk I, II, III); S. Abel and B. Simson, *Jahrbücher des fränkischen Reichs unter Karl dem Grossen* I, II (Leipzig, 2nd ed. 1888 and 1883); A. Kleinclausz, *Charlemagne* (Paris 1934); J. Calmette, *Charlemagne. Sa vie et son œuvre* (Paris 1945); L. Halphen, *Charlemagne et l'empire carolingien* (1948) [= Évolution de l'Humanité 33]; H. v. Fichtenau, *Das karolingische Imperium. Soziale und geistige Problematik eines Grossreiches* (Zürich 1949); R. Folz, *Le couronnement impérial de Charlemagne* (Paris 1964); F. Ganshof, *The Imperial Coronation of Charlemagne* (Glasgow 1949).

SHORT SURVEYS: F. L. Ganshof, "Charlemagne" in *Speculum* 24 (1949), 520–28; E. Delaruelle, "Charlemagne et l'Église" in *RHEF* 39 (1953), 165–99; P. E. Schramm, *Karl der Grosse im Lichte der Staatssymbolik* (1957) [= *Forschungen zur Kunstgeschichte und christlichen Archäologie,* ed. by F. Gerke III].

INDIVIDUAL STUDIES CONCERNING GOVERNMENT: M. Lintzel, *Ausgewählte Schriften,* I and II (Berlin 1961).

FOR THE STRUCTURE OF THE FRANKISH STATE: E. Zöllner, *Die politische Stellung der Völker im Frankenreich* (Vienna 1950) (= *VIÖG* 13); P. Vaccari, *Studi sull'Europa precarolingia e carolingia* (Verona 1955); L. Auzias, *L'Aquitaine carolingienne* (Toulouse–Paris 1937); F. L. Ganshof, *La Belgique carolingienne* (Brussels 1958); Ewig *(Francia),* Bligny (Burgundy), Wolff (Aquitaine), Wenskus (German Tribes), Reindel (Bavaria) in *Karlswerk,* I.

FOR THE CAROLINGIAN IMPERIAL ARISTOCRACY: G. Tellenbach, *Königtum und Stämme in der Werdezeit des Deutschen Reiches* (Weimar 1939); *Studien und Vorarbeiten zur Geschichte des grossfränkischen und frühdeutschen Adels,* ed. by G. Tellenbach (Freiburg 1957) [= Forschungen zur oberrheinischen Landesgeschichte, IV]; E. Hlawitschka, *Franken, Alemannen, Bayern und Burgunder in Oberitalien 774–962* (Freiburg 1960) [= Forschungen zur oberrheinischen Landesgeschichte, VIII]; Werner in *Karlswerk,* I.

FOR FRANKLAND AND BYZANTIUM: W. Ohnsorge, *Das Zweikaiserproblem im frühen Mittelalter* (Hildesheim 1947); id., *Abendland und Byzanz* (Darmstadt 1958); id., "Byzanz und das Abendland im 9. und 10. Jahrhundert" in *Saeculum* 5 (1954), 194–220; F. Dölger, *Byzanz und die europäische Staatenwelt* (Ettal 1953); Classen in *Karlswerk,* I.

10. *Charles the Great and Italy*

LITERATURE

FOR THE CONQUEST OF ITALY AND THE ROMAN PATRICIATE: O. Bertolini, "La caduta del primicerio Cristoforo" in *RSTI* 1 (1947); M. Lintzel, *Karl der Grosse und Karlmann* (see *supra*); E. Delaruelle, "Charlemagne, Carloman, Didier et la politique du mariage franco-lombard" in *RH* 170 (1932), 213–24; E. Griffe, "Aux origines de l'État pontifical" in *BLE* (1954), 65–89; H. Loewe, "Zur Vita Hadriani" in *DA* 12 (1956), 493–98; *ibid.*, 14 (1958), 531 ff.; P. E. Schramm, "Die Anerkennung Karls des Grossen als Kaiser" in *HZ* 172 (1951), 449–515; also J. Deér, "Die Vorrechte des Kaisers in Rom 772–800" in *Schweizer Beiträge zur allgemeinen Geschichte* 15 (1957), 5–63; id., *Patricius Romanorum-Titel* (see ch. 4); Classen, *Karlswerk*, I.

FOR THE DONATION OF CONSTANTINE: P. Scheffer-Boichorst, "Neuere Forschungen über die Constantinische Schenkung" in *Gesammelte Schriften,* I (1903), 1–62; W. Levison, "Constantinische Schenkung und Silvesterlegende" in *Aus rheinischer und fränkischer Frühzeit* (1948), 390–465; W. Ohnsorge, "Die constantinische Schenkung" in *Abendland und Byzanz* (1958), 79–110; see the criticism of R. Bork, "Zu einer neuen These über die Constantinische Schenkung" in *Festschrift A. Hofmeister* (1955), 39–56; E. Ewig, "Das Bild Constantins des Grossen in den ersten Jahrhunderten des abendländischen Mittelalters" in *HJ* 75 (1956), 1–46; W. Gericke, "Wann entstand die Constantinische Schenkung?" in *ZSavRGkan* 43 (1957), 1–88; also: H. Fuhrmann, "Constantinische Schenkung und Silvesterlegende in neuer Sicht" in *DA* 15 (1959), 523–40; S. Williams, "The Oldest Text of the 'Constitutum Constantini' " in *Tr* 20 (1964), 448–61.

11. *The Completing of the Frankish Empire*

SUPPLEMENTARY SOURCES

FOR SAXON HISTORY (in addition to the sources in *MGSS* I, II, XV, *MGCap* I): Beda (cf. chap. 2); Widukind of Corvey, *Rerum gestarum Saxonicarum libri tres,* rec. Lohmann-Hirsch (1935) [= *MGGS rer. Germ.*]; Vita Lebuini antiquior: *MGSS* XXX; Altfrid, *Vita Liudgeri,* ed. by Diekamp (1881) [= *Geschichtsquellen des Bistums Münster* 4].

LITERATURE

THE SAXON PEOPLE AND THE SAXON WARS: M. Lintzel (see ch. 10), *Der sächsische Stammesstaat und seine Eroberung durch die Franken* (1933); W. Lammers, "Die Stammesbildung bei den Sachsen. Eine Forschungsbilanz" in *Westfälische Forschungen* 10 (1957), 25–57; *Der Raum Westfalen,* ed. by A. Aubin and F. Petri I, II (Münster 1952, 1955); H. Krüger, "Die vorgeschichtlichen Strassen in den Sachsenkriegen Karls des Grossen" in *Korrespondenzblatt Gesamtverein deutscher Geschichts- und Altertumsvereine* 80 (1932), 223–80; K. Brandi, "Karls des Grossen Sachsenkriege" in *Niedersächsisches Jahrbuch für Landesgeschichte* 10 (1933), 29–52; J. Ramackers, "Die rheinischen Aufmarschstrassen in den Sachsenkriegen Karls des Grossen" in *AHVNrh* 142/143 (1943), 1–27.

THE SAXON MISSION AND ECCLESIASTICAL ORGANIZATION: R. E. Sullivan, "The Carolingian Missionary and the Pagan" in *Saeculum* 28 (1953), 705–40; S. Gollub, "Zur Frage der ältesten christlichen Bestattungen in Westfalen" in *Westfälische Forschungen* 11 (1958), 10–16; K. Hauck, "Ein Utrechter Missionar auf der altsächsischen Stammesversammlung" in *Das erste Jahrtausend,* vol. of Texts II (1965), 734–45; id., "Die Herkunft der Liudger-, Lebuin- und Marklo-Überlieferung. Ein brieflicher Vorbericht" in *Festschrift für Jost Trier zum*

70. *Geburtstag* (Cologne–Graz 1965), 221–39; H. Wiedemann, *Die Sachsenbekehrung* (Hiltrup 1932); *Westfalia Sacra*, I, II (1948, 1950); G. Honselmann, "Die Annahme des Christentums durch die Sachsen im Lichte sächsischer Quellen des 9. Jahrhunderts" in *Westfälische Zschr.* 108 (1958), 201–19; A. K. Hömberg, "Das mittelalterliche Pfarrsystem des kölnischen Westfalen" in *Westfalen* 29 (1951); id., "Studien zur Entstehung der mittelalterlichen Kirchen-organisation in Westfalen" in *Westfälische Forschungen* 6 (1943/52), 46–108; H. E. Feine, "Die genossenschaftliche Gemeindekirche im germanischen Recht" in *MIÖG* 68 (1960), 171–96; G. Niemeyer, *Die Vita des ersten Bremer Bischofs Willehad und seine kirchliche Verehrung* (Münster 1953); A. Schröer, "Das geistliche Bild Liudgers" in *Das erste Jahrtausend,* vol. of texts I (Düsseldorf 1964), 194–215; A. Henkis, "Die Eingliederung Nordalbingiens in das Franken-reich" in *Schleswig-Holstein* 79 (1955), 81–104; H. Büttner in *Karlswerk,* I.

SPANISH EXPEDITION: R. de Abadal y de Vinyals, *La expedición de Carlomagno a Zaragoza. El hecho histórico, su carácter y su significación* (Saragosa 1956) [= Publ. de la Facultad de Filosofía y Letras, Serie II, no. 2]; P. Aebischer, "Le rôle de Pampelune lors de l'expédition franque de 778" in *Schweizer Zeitschrift für Geschichte* 9 (1959), 305–33.

BAVARIA: Loewe (see chap. 2); Reindel in *Karlswerk,* I.

BENEVENTO: R. Poupardin, "Études sur l'histoire des principautés lombards de l'Italie méridionale et de leurs rapports avec l'empire franc" in *MA* (1907), 1–25; J. Gay, *L'Italie méridionale et l'empire byzantin* (Paris 1904) [= Bibl. des Écoles françaises d'Athènes et de Rome]; O. Bertolini, "Langobardi e Bizantini nell'Italia meridionale" in *Atti 30 Congresso internazionale di studi sull'Alto Medioevo* (Spoleto 1959), 103–24; id., *Karlswerk,* I; H. Belting, *Studien zum beneventanischen Hof im 8. Jahrhundert* (New York–Gluckstadt 1963) [= The Dumbarton Oaks Center of Byzantine Studies].

THE AVARS: G. Stadtmüller, *Geschichte Südosteuropas* (Munich 1950); A. Kollautz, "Die Awaren. Die Schichtung einer Nomadenherrschaft" in *Saeculum* 5 (1954), 129–78; W. Fritze, "Slawen und Awaren im angelsächsischen Missionsprogramm" in *Zeitschrift für slavische Philologie* 31 (1964), 316–38; esp. J. Deér in *Karlswerk,* I.

12. *Reform of Empire and Church: The Carolingian Renaissance*

FURTHER SOURCES

PL 99 (Paulinus of Aquileia), 100 and 101 (Alcuin), 105 (Theodulf of Orléans). Also *MGEp* IV (containing among others the letters of Alcuin) and *MGPoetae* I (poets of the time of Charles the Great as well as the above mentioned authors). Cf. in *Wattenbach-Levison* and *Manitius* I.

LITERATURE

CAPITULARIES: F. L. Ganshof, *Recherches sur les capitulaires* (Paris 1958); W. E. Eckhardt, "Die capitularia missorum specialia von 802" in *DA* 12 (1956), 418–516.

CHURCH AND IMPERIAL REFORM: J. Fleckenstein, "Karl der Grosse und sein Hof" in *Karls-werk,* I, 24–50; H. Büttner, "Mission und Kirchenorganisation des Frankenreichs bis zum Tode Karls des Grossen" in *Karlswerk,* I, 454–87; F. Prinz, "Abriss der kirchlichen und monastischen Entwicklung des Frankenreiches bis zu Karl dem Grossen" in *Karlswerk,* II, 290–99; J. Semmler, "Karl der Grosse und das fränkische Mönchtum" in *Karlswerk,* II, 255–89; F. L. Ganshof, "Charlemagne et les institutions de la monarchie franque" in *Karls-werk,* I, 349–93; id., "Charlemagne et l'administration de la justice dans la monarchie franque" in *Karlswerk,* I, 394–419; id., "The Impact of Charlemagne on the Institutions of the Frankish

Realm" in *Speculum* 40 (1965), 47–62; id., *Les Liens de vassalité dans la monarchie franque* (Brussels 1958); id., *L'immunité dans la monarchie franque* (Brussels 1958); E. E. Stengel, "Grundherrschaft und Immunität" in *Abhandlungen und Untersuchungen zur mittelalterlichen Geschichte* (Cologne 1960), 35–68; F. N. Estey, "The Scabini and the Local Courts" in *Speculum* 26 (1951), 119–29; V. Krause, "Geschichte des Institutes der Missi dominici" in *MIÖG* 11 (1890), 193–300; W. Metz, *Das karolingische Reichsgut* (Berlin 1960).

THE CAROLINGIAN RENAISSANCE: W. von den Steinen, "Der Neubeginn" in *Karlswerk*, II, 9–27; id., "Karl und die Dichter" in *Karlswerk*, II, 63–94; B. Bischoff, "Die Hofbibliothek Karls des Grossen" in *Karlswerk*, II, 42–62; id., "Panorama der handschriftlichen Überlieferung aus der Zeit Karls des Grossen" in *Karlswerk*, II, 233–54; F. Brunhölzl, "Der Bildungsauftrag der Hofschule" in *Karlswerk*, II, 28–41; F. Mütherich, "Die Buchmalerei am Hofe Karls des Grossen" in *Karlswerk*, III, 9–53; W. Braunfels, "Karls des Grossen Bronzewerkstatt" in *Karlswerk*, III, 168–202; J. Beckwith, "Byzantine Influence on Art at the Court of Charlemagne" in *Karlswerk*, III, 288–300; E. Lehmann, "Die Architektur zur · Zeit Karls des Grossen" in *Karlswerk*, III, 301–19; P. Lehmann, *Erforschung des Mittelalters*, 5 vols. (Stuttgart 1941–62); id., "Das Problem der karolingischen Renaissance" in *Settimane di studio . . .* I (Spoleto 1954), 310–58; F. Heer, "Die Renaissanceideologie im früheren Mittelalter" in *MIÖG* 57 (1949), 23–81; H. Liebeschütz, "Wesen und Werden des karolingischen Rationalismus" in *AKG* 33 (1951), 17–44; H. Grundmann, "Litteratus — illitteratus. Der Wandel einer Bildungsnorm vom Altertum zum Mittelalter" in *AKG* 40 (1958), 1–65; K. Hauck, *Mittellateinische Literatur: Deutsche Philologie im Aufriss*, 2nd ed. by W. Stammler (n. d.); J. Fleckenstein, *Die Bildungsreform Karls des Grossen* (1953); P. Riché, *Éducation et culture dans l'Occident barbare, 6ᵉ–8ᵉ siècle* (Paris 1962); E. Lesne, *Les écoles de la fin du 8ᵉ à la fin du 9ᵉ siècle* [= *Hist. de la propr. eccl.*, V, see Gen. Bib. II, 8]; R. Stachnik, *Die Bildung des Klerus im Frankenreich von Karl Martell bis auf Ludwig den Frommen* (Paderborn 1956); B. Bischoff, "Das Problem der karolingischen Hofschulen" in *Beihefte zur Geschichte in Wissenschaft und Unterricht* (1956), 50 ff.; A. Hessel, "Zur Entstehung der karolingischen Minuskel" *AUF* 8 (1923), 201–14; D. W. Schwarz, *Die karolingische Schriftreform* (1946) [= Schweizer Beiträge zur allgemeinen Geschichte 4], 38–54; B. Bischoff, *Paläographie, Deutsche Philologie im Aufriss*, 2nd ed. by W. Stammler (n. d.).

LITURGICAL REFORM: See chap. 3. Also: E. Bourque, *Étude sur les sacramentaires romains*, II, 2. *Le sacramentaire d'Hadrien: Studi di antichità cristiana* 25 (Rome 1958); E. Heitz, *Recherches sur les rapports entre architecture et liturgie à l'époque carolingienne* (Paris 1963).

BIBLE REVISION: S. Berger, *Histoire de la Vulgate pendant les premiers siècles du moyen âge* (Paris (1893); B. Fischer, "Bibelausgaben des frühen Mittelalters" in *Settimane di studio del Centro Italiano di studi sull'alto medioevo*, X, *La bibbia nell'alto medioevo* (Spoleto 1963), 519–600; id., "Bibeltext und Bibelreform unter Karl dem Grossen" in *Karlswerk*, II, 156–216; R. E. McNally, *The Bible in the Early Middle Ages* (Westminster, Md., 1959).

ALCUIN: A. Kleinclausz, *Alcuin* (Paris 1948); E. S. Duckett, *Alcuin* (New York 1951); L. Wallach, *Alcuin and Charlemagne* (New York 1959); id., "The Unknown Author of the Libri Carolini" in *Didascaliae. Studies in Honor of A. M. Albareda* (New York 1961), 469–515; F. L. Ganshof, "La révision de la Bible par Alcuin" in *Bibliothèque d'Humanisme et de Renaissance* 9 (1947), 7–20; B. Fischer, *Die Alcuinbibel* (Freiburg 1957); G. Ellard, *Master Alcuin Liturgist* (Chicago 1956); G. Hocquard, "Quelques réflexions sur les idées politico-religieuses d'Alcuin" in *Bulletin des Facultés catholiques de Lyon* 74 (1952); F. C. Scheibe, "Alkuin und die Admonitio Generalis" in *DA* 14 (1958), 221–9; id., "Alkuin und die Briefe Karls des Grossen" in *DA* 15 (1959), 181–93; id., "Geschichtsbild, Zeitbewusstsein und Reformwille bei Alkuin" in *AKG* 41 (1959), 35–62; A. Chélini, *Le vocabulaire politique et social dans la correspondance d'Alcuin* (Aix en Provence 1959) [= *Travaux et mém. Fac. Lettres d'Aix* 220]; H. B. Meyer, "Alkuin zwischen Antike und Mittelalter. Ein Kapitel frühmittelalterlicher

505

Frömmigkeitsgeschichte" in *ZKTh* 81 (1959), 405–54; H. Hürten, "Alkuin und der Episkopat im Reiche Karls des Grossen" in *HJ* 82 (1963), 22–49. See also Lit. on Adoptionism and the iconoclastic controversy.

THEODULF: C. Cuissard, *Théodulphe évêque d'Orléans* (Orléans 1892); H. Liebeschütz, "Theodulf of Orléans and the Problem of the Carolingian Renaissance" in *Fritz Saxl 1890–1948. A Volume of Memorial Essays*, ed. by J. Gordon, 77–92; B. Bischoff, "Theodulf und der Ire Cadac Andreas" in *HJ* 74 (1955), 92–98; D. Schaller, "Philologische Untersuchungen zu den Gedichten Theodulfs von Orléans" in *DA* 18 (1962), 13–91; Ann Freeman, "Theodulf of Orléans and the Libri Carolini" in *Speculum* 32 (1957), 663–705; id., "Further Studies in the Libri Carolini" in *Speculum* 40 (1965), 203–89. See also Lit. on the Iconoclastic controversy (III, chap. 13).

THE BEGINNING OF GERMAN LITERATURE: H. de Boor, "Von der karolingischen zur cluniazensischen Epoche" in *Annalen der deutschen Literatur,* ed. by H. O. Burger (Stuttgart, 2nd ed. 1962); id., *Die deutsche Literatur von Karl dem Grossen bis zum Beginn der höfischen Dichtung 770–1170* (Munich, 6th ed. 1964) [= de Boor/Newald, *Geschichte der deutschen Literatur von den Anfängen bis zur Gegenwart* I]; G. Baesecke, *Vor- und Frühgeschichte des deutschen Schrifttums* (Halle 1950); H. Loewe, "Arbeo von Freising" in *Rheinische Vierteljahresblätter* 15/16 (1950–51), 87–120; J. L. Weisgerber, *Der Sinn des Wortes Deutsch* (Göttingen 1949); H. Brinkmann, *Sprachwandel und Sprachbewegungen in althochdeutscher Zeit* (Jena 1931); K. F. Freudenthal, *Arnulfingisch-karolingische Rechtswörter* (Göteborg 1949); W. Betz, "Karl der Grosse und die Lingua theodisca" in *Karlswerk,* II, 300–06.

13. *Iconoclasm; Adoptionism, and Filioque*

FURTHER SOURCES

MGConc II suppl. (Libri Carolini).

LITERATURE

ON THE ICONOCLASTIC CONTROVERSY: W. von den Steinen, "Entstehungsgeschichte der Libri Carolini" in *QFIAB* 21 (1929–30), 1–93; id., "Karl der Grosse und die Libri Carolini" in *NA* 49 (1932), 207–80; H. v. Fichtenau, "Karl der Grosse und das Kaisertum" in *MIÖG* 61 (1953), 257–334; Freeman and Wallach (see ch. 12 on Theodulf and Alcuin); M. Vieillard-Troïekouroff, "Tables de canons et stucs carolingiens" in *CahArch* 13 (1962), 154–78; P. Bloch, "Das Apsismosaik von Germigny" in *Karlswerk,* III, 234–61; H. Schnitzler, "Das Apsismosaik der Aachener Pfalzkapelle" in *Aachener Kunstblätter* 29 (1964), 1 seqq.; H. Schade, "Die Libri Carolini und ihre Stellung zum Bild" in *ZKTh* 79 (1957), 69–78; G. Haendler, *Epochen karolingischer Theologie. Untersuchungen über die karolingischen Gutachten zum byzantinischen Bilderstreit* (Berlin 1958).

ADOPTIONISM: C. S. Robles, *Elipando y San Beato de Liébana* (Madrid 1935); J. F. Rivera, *Elipando de Toledo* (Toledo 1940); E. Amann, "L'adoptianisme espagnol du 8ᵉ siècle" in *RevSR* 16 (1936), 281–317; R. de Abadal y de Vinyals, *La batalla del Adopcianismo y la desintegración de la Iglesia visigoda* (Barcelona 1949); M. del Alamo, "Los comentarios de Beato al Apocalipsis y Elipando", *MiscMercati* II in *SteT* 122 (1946), 16–33; J. Solano, "El concilio de Calcedonia y la controversia adopcionista del siglo VIII en España" in *Das Konzil von Chalkedon,* II (Würzburg 1953), 841–71; F. Ansprenger, *Untersuchungen zum adoptianischen Streit im 8. Jahrhundert* (dissertation Berlin 1952); D. Bullough, "The Dating of Codex Carolinus Nr. 95, 96, 97, Wilchar and the Beginning of the Archbishopric of Sens" in *DA* 18 (1962), 223–30; W. Heil, "Der Adoptianismus. Alkuin und Spanien" in *Karlswerk,* II, 95–155.

FRANKFURT: F. L. Ganshof, "Observations sur le synode de Francfort de 794" in *Misc. historica in honorem A. de Meyer* (Louvain–Brussels 1946), 306 seqq.

14. *From Frankish Kingdom to Christian Empire*

COLLECTED SOURCES

H. Dannenbauer, *Die Quellen zur Geschichte der Kaiserkrönung Karls des Grossen* (Berlin 1931).

LITERATURE

AACHEN: E. Lehmann (as ch. 12); *Karlswerk,* III, 301–19; G. Bandmann, "Die Vorbilder der Aachener Pfalzkapelle" in *Karlswerk,* III, 424–62; F. Kreusch, "Kirche, Atrium und Portikus der Aachener Pfalz" in *Karlswerk,* III, 463–533; L. Hugot, "Die Pfalz Karls des Grossen in Aachen" in *Karlswerk,* III, 534–72; W. Kämmerer, "Die Aachener Pfalz Karls des Grossen in Anlage und Überlieferung" in *Karlswerk,* I, 322–48; E. Ewig, "Résidence et capitale pendant le haut moyen âge" in *RH* 230 (1963), 25–72.

SECURING THE FRONTIERS: E. Klebel, "Herzogtümer und Marken bis 900" in *DA* 2 (1938), 1–53; A. Hofmeister, "Markgrafen und Markgrafschaften im italischen Königreich in der Zeit von Karl dem Grossen bis zu Otto dem Grossen" in *MIÖG* suppl. vol. 7 (1906); S. Pivano, "I ducati del regno italico nell'età carolingia" in *Studi di storia e diritto in onore di E. Besta,* IV (Milan 1939), 299 seqq.; C. G. Mor, "Dal ducato longobardo del Friuli alla Marca Franca" in *Memorie storiche Forogiuliesi* 42 (1956–57), 29–41; J. Dhondt, *Études sur la naissance des principautés territoriales en France* (Bruges 1948); R. de Abadal y de Vinyals, *Nota sobre la locución Marca Hispánica* (Barcelona 1958); M. Bathe, "Die Sicherung der Reichsgrenze an der Mittelelbe durch Karl den Grossen" in *Sachsen und Anhalt* 16 (1940), 1–44.

THE FRANKISH KINGDOM AND ITS NEIGHBOURS: H. Loewe, "Von Theoderich dem Grossen zu Karl dem Grossen" in *DA* 9 (1952), 353–401; id., "Von den Grenzen des Kaisergedankens in der Karolingerzeit" in *DA* 14 (1958), 345–74; J. Fischer, *Oriens Occidens Europa* (Wiesbaden 1957); J. H. Wallace-Hadrill, "Charlemagne and England" in *Karlswerk,* I, 683–98; H. Jankuhn, "Karl der Grosse und der Norden" in *Karlswerk,* I, 699–707; M. Hellmann, "Karl und die slawische Welt" in *Karlswerk,* I, 708–18.

THE QUESTION OF LEO III: L. Wallach, "The Genuine and the Forged Oath of Pope Leo III" in *Tr* 11 (1955), 37–63; id., The Roman Synod of December 800 and the Alleged Trial of Leo III" in *HThR* 49 (1956), 123–42; opposing view: H. Loewe in Wattenbach-Levison, *Deutschlands Geschichtsquellen im Mittelalter, Vorzeit und Karolinger,* IV, 457: H. Zimmermann, "Papstabsetzungen des Mittelalters I" in *MIÖG* 69 (1961), 1–84.

EARLY HISTORY OF THE IMPERIAL CORONATION: K. Heldmann, *Das Kaisertum Karls des Grossen, Theorie und Wirklichkeit* (1928); F. L. Ganshof, *The Imperial Coronation of Charlemagne, Theories and Facts* (Glasgow 1949); W. Ohnsorge, *Abendland und Byzanz* (see ch. 10); H. Loewe, "Eine Notiz zum Kaisertum Karls des Grossen" in *Rheinische Vierteljahrsblätter* 14 (1949), 7–34; C. Erdmann, *Forschungen zur politischen Ideenwelt des frühen Mittelalters* (Berlin 1951); E. E. Stengel, "Imperator und Imperium bei den Angelsachsen" in *DA* 16 (1960), 15–72; H. Beumann, "Die Kaiserfrage in den Paderborner Verhandlungen 799" in *Das erste Jahrtausend,* ed. by V. Elbern, vol. of texts I (1962), 296–317; id., "Romkaiser und fränkisches Reichsvolk" in *Festschrift E. E. Stengel zum 70. Geburtstag* (1952), 157–80; id., "Nomen imperatoris" in *HZ* 185 (1958), 515–49; A. Borst, "Kaisertum und Nomentheorie im Jahre 800" in *Festschrift P. E. Schramm zum 70. Geburtstag* (Wiesbaden 1964), 36–51; W. Mohr, "Karl der Grosse, Leo III. und der römische Aufstand" in *Archivum Latinitatis*

Medii Aevi 30 (1960), 39–98; H. v. Fichtenau, "Karl der Grosse und das Kaisertum" in *MIÖG* 61 (1953), 257–334; P. Grierson, "The Coronation of Charlemagne and the Coinage of Pope Leo III" in *Revue belge de phil. et d'hist.* 30 (1952), 825–33; Schramm and Deér (see chap. 10); R. Folz, *Le couronnement impérial de Charlemagne* (Paris 1964); P. Classen, "Karl der Grosse, das Papsttum und Byzanz" in *Karlswerk,* I, 537–608.

IMPERIAL TITLE: P. F. Kehr in *NA* 49 (1932), 702–3: P. Classen, "Romanum gubernans imperium" in *DA* 9 (1952), 103–21.

15. *The Development of the Carolingian Theocracy*

LITERATURE

IMPERIAL LEGISLATION AND OATHS OF FIDELITY: F. L. Ganshof, *Recherches* (see chap. 12); id., "La fin du règne de Charlemagne, une décomposition" in *Zeitschrift für schweizerische Geschichte* 28 (1948), 433–52; id., "L'échec de Charlemagne" in *Comptes rendus Acad. Inscr. et Belles Lettres* (1947), 248–54; id., "Le programme de gouvernement impérial de Charlemagne: Renovatio imperii" in *Atti della giornata internazionale di Studio per il Millenario 1961* (Faenza 1963), 63–96; F. Lot, "Le serment de fidélité à l'époque franque" in *Revue belge de phil. et d'hist.* 12 (1933), 569–82; L. Halphen, "L'idée d'État sous les Carolingiens" in *RH* 185 (1939), 59–70; C. Odegaard, "The Concept of Royal Power in Carolingian Oaths of Fidelity" in *Speculum* 20 (1945), 279–89; F. L. Ganshof, "Charlemagne et le serment" in *Mélanges Halphen* (1951), 259–70; T. Mayer, "Staatsauffassung in der Karolingerzeit" in *HZ* 173 (1952), 467–84.

MONASTIC REFORM: J. Semmler, "Karl der Grosse und das fränkische Mönchtum" in *Karlswerk,* II, 255–89.

BAGHDAD AND BYZANTIUM: F. W. Buckler, *Harunu'l Rashid and Charles the Great* (Cambridge, Mass. 1931) [= The medieval academy of America, no. 7]; W. Björkman, "Karl und der Islam" in *Karlswerk,* I, 672–82; O. Bertolini, "Carlomagno e Benevento" in *Karlswerk,* I, 609–71; Ohnsorge (see ch. 10); R. Cessi, *Le origini del ducato veneziano* (Naples n. d.) [= *Collectanea storica* 4]; F. Dölger (see ch. 10); P. Classen (see ch. 14).

THE PROBLEM OF SUCCESSION: Ohnsorge (see ch. 10); W. Schlesinger, "Kaisertum und Reichsteilung" in *Forschungen zu Staat und Verfassung. Festgabe für F. Hartung* (Berlin 1958), 9–51; id., *Karolingische Königswahlen* (Berlin 1958); W. Mohr, "Reichspolitik und Kaiserkrönung in den Jahren 813 und 816" in *Welt als Geschichte* 20 (1960), 168–86; Classen (see ch. 14).

THE CAROLINGIAN LEGACY: E. Ewig, "Karl der Grosse und die karolingischen Teilungen" in *Die Europäer und ihre Geschichte* (Munich 1961), 1–18; R. Folz, *Le souvenir et la légende de Charlemagne dans l'Empire germanique médiéval* (Paris 1950) [= Publ. Univ. Dijon, VII].

SECTION FOUR

Climax and Turning Point of the Carolingian Age (814 to 840)

FURTHER SOURCES

Survey in *Wattenbach-Levison* III; Lives of Louis the Pious in *MGSS* II, 604–48 (Astronomus); *ibid.,* 585–604 (Thegan); *MGCap* II, *Ep* V and *Poetae* II (writers and poets of the 9th cent., esp. Ermoldus Nigellus); *PL* 102 (Smaragdus), 103 (Benedict of Aniane), 104

(Agobard and Claudius of Turin), 105 (Ermoldus Niggellus, Dungal, Amalarius) 106 (Hilduin, Jonas, Fréculf), 107–12 (Rhabanus Maurus), 113–14 (Walafrid Strabo), 119 (Florus of Lyons), 120 (Paschasius Radbertus); Jonas, *De institutione regia,* ed. by Reviron (see ch. 17); Vita Anscarii in *MGSS rer. Germ.* (rec. Waitz).

16. *Reform in Empire and Church from 814 to 828*

LITERATURE

ON LOUIS THE PIOUS AND HIS REIGN: H. Kuhn, *Das literarische Porträt Ludwigs des Frommen* (dissertation Basle 1930); F. L. Ganshof, "Louis the Pious Reconsidered" in *History* 42 (1957), 171–80; T. Schieffer, "Die Krise des karolingischen Imperiums" in *Aus Mittelalter und Neuzeit. Festschrift zum 70. Geburtstag von G. Kallen* (Bonn 1957), 1–15.

ON THE ORDINATIO IMPERII OF 817: F. L. Ganshof, "Over het idee van het kaizerschap bij Lodewijk de Vrome tijdens het eerste deel van zijn regering" in *Mededelingen der koninklijke vlaamse Academie, Klasse der Letteren* 15 (Brussels 1953); id., "Observations sur l'Ordinatio imperii de 817" in *Festschrift G. Kisch* (Stuttgart 1955), 15–32; W. Schlesinger, *Karolingische Königswahlen* (Berlin 1958).

ON THE CONSTITUTIO ROMANA: O. Bertolini, "Osservazioni sulla Constitutio Romana e sul Sacramentum cleri et populi Romani dell' 824" in *Studi medioevali in onore di A. Stefano* (Palermo 1956), 43 ⁻8.

IDEAS OF STATE AND POLITICAL IDEOLOGIES: W. Ohnsorge (see chap. 10); H. Lilienfein, *Die Anschauungen von Staat und Kirche im Staat der Karolinger* (Heidelberg 1902); R. Faulhaber, *Der Reichseinheitsgedanke in der Literatur der Karolingerzeit bis zum Vertrag von Verdun* (Berlin 1931); P. Vaccari, "L'unità carolingia" in *Annali di scienze politiche* 6/7 (1933); Lester K. Born, "The specula principis of the Carolingian Renaissance" in *Revue belge de phil. et d'hist.* 12 (1933), 583–612; H. M. Klinkenberg, "Über karolingische Fürstenspiegel" in *Geschichte in Wissenschaft und Unterricht* 7 (1956), 82–98; J. Hashagen, "Spätkarolingische Staats- und Soziallehren" in *DVfLG* (1939).

REFORM: J. Narberhaus, *Benedikt von Aniane* (Münster 1930) [= Beiträge zur Geschichte des alten Mönchtums 16]; J. Winandy, "L'œuvre monastique de Benoît d'Aniane" in *Mélanges bénédictins . . . à l'occasion du 14e centenaire de la mort de St. Benoît* (Fontenelle 1947); A. E. Verhulst and J. Semmler, "Les statuts d'Adalhard de Corbie de l'an 822" in *MA* (1962), 92–123, 233–69; E. Lesne, "Les ordonnances monastiques de Louis le Pieux et la Notitia de servitio monasteriorum" in *RHEF* 6 (1920), 161–75, 321–38, 448–88; J. Semmler, "Traditio und Königsschutz" in *ZSavRGkan* 45 (1959), 1–33; id., "Reichsidee und kirchliche Gesetzgebung bei Ludwig dem Frommen" in *ZKG* 71 (1960), 37–65; id., "Zur Überlieferung der monastischen Gesetzgebung Ludwigs des Frommen" in *DA* 16 (1960), 309–88; id., "Die Beschlüsse des Aachener Konzils im Jahre 816" in *ZKG* 74 (1963), 15–82; id., "Karl der Grosse und das fränkische Mönchtum" in *Karlswerk,* II, 255–89; J. Hubert, "La renaissance carolingienne et la topographie religieuse des citées épiscopales" in *I problemi della civiltà carolingia* (Spoleto 1954) [= Settimane di studio del Centro italiano di studi sull'alto medioevo, I], 219–26; id., "Évolution de la topographie et de l'aspect des villes de Gaule du 5e au 10e siècle" in *La città nell'alto medioevo* (Spoleto 1959) [= Settimane di studio del Centro italiano di studi sull'alto medioevo, VI], 549–58; E. Lehmann, "Von der Kirchenfamilie zur Kathedrale" in *Festschrift F. Gerke* (Baden-Baden 1962), 21–37; E. Heitz (as in chap. 12).

SCANDINAVIAN MISSION: E. de Moreau, *St. Anschaire, missionnaire en Scandinavie au 9e siècle* (Louvain 1930).

17. *The Carolingian Renaissance under Louis the Pious*

LITERATURE

FOR THE CAROLINGIAN RENAISSANCE (see also lit. cited in chap. 12): E. K. Rand, *A Survey of the Manuscripts of Tours,* 2 vols. (Cambridge, Mass. 1929); S. Tafel, "The Lyons scriptorium" in *Palaeographia latina* 2 and 4 (1923, 1925) [= St. Andrews Univ. Publications 20]; F. M. Carey, *De scriptura Floriacensi* (1923) [= Harvard studies in classical philology 34]; L. W. Jones, "The Scriptorium at Corbie" in *Speculum* 22 (1947), 191–204; id., *The Script of Cologne* (Cambridge, Mass. 1932); W. M. Lindsay and P. Lehmann, "The Early Mayence Scriptorium" in *Palaeographia latina* 4 (1925); W. M. Lindsay, "The Early Lorsch Scriptorium" in *Palaeographia latina* 3 (1924); B. Bischoff, *Die südostdeutschen Schreibschulen und Bibliotheken in der Karolingerzeit,* I (1940); G. Baesecke, *Das Schrifttum der Reichenau* (1927) [= Beiträge zur Geschichte der deutschen Sprache und Literatur 51]; G. Théry, *Études dionysiennes* 1 and 2 (Paris 1932, 1937) [= Études de phil. médiévale 16 and 19]; B. Bischoff, "Das griechische Element in der abendländischen Bildung des Mittelalters" in *ByZ* 44 (1951), 27–55.

MONOGRAPHS: Benedict of Aniane (see chap. 16); L. Weinrich, *Wala. Graf, Mönch und Rebell* (Lübeck–Hamburg 1963) [= Historische Studien 386]; A. Bressolles, *St. Agobard, évêque de Lyon* (Paris 1949); A. Cabaniss, *Agobard of Lyons, Churchman and Critic* (Syracuse Univ. Press 1953); id., "Florus of Lyons" in *Classica et mediaevalia* 19 (1958), 212–32; id., *Amalarius of Metz* (Amsterdam 1954); H. Peltier, *Pascase Radbert* (Amiens 1938); J. Reviron, *Les idées politico-religieuses d'un évêque du 9ᵉ siècle. Jonas d'Orléans et son De institutione regia* (Paris 1930); W. Goez, "Zur Weltchronik des Bischofs Frechulf von Lisieux" in *Festgabe für P. Kirn zum 70. Geburtstag* (1961), 93–110; R. Drögereit, "Der Heliand. Entstehungsort und Entstehungszeit" in *Das erste Jahrtausend,* vol. of texts II (Düsseldorf 1964), 762–84 (with older lit.).

18. *The Crisis of Empire and Church (828 to 840)*

FURTHER SOURCES

Paschasius Radbertus, "Epitaphium Arsenii (= Vita Walae)", ed. by E. Dümmler in *AAB* (1900), 3–98; Nithard, "Historiarum libri IV" in *MGSS* II, 649–782; *SS rer. Germ.* 1907 (ed. by Müller); *Class. Fr.* (1926) (ed. by Lauer); "Annales Bertiniani" in *SS rer. Germ.* (rec. Waitz).

LITERATURE

For Wala, Agobard, Jonas, see ch. 17; H. Zatschek, "Die Reichsteilungen unter Kaiser Ludwig dem Frommen" in *MIÖG* 49 (1935), 186–224.

SECTION FIVE

The Western Church from the Death of Louis the Pious to the End of the Carolingian Period

19. *The Frankish Empire from 840 to 875*

FURTHER SOURCES

The earlier work of Wattenbach is still reliable for the over-all coverage. The new edition *Wattenbach-Levison* IV treats only Italy and the Papacy from the Treaty of Verdun to the end of the Carolingian period. *MGDD regum et imperatorum Germaniae e stirpe Carolinorum,* I

(Louis the German); L. Levillain, *Recueil des actes de Pépin Ier et Pépin II d'Aquitaine* (Paris 1926); G. Tessier, *Recueil des actes de Charles II le Chauve*, I–III (Paris 1946–55); *MGEp.*, *Nithard* and *Annales Bertiniani* (see chap. 18); *Annales Fuldenses* rec. Kurze in *SS rer. Germ.*; *Annales Xantenses*, rec. B. de Simson in *SS rer. Germ.*; *Regino of Prüm, Chronicon*, rec. Kurze in *SS rer. Germ.*; see further sources in the next chapters.

LITERATURE

W. Schlesinger, "Die Auflösung des Karlsreiches" in *Karlswerk*, I, 792–857; E. Dümmler, *Geschichte des ostfränkischen Reiches*, 3 vols. (Leipzig 1887–88); J. Calmette, *L'effondrement d'un empire et la naissance d'une Europe* (Paris 1941); *Der Vertrag von Verdun 843. Neun Aufsätze zur Begründung der europäischen Völker- und Staatenwelt*, ed. by T. Mayer (Leipzig 1943); P. E. Hübinger, "Der Vertrag von Verdun und sein Rang in der abendländischen Geschichte" in *Düsseldorfer Jahrbuch* 44 (1947), 1–16; F. L. Ganshof, "Zur Entstehungsgeschichte und Bedeutung des Vertrags von Versun" in *DA* 12 (1956), 313–30; R. Schneider, *Brüdergemeine und Schwurfreundschaft. Der Auflösungsprozess des Karolingerreiches im Spiegel der Caritas-Terminologie in den Verträgen der karolingischen Teilkönige des 9. Jahrhunderts* (Lübeck–Hamburg 1964) [= Historische Studien 388]; G. Tellenbach, *Die Entstehung des deutschen Reiches* (Munich, 3rd ed. 1946); R. Parisot, *Le royaume de Lorraine sous les Carolingiens (843–923)* (Paris 1898); R. Poupardin, *Le royaume de Provence sous les Carolingiens* (Paris 1901); L. M. Hartmann, *Geschichte Italiens im Mittelalter*, III, 1, 2 (Gotha 1908, 1911); F. Lot and L. Halphen, "Le règne de Charles le Chauve" (only to 851) in *BÉH* 175 (Paris 1909); P. Zumthor, *Charles le Chauve* (Strasbourg 1957); P. Classen, "Die Verträge von Verdun und Coulaines 843 als politische Grundlagen des westfränkischen Reiches" in *HZ* 196 (1963), 1–35; P. E. Schramm, *Der König von Frankreich. Das Wesen der Monarchie vom 9. bis zum 16. Jahrhundert*, 2 vols. (Darmstadt, 2nd ed. 1960); M. David, *Le serment du sacre du 9e au 15e siècle* (Strasbourg 1951).

THE CHURCH IN THE PARTITIONED EMPIRE: J. Schur, *Königtum und Kirche im ostfränkischen Reich* (dissertation, Berlin 1931); K. Voigt, "Die karolingische Klosterpolitik und der Niedergang des westfränkischen Königtums" in *KRA* 90/91 (1917).

THE MARRIAGE CONTROVERSY IN LOTHARINGIA: E. Perels, "Propagandatechnik im 9. Jahrhundert. Ein Originalaktenstück für Erzbischof Gunthar von Köln" in *AUF* 15 (1938), 423–25; H. Fuhrmann, "Eine im Original erhaltene Propagandaschrift des Erzbischofs Gunthar von Köln" in *ADipl* 4 (1958), 1–51; see also lit. on Nicholas I (chap. 21) and on Hincmar of Reims (chap. 23).

20. *Spain and the British Isles. The Muslim and Viking Attacks on the West*

FURTHER LITERATURE

SPAIN: M. Díaz y Díaz, "Die spanische Jacobuslegende bei Isidor von Sevilla" in *HJ* 77 (1958), 467–72; J. Pérez de Urbel, *San Eulogio de Córdoba o la vida andaluza en el siglo IX* (Madrid 1942); F. R. Franke, "Die freiwilligen Märtyrer von Córdoba und das Verhältnis der Mozaraber zum Islam" in *Gesammelte Aufsätze zur Geschichte Spaniens* 13 (1958), 1–170; A. Sánchez-Cadeira, *El regnum — imperium leonés hasta 1037* (Madrid 1951); *Historia de España VI. España cristiana* (Madrid 1956).

ENGLAND: Ebanon S. Duckett, *Alfred the Great* (Chicago 1956).

IRELAND: E. Curtis, *A History of Ireland* (Oxford, 2nd ed. 1950).

VIKINGS: W. Vogel, "Die Normannen und das fränkische Reich (799–911)" in *Heidelberger Abhandlungen zur mittleren und neueren Geschichte* 14 (1906); U. Noack, *Nordische Frühgeschichte und Wikingerzeit* (Munich–Berlin 1941); L. Musset, *Les peuples scandinaves au moyen âge* (Paris

1951); F. Lot, "La grande invasion normande 856–862" in *BÉCh* 69 (1908), 5–62; id., "La Loire, l'Aquitaine et la Seine 862–866" in *BECh* 76 (1915), 473–510.
Muslims (see also monographs on the regions concerned): J. Gay, "L'Italie méridionale et l'empire byzantin" in *Bibl. des Écoles françaises d'Athènes et de Rome* 90 (1904).

21. The Papacy and the West from 840 to 875

FURTHER SOURCES

Wattenbach-Levison IV with selected lit.; *LP,* papal documents and registers (Jaffé and Kehr) see Gen. Bib. I, 5; *MGEp* VI and VII (Nicholas I, Hadrian II, John VIII, Anast. Bib.); "Libellus de imperatoria potestate in urbe Roma" in *MGSS* III 719–22. — See also chapters 19 and 23.

MISSION TO THE SLAVS: F. Grivec, *Konstantin und Method, Lehrer der Slawen* (Wiesbaden 1960); *Zwischen Rom und Byzanz. Leben und Wirken der Slawenapostel Kyrillos und Methodius nach den Pannonischen Legenden und der Clemensvita* . . . translated with introduction and commentary by J. Bujnoch in *Slawische Geschichtsschreiber,* ed. by G. Stökl, 1 (Graz 1958); H. Loewe, "Der Streit um Methodius. Quellen zu den nationalkirchlichen Bestrebungen in Mähren und Pannonien im 9. Jahrhundert" in *Kölner Hefte für den akademischen Unterricht, Historische Reihe* 2 (1948) with lit.; F. Dvornik, *The Slavs. Their Early History and Civilization* (Boston 1956); id., *Les Slaves, Byzance et Rome au 9ᵉ siècle* (Paris 1926); id., "La lutte entre Byzance et Rome à propos d'Illyricum au 9ᵉ siècle" in *Mélanges Diehl,* I (1930); id., *Les légendes de Constantin et de Méthode vues de Byzance* (1933); P. Duthilleul, *L'évangélisation des Slaves. Cyrille et Méthode* (Tournai 1963); F. Zagiba, "Neue Probleme der kyrillomethodianischen Forschung" in *OstKSt* 11 (Würzburg 1962); id., "Das abendländische Bildungswesen bei den Slawen im 8./9. Jahrhundert" in *Jahrbuch für altbayerische Kirchengeschichte* (1962), 15–44; id., "Die bayrische Slawenmission und ihre Fortsetzung durch Kyrill und Method" in *Jahrbuch für Geschichte Osteuropas* 9 (1961), 1–56, 247–76; K. Bosl, "Der Eintritt Böhmens in den westlichen Kulturkreis im Licht der Missionsgeschichte" in *Collegium Carolinum,* I, *Böhmen und Bayern* (Munich 1957), 43–64; W. Fritze (see chap. 11); *Cyrillo-Methodiana. Zur Frühgeschichte des Christentums bei den Slawen,* pub. by the commission of the Goerres-Gesellschaft ed. by M. Hellmann, R. Olesch, B. Stasiewski and F. Zagiba (Cologne 1964), with contributions by Bosl, Burr, Dvornik, Grivec, Hellmann, Kniczsa, Sós, Zagiba *et al.* Also Loewe's survey in *Wattenbach-Levison,* IV, 471, nn. 337, 338, 339.

LITERATURE

Dölger (see chap. 10); Ohnsorge (see chap. 10); A. Henggeler, *Die Salbungen und Krönungen des Königs und Kaisers Ludwig II.* (dissertation, Fribourg 1934); A. Lapôtre, *De Anastasio bibliothecario sedis apostolicae* (Paris 1885); E. Perels, *Papst Nikolaus I. und Anastasius Bibliothecarius* (Berlin 1920); N. Ertl, "Briefdiktatoren frühmittelalterlicher Papstbriefe" (Anast. Bibl.) in *AUF* 15 (1938), 56–132; J. Haller, *Nikolaus I. und Pseudo-Isidor* (Stuttgart 1936); K. Brandi, "Ravenna und Rom" in *AUF* 9 (1926), 1–38; H. Fuhrmann, "Nikolaus I. und die Absetzung des Erzbischofs Johann von Ravenna" in *ZSavRGkan* 44 (1958), 353–58. — See also Hincmar (chap. 23).

22. The Degradation of the Papacy and the Empire (875 to 904)

LITERATURE

C. G. Mor, *L'età feudale 887–1024,* I: *Storia politica d' Italia* (Milan 1952); A. Lapôtre, *L'Europe et le St. Siège à l'époque carolingienne,* I (Paris 1895); H. Steinacker, "Das Register Papst Johannes' VIII" in *MIÖG* 52 (1938), 171–94; D. Pop, *La défense du pape Formose* (Strasbourg 1933); G. Arnaldi, "Papa Formoso e gli imperatori della casa di Spoleto" in *Annali Fac. Lett. e Filos. Univ. Napoli* 1 (1951), 85–104; E. E. Stengel, "Die Entwicklung des Kaiserprivilegs für die römische Kirche" in *HZ* 134 (1926), 216–41.

23. *Reform, Theology, and Education under the Later Carolingians*

FURTHER SOURCES

Surveys in *Wattenbach, Manitius* and esp. (for Rome and Italy) in *Wattenbach-Levison* IV. For Notker Balbulus and the group at St. Gall (Iso, Marcellus, Ratpert, Tutilo, Hartmann, Waldo, and Salomo): W. v. den Steinen, *Notker der Dichter* (Bern 1948), 519 ff.

THE WRITING OF HISTORY (see also Poetry): *LP,* general chronicles, annals, etc. see chap. 19 and chap. 21. Also: *MGSS rer. Lang.* (Angellus of Ravenna, Erchempert of Monte Cassino, Andreas of Bergamo, Gesta epp. Neapolitanorum); G. Busson and A. Ledru, *Actus pontificum Cenomanis in urbe degentium* (Le Mans 1901); R. Charles and E. Froger, *Gesta domini Aldrici Cenom. urbis episcopi* (Mamers 1889); Flodoard, "Historia Remensis ecclesiae" in *MGSS* XIII, 405–599; "Vita Anscari und Vita Rimberti", rec. G. Waitz in *MGSS rer. Germ.;* "Notker Balbulus, Gesta Karoli Magni", rec. Hans F. Haefele in *MGSS rer Germ.,* NS 12; Agius, "Vita Hathumodae" in *MGSS* IV, 165–89.

POETRY: *MG Poetae Latini,* II (Wandalbert of Prüm), III (Paschasius Radberus, Gottschalk, Hincmar, John Scotus, Sedulius Scotus, Heiric of Auxerre, Audradus, Milo of St-Amand, Agius of Corvey, Carmen de Ludovico II imperator etc.), IV (Gottschalk, Hucbald of St-Amand, Salomo and Waldram, John The Deacon, Eugenius Vulgarius, Poeta Saxo, *Abbo de bello Parisiaco, Gesta Berengarii* etc.), VI (Gottschalk, Waltharius); G. M. Dreves, C. Blume and H. M. Bannister, *Analecta hymnica medii aevi* 7–10 34 53 (also W. v. d. Steinen, *Notker der Dichter,* 530); Notker's Sequences in W. v. d. Steinen, *Notker der Dichter,* vol. of edition (Bern 1948).

CORRESPONDENCE: *MGEp* V–VIII (Amalarius, Angelomus of Luxeuil, Lupus of Ferrières, Anastasius Bibliothecarius, Hincmar of Reims; Emperor Louis II, Popes Stephen V and Formosus); see also sources for chap. 21. — Correspondance de Loup de Ferrières, ed. by L. Levillain: *Les Classiques de l'histoire de France* 10 (1927); *ibid.* 16 (1935).

INDIVIDUAL AUTHORS IN MIGNE: Rhabanus, Amalarius, Walafrid, Florus, Paschasius Radbertus, see chap. 16. Also: *PL* 75 (John The Deacon), 103 (Sedulius Scotus), 115 (Angelomus of Luxeuil, Prudentius of Troyes), 116 (Amolo of Lyons), 116–18 (Haimo of Halberstadt), 121 (Ratramnus of Corbie, Aeneas of Paris), 122 (John Scotus), 123–24 (Ado of Vienne and Usuard of St-Germain), 125–26 (Hincmar of Reims), 127–29 (Anastasius Bibliothecarius), 129 (Auxilius and Eugenius Vulgarius), 131 (Remigius of Auxerre), 132 (Hucbald of St-Amand).

SPECIAL EDITIONS: C. Lambot, *Œuvres théologiques et grammaticales de Godescalc d'Orbais* (Louvain 1945); W. Gundlach, "Zwei Schriften des Erzbischofs Hinkmar von Reims und De ecclesiis et capellis" in *ZKG* 10 (1889), 258–310. — *MGCap* II (De ordine palatii) and *MGSS rer Mer.* III (Vita Remigii); Sedulius Scotus. *Liber de rectoribus christianis* in S. Hellmann, *Sedulius Scotus,* in *Quellen und Untersuchungen zur lateinischen Philologie des Mittelalters,* I, 1 (Munich 1906), 1–91; E. Dümmler, *Auxilius und Vulgarius, Quellen und Forschungen zur Geschichte des Papsttums im Anfang des 10. Jahrhunderts* (Leipzig 1866).

SOURCES FOR LAW: *Decretales Pseudo-Isidorianae et Capitula Angilramni,* ed. by P. Hinschius (Leipzig 1863; new impr. Aalen 1963); Benedictus Levita, *Capitularium Collectio* in *PL* 97.

LITERATURE

EDUCATION OF THE LAITY: E. Bondurand, *L'éducation carolingienne. Le Manuel de Dhuoda*
(Paris 1887); J. Wollasch, "Eine adlige Familie des frühen Mittelalters. Ihr Selbstverständnis
und ihre Wirklichkeit" in *AKG* 39 (1957), 150–88; P. Riché, "Recherches sur l'instruction
des laïcs du 9ᵉ au 12ᵉ siècle" in *CCivMéd* 5 (1962), 175–82; id., "Les bibliothèques de trois
aristocrates carolingiens" in *MA* (1963), 87–104.

PERSONALITIES: E. v. Severus, *Lupus von Ferrières, Beiträge zur Geschichte des alten Mönchtums*
21 (Munich 1940); E. Pellegrin, "Les manuscrits de Loup de Ferrières" in *BÉCh* 115 (1957),
5–31; J. Wollasch, "Zu den persönlichen Notizen des Heiricus von St-Germain d'Auxerre"
in *DA* (1959), 24–26; B. de Caiffier, "Le calendrier d'Héric d'Auxerre" in *AnBoll* 77 (1959),
392–425; M. Cappuyns, *Jean Scot Érigène* (Louvain 1933); H. Liebeschütz, "Texterklä-
rung und Weltdeutung bei Johannes Eriugena" in *AKG* 40 (1958), 66–96; J. Huber,
Johannes Scotus Erigene, Beitr GPhMA (1960); H. Peltier, *Pascase Radbert* (Amiens 1938);
A. Ripberger, "Der Pseudo-Hieronymusbrief IX Cogitis me. Ein erster marianischer
Traktat des Mittelalters von Paschasius Radbert" in *Spicilegium Friburgense* 9 (1962); K. Viel-
haber, "Gottschalk der Sachse" in *Bonner historische Forschungen* 5 (Bonn 1956); C. Lambot,
"Lettre inédite de Godescalc d'Orbais" in *RBén* 68 (1958), 41–51; H. Schrörs, *Hinkmar von
Reims* (Freiburg 1884); E. Perels, "Eine Denkschrift Hinkmars von Reims im Prozess
Rothads von Soissons" in *NA* 44 (1922), 43–100; G. Ehrenforth, "Hinkmar von Reims und
Ludwig III. von Westfranken" in *ZKG* 44 (1925), 65–98; M. Andrieu, "Le sacre épiscopal
d'après Hincmar de Reims" in *RHE* 48 (1953), 22–73; J. Devisse, "Hincmar et la Loi" in
Univ. de Dakar, Fac. des Lettres. Publications de la Section Histoire 5 (Dakar 1962); A. Pothmann,
"Altfrid. Ein Charakterbild seiner Persönlichkeit" in *Das erste Jahrtausend,* text vol. I (Düssel-
dorf 1964) 746–61; Van der Essen, "Hucbald de St-Amand et sa place dans le mouvement
hagiographique médiéval" in *RHEF* 19 (1923), 522ff.; H. Löwe, "Regino von Prüm und
das historische Weltbild der Karolingerzeit" in *Rheinisches Vierteljahrsblatt* 17 (1952), 151–79;
K. F. Werner, "Zur Arbeitsweise des Regino von Prüm" in *WaG* 19 (1959), 96–116; W. v. den
Steinen, *Notker der Dichter,* 2 vols. (Bern 1948); H. F. Haefele, "Studien zu Notkers Gesta
Karoli" in *DA* 15 (1959), 358–92; W. v. den Steinen, "Der Waltharius und sein Dichter" in
ZdAdL 84 (1952–3), 1–46; K. Hauck, "Das Waltachariusepos des Bruders Gerald von Eich-
stätt" in *GRM* 35 (1954), 1–27; D. Schaller, "Geraldus und St. Gallen" in *Mittellateinisches
Jahrbuch* 2 (1965), 74–84.

ROME AND LOWER ITALY: G. Arnaldi, "Giovanni Immonide e la cultura di Giovanni VIII" in
BISIIAM 68 (1956), 33–89; U. Westerbergh, "Beneventan Ninth Century Poetry" in *Acta
univ. Stockholmiensis. Studia Latina Stockholmiensia* 4 (Stockholm 1947); see also Löwe: *Wattenbach-Levison* IV.

THEOLOGY: J. Geiselmann, *Die Eucharistielehre der Vorscholastik* (Paderborn 1926); id.,
Studien zu den frühmittelalterlichen Abendmahlsschriften (Paderborn 1926); C. Gliozzo, *La
dottrina della conversione eucharistica in Passasio Radberto e Ratramno, Ignatianum.* Serie Teol. 1
(Palermo 1945); J. Brinktrine, "Zur Lehre der mittelalterlichen Theologen über die Konse-
krationsform der Eucharistie" in *ThGl* 45 (1955), 188–206; R. Schulte, "Die Messe als Opfer
der Kirche. Die Lehre frühmittelalterlicher Autoren über das eucharistische Opfer" in *LQF*
35 (1959); E. Aegerter, "Gottschalk et le problème de la prédestination au 9ᵉ siècle" in *RHR*
116 (1937), 187–223.

CANON LAW AND THE PSEUDO-ISIDOREAN DECRETALS: F. Lot, "Textes manceaux et fausses
décrétales" in *BÉCh* 101 (1940), 5–48; *ibid.,* 102 (1941), 5–34; H. Fuhrmann, "Studien zur
Geschichte der mittelalterlichen Patriarchate" in *ZSavRGkan* 40 (1954), 1–84; id., "Pseudo-
Isidor und die Abbreviatio Ansegisi et Benedicti Levitae" in *ZKG* 69 (1958), 309–11;
E. Seckel, "Die erste Zeile Pseudo-Isidors, die Hadrianarezension In nomine Domini . . .
und die Geschichte der Invokationen in den Rechtsquellen" (completed edition of H. Fuhr-

mann) in *SAB,* Klasse für Philosophie . . . (1959), n. 4; Schafer-Williams, "The Pseudo-Isidorian Problem today" in *Speculum* 29 (1954), 702–07; Use in Rome: Löwe in *Wattenbach-Levison* IV, 464 ff.

DIOCESAN CONSTITUTIONS: F. Gescher, "Der kölnische Dekanat und Archidiakonat in ihrer Entstehung und ersten Entwicklung" in *KRA* 95 (1919); E. Griffe, "Les origines de l'archiprêtre de district" in *RHEF* (1927), 16–50; F. Arnold, *Das Diözesanrecht nach den Schriften Hinkmars von Reims* (Vienna 1935); A. Heintz, *Die Anfänge des Landdekanats im Rahmen der kirchlichen Verfassungsgeschichte des Erzbistums Trier* (Trier 1951).

SECTION SIX

The Byzantine Church in the Age of Photius

SOURCES

The most important papal communications addressed to the Byzantine Emperor and the Patriarchs: Nicolai I "Epistolae" in *MGEp* VI, 257–690 (ed. by E. Perels); Hadriani II "Epistolae", *ibid.* VI, 691–765; Joannis VIII, "Epistolae", *ibid.* VII, 1–133 (ed. by E. Caspar); Stephani V "Epistolae", *ibid.* VII 334–365; "Formosi papae epistola ad Stylianum ep." in *Mansi* XVI, 456–58.

SYNODAL DECREES: Constantinople 861: The original Acts are lost. There are Latin extracts in the *Collection of Card. Deusdedit,* ed. by W. v. Glanvell (Paderborn 1905), 664 ff. The canons are found in *Mansi* XVI, 536–49, Rhallis II, 647–704, and *Joannou* I, 2, 447–79 — Constantinople 867: The Acts are lost. — Constantinople 869–870: The original Acts still lost; a Greek epitome: *Mansi* XVI, 320–409; the Acts in the translation of Anastasius: *Mansi* XVI, 1–208; the Canons: *Mansi* XVI, 397–406, *Joannou* I, 1, 293–342. — Constantinople 879–880: *Mansi* XVII, 373–526; Latin extracts of Deusdedit: Glanvell 610–17; Canons: *Rhallis* II, 705–12, and *Joannou* I, 2, 482–6. — An important collection of propaganda Acts by the opponents of Photius for the so-called second Photian Schism: *Mansi* XVI, 409–57. — "Anastasii Bibliothecarii epistolae" in *MGEp* VII, 395–412; „Vita Ignatii patr." in *Mansi* XVI, 209–92, *PG* 105, 487–574. Letters of the Patriarch Photius: ed. by J. N. Balettas (London 1864), *PG,* 102, 585–989; additional letters of the Patriarchs: ed. by A. Papadopulos-Kerameus (St. Petersburg 1896). Particulars will be cited in individual cases; J. Hergenröther, *Monumenta graeca ad Photium eiusque historiam pertinentia* (Regensburg 1860); A. Papadopulos-Kerameus, *Monumenta graeca et latina ad historiam Photii patriarchae pertinentia,* 2 vols. (St. Petersburg 1899–1901); G. Hofmann, *Photius et ecclesia romana. Textus et documenta,* 2 vols. (Rome 1932); J. N. Karmires, Δύο Βυζαντινοὶ ἱεράρχαι καὶ τὸ σχίσμα τῆς Ῥωμαϊκῆς ἐκκλησίας (Athens 1951).

SELECTED LITERATURE: R. Janin, "Ignace" in *DThC* VII, 713–22; V. Grumel, "Ignace" in *Catholicisme* V, 1192–95; *Grumel Reg* nn. 444–589; J. Hergenröther, *Photius, Patriarch von Konstantinopel,* 3 vols. (Regensburg 1867–69); M. Jugie, *Le schisme byzantin* (Paris 1941); F. Dvornik, *The Photian Schism. History and Legend* (Cambridge 1948); E. Amann, "Photius" in *DThC* XII, 1536–1604; F. Dvornik, *The Patriarch in the Light of Recent Research. Report to the XI International Byzantine Congress* (Munich 1958), vol III, 2. Also in the same report: Responses by P. Stéphanou and K. Bonis, 17–26, and the *Proceedings of the XI International Byzantine Congress* (Munich 1961), 41–54.

The Church and the Western Kingdoms from 900 to 1046

SOURCES

Mansi XVIII, 249 – XIX, 620; *Hefele-Leclercq* IV, 2, 721–994; further source material in individual chapters.

LITERATURE

General treatment found in the universal history cited in Gen. Bib. II, 1, a–b, esp. *Glotz* II; *Historia Mundi* V–VI; Cartellieri, *Weltstellung des deutschen Reiches;* Hampe, *Hochmittelalter; The Cambridge Medieval History;* N. F. Cantor's *Medieval History* in an excellent analysis. For ecclesiastical history see Gen. Bib. II, 3; esp. *Fliche-Martin* VII; Gen. Bib. II, 5, above all *Haller* II and *Hauck KD* III.

STATE AND SOCIETY: Gen. Bib. II, 8, a–b, esp. Mitteis, *Staat des hohen Mittelalters* and Erdmann, *Zur politischen Ideenwelt. — Settimane di studio del Centro italiano di studi sull'alto medio evo*, II: *I problemi dell'Europa postcarolingia* (Spoleto 1955); VII: *La città nell'alto medio evo* (Spoleto 1959); *Studien zu den Anfängen des europäischen Städtewesens, Vorträge und Forschungen* IV (Lindau–Constance 1958).

THEOCRATIC IDEAS: Gen. Bib. II, 8c. H. Beumann, "Die sakrale Legitimierung des Herrschers im Denken der ottonischen Zeit" in *ZSavRGgerm* 66 (1948), 1–45; C. Erdmann, "Der Heidenkrieg in der Liturgie und die Kaiserkrönung Ottos I." in *MIÖG* 46 (1932), 129–42; J. Kirschberg, *Kaiseridee und Mission unter den Sachsenkaisern und den ersten Saliern* (Berlin 1934); H. Bünding, *Das Imperium christianum und die deutschen Ostkriege vom 10.–12. Jahrhundert* (Berlin 1940).

THEORIES ON THE RENOVATION OF THE EMPIRE: P. E. Schramm, *Kaiser, Rom und Renovatio* (Darmstadt, 2nd ed. 1957), still basic; F. Heer, "Die 'Renaissance'-Ideologie im frühen Mittelalter" in *MIÖG* 57 (1949), 23–81; G. Ladner, "Die mittelalterliche Reformidee und ihr Verhältnis zur Renaissance" in *MIÖG* 60 (1952), 31–59; E. Anagnino, *Il concetto di rinascita attraverso il medio evo, V–X secolo* (Milan–Naples 1958); for further literature see chap. 28.

27. The New Kingdoms

SOURCES

FRANCE: Flodoard, *Annales* (919–966), *CollText* 39, ed. by M. P. Lauer (1905), *MGSS* III, 363–408; Flodoard, *Historia Remensis ecclesiae* (to 948), *MGSS* XIII, 405–599; Richer, *Historiarum libri IV* (to 995 or 998, not entirely reliable), *Class Hist* 12, 17, ed. by R. Latouche (1930, 1937); *MGSS rer. Germ.*, ed. by G. Waitz (1877); Raoul Glaber, *Historiarum libri* V (1000–45; filled with fables of the miraculous and of little historical value), *CollText* 1, ed. by M. Prou (1886); Selections in *MGSS* VII, 48–72; Ademar of Chabannes, *Chronicon* (to 1028), *Coll Text* 20, ed. by J. Chavanon (1897); *MGSS* IV, 106–48; for Gerbert's letters see the following chapter. Royal documents: *Recueil des actes de Charles III,* ed. by Lauer (Paris 1949); . . . *de Louis IV,* ed. by Lauer (Paris 1914); . . . *de Lothaire et de Louis V,* ed. by M. L. Halphen (Paris 1907); see Gen. Bib. I, 3, *Académie,* etc., *Chartes et diplômes;* C. Pfister, *Études sur le règne de Robert le Pieux* (Paris 1885); F. Soehnée, *Catalogue des actes d'Henri Ier* (Paris 1907).

GERMANY: Widukind of Corvey, *Rerum gestarum Saxonicarum Libri III* (to 957–58: Supplement 973), *MGSS rer. Germ.*, ed. by. P. Hirsch and A. E. Lohmann (5th ed. 1935); *Continuator*

Reginonis (907–67, probably by Adalbert, then Abbot of Weissenburg, later Archbishop of Magdeburg), *MGSS rer. Germ.,* ed. by F. Kurze (1890, with Regino); *Annales Hildesheimenses* (esp. important for 974–1040), *MGSS rer. Germ.,* ed by G. Waitz (1878); *Annales Quedling-burgenses* (important for Otto III and Henry II), *MGSS* III, 22–90; *Annales Sangallenses maiores* (to 1024; continued to 1044), *MGSS* I, 73–85; Ruotger, *Vita Brunonis* (Archbishop of Cologne 953–65), *MGSS rer. Germ.,* NS 10, ed. by I. Ott (1951); Gerhard, *Vita Udalrici* (Bishop of Augsburg 923–73), *MGSS* IV, 377–428; *PL* 135, 1001–70; Thietmar of Merseburg, *Chronicon* (to 1018), *MGSS rer. Germ.,* NS 9, ed. by R. Holtzmann (1935). — Royal and Imperial documents: *MGDD* I (Conrad I – Otto I); II (Otto II – Otto III); J. F. Böhmer, *Regesta imperii,* I (for the Carolingians to 918), new ed. by E. Mühlbacher and J. Lechner (Innsbruck, 2nd ed. 1908); II (for the Saxon house), part 1 (Henry I – Otto I), new ed. by E. V. Ottenthal (Innsbruck, 2nd ed. 1893); part 2 (Otto II), ed. by H.-L. Mikoletzky (Graz 1950); part 3 (Otto III), ed. by M. Uhlirz (Graz 1956–57). For the succeeding rulers see chap. 32. Councils: M. Boye, "Quellenkatalog der Synoden Deutschlands und Reichsitaliens 922–1059" in *NA* 48 (1903), 45–96.

THE PAPACY: Rome – Italy: *Duchesne LP* II, pp. IX–XX, 236–64; *Watterich* I, 32—90; Benedict of St. Andrea, *Chronicon* (to 968), *FontiStIt* 50 (1020), ed. by G. Zucchetti; *MGSS* III 695–722; Liutprand of Cremona, *Antapodosis* (888–949), *MGSS rer. Germ.,* ed. by J. Becker (3rd ed. 1915); *Chronicon Salernitanum* (to 974), ed. by U. Westerbergh (Stockholm 1956), *MGSS* III, 467–561.

ROYAL DOCUMENTS: all ed. by L. Schiaparelli, *I diplomi de Berengario I, FontiStIt* 35 (1903); ... *de Guido e di Lamberto, ibid.* 36 (1906); ... *di Lodovico III e di Rodolfo II, ibid.* 37 (1910); ... *di Ugo e di Lotario, di Berengario II e di Adalberto, ibid.* 38 (1924). For more particulars on the sources see *Wattenbach-Holtzmann* I, 1–2; *Jacob-Hohenleutner* II.

LITERATURE

FRANCE: The work of E. Lavisse, *Histoire de France,* II, 1–2 (Gen. Bib. II, 2) is standard; see monographs for individual rulers in *Fliche-Martin* VII, 11. — P. Poupardin, *Le royaume de Provence sous les Carolingiens 855–933* (Paris 1901); id., *Le royaume de Bourgogne 888–1038* (Paris 1907); A. Hofmeister, *Deutschland und Burgund im frühen Mittelalter* (Leipzig 1914); F. Lot and R. Fawtier, *Histoire des institutions françaises au moyen âge,* I: *Institutions seigneuriales* (Paris 1957); K. F. Werner, "Untersuchungen zur Frühzeit des französischen Königtums" in *WaG* 18 (1958), 256–89; *ibid.* 19 (1959), 146–93; *ibid.* 20 (1960), 87–119; P. E. Schramm, *Der König von Frankreich,* 2 vols. (Weimar, 2nd ed. 1960). – Ecclesiastical history: Gen. Bib. II, 4; D. W. Lowis, *The History of the Church in France 950–1000* (London 1926); E. Lesne, *Histoire de la propriété ecclésiastique en France du IXe au XIe siècle,* II: *La propriété ecclésiastique et les droits régaliens à l'époque carolingienne* (4 sections, Paris 1922–36); T. Schieffer, *Die päpstlichen Legaten in Frankreich 870–1130* (Berlin 1953); for the elections of bishops see chap. 35.

GERMANY: Gen. Bib. II, 2. — *Giesebrecht* I; JbbDG (see Gen. Bib. II, 2): for Conrad I by E. Dümmler, *Geschichte des ostfränkischen Reiches,* III (Leipzig, 2nd ed. 1888); for Henry I by G. Waitz (Leipzig, 3rd ed. 1885); for Otto I by R. Köpke and E. Dümmler (Leipzig 1876); for Otto II by M. Uhlirz (Leipzig 1902); for Otto III by M. Uhlirz (Berlin 1954); basic is R. Holtzmann, *Geschichte der sächsischen Kaiserzeit 900–1024* (Munich, 3rd ed. 1955); further lit. on political history: *Gebhardt-Grundmann* I, 48–65; *Hauck* III, 1–388; L. Santifaller, *Zur Geschichte des ottonisch-salischen Reichskirchensystems, SAWPhil.-Hist. Kl* 229, 1 (Vienna, 2nd ed. 1964), an excellent survey on royal and papal privileges and detailed sources and literature on the popes from 955–1057; M. Boye, "Die Synoden Deutschlands und Reichsitaliens 922–1059" in *ZSavRGkan* 49 (1929), 131–284; H. Barion, *Das fränkisch-deutsche Synodalrecht des Frühmittelalters* (Bonn–Cologne 1931); O. Engelmann, *Die päpstlichen Legaten in Deutschland bis zur Mitte des 11. Jahrhunderts* (dissertation, Marburg 1911); see also literature for chap. 28, 30, 31.

ITALY: Gen. Bib. II, 2, esp. *Hartmann* III–IV; further lit. for Italy and Rome in ch. 28; J. Ficker, *Forschungen zur Reichs- und Rechtsgeschichte Italiens*, 4 vols. (Innsbruck 1868–74); *I ad Arduino 880–1015* (Turin 1908); G. Fasoli, *I re d'Italia 888–962* (Florence 1949); A. Hof-P. S. Leicht, *Storia del diritto pubblico italiano* (Milano 1938); S. Pivano, *Stato e Chiesa da Berengario* meister, "Markgrafen und Markgrafschaften im italienischen Königsreich 774–962" in *MIÖG*, supplement. vol. 7 (1907), 215–435; E. Hlawitschka, *Franken, Alemannen, Bayern und Burgunder in Oberitalien 774–962* (Freiburg in Br. 1960); J. Gay, *L'Italie méridionale et l'empire byzantin* (Paris 1904); P. Lamma, "Il problema dei due imperi e dell'Italia meridionale nel giudizio delle fonti letterarie dei secoli IX–X" in *Atti del 3⁰ congresso internazionale di studi sull'alto medio evo* (Spoleto 1959), 155–253; G. Dilcher, "Bischof und Stadtverfassung in Oberitalien" in *ZSavRGgerm* 81 (1964), 225–66; *Vescovi e diocesi in Italia nel medioevo, sec. IX–XIII, Atti del II convegno di Storia della Chiesa in Italia* (Padua 1964); G. Musca and L. Musca, *L'Emirato de Bari, 847–871* (Bari 1964) contains excellent survey of secondary lit. on South Italian history in the ninth century.

ROME: Gen. Bib. II, 5; W. Kölmel, *Rom und der Kirchenstaat im 10. und 11. Jahrhundert bis in die Anfänge der Reform* (Berlin 1935); O. Gerstenberg, *Die politische Entwicklung des römischen Adels im 10. und 11. Jahrhundert* (Berlin 1933); A. Solmi, *Il senato romano nell'alto medioevo 757–1143* (Rome 1944); P. E. Schramm, *Kaiser, Rom und Renovatio* (Darmstadt, 2nd ed. 1957).

28. *Rome, the Papacy, and the Empire: 962 to 1002*

SOURCES

Cited for most part for sect. 7 and ch. 27; R. Elze, *Die Ordines für die Weihe und Krönung des Kaisers und der Kaiserin, MG Fontes iuris germ. antiqui in us. schol.* 9 (Hanover 1960); Liutprand of Cremona, *Historia Ottonis* (960–964) and *Relatio de legatione Constantinopolitana* (mission of 968) in *Luitprandi opera* ed. by J. Becker, *MGSS rer. Germ.* (3rd ed. 1915); John The Deacon, *Chronicon Venetum* (to 1008), *FontiStIt* 9, ed. by G. Monticolo (1890); *MGSS* VII, 4–38; Gerbert of Aurillac, *Lettres* (983–997), *CollText* 6, ed. by J. Havet (1889), new ed. in preparation by W. Weigle; see progress accounts in *DA* 10 (1953–54), 19–70; *DA* 11 (1954–55); 393–421; *DA* 14 (1958), 149–220; *DA* 17 (1961) 385–419; M. Uhlirz, *Untersuchungen über Inhalt und Datierung der Briefe Gerberts* (Göttingen 1957); on the *Vitae* of Adalbert of Prague see chap. 31.

LITERATURE

See sect. 7 and chap. 27. Also E. Eichmann, *Die Kaiserkrönung im Abendland,* 2 vols. (Würzburg 1942); recent literature in the above cited edition of Elze. R. Folz, *L'idée d'empire en occident du Vᵉ au XIVᵉ siècle* (Paris 1953); on the *imperium* see also G. Ladner in *WaG* 11 (1951), 143–53; F. Kempf, *Das Königtum,* Vorträge und Forschungen 3 (Lindau - Constance 1956), 225–42; J. Spörl in *Festschr. H. Kunisch* (Berlin 1961), 331–53; W. Holtzmann, *Imperium und Nationen* (Cologne–Opladen 1953); id., in *X Congresso internazionale di scienze storiche, Relazione* III (Florence 1955), 271–303; R. Holtzmann, "Der Weltherrschaftsgedanke des mittelalterlichen Kaisertums und die Souveränität der europäischen Staaten" in *HZ* 159 (1939), 251–64; H. Beumann, "Das imperiale Königtum im 10. Jahrhundert" in *WaG* 10 (1950), 117–30; H. Keller, "Das Kaisertum Ottos des Grossen im Verständnis seiner Zeit" in *DA* 20 (1964), 325–88; H. Löwe, "Kaisertum und Abendland in ottonischer und frühsalischer Zeit" in *HZ* 196 (1963), 529–62; H. Beumann, "Das Imperium und die Regna bei Wipo" in *Festschr. Fr. Steinbach* (Bonn 1961), 11–36; W. Ohnsorge, *Das Zweikaiserproblem. Die Bedeutung des byzantinischen Reiches für die Entwicklung der Staatsidee in Europa* (Hildesheim 1947); id., "Byzanz und das Abendland im 9. und 10. Jahrhundert" in *Saeculum* 5 (1954), 194–220; *Festschr. zur Jahrhundertfeier der Kaiserkrönung Ottos d. Gr., MIÖG,* supplem. vol. 20 (1962), in section I: P. E. Schramm, State symbolism and the Saxon Emperor, E. Dupré-Theseider, Otto and Italy, H. F. Schmid, Otto and the East, W. Ohnsorge, Otto and Byzantium; *Renovatio imperii, Atti della giornata internazionale di studio per il millenario* (Faenza 1963); M. Lintzel, *Die Kaiserpolitik Ottos des Grossen* (Munich - Berlin 1943); also F. Rörig in *Festschr. E. E. Stengel* (Münster - Cologne 1952), 203–22; see also chap. 27, footnote 17; G. A. Bezzola, *Das ottonische Kaisertum in der französischen Geschichtsschreibung des 10. und beginnenden 11. Jahrhunderts, VIÖG* 18 (1956); W. L. Grünewald, *Das fränkisch-deutsche Kaisertum in der Auffassung englischer Geschichtsschreiber 800–1273* (dissertation, Frankfurt 1961); K. F. Werner in *HZ* 200 (1965), 1–60 (*imperium* in French thought from 10th to 12th cent.).

THE EMPIRE, ITALY AND ROME: Lit. for chap. 27; H. *Zimmermann,* "Papstabsetzungen des Mittelalters, II: Die Zeit der Ottonen" in *MIÖG* 69 (1961) 241–91 (important); P. E. Schramm, "Kaiser, Basileus und Papst in der Zeit der Ottonen" in *HZ* 129 (1924), 424–75; G. Schwarz, *Die Besetzung der Bistümer Reichsitaliens unter den sächsischen und salischen Kaisern* (Leipzig–Berlin 1913); H. Pahnke, *Geschichte der Bischöfe Italiens deutscher Nation 951–1264* (Berlin 1913); M. Uhlirz, "Die italienische Kirchenpolitik der Ottonen" in *MIÖG* 48 (1934), 201–321; id., "Die Restitution des Exarchates Ravenna durch die Ottonen" *MIÖG* 50 (1936), 1–34; G. Graf, *Die weltlichen Widerstände in Reichsitalien gegen die Herrschaft der Ottonen und die beiden ersten Salier 951–1056* (Erlangen 1936); M. Uhlirz, "Die staatsrechtliche Stellung Venedigs zur Zeit Ottos III." in *ZSavRGgerm* 76 (1959), 82–110.

OTTO III: M. Ter Braak, *Kaiser Otto III.* (dissertation, Amsterdam 1928). Indispensable is P. E. Schramm, *Kaiser, Rom und Renovatio* (see lit. for sect. 7) I, 87–187; *ibid.,* I, 3–33; and *JbbDG, Jahrbücher des deutschen Reiches unter Otto III.* ed. by M. Uhlirz (Berlin 1954); cf. also M. Uhlirz, "Otto III. und das Papsttum" in *HZ* 162 (1940), 258–68; see ref. to research on the 'renovatio' idea in *Settimane di studio,* II (sect. 7), 201–9; R. Morghen, "Otto III., servus apostolorum" in *Settimane di studio,* II, 13–25.

29. *The Church in Spain, Ireland, and England: 900 to 1046*

SOURCES

SPAIN: See the bibliography by B. Sánchez Alonso, *Fuentes de Historia Española e Hispano-Americana* (Madrid, 2nd ed. 1927); *RepFont* I, 803f. (Register of source collections); P. Kehr, *Papsturkunden in Spanien,* I: Catalonia, II: Navarre and Aragón: *AGG* 18, 2 (1926), *ibid.,* 22, 1 (1928), and C. Erdmann, *Papsturkunden in Portugal, AGG* 20, 3 (1927), both with a wealth of archival and bibliographical material; M. C. Díaz y Díaz, *Index scriptorum latinorum medii aevi hispanorum* (Salamanca 1958–59). — Indispensable are the geographically arranged great source works: Henrique Flórez, *España Sagrada,* and J. Villanueva, *Viage literario a las iglesias de España* (Gen. Bib. I, 7); also important, *Marca Hispanica, auctore P. de Marca,* ed. by E. Baluze (Paris 1688). C. Sánchez Albornoz, *La España musulmana, según los autores islamistas y cristianos medievales,* 2 vols. (Buenos Aires 1946); A. Huici, *Las crónicas latinas de la reconquista,* 2 vols. (Valencia 1913); M. Gómez-Moreno, *Las primeras crónicas de la reconquista: El ciclo de Alfonso III, Boletín de la Academia de la Historia* 100 (1932); J. M. Lacarra, "Documentos para el estudio de la reconquista y repoblación del valle de Ebro", *Estudios de Edad Media de la Corona de Aragón,* I, II, series 2 (1946), series 3 (1947–48); A. Huici Miranda, *Colección de crónicas árabes de la Reconquista,* presently in 4 vols. (Tetuán 1951ff.); cf. *RepFont* I, 335.

Ireland and Scotland: J. Kenney, *Sources for the Early History of Ireland,* I: *Ecclesiastical* (New York 1929), narrative as well as bibliographical. The most important editions found in *Rolls Series,* see *Kenney* and *RepFont* I, 803 (Register of all Irish source collections); F. W. H. Wasserschleben, *Die irische Kanonessammlung* (Giessen, 2nd ed. 1874); L. Bieler and D. Binchy, *Irish Penitentials* (Dublin 1963). W. C. Dickinson, G. Donaldson and I. A. Miller, *A Source Book of Scottish History,* I: to 1424 (London 1952); A. Orr Anderson, *Early Sources of Scottish History 500–1286,* 2 vols. (Edinburgh 1922); id., *Scottish Annals from English Chronicles 500–1286* (London 1908); A. W. Haddan and W. Stubbs, *Councils and Ecclesiastical Documents relating to Great Britain and Ireland,* I–III in 4 vols. (Oxford 1869–78), vol. II contains the sources for Scotland to 1188 and for Ireland to 665.

England: Bibliographies by C. Gross, *Sources and Literature of English History* (London, 2nd ed. 1915); W. Bonser, *An Anglo-Saxon and Celtic Bibliography 450–1087,* 2 vols. (Oxford 1957); for the monastic reform see the survey by Eleanor S. Duckett, *Saint Dunstan;* W. Holtzmann, *Papsturkunden in England,* 3 vols. in *AGG* 25 (1930–31), *AGG,* 3rd series, 14 (1935), *AGG* 33 (1952), useful for introduction to present state for research, etc.; The collection of councils by Haddan and Stubbs III *(v. supra)* extends only to 870; B. Thorpe, *Ancient Laws and Institutes, also Monumenta ecclesiastica,* 2 vols. (London 1840); F. Liebermann, *Die Gesetze der Angelsachsen,* 3 vols. (Halle 1898–1916); F. W. H. Wasserschleben, *Die Bussordnungen der abendländischen Kirche* (Halle 1851), for Ireland and England, pp. 101–352; see also W. J. Schmitz, *Die Bussbücher und die Bussdisziplin der Kirche,* 2 vols. (Mainz 1883–98), for the Anglo-Saxons I, 490–587 and II, 645–701; for the editions of royal documents see *Santifaller NE* 21–24. Although written in the early 12th cent. the works of William of Malmesbury and Simeon of Durham are important because of their use of lost sources: see *Historia Dunelmensis ecclesiae* and *Historia regum,* ed. by T. Arnold, *Rolls Series* 75, 1–2 (1882–85); on reform see *Memorials of St. Dunstan* (vitae and other material), ed. by W. Stubbs, *Rolls Series* 63 (London 1874); Aelfric, *Vita S. Aethelwoldi episcopi Wintonensis* in *Chronicon monasterii de Abingdon,* ed. by J. Stevenson, *Rolls Series* 2, vol. II (London 1858), 253–66; continued by Wulfstan, *PL* 137, 79–108; *Vita Oswaldi, archiepiscopi Eboracensis* in *Historians of the Church of York,* ed. by S. Raine, *Rolls Series* 71, vol. I (London 1879), 399–475. — "Cnutonis regis gesta sive Encomium Emmae" in *MGSS* XIX, 509–25; *Wulfstan,* collection of homilies attributed to him, ed. by A. Napier (Berlin 1883), see especially as indicative of the spirit of the time his *Sermo lupi ad Anglos* written c. 1014, in *Lives of Edward the Confessor,* ed. by H. R. Luard, *Rolls Series* 3 (London (1858).

Literature

Spain: For ecclesiastical history see Gen. Bib. II, 4; Amann in *Fliche-Martin* VII, 417–27. — For profane history see Gen. Bib. II, 2; R. P. A. Dozy, *Histoire des musulmans d'Espagne jusqu'à la conquête de l'Andalousie par les Almoravides* (Leiden, 2nd ed. 1932); E. Lévi-Provençal, *Histoire de l'Espagne musulmane,* 2 vols. (Paris 1951), the Spanish translation found in Gen. Bib. II, 2; L. de las Cagidas, *Los Mozárabes,* 2 vols. (Madrid 1946–48). J. A. Maravall, *El concepto de España en la edad media* (Madrid 1954); E. Herrera Oria, *Historia de la reconquista de España* (Madrid, 2nd ed. 1943); J. Pérez de Urbel and R. del Arco y Garay, *España cristiana. Comienzo de la reconquista 711–1038* (see. Gen. Bib. II, 2); A. Sánchez Candeira, *El 'Regnum-Imperium' Leonés hasta 1037* (Madrid 1951); J. Pérez de Urbel, *Historia del condado de Castilla,* 3 vols. (Madrid 1945); L. Serrano, *El obispado de Burgos y la Castilla primitiva desde el siglo V al XIII,* 3 vols. (Madrid 1936); R. Menéndez Pidal, *La España del Cid,* 2 vols. (Madrid, 2nd ed. 1947); J. Descola, *Histoire de l'Espagne chrétienne* (Paris 1951); P. David, *Études historiques sur la Galice et le Portugal du VIᵉ au XIIᵉ siècle* (Lisbon–Paris 1947); A. Ubieto Arteta, "Las diócesis navarro-aragonesas durante los siglos IX y X" un *Pirineos* 10 (1954), 179–99; A. Durán Gudiol, "La iglesia en Aragón durante el siglo XI" in *Estudios de edad media de la Corona de Aragón* 4 (1951), 7–68; P. Kehr, *Das Papsttum und der Katalanische Prinzipat bis zur Vereinigung mit Aragón; AAB* 1 (1926); for the councils see note 6 of this chapter.

IRELAND AND SCOTLAND: For ecclesiastical history see Gen. Bib. II, 4; M. Leclercq in *DACL* VII, 1461–1552; Amann in *Fliche-Martin* VII, 404–07. — Gen. Histories: E. Curtis, *A History of Medieval Ireland* (London, 2nd ed. 1938); E. MacNeill, *Early Irish Laws and Institutions* (Dublin 1935); W. Nugent, *Church and State in Early Christian Ireland* (dissertation, Dublin 1949); L. Bieler, "Irland, Wegbereiter des Mittelalters" in *Stätten des Geistes* (Olten 1963).

ENGLAND: For ecclesiastical history see Gen. Bib. II, 4; Amann in *Fliche-Martin* VII, 407–15; F. Barlow, *The English Church 1000–1066. A Constitutional History* (London 1963). — Poltical history: Gen. Bib. II, 2; R. H. Hodgkin, *A History of the Anglo-Saxons*, 2 vols. (London, 3rd ed. 1952); P. E. Schramm, *A History of the English Coronation* (Oxford 1937); H. Böhmer, *Kirche und Staat in England im 10. und 11. Jahrhundert* (Leipzig 1899); H. Tillmann, *Die päpstlichen Legaten in England bis zur Beendigung der Legation Gualas 1218* (dissertation, Bonn 1926); D. Knowles, *The Monastic Order in England 940–1216* (Cambridge, 2nd ed. 1949, new impression 1963); id., with R. Neville Hadcock, *Medieval Religious Houses, England and Wales* (London 1953); F. Cabrol, *L'Angleterre chrétienne avant les Normands* (Paris 1909); E. John, "The King and the Monks in the 10th Century Reformation" in *BJRL* 42 (1959–60), 61–87; J. A. Robinson, *The Times of St. Dunstan* (Oxford 1923); Eleanor S. Duckett, *Saint Dunstan of Canterbury* (New York 1955); K. Jost, *Wulfstanstudien* (Bern 1950); D. Whitelock in *Transact. of the Royal Hist. Soc.*, 4. ser. 24 (1942), 25–42 (Wulfstan in homiletics and state-craft); id. in *EHR* 69 (1955), 72–85 (Wulfstan's influence in the legislation of Knut).

30. The Spread of Christianity Among the Scandinavians in the Tenth and Eleventh Centuries

SOURCES

Adam of Bremen, *Gesta Hammaburgensis ecclesiae pontificum, MGSS rer. Germ.*, ed. by B. Schneider (3rd. ed. 1917), an important history composed between 1074 and 1076, later extended to 1080, esp. important for the time of Archbishop Adalbert (3rd book) and for the peoples and lands of northern Europe (4th book); Saxo Grammaticus, *Historia Danica (Gesta Danorum)*, ed. by A. Holder (Strasbourg 1886); Another ed. by J. Olrik and H. Raeder in 2 vols. (Copenhagen 1931); P. Herrmann, Interpretation of the first 9 books, I: Translation (German), II: Commentary (Leipzig 1922); although not recorded until the 13th cent., the Eddas and Sagas form a valuable source of our knowledge of early Christianity in the North. Saxo's account to 1168 is based upon these. A still worthwhile account of Icelandic literature with information on texts and manuscripts is the Prolegomena to the edition of *Sturlunga saga* by G. Vigfusson (Oxford 1878); also F. Y. Powell, *Origines Islandicae* (Oxford 1905) which contains lives of bishops Jon, Pal, and Thorlak; cf. W. A. Craigie, *The Icelandic Sagas* (Cambridge, 2nd ed. 1933); *Altnordische Sagenbibliothek*, ed. by G. Cederskjöld, G. Gering and E. Mogk, 18 vols. (Halle 1922–29); cf. *RepFont* I, 25, 743; D. H. May, *Regesten der Erzbischöfe von Bremen* (Hanover 1937); extends to 1306.

LITERATURE

See research report by H. Kellenbenz in *HZ* 190 (1960), 618–55. — O. Scheel, *Die Wikinger* (Stuttgart 1939); U. Noack, *Geschichte der nordischen Völker*, I: *Nordische Frühgeschichte und Wikingerzeit* (Munich 1941); L. Musset, *Les peuples scandinaves au moyen âge* (Paris 1951). H. Ljunsberg, *Die nordische Religion und das Christentum. Studien über den nordischen Religionswechsel zur Wikingerzeit*, German trans. by H. W. Schomerus (Gütersloh 1941); in contrast W. Baetke minimizes the worth of the sagas as sources, "Christliches Lehrgut in der Sagareligion" in *BAL* 98, 6 (1951); W. Lange, *Studien zur christlichen Dichtung der Nordgermanen 1000–1200* (Göttingen 1958); W. Trillmich, "Die Krise des nordgermanischen Heidentums" in *WaG* 12 (1952), 27–43.

MISSIONS AND CHURCH HISTORY: G. Haendler in *Die Kirche in ihrer Geschichte*, II, sect. E (Gen. Bib. II, 3), E 69 to R 73 (good literature); for principal works see Gen. Bib. II, 4. — W. Trillmich, "Missionsbewegungen im Ostseeraum" in *Festgabe W. Aubin* (Hamburg 1950), 229–40; W. Göbell, "Die Christianisierung des Nordens und das Werden der mittelalterlichen Kirche bis zur Errichtung des Erzbistums Lund (1103)" in *ÖAKR* 15 (1964), 8–22, 97–102; H. v. Schubert, *Kirchengeschichte Schleswig-Holsteins*, I (Kiel 1907); K. Maurer, *Die Bekehrung des norwegischen Stammes zum Christentum*, 2 vols. (Munich 1855–56), still worthwhile; P. Zorn, *Staat und Kirche in Norwegen bis zum Schluss des 13. Jahrhunderts* (Munich 1875); J. Dehio, *Geschichte des Erzbistums Hamburg-Bremen bis zum Ausgang der Mission*, 2 vols. (Berlin 1877); J. G. Schröffel, *Kirchengeschichte Hamburgs*, I (Hamburg 1929); B. Schmeidler, *Hamburg-Bremen und Nordost-Europa vom 9. bis 11. Jahrhundert* (Leipzig 1918); F. J. Tschan, *History of the Archbishops of Hamburg-Bremen* (New York 1959); C. J. A. Oppermann, *The English Missionaries in Sweden and Finland* (London 1937); K. Maurer, *Altnordische Kirchenverfassung und Eherecht. Vorlesungen über altnordische Rechtsgeschichte*, II (Leipzig 1908); K. Haff, "Das Grosskirchspiel im nordischen und niederdeutschen Rechte des Mittelalters" in *ZSavRGkan* 63 (1943), 1–63; T. J. Oleson, *Early Voyages and Approaches* (Toronto 1963) (excellent survey of literature on Greenland during the Middle Ages).

31. *Evangelization of the Slavs and the Magyars in the Tenth and Eleventh Centuries*

SOURCES

WENDS-BOHEMIA-POLAND: G. Jakob, *Ibrahim ibn Jaqub's Bericht über die Slavenländer aus dem Jahre 973;* Anhang zu Widukinds Sachsengeschichte, trans. by P. Hirsch in *GdV* 33 (Leipzig 1931), 177ff.; Adam of Bremen, *Gesta Hammaburgensis ecclesiae pontificum* (see chap. 30); for the eastern policy of the Saxon Emperors see chap. 29: *Annales Quedlinburgenses, Hildesheimenses* and Thietmar of Merseburg, *Chronicon;* for Adalbert of Prague: John Canaparius (?), "Vita S. Adalberti" in *MGSS* IV, 581–95; Bruno of Querfurt, "Vita et passio S. Adalberti" in *Monum. Polon. hist.,* I, ed. by A. Bielowski, 184–222 (1st version) and *MGSS* IV, 596–612 (2nd version with variations); important is Bruno's letter to Henry II in *Giesebrecht,* II (5th ed.), 702–05 and his "Vita quinque fratrum" in *MGSS* XV, 709–38; also the Vita et Passio ascribed to him in *MGSS* XXX, 1350–67; Cosmas of Prague, *Cronica Boemorum* (written about 1110, until 1125), *MGSS rer. Germ.* NS 2, ed. by B. Bretholz (1923), mostly fiction; *Annales Poloniae* (from the 11th century on) in *MGSS* XIX, 612–65; *ibid.,* XXIX, 421–70 (supplement); Anonymus Gallus, *Chronicae Polonorum* (from the 1st decade of the 12th century) in *MGSS* IX, 423–78.

RUSSIA: Aside from the references in Byzantine and Latin sources, the old Russian Chronicles are of great value; the best edition is: *Polnoe sobranie russkich letopisej* [Complete Collection of Russian Chronicles] (Leningrad 1926); in vol. I the so-called Laurentius Chronicle (ed. by E. F. Karskij) is important; its oldest version, the Chronicle of Nestor, has been recently edited with commentary by D. S. Lichčev, *Povest' vremenniych let* [Stories from Bygone Years], 2 vols. (Moscow–Leningrad 1950); cf. also id., *Russkiia letopsi i ikh kulturno-istorichekoe znachenie* [Russian Chronicles and Their Cultural Significance] (Moscow–Leningrad 1947); also M. D. Priselkov, *Nestor Letopisets* [Nestor the Chronicler] (St. Petersburg 1923).

HUNGARY: Collected sources in *SS. rer. Hung.,* ed. by E. Szentpétery, 2 vols. (Budapest 1937–38); the work of L. Endlicher, *Rerum Hungaricarum Monumenta Arpadiana* (Leipzig, 2nd ed. 1931) is still indispensable for the Leges; historical writing does not appear until the end of the 11th cent.; it is mostly hagiographical; also the short *Annales Posonienses* in *SS. rer. Hung.* I, 119ff.; *MGSS* XIX, 571ff.; the remainder of the *Gesta Hungarorum* in *SS. rer. Hung.* I, 13ff.

For Bohemia-Poland-Russia-Hungary: Cf. *Wattenbach-Holtzmann* I, 798–820; also sources in the works cited below: F. Dvornik, *The Slavs;* G. Stökl, *Slavenmission;* P. David, *Les sources de l'histoire de Pologne à l'époque des Piasts* (Paris 1924); C. M. Macartney, *The Medieval Hungarian Historians. A Critical and Analytical Guide* (Cambridge 1953).

General: L. I. Strakhovsky, *A Handbook of Slavic Studies* (Cambridge, Mass., 1949); R. Trautmann, *Die slavischen Völker und Sprachen. Eine Einführung in die Slavistik* (Göttingen 1947); F. Dvornik, *The Making of Central and Eastern Europe* (London 1949); id., *The Slavs. Their Early History and Civilization* (Boston, 2nd ed. 1959); G. Stökl, *Geschichte der Slavenmission* in *Die Kirche in ihrer Geschichte,* II, section E. (Gen. Bib. II, 3), E 75 – E 91 (with good literature); O. Halecki, *The Limits and Divisions of European History* (London 1951); M. Hellmann, "Slavisches, insbesondere ostslavisches Herrschertum des Mittelalters" in *Das Königtum, Vorträge und Forschungen,* 3 (Lindau–Constance 1956), 243–77; F. Baethgen, "Die Kurie und der Osten" in *Deutsche Ostforschung,* I (Leipzig 1942), 310–39; H. Ludat, "Die ältesten geschichtlichen Grundlagen für das deutsch-slavische Verhältnis" in *Das östliche Deutschland* (Würzburg 1959), 127–60; (on the Emperor and the idea of kingship and mission cf. lit. for sec. 7 and chap. 28); T. Mayer, "Das Kaisertum und der Osten im Mittelalter" in *Deutsche Ostforschung,* I (Leipzig 1942), 291–309; W. Füllner, *Der Stand der deutsch-slavischen Auseinandersetzung zur Zeit Thietmars von Merseburg* (Jena 1937).

Wends: M. Hellmann, "Ostpolitik Kaiser Ottos II" in *Festschrift H. Aubin* (Lindau–Constance 1956), 46–76; G. Lukas, *Die deutsche Politik gegen die Elbslaven von 982 bis Ende der Polenkriege Heinrichs II.* (dissertation, Halle 1940); A. Dieck, *Die Errichtung der Havelbistümer unter Otto dem Grossen* (dissertation, Heidelberg 1944); K. Schmaltz, *Kirchengeschichte Mecklenburgs,* I (Schwerin 1935); W. Schlesinger, *Kirchengeschichte Sachsens im Mittelalter,* I: *Von den Anfängen christlicher Verkündigung bis zum Ende des Investiturstreites* (Cologne–Graz 1962); H. Herrmann, *Thüringische Kirchengeschichte,* I (Jena 1937); H. F. Schmid, *Die rechtlichen Grundlagen der Pfarrorganisation auf westslavischem Boden und ihre Entwicklung während des Mittelalters* (Weimar 1938); for criticism cf. W. Schlesinger, "Die deutsche Kirche im Sorbenland und die Kirchenverfassung auf westslavischem Boden" in *Zeitschrift für Ostforschung* 1 (1952), 345–71; H. Beumann and W. Schlesinger, "Urkundenstudien zur deutschen Ostpolitik unter Otto III." in *ADipl* I (1955), 132–256.

Bohemia: B. Bretholz, *Geschichte Böhmens und Mährens,* I (Reichenberg 1921); A. Naegle, *Kirchengeschichte Böhmens,* I, 1–2 (Vienna–Leipzig 1915–18); W. Wegener, *Böhmen, Mähren und das Reich im Hochmittelalter* (Cologne 1959); K. Bosl, "Der Eintritt Böhmens und Mährens in den westlichen Kulturraum im Lichte der Missionsgeschichte" in *Collegium Carolinum,* II: *Böhmen und Bayern* (Munich 1958), 43–64.

Poland: *Cambridge History of Poland from the Origins to Sobieski 1696* (Cambridge 1950); cf. F. Baethgen in *DA* 9 (1951), 240f.; K. Völker, *Kirchengeschichte Polens* (Berlin–Leipzig 1930); a summary in above mentioned *Cambridge History* by P. David, 60–85; B. Stasiewski, "Die ersten Spuren des Christentums in Polen" in *Zeitschrift für osteuropäische Geschichte* NF 4 (1934), 238–60; *ibid.,* 5 (1935), 572–604; also L. Koczy in *Sacrum Poloniae Millennium,* I (Rome 1954), 9–69; B. Stasiewski, *Untersuchungen über drei Quellen zur ältesten Geschichte und Kirchengeschichte Polens* (Breslau 1933); id., *Kirchengeschichtliche Beiträge zur Entwicklung des deutsch-polnischen Grenzraums im Hochmittelalter* (Berlin 1955); P. Fabre, *La Pologne et le Saint Siège du Xe au XIIe siècle* (Paris 1896); L. Kulczycki, *L'organisation de l'église de Pologne avant le XIIIe siècle* (dissertation, Strasbourg 1928).

Russia: G. Stökl, "Russisches Mittelalter und sowjetische Mediävistik" in *Jahrbücher für Geschichte Osteuropas* NF 3 (1955), 1–40, 105–22; K. Stählin, *Geschichte Russlands,* I (Berlin–Leipzig 1923); P. Miliunow, C. Seignobos and C. Eisenmann, *Histoire de Russie,* I (Paris 1932); G. Vernadsky, *Kievan Russia* (New Haven 1948); H. Paszkiewicz, *The Origins of Russia*

(London 1954); G. Vernadsky, *The Origins of Russia* (Oxford 1959); A. M. Ammann, *Abriss der ostslavischen Kirchengeschichte* (Vienna 1950); S. H. Cross, *Medieval Russian Churches* (Cambridge, Mass. 1949); G. P. Fedotov, *The Russian Religious Mind. Kievan Christianity* (Cambridge, Mass. 1946); M. Vladimirskij-Budanow, Germ. trans. by L. K. Goetz, *Staat und Kirche in Altrussland* (Berlin 1908); L. K. Goetz, *Kirchengeschichtliche und kulturgeschichtliche Denkmäler Altrusslands nebst Geschichte des russischen Kirchenrechts* (Stuttgart 1905); A. Pszywyi, *Die Rechtslage der Kirche im Kiewer Staat auf Grund der fürstlichen Statuten* (typed dissertation, Graz 1950); A. M. Ammann, *Die ostslavische Kirche im jurisdiktionellen Verband der byzantinischen Grosskirche 988 to 1459* (Würzburg 1955); A. Herman, *De fontibus iuris ecclesiastici Russorum* (Vatican City 1936); R. P. Casey, "Early Russian Monasticism" in *OrChrP* 19 (1953), 373–423.

YUGOSLAVS: G. Stadtmüller, *Geschichte Südosteuropas* (Vienna 1950); C. Jireček, *Geschichte der Serben*, I (Gotha 1911); F. Sišic, *Geschichte der Kroaten* (Zagreb 1917) (an expanded Croatian edition in 1925); F. R. Preveden, *A History of the Croatian People*, I: *Prehistory and Early Period until 1397* (New York 1955); L. Vojnović, *Histoire de Dalmatie* (Paris 1934); A. Maier, *Kirchengeschichte von Kärnten*, Heft 2: *Mittelalter* (Klagenfurt 1953); E. Tomek, *Kirchengeschichte Österreichs*, I (Innsbruck–Vienna–Leipzig 1925); J. Wodka, *Kirche in Österreich. Wegweiser durch ihre Geschichte* (Vienna 1959); F. Valjavec, *Geschichte der deutschen Kulturbeziehungen zu Südosteuropa*, I: *Mittelalter* (Munich, 2nd ed. 1953); G. Stadtmüller, "Die Christianisierung Südosteuropas als Forschungsproblem" in *Kyrios* 6 (1942–43), 61–102.

HUNGARY: B. Hóman, *Geschichte des ungarischen Mittelalters* (Berlin 1940); P. v. Váczy, *Die erste Epoche des ungarischen Königtums* (Pécs 1936); B. Hóman, *König Stephan I. der Heilige. Die Gründung des ungarischen Staates* (Breslau 1941); A. Szentirmai, "Die 'apostolische Legation' des Ungarnkönigs Stephan des Heiligen" in *ÖAKR* 8 (1957), 253–67; G. Bónis, "Die Entwicklung der geistlichen Gerichtsbarkeit in Ungarn" in *ZSavRGkan* (1963), 174–235.

32. *The Papacy and the Empire from 1002 to 1046*

SOURCES

See material for Section 7 and chapter 27.

FOR THE PAPACY AND ITALY: see Part II, Section I for the sources on the Gregorian Reform and the decades preceeding; cf. also L. Santifaller, "Chronologisches Verzeichnis der Urkunden Papst Johannes' XIX." in *Römische Historische Mitteilungen* I (1956–57), 35–76; good bibliography of sources and literature for the individual popes in L. Santifaller, *Ottonischsalisches Reichskirchensystem* (Gen. Bib. II, 8a), 193–205.

THE EMPIRE AND GERMANY: The imperial and royal documents: *MGDD* III (Henry II and Arduin), IV (Conrad II), V (Henry III); J. F. Böhmer, *Regesta imperii* III (Salian): Konrad II., revised by H. Appelt and N. v. Bischoff (Graz 1951); for the registers of Henry II and Henry III, cf. K. Stumpf-Brentano, *Die Reichskanzler vornehmlich des X., XI. und XII. Jahrhunderts*, II (Innsbruck 1879; reprint, Aalen 1960), 151–208; sources for the time of Henry II *supra* in chapter 27; sources for the Salian kings: Wipo, *Gesta Chuonradi II imperatoris*, ed. by H. Bresslau, *Wiponis opera* in *MGSS rer. Germ.* (3rd ed. 1915, reprint 1956); Hermann of Reichenau, *Chronicon* (to 1054); Anselm of St. Lambert, *Gesta episcoporum Leodiensium* (for the 11th cent.) in *MGSS* XIV, 108–20 (to the death of Bishop Wazo 1048).

LITERATURE

See material for Section 7 and chapters 27 and 28; *JbbDG, Jahrbücher des Deutschen Reiches unter Heinrich II.*, ed. by S. Hirsch, H. Pabst and H. Bresslau, 3 vols. (Leipzig 1862–75); *unter Konrad II.*, ed. by H. Bresslau, 2 vols. (Leipzig 1879–84); *unter Heinrich III.*, ed. by E. Steindorff, 2 vols. (Leipzig 1874–81); K. Hampe and F. Baethgen, *Deutsche Kaisergeschichte in der Zeit der Salier und Staufer* (Heidelberg, 10th ed. 1949); H. L. Mikoletzky, *Kaiser Heinrich II. und die Kirche* (Vienna 1946); T. H. Graff, *Beiträge zur deutschen Kirchenpolitik Heinrichs II.* (typed dissertation, Graz 1959); C. Violini, *Arduino d'Ivrea, re d'Italia, e il dramma del suo secolo* (Turin 1942); T. Schieffer, "Heinrich II. und Konrad II. Die Umprägung des Geschichtsbildes durch die Kirchenreform des 11. Jahrhunderts" in *DA* 8 (1951), 384–437; M. L. Bulst-Tiele, *Kaiserin Agnes* (Berlin 1933); P. Kehr, "Vier Kapitel aus der Geschichte Kaiser Heinrichs III." in *AAB* (1930), no. 3; G. Ladner, "Theologie und Politik vor dem Investiturstreit. Abendmahlsstreit, Kirchenreform, Cluny und Heinrich III." in *VIÖG* 2 (1936); G. Tellenbach, *Church, State, and Christian Society at the Time of the Investiture Contest* (Oxford, 3rd ed. 1959); P. Funk, "Ps.-Isidor gegen Heinrich III. Kirchenhoheit" in *HJ* 56 (1936), 305–30; J. Gay, *Les papes du XIᵉ siècle et la chrétienté* (Paris 1926); P. Brezzi, "Aspetti di vita politica e religiosa di Roma tra la fine del sec. X e la prima metà del sec. XI" in *Bolletino di Badia greca di Grottaferrata* 9 (1955), 115–26; C. Violante, "Aspetti di politica italiana di Enrico III prima della sua discesa in Italia" in *RSIt* 64 (1952), 157–76, 293–314; A. Mathis, *Il pontefice Benedetto IX* in *CivCatt* 66 (1915), 549–71; *ibid.* 67 (1916), 285–96, 535–48; S. Messina, *Benedetto IX pontefice Romano* (Catania 1922); G. B. Borino, "L'elezione e la deposizione di Gregorio VI" in *AS Romana* 39 (1916), 141–410; R. L. Poole, "Benedict IX and Gregory VI" in *Proceedings of the British Academy* 8 (1917–18), 200–35; C. Violante, *La pataria milanese e la riforma ecclesiastica,* I (Milan 1955), 43–84 (important chapter on the religious-political Italian policies of Henry III); H. Zimmermann, *Papstabsetzungen des Mittelalters,* III in *MIÖG* 70 (1962), 60–83 (with complete literature on Sutri).

SECTION EIGHT

Constitution of the Church, Worship, Pastoral Care, and Piety: 700 to 1050

33. Diocesan Organization

SOURCES

For the Carolingian period *MGLL* sect. II, *Capitularia regum Francorum,* 2 vols. (1883–97); sect. III, *Concilia,* 2 vols. extending to 843 (1893–1908); after 844 *Mansi* XIV, 799 to XIX, 620; for the synods of Germany and Italy 922–1059 see the catalogue of sources in M. Boye in *NA* 48 (1930), 45–96; basic is C. de Clercq, *La Législation religieuse franque,* 2 vols. (Louvain 1936, Antwerp 1958).

COLLECTIONS OF LAWS: Benedictus Levita in *MGLL,* sect. I, vol. II, 2 (Leipzig 1963); *PL* 97, 698–912; P. Hinschius, *Decretales Pseudo-Isidorianae et Capitula Angilramni* (Leipzig 1863); on Regino of Prüm and Burchard of Worms see ch. 40; for works on the sources of ecclesiastical law see Gen. Bib. I, 4.

LITERATURE

Always reliable also for the two following chapters are the manuals of both the general history of law and of canon law, cited in Gen. Bib. II, 6–7; for practical reasons *Feine* especially is cited in what follows, but the account by A. Dumas in *Fliche-Martin* VII, 177–316 is good; for the Frankish-German synodal decrees cf. in chap. 27 the basic work by H. Barion and the study by M. Boye in lit. for Germany.

CHURCH PROPERTIES AND THE PROPRIETARY CHURCHES: J. Balon, *Jus medii aevi,* I: *La structure et la gestion du domaine de l'église au moyen-âge dans l'Europe des Francs,* 2 vols. (Namur, 2nd ed.

1963); E. Lesne, *Histoire de la propriété ecclésiastique en France,* 6 vols. (Paris–Lille 1910–43); A. Dumas, "La notion de la propriété ecclésiastique du IX^c au XI^c siècle" in *RHEF* 26 (1940), 14–34. In spite of a certain bias the following are basic for the history of the proprietary church system: U. Stutz, *Die Eigenkirche als Element des mittelalterlich-germanischen Kirchenrechts* (Berlin 1895); id., *Geschichte des kirchlichen Benefizialwesens von seinen Anfängen bis auf Alexander III.,* part I (Berlin 1895); id., "Eigenkirche und Eigenklöster" in *RE* 23 (1913), 363–77; id., *ZSavRGkan* 57 (1937), 1–85 (selected chapters on history), followed in somewhat different presentation by *Feine RG* X, 18, cf. also X, 19 I–II and X, 20; F. Fournier, *Le droit de propriété, exercé par les laïques sur les biens de l'église dans le haut moyen-âge* (Lille 1943); for the proprietary system in various regions cf. *Feine RG* X, 18 (with lit.); very important is H. E. Feine, "Studien zum langobardisch-italischen Eigenkirchenrecht", I–III in *ZSavRGkan* 61 (1941), 1–95; *ibid.* 62 (1942), 1–105; *ibid.* 63 (1943), 64–190.

RURAL PARISHES: P. Imbart de la Tour, *Les paroisses rurales dans l'ancienne France du IVe au XIe siècle* (Paris 1900); S. Zorell, "Die Entwicklung des Parochialsystems bis zum Ende der Karolingerzeit" in *AkathKR* 82 (1902), 74–98; G. Forchielli, *La pieve rurale. Ricerche sulla storia della chiesa in Italia e particolarmente nel Veronese* (Rome 1931, new impr. 1938); H. E. Feine, "Die genossenschaftliche Gemeindekirche im germanischen Recht" in *MIÖG* 68 (1960), 171–96; H. F. Schmid, "Gemeinschaftskirchen in Italien und Dalmatien" in *ZSavRGkan* 77 (1960), 1–61; additional lit. for individual regions in *Feine RG* X, 19, I and X, 18, II, V.

BENEFICES: L. Thomassinus, *Vetus et nova disciplina circa beneficia et beneficiarios* (Paris 1688); in French (Lyons 1676–79); U. Stutz, *Benefizialwesen (v. supra);* id., "Leben und Pfründe" in *ZSavRGgerm* 20 (1899), 213 ff., for a different interpretation see A. Pöschl, "Die Entstehung des geistlichen Benefiziums" in *AkathKR* 106 (1926), 3–121, 363–471; see also H. E. Feine, "Kirchleihe und kirchliches Benefizium nach italienischen Rechtsquellen des frühen Mittelalters" in *HJ* 72 (1953), 101–11; additional lit. cf. *Feine RG* X, 20, I.

INCOME OF RURAL PARISHES: F. de Berlendis, *De oblationibus ad altare communibus et particularibus* (Venice 1743); U. Stutz, "Stolgebühren" in *RE* 19 (1906), 67–75; G. Schreiber in *ZSavRGkan* 36 (1915), 414–83; *ibid.* 63 (1943), 191–299; *ibid.* 65 (1947), 31–171 (for fees with regard to blessings, and the position of Gregory VII on the question of Mass oblations, etc.), also G. Schreiber, *Gemeinschaftsformen des Mittelalters,* Art. IV–VI (Münster 1948); for tithes see footnote 5; for *regalia* and *spolia* see the following chapter.

URBAN PARISHES AND CHAPTERS: Cf. lit. for chap. 39; P. Schneider, *Die bischöflichen Domkapitel* (Mainz 1885); E. Mayer, "Der Ursprung der Domkapitel" in *ZSavRGkan* 38 (1917), 1–33; see also footnote 8; J. Siegwart, *Die Chorherren- und Chorfrauengemeinschaften in der deutschsprachigen Schweiz vom 6. Jahrhundert bis 1160. Mit einem Überblick über die deutsche Kanonikerreform des 10. und 11. Jahrhunderts* (Fribourg 1962); A. Pöschl, *Bischofsgut und mensa episcopalis,* 3 vols. (Bonn 1908–12); K. H. Schäfer, *Pfarrkirche und Stift im deutschen Mittelalter* (Stuttgart 1903); additional lit. in *Feine RG* X, 19, II; for city prebends *ibid.,* X, 20, II.

DIOCESAN ORGANIZATION: J. Leclef, "Chorévêque" in *DDC* III (1942), 686–95; T. Gottlob, *Der abendländische Chorepiskopat* (Bonn 1928); critical revision by F. Gillmann in *AkathKR* 108 (1928), 712–23, by F. Gescher in *ZSavRGkan* 50 (1930), 708–17; A. Amanieu, "Archiprêtre" in *DDC* I (1935), 1004–26; P. Andrieu-Guitrancourt, *Histoire du décanat rural de son commencement jusqu'au XIIIe siècle* (Paris 1932); J. Faure, *L'archiprêtre des origines au droit décrétalien* (Paris 1911); J. B. Sägmüller, *Die Entwicklung des Archipresbyterats und Dekanats bis zum Ende des Karolingerreiches* (Progr. Tübingen 1898); A. Hamilton Thompson, "Diocesan Organization in the Middle Ages: Archdeacon and Rural Deans", Raleigh Lecture on History 1949 in *Proc. of the Brit. Acad.* 29; A. Amanieu, "Archidiacre" in *DDC* I (1935), 948–1004; A. Schröder, *Die Entwicklung des Archidiakonats bis zum 11. Jahrhundert* (Augsburg 1890); *Feine RG,* 19, III; *ibid.,* 21, I–IV (good lit.).

34. *Prelacies and the Secular Powers*

LITERATURE

Comprehensive resumé in K. Voigt, *Staat und Kirche von Konstantin dem Grossen bis zum Ende der Karolingerzeit* (Stuttgart 1936); L. Santifaller, *Zur Geschichte des ottonisch-salischen Reichskirchensystems*, *SAW* 229, Suppl. 1 (2nd. ed. 1964) includes besides the survey a worthwhile list of election privileges of the churches, sovereign rights, etc.; A. Pöschl, *Die Regalien der mittelalterlichen Kirchen* (Graz 1928); J. Flach, "La royauté et l'église en France du IXᵉ au XIᵉ siècle" in *RHE* 4 (1903), 432–47; K. Voigt, *Die karolingische Klosterpolitik und der Niedergang des westfränkischen Königtums* (Stuttgart 1917); H. Ganahl, *Studien zur Geschichte des kirchlichen Verfassungsrechtes im 10. und 11. Jahrhundert* (Innsbruck–Vienna–Munich 1935); further lit. in the chapters in sect. 7.

IMMUNITIES, ROYAL PROTECTION AND ADVOCACY: Cf. manuals of legal and constitutional history in Gen. Bib. II, 6–7 as well as the monographs: *ibid*. II, 8a, esp. T. Mayer, *Fürsten und Staat;* E. Magnin, "Immunités ecclésiastiques" in *DThC* VII (1922), 1218–62; M. Kroell, *L'immunité franque* (Paris 1910); E. E. Stengel, *Diplomatik der deutschen Immunitätsprivilegien vom 9. bis zum Ende des 11. Jahrhunderts* (Innsbruck 1910); id., *Abhandlungen und Untersuchungen zur mittelalterlichen Geschichte* (Cologne–Graz 1960), 30–34 (immunities), 35–68 (manorial control and immunity); J. Ficker, "Über das Eigentum des Reiches am Reichskirchengut" in *SAW* 72 (1872), 381–450; Registers and catalogues in Santifaller, *Reichskirchensystem*, 78–115; J. Semmler, "Traditio und Königsschutz" in *ZSavRGkan* 76 (1959), 1–33; A. Waas, *Vogtei und Bede in der deutschen Kaiserzeit*, 2 parts (Berlin 1919–23); H. Hirsch, *Die hohe Gerichtsbarkeit im deutschen Mittelalter* (Prague 1922); E. F. Otto, *Die Entwicklung der deutschen Kirchenvogtei im 10. Jahrhundert* (Berlin 1933); F. Senn, *L'institution des avoueries ecclésiastiques* (Paris 1903); H. Dubled in *Archives de l'église d'Alsace* 26 (1959), 1–88 (monastic advocacy in Alsace).

SECULAR POWER OF BISHOPS: there is no comprehensive work on this subject. *Fliche-Martin* VII, 220 contains bibliography on various dioceses as does the indispensable work on Germany, A. Werminghoff, *Verfassungsgeschichte der deutschen Kirche* § 26 and § 25; for the development of the idea of the episcopacy as an ecclesiastical benefice cf. E. Lesne, "Évêché et abbaye. Les origines du bénéfice ecclésiastique" in *RHEF* 5 (1914), 15–20; A. Pöschl, *Bischofsgut und mensa,* esp. vol. III (see lit. in ch. 33); A. Dumas in *RHEF* 26 (1940), 14–34.

For the legal position of the monasteries cf. Lit. in *Feine RG* § 18, III; also Dumas in *Fliche-Martin* VII, 293–316.

ELECTION AND INSTALLATION OF BISHOPS AND ABBOTS: G. Weise, *Königtum und Bischofswahlen im fränkischen und deutschen Reich vor dem Investiturstreit* (Berlin 1912); P. Imbart de la Tour, *Les élections épiscopales dans l'église de France du IXᵉ au XIIᵉ siècle* (Paris 1891); E. Laehns, *Die Bischofswahlen in Deutschland 936–1056* (dissertation, Greifswald 1909); P. Schmid, *Der Begriff der kanonischen Wahl in den Anfängen des Investiturstreites* (Stuttgart 1926); C. Magni, *Ricerche sopra le elezioni episcopali in Italia durante l'alte medio evo*, 2 vols. (Rome 1928–30); G. Schwarz, *Die Besetzung der italienischen Bistümer* (lit. for chap. 28); J. Polzin, *Die Abtswahlen in den Reichsabteien 1024–1054* (dissertation, Greifswald 1908); H. Lévy-Bruhl, *Les élections abbatiales en France* (Paris 1913); on the position of the German rulers regarding election rights, cf. H. Claus (dissertation, Greifswald 1911) and the catalogues in Santifaller, *Reichskirchensystem,* 51–58; A. Scharnagl, *Der Begriff der Investitur in den Quellen und in der Literatur des Investiturstreites* (Stuttgart 1908).

RIGHTS OF REGALIA AND SPOLIA: U. Stutz, "Regalie" in *RE* XVI (1905), 536–44; E. Lesne, "Les origines du droit de régale" in *Nouv. rev. d'hist. de droit franc. et étr.* 45 (1921), 5–52; J. Gaudement, *La collation par le roi de France des bénéfices vacants en régale des origines à la fin du*

XIVe siècle (Paris 1935); E. Friedberg, "Spolienrecht" in *RE* XVIII (1906), 861–86; F. Prochnov, *Das Spolienrecht und die Testierfähigkeit der Geistlichen im Abendland bis zum 13. Jahrhundert* (Berlin 1919); on both rights cf. G. Forchielli in *Festschr. Joh. Heckel* (Cologne–Graz 1959), 13–53; Werminghoff, *Verfassungsgeschichte*, 57–9; lit. in *Feine RG* § 19, I, a–c.

SERVITIUM REGIS: B. Heusinger, "Das servitium regis in der deutschen Kaiserzeit" in *AUF* 8 (1923), 26–159.

THE PAPACY AND THE PAPAL STATE: The works of P. Brezzi, L. Duchesne, L. Halphen in Gen. Bib. II, 5, and W. Kölmel and Gerstenberg in Lit. for chap. 27; T. Hirschfeld, "Das Gerichtswesen der Stadt Rom vom 8. bis 12. Jahrhundert" in *AUF* 4 (1912), 419–562; K. Jordan, "Das Eindringen des Lehenswesens in das Rechtsleben der römischen Kurie" in *AUF* 12 (1932), 13–110; id., "Die päpstliche Verwaltung im Zeitalter Gregors VII." in *StudGreg* I (1947), 111–35; D. B. Zema, "Economic Reorganization of the Roman See during the Gregorian Reform" in *StudGreg* I (1947), 169–81 (both works offer comprehensive surveys and literature for the pre-Gregorian period); R. Elze, "Das 'sacrum palatium Lateranense' im 10. und 11. Jahrhundert" in *StudGreg* IV (1952), 27–54; M. Hartmann in *Vierteljahrschrift für Sozial- und Wirtschaftsgeschichte* 7 (1909), 142–58 (manorial control and bureaucracy in the Papal State); W. Sickel in *MIÖG* 23 (1902), 50–126 (Alberic and the Papal State).

THE PAPAL CHANCERY: H. Breslau, *Handbuch der Urkundenlehre für Deutschland und Italien,* I (Leipzig, 2nd ed. 1912), 76–78, 191–240, 226–69; *ibid.,* II, 2 (Berlin–Leipzig, 2nd ed. 1931), 518–20, 531–33; L. Santifaller, "Saggio di un elenco dei funzionari, impiegati e scrittori della cancellaria Pontificia dell'inizio all' anno 1099" in *BIStIAM* 56 (1940), 1–865; P. Rabikauskas, *Die römische Kuriale in der päpstlichen Kanzlei* (Rome 1958), contains good survey of the history of the chancery; for the 11th cent. basic are the articles by Kehr, "Scrinium und Palatium" in *MIÖG* Suppl. vol. 6 (1901), 70–112; id., "Die ältesten Papsturkunden Spaniens" in *AAB* (1926), no. 2.

35. *Metropolitans, Primates, and Papacy*

LITERATURE

METROPOLITAN CONSTITUTION: *Feine RG* §§ 6 I, 13 I, 22; E. Lesne, *La hiérarchie épiscopale. Provinces, métropolitains, primats en Gaule et Germanie, 742 à 882* (Paris 1905); useful references in P. Imbart de la Tour, *Les élections épiscopales dans l'église de France du IXe au XIIe siècle* (Paris 1891); A. Werminghoff, *Verfassungsgeschichte der deutschen Kirche im Mittelalter* (Berlin, 2nd ed. 1913) §§ 9, 11, 31, 33; P. Wagner, *Die geschichtliche Entwicklung der Metropolitangewalt bis zum Zeitalter der dekretalen Gesetzgebung* (typed dissertation, Bonn 1917); H. Barion, *Das fränkisch-deutsche Synodalrecht des Frühmittelalters* (Bonn–Cologne 1931).

PRIMATES, APOSTOLIC VICARS: H. Fuhrmann, "Studien zur Geschichte der mittelalterlichen Patriarchate" in *ZSavRGkan* 70 (1953), 112–76; *ibid.,* 71 (1954), 1–84; *ibid.,* 72 (1955), 95–183

PAPACY: *Haller* II, 235–61; Z. N. Brooke, *The English Church and the Papacy* (Cambridge 1931); H. M. Klinkenberg, "Der römische Primat im 10. Jahrhundert" in *ZSavRGkan* 72 (1955), 1–57; (the following is used with permission of the author) S. Lindemans, *La primauté du pape dans la tradition littéraire de la fin du IXe au début du XIe siècle* (dissertation, Rome-Gregoriana 1959). — For the establishing of bishoprics by the papacy cf. the survey with literature in L. Santifaller, *Reichskirchensystem* (see lit. for chap. 34), 217–23.

PAPACY AND MONASTERIES: P. Fabre, *Étude sur le liber censuum de l'église Romaine* (Paris 1892); H. Hirsch, "Untersuchungen zur Geschichte des päpstlichen Schutzes" in *MIÖG* 54 (1942),

363–433; H. Appelt, "Die Anfänge des päpstlichen Schutzes" in *MIÖG* 62 (1954), 101–11; W. Szaivert, "Die Entstehung und Entwicklung der Klosterexemtion" in *MIÖG* 59 (1951), 265–98; J. F. Lemarignier, "L'exemption monastique et les origines de la réforme Grégorienne" in *À Cluny. Congrès scientifique* (Dijon 1950), 280–340; W. Schwarz, "Jurisdictio und Condicio. Eine Untersuchung zu den Privilegia libertatis der Klöster" in *ZSavRGkan* 76 (1959), 34–98; more lit. in *Feine RG* § 18, III, especially note 15.

CANONIZATION: E. W. Kemp, *Canonization and Authority in the Western Church* (London 1948); R. Klauser, "Zur Entwicklung des Heiligsprechungsverfahrens bis zum 13. Jahrhundert" in *ZSavRGkan* 71 (1954), 85–101 (with lit.).

PENANCE: E. Göller, *Papsttum und Bussgewalt in spätrömischer und frühmittelalterlicher Zeit* (Freiburg 1933).

LEGATES: K. Ruess, *Die rechtliche Stellung der päpstlichen Legaten bis zu Bonifaz VIII.* (Paderborn 1912); O. Engelmann, *Die päpstlichen Legaten in Deutschland bis zur Mitte des 11. Jahrhunderts* (dissertation, Marburg 1913); T. Schieffer, *Die päpstlichen Legaten in Frankreich vom Vertrag in Meersen (870) bis zum Schisma 1130* (Berlin 1935).

REIMS QUARREL (989–997): *Fliche-Martin* VII, 68–75; M. Uhlirz, *JbbDG unter Otto III.* (passim); P. Cousin, *Abbon de Fleury-sur-Loire* (Paris 1954); on Gerbert cf. lit. in chap. 28, note 16.

36. *The Sacraments and the Mass*

SOURCES

For particulars see the manuals by Eisenhofer, Righetti *et al.;* also see Baumstark, *Missale Romanum (v. infra);* E. Dekkers, *Clavis Patrum latinorum* (Steenbrügge 1951), 325–45; K. Gamber, *Codices liturgici antiquiores* (Fribourg 1963); Continuous survey of lit. (since 1921) in *Jahrbuch für Liturgiewissenschaft* and (since 1950) in *Archiv für Liturgiewissenschaft.* Here only basic texts are mentioned.

SACRAMENTARIES: *Mohlberg; Lietzmann SG;* (the same Sacramentary with that of Alcuin appended:) H. A. Wilson, *The Gregorian Sacramentary under Charles the Great* (London 1915); G. Richter and A. Schönfelder, *Sacramentarium Fuldense saec. X* (Fulda 1912); C. Vogel, "Le Pontifical Romano-germanique" in *SteT* 226/7 (Rome 1963).

LECTIONARIES: S. Beissel, *Entstehung der Perikopen des römischen Messbuches* (Freiburg 1907); T. Klauser, *Das römische Capitulare evangeliorum,* I (Münster 1935); W. H. Frere, *The Roman Epistle-Lectionary* (Oxford 1935); G. Godu, "Épître" in *DACL,* V, 245–344.

CHORAL (SUNG) MASSES: *Hesbert;* for early ritual: *Andrien OR; Amalarii episcopi opera liturgica omnia,* ed. by J. M. Hanssens, 3 vols. (Rome 1948–50); *Martène R.*

LITERATURE

Eisenhofer; Righetti; L. Duchesne, *Origines du culte chrétien* (Paris 1925); A. Baumstark, *Vom geschichtlichen Werden der Liturgie* (Freiburg 1923); H. Netzer, *L'introduction de la Messe Romaine en France* (Paris 1910); G. Ellard, *Master Alcuin Liturgist* (Chicago 1956); F. Cabrol, "Charlemagne et la liturgie" in *DACL* III, 807–25; A. L. Mayer, "Altchristliche Liturgie und Germanentum" in *JLW* 5 (1925), 80–96; I. Herwegen, *Germanische Rechtssymbolik in der römischen Liturgie* (Heidelberg 1913); T. Klauser, "Die liturgischen Austauschbeziehungen zwischen der römischen und der fränkisch-deutschen Kirche vom 8. bis zum 11. Jahrhundert" in *HJ* 53 (1933), 169–89.

SACRAMENTS: A. Stenzel, *Die Taufe. Eine genetische Erklärung der Taufliturgie* (Innsbruck 1958); H. J. Schmitz, *Die Bussbücher und die Bussdisziplin der Kirche* (Mainz 1883); id., *Die Bussbücher und das kanonische Bussverfahren* (Düsseldorf 1898); L. Bieler, *The Irish Penitentials* (Dublin 1963); B. Poschmann, *Die abendländische Kirchenbusse im frühen Mittelalter* (Breslau 1930); id., *Penance and the Annointing of the Sick* (New York 1964); J. A. Jungmann, *Die lateinischen Bussriten* (Innsbruck 1932); K. Ritzer, *Formen, Riten und religiöses Brauchtum der Eheschliessung in den christlichen Kirchen des ersten Jahrtausends* (Münster 1962); H. Mayer, "Geschichte der Spendung der Sakramente in der alten Kirchenprovinz Salzburg" in *ZKTh* 37 (1913), 760–804; *ibid.* 38 (1914), 1–36, 267–96; P. de Puniet, *Le Pontifical Romain,* 2 vols. (Louvain 1930–31).

MASS: A. Baumstark, *Missale Romanum. Seine Entwicklung, ihre wichtigsten Urkunden und Probleme* (Eindhoven–Nijmegen 1929); *Jungmann MS;* B. Luykx, "Der Ursprung der gleichbleibenden Teile der Heiligen Messe" in *LuM* 29 (1961), 72–119; P. Browe, *Die häufige Kommunion im Mittelalter* (Münster 1938); id., *Die Pflichtkommunion im Mittelalter* (Münster 1940); G. Nickl, *Der Anteil des Volkes an der Messliturgie im Frankenreiche von Chlodwig bis auf Karl den Grossen* (Innsbruck 1930); C. De Clercq, "Gebed en sacramenten bij 't volk ten tijde van Karel den Groote" in *OGE* 3 (1929), 278–90, 375–93.

37. *The Clergy and the Care of Souls*

SOURCES

The capitularies *(MGCap)* and councils (*MGConc aevi Karolini; Mansi* XII–XIX); Regino of Prüm, *De synodalibus causis et disciplinis ecclesiasticis,* ed. by Wasserschleben (Leipzig 1840); Burchard of Worms, *Decretum* (*PL* 140, 337–1058); id., *Admonitio synodalis* (one of the original texts: *PL* 96, 1375–80).

LITERATURE

R. Stachnik, *Die Bildung des Weltklerus im Frankenreiche von Karl Martell bis auf Ludwig den Frommen* (Paderborn 1926); G. H. Hörle, *Frühmittelalterliche Mönchs- und Klerikerbildung in Italien* (Freiburg 1914); G. Flade, *Die Erziehung des Klerus durch die Visitationen bis zum 10. Jahrhundert* (Berlin 1933); A. M. Königer, *Die Sendgerichte in Deutschland,* I (Munich 1907), 7–28; P. Imbart de la Tour, *Les paroisses rurales dans l'ancienne France du IVe au XIe siècle* (Paris 1900); L. Pfleger, *Die Entstehung und Entwicklung der elsässischen Pfarrei* (Strasbourg 1936); S. Zorell, "Die Entwicklung des Parochialsystems bis zum Ende der Karolingerzeit II" in *AkathKR* 82 (1902), 258–89; L. Nanni, "L'evoluzione storica della parrocchia" in *SC* 81 (1953), 475–544; A. Heintz, *Die Anfänge des Landdekanates im Rahmen der kirchlichen Verfassungsgeschichte des Bistums Trier* (Trier 1951); H. Leclercq, "Chanoines" in *DACL* III, 223–48; L. Hertling, "Kanoniker, Augustinusregel und Augustinerorden" in *ZKTh* 54 (1930), 335–59; G. G. Meersseman, "Die Klerikervereine von Karl dem Grossen bis Innocenz III." in *ZSKG* 46 (1952), 1–42, 81–112; A. Linsenmayer, *Geschichte der Predigt in Deutschland bis zum Ende des 14. Jahrhunderts* (Munich 1886); F. Wiegand, *Das Homiliarium Karls des Grossen* (Leipzig 1897); *Schnürer* II; J. B. Schneyer, "Die Predigt im MA" in *LThK* VIII (2nd ed. 1963), 708–13.

38. *Forms of Devotion*

LITERATURE

As most of this subject is treated in the chapter on the liturgy (36) only the following are listed: S. Bäumer, *Geschichte des Breviers* (Freiburg 1895); J. Stadlhuber, "Das Laienstundengebet vom Leiden Christi in seinem mittelalterlichen Fortleben" in *ZKTh* 72 (1950), 282–325.

ON THE BASIC SUBJECT OF PIETY: E. Dumoutet, *Le Christ selon la chair et la vie liturgique au moyen-âge* (Paris 1932), 1–27; R. Berger, *Die Darstellung des thronenden Christus in der romanischen Kunst* (Reutlingen 1926); *Jungmann LE* (esp.: "Die Abwehr des germanischen Arianismus und der Umbruch der religiösen Kultur im frühen Mittelalter", 3–86; "Beiträge zur Struktur des Stundengebetes", 208–64; "Der liturgische Wochenzyklus", 332–65); S. Beissel, *Geschichte der Verehrung Marias in Deutschland während des Mittelalters* (Freiburg 1909); id., *Die Verehrung der Heiligen und ihrer Reliquien in Deutschland bis zum Beginn des 13. Jahrhunderts* (Freiburg 1890).

FOR THE BEGINNINGS OF PRAYER BOOKS: A. Wilmart, *Precum libri quattuor aevi Karolini* (Rome 1940); id., *Auteurs spirituels et textes dévots du moyen-âge latin* (Paris 1932); id., "Prières médiévales pour l'adoration de la Croix" in *ELit* 46 (1932), 22–65; id., "Le manuel de prières de S. Jean Gualbert" in *RBén* 48 (1936), 259–99 (with proof that it derives from the collected prayers of 9th cent. Nonantola); A. Salvini, *Manuale precum S. Joannis Gualberti* (Rome 1933); F. X. Haimerl, *Mittelalterliche Frömmigkeit im Spiegel der Gebetbuchliteratur Süddeutschlands* (Munich 1952); W. Godel, "Irisches Beten im frühen Mittelalter" in *ZKTh* 85 (1963), 261–321, 389–439; E. Iserloh, "Die Kontinuität des Christentums beim Übergang von der Antike zum Mittelalter im Lichte der Glaubensverkündigung des heiligen Bonifatius" in *TThZ* 63 (1954), 193–205; H. B. Meyer, "Alkuin zwischen Antike und Mittelalter. Ein Kapitel frühmittelalterlicher Frömmigkeitsgeschichte" in *ZKTh* 81 (1959), 306–50, 405–54; U. Berlière, *L'ascèse bénédictine des origines à la fin du XIIᵉ siècle* (Paris 1927); L. Gougaud, *Dévotions et pratiques ascétiques du moyen âge* (Paris 1925); *Veit; Künstle.*

SECTION NINE

Renewal and Reform from 900 to 1050

39. *The Renewal of Monastic and Canonical Life*

SOURCES

RULES OF THE ORDERS: See Gen. Bib. I, 8, the editions by *Holstenius, Albers, Hallinger* I (with the newly edited Monks' Rule of Aachen). The Canons' Rule of Chrodegang of Metz is edited in *PL* 89, 1097–1120 (extended version), 1057–1108 (interpolated version); also by W. Schmitz (Hanover 1889) and Napier (London 1917); *Institutio canonicorum Aquisgranensis* in *MGConc* II, 307–421.

CLUNY: M. Marrier, *Bibliotheca Cluniacensis* (Paris 1614; new imp. Mâcon 1915); A. Bernard and A. Bruel, *Recueil des chartes de l'abbaye de Cluny,* 6 vols. (Paris 1876–1903); G. F. Ducket, *Charters and Records among the Archives of the Ancient Abbey of Cluny 1077–1534,* 2 vols. (Lewes 1890); John of Salerno, *Vita Odonis* in *PL* 133, 43–89; Eng. trans. by G. Sitwell; *St Odo of Cluny (Life of St Odo by John of Salerno and Life of St Gerald of Aurillac by St Odo)* (Oxford 1958); Odilo, *Vita Maioli* in *ActaSS,* Maii II, 683–8; Nalgold and Syrus, *Vita Maioli* in *ActaSS,* Maii II, 657–83; Jotsaldus, *Vita Odilonis* in *PL* 142, 897–940; Gilo, *Vita Hugonis* in A. L'Huillier, *Vie de Saint Hugues* (Solesmes 1888), 565–618. For other centres of reform cf. *Heimbucher* I (Gen. Bib. II, 9).

Literature

For the history of monasticism cf. Gen. Bib. II, 9; *Kalendarium Benedictinum. Die Heiligen und Seligen des Benediktinerordens und seiner Zweige,* 4 vols. (Metten 1933–39); R. Molitor, *Aus der Rechtsgeschichte benediktinischer Verbände,* 3 vols. (Münster 1928–33). For various regions cf. Gen. Bib. II, 9; also: *L'Italia benedittina,* ed. by P. Lugano (Rome 1929); P. Grossi, *Le abbazie benedettine nell'alto medioevo italiano. Struttura giuridica, amministrazione e giurisdizione* (Florence 1957); for Germany and Belgium cf. *Hauck* and E. de Moreau (Gen. Bib. II, 4); L. J. Daly, *Benedictine Monasticism. Its Formation and Development through the 12th Cent.* (New York 1965) intended for the beginner, overlooks the present controversy on early Cistercian history, contains English trans. of the so-called Rule of St Augustine, the Prologue of the Benedictine Rule and the Cistercian Carta Caritatis.

MONASTIC RENEWAL IN THE 10TH AND 11TH CENTURIES: E. Sackur, *Die Cluniacenser in ihrer kirchlichen und allgemeingeschichtlichen Wirksamkeit bis zur Mitte des 11. Jahrhunderts,* 2 vols. (Halle 1892–94, new impression, Darmstadt 1965), basic, on Cluny's far-reaching influence; K. Hallinger, *Gorze-Cluny. Studien zu den monastischen Lebensformen und Gegensätzen im Hochmittelalter,* 2 vols. (Rome 1950–51); cf. T. Schieffer in *AMrhKG* 4 (1952), 24–44; E. Werner, *Die gesellschaftlichen Grundlagen der Klosterreform im 11. Jahrhundert* (Berlin 1953); on this Marxist interpretation cf. K. Hallinger in *AMrhKG* 9 (1957), 19–32; P. Doyère, "Érémitisme en Occident" in *DSAM* IV (1961), 953–82; J. Sainsaulieu, "Ermites" in *DHGE* XV (1963), 766–87; id., *L'eremitismo in occidente nei secoli XI e XII: Atti della settimana di studio, Mendola 1962* (Milan 1965).

LOTHARINGIA AND GERMANY: E. Tomek, *Studien zur Reform der deutschen Klöster im 11. Jahrhundert,* I: *Die Frühreform* (Vienna 1910); H. Büttner, "Verfassungsgeschichte und lothringische Klosterreform" in *Festschrift G. Kallen* (Bonn 1957), 17–27; R. Blouard, *S. Gérard de Brogne* (Namur 1959); the contributions to the congress commemorating the 900th anniversary of the death of Gerard held in Maredsous in 1959 are published in *RBén* 70 (1960); for Gorze cf. esp. Hallinger, *Gorze-Cluny (supra);* H. Dauphin, *Le b. Richard, abbé de Saint-Vanne de Verdun* (Louvain–Paris 1946); H. Glaesener, "Saint Poppon, abbé de Stavelot-Malmédy" in *RBén* 60 (1950), 163–79. For Burgundy: B. Bligny, *L'Église et les ordres religieux dans le royaume de Bourgogne aux XIᵉ et XIIᵉ siècles* (Paris 1960).

CLUNY: Sources *(v. supra);* K. Hallinger in *ECatt* III (1949), 1883–93; G. de Valous in *DHGE* XIII (1956), 35–174; A. Chagny, *Cluny et son empire* (Paris, 4th ed. 1949); E. Sackur, K. Hallinger *(v. supra);* G. de Valous, *Le monachisme clunisien des origines au XVᵉ siècle,* 2 vols. (Paris 1935), basic work; L. M. Smith, *Cluny in the XIth and XIIth Cent.* (London 1930); J. Evans, *Monastic Life at Cluny 910–1157* (Oxford 1931); P. Lamma, *Momenti di storiografia cluniacense* (Rome 1961); W. Jorden, *Das cluniacensische Totengedächtniswesen, vornehmlich unter den ersten Äbten* (Münster 1930).

COLLECTED WORKS: *A Cluny, Congrès scientifique . . . en honneur des saints abbés Odon et Odilon* (Dijon 1950); *Spiritualità cluniacense, Convegni del Centro sulla Spiritualità Medievale,* 2 (Todi 1960); *Neue Forschungen über Cluny und die Cluniacenser,* ed. by G. Tellenbach (Freiburg 1959), cf. the collected articles by G. Schreiber, *Gemeinschaftsformen des Mittelalters* (Münster 1948), also the congress contributions of various authors in *Il monachesimo nell'alto medio evo* (Gen. Bib. II, 9).

INDIVIDUAL STUDIES: M. Chaume, "En marge de l'histoire de Cluny" in *RMab* 29 (1939), 41–61; *ibid.* 30 (1940), 33–62; K. Hallinger, "Zur geistigen Welt der Anfänge Clunys" in *DA* 10 (1954), 417–45; continued in *RMab* 46 (1956), 117–41; H. E. Mager, "Studien über das Verhältnis der Cluniacenser zum Eigenkirchenwesen" in *Neue Forschungen über Cluny (v. supra),* 167–217; H. Diener, "Das Verhältnis Clunys zu den Bischöfen" in *Neue Forschungen über Cluny,* 219–352; J. F. Lemarignier, "L'exemption monastique et les origines de la réforme grégorienne" in *A Cluny (v. supra)*, 288–334; id., "Structures monastiques et structures politiques dans la France de la fin du Xe et des débuts du XIe siècle" in *Il monachesimo nell'alto medio evo* (Gen. Bib. II, 9), 357–400; id., "Hiérarchie monastique et hiérarchie féodale" in *Rev. d'hist. de droit franç. et étrang.*, 4e sér. 31 (1953), 171–74; C. Violante, "Il monachesimo cluniacense di fronte al mondo politico ed ecclesiastico (sec. X e XI)" in *Spiritualità cluniacense (v. supra)*, 155–242. On Cluny's *Consuetudines* cf. H. R. Philippeau in *RMab* 44 (1954), 141–51, and K. Hallinger in *ZSavRGkan* 76 (1959), 99–140. T. Schieffer, "Cluny et la querelle des investitures" in *RH* 225 (1961), 47–72; H. Hoffmann, "Cluny und gregorianische Reform" in *AKG* 45 (1963), 165–209.

OTHER FRENCH MONASTIC CENTRES: H. Leclercq, *Saint-Benôit-sur-Loire* (Paris 1925), and with the same title M. Thibout and J. Leclercq (Paris 1945); P. Cousin, *Abbon de Fleury-sur-Loire* (Paris 1954). On Dijon cf. E. Sackur, *Die Cluniacenser (v. supra)*, I, 257–69 and *passim;* for Fruttuaria *ibid.* II, 1–16. Normandy: good survey in H. Wolter, *Ordericus Vitalis* (Wiesbaden 1955), 17–46; J. F. Lemarignier, *Études sur les privilèges d'exemption et de juridiction des abbayes normandes depuis les origines jusqu'à 1140* (Paris 1937). St-Victor: P. Schmid, "Die Entstehung des Marseiller Kirchenstaates" in *AUF* 10 (1928), 176–207; *ibid.* 11 (1930), 138–52.

ITALY: P. Kehr, *Italia Pontificia* (Gen. Bib. I, 5) is indispensable for individual monasteries; organized presentation by Sackur, Grossi, Lugano *(v. supra)* and esp. Penco (Gen. Bib. II, 9); cf. K. Hallinger in *AMrhKG* 9 (1957), 13–19.

SOUTHERN ITALY AND NILUS: Penco, 22–229 (with lit.); A. Boise, *Il monachesimo in Calabria, Sue origini e suo progresso* (Cosenza 1947); A. Guillou, "Il monachesimo greco in Italia meridionale e in Sicilia" in *L'eremitismo in occidente (v. supra:* Monastic Renewal), 355–79; A. Pertusi in *L'eremitismo in occidente,* 382–426 (organizational and cultural aspects); P. Batiffol, *L'abbaye de Rossano* (Paris 1891); for the beginnings in Rossano cf. B. Cappelli, *Bollet. d. Badia greca di Grottaferrata* in NS 9 (1955), 3–26; A. Rocchi, *La Badia di Grottaferrata* (Rome 1904).

ROMUALD: Penco, 211–19; W. Franke, *Romuald von Camaldoli und seine Reformtätigkeit zur Zeit Ottos III.* (Berlin 1913); A. Pagnani, *Vita di S. Romualdo abbate, fondatore dei Camaldolesi* (Sassoferrato 1927); id., *Storia dei benedittini Camaldolesi* (Sassoferrato 1949); G. Palazzini, "S. Romualdo e le sue fondazioni tra i monti del Cagliese" in *Studia Picena* 18 (1948), 61–76.

PETER DAMIANI: Biographical lit. in chap. 42; P. M. Della Santa, *Ricerche sull'idea monastica di S. Pier Damiani* (Camaldoli 1961); also O. Capitani in *L'eremitismo in occidente (v. supra)* 122–63; C. Roggi, "Vita e costumanza dei Romualdini del Pereo, di Fonte Avellana e di Camaldoli" in *Benedictina* 4 (1951), 69–86.

CANONS: For development and organization of the chapters *v. supra* chapter 33 with lit. — Excellent comprehensive history by C. Dereine in *DHGE* XII (1953), 353–405; cf. also L. Hertling, "Kanoniker, Augustinerregel, Augustinerorden" in *ZKTh* 53 (1930), 335–69; G. G. Meersseman, "Die Klerikervereine von Karl dem Grossen bis Innocenz III." in *ZSKG* 46 (1952), 1–42, 81–112; J. Siegwart, *Die Chorherren- und Chorfrauengemeinschaften in der deutschsprachigen Schweiz vom 6. Jahrhundert bis 1160. Mit einem Überblick über die deutsche Kanonikerreform des 10. und 11. Jahrhunderts* (Fribourg 1962). A. Werminghoff, "Die Beschlüsse des Aachener Konzils im Jahre 816" in *NA* 27 (1902), 605–75; O. Hannemann, *Die Kanonikerregeln Chrodegangs von Metz und der Aachener Synode von 816 und das Verhältnis Gregors VII. dazu* (dissertation, Greifswald 1914); L. Musset, "Recherches sur des communautés des clercs réguliers en Normandie au XIe siècle" in *Bull. de la Soc. des Antiquaires de Normandie* 55 (1959–60), 5–38; scattered material on the pre-Gregorian era found in: *La vita comune del clero nei sec. XI e XII, Atti della settimana di studio, Mendola* 1959, 2 vols. (Milan 1962), esp. J. F. Lemarignier, "Aspects politiques de fondations de collégiales dans le royaume de

France en XIe siècle", *ibid.* 19–40; G. Duby, "Les chanoines réguliers et la vie économique des XIe et XIIe siècles", *ibid.* 72–81. H. E. Salter, *Chapters of the Aug. Canons* (Oxford 1922); E. A. Foran, *The Augustinians from St. Augustine to the Union of 1256* (London 1938); J. C. Dickinson, *The Origins of the Austins Canons and their Introduction into England* (London 1951).

40. Education and Learning

LITERATURE

The works cited in Gen. Bib. II, 11 are basic for Latin literature and cultural history; cf. esp. *Manitius* II; De Ghellinck, *Littérature latine au moyen âge*, II; Curtius, *European Literature*, 45–78; also E. R. Curtius, "Das mittelalterliche Bildungswesen und die Grammatik" in *Romanische Forschungen* 60 (1947), 1–26; E. Faral, "Les conditions générales de la production littéraire en Europe occidentale pendant les IXe et Xe siècles" in *I problemi comuni dell'Europa postcarolingia* (Spoleto 1955), 247–94; A. Auerbach, "Lateinische Prosa des 9. und 10. Jahrhunderts. Sermo humilis" in *Romanische Forschungen* 66 (1954), 1–64.

THEOLOGY AND PHILOSOPHY: Contents of works and lit. in *Manitius* II, also to some extent in De Ghellinck *(supra);* for the development of teaching methods cf. basic works in Gen. Bib. II, 12.

CANON LAW: Among the works cited in Gen. Bib. I, 4 *Fournier - Le Bras* I, 268–456, is esp. important; the manuals on the history of ecclesiastical law in Gen. Bib. II, 6; further lit. for this period in *Feine RG* § 17, III.

THE WRITING OF HISTORY: In addition to *Manitius* II cf. *Wattenbach-Holtzmann,* 1–2, and *Jacob-Hohenleutner* II, 1–50.

41. Heretical and Reform Movements among Clergy and Laity (1000 to 1050)

LITERATURE

HERESIES: excellent summary in H. Grundmann, "Ketzergeschichte des Mittelalters" in *Die Kirche in ihrer Geschichte* (Gen. Bib. II, 3), II, G 8 – G 11 (1963); cf. also H. Grundmann, *Religiöse Bewegungen im Mittelalter* (Berlin 1935; new impression 1961), 476–83; A. Borst, *Die Katharer* (Stuttgart 1953), 71–80; P. Ilarino da Milano, "Le eresie populari del sec. XI nell'Europa occidentale" in *StudGreg* II (Rome 1947), 43–89; R. Morghen, *Medioevo cristiano* (Bari 1951), 212–86; a criticism by A. Dondaine, "L'origine de l'hérésie médiévale" in *RSTI* 6 (1952), 47–78; R. Morghen, "Movimenti religiosi popolari nel periodo della riforma della Chiesa" in *X Congresso Internaz. di Scienze Storiche,* Relazioni III (Florence 1955), 333–56; id., "Il cosidetto neo-manicheismo occidentale del sec. XI" in *Acad. nazion. dei Lincei,* Convegno "Volta" (Rome 1957), 84–104; E. Werner, *Klosterreform* (lit. for chap. 39), 71–79; H. J. Warner, *The Albigensian Heresy* (London 1922); S. Runciman, *The Medieval Manichee. A Study of the Christian Dualist Heresy* (Cambridge 1946, new impression 1961); D. Obolensky, *The Bogomils* (Cambridge 1948).

OPPOSITION TO ABUSES: *Hauck KD (passim)* ; *Fliche-Martin* VII *(passim)* ; A. Dresdner, *Kultur- und Sittengeschichte der italienischen Geistlichkeit im 10. und 11. Jahrhundert* (Breslau 1890); useful but somewhat artificial is the survey in A. Fliche, *La réforme grégorienne,* I (Louvain–Paris 1924), 1–128; G. Tellenbach, *Church, State and Christian Society* (Oxford 1959) is important, esp. chapters I–III and the appendix.

SIMONY: H. Meier-Welcker, "Die Simonie im frühen Mittelalter" in ZKG 64 (1952–53), 61–93; A. Kupper, *Beiträge zum Problem der Simonie im 11. Jahrhundert* (typed dissertation, Mainz 1954); J. Leclercq, "Simoniaca haeresis" in *StudGreg* I (1947), 523–30; E. Hirsch, "Der Simoniebegriff und die angebliche Erweiterung im 11. Jahrhundert" in *AkathKR* 86 (1906), 3–19.

THE PEACE OF GOD AND THE TRUCE OF GOD: The earlier works by A. Kluckhohn (1857), E. Sémichon (1869), L. Huberti (1892 well documented), G. C. W. Görris (1912) *et al.* are now superseded by H. Hoffmann, *Gottesfriede und Treuga Dei* (Stuttgart 1964); a worthwhile Marxist interpretation is B. Töpfer, *Volk und Kirche zur Zeit der beginnenden Gottesfriedensbewegung in Frankreich* (Berlin 1957).

HOLY WAR AND CHRISTIAN KNIGHTHOOD: C. Erdmann, *Die Entstehung des Kreuzzugsgedankens* (Stuttgart 1935); contains details on the Peace of God.

Part Two:
The Struggle for the Freedom of the Church

SECTION ONE

The Gregorian Reform

Sources

GENERAL: The polemical literature: *MGLiblit,* 3 vols.; *Manitius* III, 21–57; *Wattenbach-Holtzmann* I, 394–414; C. Mirbt, *Die Publizistik im Zeitalter Gregors VII.* (Leipzig 1894); A. Fauser, *Die Publizisten des Investiturstreites* (dissertation, Munich 1935).

ITALY: unreliable but of some value is Bonzio of Sutri, *Liber ad amicum* (—1085): *MGLiblit* I, 568–620; important is Leo of Marsica, *Chronicon s. monasterii Casinensis* (—1087), continued (—1127) by the monk Guido, revised and continued, not without falsification (–1138) by Petrus Diaconus, *MGSS* 574–844; for a survey of present research see W. Wühr in *StudGreg* III (1948), 399–401; Amatus of Montecassino, *Historia Normannorum,* old French translation in *FontiStIt,* 76 ed. by V. de Bartolomeis (1935); cf. W. Smidt in *StudGreg* III (1948), 173–231; Gaufred Malaterra, *De rebus gestis Rogerii . . . comitis et Roberti Guiscardi ducis* (—1099) in *Muratori* 2nd ed., *SS* V, 1, ed. by E. Pontieri (1925–28); William of Apulia, *Gesta Roberti Wiscardi* in *MGSS* IX, 239–98; Donizo of Canossa, *Vita Mathildis, carmine scripta, Muratori,* 2nd ed., *SS* V, 2, ed. by L. Simeoni, with other sources on the history of the marchioness (1930–40); *MGSS* XII, 348–409; Landulf the Elder, *Historia Mediolanensis* (—1085), *Muratori,* 2nd ed., *SS* IV, 2, ed. by A. Cutolo (1942); *MGSS* VIII, 32–100; more objective is Arnulf, *Gesta archiepiscoporum Mediolanensium* (—1077), *MGSS* VIII, 6–31; cf. *Manitius* III and *Jacob-Hohenleutner* II.

GERMANY AND LOTHARINGIA: *MGDD regum et imperatorum Germaniae,* V: *Die Urkunden Heinrichs III.* (1931; new impression 1957); *ibid.* VI, 1–2: *Die Urkunden Heinrichs IV.* (1941–59); *MGConst* I. *Die Briefe Heinrichs IV.,* ed. by C. Erdmann in *MG Deutsches MA,* 1 (1937); *Briefsammlungen der Zeit Heinrichs IV.,* ed. by Erdmann-Fickermann in *MG Die Briefe der deutschen Kaiserzeit* 5 (1950); *Codex Udalrici* (—1125, with supplements —1134) in *Jaffé, Bibl. rer. germ.* (Gen. Bib. I, 3), V, 17–469; *Vita Heinrici IV* (important for the later years) in *MGSS rer. Germ.* 58, ed. by W. Eberhard (3rd ed. 1899; new imp. 1949); Bruno, *De bello saxonico* in *MG Deutsches MA,* 2, ed. by H. E. Lohmann (1937); among the World Chronicles which began to appear at this time the following are important: Hugh of Flavigny (—1102) in *MGSS* VIII, 288–502; Sigebert of Gembloux (—1111, then continued) in *MGSS* VI, 300–74; Frutolf of Michelsberg (—1101), revised and continued (—1125) by Ekkehard of Aura in *MGSS* VI, 33–265; Berthold of Reichenau, continuator of the Chronicle of Hermann the Lame (—1180) in *MGSS* V, 264–326, and XIII, 730–32; Bernold of St Blasien (—1100) in *MGSS* V, 385–467; Annals: of Niederaltaich (—1073) in *MGSS rer. Germ.* 4, ed. by E. v. Oefele (2nd ed. 1892); Lampert of Hersfeld (—1077) in *MGSS rer. Germ.* 38, ed. by Holder-Egger (3rd ed. 1894; new impression 1956). Important for the northern mission is Adam of Bremen, *Gesta Hammaburgensis ecclesiae pontificum* in *MGSS rer. Germ.,* 2, ed. by

B. Schmeidler (3rd ed. 1917). For the problem of the sources and their worth, cf. *Wattenbach-Holtzmann* I; *Jacob-Hohenleutner* II.

FRANCE (with the exception of the Crusade literature and Normandy): *Recueil des Actes de Philippe Ier (1059–1108), Chart Dipl,* ed. by M. Prou (1908); for the regesta: A. Luchaire, *Louis le Gros, Annales de sa vie et de son règne 1081–1137* (Paris 1890); Suger of Saint Denis, *Vita Ludovici Grossi* in *ClassHist* 11, ed. by H. Waquet (1929); *CollText* 4, ed. by A. Molinier (1887); Hugh of Fleury, *Liber modernorum regum Francorum* (—1108) in *MGSS* IX, 376–95. A good survey with lit. in *Wattenbach-Holtzmann* I, 765–97.

ENGLAND AND NORMANDY: *Regesta regum Anglo-Normannorum 1066–1154,* vol. I, 1–2 (for William I and II), ed. by Davis and Whitwell (Oxford 1913–56); vol. II (for Henry I), ed. by Johnson and Cronne (London 1956); Eadmer, *Historia novorum in Anglia* (—1122) and *Vita Anselmi* in *Rolls Series* 81, ed. by M. Rule (1884); *PL* 159, 347–524; *PL* 158, 49–118; William of Malmesbury, *Historia regum Anglorum* (—1128 with his own additions —1140) in *Rolls Series* 90, 2 vols., ed. by W. Stubbs (1887); William of Malmesbury, *Gesta pontificum Anglorum* (—1125, in 2nd redaction —1140) in *Rolls Series* 52, ed. by N. Hamilton (1870); *PL* 179, 1441–1680; Ordericus Vitalis, *Historiae ecclesiasticae libri XIII* (—1141), ed. by Le Prevost-Guérard-Delisle, 5 vols. (Paris 1838–55); *PL* 188, 15–984; critical study by H. Wolter, *Ordericus Vitalis* (Wiesbaden 1955). Cf. *Manitius* III and *Jacob-Hohenleutner.*

BOHEMIA, POLAND, HUNGARY: Cf. Sources for chap. 31; good survey with lit. in *Wattenbach-Holtzmann* I, 798–820.

GENERAL LITERATURE

For universal histories cf. Gen. Bib. II, 1a, esp. *Peuples et Civilisations,* VI; *Glotz* II, III, VIII, IX, 1; *The Cambridge Med. History,* V; *Historia Mundi,* VI, Cartellieri, *Aufstieg des Papsttums,* and *Vorrang des Papsttums;* also: K. Jordan, "Das Reformpapsttum und die abendländische Staatenwelt" in *WaG* 18 (1958), 122–37.

ECCLESIASTICAL HISTORY: Cf. Gen. Bib. II, 3: *Fliche-Martin* VII, 92–110 and *passim* (—1057), VIII (—1125); also A. Fliche, *La réforme grégorienne,* 3 vols. (Louvain 1924–37); id., *La querelle des investitures* (Paris 1946); G. Tellenbach, *Church, State and Christian Society at the Time of the Investiture Contest* (Oxford, 3rd ed. 1959), trans. with intro. by R. F. Bennett; series *StudGreg,* 7 vols., for an excellent analysis of the first 6 vols. cf. P. E. Schramm in *GGA* 207 (1953), 62–140.

COUNCILS AND PAPAL HISTORY: cf. Gen. Bib. II, 5; *Hefele-Leclercq* IV–V; Haller, *Papsttum,* II, 283 to end; *Seppelt* III, 1–164; J. Gay, *Les papes du XIe siècle et la chrétienté* (Paris 1926), 134 to end.

INDIVIDUAL PROBLEMS: C. Erdmann, *Die Entstehung des Kreuzzugsgedankens* (Stuttgart 1935). Simony: cf. lit. for chap. 41; Reordination: cf. lit. for chap. 53. A. Scharnagl, *Der Begriff der Investitur in den Quellen und in der Literatur des Investiturstreites,* 2 vols. (Stuttgart 1908–09); G. Kallen, *Der Investiturstreit als Kampf zwischen germanischem und romanischem Denken* (Cologne 1937); N. Brooke, *Lay Investiture and its Relation to the Conflict of Empire and Papacy* (Oxford 1939); H. E. Feine, "Kirchenreform und Niederkirchenwesen. Beiträge zur Reformfrage, vornehmlich im Bistum Lucca im 11. Jahrhundert" in *StudGreg* III (1948), 505–24; P. Schmid, *Der Begriff der kanonischen Wahl in den Anfängen des Investiturstreites* (Stuttgart 1926).

GERMANY AND IMPERIAL ITALY: Cf. Gen. Bib. II, 2, esp.: *JbbDG, Unter Heinrich III.,* ed. by E. Steindorff, 2 vols. (Leipzig 1874–81), *Unter Heinrich IV. und Heinrich V.,* ed. by G. Meyer v. Knonau, 7 vols. (Leipzig 1890–1909); *Giesebrecht* II, 419 – III, 963; Hambe-Baethgen, *Kaisergeschichte,* 25–103; *Hauck KD* III, 522 to end; also M. L. Bulst-Thiele, *Kaiserin Agnes*

(Leipzig 1933); O. Schumann, *Die päpstlichen Legaten in Deutschland zur Zeit Heinrichs IV. und Heinrichs V.* (Marburg 1912).

SOUTHERN ITALY: L. v. Heinemann, *Geschichte der Normannen in Unteritalien und Sizilien bis zum Aussterben des normannischen Königshauses* (Leipzig 1894); F. Chalandon, *Histoire de la domination normande en Italie et en Sicile*, 2 vols. (Paris 1907); P. Kehr, "Die Belehnungen der süditalienischen Normannenfürsten durch die Päpste 1059–1192" in *SAB* (1934), no. 1. H. W. Klewitz, "Studien zur Wiederherstellung der römischen Kirche in Süditalien durch das Reformpapsttum" in *QFIAB* 25 (1933–4), 105–57; W. Holtzmann, "Papsttum, Normannen und griechische Kirche" in *Miscellanea Bibliothecae Hertzianae* (Munich 1961), 69–76; L. R. Ménager, "La byzantinisation religieuse de l'Italie méridionale (IXe–XIIe siècle) et la politique monastique des Normands d'Italie" in *RHE* 53 (1958), 747–74; *ibid.* 54 (1959), 5–40; L. T. White, *Latin Monasticism in Norman Sicily* (Cambridge, Mass. 1938); M. Scaduto, *Il monachismo basiliano nella Sicilia medioevale. Rinascita e decadenza sec. XI–XIV* (Rome 1947).

FRANCE: A. Fliche, *Le règne de Philippe Ier, roi de France 1060–1108* (Paris 1912); *Lavisse* II, 2 (Gen. Bib. II, 2). W. Schwarz, "Der Investiturstreit in Frankreich" in *ZKG* 42 (1923), 255–328; *ibid.* 43 (1924), 92–150; A. Becker, *Studien zum Investiturproblem in Frankreich: Papsttum, Königtum und Episkopat im Zeitalter der gregor. Kirchenreform* (dissertation, Saarbrücken 1955); T. Schieffer, *Die päpstlichen Legaten in Frankreich vom Vertrag von Meersen bis zum Schisma von 1130* (Berlin 1935); A. Fliche, "Premiers résultats d'une enquête sur la réforme grégorienne, dans les diocèses français" (completed for the ecclesiastical province of Narbonne) in *Comptes rendus des séances de l'Acad. d. Inscript. et Bell. Lettr.* (1934), 152–80.

ENGLAND, IRELAND AND SCOTLAND: For English national history see Gen. Bib. II, 2, and F. Barlow, *The Feudal Kingdom of England 1042–1216* (London 1955); for Irish and Scottish history see lit. for chap. 29 and E. Curtis, *A History of Medieval Ireland from 1086 to 1513* (Forest-Hills 1944).

For ecclesiastical history cf. Gen. Bib. II, 4; also Z. N. Brooke, *The English Church and the Papacy fom the Conquest to the Reign of John* (Cambridge 1932); H. Böhmer, *Kirche und Staat in England und in der Normandie im 11. und 12. Jahrhundert* (Leipzig 1899); J. Tracy Ellis, *Anti-Papal Legislation in Medieval England 1066–1377* (dissertation, Cath. Univ. Wash. D.C. 1930); H. Tillmann, *Die päpstlichen Legaten in England bis zur Beendigung der Legation Gualas* (dissertation, Bonn 1925); C. N. L. Brooke, "Gregorian Reform in Action. Clerical marriage in England 1050–1200" in *CambrHJ* 12 (1956), 1–21; A. Gwynn in *IER* 57 (1941), 213–33 (Ireland and Rome in the 11th cent.); *ibid.* 481–500, *ibid.* 58 (1941), 1–15 (Lanfranc and the Irish Church), *ibid.* 59 (1942), 1–14 (Anselm and the Irish Church).

SPAIN: Gen. Bib. II, 2 and 4: also R. Ménendez Pidal, *La España del Cid*, 2 vols. (Madrid 1929); L. de la Calzada, "Alfonso VI y la crisis occidental del siglo XI" in *An. de la Univ. de Murcia* 12 (1953–54), 9–86; G. Säbekow, *Die päpstlichen Legationen nach Spanien und Portugal bis zum Ausgang des 12. Jahrhunderts* (dissertation, Berlin 1931); D. Mansilla, *La curia Romana y el reino de Castilla en un momento decisivo de su historia 1061–1085* (Burgos 1944); C. Erdmann, "Das Papsttum und Portugal im ersten Jahrhundert der portugiesischen Geschichte" in *AAB* (1928), no. 5; P. Kehr, "Das Papsttum und der Katalanische Prinzipat bis zur Vereinigung mit Aragón" in *AAB* (1926), 1–91; id., "Das Papsttum und die Königreiche Navarra und Aragón bis zur Mitte des 12. Jahrhunderts" in *AAB* (1928), 1–58; id., "Wie und wann wurde das Reich Aragón ein Lehen der römischen Kirche" in *AAB* (1928), 196–233; J. Vincke, *Kirche und Staat in Katalonien und Aragón während des Mittelalters*, I (Münster 1931); id., "Der Übergang vom Eigenkirchenrecht zum Patronatsrecht bezüglich der Niederkirchen in Katalonien und Aragón" in *StudGreg* III (1948), 451–61. Cf. lit. for chap. 29 and *infra* chapters 43–44.

42. Beginning of the Reform: The German Popes (1046 to 1057)

SOURCES

Watterich I, 93–188; *Duchesne LP* II, 273–7, 332–4; cf. H. Tritz, "Die hagiographischen Quellen zur Geschichte Papst Leos IX." in *StudGreg* IV (1952), 191–353; the very important Vita generally ascribed to Wibert: *ActaSS* Apr. II, 648–65, *PL* 143, 465–504, is considered by Tritz to be the work of Humbert of Silva Candida; for a well supported contrary view, H. Hoffmann in *AKG* 45 (1963), 203–09. — *Mansi* XIX, 619–862; *Hefele-Leclercq* IV, 2, 995–1125; other sources in the footnotes.

LITERATURE

See literature at the beginning of this section.

PAPACY: good bibliography with lit. in Snatifaller, *Reichskirchensystem* (Gen. Bib. II, 8a), 205–16; C. Höfler, *Die deutschen Päpste*, 2 vols. (Regensburg 1839), still valuable; P. Brucker, *L'Alsace et l'Église au temps du pape Saint Léon IX*, 2 vols. (Paris 1889), E. Martin, *Saint Léon IX* (Paris 1904); L. Sittler and P. Stintzi, *Saint Léon, le pape alsacien* (Colmar 1951); Larose, *Étude sur les origines du pape Saint Léon IX* (Metz 1954); Centenaire de la mort de Saint Léon (Colmar 1954); J. Drehmann, *Leo IX. und die Simonie* (Leipzig 1908), not always correct; N. N. Hugghebaert in *StudGreg* I (1947) 417–32 (Leo and the struggle against simony in Verdun); G. Drioux in *StudGreg* II (1947), 31–41 (Leo and the bishops of Langres).

HUMBERT OF SILVA CANDIDA: A. Michel, "Die Anfänge des Kard. Humbert bei Bruno von Toul" in *StudGreg* III (1948), 299–319; id., "Die folgenschweren Ideen des Kard. Humbert und ihr Einfluss auf Gregor VII." in *StudGreg* I (1947), 65–92; id., "Humbert von Silva Candida bei Gratian. Eine Zusammenfassung" in *Studia Gratiana* I (Bologna 1953), 83–117; more in the footnotes.

PETER DAMIAN: F. Dressler, *Petrus Damiani. Leben und Werk* (Rome 1954); J. Leclercq, *Saint Pierre Damien, ermite et Homme d'Église* (Rome 1960); O. J. Blume, *St. Peter Damian. His Teaching on the Spiritual Life* (Washington 1947); id., "The Monitor of the Popes: St. Peter Damian" in *StudGreg* II (1947), 459–76; J. Ryan, *Saint Peter Damiani and his Canonical Sources* (Toronto 1956); good bibliographical survey by K. Reindel in *DA* 15 (1959), 23 n. 1; further lit. *infra* in footnotes.

43. Progress of the Reform: The Lotharingian and Tuscan Popes (1057 to 1073)

SOURCES

Cf. sources cited at the beginning of this section; *Watterich* I, 188–290; *Duchesne LP* II, 278–81, 334–37; *Mansi* XIX, 861 – XX, 56; synods of Nicholas II also in *MGConst* I, 537–51; *Hefele-Leclercq* IV, 2, 1125–1289; for the *Pataria*, in addition to the works of Landulf and Arnulf of Milan cited at the beginning of this Sect., cf. also Andrew of Strumi, "Vita S. Arialdi" in *ActaSS* Junii, V, 281–303.

LITERATURE

PAPACY: G. Despy, "La carrière lotharingienne du pape Étienne IX" in *Revue belge de phil. et d'hist.* 31 (1953), 955–72; G. B. Borino, "L'arcidiaconato di Ildebrando" in *StudGreg* III (1948), 463–516; A. Michel, "Humbert und Hildebrand bei Nikolaus II." in *HJ* 72 (1953), 133–61; R. Scheffer-Boichorst, *Die Neuordnung der Papstwahl durch Nikolaus II.* (Strasbourg 1879); A. Michel, *Papstwahl und Königsrecht oder das Papstwahlkonkordat von 1059* (Munich 1936); id., "Das Papstwahlpactum von 1059" in *HJ* 59 (1939), 291–351; H. G. Krause, "Das Papstwahldekret von 1059 und seine Rolle im Investiturstreit" in *StudGreg* VII (1960);

F. Kempf, "Pier Damiani und das Papstwahldekret von 1059" in *ArchHP* 2 (1964), 73–89; F. Heberhold, "Die Beziehungen des Cadalus von Parma zu Deutschland" in *HJ* 54 (1934), 84–104; id., "Die Angriffe des Cadalus von Parma auf Rom 1062–1063"in *StudGreg* II (1947), 447–503; G. B. Borino, "Cencio del prefetto, l'attentatore di Gregorio VII" in *StudGreg* IV (1952), 373–410.

INDIVIDUAL LANDS: On the military action in England, Spain, Sicily and Milan and its relation to the reform papacy, cf. esp. Erdmann, *Kreuzzugsgedanke,* 116–30, 137–41, 167–9, as well as the lit. in the bibliography for this section corresponding to various lands. Further lit. on Italy: H. Glaesener, "Un mariage fertile en conséquences: Godefroid le Barbu et Béatrix de Toscana" in *RHE* 42 (1947), 379–416; A. Violante, *La Pataria milanese e la riforma ecclesiastica,* I: *Le premesse 1045–1057* (Rome 1955); G. Miccoli, "Per la storia della Pataria milanese" in *BIStIAM* 70 (1958), 43–123; id., *StudGreg* V (1956), 33–81 (see footnote 9 in this chapter). For England: T. J. Oleson, "Edward the Confessor's Promise of the Throne to Duke William of Normandy" in *EHR* 72 (1957), 221–28; cf. D. Douglas in *EHR* 69 (1953), 526–45. For Spain: P. Boissonade, "Cluny, la papauté et la première croisade internationale contre les Sarrasins: Barbastro 1063/64" in *RQH* 117 (1932), 257–301; for the Mozarabic rite cf. lit. for next chapter.

44. *Pope Gregory VII (1073 to 1085)*

SOURCES

Mansi XX, 55–630; *Hefele-Leclercq* V, 1, 13–323. — The Register of Gregory VII: *MGEp* sel. 2, ed. by E. Caspar, 2 vols. (1920–23); further letters: *Jaffé; Bibl. rer. germ.* (Gen. Bib. I, 3), II, 520 seqq.; Privileges: L. Santifaller, *Quellen und Forschungen zum Urkunden- und Kanzleiwesen Gregors VII.:* I. *Quellen, Urkunden, Regesten, Facsimilia* (Vatican City 1957); W. M. Peitz, "Das Originalregister Gregors VII. im Vatikanischen Archiv in *SAW* 145, 5 (1911); E. Caspar, "Studien zum Register Gregors VII." in *NA* 38 (1913), 143–226; H. W. Klewitz, "Das 'Privilegienregister' Gregors VII." in *AUF* 16 (1939), 385–424; the well founded opinion of Peitz and Caspar that the Vatican Archives possessed an original register placed in the chancery has been recently contested by F. Bock in *StudGreg* V (1956), 243–79; G. M. Borino in *StudGreg* V, 391–402; *ibid.* VI (1959–61), 363–89; R. Morghen, "Ricerche sulla formazione del Registro di Gregorio VII" in *Annali di storia di Diritto* 3/4 (1959–60), 35–65. The latter accepts it as a selection from a memoire dictated by Gregory; the entire problem must be newly researched using the paleographical and documentary criteria of Peitz and Caspar.

BIOGRAPHICAL: *Watterich* I, 239–543; *Duchesne LP* II, 282–91; for the *Vita* of Paul of Bernried (besides Watterich *ActaSS* Maii, VI, 113–43) H. Fuhrmann in *StudGreg* V (1956), 299–312. The *Vita Anselmi ep. Lucensis* in *MGSS* XII, 13–35 is useful; Rangerius of Lucca, *Vita metrica S. Anselmi* in *MGSS* XXX, 1152–55; cf. P. Guidi in *StudGreg* I (1947), 263–80 (Rangerius's home). For Bonizo of Sutri, Donizo of Canossa and others see sources for this sect.

LITERATURE

GENERAL WORKS, see lit. at the beginning of this section; W. Martens, *Gregor VII. Sein Leben und Wirken,* 2 vols. (Leipzig 1894); E. Caspar, "Gregor VII. in seinen Briefen" in *HZ* 130 (1924), 1–30; A. Fliche, *Grégoire VII* (Paris, 4th ed. 1928); W. Wühr, *Studien zu Gregor VII. Kirchenreform* und *Weltpolitik* (Munich-Freising 1930); M. J. MacDonald, *Hildebrand. Life of Gregory VII* (London 1932); J. P. Whitney, *Hildebrandine Essays* (Cambridge 1932); A. B. Cavanagh, *Pope Gregory VII and the Theocratic State* (dissertation, Cath. Univ. Wash. D.C. 1934); H. X. Arquillière, *Saint Grégoire. Essai sur sa conception du pouvoir pontifical* (Paris 1934); R. Morghen, *Gregorio VII* (Turin 1942). E. Bernheim, *Mittelalterliche Zeitanschauungen in ihrem Einfluss auf Politik und Geschichtsschreibung* (Tübingen 1918), 202–21; A. Nischke,

"Die Wirksamkeit Gottes in der Welt Gregors VII." in *StudGreg* V (1956), 115–219; H. X. Arquillière, "La signification théologique du pontificat de Grégoire VII" in *Rev. de l'Univ. d'Ottawa* 20 (1950), 140–61; G. Soranzo, "Aspetti del pensiero dell'opera di Gregorio VII e lo spirito dei tempi" in *Aevum* 22 (1948), 309–32; id., "Gregorio VII e gli Stati vasalli della Chiesa" *ibid.* (1949), 131–58; V. Ussani in *StudGreg* II (1947), 341–59 (Gregory's style); P. S. Leicht in *StudGreg* I (1947), 93–110 (Gregory and Roman law); L. F. J. Meulenberg, *Der Primat der römischen Kirche im Denken und Handeln Gregors VII.* ('s Gravenhage 1965).

THE CHRISTIAN EAST: G. Hofmann, "Papst Gregor und der christliche Osten" in *StudGreg* I (1947), 169–81; W. Ziegler, "Gregor VII. und der Kijewer Grossfürst Izjaslav" in *StudGreg* I (1947), 387–411; V. Meystowicz, "L'union de Kiew avec Rome sous Grégoire VII. Avec notes sur les précédents et sur le rôle de Pologne" in *StudGreg* V (1956), 83–108; D. Oljančyn, "Zur Regierung des Grossfürsten Izjaslav-Demeter von Kiev" in *Jahrbücher für Geschichte Osteuropas* NS 8 (1960), 397–410; W. Holtzmann, "Studien zur Orientpolitik und zur Entstehung des ersten Kreuzzugs" in *HV* 22 (1924), 167–99; id., *Beiträge zur Reichs- und Verfassungsgeschichte des hohen Mittelalters* (Bonn 1957), 51–78.

INDIVIDUAL LANDS OF THE WEST: Cf. at the beginning of this section.

IRELAND: A. Gwynn, "Gregory and the Irish Church" in *StudGreg* III (1948), 105–28.

SPAIN: L. de la Calzada, "La proyección del pensamiento de Gregorio VII en los reinos de Castilla y León" in *StudGreg* III (1948), 1–87; B. Llorca, "Derechos de la Santa Sede sobre España. El pensamiento de Gregorio VII" in *Sacerdozio e Regno da Gregorio VII a Bonifacio VIII* (Rome 1954), 79–105; J. F. Rivera, "Gregorio VII y la liturgia mozárabe" in *RET* 2 (1942), 3–33; F. Pérez, "San Gregorio VII y la liturgia española" in *Liturgia* 3 (1948), 105–13; 323–30; A. Urbieto Arteta, "La introducción de rito romano en Aragón y Navarra" in *HS* 1 (1948), 299–324; R. B. Donovan, *The Liturgical Drama in Medieval Spain* (Toronto 1958); P. David, *Études historiques* (lit. for chap. 29), 341–439 (Gregory, Cluny and Alphonso VI).

FRANCE: O. Meyer, "Reims und Rom unter Gregor VII." in *ZSavRGkan* 59 (1939), 418–52; H. Gaul, *Manasses I., Erzbischof von Reims,* I (Essen 1940); J. R. Williams in *AHR* 54 (1949), 804–29 (Manasses and Gregory).

ITALY: G. B. Borino, "Cencio del Prefetto, l'attentatore di Gregorio VII" in *StudGreg* IV (1952), 373–440; *ibid.* 456–65 (actual time of the excommunication of Hugh the White and Guibert of Ravenna); A. Overmann, *Gräfin Mathilde von Canossa* (Innsbruck 1895); G. Nencioni, *Matilde di Canossa* (Milan, 2nd ed. 1940); L. Simeoni, "Il contributo della contessa Matilde nella lotta per le investiture" in *StudGreg* I (1947), 353–72; on the Donations: P. Scheffer-Boichorst, *Gesammelte Schriften,* I (Berlin 1903), 87 seqq.; T. Leccisotti in *StudGreg* I (1947), 306–19 (meeting of Desiderius of Montecassino with Henry IV in Albano).

GERMANY: A. Brackmann, "Gregor VII. und die kirchliche Reformbewegung in Deutschland" in *StudGreg* II (1947), 7–30; C. Erdmann, *Studien zur Briefliteratur Deutschlands im 11. Jahrhundert* (Leipzig 1938), 225–81 (Gregory and Germany in the years 1073–75); A. Mayer-Pfannholz, "Die Wende von Canossa" in *Hochland* 30 (1933), 385–404; R. Wahl, *Der Gang nach Canossa, Kaiser Heinrich IV. Eine Historie* (Munich, 2nd ed. 1951); W. von den Steinen, *Canossa. Heinrich IV. und die Kirche* (Munich 1957).

45. *Stubborn Fight and Victory: From Victor III to Calixtus II*

SOURCES

Watterich I, 559 – II, 153; *Duchesne LP* II, 292–326, 338–48, 369–79, III (also Gen. Bib. I, 5) 143–69. — *Mansi* XX, 629 - XXI, 318; *Hefele-Leclercq* V, 1, 325–644. Further sources pp. 536 f.

LITERATURE

See the literature cited on pp. 537f.

CLEMENT III: O. Köhncke, *Wibert von Ravenna: Papst Clemens III.* (Leipzig 1888); P. Kehr, "Zur Geschichte Wiberts von Ravenna" in *SAB* (1921), 355–68, 973–88; K. Jordan, "Die Stellung Wiberts von Ravenna in der Publizistik des Investiturstreites" in *MIÖG* 62 (1954), 155–64.

VICTOR III: A. Fliche, "Le pontificat de Victor III" in *RHE* 20 (1924), 387–412; A. Rony, "L'élection de Victor III. Conflit entre le nouveau pape et Hugues, archevêque de Lyon" in *RHEF* 14 (1928), 145–60.

PONTIFICATE OF URBAN II: All available literature contained in the basic work of A. Becker, *Papst Urban II.,* part I: *Herkunft und kirchliche Laufbahn. Der Papst und die lateinische Christenheit* (Stuttgart 1964); F. J. Gossman, *Pope Urban II and Canon Law* (dissertation, Washington, Cath. Univ. 1960); R. Crozet, "Le voyage d'Urbain II et ses négotiations avec le clergé de France 1095/96" in *RH* 179 (1937), 271–310. For southern Italy cf. literature on page 538, especially Klewitz in *QFIAB* 25 (1934–5), 105–57; also E. Caspar, *Roger II. und die Gründung der normannisch-sizilischen Monarchie* (Innsbruck 1904); E. Jordan, "La politique ecclésiastique de Roger Ier et les origines de la 'légation sicilienne'" in *MA* 24 (1922), 237–73; *ibid.* 25 (1923), 32–65; on his relations with Byzantium relating to the First Crusade cf. lit. for chap. 51.

PASCHAL II AND THE INVESTITURE PROBLEM: B. Monod, *Essai sur les rapports de Pascal II et de Philippe Ier* (Paris 1907); H. Hoffmann, "Ivo von Chartres und die Lösung des Investiturproblems" in *DA* 15 (1959), 393–440; R. Sprandel, *Ivo von Chartres und seine Stellung in der Kirchengeschichte* (Stuttgart 1962); I. Ott, "Der Regalienbegriff im 12. Jahrhundert" in *ZSavRGkan* 66 (1948), 234–304; N. F. Cantor, *Church, Kingship and Lay Investiture in England 1098–1135* (Princeton, N. J., 1958); K. Pivec, "Die Bedeutung des ersten Romzugs Heinrichs V." in *MIÖG* 52 (1938), 217–25; W. Kratz, *Der Armutsgedanke im Entäußerungsplan des Papstes Paschalis II.* (dissertation, Freiburg 1933).

PONTIFICATES OF GELASIUS II AND CALIXTUS II: R. Krohn, *Der päpstliche Kanzler Johannes von Gaeta: Gelasius II.* (Berlin 1918); O. Engels, "Papst Gelasius II. als Hagiograph" in *QFIAB* 35 (1935), 1–45; C. Erdmann, "Mauritius Burdinus (Gregor VIII.)" in *QFIAB* 19 (1927), 205–61; P. David, *Études historiques* (lit. for chap. 28), 441–501 (L'énigme de Maurice Bourdin); A. Maurer, *Papst Calixt II.,* 2 parts (Munich 1886–89); U. Robert, *Histoire du pape Calixte II* (Paris 1891); T. Schieffer, "Nochmals die Verhandlungen von Mouzon" in *Festschrift E. E. Stengel* (Münster–Cologne 1952), 324–41; E. Bernheim, *Das Wormser Konkordat und seine Vorurkunde* (Breslau 1906); A. Hofmeister, "Das Wormser Konkordat. Zum Streit um seine Bedeutung" in *Festschrift Dietr. Schäfer* (Jena 1915), 64–148.

SECTION TWO

The Byzantine Church from 886 to 1054

47. *The Road to Schism*

SOURCES

C. Will, *Acta et scripta quae de controversiis ecclesiae grecae et latinae saeculo XI extant* (Leipzig 1861). Denunciation of Caerularius by Psellus = L. Bréhier, "Un discours inédit de Psellos" in *RÉG* 16 (1903), 375–416, and 17 (1904), 34–76; J. Hergenröther, *Monumenta graeca ad Photium eiusque historiam pertinentia* (Regensburg 1869), contains sources for the 11th century; A. Demetrakopulos, *Bibliotheca Ecclesiastica,* I (Leipzig 1866).

LITERATURE

L. Bréhier, *Le schisme oriental du XIᵉ siècle* (Paris 1899); A. Michel, *Humbert und Kerullarios,* 2 vols. (Paderborn 1924–30); id., "Schisma und Kaiserhof im Jahre 1054" in *L'église et les églises,* I (Chevetogne 1954), 351–440; S. Runciman, *The Eastern Schism: A Study of the Papacy and the Eastern Churches During the XIth and XIIth Centuries* (Oxford 1955).

SECTION THREE

Changes in the Christian West during the Gregorian Reform

49. *The New Shape of the Church: Law and Organization before Gratian*

SOURCES OF LAW

Atto of Milan, *Breviarium,* ed. by A. Mai, *Scriptorum veterum nova collectio,* VI, 2 (Rome 1832), 60–102; *Anselmi episcopi Lucensis collectio,* ed. by F. Thaner (Innsbruck 1906–15), lacking here are a part of lib. XI and all of XII–XIII; *Die Kanonessammlung des Kardinals Deusdedit,* ed. by Wolf v. Glanvel (Paderborn 1905); P. Martinucci, *Deusdedit presbyteri cardinalis collectio* (Venice 1869); Bonizo of Sutri, *Liber de vita christiana,* ed. by E. Perels (Berlin 1930); Cardinalis Gregorius, *Polycarpus,* ed. Ballerini, *De antiquis collectionibus,* IV, c. 17: A. Gallandius, *De vetustis canonum collectionibus sylloge,* I (Mainz 1790); Ivo of Chartres, *Decretum* in *PL* 161, 47–1022, *Panormia, ibid.,* 1041–1344 (Ivo's *Collectio Tripartita* remains unedited); *Collectio Caesaraugustana,* ed. by Ballerini *(v. supra)* IV, c. 18.

LITERATURE

FOR THE SOURCES AND DEVELOPMENT OF CANON LAW: Fournier – Le Bras, *Histoire des collections,* II (Gen. Bib. I, 4); Stickler, *Historia Fontium* (Gen. Bib. I, 4), 160–95; *Feine RG* § 17, III; Plöchl, *Kirchenrecht* (Gen. Bib. II, 6) II (1955), 405–11; A. Michel, *Die Sentenzen des Kardinals Humbert. Das erste Rechtsbuch der päpstlichen Reform* (Stuttgart 1943), and Michel's response to objections of J. Haller and F. Pelster in *StudGreg* III (1948), 149–61; A. Authenrieth, "Bernold von Konstanz und die erweiterte 74-Titel-Sammlung" in *DA* 14 (1958), 375–94; R. Montanari, *La "collectio canonum" di S. Anselmo di Lucca e la riforma gregoriana* (Mantua 1941); A. Fliche, "La valeur historique de la collectio canonum d'Anselme de Lucques" in *Misc. hist. in honor. A. De Meyer,* I (Louvain 1946), 348–57; U. Lewald, *An der Schwelle der Scholastik. Bonizo von Sutri und das Kirchenrecht seiner Tage* (Weimar 1938). For Bonizo also E. Nasalli-Rocca di Corneliano in *StudGreg* II (1947), 151–62; J. T. Gilchrist, "Canon Law Aspects of the 11th Century Reform" in *JEH* 13 (1962), 21–38.

ON LAYMEN IN THE CHURCH: Plöchl, *Kirchenrecht* (Gen. Bib. II, 6) II (1955), 160 seqq.; *Feine RG* § 34; both manuals contain further material in the chapters on parishes.

PATRONATUS: *Feine RG* § 24, II, § 32, II; Plöchl, *Kirchenrecht,* 368–71; U. Stutz, "Patronat" in *RE* 15 (1904), 13–26; id., "Eigenkirche", *ibid.* 23 (1913), 375–77; id., "Gratian und die Eigenkirche" in *ZSavRGkan* 32 (1911), 1–33, and 33 (1912), 342 seq.

BISHOPS, METROPOLITANS, PRIMATES: Werminghoff, *Verfassungsgeschichte* (Gen. Bib. II, 6), 118–59; *Feine RG* § 31, § 24, III (with lit.); Plöchl, *Kirchenrecht,* 126–59; H. Fuhrmann, "Studien zur Geschichte mittelalterlicher Patriarchate II–III" in *ZSavRGkan* 71 (1954), 1–84; *ibid.* 72 (1955), 95–183; A. Felbinger, "Die Primatialprivilegien von Gregor VII. bis Innozenz III." in *ZSavRGkan* 68 (1951), 15–163.

PAPACY: *Feine RG* § 28–30 (with lit.); Plöchl, *Kirchenrecht,* 20–100; R. Zoepffel, *Die Papstwahlen vom 11. bis 14. Jahrhundert* (Göttingen 1872); F. Wasner, *De consecratione, inthronisatione, coronatione Summi Pontificis* (Rome 1936); E. Eichmann, *Weihe und Krönung des Papstes im Mittelalter* (Munich 1951); A. Hauck, "Rezeption und Umbildung der allgemeinen Synoden im Mittelalter" in *HV* 10 (1907), 465–82; E. Voosen, *Papauté et pouvoir civil à l'époque de Grégoire VII* (Gembloux 1927), 94–157 (the Primacy); H. Weisweiler, "Die päpstliche Gewalt in den Schriften Bernolds von St. Blasien" in *StudGreg* IV (1952), 129–47; K. Hofmann, *Der "Dictatus Papae" Gregors VII.* (Paderborn 1933).

PAPAL LEGATES: K. Ruess, *Die rechtliche Stellung der päpstlichen Legaten bis Bonifaz VIII.* (Paderborn 1912); important is the lit. for Part II, Section one, with works on the legations in Germany (O. Schumann), in England (H. Tillmann), France (T. Schieffer), Spain (G. Säbekow).

CARDINALS: V. Martin, *Les cardinaux et la curie* (Paris 1930); J. B. Sägmüller, *Die Tätigkeit und Stellung der Kardinäle bis Papst Bonifaz VIII.* (Freiburg 1896); H. W. Klewitz, "Die Entstehung des Kardinalkollegiums" in *ZSavRGkan* 56 (1936), 115–221, new impression in Klewitz, *Reformpapsttum und Kardinalkolleg* (Darmstadt 1957), 1–134; S. Kuttner, "Cardinalis. The History of a Canonical Concept" in *Tr* 3 (1945), 129–214; M. Andrieu, "L'origine du titre de Cardinal" in *MiscMercati* V (Vatican City 1946), 113–44; K. Ganzer, *Die Entwicklung des auswärtigen Kardinalats im hohen Mittelalter* (Tübingen 1963); further lit. in *Feine RG* § 28, II.

ROMAN CURIA: K. Jordan, "Die Entstehung der römischen Kurie" in *ZSavRGkan* 59 (1939), 96–152; id., "Die päpstliche Verwaltung im Zeitalter Gregors VII." in *StudGreg* I (1947), 111–35; J. Sydow, "Untersuchungen zur kurialen Verwaltungsgeschichte im Zeitalter des Reformpapsttums" in *DA* 11 (1954), 18–73; R. Elze, "Die päpstliche Kapelle im 12.–13. Jahrhundert" in *ZSavRGkan* 67 (1950), 145–204; J. Sydow, "Cluny und die Anfänge der Apostol. Kammer" in *SM* 63 (1951), 45–66; D. B. Zema, "Economic Reorganisation of the Roman See during the Gregorian Reform" in *StudGreg* I (1947), 137–68.

50. *The New Relationship of the Church to Western Christendom*

LITERATURE

For political ideologies cf. works in Gen. Bib. II, 8b; *ibid.*, II, 8a citations by Kern, *Gottesgnadentum*, David, *La souveraineté*, and O. Gierke, *Genossenschaftsrecht*, esp. vol. III, 502–644, on the publicists of the Middle Ages. Also L. Knabe, *Die gelasianische Zweigewaltenlehre bis zum Ende des Investiturstreites* (Berlin 1936); cf. Maitland's work, *Political Theories of the Middle Ages* (Cambridge 1900) containing one of the sections of Gierke's *The German Law of Associations;* E. Lewis, *Medieval Political Ideas,* 2 vols. (London 1954); C. H. McIlwain, *The Growth of Political Thought in the West from the Greeks to the End of the Middle Ages* (New York 1932); G. Tellenbach, *Church, State and Christian Society* (Lit. Sect. I), 48–76, 175–92; W. Ullmann, *The Growth of Papal Government* (Gen. Bib. II, 5) 253–412, and also F. Kempf *(ibid.),* 135–53; E. Voosen, *Papauté et pouvoir civil à l'époque de Grégoire VII. Contribution à l'histoire du droit public* (Gembloux 1927); A. Fliche, "Les théories germaniques de la souveraineté à la fin du XIᵉ siècle" in *RH* 125 (1917), 1–67; G. Ladner, "Aspects of Medieval Thought on Church and State" in *Review of Politics* 9 (1947), 403–22; F. Kempf, "Zur politischen Lehre der früh- und hochmittelalterlichen Kirche" in *ZSavRGkan* 78 (1961), 403–22; id., "Kanonistik und kuriale Politik im 12. Jahrhundert" in *AHPont* 1 (1963), 11–52.

ON CHRISTENDOM: G. Tellenbach, "Die Bedeutung des Reformpapsttums für die Einigung des Abendlandes" in *StudGreg* II (1947), 125–49; J. Rupp, *L'idée de chrétienté dans la pensée Pontificale des origines à Innocent III* (Paris 1939); É. Gilson, *Les métamorphoses de la Cité de Dieu* (Louvain–Paris 1952); G. Ladner, "The Concepts of 'Ecclesia' and 'Christianitas' and their Relation to the Idea of Papal 'Plenitudo potestatis' from Gregory VII to Boniface VIII" in *Sacerdozio e Regno da Gregorio VII a Bonifacio VIII* (Rome 1954), 49–77; F. Kempf, "Das

Problem der Christianitas im 12.–13. Jahrhundert" in *HJ* 79 (1960), 104–23; J. van Laarhoven, "'Christianitas' et réforme grégorienne" in *StudGreg* VI (1959–61), 1–98.

IMPERIAL INSIGNIA OF THE POPES: H. W. Klewitz, "Die Krönung des Papstes" in *ZSavRGkan* 61 (1941), 96–130; P. E. Schramm, "Sacerdotium und Regnum im Austausch ihrer Vorrechte" in *StudGreg* II (1947), 403–57; cf. also footnote 8 of this chapter and the lit. cited in previous chapter by Zoepffel, Wasner, Eichmann on election and enthronement.

PAPACY AND STATES: K. Bierbach, *Kurie und nationale Staaten im frühen Mittelalter* (Dresden 1938); K. Jordan, "Das Eindringen des Lehnwesens in das Rechtsleben der römischen Kurie" in *AUF* 12 (1932), 13–110; id., "Das Reformpapsttum und die abendländische Staatenwelt" in *WaG* 18 (1958), 122–37; for individual states cf. lit. in section two.

51. *The Papacy, the Holy Wars, and the First Crusade*

SOURCES

For sources and literature H. E. Mayer, *Bibliographie zur Geschichte der Kreuzzüge* (Hanover 1960) is always reliable; cf. also A. S. Atiya, *The Crusade. Historiography and Bibliography* (Bloomington, Ind., 1962).

DOCUMENTS AND LETTERS: R. Röhricht, *Regesta regni Hierosolimitani 1097–1291* (Innsbruck 1893) with Additamentum (1904); *Epistolae et chartae historiam primi belli sacri spectantes*, ed. by H. Hagenmeyer (Innsbruck 1901); H. Hagenmeyer, *Chronologie de la première croisade* (Paris 1901).

REPORTS: *Anonymi Gesta Francorum et aliorum Hierosolimitanorum*, ed. by H. Hagenmeyer (Heidelberg 1890), new editions by R. Hill (London 1962); Fulcher of Chartres, *Historia Hierosolymitana* in *Recueil des historiens des croisades* (Gen. Bib. I, 3: *Acad. des Inscr.*), *Historiens occid.*, III, 319–485; Radulf of Caen, *Gesta Tancredi in expeditione Hierosolymitana* in *Historiens occid.*, III, 603–716; Raymund of Aguilers, *Historia Francorum qui ceperunt Hierusalem* in *Historiens occid.*, III, 235–309; Albert of Aachen, *Historia Hierosolymitana* in *Historiens occid.*, IV; Ekkehard of Aura, *Hierosolymitica*, ed. by H. Hagenmeyer (Heidelberg 1877); Anna Comnena, *Alexiade. Règne de l'empereur Alexis I Comnène*, ed. by B. Leib (with French translation), 3 vols. (Paris 1937–45); for Arabic, Persian, Armenian, and other sources cf. bibliography by H. Mayer and S. Runciman, *A History of the Crusades*, I (Cambridge, 6th ed. 1962), 342–60.

LITERATURE

GENERAL HISTORIES OF THE CRUSADES: Mayer and Runciman *(v. supra);* the brilliant but at times francophile work of R. Grousset, *Histoire des croisades et du royaume franc de Jérusalem,* 3 vols. (Paris 1934–36) is now superseded by S. Runciman, *A History of the Crusades*, 3 vols. (Cambridge, 6th ed. 1962), German transl. by P. de Mendelsohn, *Geschichte der Kreuzzüge,* 3 vols. (Munich 1957–60); *A History of the Crusades*, Editor-in-Chief K. M. Setton: vol. I, ed. by H. W. Baldwin: *The First Hundred Years* (Philadelphia 1955), vol. II, ed. by R. L. Wolf and H. W. Hazard: *The Later Crusades 1189–1311* (1962), three more volumes will follow; A. Waas, *Geschichte der Kreuzzüge,* 2 vols. (Freiburg 1956). On these three works cf. H. E. Mayer in *GGA* 211 (1957), 234–46 (critique of Waas), *ibid.,* 214 (1960), 42–63 (critique of Runciman); still valuable is P. Rousset, *Histoire des croisades* (Paris 1957); A. S. Atiya, *Crusade, Commerce and Culture* (Bloomington, Ind., 1962); H. E. Mayer, *Geschichte der Kreuzzüge* (Stuttgart 1965), a critical and penetrating analysis of previous works.

THE FIRST CRUSADE: Mayer, *Bibliographie (v. supra),* 1902–2007; Runciman, *A History of the Crusades,* I, 342–60; F. Chalandon, *Histoire de la première croisade jusqu'à l'élection de Godefroi de Bouillon* (Paris 1924); C. D. J. Brandt, *Kruisvaarders naar Jeruzalem. Geschiedenis van de eerste kruistocht* (Utrecht 1950); R. Rousset, *Les origines et les caractères de la première croisade* (dissertation, Neuchâtel 1945).

CRUSADING IDEA AND THE ORIGIN OF THE CRUSADES: C. Erdmann, *Die Entstehung des Kreuzzugsgedankens* (Stuttgart 1935, reprinted 1955); P. Alphandéry and A. Dupront, *La chrétienté et l'idée de croisade*, I: *Les premières croisades* (Paris 1954); M. Villey, *La croisade. Essai sur la formation d'une théorie juridique* (Paris 1942); W. Holtzmann, "Studien zur Orientpolitik des Reformpapsttums und zur Entstehung des 1. Kreuzzugs" in *HV* 22 (1924–25), 167–99; id., "Die Unionsverhandlungen zwischen Kaiser Alexios I. und Papst Urban II. im Jahre 1089" in *ByZ* 28 (1928), 38–67.

THE KINGDOM OF JERUSALEM AND THE OTHER STATES: Mayer, *Bibliographie,* 2958–3099 and Runciman, II, 493–99; R. Röhricht, *Geschichte des Königreichs Jerusalem 1100–1291* (Innsbruck 1898); J. L. La Monte, *Feudal Monarchy in the Latin Kingdom of Jerusalem* (Cambridge, Mass. 1932); D. C. Munro, *The Kingdom of the Crusaders* (New York 1935); J. Richard, *Le royaume latin de Jérusalem* (Paris 1953); J. Prawer, *History of the Latin Kingdom of Jerusalem* (Hebrew) 2 vols. (Jerusalem 1963); C. Cahen, *La Syrie du Nord à l'époque des croisades et la principauté franque d'Antioche* (Paris 1940); J. Richard, *Le comté de Tripoli sous la dynastie toulousaine 1102–1187* (Paris 1945); R. L. Nicholson, *Jocelin I, Prince of Edessa* (Urbana 1954); W. Hotzelt, *Kirchengeschichte Palästinas im Zeitalter der Kreuzzüge 1099–1291* (Cologne 1940). For ecclesiastical history in the East cf. Mayer, *Bibliographie,* 3913–4090.

52. The "Vita Evangelica" Movement and The Appearance of New Orders

SOURCES

Editions of rules and constitutions by Holstenius-Brockie, Albers and Hallinger cf. Gen. Bib. I, 8; for individual orders or monasteries cf. sources in Heimbucher (Gen. Bib. II, 9) and Cottineau (Gen. Bib. I, 7), some references also in the literature and footnotes in this chapter.

LITERATURE

Cf. Gen. Bib. II, 9, and lit. to chap. 39.

VITA-APOSTOLICA MOVEMENT, HERMITS AND ITINERANT PREACHERS: H. Grundmann, *Religiöse Bewegungen im Mittelalter* (Berlin, 2nd ed. 1961), id., "Neue Beiträge zur Geschichte der religiösen Bewegungen im Mittelalter" in *AKG* 37 (1955), 129–82, esp. 147–57; E. Mens, *Oorsprong en betekenis van de Nederlandse Begijnen- en Begardenbeweging* (Brussels 1947), contains much on the entire religious movement; E. Werner, *Pauperes Christi. Studien zu sozial-religiösen Bewegungen in der Zeit des Reformpapsttums* (Leipzig 1956), worthwhile in spite of its Marxist views; M. D. Chenu, "Moines, clercs, laïcs au carrefour de la vie évangélique (XIIᵉ siècle)" in *RHE* 49 (1954), 59–89; "Érémitisme" in *DSAM* IV (1960), 953–82; "Ermites" in *DHGE* XV (1963), 766–87; *L'eremitismo in occidente nei secoli XI e XII in Atti della 2ᵉ Settimana internazionale di studio, Mendola 1962* (Milan 1965), esp. L. Génicot, "L'érémitisme du XIᵉ siècle dans son contexte économique et social" (45–69), G. G. Meersseman, "L'eremitismo e la predicazione itinerante" (164–79), J. Becquet, "L'érémitisme clérical et laïque dans l'ouest de la France" (182–202), E. Delaruelle, "Les ermites et la spiritualité populaire" (212–41); J. v. Walter, "Die ersten Wanderprediger Frankreichs I" in *StGThK* 9, no. 3 (Leipzig 1903), 1–195; II as supplement to vol. 9 *ibid.* (1906); L. Spätling, *De apostolis, pseudoapostolis, apostolinis* (dissertation, Rome 1947); J. Leclercq, "La crise du monachisme aux XIᵉ et XIIᵉ siècles" in *BIStIAM* 70 (1958), 19–41; N. F. Cantor, "The Crisis of Western Monasticism 1050–1130" in *AHR* 66 (1960–1), 47–67.

VALLOMBROSA: *L'abbazia di Vallombrosa nel pensiero contemporaneo* (Livorno 1953), contains Congress reports; B. Quilici, *Giovanni Gualberto e la sua riforma monastica* (Florence 1943);

further biographies by A. Salvini (Rome 1950) and by E. Lucchesi (Florence 1959); G. Miccoli, *Pietro Igneo* (Rome 1960), the beginning of the Congregation 133–38; S. Boesch Gajano, "Storia e tradizione Vallombrosiane" in *BIStIAM* 76 (1964), 99–215.

CARTHUSIANS: B. Bligny, *Recueil des plus anciens actes de la Grande-Chartreuse 1086–1196* (Grenoble 1958); A. De Mayer and J. M. De Smet, *Guigo's Consuetudines van de eerste Kartuizers* (Brussels 1951); Y. Gourdel, "Chartreux" in *DSAM* II (1937), 705–76 (with lit.); E. Baumann, *Les Chartreux* (Paris 1928); B. Bligny, "Les premiers Chartreux et la pauvreté" in *MA* 4 Series, 6 (1951), 27–60; id., "L'érémitisme et les Chartreux" in *L'eremitismo (v. supra)*, 248–63; H. Löbbel, *Der Stifter des Karthäuserordens, der hl. Bruno von Köln* (Münster 1899), still indispensable.

CISTERCIANS: J. M. Canivez, *Statuta capitulorum generalium O. Cist. 1116–1787,* 8 vols. (Louvain 1933–41); J. Turk, "Carta caritatis prior" in *Analecta S. O. Cist.* 1 (1945), 11–61; id., "Cistercii statuta antiquissima", *ibid.* 4 (1948), 1–159; J. B. van Damme, *Documenta pro Ord. Cist. collecta* (Westmalle 1959). For the confusing recent source studies on the early development of the order advanced especially by J. A. Lefèvre and J. B. van Damme, cf. the critical literature survey in P. Zakar, "Die Anfänge des Zisterzienserordens" in *Analecta S. O. Cist.* 20 (1964), 103–38 and *ibid.,* 21 (1965), 138–66 (answer to van Damme); E. Pásztor in *Annali di scuola spec. per arch. e bibl.* 4 (1964), 137–44; J. M. Canivez, "Cîteaux: Abbaye; Ordre" in *DHGE* XII (1953), 852–74, 874–997; J. B. Mahn, *L'ordre cistercien et son gouvernement 1098–1265* (Paris, 2nd ed., 1951); L. J. A. Lekai and A. Schneider, *Geschichte und Wirken der Weissen Mönche* (Cologne 1958); L. Bouyer, *La spiritualité de Cîteaux* (Paris 1955); F. Delehaye in *Collect. Ord. Cist. Ref.* 14 (1952), 83–106 (on Robert as founder of Citeaux); R. Duvernay, "Citeaux, Vallombreuse et Étienne Hardin" in *Analecta S. O. Cist.* 8 (1952), 379–495; on Bernard of Clairvaux cf. next volume; A. King, *Cîteaux and her Elder Daughters* (London 1954); P. Salmon, "L'ascèse monastique et les origines de Cîteaux" in *Mélanges Saint-Bernard* (Dijon 1954), 268–83.

CANONS REGULAR: Cf. Literature for chap. 39. The latest research is found in a wealth of monographs and articles: basic is C. Dereine, "Chanoines" in *DHGE* XII (1953), 353–405; J. C. Dickinson, *The Origins of the Austin Canons and their Introduction into England* (London 1950); M. Mois, *Das Stift Rottenburg in der Kirchenreform des 11.–12. Jahrhunderts* (Munich–Freising 1953); A. van Ette, *Les chanoines réguliers de Saint-Augustin. Aperçu historique* (Bressoux–Liège 1953); J. Siegwart, for Switzerland and Germany (lit. for chap. 39); *La vita comune del clero nei secoli XI–XII, Atti di Settimana di studio, Mendola 1959,* 2 vols. (Milan 1962), an excellent survey of present research and well oriented. On its contents cf. T. Schieffer in *HZ* 200 (1965), 632–41. Important particular studies are C. Dereine, "Vie commune, règle de Saint Augustin et chanoines réguliers au XIe siècle" in *RHE* 41 (1946), 365–406; G. Bardy, "Saint Grégoire et la réforme canonicale" in *StudGreg* I (1947), 47–64; C. Dereine, "Le problème de la vie commune chez les canonistes réguliers d'Anselme de Lucques à Gratien", *ibid.* III (1948), 287–98; id., "L'élaboration du statut canonique des chanoines réguliers, spécialement sous Urbaine II" in *RHE* 46 (1951), 534–65; G. Schreiber, "Gregor VII., Cluny, Cîteaux, Prémontré zu Eigenkirche, Parochie, Seelsorge" in *ZSavRGkan* 65 (1947), 51–171; F. J. Schmale, "Kanonie, Seelsorge, Eigenkirche" in *HJ* 78 (1959), 38–63.

PREMONSTRATENSIANS: N. Backmund, *Monasticon Praemonstratense,* 3 vols. (Straubing 1949–56); F. Petit, *L'ordre de Prémontré* (Paris 1926); B. F. Grassl, *Der Prämonstratenser-Orden* (Tongerloo 1934); F. Petit, *La spiritualité des Prémontrés aux XIIe et XIIIe siècles* (Paris 1947); P. F. Lefèvre, *La liturgie de Prémontré* (Louvain 1946); C. Dereine, "Les origines de Prémontré" in *RHE* 42 (1947), 352–78; id., "Le premier 'ordo' de Prémontré" in *RBén* 58 (1948), 84–92; G. Madelaine, *Histoire de Saint Norbert,* 2 vols. (Tongerloo, 2nd ed. 1928); additional biographies by A. Zák (Vienna 1930) and by W. P. Romain (Paris 1960); P. Lefèvre in *RHE* 56 (1961) on Norbert's conversion.

On the Military Orders H. E. Mayer, *Bibliographie zur Geschichte der Kreuzzüge* (Hanover 1960), 3460–77 (gen. lit.); 3561–3621 (Templars); 3478–3560 (Hospitallers). Still valuable is Héliot (Gen. Bib. II, 9); G. A. Campbell, *The Knights Templars. Their Rise and Fall* (London 1937); G. Schnürer, *Die ursprüngliche Templerregel* (Freiburg 1903); J. Delaville Le Roulx, *Les Hospitaliers en Terre-Sainte et à Chypre* (Paris 1904); G. Bottarelli and M. Montersi, *Storia politica e militare del ordine di S. Giovanni di Gerusalemme,* 2 vols. (Milan 1940); E. J. King, *The Rule, Status and Customs of the Hospitallers 1099–1310* (London 1934).

53. *The Beginnings of Scholasticism*

Sources

Dialecticians and Anti-Dialecticians: Anselm of Besata, *Rhetorimachia,* ed. by K. Manitius in *MG Quellen zur Geistesgeschichte* 2 (1958); Otloh of St Emmeran, Complete works in *PL* 146, 27–434, esp. his *Dialogus de tribus questionibus, ibid.* 59–136, and the autobiographical work *Liber de tentationibus suis et scriptis, ibid.* 27–58; Manegold of Lautenbach, *Opusculum contra Wolfelmum Coloniensem* in *PL* 155, 147–76; Peter Damiani, Complete works in *PL* 144–45; esp. Op. 45, *ibid.* 145, 695–704, Op. 58, *ibid.* 831–38, and the work on the Principle of Contradiction, Op. 36; *De divina omnipotentia in reparatione corruptae et factis infectis reddendis, ibid.* 595–622.

Eucharistic Controversy: *Berengarii Turonensis opera quae supersunt,* ed. by A. F.-F. T. Vischer (Berlin 1834); the work *De sacra coena adversus Lanfrancum,* here contained, is newly edited by W. H. Beekenkamp (The Hague 1941); Berengar's Letters to Adelmann in Martène-Durand, *Thesaurus novus anecdotorum,* IV (Paris 1717), 109–13, to Jocelin of Bordeaux, ed. by G. Morin in *RBén* 46 (1934), 220–6; Lanfranc, *De corpore et sanguine Domini adversus Berengarium Turonensem* in *PL* 150, 407–22; Guitmund of Aversa, *De corpore et sanguine Christi Libri tres* in *PL* 159, 1427–94; Anselm of Laon, *Systematische Sentenzen,* ed. by F. P. Bliemetzrieder in *BeitrGPhMA* 18, 2–3 (1919); additional tractus in J. Geiselmann (lit. *infra*).

Quarrel over Ordinations: Peter Damian, *Liber Gratissimus* in *MGLiblit* I, 15–75; Humbert of Silva Candida, *Adversus simoniacos libri tres, ibid.* 95–253; for tracts written by later authors cf. A. Schebler (lit. *infra*).

Anselm of Canterbury: The earlier edition in *PL* 158–59 now superseded by *S. Anselmi opera omnia,* ed. by F. S. Schmitt, I–V in 6 vols. (London 1938–51); Schmitt previously edited *Cur Deus Homo, Monologion, De incarnatione Verbi, Proslogion* in *FlorPatr* (Gen. Bib. I, 11), 18 (1929), 20 (1929), 28 (1931), 29 (1931); also: *Cur Deus homo* (Munich 1956), Latin and Germ.

Literature

For important comprehensive lit. see Gen. Bib. II, 12; esp. useful are the bibliographical accounts in *Ueberweg* II; always reliable is Gen. Bib. II, 11, esp. *Manitius* and J. de Ghellinck, also by de Ghellinck, *Le mouvement théologique du XIIe siècle* (Paris, 2nd ed. 1948).

Quarrel over Dialectics and the Beginnings of Early Scholasticism: J. Endres, *Forschungen zur Geschichte der frühmittelalterlichen Philosophie* (Münster 1915); M. Grabmann, *Geschichte der scholastischen Methode,* 2 vols. (Freiburg 1909–11); A. J. Macdonald, *Authority and Reason in the Early Middle Ages* (Oxford 1933); for Peter Damian cf. lit. for chap. 42 and J. Endres, *Petrus Damiani und die weltliche Wissenschaft* (Münster 1910).

The Eucharistic Controversy: J. Geiselmann, *Eucharistielehre der Vorscholastik* (Paderborn 1926), basic treatment to 1100; C. E. Sheedy, *The Eucharistic Controversy of the 11th Century*

(Washington 1948); A. J. Macdonald, *Berengar and the Reform of Sacramental Doctrine* (London 1930); M. Cappuyns in *DHGE* VIII (1935), 385–407; G. Ladner, *Theologie und Politik vor dem Investiturstreit* (Baden bei Wien 1936), 14–41; W. H. Beekenkamp, *De avondmaalsleer van Berengarius v. Tours* ('s Gravenhage 1941); N. M. Haring, "Berengar's Definitions of Sacramentum and their Influence on Mediaeval Sacramentology in *MS* 29 (1951), 109–46; O. Capitani, "Studi per Berengario di Tours" in *BIStIAM* 69 (1957), 67–173; id., "Per la storia dei rapporti tra Gregorio VII e Berengario di Tours" in *StudGreg* VI (1959–61), 99–145.

QUARREL OVER THE SACRAMENT OF ORDERS: L. Saltet, *Les réordinations* (Paris 1907); A. Schebler, *Die Reordinationen in der 'altkatholischen Kirche'* (Bonn 1936); V. Fuchs, *Der Ordinationstitel von seiner Entstehung bis auf Innozenz III.* (Bonn 1930); the latter two written from the viewpoint of R. Sohms; still useful today is E. Hirsch, "Die Auffassungen der simonistischen und schismatischen Weihen im 11. Jahrhundert", esp. for Card. Deusdedit, in *AkathKR* 87 (1907), 25–70; cf. also the useful work of M. Rosati, *La teologia sacramentaria nella lotta contro la simonia e l'investitura laica del secolo XI* (dissertation, Rome, Gregoriana, 1951).

ANSELM OF CANTERBURY: In addition to *Ueberweg* II, 192–203, 698–700 (lit.); *Fliche-Martin* XIII, 49–66; *DHGE* III (1924) 464–85; *DThC* I (1923), 1327–60; G. Ceriani, *S. Anselmo* (Brescia 1946); *Specilegium Beccense* (Paris 1959), report of the International Congress Commemorating the 900th Anniversary of Anselm's arrival at Bec; S. Vanni Rovighi, *S. Anselmo e la filosofia del secolo XI* (Milan 1949); G. Söhngen, *Die Einheit der Theologie in Anselms Proslogion* (Bonn 1938); K. Barth, *Fides quaerens intellectum. Anselms Beweis der Existenz Gottes* (Munich, 2nd ed. 1958), on 1st ed. (1931) cf. A. Stolz in *Catholica* 2 (1933), 1–24, and É. Gilson in *AHD* 9 (1934), 5–51; A. Kolping, *Anselms Proslogion-Beweis der Existenz Gottes* (Bonn 1939); J. McIntyre, *St. Anselm and his Critics. Re-Interpretation of the Cur Deus homo* (London 1954); R. Perino, *La dottrina trinitaria di S. Anselmo* (Rome 1951); J. Rivière, *Le dogme de la rédemption au début du moyen âge* (Paris 1934); A. Schmitt, "La Meditatio redemptionis humanae di s. Anselmo in relazione al Cur Deus homo" in *Benedittina* 9 (1955), 197–213; H. Ott, "Anselms Versöhnungslehre" in *ThZ* (1957), 183–99.

LIST OF POPES IN THE EARLY MIDDLE AGES

Antipopes are preceded by an asterisk

St. Sergius I	687–701	John IX	898–900
John VI	701–705	Benedict IV	900–903
John VII	705–707	Leo V	903
Sisinnius	708	*Christopher	903
Constantine I	708–715	Sergius III	904–911
St. Gregory II	715–731	Anastasius III	911–913
St. Gregory III	731–741	Lando	913–914
St. Zachary	741–752	John X	914–928
Stephen II	752	Leo VI	928
Stephen II (III)	752–757	Stephen VII (VIII)	928–931
St. Paul I	757–767	John XI	931–935
*Constantine II	767–768	Leo VII	936–939
*Philip	768	Stephen VIII (IX)	939–942
Stephen III (IV)	768–772	Marinus II (Martin III)	942–946
Hadrian	772–795	Agapitus II	946–955
St. Leo III	795–816	John XII	955–964
Stephen IV (V)	816–817	Benedict V	964
St. Paschal I	817–824	Leo VIII	964–965
Eugene II	824–827	John XIII	965–972
Valentine	827	Benedict VI	973–974
Gregory IV	827–844	*Boniface VII (Franco)	974
*John	844	Benedict VII	974–983
Sergius II	844–847	John XIV	983–984
St. Leo IV	847–855	Boniface VII	984–985
Benedict III	855–858	John XV	985–996
*Anastasius III	855	Gregory V	996–999
St. Nicholas I	858–867	*John XVI	997–998
Hadrian II	867–872	Silvester II	999–1003
John VIII	872–882	John XVII	1003
Marinus I (Martin II)	882–884	John XVIII	1003/04–1009
St. Hadrian III	884–885	Sergius IV	1009–1012
Stephen V (VI)	885–891	Benedict VIII	1012–1024
Formosus	891–896	*Gregory VI	1012
Boniface VI	896	John XIX	1024–1032
Stephen VI (VII)	896–897	Benedict IX	1032–1045
Romanus	897	*Silvester III	1045
Theodore II	897	Gregory VI	1045–1046

Clement II	1046–1047	*Clement III	1080–1100
Damasus II	1048	Bl. Victor III	1086–1087
St. Leo IX	1049–1054	Bl. Urban II	1088–1099
Victor II	1055–1057	Paschal II	1099–1118
Stephen IX (X)	1057–1058	*Dietrich	1100–1102
*Benedict X	1058–1059	*Albert	1102
Nicholas II	1059–1061	*Silvester IV	1105–1111
Alexander II	1061–1073	Gelasius II	1118–1119
*Honorius II	1061–1071/72	*GregorvVIII	1118–1121
St. Gregory VII	1073–1085	Calixtus II	1119–1124

GENERAL INDEX

Figures in italics denote pages where the subject receives more intensive treatment.

557

559

569